The
RIGHT
Doctrine
from the
WRONG
Texts?

The RIGHT Doctrine from the WRONG Texts?

Essays on the Use of the Old Testament in the New

Edited by G. K. Beale

Baker Academic
Grand Rapids, Michigan

© 1994 by G. K. Beale

Published by Baker Academic
a division of Baker Publishing Group
P.O. Box 6287, Grand Rapids, MI 49516-6287
www.bakeracademic.com

Fourteenth printing, February 2007

Printed in the United States of America

Library of Congress Cataloging-in-Publication Data
The right doctrine from the wrong texts? / essays on the use of the Old Testament in the New / edited by G. K. Beale
    p.   cm.
    Includes bibliographical references and indexes.
    ISBN 10: 0-8010-1088-8
    ISBN 978-0-8010-1088-0
    1. Bible. N.T.—Relation to the Old Testament. 2. Bible O.T.—Quotations in the New Testament. 3. Typology (Theology) I. Beale, G. K. (Gregory K.)
BS2387.R54   1994
225.6—dc20   94-33709

Contents

Introduction

G. K. Beale

The purpose of this book is to present various perspectives concerning the hermeneutical issue of whether or not Jesus and the apostles quoted Old Testament texts with respect for their broader Old Testament context. Did they refer to Old Testament passages in a way that is inconsistent with or contradictory to the original intention of an Old Testament passage?

The articles assembled here represent different perspectives on this basic question and are written by authors from diverse theological backgrounds. The book is organized into seven sections. Each discusses major issues in the study of the Old Testament in the New. Part 1 consists of articles that provide introductory overviews of the use of the Old in the New. Each of the remaining parts address one major issue of the hermeneutical debate.

Part 2 analyzes the problem of authorial intention. Can an Old Testament text be understood by New Testament authors with a *fuller meaning* (i.e., *sensus plenior*) than was understood by the original Old Testament author? Or, do Old Testament texts retain the same meaning in the New Testament, so that there is merely a different application in the New Testament than in the Old Testament?

Parts 3, 4, and 5 examine the problem of hermeneutical integrity. Did Jesus and the apostles quote Old Testament texts with exegetical respect for the broader context? This matter is at the heart of the book and is crucial for any study of the Old Testament in the New. The majority of the essays in these three sections address this issue from a variety of perspectives. The essays in part 3 argue that the New Testament uses the Old Testament without regard for its original contextual meaning. In response, the essays in part 4 assert that the Old Testament is interpreted with contextual respect. Two studies in part 5 focus on one much debated text as a test case. One essay contends that Paul's creativity in 2 Corinthians 3 goes beyond the bounds of the original meaning of the Old Testament text used there and contradicts its intent. The other article argues that Paul exegetes the Old Testament background of 2 Corinthians 3 creatively, yet consistently with the original intent of Exodus 34.

Part 6 of the book presents the problem of typology. A number of questions must be addressed. First, what is the definition of typology? Is typology merely an analogy between an Old Testament text and a New Testament passage? Or, does typology have both an analogous and a prophetic nature? Second, if New Testament authors understand certain Old Testament events to foreshadow prophetically events in the New Testament, how does this relate to the original Old Testament author's intention in recording the Old Testament event, and how can this be contextual interpretation of the Old Testament?

Part 7, the conclusion of the book, inquires whether or not twentieth-century interpreters should emulate all of the exegetical methods used by Jesus and his followers. Were the New Testament writers so immersed in Jewish interpretative methods that they employed both the contextual and the non-contextual? If they sometimes employed non-contextual interpretative procedures in using the Old Testament, did they err in doing so or did the Holy Spirit guarantee the truth of their doctrinal conclusions for the church of following generations? Put another way, did Jesus and the apostles preach the right doctrine from the wrong Old Testament texts? If so, did apostolic inspiration make their exegetical methods unique and unrepeatable? Or did inspiration give the New Testament writers unique and greater epistemological certainty about their interpretative conclusions than twentieth-century interpreters could ever hope to attain concerning their interpretations?

The issue of typology is of special interest here as well. On numbers of occasions New Testament authors see events in Old Testament narratives as being prophetic of events in the life of Christ. Even if one judges such interpretation legitimate, is it an exegetical method that interpreters should attempt to use today? Should we attempt to discover "prophetic types" in the Old Testament even where New Testament writers did not find them? This is a debate which has generated much discussion, especially in the twentieth century.

All of the preceding issues should be of interest to anyone with a serious interest in the way the New Testament uses the Old Testament, a question which has generated much debate in the twentieth century. There is no editorial evaluation of the essays. They stand on their own, and the reader has the responsibility of evaluation. However, some of the essays evaluate prior work done in the field on the issues at hand, and these will be of particular value. Additional bibliography can be found in the notes at the conclusion of the studies which further discuss the various topics debated (the chapter by Snodgrass is a good example of this).

The reader may notice that there is more space devoted to articles arguing in favor of the New Testament's contextual approach to the Old (in part 4) than to the opposing perspective (most of which is found in part 3). The reason for this is threefold. First, the articles have been chosen primarily for their clarity in setting out the issues of debate. Second, some of the essays have also been selected because of their "classical" nature and significant impact on Old Testament in New Testament studies. Included are some which are often sought, but hard to find (note especially the essays by Dodd, Foulkes, and Kaiser). Third, there is a consensus among the significant group of New Testament scholars, if not a majority, that the New Testament uses the Old without regard for its original meaning. The collection of essays here is intentionally lopsided in order that there be fuller exposure for the "minority view" in the public forum. Nevertheless, the following books and articles, together with other references in the concluding bibliography, should be consulted, if the reader wants more samples of representative works arguing for the non-contextual interpretation of the Old in the New (for full citations of the references below see the bibliography at the end of the book).

(1) K. Stendahl, *The School of St. Matthew and Its Use of the Old Testament*.

(2) B. Lindars, *New Testament Apologetic*.

(3) A. T. Hanson, *The Living Utterances of God: The New Testament Exegesis of the Old*.

(4) D. Juel, *Messianic Exegesis. A Christological Interpretation of the Old Testament in Early Christianity*.

There is no book which addresses the crucial issues revolving around the use of the Old Testament in the New in the manner in which this book does. The uniqueness of the book especially lies in its unswerving focus on exegetical methodology instead of theology, as this pertains to the use of the Old Testament in the New. In this respect, the presuppositions and assumptions which underlie Jesus' and the apostles' exegetical method will be examined and compared with the presuppositions underlying typical twentieth-century methods of exegesis.

The essays collected in this volume represent some of the best in scholarship on the various subjects written since the middle of the twentieth century. To have all of these essays finally gathered into one volume should be a service for scholars, teachers, and other interested readers.

More specific treatments of some of the above issues can be found in the following books, though many others could also be cited:

1) On the use of the Old Testament in the Gospels see
   a) R. T. France, *Jesus and the Old Testament*
   b) R. Gundry, *Use of the Old Testament in Matthew*

     c)   D. Moessner, *The Lord of the Banquet* (on Luke)
     d)   D. L. Bock, *Proclamation from Prophecy and Pattern: Lucan Old Testament Christology*.

  2) On the use of the Old Testament in Paul see
     a)   E. E. Ellis, *Paul's Use of the Old Testament* (and a spate of others recently published on this topic).

  3) On the use of the Old Testament in Revelation see
     a)   G. K. Beale, *The Use of Daniel in Jewish Apocalyptic Literature and in John's Apocalypse*
     b)   J. Fekkes, *Isaiah and Prophetic Traditions in the Book of Revelation*.

  4) On themes which have bearing on the use of the Old Testament in the New Testament see
     a)   J. S. Feinberg (editor), *Continuity and Discontinuity,* which discusses how such Old Testament theological themes as covenant, salvation, the law, kingdom, and Israel are related to the New Testament.

There are other selected studies on the use of the Old Testament in the New Testament (e.g., see Ellis's other works cited in the bibliography at the end of the book). Other studies significant to mention are W. C. Kaiser's *The Uses of the Old Testament in the New Testament and It Is Written: Scripture Citing Scripture: Essays in Honor of Barnabas Lindars*, ed. D. A. Carson and H. G. M. Williamson. Only half of the latter volume concerns Old Testament in New Testament studies, which attempt to cover each corpus in the New Testament canon. Some of the studies are more technical or focus on narrow aspects of the use of the Old Testament in the New, while others are of a more general nature.

The essays in this volume have been selected from a larger collection of works which have been gathered over a ten-year period for a class on "The Use of the Old Testament in the New Testament," which I have taught annually at Gordon-Conwell Theological Seminary since 1985.

Part **1**

Introductory
Issues

1

The New Testament Use of the Old Testament

Roger Nicole

From Roger Nicole, "The New Testament Use of the Old Testament," in *Revelation and the Bible*, ed. Carl F. H. Henry (Grand Rapids: Baker, 1958), 135–51.

The New Testament contains an extraordinarily large number of Old Testament quotations. It is difficult to give an accurate figure since the variation in use ranges all the way from a distant allusion to a definite quotation introduced by an explicit formula stating the citation's source. As a result, the figures given by various authors often reflect a startling discrepancy.

Range of Old Testament References

The present writer has counted 224 direct citations introduced by a definite formula indicating the writer purposed to quote. To these must be added 7 cases where a second quotation is introduced by the conjunction "and," and 19 cases where a paraphrase or summary rather than a direct quotation follows the introductory formula. We may further note at least 45 instances where the similarity with certain Old Testament passages is so pronounced that, although no explicit indication is given that the New Testament author was referring to Old Testament Scripture, his intention to do so can scarcely be doubted. Thus a very conservative count discloses unquestionably at least 295 separate references to the Old Testament. These occupy some 352 verses of the New Testament, or more than 4.4 percent. Therefore one verse in 22.5 verses of the New Testament is a quotation.

If clear allusions are taken into consideration, the figures are much higher: C. H. Toy lists 613 such instances, Wilhelm Dittmar goes as high as 1640, while Eugen Huehn indicates 4105 passages reminiscent of Old Testament Scripture. It can therefore be asserted, without exaggeration, that more than 10 percent of the New Testament text is made up of citations or direct allusions to the Old Testament. The recorded words of Jesus disclose a similar percentage. Certain books like Revelation, Hebrews, Romans are well nigh saturated with Old Testament forms of language, allusions, and quotations. Perusal of Nestle's edition of the Greek New Testament, in which the Old Testament material is printed in bold face type, will reveal at a glance the extent of this practice. These facts appear even more impressive when one remembers that in New Testament times the Old Testament was not, as today, duplicated by the million but could be obtained only in expensive handwritten copies.

If we limit ourselves to the specific quotations and direct allusions which form the basis of our previous reckoning, we shall note that 278 different Old Testament verses are cited in the New Testament: 94 from the Pentateuch, 99 from the Prophets, and 85 from the Writings. Out of the 22 books in the Hebrew reckoning of the canon only 6 (Judges–Ruth, Song of Solomon, Ecclesiastes, Esther, Ezra–Nehemiah, Chronicles) are not explicitly referred to. The more extensive lists of Dittmar and Huehn show passages reminiscent of all Old Testament books without exception.

It is to be noted that the whole New Testament contains not even one explicit citation of any of the Old Testament Apocrypha which are considered as canonical by the Roman Catholic Church. This omission can scarcely be viewed as accidental.

Authority of Old Testament References

From beginning to end, the New Testament authors ascribe unqualified authority to Old Testament Scripture. Whenever advanced, a quotation is viewed as normative. Nowhere do we find a tendency to question, argue, or repudiate the truth of any Scripture utterance. Passages sometimes alleged to prove that the Lord and his apostles challenged at times the authority of the Old Testament, when carefully examined, turn out to bolster rather than to impair the evidence for their acceptance of Scripture as the Word of God. In Matthew 5:21–43 and 19:3–9, our Lord, far from setting aside the commandments of the Old Testament, really engages in a searching analysis of the spiritual meaning and original intent of the divine precepts, and from this vantage point he applies it in a deeper and broader way than had been done before him. In some passages in which comparison is made between the revelation of the Old Testament and that of the New (John 1:17; 2 Cor. 3:6; Gal. 3:19ff.; Heb. 1:1–2, and so forth), the superior glory of the New Testament is emphasized, not as in conflict with the Old, but as the perfect fulfillment of a revelation still incomplete, yet sanctioned by divine authority.

It is noteworthy that the New Testament writers and the Lord Jesus himself did not hesitate on occasion to base their whole argumentation upon one single word of Old Testament Scripture (Matt. 2:15; 4:10; 13:35; 22:44; Mark 12:36; Luke 4:8; 20:42–43; John 8:17; 10:34; 19:37; Acts 23:5; Rom. 4:3, 9, 23; 15:9–12; 1 Cor. 6:16; Gal. 3:8, 10, 13; Heb. 1:7; 2:12; 3:13; 4:7; 12:26), or even on the grammatical form of one word (Gal. 3:16).

Of special interest are the formulas by which the New Testament writers introduce their quotations. In a particularly significant way these formulas reflect their view of the Old Testament Scriptures, since they do not manifest any design to set forth a doctrine of Scripture, but are rather the instinctive expression of their approach to the sacred writings.

The formulas emphasize strongly the divine origin of the Old Testament, and commonly (at least 56 times) refer to God as the author. In a number of passages God is represented as the speaker when the quotation is not a saying of God recorded as such in the Old Testament, but the word of Scripture itself, in fact, at times a word addressed to God by man (Matt. 19:5; Acts 4:25; 13:35; Heb. 1:5–8, 13; 3:7; 4:4). These "can be treated as a declaration of God's only on the hypothesis that all Scripture is a declaration of God's" (B. B. Warfield, *The Inspiration and Authority of the Bible*, 143).

Often passages of the Old Testament are simply attributed to the Scripture, which is thus personified as speaking (John 7:38, 42; 15:25; 19:37; Rom. 4:3; 7:7; 9:17; 10:11; 11:2; 1 Cor. 14:24; 2 Cor. 6:2; Gal. 3:8; 4:30; 1 Tim. 5:18; James 2:23; 4:5). In Romans 9:17 and Galatians 3:8 the identification between the text of Scripture and God as speaking is carried so far that the actions of God are actually ascribed to Scripture, which is represented as speaking to Pharaoh and as foreseeing justification by faith. Warfield urges that "These acts could be attributed to Scripture only as the result of such a habitual identification, in the mind of the writer, of the text of Scripture with God as speaking that it became natural to use the term 'Scripture says,' when what was really intended was 'God, as recorded in Scripture, said'" (ibid., 299–300).

The collaboration of man in the writing of Scripture is also emphasized. The names of Moses, David, Isaiah, Jeremiah, Daniel, Joel, and Hosea appear in the formulas of quotation. It is noteworthy that, in the majority of the cases where the human author is named, reference is made not to a personal statement recorded in Scripture but to an utterance of God, which the writer was commissioned to transmit as such. In a number of passages both the divine and the human authorship appear side by side.

> ". . . which was spoken by the Lord through the prophet . . ." (Matt. 1:22). "David himself said in the Holy Spirit" (Mark 12:36; cf. Matt. 22:43). ". . . the Holy Spirit spake before by the mouth of David" (Acts 1:16; cf. 4:25). "Well spake the Holy Spirit through Isaiah the prophet . . ." (Acts 28:25). "He saith also in Hosea . . ." (Rom. 9:25).

These passages supply clear evidence that the divine superintendence was not viewed as obliterating the human agency and characteristics of the writers, but rather, that God secured a perfectly adequate presentation of the truth through the responsible and personal agency of the men he called and prepared for this sacred task.

"It is written" is one of the frequent formulas of introduction, the one, in fact, which our Lord used three times in his temptation (Matt. 4:4, 7, 10). This expression does not connote merely that an appeal is made to the written text of Scripture but, as Warfield so aptly has said, "The simple adduction in this solemn and decisive manner of a written authority carries with it the implication that the appeal is made to the indefectible authority of the Scriptures of God, which in all their parts and in every one of their declarations are clothed with the authority of God Himself" (ibid., 240).

The use of the terms "law" (John 10:34; 15:25; Rom. 3:19; 1 Cor. 14:21), or "prophets" (Matt. 13:35), where reference is made to passages belonging, strictly speaking, to other parts of the Hebrew canon, indicates that the New Testament writers viewed the whole Old Testament Scripture as having legal authority and prophetic character.

In their formulas of quotation the New Testament writers give expression to their conviction as to the eternal contemporaneity of Scripture. This is manifest in particular in the many (41) instances where the introductory verb is in the present: "He says," and not "he said." This is reinforced by the use of the pronouns "we," "you," in connection with ancient sayings: "That which was spoken unto you by God" (Matt. 22:31); "The Holy Spirit also beareth witness to us" (Heb. 10:15; cf. also Matt. 15:7; Mark 7:6; 12:19; Acts 4:11; 13:47; Heb. 12:5). This implication gains explicit statement in Romans 15:4: "Whatsoever things were written aforetime were written for our learning" (cf. also Rom. 4:23, 24; 1 Cor. 9:10; 10:11).

The New Testament writers used quotations in their sermons, in their histories, in their letters, in their prayers. They used them when addressing Jews or Gentiles, churches or individuals, friends or antagonists, new converts or seasoned Christians. They used them for argumentation, for illustration, for instruction, for documentation, for prophecy, for reproof. They used them in times of stress and in hours of mature thinking, in liberty and in prison, at home and abroad. Everywhere and always they were ready to refer to the impregnable authority of Scripture.

Jesus Christ himself provides a most arresting example in this respect. At the very threshold of his public ministry, our Lord, in his dramatic victory over Satan's threefold onslaught, rested his whole defense on the authority of three passages of Scripture. He quoted the Old Testament in support of his teaching to the crowds; he quoted it in his discussions with antagonistic Jews; he quoted it in answer to questions both captious and sincere; he quoted it in instructing the disciples who would have readily accepted his teaching on his own authority; he referred to it in his prayers, when alone in the presence of the Father; he quoted it on the cross, when his sufferings could easily have drawn his attention elsewhere; he quoted it in his resurrection glory, when any limitation, real or alleged, of the days of his flesh was clearly superseded. Whatever may be the differences between the pictures of Jesus drawn by the four Gospels, they certainly agree in their representation of our Lord's attitude toward the Old Testament: one of constant use and of unquestioning endorsement of its authority.

Accuracy of Old Testament References[1]

A difficulty comes to the fore, however, when the New Testament citations are carefully compared with the original Old Testament texts. In their quotations the New Testament writers, it would appear, use considerable freedom, touching both the letter and the meaning of the Old Testament passages.

Opponents of verbal inspiration repeatedly have brought forward this objection mainly in two forms:

1) The New Testament writers, not having taken care to quote in absolute agreement with the original text of the Old Testament, it is urged,

---

1. The material to be found under this heading has in substance been set forth with more detail in a paper presented to the sixth annual meeting of the Evangelical Theological Society, December 30, 1954, at Ringwood, New Jersey. This paper was published in volume 1 of the *Gordon Review*, February and May 1955. Further detail and discussion of the actual quotations in the New Testament, especially in Matthew, were presented in an S.T.M. thesis submitted by the present writer to the faculty of Gordon Divinity School in 1940 under the title: "The Old Testament Quotations in the New with special reference to the Doctrine of the Plenary Inspiration of the Bible."

cannot have held the doctrine of plenary inspiration. Otherwise they would have shown greater respect for the letter of Scripture.

2) The New Testament writers, in quoting the Old "inaccurately" as to its letter, or "improperly" as to its sense, or both, cannot have been directed to do so by the Spirit of God.

The first argument impugns mainly the inspiration of the Old Testament, the second mainly that of the New. Both will be met if it can be shown that the New Testament method of quotation is entirely proper and consistent with the highest regard for the texts cited. In the present treatment it is possible only to delineate the main principles involved, without showing their application to particular cases. We shall consider first, principles involved in the solution of difficulties arising from the New Testament manner of quoting, after which brief comments will be offered regarding the methods of interpretation exhibited by the New Testament authors in their application of Old Testament passages.

Form of Quotation

It must be recognized that each of the following principles does not find application in every case, but the writer is of the opinion that, singly or in combination, as the case may be, they provide a very satisfactory explanation of apparent discrepancies in almost all cases, and a possible solution in all cases.

The New Testament writers had to translate their quotations. They wrote in Greek and their source of quotations was in Hebrew. They needed therefore either to translate for themselves or to use existing translations. Now no translation can give a completely adequate and coextensive rendering of the original. A certain measure of change is inevitable, even when one is quoting by divine inspiration.

When the New Testament writers wrote, there was one Greek version of the Old Testament, the Septuagint. It was widespread, well known, and respected in spite of some obvious defects when appraised from the standpoint of modern scholarship. In most cases, it was a fair translation of the Hebrew text, and possessed distinctive literary qualities. Its position in the ancient world is comparable to that of the Authorized Version before the Revised was published. A conscientious scholar writing nowadays in a certain language will use for his quotations from foreign sources the translations which his readers generally use. He will not attempt to correct or change them unless some mistake bears directly on his point. When slight errors or mistranslations occur, generally he will neither discuss them, for in so doing he would tend to direct the reader's attention away from his point, nor correct them without giving notice, for this might tend to arouse the reader's suspicion. This practice is followed by many preachers and writers who use the Authorized Version in English or Luther's translation in German. They are often well aware that some verses rather inadequately render the Hebrew or the Greek, but no blame can be laid on them as long as they base no argument on what is mistaken in the translation. Similarly, the writers of the New Testament could use the Septuagint, the only Greek version then existing, in spite of its occasional inaccuracy, and even quote passages which were somewhat inaccurately translated. To take advantage of its errors, however, would have been inadmissible. We do not find any example of a New Testament deduction or application logically inferred from the Septuagint and which cannot be maintained on the basis of the Hebrew text.

Some of the recently discovered Dead Sea scrolls at times provide the Hebrew text which underlay the Septuagint where it differs from the Masoretic Text. This is the case, for instance, in Isaiah 53:11, where the scroll Isaiah A reads "He shall see light," thus supporting the Septuagint rendering. While great caution is still necessary in any textual emendation of the Massoretic text, the possibility that in some divergent translations the Septuagint occasionally represents the primitive Hebrew original may be held to have received some support from these discoveries. In such cases, of course, it would not only have been proper for the New Testament writers to quote from the Septuagint, but this would actually have been preferable.

The use of the Septuagint in quoting does not indicate that the New Testament writers have thought of this version as inspired in itself. *A fortiori* they did not confer inspiration upon the translation of the passages they have used. Samuel Davidson was laboring under a regrettable confusion when he wrote: "It will ever remain inexplicable by the supporters of verbal inspiration that the words of the Septuagint became literally inspired as soon as they were taken from that version and transferred to the New Testament pages" (*Sacred Hermeneutics* [Edinburgh: Clark, 1843], 515). This statement misconstrues verbal inspiration. When the New Testament authors appealed to Scripture as the Word of God, it is not claimed that they viewed anything but the original communication as vested in full with divine inerrancy. Yet their willingness to make use of the Septuagint, in spite of its occasional defects, teaches the important lesson that the basic message which God purposed to deliver can be conveyed even through a translation, and that appeal can be made to a version insofar as it agrees with the original. It would be precarious, however, to rest an argument on any part of the Septuagint quotations which appears not to be conformed to the Hebrew original nor to the point of the New Testament writers, for the mere fact that the quotation was adduced in this fashion was not meant as a divine sanction upon incidental departures from the autographs.

In the quotations made from the Septuagint we have indeed God's seal of approval upon the contents of the Old Testament passage, but the form of the citation is affected by the language and conditions of those to whom the New Testament was first addressed. Such use of the Septuagint was not a case of objectionable accommodation. That the inspired Word is accommodated to humanity is an obvious fact: it is written in human languages, uses human comparisons, its parts are conditioned by the circumstances of those to whom they were at first destined, and so forth. But we cannot admit of an accommodation in which inspired writers would give formal assent to error. In their use of the Septuagint, however, the New Testament authors were so far from actual endorsement of error that the best scholars of all times have used similar methods in adducing translated quotations, as noted above.[2]

The frequent use of the Septuagint, it must also be noted, did not impose upon the New Testament authors the obligation to quote always in accordance with this version. Whenever they wanted to emphasize an idea which was insufficiently or inadequately rendered in the Septuagint, they may have retranslated in whole or in part the passage in question. In certain cases the reason for their introduction of changes may remain unknown to us, but we are not on that account in a position to say either that a careful reproduction of the Septuagint is illegitimate or that a modification of that text is unjustifiable.

The New Testament writers did not have the same rules for quotations as are nowadays enforced in works of a scientific character. In particular, they did not have any punctuation signs which are so important in modern usage.

They did not have any quotation marks, and thus it is not always possible to ascertain the exact beginning, or the real extent of quotations. They were not obliged to start actual citations immediately after an introductory formula, nor have we a right to affirm that their quotations do not end until every resemblance with the Old Testament text disappears. In certain cases they may very well have made shorter citations than is generally believed, and also may have added developments of

---

2. If it be urged that these scholars were not inspired and that therefore their writings can scarcely be compared to Holy Writ, this point will be freely granted. What is significant here, however, is the fact that methods of quotation similar to those of the New Testament writers were used and are still now being used by men who can hardly be viewed as ignorant of the minor differences between the original text and the translations they adduce, and still less as intending to authenticate by their citation what they know to be divergent. These men's unquestioned competence, integrity, and attachment to truth prove, for themselves as well as for the inspired authors, that the methods in question do not connote an endorsement of error.

their own, retaining some words taken from the original source but not actually intended as part of a quotation. Criticism of such passages if they were not intended as actual citations is manifestly unfair.

They did not have any ellipsis marks. Thus special attention is not drawn to the numerous omissions they made. These ellipses, however, are not to be considered as illegitimate on that account.

They did not have any brackets to indicate editorial comments introduced in the quotation. Thus we should not be surprised to find intentional additions, sometimes merely of one word, sometimes more extended (cf. Eph. 6:2).

They did not have any footnote references by which to differentiate quotations from various sources. Sometimes we find a mixture of passages of analogous content or wording, but we are not justified on that account in charging the writers with mishandling or misusing the Old Testament.

We readily recognize that the New Testament writers fell into these patterns, whose legitimacy is universally granted, much more than a present-day author would. Modern punctuation rules make such practices tiresome and awkward. One tries nowadays to omit, insert, or modify as little as possible in quotations, in order to avoid the complexity of repeated quotation marks, ellipsis marks, brackets, and so forth. Yet this common present usage is by no means a standard by which to judge the ancient writers.

The New Testament writers sometimes paraphrased their quotations.

Under this heading we might first mention certain cases where we find a free translation of the Hebrew rather than a real paraphrase. Such a procedure certainly needs no justification, since a free translation sometimes renders the sense and impression of the original better than a more literal one.

Slight modifications, such as a change of pronouns, a substitution of a noun for a pronoun or vice versa, transformations in the person, the tense, the mood, or the voice of verbs, are sometimes introduced in order to better suit the connection in the New Testament. These paraphrases are perhaps the most obviously legitimate of all.

There are cases in which the New Testament writers obviously forsake the actual tenor of the Old Testament passage in order to manifest more clearly in what sense they were construing it. In this they are quite in agreement with the best modern usage, as represented, for example, in W. G. Campbell, *A Form Book for Thesis Writing* (New York: Houghton Mifflin, 1939): "A careful paraphrase that does complete justice to the source is preferable to a long quotation" (p. 15).

In certain cases the New Testament writers do not refer to a single passage, but rather summarize the general teaching of the canonical books on certain subjects in phrasing appropriate to the New Testament, although as to the essential thought they express indebtedness to, or agreement with, the Old Testament. This method of referring to the Old Testament teachings is obviously legitimate. The following passages might be viewed as examples of "quotations of substance," as Franklin Johnson calls them in his able treatise on *The Quotations of the New Testament from the Old Considered in the Light of General Literature* (London: Baptist Tract and Book Society, 1896): Matthew 2:23; 5:31, 33; 12:3, 5; 19:7; 22:24; 24:15; 26:24, 54, 56; Mark 2:25; 9:12, 13; 10:4; 12:19; 14:21, 49; Luke 2:22; 6:3; 11:49; 18:31; 20:28; 21:22; 24:27, 32, 44–46; John 1:45; 5:39, 46; 7:38, 42; 8:17; 17:12; 19:7, 28; 20:9; Acts 1:16; 3:18; 7:51; 13:22, 29; 17:2–3; Romans 3:10; 1 Corinthians 2:9; 14:34; 15:3–4, 25–27; 2 Corinthians 4:6; Galatians 3:22; 4:22; Ephesians 5:14; James 4:5; 2 Peter 3:12–13.

Finally, we must consider the possibility that the writers of the New Testament, writing or speaking for people well acquainted with the Old, may in certain cases have intended simply to refer their readers or hearers to a well-known passage of Scripture. Then, in order to suggest it to their memory they may have accurately cited therefrom some expressions, which they then placed in a general frame different from that of the original. At times the actual words quoted may have been intended merely or primarily to indicate the location of a passage, as the general context of the Old Testament in which the stipulated truth could be found, rather than as an express citation.

The New Testament writers often simply alluded to Old Testament passages without intending to quote them. It was quite natural that people nurtured and steeped in the oracles of God should instinctively use forms of language and turns of thought reminiscent of Old Testament Scripture.

> The speakers or writers, in such cases, do not profess to give forth the precise words and meaning of former revelations; their thoughts and language merely derived from these the form and direction, which by a kind of sacred instinct they took; and it does not matter for any purpose, for which the inspired oracles were given, whether the portions thus appropriated might or might not be very closely followed, and used in connections somewhat different from those in which they originally stood (Patrick Fairbairn, *Hermeneutical Manual* [Edinburgh: T. & T. Clark, 1858], 355).

Only in cases where the New Testament authors definitely manifest the intention of citing by the use of a formula of introduction can we require any strong degree of conformity.

With respect to what might be viewed as formulas of introduction, the following remarks may be made:

Only a quotation which immediately follows such a formula is to be certainly considered as a formal citation. In cases of successive quotations "and again" always introduces an actual citation (Rom. 15:11; 1 Cor. 3:20; Heb. 1:5; 2:13; 10:30), but in the case of "and" or "but," or of successive quotations without any intervening link, criticisms are quite precarious, since no formal quotation may be intended.

Even when a definite formula points directly to an Old Testament passage, we may not expect strict adherence to the letter of the source when this quotation is recorded in indirect rather than in direct discourse. In such cases we often find remarkable verbal accuracy, but we cannot criticize departure from the original when the very form of the sentence so naturally allows for it.

When what may appear to be a citation is introduced by a form of the verbs "say" or "speak," it is not always certain that the writer actually intended to quote. Rather, the possibility must at times be taken into consideration that we are facing an informal reference to some saying recorded in Scripture. Perhaps some of the clearest examples along this line may be found in the discourse of Stephen in Acts 7, in which free references are made to sayings of God, of Moses, and of the Jews, woven in the survey of covenant history presented by the first martyr. In Acts 7:26, a declaration of Moses is mentioned which is not found at all in the Old Testament and obviously was not intended as an actual quotation. In all cases of this type it must certainly be acknowledged that a considerable measure of freedom is legitimate and that one could scarcely expect here the exactness looked for in actual citations. The following may belong to this category: Matthew 2:23; 15:4; 22:32; 24:15; Mark 12:26; Acts 3:25; 7:3, 5–7, 26–28, 32–35, 40; 13:22; Romans 9:15; 11:4; 2 Corinthians 4:6; Galatians 3:8; Hebrews 1:5, 13; 6:14; 8:5; 10:30; 12:21, 26; 13:5; James 2:11; 1 Peter 3:6; Jude 14.

The New Testament authors sometimes recorded quotations made by others. Not all quotations in the New Testament are introduced by the writers themselves for the purpose of illustrating their narrative or bolstering their argument. Sometimes they record quotations made by the personalities who appear in the history, as by Jesus, Paul, Peter, James, Stephen, the Jews, and Satan. In two cases we have a record of a reading—Luke 4:18–19 and Acts 8:32–33. The New Testament writers had at their disposal at least three legitimate methods of recording such quotations:

1) They could translate them directly from the original text;

2) They could use the existing Septuagint and quote according to this version, as suggested earlier;

3) They could translate directly from the form used by the person quoting, often presumably an Aramaic translation of the Hebrew text. A few words are needed here only with reference to the last possibility. Of course, we expect the persons quoting, at least those who were inspired (Jesus, Paul, Peter, James, and probably Stephen), to quote accurately, so that in these cases no divergence from the original can be explained by the mere fact that somebody else's quotation is recorded. Since, however, probably most of these quotations were originally made in Aramaic according to a current oral or written Aramaic translation, certain discrepancies between the Old Testament and the New, which cannot be accounted for on the basis of the Septuagint, may have their true explanation in the use of this probable Aramaic version.

Other principles whose application must be limited. Under this heading we need to consider briefly three additional principles of explanation of apparent discrepancies between the text of the Old Testament and that of the New. These principles, in the writer's opinion, may well be at times the ground of a legitimate explanation, but they ought to be handled with utmost discrimination, lest the assured present authority of Scripture appear to be placed in jeopardy.

1) *The texts may have been altered in the process of transmission.* We have ample reasons to be grateful for the marvelous state of conservation of the text of Scripture: the New Testament possesses a degree of certainty no doubt unequalled by any other ancient text transmitted to us by manuscript; the Hebrew Old Testament has been the object of the loving and painstaking watchcare of the Jews and the accuracy of the Massoretic text has been confirmed in a striking way by the Dead Sea Scrolls. Nevertheless, it is conceivable that at times an early mistake in copying may have vitiated our texts, thereby introducing a discrepancy which was not present in the autographs. Still, it would be very injudicious to indulge in unrestrained corrections of the texts on the ground of the quotations, and the present writer has not found any instance in the New Testament where such a correction might appear as the only possible legitimate explanation of a quotation difficulty.

2) *In the quotations, as well as in other inspired texts, the personality of the writers has been respected.* It is an unsearchable mystery that the Holy Spirit could inspire the sacred writings so as to communicate his inerrancy to their very words and, at the same time, respect the freedom and personality of the writers so that we might easily recognize their style and their characteristics. The same thing is true of the quotations, for there also we may discern the individuality of the writers in their use of them, in the sources quoted, and in the method of quoting. There is, however, a dangerous distortion of this principle in the appeal made by some to slips of memory in order to explain certain difficulties

in the quotations. Now the very idea of a slip of memory undermines seriously the whole structure of inerrancy and is therefore out of keeping with a consistent upholding of plenary verbal inspiration. In fact, as C. H. Toy himself recognized—and he cannot easily be charged with undue bias in favor of the conservative view of Scripture!—so many quotations show verbal agreement with the Septuagint "that we must suppose either that they were made from a written text, or, if not, that the memory of the writers was very accurate" (*Quotations in the New Testament*, xx).

3) *The Spirit of God was free to modify the expressions that he inspired in the Old Testament.* While this is no doubt true with respect to the interpretation of Old Testament passages and with respect to allusions or distant references, the statement should not be made too glibly with respect to quotations, and some conservative writers may have been too prone to advocate this approach when other less precarious solutions might be advanced. Nevertheless, in this connection, one may well give assent to the judgment of Patrick Fairbairn:

> Even in those cases in which, for anything we can see, a closer translation would have served equally well the purpose of the writer, it may have been worthy of the inspiring Spirit, and perfectly consistent with the fullest inspiration of the original Scriptures, that the sense should have been given in a free current translation; for the principle was thereby sanctioned of a rational freedom in the handling of Scripture, as opposed to the rigid formalism and superstitious regard to the letter, which prevailed among the Rabbinical Jews. . . . The stress occasionally laid in the New Testament upon particular words in passages of the Old . . . sufficiently proves what a value attaches to the very form of the Divine communication, and how necessary it is to connect the element of inspiration with the written record as it stands. It shows that God's words are pure words, and that, if fairly interpreted, they cannot be too closely pressed. But in other cases, when nothing depended upon a rigid adherence to the letter, the practice of the sacred writers, not scrupulously to stickle about this, but to give prominence simply to the substance of the revelation, is fraught also with an important lesson; since it teaches us, that the letter is valuable only for the truth couched in it, and that the one is no further to be prized and contended for, than may be required for the exhibition of the other (*Hermeneutical Manual*, 413–14).

Meaning of the Old Testament Passages

It has been urged at times that the New Testament writers have flouted the proper laws of hermeneutics, have been guilty of artificial and rabbinical exegesis, and thus have repeatedly distorted the meaning of the Old Testament passages which they quote.

This type of objection may appear at first more weighty than those which affect merely the wording of the quotations, since an alleged discrepancy in meaning is more grievous than a mere divergence of form. Yet the problems raised in this area are probably less embarrassing to the advocates of plenary inspiration, since a verbal comparison is largely a matter of plain fact, while the assessment of the full extent of the meaning of a passage calls for the exercise of human individual judgment and fallible opinion. Few Christians, it is hoped, will have the presumption of setting forth their own interpretation as normative, when it runs directly counter to that of the Lord Jesus or of his apostles.

There is obviously a deep underlying relationship between the Old Testament and the New: one purpose pervades the whole Bible and also the various phases of human history, more especially of Israel. Thus the Old Testament can and must be considered, even in its historical narratives, as a source of prefigurements and of prophecies. It has been widely acknowledged that, in spite of certain difficult passages, the New Testament interpretation of the Old manifests a strikingly illuminating understanding of Old Testament Scripture. C. H. Dodd, although not a defender of verbal inspiration, could write: "In general . . . the writers of the New Testament, in making use of passages from the Old Testament, remain true to the main intention of their writers" (*According to the Scriptures* [London: Nisbet, 1952], 130). And again: "We have before us a considerable intellectual feat. The various scriptures are acutely interpreted along lines already discernible within the Old Testament canon itself or in pre-Christian Judaism—in many cases, I believe, lines which start from their first, historical, intention—and these lines are carried forward to fresh results" (ibid., 109).

There are certain Old Testament passages in which the connection with the New Testament is so clear that there can hardly be doubt about their applicability and about the fact that the Old Testament writers foresaw some events or some principles of the new covenant. This is not necessary in every case, however, and the Spirit of God may very well have inspired expressions which potentially transcended the thoughts of the sacred writers and of those to whom they addressed themselves. This certainly occurred in the case of Caiaphas (John 11:49–52), and there is no ground to deny the possibility of such a process in the inspiration of the Old Testament Scripture.

While the doctrine of verbal inspiration requires that we should accept any New Testament interpretation of an Old Testament text as legitimate, it does not require that such interpretation be necessarily viewed as exclusive or exhaustive of the full Old Testament meaning. In many cases the New Testament makes a particular application of principles stated in the Old, whose fulfillment is accomplished in more than a single event. Thus certain Old Testament prophecies may have conveyed to the original hearers a meaning more restricted than the perspective opened in the New Testament pages. The original understanding was a legitimate interpretation of the prophecy, yet one which does not preclude the propriety of the larger vistas, authoritatively revealed in the New Testament.

Not all the passages quoted in the New Testament are necessarily to be considered as definite prophecies, but many are cited as simply characterizing in a striking way the New Testament situation. At times the New Testament writers may have simply used Old Testament language without intending to imply that there is a distinct relationship of prophecy to fulfillment, or of antitype to type.

Writing about this subject, C. H. Toy makes a remark which he apparently intends only with respect to apostolic times, but which may well be viewed as having more general reference: "The deeper the reverence for the departed Lord and for the divine word, the greater the disposition to find him everywhere" (quotations in the *New Testament*, xxv). Conservatives hope that, judged by this standard, they will not be found to have less reverence for their Lord and for the divine Word than the New Testament writers!

In conclusion, one could wish to quote at length some remarks of B. B. Warfield (*The Inspiration and Authority of the Bible*, 218–20), which for the sake of brevity we shall be constrained to summarize here. The student of Scripture is not bound to provide the solution of all the difficulties which he encounters in the Bible. It is better to leave matters unharmonized than to have recourse to strained or artificial exegesis. Even when no solution of a difficulty is offered, we are not thereby driven to assume that the problem is insoluble.

> Every unharmonized passage remains a case of difficult harmony and does not pass into the category of objections to plenary inspiration. It can pass into the category of objections only if we are prepared to affirm that we clearly see that it is, on any conceivable hypothesis of its meaning, clearly inconsistent with the Biblical doctrine of inspiration. In that case we would no doubt need to give up the Biblical doctrine of inspiration; but with it we must also give up our confidence in the Biblical writers as teachers of doctrine" (ibid., 220).

It has been the writer's privilege to devote substantial time to the consideration of all quotations of the Old Testament in the New. This study has led him to the conclusion that the principles mentioned above can provide in every case a possible explanation of the difficulties at hand in perfect harmony with the doctrine of the inerrancy of Scripture. There is no claim here that all the difficulties are readily dispelled, or that we are in possession of the final solution of every problem. Nevertheless, possible if not plausible explanations are at hand in every case known to the present writer. It is therefore with some confidence that this presentation is made. In fact, the quotations, which are often spoken of as raising one of the major difficulties against the view of plenary inspiration, upon examination turn out to be a confirmation of this doctrine rather than an invalidation of it. To this concurs the judgment of men who can surely be quoted as impartial witnesses, in statements such as the following, made precisely with reference to Old Testament quotations in the New:

> We know, from the general tone of the New Testament, that it regards the Old Testament, as all the Jews then did, as the revealed and inspired word of God, and clothed with his authority (C. H. Toy, *Quotations,* xxx).
>
> Our authors view the words of the Old Testament as *immediate* words of God, and introduce them explicitly as such, even those which are not in the least related as sayings of God. They see nothing in the sacred book, which is merely the word of the human authors and not at the same time the very word of God Himself. In everything that stands "written," God Himself is speaking to them (R. Rothe, *Zur Dogmatik* [Gotha: Perthes, 1869], 177–78).
>
> In quoting the Old Testament, the New Testament writers proceed consistently from the presupposition that they have Holy Scripture in hand. . . . The actual author is God or the Holy Spirit, and both, as also frequently the *graphe,* are represented as speaking either directly or through the Old Testament writers (E. Huehn, *Die Alttestamentlichen Citate . . . im Neuen Testament* [Tübingen: Mohr, 1900], 272).

Such statements, coming as they are from the pen of men who were not at all inclined to favor the conservative approach to the Scripture, are no doubt more impressive than anything a conservative scholar could say. They may be allowed to stand at the end of this study as expressing in a striking way the writer's own conclusions on the subject.

2

The Use of the Old Testament in the New

Klyne Snodgrass

Taken from the book, *New Testament Criticism and Interpretation* by David Alan Black and David S. Dockery. Copyright © 1991 by David Alan Black and David S. Dockery. Used by permission of Zondervan Publishing House.

No subject is perhaps more important for the understanding of the Christian faith than the use of the Old Testament in the New Testament. The Hebrew and Aramaic Scriptures were, of course, the only Bible the early Christian thinkers and writers had. Many of these Christians were transformed Jews and would have known Hebrew. Other early Christians would have known the Jewish Scriptures only in Greek translation. Regardless of their language, however, all Christians would have been engaged in relating the two most important realities of their lives—the Scriptures and Jesus Christ.

At every point early Christians attempted to understand their Scriptures in the new light of the ministry, death, and resurrection of Jesus Christ. They used the Old Testament to prove their Christian theology and to solve Christian problems. The Old Testament provided the substructure of the New Testament theology.[1] The Old Testament also provided the language and imagery for much of New Testament thought, although this is not always obvious to a casual reader. Therefore, New Testament concepts must be understood from Old Testament passages. Virtually every New Testament subject must be approached through

1. C. H. Dodd, *According to the Scriptures: The Sub-structure of New Testament Theology* (London: Nisbet, 1952).

the contribution of the Old Testament. As Augustine observed, "The New Testament is in the Old concealed; the Old Testament is in the New revealed."[2]

However, not everything in the Old Testament is brought into the new faith. There is both continuity and discontinuity between the Old Testament and the New Testament. That is, while some parts of the New Testament are direct extensions of the Old Testament message, some parts of the Old Testament message have been superseded. Even so, none of the New Testament writers ever suggests that the Old Testament is less than fully the Word of God.

The analysis of this continuity and discontinuity is a much more fascinating and intriguing study than many people have realized. Too often Old Testament texts are considered as only so many prophecies to be calculated and at which to marvel. Any serious reading will show that the way the New Testament uses the Old Testament is far different from what we expected or have been led to believe. The New Testament writers have been disturbingly creative in their use of the Old Testament. Not only do New Testament quotations of the Old Testament sometimes differ from the Hebrew and Aramaic Scriptures on which our translations are based, the New Testament writers also have applied texts in surprising ways. For example, why does Matthew 2:18 view Jeremiah 31:15 as a prophecy of Herod's slaying of innocent babies, while Jeremiah's words obviously relate to the Babylonian invasion of Judea? Do the New Testament writers twist the Old Testament Scriptures, as some have charged?[3]

In addition to being fascinating, the study of the use of the Old Testament in the New Testament is comprehensive and demanding. To enter this arena is to be engaged in studies on the history of the text. Serious study requires the knowledge of Hebrew, Greek, and Aramaic because one has to compare the New Testament wording with the Masoretic Hebrew text, the Septuagint (the translation of the Old Testament into Greek), information from the Dead Sea Scrolls, the targums (Aramaic paraphrases of the Old Testament), and other Jewish or Christian uses of the Old Testament. Do not think that this is an exercise in tedium, however, for the use of the Old Testament in the New Testament also engages a person in hermeneutics, exegesis, and theology, study that in many cases will require adjustment of previous conclusions. How the Old Testament is viewed is *the* theological issue dividing many Christians. Dispensational theology, which views God as operating in different ways in different eras, and covenant theology, which

---

2. Augustine, *Quaestionum in Heptateuchum libri Septem* 2.73.
3. See S. Vernon McCasland, "Matthew Twists the Scriptures," *JBL* 80 (1961): 143–48.

emphasizes the unity of God's action throughout history, divide from each other and also from other approaches specifically over this issue.[4]

Our subject also has the potential of being a troublesome one. There are issues here that have not been treated adequately. We often proclaim our theories about Scripture in the abstract, but the use of the Old Testament by New Testament writers raises questions about our theories. Are all the discussions about inerrancy or other labels irrelevant in view of the selectivity by which the New Testament writers use the Old Testament? Obviously there are numerous Old Testament texts that were and are ignored by Christians, and we would argue that many are not to be implemented.[5] Why?

Brief Historical Considerations

The question of how the Old Testament should be appropriated exists already with the teaching of Jesus. His way of reading the Old Testament angered the religious authorities, for he did not focus on sabbath keeping and laws of purity as they did. In fact, according to the Gospels, Jesus appeared to flaunt violation of the purity code by touching lepers, a woman with an issue of blood, and corpses, and by eating with defiled people (note especially Matt. 8–9 in contrast with Lev. 13; 15:19–20; and Ezra 10:11). He argued that *sin* defiled a person, not eating with unclean hands (Matt. 15:10–20). Mark 7:19 extends Jesus' teaching so that all foods are clean.[6] So much for dietary laws! Jesus focused on the intent of the law in the love commands and on the theme of mercy. Still, he claimed that none of the Scripture was set aside (Matt. 5:17–20) and complained that the Jewish authorities substituted human traditions for the commands of God (Matt. 15:3).[7] In Luke 24:44–45 the risen Christ claimed that all three sections of the Hebrew Scriptures (Law, Prophets, and Writings) find their fulfillment in him. He then opened the mind of his disciples to understand the Scriptures. Clearly the issue both for the earthly and risen Christ is *how* the Hebrew

---

4. See the collection of essays edited by John S. Feinberg, *Continuity and Discontinuity: Perspectives on the Relationship Between the Old and New Testaments* (Westchester, Ill.: Crossway, 1988). The main problem is how promises to the nation of Israel should be treated.

5. No one would argue that we should test a suspected adulteress with "bitter waters" (Num. 5:11–12) or that we should execute heretics (Deut. 13:6–7) or Sabbath breakers (Exod. 31:15). The number of such texts is not small.

6. See Robert Banks, *Jesus and the Law in the Synoptic Tradition* (Cambridge: Cambridge University Press, 1975), 132–46. Is Jesus' thought from Prov. 4:23? See also Acts 10:9–16; Rom. 14:14; 1 Cor. 10:26–27; and 1 Tim. 4:4, which place Christian conclusions in opposition with dietary restrictions in the Old Testament.

7. On the question of Jesus and the law in Matthew, see my "Matthew and the Law," *Society of Biblical Literature 1988 Seminar Papers,* ed. David J. Lull (Atlanta: Scholars, 1988), 536–54.

Scriptures are to be interpreted correctly. The usual reading of the religious authorities was not sufficient.

The same question dominated the life of the early church. When asked whether he understood the text from Isaiah 53, the Ethiopian eunuch replied, "How am I able unless someone should guide me?" Beginning from that text Philip then proclaimed Christ to him (Acts 8:26–35). This account points both to the Christological way in which the early church interpreted the Old Testament and to the need of guidance in understanding.

One crucial issue for the early church was the question how to treat the Old Testament commands on circumcision. At the "Jerusalem Council," surprisingly, explicit Old Testament commands on circumcision were set aside because of Christian experience *and other Old Testament texts* focusing on the inclusion of the Gentiles (Acts 15). One can well ask how Paul could say, "Circumcision is nothing and uncircumcision is nothing, but keeping the commands of God is what counts" (1 Cor. 7:19), when circumcision was obviously an Old Testament command. Clearly it was no longer a relevant command for him. Still, the discussions of law in the epistles to the Galatians and to the Romans show how much the debate continued over the right use of the Old Testament. However, even when conclusions were drawn that a command was not binding, they were made from the Old Testament itself and with no thought of nullifying the Word of God.

In the second century a radical solution to the problem of the Old Testament emerged. Marcion of Sinope, influenced by Gnosticism, argued that the whole Old Testament should be rejected, even though he found value in some sections of the Old Testament. Marcion repudiated the God of the Old Testament as the creator of evil and sought to separate Christianity from anything Jewish. Consequently, he accepted as canonical only Paul's epistles (excluding the Pastorals) and the Gospel of Luke. In addition, he expurgated sections of these books that he felt were influenced too much by the Old Testament.[8] Unfortunately, there are still those around who are essentially Marcionite in their approach.

Most Christians, thankfully, did not follow Marcion. Instead, they sought to extend the interpretive practices of the New Testament writers and appropriate the Old Testament for Christian purposes in new ways. The Old Testament was combed for passages that could be under-

---

8. See Irenaeus, *Against Heresies* 1.27.2; Tertullian, *Against Marcion* 4.5–7 and 5.2–4; Richard N. Longenecker, "Three Ways of Understanding Relations Between the Testaments: Historically and Today," *Tradition and Interpretation in the New Testament*, ed. Gerald F. Hawthorne with Otto Betz (Grand Rapids: Eerdmans, 1987), 22–23; and E. C. Blackman, *Marcion and His Influence* (London: SPCK, 1948), 23–24, 42–43, and 113–24.

stood of Christ and his church. Christians used the Old Testament to teach morality, to explain who Jesus was, and to provide illustrations of Christian thought. Unfortunately, however, usually there was little historical sensitivity or treatment of extended texts. Instead, the Old Testament was viewed as prophecy about Christ, as providing types of Christ, or as holding hidden ideas and symbols that may be spiritually understood through allegory.[9] Justin Martyr, for example, and numerous others found references to Christ in places most of us could hardly imagine. The stone cut out without hands in Daniel 2:45 was understood as a reference to the virgin birth. Nearly every stick, piece of wood, or tree was understood as pointing to the crucifixion.[10]

In the centuries that followed, the Old Testament and New Testament were interpreted along two diverse New Testament paths. The Antiochean School, represented by John Chrysostom and Theodore of Mopsuestia, argued against allegorizing and engaged in fairly straightforward exegesis. Far more influential, but far more unacceptable from a modern viewpoint, was the Alexandrian School represented by Origen and Augustine. This school engaged in allegorical exegesis, by which a spiritual meaning could be assigned to a text, especially if that text were troublesome.[11] Allegorizing made it easy to read Christian theology into Old Testament texts. Allegorical exegesis was dominant until the Reformation and is still encountered today as pastors read into texts spiritual meanings that have nothing to do with the original purposes of the authors.

The Protestant reformers turned away from allegorical exegesis to focus on the plain meaning of the text, although Martin Luther on occasion still allegorized. Both Luther and John Calvin were aware of the unity and the differences between the Testaments. Luther stressed the discontinuity between the Testaments because of his distinction between law and gospel. Calvin, on the other hand, focused on continuity between the Testaments and argued for a "third use" of the law.[12] By this he argued what Luther was not ready to accept, that the law still has a role in guiding Christian morality. These differences in under-

9. For information on the early church's treatment of the Old Testament, see R. P. C. Hanson, "Biblical Exegesis in the Early Church," *The Cambridge History of the Bible*, ed. P. R. Ackroyd and C. F. Evans (Cambridge: Cambridge University Press, 1970), 1:412–53; Robert M. Grant with David Tracy, *A Short History of the Interpretation of the Bible* (Philadelphia: Fortress, 1984); Karlfried Froehlich, *Biblical Interpretation in the Early Church* (Philadelphia: Fortress, 1984); and James L. Kugel and Rowan A. Greer, *Early Biblical Interpretation* (Philadelphia: Westminster, 1986).

10. See Justin, *Dialogue with Trypho* 70 and 76 (on the stone of Dan. 2) and 86 and 90–91 (on wood and trees and other symbols of the cross).

11. On the Antiochean and Alexandrian schools of interpretation, see Richard N. Longenecker, "Three Ways of Understanding Relations between the Testaments: Historically and Today," 22–32; and Grant with Tracy, 52–72.

standing the Old Testament have characterized the followers of Luther and Calvin to the present day.

How the Old Testament should be viewed in relation to the New Testament is still a matter of debate. In his *Two Testaments: One Bible,* D. L. Baker presented eight modern solutions to the problem of the relation of the Testaments.[13] Some of these solutions, such as that by A. A. Van Ruler, place priority on the Old Testament.[14] Some are much more negative in the assessment of the Old Testament, such as the view of Rudolf Bultmann, for whom the Old Testament is the necessary presupposition of the New Testament, but in actuality is only a history of Israel's *failure.*[15] The other solutions all view both Testaments positively, but vary in the degree to which they see the Old Testament as Christological, how they deal with Old Testament history, and how they balance continuity and discontinuity.

The main problem for modern readers in the New Testament use of the Old Testament is the tendency of New Testament writers to use Old Testament texts in ways different from their original intention. A particular expression came into use to provide a solution. *Sensus plenior* is a Latin term popular among Roman Catholics and also among some evangelicals. It refers to the "fuller sense" God intended for a text beyond the human author's intention. The New Testament writers are viewed as inspired by the Spirit to understand and apply this fuller sense.[16] For some this is a solution; for others it is an obfuscation.

12. For the approaches of Luther and Calvin, see Grant with Tracy, 92–99; Roland Bainton, "The Bible in the Reformation," *The Cambridge History of the Bible,* ed. S. L. Greenslade (Cambridge: Cambridge University Press, 1963), 3:1–37; Paul Althaus, *The Theology of Martin Luther,* trans. Robert C. Schultz (Philadelphia: Fortress, 1966), 86–102; Wilhelm Niesel, *The Theology of Calvin,* trans. Harold Knight (Philadelphia: Westminster, 1956), 104–9. On the third use of the law, see Calvin, *The Institutes of the Christian Religion,* ed. John T. McNeill, trans. Ford Lewis Battles (Philadelphia: Westminster), 2.7.12.

13. D. L. Baker, *Two Testaments: One Bible* (Downers Grove, Ill.: InterVarsity, 1976).

14. Arnold A. van Ruler, *The Christian Church and the Old Testament,* trans. Geoffrey W. Bromiley (Grand Rapids: Eerdmans, 1971).

15. Rudolf Bultmann, "The Significance of the Old Testament for the Christian Faith," *The Old Testament and Christian Faith,* ed. Bernhard W. Anderson (New York: Herder and Herder, 1969), 8–35, especially 14–15; and "Prophecy and Fulfillment," *Essays on Old Testament Hermeneutics,* ed. Claus Westermann; English trans. ed. James Luther Mays (Richmond: John Knox, 1963), 50–75, especially 75.

16. On *sensus plenior,* see Raymond Edward Brown, *The Sensus Plenior of Sacred Scripture* (Baltimore: St. Mary's University, 1955); "The History and Development of the Theory of a Sensus Plenior," *CBQ* 15 (1953): 141–62; "The *Sensus Plenior* in the Last Ten Years," *CBQ* 25 (1963): 262–85; William Sanford LaSor, "The *Sensus Plenior* and Biblical Interpretation," *Scripture, Tradition, and Interpretation,* ed. W. Ward Gasque and William Sanford LaSor (Grand Rapids: Eerdmans, 1978), 260–77; and Douglas Moo, "The Problem of *Sensus Plenior,*" *Hermeneutics, Authority, and Canon,* ed. D. A. Carson and John D. Woodbridge (Grand Rapids: Zondervan, 1986), 179–211.

The questions that emerge from this historical overview cannot be neglected. Is the Old Testament really revelation for Christians? Can it be appropriated without being violated? To what degree does it tell of Jesus Christ? How do we deal with the discontinuity?

Distribution and Frequency of the Use of the Old Testament in the New Testament

Interesting results derive from an examination of Old Testament quotations and allusions printed in bold print in the United Bible Society's first edition of *The Greek New Testament*.[17] Three-fourths of the 401 quotations and allusions appear in the Gospels, Acts, Romans, and Hebrews. Of those 401 uses of the Old Testament, 195 have some type of accompanying formula such as "it is written" to inform the reader that a Scripture text is being cited.[18] In the remaining uses the only way the reader would know the Old Testament was being cited is by knowing the wording from the Old Testament text.

How and where the Old Testament is used depends on the author's purposes. Whereas Matthew focused on Jesus as the fulfillment of the

17. The first edition UBS Greek New Testament has more passages in bold print and a much better index than later editions.

18. The actual statistics of usage in the first edition UBS text are: Matthew, sixty-two quotations or allusions in bold print with thirty-two of them having an introductory formula; Mark, thirty with eleven having an introductory formula; Luke, thirty-nine with fifteen; John, eighteen with fourteen; Acts, thirty-seven with twenty-three; Romans, fifty-four with forty; 1 Corinthians, sixteen with ten; 2 Corinthians, twelve with five; Galatians, eleven with five; Ephesians, ten with one; Philippians, one with zero; Colossians, zero; 1 Thessalonians, one with zero; 2 Thessalonians, four with zero; 1 Timothy, two with one; 2 Timothy, one with zero; Titus, zero; Philemon, zero; Hebrews, fifty-nine with thirty; James, six with four; 1 Peter, fifteen with three; 2 Peter, two with zero; 1 John, zero; 2 John, zero; 3 John, zero; Jude, one with one; Revelation, twenty with zero. There are, of course, other allusions besides the ones in bold print in the UBS text, and other editions will assess quotations differently. There are a variety of introductory formulae. See Joseph A. Fitzmyer, "The Use of Explicit Old Testament Quotations in Qumran Literature and in the New Testament," *NTS* 7 (1960–1961): 299–305.

On the extent of the canon in the first century, see Roger Beckwith, *The Old Testament Canon of the New Testament Church* (Grand Rapids: Eerdmans, 1985). It is significant that there are no quotations from the apocryphal and pseudepigraphal writings. There are, however, allusions to these writings.

Helpful treatments of the use of the Old Testament in the New Testament can be found in C. K. Barrett, "The Interpretation of the Old Testament in the New," *The Cambridge History of the Bible*, ed. P. R. Ackroyd and C. F. Evans (Cambridge: Cambridge University Press, 1970), 1:377–411; E. Earle Ellis, "How the New Testament Uses the Old," *New Testament Interpretation* (Grand Rapids: Eerdmans, 1978), 199–219; and D. Moody Smith, "The Use of the Old Testament in the New," *The Use of the Old Testament in the New and Other Essays*, ed. James M. Efird (Durham: Duke University Press, 1972), 3–65.

Old Testament, Paul did not use this language, even though he believed it (Rom. 1:2). Paul's use of the Old Testament is clearly circumstantial. When he discussed the relation of Jews to salvation in Christ in the epistle to the Romans, he quoted the Old Testament fifty-four times. But in several of his letters he makes little or no reference to the Old Testament. Colossians, for example, does not have any explicit reference to the Old Testament. The author of Revelation never quotes the Old Testament, but he uses wording of the Old Testament as much as any other writer. He merely reuses Old Testament language and images to make his point. The more an author attempts to explain the identity of Jesus or address Jews, the more likely the Old Testament will be used. To the degree that the identity of Jesus is assumed or that Gentiles are addressed, there is usually less use of the Old Testament.[19] The New Testament books with the most dependence on the Old Testament are Hebrews, Revelation, and 1 Peter.

Methods and Hermeneutical Assumptions

The fascinating aspect of this subject is the *way* in which Old Testament texts are used. As is clear already, not all New Testament writers use the Old Testament in what we would consider straightforward ways. Straightforward uses do occur, of course. Old Testament texts are used as direct prophecy (Matt. 2:5–6) or as direct logical proof of an argument (Matt. 4:4–5; Rom. 4). New Testament writers adapt the words of the Old Testament for new purposes in easily understood ways. Analogies to the ministry of Jesus are found in Old Testament events (John 3:14). Words of judgment in Hosea 13:14 become words of victory in 1 Corinthians 15:54–55.[20] Such uses are easily justified as merely the rhetorical adaptation of familiar language. It is easy to understand the use of an Old Testament text as an illustration (1 Cor. 10:7–8). It is not so easy to understand how a text that was not intended as messianic (Deut. 18:15) becomes understood as messianic (Acts 3:22–23).[21] This is not a straightforward use. It is also not easy to see how Hosea 11:1, which refers to the exodus of Israel from Egypt, can be fulfilled by Joseph taking Jesus and Mary to Egypt (Matt. 2:15). Nor is it easy to see how words clearly addressed to Isaiah (6:9–10) are seen as fulfilled in Jesus (John 12:39–41). Such examples of unexpected uses of the Old Testament could be multiplied easily.

19. First Corinthians is an exception.
20. Hos. 13:14 should be translated, as in the New English Bible, with questions and call for death to bring its plagues. The passage expects judgment.
21. Deut. 18:15–16 refers to prophets in general who serve as spokespersons for God to the community. Note that 18:20–21 refers to prophets who speak falsely.

The key to understanding the New Testament writers' use of the Old Testament is in understanding the presuppositions and exegetical methods by which they operated. Most of this necessary framework can be gleaned from the New Testament itself, but the discovery of the Qumran Scrolls has provided helpful insight and parallels to the practices of the New Testament writers.

The first presupposition about which we need to know is *corporate solidarity*.[22] This expression refers to the oscillation or reciprocal relation between the individual and the community that existed in the Semitic mind. The act of the individual is not merely an individual act, for it affects the community and vice versa. The individual is often representative of the community and vice versa. Achan sinned and the nation suffered (Josh. 7). An individual speaks in Psalm 118:10, but almost certainly he is representative of the nation. The "servant" is a collective term for the nation (Isa. 44:1), but it also refers to the remnant (Isa. 49:5) and probably also to an individual. Corporate solidarity should not be viewed as strange, for it is the basis for Paul's understanding of the atonement: "One died for all; therefore, all died" (2 Cor. 5:14).

The representative character of Jesus' ministry, which is closely related to corporate solidarity, is one of the most important keys in understanding him and the way Old Testament texts are applied to him. The christological titles "Servant," "Son of man," and "Son of God" were all representative titles that were applied to Israel first. Jesus took on these titles because he had taken Israel's task.[23] He was representative of Israel and in solidarity with her. God's purposes for Israel were now taken up in his ministry. If this were true, what had been used to describe Israel could legitimately be used of him.

The second presupposition is *correspondence in history*, which is sometimes referred to as "typology."[24] Correspondence in history is ac-

22. See Richard N. Longenecker, *Biblical Exegesis in the Apostolic Period* (Grand Rapids: Eerdmans, 1975), 93–94; E. Earle Ellis, "Biblical Interpretation in the New Testament Church," *Mikra,* ed. Martin Jan Mulder and Harry Sysling; *Compendia Rerum Iudaicarum ad Novum Testamentum,* sec. 2, pt. 1 (Philadelphia: Fortress, 1988), 716–20; H. Wheeler Robinson, *Corporate Personality in Ancient Israel* (Philadelphia: Fortress, 1964); and Russell Philip Shedd, *Man in Community* (Grand Rapids: Eerdmans, 1964).

23. N. T. Wright, "Jesus, Israel, and the Cross," *Society of Biblical Literature 1985 Seminar Papers,* ed. Kent Harold Richards (Atlanta: Scholars, 1985), 75–96, especially 83–84.

24. On correspondence in history, see Ellis, "Biblical Interpretation in the New Testament Church," 713–16; Baker, 239–70; Gerhard von Rad, "Typological Interpretation of the Old Testament," *Essays on Old Testament Hermeneutics,* ed. Claus Westermann; English trans. ed. James Luther Mays (Richmond: John Knox, 1963), 17–39; Leonhard Goppelt, *Typos: The Typological Interpretation of the Old Testament in the New,* trans. Donald H. Madvig (Grand Rapids: Eerdmans, 1982). "Correspondence in history" is to be preferred to "typology"; the latter is too restricting and too associated with abuse.

tually a conviction about God and the way he works. The presupposition is that the way God worked in the past is mirrored in the way he works in the present and future. There is a correspondence between what happened to God's people in the past and what happens now or in the future. Climactic events in Israel's history become the paradigms by which new events are explained. For example, the exodus was the climactic event by which God saved his people. Later writers use exodus terminology to describe God's saving his people from Assyria (Isa. 11:6) or salvation generally. The suffering of a righteous person (Ps. 22) finds correspondence in the crucifixion of Jesus (Matt. 22:39–46).[25]

The important point about correspondence in history is that the text is not used *up* by a single event. Isaiah 40:3 was understood as a classic expression of God's salvation from Babylon. Malachi 3:1 reused the language to express the promise of future salvation. The New Testament writers saw John the Baptist as the one in whom this verse finds its climax.[26] He was the voice crying in the wilderness to prepare the way before the Lord for ultimate salvation (Luke 3:4–6). Still, Luke 9:52 can adapt the words of Isaiah 40:3 to the disciples who prepare the way for Jesus as he goes to Jerusalem.[27] Those same words from Isaiah can even be applied to others who prepare the way.[28] Often words that find their climax in Jesus find further correspondence in his followers. If Jesus is the fulfillment of Isaiah 49:6 as the light to the Gentiles (Luke 2:32), the words can still be applied to Paul (Acts 13:47). If Jesus is a living stone, partly on the basis of Isaiah 28:16 and Psalm 118:22, his followers are living stones (1 Pet. 2:4–5). If he is the anointed One, they too are anointed (2 Cor. 1:21). If 2 Samuel 7:14 can be interpreted of Jesus in Hebrews 1:5, it can also be applied to Christians in 2 Corinthians 6:18. We have not interpreted a text appropriately until we have determined how it corresponds or does not correspond with our present situation.

A third presupposition of the early church is that they lived in the days of *eschatological fulfillment*.[29] They believed that the end time had

---

25. Jesus' cry of dereliction no doubt expressed the initial awareness of correspondence with Ps. 22. This psalm must be seen as the lament of a righteous sufferer and not as a prophecy of Jesus' death.

26. In John 1:23 it is John the Baptist himself who uses Isa. 40:3 as a description of his role.

27. Isa. 40:3 was also used at Qumran as a description of the role of the community. See my "Streams of Tradition Emerging from Isaiah 40:1–5 and Their Adaptation in the New Testament," *JSNT* 8 (1980): 24–45, for a discussion of the use of Isa. 40:3.

28. Even if they are not applied in the same way.

29. On eschatological fulfillment as a hermeneutical presupposition, see Ellis, "Biblical Interpretation in the New Testament Church," 710–13; Longenecker, *Biblical Exegesis in the Apostolic Period*, 95; Donald Juel, *Messianic Exegesis* (Philadelphia: Fortress,

dawned upon them (1 Cor. 10:11). This presupposition has a near parallel in the beliefs of the people of the Qumran community. They and many other Jews had an eschatological focus in their reading of the Hebrew Scriptures. Whereas for some Jews the end time belonged to an unknown future, the people at Qumran believed they were an end-time community from whose gates God would break out very soon in victorious conquest over his enemies. The early Christians viewed themselves as an end-time community as well, but there are major differences. For Christians, the end time was not just soon to appear. It had *already* appeared in the ministry of Jesus and especially in his resurrection and the pouring out of the Spirit. They could look at these events and know that God's kingdom had broken into their midst, even though its full realization was yet to come.

Old Testament texts that were viewed eschatologically were, therefore, texts that were descriptive of the reality they experienced. This presupposition can be seen clearly in a text like 1 Peter 1:12, where the author states that it was revealed to Old Testament prophets that, not to themselves but to his readers, they were ministering their prophecies. If the Scriptures find their *climax* in Christ, surely what is written there is especially for his followers. Similar expressions of this hermeneutical presupposition are seen in Romans 15:4, 1 Corinthians 9:10, and especially 10:11 ("These things happened to those people as an example, and they were written for our admonition upon whom the ends of the ages has come").[30]

The fourth presupposition is actually inherent in the third, but needs to be made explicit. The early church, like most of Judaism, assumed that the Scriptures were *christological.* Texts that may have been general statements about the nation, prophets, priests, or kings were often *idealized* in anticipation of God's end-time deliverer who would fill the categories as no one else had. David had been the king *par excellence*, but one day there would be a king like him, only better.[31] The early church applied such texts to Jesus because of their conviction about his identity. The conviction about his identity did *not* derive from the Old Testament. They did not find texts and then find Jesus. They found Jesus and then saw how the Scriptures fit with him. They were not *proving* his identity in the technical sense so much as they were demonstrat-

---

1988), 49–56; F. F. Bruce, *Biblical Exegesis in the Qumran Texts* (London: Tyndale, 1960), especially 9–19.

30. Rom. 4:23–24 is slightly different, but also represents an eschatological presupposition.

31. The Jews' expectation of an idealized Davidic king is well known. Note especially Jer. 23:5–8; 33:15–18; Ps. 89; and 4Q Florilegium. See Jeul, 59–88.

ing how the Scriptures fit with him. Often they were merely following his lead in pointing to texts that summarized his ministry.[32]

Before examples of how these presuppositions are evidenced in specific New Testament quotations of Old Testament texts, another point needs to be made. Too often people look only at Old Testament texts and New Testament quotations without asking what those Old Testament texts had become in the history of Judaism. Specifically because of christological or eschatological concerns, texts had a "life" in Judaism that led to their being understood in specific ways. These traditional interpretations have influenced the way Jesus and the early church adapted texts. Many times they are only picking up or adapting common understandings so as to make their point. They were only entering into the conversation of their hearers. The Dead Sea Scrolls have been particularly helpful in showing how texts were understood in the time of Jesus.

With these presuppositions, and with the awareness that there were traditional interpretations, we can understand why Old Testament texts were adapted the way they were. The presuppositions of corporate solidarity and correspondence in history are both at work in the application to Jesus of Hosea 11:1 ("Out of Egypt I called my son," Matt. 2:15). Since Jesus, like Israel, is Son of God, there is parallelism between what happens to these two "sons." The application of Jeremiah 31:15 to the slaying of babies by Herod is also understandable. This is not merely correspondence between two sets of mothers who cry. Jeremiah 31 is an eschatological text, and the words immediately following 31:15 are words of comfort and hope for salvation that climax in 31:31–34 with the focus on the new covenant. Matthew and his readers know that Jesus has ushered in that eschatological time.[33] There is both correspondence and fulfillment.

The application of Isaiah 6:9–10 to the ministry of Jesus is another example of correspondence in history. This Old Testament text was spoken specifically to Isaiah about the hardness of heart of his hearers. Other Old Testament prophets picked up the language of Isaiah 6:9–10 so that these words became the classic expression of hardness of heart (cf. Jer. 5:21; Ezek. 12:2). In the synoptic Gospels the words are applied to Jesus' ministry as evidence of the hardness of heart of Jews in not responding to his teaching in parables (Matt. 13:14–15/Mark 4:12/Luke 8:10). They are applied in a similar way in John 12:39–40 as a summary

32. There are several Old Testament texts that seem to have provided the framework for Jesus' understanding of his ministry. Of primary significance are Ps. 118:22–26; Isa. 61:1–3; Dan. 7:13–14. The impact of Isa. 53 is debated but seems probable.

33. On the infancy quotations in Matthew, see Longenecker, *Biblical Exegesis in the Apostolic Period*, 140–47; Raymond E. Brown, *The Birth of the Messiah* (Garden City: Doubleday, 1979), 96–116, 143–53, 184–88, and 219–25.

statement marking the rejection of Jesus by the Jews. Interestingly, these words are also addressed to the *disciples* in Mark 8:18 to ask whether they have hardened hearts. Isaiah 6:9–10 finds further correspondence as a description of the rejection of the Jews in Paul's ministry (Acts 28:26–27).[34]

Such examples suggest that the statement "Jesus is the fulfillment of the Scriptures" might be more adequately expressed as "Jesus is the *climax* of the Scriptures." His identity and ministry are mirrored there in unique ways, but "fulfillment" suggests a singularity and a focus on predictive prophecy that does justice only to some texts. Many Old Testament texts had other initial referents and also found later referents after Jesus. They find their coherence and true brilliance in him. This suggestion is not an effort to diminish the importance of predictive prophecy. It is merely a recognition that other uses of the Old Testament are common in the New Testament.

The use of Deuteronomy 18:15–19 is a good example of a text that had a life in Judaism. This text was not messianic originally, but the promise of a prophet like Moses became idealized (possibly because of Deut. 34:10) so that hope emerged for an eschatological prophet. In both the Samaritan Pentateuch and in 4Q Testimonia of the Dead Sea Scrolls, Deuteronomy 18:18 is understood messianically. This expectation of an eschatological prophet is obvious in John 1:21, where John the Baptist is asked whether he is *the* prophet, and in 6:14, where people exclaim that Jesus is "truly *the* prophet, the one coming into the world." In Acts 3:22 Peter uses this expectation to define the identity of Jesus for his hearers.[35] Such usage arises from a context where certain assumptions were held about a text and where those assumptions become the tools to describe something else.

Pesher and Midrash

In addition to the Jewish presuppositions we have mentioned, an interpreter of the New Testament's use of the Old Testament needs to be aware of other Jewish methods of treating the Scriptures. One method of appropriating Scripture for some Jews, particularly Jews from Qumran, was *pesher*. This practice does not seek to explain a text so much as it seeks to show where a text fits. The word *pesher* derives from an Aramaic root meaning "solution." The presupposition is that the text contains a mystery communicated by God that is not understood until the

---

34. See Craig A. Evans, *To See and Not Perceive: Isaiah 6:9–10 in Early Jewish and Christian Interpretation* (Sheffield: JSOT, 1989).

35. See Richard N. Longenecker, *The Christology of Early Jewish Christianity* (London: SCM, 1970), 32–38; and Howard M. Teeple, *The Mosaic Eschatological Prophet* (Philadelphia: Society of Biblical Literature, 1957). Note also John 7:40.

solution is made known by an inspired interpreter. With *pesher,* the starting point for understanding is not the Old Testament text, but a historical event or person. By viewing a text in the framework of an event, a *pesher* interpretation provides a solution to the mystery involved in understanding. In effect, *pesher* says "This [event or person] is that [of which the Scripture speaks]."[36] For example, the Qumran *Pesher* on Habakkuk understands the judgment spoken against Babylon (Hab. 2:7–8) to refer to a wicked priest in Jerusalem who caused trouble for the Qumran community (1QpH 8:13–14).

Pesher also occurs in the New Testament. The most obvious example is Acts 2:17.[37] The event of the pouring out of the Spirit provided a framework for understanding Joel 2:28–29. The event is seen as an actualization of the text.

The more common method of interpreting Scripture among Jews, however, was *midrash. Midrash* derives from a Hebrew word meaning "to seek" and refers to interpretive exposition. The starting point is the text itself, and the concern is to provide practical instruction so that people may understand God's Word and live accordingly. If *pesher* says "This is that," *midrash* says "That [Scripture] has relevance to this [aspect of life]." In the earlier rabbinic material, midrashic interpretation is fairly straightforward, but later rabbinic practices often focused more on individual words and even letters. The result is a "creative" exegesis in which the original concern of the text is often lost.[38] Even where the midrashic interpretation is fairly straightforward, the focus with *midrash* is on the application of the text rather than with understanding the text itself. *Midrash* is not usually a commentary on the text.

Still, *midrash* is not arbitrary application of the text. There are rules to guide an interpreter that legitimated an interpretation. The early rabbinic practices were guided by seven rules of exposition, which later were expanded until eventually there were thirty-two.[39] The seven rules

36. See Bruce, 7–11; and Longenecker, *Biblical Exegesis in the Apostolic Period,* 39–45. On the interpretation of Scripture more generally at Qumran, see Daniel Patte, *Early Jewish Hermeneutic in Palestine* (Missoula, Mont.: Scholars, 1975), 211–314.

37. Note also Acts 4:11 and Luke 4:18–21. Longenecker, *Biblical Exegesis in the Apostolic Period,* 70–75 and 100–101, lists several other passages that he would categorize as New Testament *pesher* interpretations of Old Testament texts.

38. On *midrash,* Rimon Kasher, "The Interpretation of Scripture in Rabbinic Literature," *Mikra,* ed. Martin Jan Mulder and Harry Sysling; *Compendia Rerum Iudaicarum ad Novum Testamentum,* sec. 2, pt. 1 (Philadelphia: Fortress, 1988), 560–77; Longenecker, *Biblical Exegesis in the Apostolic Period,* 32–38; Ellis, "Biblical Interpretation in the New Testament Church," 702–9.

39. On hermeneutical rules for exposition, see Kasher, 584–94; Ellis, "Biblical Interpretation in the New Testament Church," 699–702; and Hermann L. Strack, *Introduction to the Talmud and Midrash* (Cleveland: World, 1963), 93–98.

are fairly logical and may have derived from Hellenistic rhetoric.[40] Such procedures have frequently been adopted by expositors of texts. These seven rules merit repetition and consideration, for at least some of them are observable in the New Testament.[41]

1 *Qal wahomer*—"light and heavy," meaning what applies in a less important case applies also in a more important case and vice versa.
2 *Gezerah shawa*—"an equivalent regulation," meaning where the same words are applied in two separate cases the same considerations apply.
3 *Binyan ab mikathub 'ehad*—"constructing a family from one passage," meaning that where texts are similar a principle derived from one of them applies to the others.
4 *Binyan ab mishene kethubim*—"constructing a family from two texts," meaning that where texts are similar a principle derived from two texts can be applied to the others.
5. *Kelal uferat*—"general and particular," meaning that a general rule may be applied to a particular situation and vice versa.
6. *Kayotse bo bemaqom 'aher*—"something similar in another passage," meaning that a text may be interpreted by comparison with a similar text.
7. *Dabar halamed me 'inyano*—"explanation from the context."

Such midrashic techniques are observable in the New Testament. When Jesus argued that if God cared for the birds, surely he cared much more for humans (Matt. 6:26), he was arguing in good rabbinic fashion from the less important case to the more important. Similarly, when Jesus justified his disciples' eating grain on the Sabbath by pointing to the eating of the showbread by David and his men, he was arguing on the basis of an equivalent regulation (or possibly also from a less important case to a more important).[42] When Paul quoted several Old Testament texts with common key words, as he does in Galatians 3:8–14,[43] he was following the midrashic technique of bringing texts together to

40. See David Daube, "Rabbinic Methods of Interpretation and Hellenistic Rhetoric," *HUCA* 22 (1949): 239–64.
41. Ellis, "Biblical Interpretation in the New Testament Church," 700–702, would argue that all seven are used in the New Testament.
42. Matt. 12:1–8; see Ellis, "Biblical Interpretation in the New Testament Church," 700.
43. Note the use of *epikataratos* in Gal. 3:10 (quoting Deut. 27:26) and 3:13 (quoting Deut. 21:23), *poiēmsas auta* in 3:10 (from Deut. 27:26) and *poiēmsas auta* in 3:12 (from Lev. 18:5), and *zēmsetai* in 3:11 (quoting Hab. 2:4) and 3:12 (quoting Lev. 18:5).

provide explanation. Such grouping of texts as a method of argumentation occurs often.[44]

Testimonia

One further Jewish practice that must be noted is the use of testimonia. If one analyzes the use of Old Testament passages in the New Testament, very quickly one sees that certain Old Testament passages are quoted by several New Testament writers. In addition, sometimes the New Testament writers agree in using combinations of texts, and sometimes they even agree in wording that does not agree with the Septuagint or other known texts. The best example of these interesting phenomena is the agreement between 1 Peter 2 and Romans 9. First Peter 2:6–10 uses Isaiah 28:16; Psalm 118:22, Isaiah 8:14; parts of several other texts and Hosea 2:23. Romans 9:25–33 uses Hosea 2:23, other texts from Isaiah, and then a conflation of Isaiah 28:16 and 8:14 in the same non-Septuagintal form that 1 Peter has.[45] Should we account for such instances by arguing that one writer copied from the other?[46] Furthermore, there are a few places where Old Testament texts seem to have been joined in unexpected ways. For example, Mark 1:2–3 attributes to Isaiah words that appear to be a combination of Exodus 23:20, Malachi 3:1, and Isaiah 40:3.[47]

An attractive explanation of these phenomena is the argument that early Christians used *testimonia*. That is, they used collections of Old Testament texts that had been grouped thematically for apologetic, liturgical, and catechetical purposes. While it would be easy to overstate the case for *testimonia*,[48] their existence and use seem to be beyond doubt. Pre-Christian Jewish *testimonia* have been found at Qumran.[49] Evidence of the continued use and growth of *testimonia* in the patristic period also is without question.[50] For the New Testament itself, the ar-

---

44. Note Acts 2:25, 30, and 34; 13:34–35; Rom. 4:2 and 7; 9:33 and 11:9; 1 Cor. 15:54–55; and Heb. 1:5, 6–7.

45. Ps. 118:22 also occurs in Matt. 21:42 and parallels and in Barnabas 6.4.

46. See, for example, C. Leslie Mitton, *The Epistle to the Ephesians* (Oxford: Clarendon Press, 1951), 186–89.

47. Note a similar example in Matt. 27:9–10, where a conflation of Zech. 11:12–13 and Jer. 32:6–9 is attributed to Jeremiah. Such combinations of texts and their attributions to a specific author ought not be considered "errors."

48. As Rendel Harris did with his "testimony book" hypothesis. See Rendel Harris, with the assistance of Vacher Burch, *Testimonies* (Cambridge: Cambridge University Press, 1916–1920), 2 vols.

49. Note 4Q Testimonia and 4Q Florilegium. See Joseph A. Fitzmyer, "'4Q Testimonia' and the New Testament," *TS* 18 (1957): 513–37.

50. See Barnabas 6.2–4 for an example, and cf. Pierre Prigent, *Les Testimonia dans le christianisme primitif: L'Epître de Barnabé I–XVI et ses sources* (Paris: J. Gabalda et Cie, 1961), passim. Note also Cyprian, Treatise 12 ("Three Books of Testimonies Against the Jews").

gument that one author copied from the other is often far too simplistic to account for the data.[51] Rather, there were collections of Old Testament texts that were useful to the church in a variety of ways. Such collections would have circulated in *both* written and oral forms and would have offered practical resources for both itinerant preachers and gentile congregations.

The stone *testimonia*, then, would have been a pre-Christian Jewish collection that was adopted by Christians. The frequent use of Psalm 8 and Psalm 110 in combination reflects christological *testimonia* brought together by the church.[52] The most common uses of *testimonia* were christological and apologetic, but catechetical and liturgical uses are present as well. Romans 3:10–18 possibly is a grouping of *testimonia* on sin.[53] Romans 15:9–12 may reflect *testimonia* thematically arranged around the subject of the Gentiles.

Testimonia provide a window into the way the early church did its theology and ministry. They also provide insight into Old Testament quotations that are otherwise anomalies. Therefore, when an Old Testament quotation occurs, one must inquire about its use and textual form elsewhere in the New Testament and, if possible, in Judaism and the patristic period as well.

Example One—An Important Allusion
John 1:14–18

John 1:14–18 is a marvelously rich theological text on almost any reading, but a reading that does justice to the Old Testament background increases the significance of this text considerably. There is no Old Testament quotation in these verses, but there is an important allusion. Without an awareness of the Old Testament background on which the author frames his material, not only will much of the theological significance of this passage be lost, but one will not know why the author has chosen these words. There often is argument about whether a New Testament writer is alluding to an Old Testament

51. See my "1 Peter 2: 1–10: Its Formation and Literary Affinities," *NTS* 24 (1978): 97–106, especially 101–3.

52. Note 1 Cor. 15:25–27; Eph. 1:20–22; and Heb. 1:13 and 2:6–8. Ps. 110:1 is used in several other places, and is used in the New Testament more than any other Old Testament text. On the use of Ps. 110, see David M. Hay, *Glory at the Right Hand* (Nashville: Abingdon, 1973).

53. As several commentators have suggested. See, e.g., Ernst Käsemann, *Commentary on Romans,* trans. Geoffrey W. Bromiley (Grand Rapids: Eerdmans, 1980), 86. Note that this grouping of Old Testament texts on sin is present in the Septaugint version of Ps. 14:2–3. This could be due to Christian influence, but it seems more likely that these verses had earlier been collected in Judaism.

text,[54] but there is such a constellation of words drawn from Exodus 33:17–34:6 that there can be no doubt that John 1:14–18 is based on this passage.[55]

Exodus 33:17–18 is about Moses seeking a revelation of God's glory. Moses was told that neither he nor any other human could see God and live. He was allowed to see all God's goodness pass before him and, as it were, also to see the "back" of God. In this context Moses received the two tables of the law and was told that God is, among other things, full of lovingkindness and truth *(ḥesed vᵉ'emet)*. More than any text, this Old Testament passage defined who God was for Israel, and this event was viewed by Jews as the supreme revelation of God.

In John 1:14 the author claims to have seen the glory of the Word *(logos)*, who was full of grace and truth. "Glory" is frequently to be understood as that which makes God visible.[56] Although "grace" *(charis)* is not often used to render the Hebrew word for lovingkindness *(ḥesed)*, clearly the intention in John 1:14 is to say that in the *logos* made flesh, we encounter a revelation of God. He is the unique one from the Father in whom we encounter the very character of the Father, grace and truth.

Similarly in John 1:17, the intention of the author is clear with an awareness of the background in Exodus. The law, a valid revelation, was given through Moses. The true revelation of the Father, however, was given through Jesus Christ. There is a contrast with the revelation of Moses, but there is not a rejection of that revelation. In effect, this verse says, "Revelation did take place through Moses, but the supreme revelation of God is to be found in Jesus Christ."

John 1:18 expresses the whole of Johannine theology in a nutshell. The assertion that no human can see God and live is drawn from Exodus 33:20 and is an important theme throughout the Gospel.[57] No one, not even Moses, has ever seen God, but the unique God,[58] the one in the bosom of the Father, has revealed him. To see him is to see the Father (John 14:9).

---

54. What constitutes an allusion? Is one word in common between New Testament and Old Testament texts sufficient? Certainly not unless there is something in the New Testament context that suggests dependence on the Old Testament text. Does an allusion have to be a conscious allusion? Does it have to be an allusion that one could expect the readers to recognize? Frequently allusions are suggested that require a stretch of the imagination to accept.

55. See Morna Hooker, "The Johannine Prologue and the Messianic Secret," *NTS* 21 (1975): 52–56; and Anthony T. Hanson, "John 1:14–18 and Exodus XXXIV," *NTS* 23 (1977): 90–101.

56. S. Aalen, "Glory, Honour," *The New International Dictionary of New Testament Theology*, ed. Colin Brown (Grand Rapids: Zondervan, 1976), 2:45.

57. Cf. 5:37; 6:46; 12:41; and 14:8–9. Note also 1 John 4:12–20.

58. *Theos*, not *huios*, is the correct reading.

Example Two—An Important Quotation
Luke 4:18–19

Like John, the other Gospel writers use Old Testament quotations early in their writing to establish the identity of Jesus. The reader knows who Jesus is right from the start in every Gospel. In addition, Luke 4:18–19 established the character of Jesus' ministry through the quotation of Isaiah 61:1–2. This Old Testament text was the focus of Jesus' preaching in Nazareth.[59] Luke has placed this incident first in his account of Jesus' ministry to provide a programmatic description of Jesus' task. The importance of Isaiah 61:1–2 for Luke is obvious. He has moved this narrative to the beginning of his account of Jesus' ministry, whereas Matthew and Mark had it much later. Also, many of the main themes of Lukan theology are evidenced in this quotation (the Spirit, proclamation of the good news, the *aphesis*—which is both release and forgiveness, the poor and oppressed, and eschatology).

The words of Isaiah 61 are obviously important, but this text is another example of an Old Testament passage with a life in Judaism. The ideas associated with this text would have made it even more significant for Jesus and his hearers. Isaiah 61, with its focus on the "acceptable year of the Lord," would have alluded both to the "Year of Jubilee" described in Leviticus 25 and to God's end-time salvation.[60] The interpretation of Isaiah 61 in 11Q Melchizedek with reference to the "end of days" is clear proof of the eschatological association this text had. When people heard Isaiah 61, they understood it as a classic text describing end-time salvation. In effect, Jesus proclaimed to his hearers that God's end-time salvation had been fulfilled in their hearing. Their surprise is understandable.[61]

Guidelines

We have looked at a few examples of the significance of the Old Testament quotations in the New Testament. Other examples could be multiplied easily. Given that the use of the Old Testament in the New Testament is one of the most important issues in understanding the New Testament, certain guidelines will be helpful for studying those quotations.

---

59. Note that while Luke's quotation is basically septuagintal, part of Isa. 61:1 is omitted and part of Isa. 58:6 is inserted.

60. The Jubilee included four elements: 1) return of all property to the original owner; 2) release of all Jewish slaves; 3) cancellation of all debts; 4) allowing the land to lie fallow.

61. See the discussion of this text in Robert B. Sloan, Jr., *The Favorable Year of the Lord* (Austin, Tex.: Schola Press, 1977); John Howard Yoder, *The Politics of Jesus* (Grand Rapids: Eerdmans, 1972), 34–40 and 64–77.

'mine the original intention of the Old Testament passage.
attention must be given to the context and to the theology
rk in the Old Testament text.

ze the form of the text. To the degree that one is able, com-
ρⱥ₁₁ₒᵤn should be made between the New Testament quotation
and Old Testament text and various witnesses to it. Is the New
Testament reference a precise quotation, a quotation from
memory, a paraphrase, or an allusion? Does the New Testament agree with the Masoretic text or the Septuagint or some
other witness such as a targum? Are any insights to be gained
from the form of the quotation? Even when one cannot make
an independent comparison of other forms of the text, good
commentaries will provide summaries of such comparisons.

3) Determine, if possible, how the Old Testament text was understood and used in Judaism. Again, where personal investigation is not practical, good commentaries will provide such
information.

4) Determine the hermeneutical or exegetical assumptions that
enabled the use of the Old Testament text. Is the use straightforward from our standpoint, or is there an assumption such as
corporate solidarity or correspondence in history that makes
the usage possible? Have any rabbinic techniques or wordplays
made the Old Testament text attractive?

5) Analyze the *way* the New Testament writer uses the Old Testament text. Is the text being used as divine proof of the validity of
his statement? Are words from the Old Testament used to en-
lighten, but with no thought of providing validation (as John
1:14–18)? Are the words adapted and used for rhetorical effect in
the writer's own argument (as in 1 Pet. 1:3)? Is the New Testament writer only using an analogy based on an Old Testament
text (John 3:14)?

6) Determine the theological significance and relevance of the use
of the Old Testament text. For example, the christological importance of the adaptation of Isaiah 8:12–13 to Christ in 1 Peter
3:14–15 is enormous. An Old Testament text that was explicitly
about "*Yahweh* of hosts" has been applied to Christ without
hesitation or any sense of need for explanation. That Paul could
interpret Isaiah 49:8 eschatologically of his own ministry
(2 Cor. 6:2) is important in understanding both him and our
own ministries.

7) Note which Old Testament texts are used in the New Testament and which are not.[62] Most of the New Testament refer-

---

62. Note Dodd's summary, *According to the Scriptures*, 107–8.

ences to the Old Testament come from parts of the Pentateuch, the Psalms, and a few of the prophets, especially Isaiah. Clearly all the Hebrew Scriptures were considered the Word of God, but what theological conclusions should be drawn with regard to texts that were set aside (as the food laws) or ignored? On what ground did Jesus and the New Testament writers find the essence of their gospel in certain texts, especially those that focused on God's promises, love, and mercy rather than those that focused on separation and the exclusiveness of Israel?

Beyond these guidelines, a further question must be mentioned. In view of the fact that the New Testament writers use Old Testament passages in ways that we find surprising, should we interpret the Old Testament the same way they did? In other words, can we use their technique to find Christian significance in Old Testament texts, or were they operating from a revelatory stance in ways that we cannot?[63] This question is crucial, for the abuse of the Old Testament message is all too common in Christian history. Clearly the proximity of the apostles to the ministry, death, and resurrection of Jesus places them in a unique category. Also, the eschatological significance of Jesus' ministry and his identity have been marked out in ways that, even though they may be enhanced, do not need improvement. We should not expect to see new instances of verses applied to Jesus on the basis of corporate solidarity or eschatological or messianic presuppositions.

With great fear of possible abuse, however, I would not want to argue that the apostles could be creative because of their context, but that we are confined to more mundane methods. In terms of approaching the text, whether Old Testament or New Testament, we must be guided by the author's intention. We do also, however, read the Scriptures in light of the person and work of Christ. We must resist superimposing Christian theology on Old Testament texts and should feel no compulsion to give every Old Testament text, or even most of them, a christological conclusion. But we will have failed if we do not ask how Old Testament texts function in the whole context of Scripture. Without allegorizing the Old Testament, we must seek to understand God's overall purpose with his people. I am not impressed with the concept of *sensus plenior*, but neither am I willing to isolate texts from God's overall purpose.

63. Note the discussions in Longenecker, *Biblical Exegesis in the Apostolic Period*, 214–20; "Can We Reproduce the Exegesis of the Apostles," *Tyndale Bulletin* 21 (1970): 3–38; and G. K. Beale, "Did Jesus and His Followers Preach the Right Doctrine from the Wrong Texts?" *Themelios* 14 (1989): 89–96.

Specifically, I have become convinced that the concept of correspondence in history is particularly valuable in interpretation. We have not completed the interpretive task until we have determined how a text does or does not correspond with Jesus' ministry or the ministry of the church.[64] The writers of the New Testament seem to have looked for patterns of God's working in the Hebrew Scriptures, in the life of Jesus, and in their own experience. Our reading of the Scriptures should do no less. Noting such patterns is a far cry from the abusive interpretation of allegorizing.

The New Testament writers were immersed in their Scriptures. The Scriptures were the frame of reference for their theology and provided many of the tools for their thinking. The same should be true of us.

Bibliography

Anderson, Bernhard W., ed. *The Old Testament and Christian Faith*. New York: Herder and Herder, 1969.

Baker, D. L. *Two Testaments: One Bible*. Downers Grove, Ill.: InterVarsity, 1976.

Bock, Darrell L. *Proclamation From Prophecy and Pattern*. Sheffield: JSOT, 1987.

Bruce, F. F. *The New Testament Development of Old Testament Themes*. Grand Rapids: Eerdmans, 1968.

Carson, D. A., and H. G. M. Williamson. *It Is Written: Scripture Citing Scripture*. Cambridge: Cambridge University Press, 1988.

Dodd, C. H. *According to the Scriptures*. New York: Scribner's, 1952.

Efird, James M., ed. *The Use of the Old Testament in the New*. Durham, N.C.: Duke University Press, 1972.

Ellis, Earle E. *Paul's Use of the Old Testament*. Grand Rapids: Eerdmans, 1957.

———. *Prophecy and Hermeneutic in Earliest Christianity*. Grand Rapids: Eerdmans, 1978.

Feinberg, John S., ed. *Continuity and Discontinuity: Perspectives on the Relationship Between the Old and New Testaments*. Westchester, Ill.: Crossway, 1988.

France, R. T. *Jesus and the Old Testament*. London: Tyndale, 1971.

Goppelt, Leonhard. *Typos: The Typological Interpretation of the Old Testament in the New*. Translated by Donald H. Madvig. Grand Rapids: Eerdmans, 1982.

Juel, Donald. *Messianic Exegesis: Christological Interpretation of the Old Testament in Early Christianity*. Philadelphia: Fortress, 1988.

64. See my "Streams of Tradition Emerging from Isaiah 40:1–5 and Their Adaptation in the New Testament," 39–40. For example, I would argue that the application of Lam. 1:12 to the ministry of Jesus is legitimate on the basis of correspondence between the suffering of the nation and the suffering of Christ. This is not a text referring to Christ; it is a text applicable to Christ.

Lindars, B. *New Testament Apologetic.* Philadelphia: Westminster, 1961.
Longenecker, Richard N. *Biblical Exegesis in the Apostolic Period.* Grand Rap-
    ids: Eerdmans, 1975.
Westermann, Claus, ed. *Essays on Old Testament Hermeneutics.* English trans.,
    edited by James Luther Mays. Richmond: John Knox, 1963.

Were the New Testament Authors Faithful to the Old Testament Authors' Intention?

3

The Single Intent of Scripture

Walter C. Kaiser, Jr.

From Walter C. Kaiser, Jr., "The Single Intent of Scripture," in *Evangelical Roots: A Tribute to Wilbur Smith*, ed. K. S. Kantzer (Nashville: Nelson, 1978), 123–41. Reprinted by permission.

Even before T. S. Eliot, Ezra Pound, and their associates began to argue on literary grounds that the meaning of a biblical text was independent of an author's verbal meanings, evangelical exegetical practice had likewise begun to slip into an easygoing subjectivism. Words, events, persons, places, and things in Scripture were allowed to signify all they could be made to signify apart from any authorial controls of those prophets and apostles who claimed to have stood in the divine council and received this intelligible revelation.

Almost as if to prepare for the banishment of the author in later theories of literary criticism, evangelicals began to excuse their multiple interpretations of a single text as logical outgrowths of the fact that 1) Scripture had two authors (God and the human writer); 2) prophecy had at least two meanings (the prophet's understanding and God's surprise meaning in the distant fulfillment); and 3) interpreters are divided into two groups: the natural man who fails to "receive the things of God" (1 Cor. 2:14) and the spiritual man who understands the deep things of God.

But such views were so antithetical to the actual statements and claims of Scripture that if any or all of them were consistently pressed, they would lead to outright departure from the concept of an intelligible revelation from God. Bishop Ryle likewise commented:

I hold it to be a most dangerous mode of interpreting Scripture, to regard everything which its words may be tortured into meaning as a lawful interpretation of the words. I hold undoubtedly that there is a mighty depth in all Scripture, and that in this respect it stands alone. But I also hold that the words of Scripture were intended to have one definite sense, and that our first object should be to discover that sense, and adhere rigidly to it. I believe that, as a general rule, the words of Scripture are intended to have, like all other language, one plain definite meaning, and that to say that words *do* mean a thing, merely because they *can* be tortured into meaning it, is a most dishonourable and dangerous way of handling Scripture.[1]

While few would directly challenge the general legitimacy of Ryle's principles, many would conveniently escape its full application to personal Bible study and the practical needs of the professional ministry. For this group of unconvinced evangelical exegetes, there are parts of the Bible that are given in terms unintelligible to the sacred writers themselves and, as a consequence, to their original listeners. Accordingly, on this line of reasoning, there must be parts of the Bible incapable of being interpreted by the ordinary aids and procedures of exegesis. These texts then become the exceptions that prove the rule that, by and large, biblical exegesis is to be placed outside the pale of the ordinary conventions of literary interpretation. Therefore, before any progress can be made in the area of general hermeneutics or any practical applications can be implemented in preaching and teaching, an examination must be made of a representative number of texts that point to the biblical writers' alleged ignorance, passivity, or mundane apprehension of the messages they were receiving and delivering to Israel and the church.

Alleged Proof Texts for "Double Meaning"

1 Peter 1:10–12

No text has appeared more frequently in the argument against the single meaning of the text as found in the author's verbal meanings than 1 Peter 1:10–12. I have treated this text at some length already,[2] but it must be included here because of its central place in the debate.

Of which salvation the prophets have enquired and searched diligently, who prophesied of the grace that should come unto you:
Searching what, or what manner of time the Spirit of Christ which was

---

1. *Expository Thoughts on the Gospels,* vol. 2 (Grand Rapids: Zondervan, 1953), 383.
2. For example, Walter C. Kaiser, Jr., "The Eschatological Hermeneutics of Evangelicalism: Promise Theology," *Journal of Evangelical Theological Society* 13 (1970): 94–96.

in them did signify, when it testified beforehand the sufferings of Christ, and the glory that should follow.

Unto whom it was revealed, that not unto themselves, but unto us they did minister the things, which are now reported unto you by them that have preached the gospel unto you with the Holy Ghost sent down from heaven; which things the angels desire to look into.

Does this text teach that the writers of Scripture "wrote better than they knew"? Indeed it does not. On the contrary, it decisively affirms that the prophets spoke knowingly on five rather precise topics: 1) the Messiah, 2) his sufferings, 3) his glory, 4) the sequence of events (for example, suffering was followed by the Messiah's glorification), and 5) that the salvation announced in those pre-Christian days was not limited to the prophets' audiences, but it also included the readers of Peter's day (v. 12).

What they "enquired and searched diligently for" without any success was the *time* when these things would take place. The Greek phrase that gives the object of their searching was "what" [time] or "what manner of time" [*eis tina ē poion kairon*] this salvation would be accomplished. In no case can the first interrogative "what" [*tina*] be translated as the RSV, NASB, the Berkeley, the Amplified, and the NEB footnote have it—"what person." Greek grammarians such as A. T. Robertson;[3] Blass, DeBrunner, and Funk;[4] the lexicon by Baur, Arndt, and Gingrich;[5] and Moulton, along with such important commentaries as Charles Briggs and Edward G. Selwyn,[6] are all emphatic on the point: *tina* and *poion* are "a tautology for emphasis"[7] and both modify the word "time."

This passage does not teach that these men were curious and often ignorant of the exact meaning of what they wrote and predicted. Theirs was not a search for the *meaning* of what they wrote; it was an inquiry into the *temporal* aspects of the *subject*, which went beyond what they wrote. Let it be noted then that the *subject* is invariably larger than the verbal meaning communicated on any subject; nevertheless, one can know *adequately* and truly even if he does not know comprehensively and totally all the parts of a subject.

3. *A Grammar of the Greek New Testament in Light of Historical Research,* 4th ed. (1923), 735–36.

4. F. Blass and A. DeBrunner, *A Greek Grammar of the New Testament,* rev. and trans. Robert W. Funk (Chicago: University of Chicago Press, 1961), 155.

5. W. F. Arndt and F. W. Gingrich, *A Greek-English Lexicon of the New Testament* (Chicago: University of Chicago Press, 1957), 691.

6. Briggs, *International Critical Commentary on 1 Peter* (Edinburgh: T. & T. Clark), 107–8; Selwyn, *The First Epistles of St. Peter* (London: Macmillan & Co., 1955), 134–38.

7. Blass, DeBrunner, and Funk, *Greek Grammar,* 155.

Daniel 12:6–8

> And one said to the man clothed in linen, which was upon the waters of the river, How long shall it be to the end of these wonders?
>
> And I heard the man clothed in linen, which was upon the waters of the river, when he held up his right hand and his left hand unto heaven, and sware by him that liveth for ever that it shall be for a time, times, and an half; and when he shall have accomplished to scatter the power of the holy people, all these things shall be finished.
>
> And I heard, but I understood not: then said I, O my Lord, what shall be the end of these things?

Attention usually moves from 2 Peter 1:10–12 to this statement of Daniel. "I heard, but I understood not." But again, what was it that Daniel did not understand? Was it the words he was speaking? Not at all; the words he did not understand were those of the angel, not his own! Furthermore, the fact that these words of the angel were to be "closed up and sealed until the time of the end" was no more a sign that these events were to remain *unexplained* until the end time than was the equivalent expression used in Isaiah 8:16, "Bind up the testimony, seal the law." There, as here, the "sealing" of the testimonies was a reference primarily to the certainty of the predicted events.

Moreover, Daniel's question in verse 8 involved the temporal aspect and consequences of the angel's prophecy: "What shall be the end of these things?" One of the angels had asked in verse 6, "How long shall it be to the end of these wonders?" But Daniel asked a different question: "What" would be the state of affairs at the close of "the time, times, and an half?" Concerning this question he was given no further revelation. Therefore the "sealing up" of the prophecy only indicated its *certainty*, not its hiddenness.

Let it be admitted, however, that whenever the prophet received his revelation in a vision (for example, Dan. 8 or Zech. 1–6), the objects presented to his mind's eye were usually a preparation for the verbal prediction that accompanied that vision. Thus, in those cases the interpreting angel did not refuse to clarify the prophecy. So clear was Daniel's understanding of the meaning of his prophecy and so dramatic was its effect on him that he "was overcome and lay sick for some days" (Dan. 8:27 RSV).

To say that we now understand the predictions of the apostles and prophets better than they did contributes nothing to the present debate about authorial controls over meanings. Certainly a man who visits a country can understand the description of a place better than one who never personally saw it. But this is to confuse fullness of consequences or fullness of a total subject with the validity, truthfulness, and accuracy of contributions to that subject. And should this lead to the argument that God is the real Author of Scripture, it would still make no important difference. God did not make the writers omniscient. Rather, he imparted just as much as they needed to make their message effective for that moment in history and for the future contribution to the whole progress of revelation.[8]

John 11:49–52

And one of them, named Caiaphas, being the high priest that same year, said unto them, Ye know nothing at all,

Nor consider that it is expedient for us, that one man should die for the people, and that the whole nation perish not.

And this spake he not of himself: but being high priest that year, he prophesied that Jesus should die for that nation;

And not for that nation only, but that also he should gather together in one the children of God that were scattered abroad.

Relentlessly the argument is pressed into the New Testament. There it is hoped that Caiaphas could be a witness for the double-author theory of hermeneutics.

Caiaphas pronounced an accurate judgment on his colleagues, "You know nothing at all" (John 11:49). But as Rudolf Stier asked, "What better, then, [did Caiaphas] know?"[9] His suggestion was one of political expediency: it is better to let one man be a sacrificial lamb to save the Jewish cause than to have everyone implicated, with Rome's wrath falling on the whole body politic.

John's comment on Caiaphas's speech was: "And this spake he not of himself: but being high priest that year, he prophesied. . . ."

Now, several things must be observed:

1) These words are not to be classed along with later rabbinic alleged examples of unintentional prophecy, as cited by Strack and Billerbeck on John 11:51 and 2 Peter 1:20–21 (11.546). Nor is this proof that the earlier prophets belonged to such a category as Rabbi Eleazar (ca. A.D. 270), who argued, "No prophets have known what they prophesied. Only Moses and Elijah knew." Indeed, according to the same line of logic, even "Sam-

---

8. For a discussion of this passage, see Moses Stuart's "On the Alleged Obscurity of Prophecy," *The Biblical Repository* 2 (1832): 239–40; "Remarks on Hahn's Definition of Interpretation and Some Topics Connected With It," *The Biblical Repository* 1 (1831): 146ff.; *Hints on the Interpretation of Prophecy*, 2d ed. (Andover: Allen, Morrill & Wardwell, 1842), 56–58.

9. *Words of the Lord Jesus* 6 (Edinburgh: T. & T. Clark, 1865), 56.

uel, the master of the prophets, did not know what he prophesied."[10] Thus it is argued that Caiaphas illustrates the same
process. But Caiaphas said what he wanted to say and mean.
There was no compulsion or constraint here any more than
there was in the superscription Pilate put over Jesus' cross.
Rather, in these words John immediately saw there was "a
grand irony of a most special Providence"[11] in the case of both
Pilate and Caiaphas.[12]

2) The truth-intention of Caiaphas (v. 50) is to be sharply contrasted with the *significance* (v. 51) John found in these words,
especially since Caiaphas was high priest when he uttered his
cynical estimate of the situation. For John there was a strong
contrast (note John's word, "on the contrary" *[alla])* between
what Caiaphas said and meant and what John under the inspiration of the Spirit of God disclosed by using many of the same
words.

3) With that John *corrected* Caiaphas's provincial statement with
its ethnocentricities and turned it into a comprehensive statement of the universal implications of Jesus' death (v. 52).
Whereas Caiaphas had used the expression, "on behalf of the
people" (v. 50), John corrected those words of cynical political
expediency and expanded them to match the value of Jesus'
death; it was now, "on behalf of the nation" (v. 51) and on behalf of the "children of God scattered abroad" (v. 52). Caiaphas
had said that the nation was going to perish—therefore Jesus
must die. John said that the people and nation were perishing—
therefore Jesus must die to unite all the children of God, including the nation, into the true "people" of God as Jesus had proclaimed in John 10:15–16 and as Paul would later describe in
Ephesians 2:14.

4) John's evaluation of Caiaphas's speech was that "he did not
speak on his own authority, but being high priest that year, he
prophesied." The expression "on his own authority" is unique to
John and occurs in six passages (John 5:19; 7:18; 11:51; 15:4;
16:13; 18:34). In three of the instances, it clearly means to say
something on one's own *authority:* "The Son can do nothing on
his own authority" (5:19), "a person who speaks on his own au-

    10. As quoted in Edwyn C. Hoskyns, *The Fourth Gospel,* 2d ed. (London: Faber and
Faber, 1947), 412; Charles K. Barrett, *Gospel According to St. John* (London SPCK, 1960),
339.
    11. Stier, *Words of Lord Jesus*, 57.
    12. Brooke F. Westcott, *Gospel According to St. John* (Grand Rapids: Eerdmans,
1967), 175. Other examples of John's use of irony are listed: John 7:41–42; 19:21.

thority" (7:18), and "The Spirit . . . will not speak on his own authority" (16:13). If this meaning is also correct for John 11:51—and we believe it is—then John's point was not the *method* in which Caiaphas spoke (unconscious or involuntary prediction), but that since he was in the office of high priest when he gave this somewhat bitter proverb, it had the *significance* of an official prediction.[13] One cannot miss the repeated emphasis of verses 49 and 51, "He being high priest that year."

5) When verse 51 comments that he (Caiaphas) was prophesying *that [hoti]* Jesus was about to die, John is not giving us the contents of Caiaphas's prophecy, but only that the significance of this otherwise witty speech could be found in *reference to the fact that* Jesus was about to die. In Caiaphas we do not have the words of a true prophet coming with authority from God. Instead we see an erring high priest giving wicked counsel. However, God was pleased to turn this advice back on the speaker as a most appropriate explication of the very principle he was intent on denying.

Thus we conclude that if Caiaphas had prophesied in the ordinary sense of the word, there would have been no need for any immediate corrections on John's part. But when an official like himself or Pilate gave a verdict that could take on a proverbial status and significance which accorded with the plan of God, only the God of providence could be praised, for now the wrath of men had been turned into the glory of God. But such examples could not be used to support a double-author view of normative revelation. Even if every part of our previous argument failed, it still remains true that Caiaphas never belonged to the class of the apostles and prophets who received revelation.

2 Peter 1:19–21

We have also a more sure word of prophecy: whereunto ye do well that ye take heed, as unto a light that shineth in a dark place, until the day dawn, and the day star arise in your hearts:

13. Three interpretations are given to this "prophesying": 1) The accidental lots or circumstances of life were echoes by which the heavenly revelation was given to men: 2) Involuntary [?] prophecy like Balaam's words in Numbers 23–24; and 3) The high priest as bearer of divine revelation—usually through the Urim and Thummim.

The second view is certainly wrong since Balaam and Scripture claimed divine authority for what he said. The first view is possible since Pharaoh, Saul, Nebuchadnezzar, and Pilate all were in act and word witnesses to the truth, but then "prophesied" would have a secondary sense in John's use. The third is likewise deficient in that the Urim and Thummim were used to obtain a yes or no answer. The office of prophet and apostle was God's channel of biblical revelation.

Knowing this first, that no prophecy of the scripture is of any private interpretation.

For the prophecy came not in old time by the will of man: but holy men of God spake as they were moved by the Holy Ghost.

Scholars of the standing and stature of E. W. Hengstenberg have appealed to 2 Peter 1:19–21 to show that the prophets did not always understand nor could they always interpret their own words. But Peter makes the opposite point. Christians, he argues, "have not followed cleverly devised fables" (v. 16), for not only was Peter among those eyewitnesses who saw Jesus' glory on the Mount of Transfiguration (2 Pet. 1:16–18), but "we have the stronger or more secure prophetic word" found in the Old Testament prophecies (v. 19a). If readers would attentively contemplate what was said in these Old Testament prophecies, they would find the day dawning and the day star rising in their own minds; they would become instructed, illuminated, and satisfied by means of the light shed from these prophecies (v. 19b).

These Old Testament Scriptures were not a matter of one's own "loosing" (*epiluseōs*, v. 20), "because prophecy came not in old time by the will of man, but holy men of God spoke as they were moved by the Holy Spirit" (v. 21).

To make the word *epiluseōs* mean in this context an "explanation" or "interpretation," as some do, would be to argue that no prophet can interpret his own message—hence he had to write better than he knew. So argued Hengstenberg.

However, the claim is too bold for the following reasons:

1) The substantive *epilusis* in classical usage is a "freeing, loosing" or "destroying"; in other words, it is an unleashing from life. The only example of this form in the New Testament is 2 Peter 1:20; the Septuagint exhibits no instances of its usage either. However, the verbal form in its original meaning would appear to be "to set at liberty, to let go, to loose," while secondarily it came to mean "to explain, unfold, or interpret," as in Mark 4:34.

2) Even if that secondary meaning were intended by Peter here, it would claim too much. Can it be said that *all* prophetic writings were closed to their writers?

3) Peter's readers are urged to give heed to the Old Testament prophecies, "as unto a light that shineth in a dark place" because the Spirit of God has revealed through these prophets what is certain, plain, and intelligible. The light offered in the text came not from the ability of men, but from the "Father of lights" above. Had Peter's logic been, "Give heed to the light shining in

a dark place since no prophet understood or could even explain what he said, but wrote as he was carried along by the Holy Spirit," then the light would have been darkness and how could any, including the prophet, give heed to that enigmatic word? No, since the prophets were enlightened, instructed, and carried along by the Holy Spirit, they too were thus enabled to understand what they wrote. Otherwise we must ask for a second miracle—the inspiration of the interpreter.

John 14:25, 26; 15:26, 27; 16:12–15

Some, of course, will not shrink from following this last suggestion to its ultimate end. After all, they say, did not the Spirit promise to "teach us all things" (John 14:26) and then take what was his and declare it to us (John 16:15)?

But as any serious New Testament student will immediately recognize, the "you" intended in these passages was not the body of believers at large but the future writers of the New Testament. This is clear from its larger contextual setting (the "upper room discourse") and from the immediate contextual notations such as:

John 14:26 ". . . he will teach you all things, and bring to your remembrance all that I have said to you when I was with you" (RSV).
John 15:27 "You also are witnesses, because you have been with me from the beginning [of my earthly ministry]" (RSV).
John 16:12–13 "I have yet many things to say to you, but you cannot bear them now [while I am still on earth with you men]. When the Spirit of truth comes, we will guide you into all the truth . . ." (RSV).

Therefore, believers must refrain from using these texts as proofs of their own inspired interpretations as against those meanings derived through the hard labor of exegesis. Almost every cult or aberration from historical Christian doctrine has appealed at one time or another to these three texts as their grounds for adding to the inscripturated Word of God, but all have failed to meet the demands of the text. They have never personally walked with the Lord while he was on earth. They have never heard from his lips his instruction, and they were not witnesses from the start of his three-year ministry. But the apostles were! Therefore, that special band of men could record the life, words, and works of Christ in the Gospels with the Spirit's aid of recollection (John 14:26); teach doctrine ("what is mine"—John 16:14–15); and predict the future (John 16:12). They were eyewitnesses of what had happened to the Christ (John 15:26–27).

If believers complain that this principle, if applied consistently, could signal the ruin of the Great Commission (Matt. 28:18–20) for contemporary believers, let it be noted that this was the precise problem William Carey faced when he launched the modern impetus for missions. Believers resisted the appeal to "go and make disciples" by arguing that that command was delivered to the disciples alone. But Carey answered wisely that the principle was extended to all, for that same text also said: "And lo, I am with you always even to the end of the age"! Hence the divine intention would admit no such easy excuses as the one Carey's generation offered at first. Such is also the solution to our texts; where the extension is made, it must be observed.

2 Corinthians 3:6; Romans 2:29; Romans 7:6

As a final line of defense, some will appeal to the contrast between the dead exegesis of the "letter" of Scripture (according to them, the author's verbal meanings) versus the freedom of viewing the text under the fresh and immediate aid of the "Spirit."[14] But this stems from a false dichotomy that pretends to use the method it assails in order to substantiate the validity of its practice, only to depart from it once it is aloft. However, it is wrongheaded on both counts.

2 Cor. 3:6 ". . . the letter kills, but the spirit gives life" (NASB).
Rom. 2:29 "But he is a Jew, which is one inwardly; and circumcision is that of the heart, in the spirit, and not in the letter . . ."
Rom. 7:6 ". . . we serve in newness of the Spirit and not in oldness of the letter" (NASB).

The Pauline word for "letter" in these verses is *gramma*, not *graphē*. Paul assails outward, fleshly, uncommitted "letterism"—a perfunctory external observance of the law which has no antecedent commitment of the life by faith to the God who has given the law. Such ceremonialism was a "serving in the oldness of the letter." But the *graphē* was sacred to Paul: it was the very Word of God.

Paul's complaint is not about the inadequacy of what was written or about what the words of the text meant grammatically and syntactically as used by individual writers. His complaint was rather with those who *by means of* observing the outward letter of the law and *by means of* [in-

---

14. See, for example, Peter Richardson, "Spirit and Letter: A Foundation for Hermeneutics," *Evangelical Quarterly* 45 (1973): 208–18. He concludes (p. 218) that while Paul based his argument on "what is written," Paul's method and results show a great deal of freedom so that there is ". . . no final and authoritative interpretation, nor even, perhaps, a final and authoritative principle of interpretation"!

strumental use of *dia* in Rom. 2:20] circumcision were actually breaking the law. Circumcision was really a matter of the heart *by means of the Spirit* and not a matter of letter-keeping *(gramma).*[15]

Once again, Scripture is abused if such contrasts as "the letter kills, but the Spirit makes alive" is turned into a slogan to allow so-called Spirit-led interpreters to bypass the authorial verbal meanings in each text in favor of more practical, personal, relational, spiritual, or sensational meanings obtained allegedly from the Holy Spirit as promised in these three texts. But the promise is nonexistent and the method is therefore subbiblical and ultimately heretical.

The work of the Holy Spirit in 2 Corinthians 3:14ff. must not be used in a dialectical way that relates understanding to an existential response or to the tension that exists between the "letter" and the "Spirit" as Peter Richardson and others have proposed. The source of our understanding in 2 Corinthians 3:14 is still located in our "reading." What Paul prescribed for the removal of the veil that prevented a personal reception and application of either Moses' or Paul's words was that men should "turn to the Lord" (v. 16), who is the Spirit (v. 17).

Now does the Spirit set us free from the verbal meanings of the Word of the text (supposedly the *gramma*)? We answer with a decisive no! The Spirit is the Unveiler of significance, relevance, personal application, but not the Releaser of additional or delayed verbal meanings. This latter ministry of the Spirit was focalized in the apostles and prophets. They received the gifts of revelation, truth, verbal meanings, and valid teachings; their readers, on the other hand, received the ministry of reception, application, and significance—sometimes called "meaning-for-me." To confuse meaning and significance is to reduce all hermeneutics to shambles.[16]

Evangelical Exegetical Procedure

If each of the above arguments can be successfully sustained (and we believe they will bear even more intense scrutiny than is possible in the short scope of this chapter), then all alleged biblical grounds for finding some sort of *superadditum* or *sensus plenior* in addition to the human writers' supposed nominal or prosaic meanings is cut away. We

15. For further discussion on these texts, see Walter C. Kaiser, Jr., "The Weightier and Lighter Matters of the Law," in *Current Issues in Biblical and Patristic Interpretation,* ed. Gerald Hawthorne (Grand Rapids: Eerdmans, 1975), 187–88.

16. Once again E. D. Hirsch, Jr. has clarified this issue best in his *Aims of Interpretation* (Chicago: University of Chicago Press, 1976), 2–4: "'meaning' refers to the whole verbal meaning of a text and 'significance' to textual meaning in relation to a larger context—another mind, another era, a wider subject matter, an alien system of values."

are back to searching for God's revelation for our generation through the verbal meanings and contexts supplied by the ancient writers of Scripture.

That is exactly where the Pauline claim of 1 Corinthians 2:9–16 figures so prominently. Indeed, this may be one of the most neglected, yet most significant texts in the whole inspiration-hermeneutical debate. Paul located the source of his inscripturated wisdom in God. It was altogether different from that wisdom found in empirical sources or from pockets of political savvy (1 Cor. 2:6–9). And this wisdom God had revealed (aorist tense) to the apostle (the "us" of v. 10 and "we" of vv. 12 and 13 are used editorially; cf. 3:1, "I") by means of the Holy Spirit. The words Paul wrote, then, were not merely the result of his own human intelligence, but the result of *"words* taught by the Spirit" as he "explained spiritual truths with *words* given by the Spirit" (note the Greek grammar here versus the misunderstanding of most modern translations on 1 Cor. 2:13). An identical claim was repeated again in 1 Thessalonians 2:13: ". . . you received the word of God which you heard from us . . . not as the word of men but as what it really is, the *word* of God" (rsv, italics mine).

But it is the organic unity between the words of the writer and the work of the Holy Spirit that is the key point of the 1 Corinthians 2:13 reference. There the Holy Spirit *teaches* the apostle in words. Consequently, the writer was not oblivious to the import or verbal meaning of his terms: he himself was taught by the Holy Spirit. Such a claim can only mean there was a living assimilation of God's intended truth into the verbalizations of the writers of Scripture, rather than a mere mechanical printout of semi-understandable verbiage.

Therefore evangelicals are urged to begin a new "hermeneutical reformation" to correct this type of growing malpractice our profession has allowed in recent years. As a contribution towards that end, it is urged that the following axioms be adopted and implemented in our preparation of lectures, sermons, home Bible studies, and personal devotions:

1) God's meaning and revelatory-intention in any passage of Scripture may be accurately and confidently ascertained only by studying the verbal meanings of the divinely delegated and inspired human writers.

2) Only one verbal meaning is to be connected with any passage of Scripture unless the writer of the text gives literary and contextual clues that he has several aims in view for this exceptional passage (for example, the two or three questions asked at the beginning of the Olivet Discourse).

3) That single, original verbal meaning of the human author may be ascertained by heeding the usual literary conventions of history, culture, grammar, syntax, and accumulated theological context. And if it cannot be ascertained by these means then it cannot be ascertained at all.

4) This authorial meaning can be understood by all readers who will allow the writer to first say what he wants to say without introducing conservative or liberal prejudices as a preunderstanding.

5) The personal impact, significance, application, reception, and value this text has for particular individuals or situations is directly linked to the illuminating ministry of the Holy Spirit. The Spirit takes the single truth-intention of the author and in his convicting, comforting, teaching, and motivating power urges us to apply the principle taught in this text to scores of different situations.

In addition to these axioms, the following clarifications should be added if exegetical practice is to be worthy of the Bible.

1) The "original meaning" of any text can be defined, as John F. A. Sawyer reminds us, in two different ways: "original" in an etymological sense, and "original" in the meaning it had in its original context.[17] Exegesis is interested in this second usage. The object of exegesis is to discern the original meaning of the present canonical shape of the text rather than the root meaning of words or even the original meaning of the text's separate units (if indeed it had such a prehistory).

2) "Theological exegesis" of a passage is most important if we are to transcend the chasm between the scientific dissecting of the text into its philological components, complete with parsings and grammatical notes. However, a premature use of the *analogia fidei*, "analogy of faith," is as destructive of true meaning as no interaction with the accumulated and antecedent theology that "informed" that text. The "analogy of faith" is the sum of the prominent teachings of Scripture gathered from all its parts without regard to any diachronic considerations. This "rule of faith" was first set forth by Augustine and further defined by men like Chemnitz (*Examen*, VIII.I) to say that the ar-

---

17. "The Original Meaning of the Text and Other Legitimate Subjects for Semantic Description," *Questions Disputees d'ancien Testament*, ed. C. Brekemans (Leuven University Press, 1974), 63–70.

ticles of faith were to be derived from clear passages and in no case was a clear passage to be set in opposition to a difficult or problematic passage. Hence a principle of harmonization or proportionality was introduced.[18]

But can the analogy of faith function as a "pre-understanding" with which the interpreter approaches his task of exegesis in a distinctively Christian way? I believe not! The interpreter must not even carry such high and worthy goods as these to his task. Only the doctrine and the theology prior to the time of the writer's composition of his revelation (which theology we propose to call here the "Analogy of Scripture"[19]) may be legitimately used in the task of theological exegesis, in other words, where the writer directly cites or obviously alludes to the theology that preceded his writing and formed a backdrop against which he cast his own message. Only the discipline of biblical theology, if it traces the buildup of doctrine from era to era within each of the Testaments, will supply the extremely important theological data necessary to rescue an otherwise dull philological and grammatical exercise.[20] The "analogy of Scripture" then was the "pre-understanding" of both the writer and of those in his audience who were alert to what God had revealed prior to this new word of revelation. Likewise, the interpreter must employ the identical method if he is to be successful in aiding modern hearers to hear the total word in a text.

Having arrived at the original historical, cultural, grammatical, syntactical, theological meaning of the text, the exegete may *now* use the analogy of faith (of the whole of Scripture) in the summaries and conclusions he offers to each section of his exegesis and to the whole message, for what is learned in this context may relate to what was later revealed in Scripture. However, our methodology must be clean and there must be no confusion about these two methods in the name of orthodox or pragmatic results.

18. For a sympathetic discussion, see John F. Johnson, "*Analogia Fidei* as Hermeneutical Principle," *The Springfielder* 36 (1972–73): 249–59.

19. Kenneth Kantzer has wisely suggested that a better name for the phenomena described here would be something like the "Analogy of the Revelational Context," in other words, that part of Scripture that served as the context of revelation received prior to the writing of the immediate context under investigation. The "Analogy of Scripture" has been employed to designate various things in the history of the church. See my limited defense of this term in "The Present State of Old Testament Studies," *JETS* 18 (1975): 73–74.

20. See the strong stand on this matter taken by George M. Landes, "Biblical Exegesis in Crisis: What Is Exegetical Task in a Theological Context?" *Union Seminary Quarterly Review* 26 (1970): 275–77. "Any exegesis that refuses to expound the theological dimensions in the writings overlooks their *raison d'etre.*"

Nowhere, then, does Scripture support the view that the Bible has a multi-track concept of meanings. If the human author did not receive by revelation the meaning in question, then exegetes and readers have no right to identify their meanings with God. Only by following the careful distinctions set forth in the authorial autonomy view can the Word of God be preserved for future generations and be handled as what it is indeed—the powerful and authoritative Word from God.

4

The Fallacy of Equating Meaning with the Human Author's Intention

Philip Barton Payne

From Philip Barton Payne, "The Fallacy of Equating Meaning with the Human Author's Intention," *Journal of the Evangelical Theological Society* 20 (1977): 243–52. Reprinted by permission.

The Importance of Intention

A fundamental question behind most biblical exegesis is and ought to be: "What was the intention of the human author?" Most of the meaning of the biblical text is identical with the human author's intention. The importance of his intention is highlighted when one considers that social context is an essential part of meaning. Often underlying the question of an author's intention, however, is a misunderstanding of the word "intention" and of its proper significance for exegesis. Some of the various ways in which the word "intention" is used and the complexity of this idea will be considered below. It will be seen how difficult it can be to demonstrate what the original intention of a biblical author was centuries ago.

But beyond specifying the problems related to the word "intention," the thesis of this chapter is that in spite of the crucial role the human author's intention has for the meaning of a text his conscious intention does not necessarily *exhaust* the meaning of his statements, especially in more poetic and predictive writings. Ultimately God is the author of Scripture, and it is his intention alone that exhaustively determines its meaning. Therefore the exegete should not necessarily restrict the meaning of the text to what he feels can be demonstrated to be the intention of the human author.

Nonetheless, interpretation of any text should not obviate the intention of the human author. He does have the right to say that certain interpretations of his words are wrong. It should be remembered, though, that God can reveal more through the words of a writer of Scripture than he fully understood. An exegete can know that God has done this only when further revelation shows that he did.

Intention should guide exegesis only tentatively and as the text opens it up. Ultimately the *text* is the source from which the exegete draws meaning. In order to draw out this meaning, the text must be considered in the light of its total context, literary and historical. The literary context of a passage includes first and foremost its immediate literary setting, then the whole book, other books by the same author, the illumination given by the rest of Scripture, and all other documents that elucidate the meaning of the text. The historical context involves primarily the immediate configuration of the author (including his intention), his audience, and their situation, which may be elucidated by other social, cultural, and historical factors.

The Social Context of Meaning

Meaning does not exist in any text apart from someone's understanding of it, whether that be the author, his audience, or even God. If there is to be a meaning at all it must have a personal point of reference. Many philosophers and linguists have shown that language is a social phenomenon and must be understood in terms of its use.[1]

The meaning of a saying depends frequently on who said it, to whom, and on what occasion. Its context helps to specify its meaning. When something is said to a particular audience, the author's intention usually concerns that audience. He chooses terms appropriate to them, and so the saying reflects the character of the audience.

> For some years we have been realizing more and more clearly that the occasion of an utterance matters seriously, and that the words used are to some extent to be "explained" by the context in which they are designed to be or have actually been spoken in a linguistic interchange.[2]

Thus meaning is related to the author's intention and may be elucidated by an understanding of his hearers and their situation. Investigation of

---

1. Cf. L. Wittgenstein, *Philosophical Investigations*, trans. G. E. M. Anscombe (Oxford: Blackwell, 1968); J. L. Austin, *How to Do Things with Words* (Oxford: Clarendon, 1962); K. L. Pike, *Language in Relation to a Unified Theory of the Structure of Human Behavior* (The Hague: Mouton, 1967), 25–36.
2. Austin, *Things*, 100.

the probable understanding of the audience can often be done more ob-jectively than investigation of the author's intention, which depends on probing his consciousness to find his purpose behind writing.

Various aspects of the social context of meaning have at times been used selectively to the exclusion of others. Two fallacies concerning the identification of meaning have become widely recognized within liter-ary circles: the "intentional fallacy,"[3] and the "affective fallacy." The former makes complete identification of a text's meaning with the au-thor's intention, the latter with its understanding by or its effect on its hearers. At an opposite pole to these two fallacies is a third fallacy, namely that of divorcing meaning from the author, his original audi-ence and the occasion of utterance. Such thinking has typified the ap-proach of the newer criticism, which characteristically treats the text as autonomous from its original situation.

The Difficulty of Demonstrating Intention

The Bible authors' intentions are an elusive matter for many reasons. We will consider only four reasons here: 1) "intention" can be under-stood at many levels; 2) an author may have more than one reason for making a statement—his intention, in other words, may be complex; 3) intention is a complex category involving mental states that are in a constant flux; intention may suggest subconscious as well as conscious factors; and 4) it is difficult to demonstrate what the intentions of the biblical authors were, since we are separated from them by many cen-turies and their thoughts are known to us only through their writings.

"Intention" can be understood at many levels. These include the in-tention of an author in writing a book, a chapter, a paragraph, a sen-tence, a phrase, or even a particular word. It is important to recognize the particular levels of intention under consideration and not to con-fuse them. Occasionally someone says that the Chronicler or an Evan-gelist did not intend to convey historical information but that in writing his book(s) he was concerned only with spiritual truths. It may be true that the Chronicler's *primary* intention in writing the books of 1 and 2 Chronicles was to convey spiritual truths, such as God's involvement with his people. But this does not exclude—indeed, it may even de-mand—*his intention through particular narratives* (chapters, para-graphs, sentences) to convey historical information that demonstrates God's involvement with his people, acting in history.

Often there are many reasons for, or intentions behind, a work. Why

3. The first detailed study of this seems to be W. K. Wimsatt, Jr., and M. C. Beardsley, "The Intentional Fallacy," *The Verbal Icon: Studies in the Meaning of Poetry*, ed. W. K. Wimsatt, Jr., and M. C. Beardsley (London: Methuen, 1970), 4–18.

did Luke write Luke and Acts? Was it as an evangelistic work, or to encourage Christians, or to propound a particular theological viewpoint, or to vindicate Paul, or out of interest in the early history of the church? No single answer would exhaust Luke's reasons for writing. Perhaps if we could ask Luke for all the reasons why he wrote, he would list several and then admit that there were probably more reasons but that he had never consciously set out to specify all of them. If he could look over what he had written, the text would probably suggest further reasons to him.

The complexity of intention applies on other levels as well as on that of books. Frequently the author has more than one reason for writing a chapter, paragraph, sentence, or word. Therefore to limit meaning to *"the* intention of the author" as if he had *only one* intention may truncate the meaning he intended to convey. This is not to deny the importance of an author's having a specific purpose in mind, one that gives his writing coherence. Nor is it to deny that it is crucial for exegetes to recognize what is primary in any given text.

Few if any writers or speakers could describe all the complex factors that contribute to the development of their work, such as why they chose the imagery they did and all they wanted their work to accomplish. Behind, and in some sense "causing," every piece of literature is a reservoir of sensory and mental experiences. The mental process, of which intention is a part, is constantly developing as a work progresses. But this progression can never be known fully, nor need it be identified in order to understand and evaluate a given work.

The elusiveness of changing intentions is further complicated by the possibility of subconscious intentions being expressed or of intentions being expressed accidentally. It is impossible to know for sure how much of an author's intention was subconscious or how his choice of words and forms was shaped by unconscious desires and patterns. In the case of the biblical writers and Jesus, the only access we have to their intentions is in the texts that survive from their time.

When we are considering men whose minds were immersed in the Hebrew Scriptures, it is difficult to distinguish conscious from unconscious allusions to the Old Testament and both of these from coincidental similarities in expression. Probably these biblical authors themselves were not aware of every allusion they made to Scripture.

This elusiveness of intention, which develops and is modified as a work unfolds, is reflected in the quest undertaken by Hardy's rustic constable, who said, "he's the man we were in search of, that's true, and yet he's not the man we were in search of. For the man we were in search of was not the man we wanted."[4]

4. Wimsatt and Beardsley, "Intentional," 4–6, 9.

Even if it were possible for an author to specify his intention(s) exhaustively and with precision, should a hearer ask him for further clarification, still in the case of biblical exegesis centuries separate us from those authors. Their thoughts are accessible to us only through their writings. Hence it is difficult if not impossible to prove exactly what the intentions of an author were. To equate "intention" with "purposes that can be demonstrated" will tend to truncate the author's original intent.

The various levels at which intention can be understood, its frequent complexity, its elusiveness, and the time gap separating us from the biblical authors all add to the difficulty of demonstrating what the intentions of the biblical authors were.

This difficulty is further complicated since the phrase "the intention of the author" is commonly understood in three different ways: 1) the author's primary intention; 2) the totality of the author's *conscious* understanding of the import of his words at the time he originally spoke them; and 3) all those factors, subconscious as well as conscious, that guided him in his choice of words and total expression. We will argue next that given any one of these three understandings of "intention," particularly of the first two, it is fallacious to assume that meaning *always* ought to be equated with the author's intention.

The Fallacy of Equating Meaning with the Human Author's Intention

Error comes when we define "intention" as the author's *primary* intention, if we then proceed to exclude on principle any other meaning from the text. This is fallacious because the author may originally have intended to convey more than his primary intention. It is also fallacious because he might originally have intended subconsciously to convey more than his primary intention. This would be confirmed if the author himself were later to recognize that originally, even though he had not verbally or consciously formulated the secondary import that is in question, he had in fact desired to convey such an import through his words.

Error also comes when we define intention as the author's *conscious* understanding of the import of his words at the time when he originally spoke them, if we then proceed to exclude on principle any other meaning from the text. This is fallacious because an author may say something that carries a meaning he might subsequently acknowledge and approve, even though this meaning had been subconscious when it first came to expression in his words. It is not uncommon for someone to be surprised by the degree of insight that appears in something one has said or written. The expression of the subconscious is so characteristic of human language that to say that the prophets could not speak better than they knew would be to consider them in this respect unhuman, unless "knew" were taken to include all their subconscious thought and perception.

The inadequacy of intention exhaustively to define meaning is compounded in the case of poetry. Poetic writings usually have a more complex meaning and are more pictorial than prose. Their depth of meaning does not lend itself easily to fitting into precise intentions, since it often grows out of emotion or intuition. The literary critic Stephen Ullmann has correctly observed that "the intention behind an image is often very difficult to determine, and one must also allow for the presence of two or three intentions in the same image."[5] The extensive poetic and parabolic material in the Scriptures should be interpreted with particular caution lest the conjectured intention of the author be used to truncate its meaning. But on the other hand one must not ignore the necessary quest for the author's intention, nor must he give an interpretation that would obviate the author's intention. Such expressions of unintended but still desired meanings are not restricted to poetic language. One common example in all sorts of writing is what is called the principle of entailment. Speakers are frequently unconscious of meanings which are *entailed* in their utterances. There is such a complexity involved in certain types of utterances that they entail things other than their primary assertions. For instance, in an ethical challenge, there may be entailed some description of the situation, an evaluation of it, a declaration of the possibility of action in the situation, and advice concerning the right course of action to take. But the person presenting the challenge is usually not conscious that he is performing all of these functions.

We may illustrate this with Nathan's parable of the ewe lamb, which urged David to repent. In this challenge to David, Nathan, at least in part, described David's situation, assessed it, declared David's situation to be open for repentance, and advised David to repent. We do not know if Nathan consciously intended to convey each of these separate yet entailed aspects of his challenge. But to deny that any one of these factors is entailed in Nathan's challenge would be to undercut the basis of its effective performance as a challenge.

Many sorts of utterances entail more than the conscious intention of their speaker: commands, calls to action, urgings, challenges, expressions of attitudes, warnings, advice, judgments, and statements of intention.[6] I. A. Richards and Christine Gibson affirm that most sen-

---

5. S. Ullmann, *Style in the French Novel* (Cambridge: Cambridge University, 1957), 216.
6. Cf. the development of the principle of entailment by Austin, *Things*, 142–60.

tences are "at least attempting to do" these sorts of work: selecting, describing, realizing, valuing, influencing, ordering, and proposing.[7] Whether or not these critics are correct in saying that most sentences attempt to do *each* of these functions, it seems to be beyond question that many of our statements perform functions of which we are unconscious at the time of utterance. From this basic insight into the nature of entailment, which characterizes so much of language, it should be evident that meaning should not be confined to the author's *conscious* intention.

Even if we were to define "intention" to include the subconscious factors at work in molding the author's expression, in the case of the biblical authors we would still be in error if we were to equate, on principle, meaning with the author's intention. This is because of the further influence of the Holy Spirit inspiring their words.

The scriptural text seems to teach that at least in certain instances the biblical writer was not aware of the *full import* of his own words. This recognition does not necessitate, as Walter Kaiser assumed in his 1970 article, "The Eschatological Hermeneutics of 'Epangelicalism': Promise Theology," that the meaning would then be "totally unknown to the human writer."[8] But the biblical text does seem to teach that there were certain things the biblical writers conveyed that they themselves did not *fully* understand.

For instance, Daniel 8:27 states: "And I, Daniel, was overcome and lay sick for some days; then I rose and went about the king's business; but I was appalled by the vision and did not understand it." Here Daniel makes it clear that he did not understand the vision of a ram, a he-goat and a horn. Even the interpretation left him baffled. Likewise in Daniel 12:8–9 we read: "I heard, but I did not understand. Then I said, 'O my lord, what shall be the issue of these things?' He said, 'Go your way, Daniel, for the words are shut up and sealed until the time of the end.'" Daniel again admits he did not understand and asks, "What shall be the issue (or as the NASB has it, "the outcome") of these things?" His question is not merely "When," as Kaiser says,[9] but *"What* will be the outcome of these events?" In context, "these events" are those of which he had been prophesying. Again, Daniel was not fully aware of the import of his prophecy.

When Abraham said to Isaac, "God will provide himself the lamb for a burnt offering, my son" (Gen. 22:8), he seems to have been anticipating the sacrifice of Isaac. But he spoke better than he knew, as could

7. *Techniques in Language Control* (Rowley, Mass.: Newbury, 1974), 137–38.
8. *JETS* 13 (1970): 94.
9. Ibid., 95.

also be said of Caiaphas in his statement, "It is expedient for you that one man should die for the people, and that the whole nation should not perish" (John 11:51).[10]

Likewise, it would be difficult to defend that every prophecy identified in the New Testament as being fulfilled by Jesus Christ, such as Psalm 16, 22, or 110, was understood in just that sense by its author or that each was on his part intended as a messianic prediction. First Peter 1:10–12 seems to indicate that this was a fairly common phenomenon:

> The prophets, who spoke of the grace that was to come to you, searched intently and with the greatest care, trying to find out the time and circumstances to which the Spirit of Christ in them was pointing when he predicted the sufferings of Christ and the glories that would follow. It was revealed to them that they were not serving themselves but you, when they spoke of the things that have now been told you by those who have preached the gospel to you by the Holy Spirit sent from heaven. Even the angels long to look into these things (NIV).

The prophets' quest concerned that "to which the Spirit of Christ in them was pointing." The text teaches that the object of their intent searching was that which the Spirit was revealing through them. All the passage clearly states that the prophets did understand is that "they were not serving themselves but you."[11]

In the light of these texts and the previous observations on the character of language, we cannot agree with the conclusion of Kaiser that the Scriptures have "one truth-intention, whose meaning is to be found in the intention of the human writer."[12] The "intention of the human writer" is *not* necessarily identical with "the sense conveyed by his words."[13]

If we were to be correct in limiting meaning to the author's intention, we would have to define "intention" to include *all* those factors, unconscious and subconscious as well as conscious, that guided him in his choice of words and total expression. In the case of the Scriptures, this would include the influence of the Holy Spirit.

---

10. Cf. further defense of this thesis from Scripture with bibliographical references in J. B. Payne, *Encyclopedia of Biblical Prophecy* (New York: Harper, 1973), 4–5.

11. Kaiser goes beyond the clear assertion of the text when he states that "the prophets knew they were predicting four things according to 1 Pet. 1:10–12:1) the sufferings of Christ, 2) the glories of Christ, 3) the order of these two events, i.e., 'the glory that should follow,' and 4) that they were ministering when we in the N.T. are"; *JETS* 13 (1970): 95.

12. Ibid., 94.

13. *Contra* ibid.; cf. "The Present State of Old Testament Studies." *JETS* 18 (1975): 71–72.

But is it appropriate to include the work of the Holy Spirit as part of the unconscious "intention" of a biblical author? In English usage "intention" generally refers to "what one has in mind to do or bring about." Hence, it is typically associated with a conscious plan. Even if we understand the term so as to include subconscious factors, it still seems to be an odd use of language to include the influence of the Holy Spirit as part of an author's "intention." In the examples mentioned above, the prophets seem not to have understood consciously or subconsciously the total import of their prophetic words. Since the influence of the Holy Spirit was not something arising from the mental framework of the speaker, we should not necessarily include his influence as part of the author's "intention." Therefore, at least in cases of prophecy in which the prophet was not fully cognizant of the import of his words, it would be fallacious to *equate* the meaning of the prophecy with the author's intention.

The Supposed Autonomy of Literature

Many modern literary critics speak of literary works of art as autonomous in the sense of being independent of their original setting in life. For instance, there is a tendency in treating the parables of Jesus as literature to divorce them from their setting in history and to subordinate their original meaning to some contemporary or timeless meaning. Dan O. Via, R. W. Funk, and J. D. Crossan deny that a parable's meaning depends on its context in Jesus' life.[14] Via claims that reapplication rather than the original reference of parables is the true goal of interpretation and that the parable itself apart from its context carries meaning.[15] He states, "I have no interest at all in even the Persona of the historical Jesus."[16]

14. D. O. Via, "A Response to Crossan, Funk and Petersen," *Semeia* 1 (1974): 222; "Parable and Example Story: A Literary-Structuralist Approach," *Semeia* 1 (1974): 119–20; *The Parables: Their Literary and Existential Dimension* (Philadelphia: Fortress, 1967), 39; R. W. Funk, "Critical Note," *Semeia* 1 (1974): 189; J. D. Crossan, "The Seed Parable of Jesus," *JBL* 92 (1973): 261 n. 62. "Structuralist Analysis and the Parables of Jesus," *Semeia* 1 (1974): 206, where Crossan rejects his earlier qualification of "the necessity of having some established idea of Jesus' 'non-parabolic' teaching so that the reader of the parables can move from the literal to the metaphorical level intended by Jesus himself," quoted from "Parable and Example in the Teaching of Jesus," *Semeia* 1 (1974): 86.

15. Cf. E. C. Blackman, "New Methods of Parable Interpretation," *CJT* 15 (1969): 7–8; N. Perrin, "The Modern Interpretation of the Parables of Jesus and the Problem of Hermeneutics," *Int* 25 (1971): 143; N. M. Wilson, *Interpretation of the Parables in Mark* (Ph.D. dissertation, Drew University, 1968), 10–11.

16. Via, "Response," 222, indicating a shift from his earlier position in *Parables* where, although affirming the autonomy of the parables, he aimed not to distort "the original intention," 23–24.

The key reason for this lack of historical concern has been exposed by one who should know, the literary critic Northrop Frye: "The commenting critic is often prejudiced against whatever restricts his freedom."[17] Such a divorce of meaning from the context of the parables in Jesus' life detracts from the interdependence of factors in the original speech event which contributed to their meaning. Our concern as exegetes should be restricted to the *original meaning* that God intended, not the contemporary impressions that the text can evoke.

When Via and others treat the parables as independent of their original setting in Jesus' life, they are not really treating them as autonomous. They merely substitute a new setting, that of their own world. It is not possible to set a piece of literature free, as "autonomous" might suggest. One can only perceive it from new vantage points, always providing it with a new setting. This can be an interesting venture as Via's existentialist interpretations demonstrate, but it is not exegesis. It is *eisegesis* of existential philosophy into the parables. When parables are used as springboards for contemporary reflection divorced from their setting in Jesus' life, they lose their peculiar power and authority as parables of *Jesus.*

Implications for the Exegete's Task

The task of the exegete, as is suggested by the term "exegesis," is to "lead" the meaning "out" of the text. Foundational in any investigation of the meaning of Scripture must be the scriptural *text.* It is the written text, the *graphē,* which the Scriptures claim to be God-breathed (2 Tim. 3:16). Throughout the teaching of Jesus there is recognition of the divine origin and authority of the written Scriptures,[18] but he never cites as authority the human author's intention.

Ultimately all argument about meaning or the author's intention must be rooted in the text if it is to be objective. Many today build on another foundation, that is, the intention of the author. But as "intention" refers to the purpose in the mind of the author, it is inevitably subjective. Roman Catholic advocates of a *sensus plenior* typically argue from church tradition, designated as divine intention, to substantiate their peculiar views, which find no obvious support from the biblical text. Such subjective interpretation is rightly criticized by Kaiser, and

---

17. *Anatomy of Criticism* (Princeton: University Press, 1957), 90.
18. "It is written": Mark 7:6; 9:12, 13; 10:17; 14:21, 27; Luke 4:4, 8, 12; 7:27; 10:25; 18:31; 19:46; 20:17; 21:22; 22:37; 24:46; John 6:45; 8:17; 10:34; "the Scriptures": Matt. 22:29; 21:42; 26:54, 56; Mark 12:10; 12:24; 14:49; Luke 4:21; 22:37; John 5:39; 7:38; 10:35; 13:18; 17:12; "God's word": Matt. 15:6; 4:4; 22:31–32; Mark 7:13; Luke 8:21; 11:28; John 10:35; "God commanded": Matt. 15:3, 4; Mark 7:8–9.

we need a hermeneutic that can effectively challenge it. If we are to be objective, the foundation must be the biblical text itself.[19]

To say that the text is foundational for meaning does not mean that we simply look at the text, and meaning issues forth. The text develops *ideas* and *arguments*. Not everything in the text is of equal importance. It is imperative for the exegete to ask what ideas and arguments are developed by the text. A question that must always be considered concerns what is most important in any text. What receives emphasis? How much emphasis does it receive? The observations of an exegete may be correct, but if he misses the overall development of thought in the passage or fails to emphasize its major point his exegesis has failed. This is applicable at each level at which a work might be considered: as a total book, a chapter, a paragraph, or a sentence.

The process by which meaning is specified is basically the scientific process. Observation leads to hypotheses which are subsequently tested and refined. The text read in its total context leads the exegete to a tentative understanding of the primary (divine) author's intention. This tentative understanding is tested through closer scrutiny of the text and adjusted to take into account any new understanding of the structure, content, and context of the text. Various meanings may be conjectured to see which best explains the text and the ideas and arguments it develops.

The exegete must be cautious lest he argue from a conjectured intention to dismiss elements of the text as insignificant. The danger is that of circular argumentation: positing an aim and dismissing as insignificant those elements that do not reinforce that aim. Concerning the parable of the sower, for example, those who interpret "the point of comparison" as the eschatological harvest tend to dismiss the parable's other details as though they were not intended to have particular significance. But until it has been established that this is indeed the major point of the parable, any deductions one might make must be done tentatively.

The correct understanding of the meaning of the text is that which accounts for all of the text, puts it together as a coherent development of ideas and arguments, and takes into account its total context.

19. The exegete who limits his discussion of the meaning of a passage to what he is convinced was the intention of the author will produce a different kind of exegesis than the exegete who lets the text within its total context determine the meaning. The danger of the exegete's attention being diverted from the text can be evident in the terms he uses to describe a work. Critics who focus on intention tend to speak of "sincerity," "fidelity," "spontaneity," "authenticity," and "genuineness." These terms focus on the author's feelings and intentions and only indirectly on his composition. The meaning of a text is explored through such categories as "integrity," "unity," "function," "maturity," and "subtlety." These categories are more capable of delineation through textual study than the categories of intention: cf. Wimsatt and Beardsley, "Intentional," 9.

Unhappily, some of those who wish to preserve objectivity and to place a limitation on uncontrolled allegorical exegesis have based their hermeneutical system on the intention of the secondary (human) author. But it is precisely the conjectured intention of this author that has been used at times to justify an interpretation the text itself cannot bear. While it is true that a proper investigation of the intention of the human author can put a check on uncontrolled exegesis, this is more effectively accomplished when the foundational role of the text is recognized and argument proceeds from the text in its total context, including any elucidation given by the rest of Scripture.

The classical hermeneutical principle of *analogia Scripturae* states that we must interpret each passage in the light of, and in harmony with, other Scriptures. As the *Westminster Confession of Faith* 1, 9 puts it:

> The infallible rule of interpretation of Scripture is the Scripture itself; and therefore, when there is a question about the true and full sense of any Scripture (which is not manifold, but one), it may be searched and known by other places that speak more clearly.

If we were to limit meaning to the human author's intention we would have no basis for using the analogy of Scripture to check present-day interpretations that conflict with other teachings of Scripture. This principle of *analogia Scripturae* assumes correctly that our primary task is to understand God's intention, not fundamentally the human author's. After all, the Bible is *God's* Word.

5

Divine Meaning of Scripture

Vern Sheridan Poythress

From Vern Sheridan Poythress, "Divine Meaning of Scripture," *Westminster Theological Journal* 48 (1986): 241–79. Reprinted by permission.

What is the relation between God and human authors of the Bible? Does God's meaning at every point coincide with the intention of the human author? Can we use the same procedures of interpretation as we would with a noninspired book?

Even if we hold an orthodox, "high" view of inspiration, the answer to these questions is not easy. Many, of course, would deny that God is the author of the Bible in any straightforward way. They argue that the books of the Bible are to be interpreted as so many human writings, subject to the errors, distortions, and moral failures of human beings everywhere else.[1]

---

1. E.g., James Barr, *The Bible in the Modern World* (London: SCM, 1973); *The Scope and Authority of the Bible* (Philadelphia: Westminster, 1980); *Holy Scripture: Canon, Authority, Criticism* (Philadelphia: Westminster, 1983); may be taken as representative of one form of this view. Barr along with many interpreters in the historical-critical tradition wants to retain a diffuse authority for the Bible. Theologians are still called upon to reflect upon the Bible, and say what they think the implications are for our doctrine. But this is not to say that they treat the Bible as what God says.

A more conservative Barthian view, or a "canonical" approach like that of Brevard Childs (*Introduction to the Old Testament as Scripture* [Philadelphia: Fortress, 1979]), would leave more room for a distinctively "theological" interpretation based on historical-critical interpretation or alongside of it. But such approaches, in my opinion, still compromise divine authorship and authority by allowing errors in the propositional content of Scripture. See, e.g., John M. Frame, "God and Biblical Language: Transcendence and Immanence," in *God's Inerrant Word*, ed. John Warwick Montgomery (Minneapolis: Bethany Fellowship, 1974), 159–77.

If, however, we believe in the testimony of Jesus Christ, the apostles, and the Old Testament, we know that books of the Bible are both God's word and the word of the human authors. The exact historical, psychological, and spiritual processes involved in the production of individual books of the Bible may, of course, have varied from book to book. In many cases we simply do not have much firm information about these processes. In all cases, however, the result was that the literary product (specifically, the autograph) was *both* what God says *and* what the human author says (see, e.g., Deut. 5:22–33; Acts 1:16; 2 Pet. 1:21).[2]

Suppose, then, that we confine ourselves to people who hold to this classic doctrine of inspiration. We still do not have agreement about the relation of God's meaning to the meaning of the human author. A recent article by Darrell Bock[3] delineates no less than four distinct approaches among evangelicals. The specific issue which Bock discusses is the question of New Testament interpretation of the Old Testament. Does New Testament use of Old Testament texts sometimes imply that God meant more than what the human author thought of? Walter C. Kaiser, Jr., says no, while S. Lewis Johnson, James I. Packer, and Elliott Johnson say yes.[4] Bruce K. Waltke introduces still a third approach emphasizing the canon as the final context for interpretation. A fourth approach, represented by E. Earle Ellis, Richard Longenecker, and Walter Dunnett, emphasizes the close relation between apostolic hermeneutics and Jewish hermeneutics of the first century.[5]

Admittedly the New Testament use of the Old Testament has some complexities of its own. We cannot here look at all of the ways in which the New Testament makes use of the Old Testament. Instead, we will concentrate on the problem of dual authorship, a problem touching on our understanding of the entire Bible, rather than on the New Testament or Old Testament specifically.

Divine Meaning and Human Meaning

Disagreements in interpretation arise from differing views of the relation of divine and human authorship. The chief question is this: What

---

2. I am aware that almost any biblical passage one could cite concerning inspiration has been disputed by deniers of inerrancy. Moreover, with few exceptions the direct statements about inspiration refer primarily to the OT (or parts of it) rather than to the NT. Hence some additional arguments are needed. But it is outside the scope of this chapter to deal with such disputations.

3. D. Bock, "Evangelicals and the Use of the Old Testament in the New," *BSac* 142 (1985): 209–23.

4. Elliott Johnson, however, wishes to express this "more" as more references ("references plenior"), not more sense ("sensus plenior").

5. Bock, "Evangelicals and the Use of the OT."

is the relationship between what God says to us through the text and what the human author says? Let us consider two simple alternatives. First, we could take the view that the meaning of the divine author has little or nothing to do with the meaning of the human author. For instance, according to an allegorical approach, commonly associated with Origen,[6] whenever the "literal" meaning is unworthy of God, it is to be rejected. And even when the "literal" meaning is unobjectionable, the heart of the matter is often to be found in another level of meaning, a "spiritual" or allegorical meaning. If we were to take such a view, we could argue that the spiritual or allegorical meaning is part of the *divine* meaning in the text. But the human author was not aware of it.

The difficulties with this view are obvious. When we detach the divine meaning from the human author, the text itself no longer exercises effective control over what meanings we derive from it. The decisive factor in what we find God to be saying is derived from our allegorical scheme and our preconceptions about what is "worthy" of God. We can read in what we afterwards read out. God's lordship over us through his word is in practice denied.

When we see the dangers of this view, we naturally become sympathetic with the opposite alternative. In this case, we say that what God says is simply what the human author says: no more, no less.[7] Sometimes, of course, there may be difficulties in determining what a particular human author says at a particular point. Moreover, sometimes what authors say may be not perfectly precise. Sometimes they may choose to be ambiguous or to hint at implications without blurting

6. Frederic W. Farrar, *History of Interpretation* (Grand Rapids: Baker, 1961), 191–98. But see R. P. C. Hanson, *Allegory and Event: A Study of the Sources and Significance of Origen's Interpretation of Scripture* (London: SCM, 1959), for a more balanced presentation of Origen. Note also the article by Dan G. McCartney in [*WTJ* 48 (1968)].

7. Walter C. Kaiser, Jr. might seem to be a representative of this "single-meaning" approach, by virtue of his strong statements in favor of the single meaning of biblical texts ("Legitimate Hermeneutics," in *Inerrancy*, ed. Norman L. Geisler [Grand Rapids: Zondervan, 1980], 125, 127; *Toward an Exegetical Theology: Biblical Exegesis for Preaching and Teaching* [Grand Rapids: Baker, 1981], 47). But Kaiser's position contains much more besides this. He provides detailed instructions for treating the question of applying the Bible to the present day (ibid., 34, 149–63). And he advises us, when interpreting a passage, to take into account "antecedent Scripture": books of the Bible composed before the composition of the passage in question (ibid., 131–47). This is not *merely* a way of saying that we should understand general historical and literary backgrounds of the passage. We must do that with any kind of text whatsoever. But, in addition, in the case of Scripture we should also devote particular attention to those texts which have the same divine author (ibid., 133–34). Finally, Kaiser acknowledges the need for systematic theology, integrating the teaching of the whole Bible (ibid., 161). This presupposes the value of viewing the whole of Scripture as the product of a single divine author. Hence Kaiser is concerned to protect the value of historical backgrounds and progressive revelation, rather than to deny the value of looking at the whole of the canon at some later stage of synthesis.

them out. But the difficulties here are the same difficulties that confront us with all interpretation of human language. Such difficulties
have never prevented us from understanding one another sufficiently to
carry on. The divine authorship of the Bible does not alter our procedure at all.

I am sympathetic with this view. With some qualifications it can
serve us well: much better, certainly, than the procedure of unbridled
allegorization. However, there are several nuances and complexities
about interpretation that this view does not handle well.

First of all, and perhaps most obviously, this view, at least as described so far, does not tell us enough about how the Bible speaks to our
situation and applies to ourselves.[8] Some of the human authors of the
Bible were, perhaps, consciously "writing for posterity," but most, at
least, were writing primarily to their contemporaries. They did not
write with us directly in view. Nor did they foresee all our circumstances and needs. We can still *overhear* what they said to people in
their own time, but that is not the same as hearing them speak *to* us.
How do we know what they want us to do with their words, if they did
not have us in mind?

A popular solution to this difficulty is to invoke E. D. Hirsch's distinction between "meaning" and "significance."[9] "Meaning," in Hirsch's
view, is what the human author expressed, including what is expressed
tacitly, allusively, or indirectly. It includes what can legitimately be inferred. "Significance" is a relation that we as readers draw between
what is said and our own (or others') situation. Interpretation of a biblical passage, narrowly speaking, determines the meaning of the human
author. Application involves the exploration of the significance *for us* of
that one meaning, and action in accordance with it.

Let us take as an example Malachi 3:8–12. Malachi here instructs his
readers that they have robbed God in tithes and offerings, and that they
are to bring the tithes to the temple storehouse, as Moses commanded.
Both the general principle of not robbing God and the specific application to keep the law of tithes are part of the "meaning." Malachi did not
have our modern situations immediately in view. Nevertheless, modern
readers are to apply Malachi's meaning to themselves. In a comprehensive way, they are to devote all their lives and substance to the Lord, and

---

8. Kaiser sees the deficiency here and presents a remedy (*Exegetical Theology,* 149–63).

9. Eric D. Hirsch, *Validity in Interpretation* (New Haven/London: Yale University,
1967); *The Aims of Interpretation* (Chicago: University of Chicago, 1976); cf. Emilio Betti,
Die Hermeneutik als allgemeine Methodik der Geisteswissenschaften (Tübingen: Mohr,
1962); Charles Altieri, *Act & Quality: A Theory of Literary Meaning and Humanistic Understanding* (Amherst: University of Massachusetts, 1981), 97–159; Kaiser, *Exegetical
Theology,* 32.

specifically they are liberally to give a portion (some would say, at least one tenth) of their gains to the church and Christian causes. These applications are "significances," based on a relation between Malachi's meaning and the modern situation.

So far this is reasonable. But there is a difficulty. "Significance" is here understood as any kind of relation that readers perceive between their own situations and the passage. There are many possible "significances," even for a single reader. There are many possible applications. What then distinguishes a good from a bad application of a passage of the Bible? Is it up to the reader's whim? In cases when we read Shakespeare, Camus, or some other human writer, we may derive "lessons" from what we read, and apply things to ourselves. But, as Hirsch and other theorists in his camp assert, it is we as readers who decide how to do this, based on our own framework or values.[10] To be sure, even a human writer may want to challenge our values. But we treat that challenge as simply a challenge from another human being, fallible like ourselves.

In the case of the Bible it is different. Precisely because it has divine authority, and for no other reason, we must allow it to challenge and reform even our most cherished assumptions and values. But how do we do this? We listen to the human author of, say, Malachi. But he speaks to the Jewish audience of his day, not to us. Hypothetically, therefore, modern readers might evade applying Malachi 3:8–12 to themselves by any of several strategies. 1) God's intention is simply Malachi's intention: that Malachi's Jewish readers repent concerning their attitude and practice in tithing. There is no implication for us. 2) God intends us to understand that we ought not to rob God, but this applies simply to our general attitude toward possessions, since there is no longer a temple in the Old Testament sense. 3) God intends us to understand that if we are remiss in our financial obligations in our day, he will send a prophet to let us know about it.

Note that these construals do not dispute the "meaning" of Malachi 3:8–12 in a Hirschian sense. They dispute only the applications ("significances"). There are several possible replies. For one thing, we could argue that the rest of Scripture, and the New Testament in particular, shows that we are to give proportionally (1 Cor. 16:1–4), and that in various other ways we are to be good stewards of God's gifts. That is not disputed. The question is whether *Malachi* shows us such applications.

Second, we may say that, in the light of the rest of the Bible, we know that God intends us to apply *Malachi* to our proportional giving. But if we say that God intends(!) each valid application of Malachi, then in an ordinary sense each valid application is part of God's meaning (=inten-

10. Hirsch, *Aims*, 95–158.

tion), even if it was not immediately in the view of the human author of Malachi. This seems to break down the idea that there is an *absolute, pure* equation between divine intention and human author's meaning. Divine intention includes more, inasmuch as God is aware of all the future applications.

Third, we may say that even though the human author did not have all the applications in mind, they are part of his "unconscious intention."[11] That is, the (valid) applications are the "kind of thing he had in mind." Once Malachi saw our circumstances, he would acknowledge the legitimacy of our applications. This is quite reasonable. But there are still some complexities. 1) Some people, with a very narrow conception of "meaning," might object that this breaks down the initial distinction between meaning and significance. I do not think that this is so, but it is sometimes hard to know where the exact line is drawn between "meaning" and "significance." 2) We still need to discuss what guidelines to use in drawing applications. How do we go about determining what Malachi would say were he confronted by a situation very different from any that he confronted in his own lifetime? We have only his text to go by. Or do we have also the rest of the biblical canon, which expresses thoughts consonant with Malachi's? But appealing to the rest of the canon as revealing the mind of God takes us beyond the mind of Malachi, unless we say that all this is in his "unconscious intention." 3) Even if Malachi were acquainted with our situation, he would never be as well acquainted with it as God is. Moreover, there is an undeniable difference between God's understanding of the text and Malachi's, since God is conscious of those aspects of Malachi's intention which are unconscious to Malachi himself.

What are we to do with these difficulties? I think it indicates that when we come to the point of application, we must somewhere along the way appeal directly to God's knowledge, authority, and presence. Otherwise, we are simply "overhearing" a human voice from long ago, a voice to which we may respond in whatever way suits our own value system. To be sure, the idea of simply equating divine and human meaning in the Bible is a useful one. It directs us away from the arbitrariness of an allegorical system. But when we use this idea in order simply to stick to human meaning, arbitrariness can still exist in the area of the application. No technical rigidity in our theory of meaning will, by itself, allow us to escape this easily, because there are an indefinite number of applications, and many of them are not *directly* anticipated in the text of Scripture.

I propose, then, to deal with this area of application. I count as "applications" both effects in the cognitive field (e.g., concluding mentally,

11. Hirsch, *Validity*, 51–57.

"I ought to have a practice of giving to my church") and effects in the field of overt action (e.g., putting money in the collection plate). "Application" in this sense *includes* all inferences about the meaning of a biblical text. Such inferences are always applications in the cognitive field. For example, to conclude that Malachi teaches tithing (inference about meaning) is simultaneously to come to *believe* that "Malachi teaches tithing" (a cognitive effect in the reasoner).

With this in mind, the central question confronting us is, "What applications of a biblical passage does God approve?" To answer this, we have to look at some characteristics of communication through language.

Interpreting Human Discourse

Let us first consider communication from one human being to another. Person A speaks discourse D to person B. Now, given almost any fixed sequence of words (D), we can plausibly interpret them in several different conflicting ways. We can do this by imagining different contexts in which they are spoken or written. "The door is open" can easily be intended to imply, "Please shut it," or "Get out," or "That is the cause of the draft," or "Someone was careless." Or it may simply convey a bit of information. To understand what another human being A is saying, in the discourse D, is not simply to explore the range of all possible interpretations of a sequence of words. Rather, it is to understand what the *speaker as a person* is saying. We do this using clues given by the situation and by what we know of the person. We must pay attention to the author and to the situation as well as to the exact choice of words.

Moreover, many different things are happening in an act of communication. For one thing, speakers make assertions about the world. They formulate hypotheses, they express assumptions, and otherwise make reference to the world. Let us call this the "referential" aspect of communication. But referring to the world is not all that speakers do. They may also be trying to bring about actions or changes of attitude on the part of their hearers. They are trying to achieve some practical result. Let us call this the "conative" aspect of communication. Next, whether they want to or not, speakers inevitably tell their hearers something about themselves and their own attitudes. Let us call this the "expressive" aspect of communication. In fact, Roman Jakobson, in analyzing communicative acts, defines no less than six planes or aspects of communication.[12] For our purposes, we may restrict ourselves to three prominent aspects: referential, conative, and expressive.

---

12. Roman Jakobson, "Closing Statement: Linguistics and Poetics," *Style in Language*, ed. Thomas A. Sebeok (Cambridge: Massachusetts Institute of Technology, 1960),

Note that most of the time a speaker is not doing only one of these. In fact, any of the three indirectly implies the others. Facts about the speaker's attitudes (expressive) are also one kind of fact about the world (referential). And facts about the speaker's goals or attempts to change the hearer (conative) are also one kind of fact about the world (referential). Conversely, any statements about the world (referential) simultaneously give information about what a speaker believes (expressive) and what the speaker wants others to believe (conative).

Interpreting Divine Speech

Now consider what is involved in interpreting speech from God to a human being. I have in mind instances such as God's speeches to Abraham (e.g., Gen. 12:1–3; 15:1–21; 17:1–21) and God's pronouncements from Mount Sinai to the people of Israel (Exod. 20:2–17). Of course, these speeches (or portions or condensations of them) are later on recorded in written form by human authors writing the books of the Bible. But for the moment let us concentrate on the original oral communication. This is useful, because no human being mediates these original acts of communication. In these cases, does interpretation proceed in the same way as with human speech? In a fundamental sense it does. For one thing, the speeches come in a human language (in this case Hebrew). They are sometimes directly compared with speech from one human being to another (Exod. 20:19). The audiences are expected to proceed in a way similar to what they do with speech from a human being. They interpret what God says in terms of the situation in which he speaks (Exod. 20:2; 20:18, 22), and in terms of what they already know about God and his purposes (Exod. 20:2; 20:11). But here lies the decisive difference, of course. The people are listening to *God*. Using the "same" interpretive process that we use with human speech is precisely what causes us to acknowledge the profound difference and uniqueness of divine speech—for God is unique.

Now consider what it means to know that God is speaking. We earlier observed that a discourse detached from any author and any situation could mean any number of things. Moreover, if we attribute a discourse to a different author or a different situation than the real one, we will often find that we interpret the same sequence of words in a different fashion. For example, if we think that the wording of Colossians 1:15 is a writing of Arius, we will interpret it differently than if we think it is a writing of the apostle Paul.

350–77. Cf. Vern S. Poythress, "A Framework for Discourse Analysis: The Components of a Discourse, from a Tagmemic Viewpoint," *Semiotica* 38–3/4 (1982): 277–98.

Likewise, if we think that the wording of God's speech at Mount Sinai is spoken by someone else, or if we have mistaken conceptions about God, this will more or less seriously affect our interpretation of the speech. What is authoritative about God's speech at Mount Sinai? Divine authority does not attach to whatever meaning other people may attach to the words. They may even choose to speak the same sequence of words as in Exodus 20:2–17, yet mean something different. In this sense, we may freely admit that many "meanings" can be attached to these same words. But that is not the issue. Rather, divine authority belongs to what *God* is saying. What is crucial is what *God* means. To find this out, we must interpret the words in accordance with what we know about God, just as we would take into account what we know of human authors when we interpret what they say.

But, someone may say, this is circular. How can we know God except by what he says and does? And how can we properly understand what he says and does unless we already know him? Well, how do we come to know another human being? In both cases there is a certain "theoretical" circularity. But in fact, it is more like a spiral, because earlier incorrect impressions may be corrected in the process of seeing and hearing more from a person.

In addition, we may say something about the application of God's words. God expects his words to be applied in many situations throughout history. He binds us to obey, not only what he says in the most direct way ("meaning"), but what he implies ("application"). Each valid application is something that God intended from the beginning, and as such has his sanction. Divine authority attaches not only to what he says most directly, but to what he implies. It attaches to the applications.

Of course, we must be careful. We may be wrong when we extend our inferences too far. We must respect the fact that our inferences are not infallible. Where we are not sure, or where good reasons exist on the other side, we must beware of insisting that our interpretation must be obeyed. But if it turns out that we did understand the implications and applications correctly, then we know that those applications also had divine sanction and authority.

This means, then, that we do not need a rigid, precise distinction between meaning and application, in the case of God's speech. To be sure, some things are said directly ("meaning"), and some things are left to be inferred in the light of seeing a relation between what is said and our situation ("significance," "application"). But the distinction, as far as I can see, is a relative one. It is a distinction between what is said *more or less directly*, and between what needs *more or less* reckoning with a larger situation in order to be inferred.

The usual way of distinguishing between meaning and application is to say that meaning has to do with what the text itself says (in itself), whereas application has to do with a *relation* between the text and the reader's situation. But we have already seen that, in general, we cannot properly assess "meaning" even in the narrowest possible sense apart from attention to the author's situation. This situation includes the hearers. *All* assessment of an author's expressed meaning must reckon with the intended hearers and their situation. In the case of divine speech, all future hearers are included, hence all their situations are included. Therefore, focus on what the text says most directly and obviously, and focus on what it is seen to say in the light of relation to a situation, are both a matter of degree.

Next, we may observe that God's speeches include referential, expressive, and conative aspects. God's speeches make assertions about the world and about ethical standards for our lives (the referential aspect). Secondly, we meet *God* when we hear him speaking (the expressive aspect). And thirdly, we are affected and transformed by what we hear (the conative aspect). God's word may empower us to do good, but it may also harden our hearts when we are rebellious.

These three aspects of God's communication are not so many isolated pieces. Rather, they are involved in one another. In fact, each one can serve as a perspective on the whole of God's communication.

First of all, all of God's speech is referential in character. In all of what God says, he is bringing us to *know* him and his world. For knowledge includes not just information (knowing that), but skills in living (knowing how) and personal communion with God (knowing a person).

Second, in all of what God says, we meet him: he "expresses" himself. God is present with his word.

Third, in all of what God says, he affects us ("conatively") for good or ill, for blessing or for cursing (e.g., 2 Cor. 2:15–16).

These three aspects of God's speech are expressions of his knowledge (referential), his presence (expressive), and his active power (conative). These are nothing less than attributes of God. It is no wonder that we find these features in all that God says.

Divine Speech as Propositional and Personal

We may already draw some conclusions with respect to modern views of revelation. Neo-orthodoxy and other modernist views of divine revelation typically argue that revelation is personal encounter and therefore not propositional. But these are not exclusive alternatives. Human communication in general is simultaneously both. That is, it simultaneously possesses a referential and an expressive aspect. To be sure, one or other aspect may be more prominent and more utilized at one time, but each tacitly implies the other. Moreover, to know a person always involves knowing true statements about the person, though it means also more than this. If the supposed "encounter" with the divine is indeed "personal," it will inevitably be propositional as well. When I say that communication is "propositional," I do not of course mean that it must be a logical treatise. I mean only that communication conveys information about states of affairs in the world. One may infer from it that certain statements about the world are true.

In our claims about divine speech we do not rely only on general arguments based on the nature of human communication. The reader of Scripture over and over again finds accounts of divine communication that involve both propositional statements and personal presence of God. (Exodus 20 may serve as well as many other examples.)

But there are lessons here also for evangelicals. Evangelicals have sometimes rebounded against modernist views into an opposite extreme. In describing biblical interpretation, they have sometimes minimized the aspect of personal encounter and divine power to transform us. There is no need to do this. The issue with modernism is rather what *sort* of divine encounter and personal transformation we are talking about: is it contentless, or does it accompany what is being said (referentially and propositionally) about the world?

Moreover, there may be a tiny grain of truth in the slanders from modernists about evangelicals "idolizing" the pages of the Bible. We say that divine speech is "propositional." To begin with, we mean only that God makes true statements referring to the world. That is correct. But then, later on, we may come to mean something else. We think that we can isolate that referential and assertive character of what God is saying into gem-like, precise, syllogistic nuggets which can be manipulated and controlled by us, from then on, without further reflection on God's presence and power at work in what we originally heard. The "proposition," now isolated from the presence of God, can become the excuse for evading God and trying to lord it over and rationally master the truth which we have isolated. And then we have become subtly idolatrous, because we aspire to be lords over God's word.

I do not mean to bar us from reasoning from Scripture. We *must* do this in order to struggle responsibly to apply the Bible to ourselves. We must take seriously its implications as well as what is said most directly. What I have in mind is this. Even with the discourses from human beings, it would be unfair not to take into account what we know of their character, their views and their aspirations when we draw out the implications of an individual sentence. A statement with no explicit qualifications, and with no explicit directions as to the way in which we are to draw implications, may nevertheless not be completely universal. It may not have all the implications that we think. A larger knowledge of the author forms one kind of guide to the drawing of implications. At least this much is true with respect to the situation where God is the author.

Speech with Two Authors

So far we have discussed speech with a single author. But of course the Bible as we have it is a product of both the divine author and various human authors. How do we deal with this situation?

Well, the Bible makes it very clear that what God says does not cease to be what God says just because a human intermediary is introduced (Deut. 5:22–33). After all, it is God who chose the human intermediary and who fashioned his personality (Ps. 139:13–16). Hence everything that we have said about divine speech, such as God's speeches to Abraham, applies also to God's speeches through human spokesmen. In particular, it applies to all of the Bible, as the written word of God.

Conversely, what human beings say to us does not cease to be what they say when they become spokesmen of God. Hence, it would appear, everything that we have said about human communication applies to all of the Bible, as the writings of men.

But now we have a complex situation. For we have just argued that interpretation of a piece of writing interprets the words in the light of what is known of the author and his situation. If the same words happen to be said by two authors, there are two separate interpretations. The interpretations may have very similar results, or they may not, depending on the differences between the two authors and the way in which those differences mesh with the wording of the text. But, in principle, there may be differences, even if only very subtle differences of nuances.

Hence it would seem to be the case that we have two separate interpretations of any particular biblical text. The first interpretation sees the words entirely in the light of the human author, his characteristics, his knowledge, his social status. The second sees the same words entirely in the light of the divine author, his characteristics, his knowledge, his status. In general, the results of these two interpretations will differ.

But couldn't we still stick to a single interpretation? Couldn't we say that interpretation in the light of the human author is all that we need? Then, after we complete the interpretation, we assert that the product is, pure and simple, what God says.

Well, that still leaves us with the earlier problems about applications. But in addition to this, there are now several further objections. First, the strongest starting point of the "single interpretation" approach is its insistence on the importance of grammatical-historical exegesis. But it has now ended by hedging on one of the principles of grammatical-historical exegesis, namely the principle of taking into account the person of the author. When we come to interpreting the Bible, we must pay attention to who God is.

Secondly, this view seems dangerously akin to the neo-orthodox view that when God speaks, his attributes of majesty are somehow wholly hidden under human words. That is why the neo-orthodox think that they need not reckon with the divine attributes when they subject Scripture to the historical-critical method. As evangelicals, we do not want to use the antisupernaturalist assumptions of historical-critical method. We will not do that when it comes to miracles described in the Bible. But are we going to do it when we deal with the actual reading of the Bible?

Third, we must remember that God's speech involves his presence and power as well as propositional affirmations. At the beginning of interpretation we cannot arbitrarily eliminate the power and presence of God in his word, in order to tack them on only at the end. That automatically distorts what is happening in biblical communication from God. Hence it is asking for skewed results at the end.

Fourth, this procedure virtually demands that, at the first stage, we *not* reckon with the fact that God is who he is in his speaking to us. We must put wholly into the background that he is speaking to us. We must simply and *exclusively* concentrate on the human author. But how can we *not* reckon with all that we know of God as we hear what he says? This seems to be at odds with the innate impulse of biblical piety.

But there may still be a way to save this "single interpretation" approach. Namely, we can claim that God in his freedom decided to "limit" what he said to the human side. Namely, God decided to say simply what we arrive at through the interpretation of biblical passages when treated as though simply human.

This is a valiant effort. It is close to the truth. But, myself, I think that it will not work. First, it is difficult to see how one can justify this from Scripture. Deuteronomy 5:22–33 is a natural passage with which to begin. It describes the nature of God's communication through Moses. Since later Scripture builds on Moses, Deuteronomy 5:22–33 indirectly illuminates the nature of all God's later communication through human beings. Now Deuteronomy 5:22–33 starts first with divine communication. The human instrument is taken up into the divine message, rather than the divine message being "trimmed down" to suit the human instrument. If we were willing to use the analogy with the person and natures of Christ, we could say that Deuteronomy 5:22–33 is analogous to the Chalcedonian view (human nature taken up into the divine person), whereas the "single interpretation" approach is analogous to a kenotic view (divine person "losing" some attributes for the sake of assuming human nature).

Second, I find it psychologically impossible to maintain the experience of God's power and presence on the one hand, and on the other to exclude all reckoning with them when we come to assessing the referential aspect of biblical communication. It is not so easy thus to separate the referential from the expressive and the conative aspects of communication. God speaks to us as whole people. Moreover, if one could separate them, one would have arrived back at an essentially neo-orthodox dichotomy between propositional content and personal encounter.

Third, I think that scholarly hesitation about emphasizing God's role in authorship, though understandable, is groundless. Perhaps some scholars are influenced by the modernist atmosphere. Since modernists disbelieve in divine authorship, naturally their hermeneutical approach will demand its exclusion. We may unknowingly have absorbed some of this atmosphere.

But scholars have another cause for hesitation. Mention of God's role easily leads to dehistoricizing the message of the Bible. Readers reason to themselves that since God wrote the book, and since God is not subject to the limitations of knowledge of any historical period, he can be expected to write to all historical periods equally. Hence the historical circumstances in which the Bible appeared are irrelevant. The Bible is just like a book dropped directly from heaven.

Against this argument we may point to Exodus 20. There God speaks without a human intermediary. But this speech is not simply a speech "for posterity." It is a speech directly to specific people in specific circumstances (Exod. 20:2, 12), people subject to specific temptations (Exod. 20:17). The most important factor leading to a historically rooted message is not the human intermediary (though this further emphasizes it), but the fact that God chooses to speak to people where they are. He can do so fluently because he is competent in Hebrew, Greek, Aramaic, and is master of all the customs of each culture into which he chooses to speak. Over against this, the dehistoricizing approach not only neglects human intermediaries. It unwittingly denies *God's* linguistic and cultural competence!

Hence, I conclude, the confinement to purely human meaning is not correct. But if this is not the answer, what is? If we do not collapse the two interpretations into one, do they simply exist side by side, with no necessary relation to one another? This would result in reproducing the problems of the old allegorical approach.

Personal Communion of Authors

The Bible itself shows the way to a more satisfactory resolution of the difficulty. In the Bible itself, the two authors, human and divine, do not simply stand side by side. Rather, each points to the other and affirms the presence and operation of the other.

First, God himself points out the importance of the human authors. For example, when God establishes Moses as the regular channel for conveying his word to the people of Israel, he makes it clear that Moses, not merely God, is to be active in teaching the people (Deut. 5:31; 6:1). Similarly, the commissioning of prophets in the Old Testament often includes a mention of their own active role, not only in speaking God's word to the people, but in actively absorbing it (Ezek. 2:8–3:3; Dan. 10:1–21; Jer. 23:18). This is still more clear in the case of Paul's writings, where his own personality is so actively involved. Now, what happens when we pay careful attention to God as the divine author? We find that we must pay attention to what he says about the role of the human authors. Sometimes he directly affirms the significance of their involvement; sometimes this is only implied. But whichever is the case, it means that God himself requires us to interpret the words of Scripture against the background of what we know about the human author. We cannot simply ignore the human author, when we concentrate on what *God* is saying.

Conversely, the human authors of the Bible indicate that they intend us to interpret their words as not merely words that they speak as ordinary persons. For example, here and there Isaiah says, "Thus says the Lord." What is the effect of such phrases? Would the inhabitants of Jerusalem in Isaiah's time say, "Now we must interpret what our friend Isaiah is saying simply in terms of everything we know about him: his relations with his family, his opinions about agriculture and politics, and so on." Certainly not! When Isaiah says, "Thus says the Lord," it is no doubt still Isaiah who is speaking. But Isaiah himself, by using these words, has told people to create a certain distance between himself, merely viewed as a private individual, and what the Lord has commissioned him to convey. In addition to this, consider what happens when Isaiah makes detailed predictions about the distant future. If the hearers treat him simply as a private human being, they would say, "Well, we know Isaiah, and we know the limits of his knowledge of the future. So, because of what we know about him, it is obvious that he is simply expressing his dreams or making artistically interesting guesses." Again, such a reaction misunderstands Isaiah's claims.

We may try to focus as much as possible on Isaiah as a human author. The more carefully we do our job, the more we will realize that he is not just any human author. He is one through whom God speaks. His own intentions are that we should reckon with this. It is not a denial of human authorship, but an affirmation of it, when we pay attention to God speaking. In particular, in the case of predictions, we pay attention to all that we know of God, God's knowledge of the future, the wisdom of his plan, and the righteousness of his intentions. This is in accord with Isaiah's intention, not contrary to it. In fact, we might say that Isaiah's intention was that we should understand whatever God intended by his words.[13] Hence there *is* a unity of meaning and a unity of application here. We do not have two diverse meanings, Isaiah's and God's, simply placed side by side with no relation to one another.

But the matter is complex. What we have here is a situation of personal communion between God and prophet. Each person affirms the significance of the other's presence for proper interpretation. On the one hand, God has formed the personality of the prophet, has spoken to him in the heavenly counsel (Jer. 23:18), has brought him into inner sympathy with the thrust of his message. What the prophet says using his own particular idiom fits exactly what God decided to say. On the other hand, the prophet affirms that what God is saying is true even where the prophet cannot see all its implications.

This situation therefore leaves open the question of how far a prophet understood God's words at any particular point. The Bible affirms the prophets' inner participation in the message. In addition extraordinary psychological experiences were sometimes involved. Because of this, it would be presumptuous to limit dogmatically a prophet's understanding to what is "ordinarily" possible. On the other hand, it seems to me equally presumptuous to insist that at every point there must be complete understanding on the part of the prophet. Particularly this is so for cases of visionary material (Dan. 7, 10; Zech. 1–6; Rev. 4:1–22:5) or historical records of divine speech (e.g., the Gospel records of Jesus' parables). Why should we have to say, in the face of Daniel 7:16; Zechariah 4:4–5; Revelation 7:14, and the like, that the prophets came to understand everything that there was to understand, by the time that they wrote their visions down? Isn't it enough to stick with what is clear? It is clear that the prophet faithfully recorded what he saw and heard. He intended that we should understand from it whatever there is to understand when we treat it as a vision from God. Similarly, there is no need to insist that Luke understood all the ramifications of each of Jesus' parables. He may have, but then again he may not

---

13. See, e.g., Ben F. Meyer, *The Aims of Jesus* (London: SCM, 1979), 246: "In prophecy what the symbol intends is identical with what God, for whom the prophet speaks, intends. This may enter the prophet's own horizon only partially and imperfectly."

have. The results for our interpretation of the parables in the Gospel of Luke will be the same.

I have spoken primarily about the role of prophets in speaking the word of God. But, of course, prophecy is not the only form in which the Bible is written. The different genres of biblical writings, prophecy, law, history, wisdom, song, each call for different nuances in our approach. The relation between divine and human participation in the writing is not always exactly the same.[14]

For instance, consider the case of Mosaic law. The background of the meeting at Mount Sinai forms a framework for Moses's later writings, and leads us to reckon more directly with the divine source of the law. On the other hand, Moses' close communion with God (Num. 12:6–8) hints at his inner understanding of the law.

In the case of prophecy, narrowly speaking, the prophet's pronouncement, "Thus says the Lord," and the predictive elements in his message frequently have the effect of highlighting the distinction between the prophet as mere human being and the prophet as channel for the Lord's message. The prophet himself steps into the background, as it were, in order to put all the emphasis on God's speaking. In visionary experiences this may be all the more the case, inasmuch as it is often not clear how much the prophet understands.

With the Psalms and the New Testament Epistles, on the other hand, the human author and his understanding come much more to the front. The apostle Paul does not continually say, "Thus says the Lord." That is not because he has no divine message. Rather, it is (largely) because he has so thoroughly absorbed the message into his own person. He has "the mind of Christ" (1 Cor. 2:16, 13), as a man indwelt by the Spirit.[15]

Here we confront still another complexity. What is human nature, and what does it mean to analyze a passage as the expression of a human author? If the human author is Paul, that means Paul filled with the Holy Spirit. We are not dealing with "bare" human nature (as if human beings ever existed outside of a relationship to God of one kind or another). We are already dealing with the divine, namely the Holy Spirit. Paul as a human being may not be immediately, analytically self-

14. Abraham Kuyper notices some of these differences and argues for a division into the categories of lyric, chokmatic, prophetic, and apostolic inspiration (*Principles of Sacred Theology* [Grand Rapids: Eerdmans, 1968], 520–44, the section on "The Forms of Inspiration").

15. See Peter R. Jones, "The Apostle Paul: A Second Moses according to 2 Corinthians 2:14–4:7" (Ph.D. dissertation, Princeton University; Ann Arbor: University Microfilms, 1974); idem, "The Apostle Paul: Second Moses to the New Covenant Community: A Study in Pauline Apostolic Authority," in *God's Inerrant Word*, ed. John Warwick Montgomery (Minneapolis: Bethany Fellowship, 1974), 219–44.

conscious of all the implications of what he is saying. But people always know more and imply more than what they are perfectly self-conscious of. How far does this "more" extend? We are dealing with a person restored in the image of Christ, filled with the Holy Spirit, having the mind of Christ. There are incalculable depths here. We cannot calculate the limits of the Holy Spirit and the wisdom of Christ. Neither can we perform a perfect analytical separation of our knowledge from our union with Christ through the Holy Spirit.

Christological Fullness in Interpretation

The complexities that we meet here are only a shadow of the greatest complexity of all: the speeches of the incarnate Christ. Here God is speaking, not through a mere human being distinct from God, but in his own person. The eternal Word of God, the Second Person of the Trinity, speaks. Hence we must interpret what he says in the light of all that we know of God the author. At the same time a man speaks, Jesus of Nazareth. With respect to his human nature, he has limited knowledge (Luke 2:52). Hence we must interpret what he says in the light of all that we know of Jesus of Nazareth in his humanity.

This is a permanent mystery! Yet we know that we do not have two antithetical interpretations, one for the human nature speaking and one for the divine nature speaking. We know that there is a unity, based on the unity of the one person of Christ. However, it is possible, with respect to his *human nature,* that Jesus Christ is not exhaustively self-conscious of all the ramifications, nuances, and implications of what he says. He nevertheless does take responsibility for those ramifications, as does any other human speaker. As the *divine* Son, Jesus Christ does know all things, including all ramifications, applications, et cetera, of his speech. There is a distinction here, but nevertheless no disharmony.

In addition to this, we may say that Jesus in his human nature was especially endowed with the Spirit to perform his prophetic work, as planned by God the Father (Luke 4:18–19; 3:22). When we interpret his speech, we should take into account that the Holy Spirit speaks through him. Thus, we are saying that we must take into account the ultimately trinitarian character of revelation, as well as the unique fullness of the Spirit's endowment in Christ's messianic calling.

In short, when we interpret Christ's speech, we interpret it (as we do all speech) in the light of the author. That is, we interpret it as the speech of the divine Son. But Christ says that the Father speaks through him (John 14:10; 12:48–50). Hence it is the speech of the Father. Since the Holy Spirit comes upon Jesus to equip him for his messianic work, we also conclude that it is the speech of the Spirit. And of course it is the speech of the man Jesus of Nazareth. Each of these aspects of inter-pretation is distinct, at least in nuance!

What we meet in Christ is verbal communication undergirded by a communion and fellowship of understanding. In Christ's being there is no pure mathematical identity of divine persons or identity of two na-tures, but harmony. The result is that there is no pure mathematical identity in the interpretive product. That is, we cannot in a pure way an-alyze simply what the words mean as (for instance) proceeding from the human nature of Christ, and then say that precisely that, no more, no less, is the exhaustive interpretation of his words.

The case of divine speech through apostles and prophets is, of course, secondary, but none the less analogous. The revelation of Jesus Christ is the pinnacle (Heb. 1:1–3). All other revelations through proph-ets and apostles are secondary to this supreme revelation. There is ulti-mately no other way to gain deeper insight into the secondary than through the pinnacle. Hence we cannot expect to collapse the richness of divine presence into a mathematical point, when we are dealing with the words of the Bible.

Progressive Understanding

A further complexity arises because the many human authors of the Bible write over a long period of time. None of the human authors ex-cept the very last can survey the entire product in order to arrive at an interpretation of the whole.

Once again, we may throw light on the situation by starting with a simpler case. Suppose that we have a single uninspired human author speaking or writing to a single audience over a period of time. Even if we are dealing with only a single long oral discourse, the discourse is spread out in time. Individual statements and individual paragraphs near the beginning of the discourse are understood first, then those near the end. Moreover, an audience is in a better position to draw more inferences from earlier parts of a discourse once they have reached the end. Typically, all the parts of a discourse qualify and color each other. We understand more by reading the whole than we do from reading any one part, or even from all the parts separately. The effect is somewhat like the effect of different parts of an artist's picture. If we just attend to small bits of paint within the picture, one by one, we may miss many implications of the whole. The "meaning" of the picture does not reside merely in a mechanical, mathematical sum of the blobs of paint. Rather, it arises from the joint effect of the individual pieces. Their joint effect arises from the relations between the pieces. Likewise, the import of an author's discourse arises partly from the reinforcements, qualifications, tensions, complementations, and other relations between the individual words and sentences, as well as from the effects of each sentence "in itself."

The overall effect of this is that an audience may understand what the first part of a discourse means, and then have that understanding modified and deepened by the last of the discourse.

Now consider a particular example of two people in communication over a long period of time. Suppose a father teaches his young son to sing "Jesus Loves Me." Later on, he tells the story of the life of Christ from a children's Bible story book. Still later, he explains how the Old Testament sacrificial system depicted aspects of Christ's purpose in dying for us. Finally, the son becomes an adult and does extended Bible study for himself. Suppose then that the son remembers how his father taught him "Jesus Loves Me." He asks, "What was my father saying in telling me the words of the song?" At the time, did I understand what he was saying? The answer may well be yes. The son understood what the father expected that he would have capacity to understand at that point. But the father knew as well that the child's initial understanding was not the end point. The father intended that the earlier words should be recalled later. He intended that the son should understand his father's mind better and better by comparing those earlier words with later words that the father would share.

Now, suppose that there was no misunderstanding, no misjudgment at any point. There is still more than one level of understanding of the father's words. There is what one may understand on the basis of those words more or less by themselves, when not supplemented by further words, and when seen as words adapted to the capacity of the young child. And there is what one may understand on the basis of comparing and relating those words to many later words (and actions) of the father. The first of these understandings is a legitimate one, an understanding not to be underestimated. As long as the child has only those words of the father, and not all the later history, it would be unfair of him to build up an exact, elaborate analysis of all the ramified implications of the statements. But once the father has said a lot more, it throws more light on what the father intended all along that those words should do: they should contribute along with many other words to form and engender an enormously rich understanding of Christ's love, an understanding capable of being evoked and alluded to by the words of the song.

The complexity arises, as before, from the dynamic and relational character of communicative meaning. The understanding we achieve from listening arises not only from individual words or sentences in the discourse but from the complex relations that they have to one another and to the larger situation, including what we know of the author himself. In particular, the song, "Jesus Loves Me," conveys meaning not simply in virtue of the internal arrangement of the words, but also in virtue of the context of who is saying it, what else is being said by way of explanation, and so on. True, there is something like a "common core" of meaning shared by all or nearly all uses of the song. But the implications that we may see around that common core may differ. (Imagine the song being used by a liberal who believes that in fact Jesus is merely human, and therefore still dead. In his mouth, the song is only a metaphorical expression of an ideal of human love.)

Progressive Revelation

Now we are ready to raise the crucial question: does something analogous to this happen with God's communication to his people over the period of time from Adam onwards? Is God like a human father speaking to his child?

The basic answer is obviously yes. But, for those who do not think it is so obvious, we can supply reasons.

1) Israel is called God's son (Exod. 4:22; Deut. 8:5), and Paul explicitly likens the Old Testament period to the time of a child's minority (Gal. 4:3–4). These passages are not directly discussing the question of biblical interpretation, but they are nevertheless suggestive.

2) From very early in the history of the human race God indicates in his speeches to us that more is to come. History and the promises of God are forward-looking. The story is yet to be completed. It is altogether natural to construe this as implying that earlier promissory statements of God may be more deeply understood once the promises begin to be fulfilled, and especially when they are completely fulfilled. Similar reflections evidently apply even to the hope we now have as Christians (1 Cor. 13:12).

3) In at least a few cases, within the pages of the Old Testament, we find prophecies whose fulfillments take unexpected form. One of the most striking is Jacob's prophecy about the dispersion of Simeon and Levi (Gen. 49:7b).[16] If we attend *only* to the immediate context (49:7a), we are bound to conclude that God undertakes to disgrace both tribes by giving them no connected spot of settlement. The actual fulfillment is therefore quite surprising in the case of Levi. But it is not out of accord with God's character of turning cursings into blessings. What we know about him includes his right to exceed our expectations. This

16. Oswald T. Allis, *Prophecy and the Church* (Philadelphia: Presbyterian and Reformed, 1945), 30.

whole affair is more easily understood when we take into account the fact that Genesis 49:7 is not an isolated word of God, but part of a long history of God's communications, yet to be completed. We are not supposed to make dogmatically precise judgments without hearing the whole.

In short, God's actual ways of bringing fulfillments may vary. Some of them may be straightforward, others may be surprising. This is true just as it is true that an author may continue a discourse in a straightforward way, or in a surprising way that causes us to reassess the exact point of the first part of what he says.

4) The symbolic aspect of Old Testament institutions proclaim their own inadequacy (Heb. 10:1, 4). They are not only *analogous* to the final revelation of God, but at some points *disanalogous* (Heb. 10:4). Suppose that people stand in the Old Testament situation, trying to understand what is symbolized. They will inevitably continue with *some* questions unanswered until they are able to *relate* what is said and done earlier to what God does at the coming of Christ. Until the point of completion, the interpretation must remain open-ended (but not contentless).

5) Likewise, the speech of God is not complete until the coming of Christ (Heb. 1:1–3). We must, as it were, hear the end of the discourse before we are in a position to weigh the total context in terms of which we may achieve the most profound understanding of each part of the discourse.

I conclude, then, that any particular passage of the Bible is to be read in three progressively larger contexts, as follows.

a) Any passage is to be read in the context of the particular book of the Bible in which it appears, and in the context of the human author and historical circumstances of the book. God speaks truly to the people in particular times and circumstances.

b) Any passage is to be read in the context of the total canon of Scripture available up to that point in time.[17] The people originally addressed by God must take into account that God's speech does not start with them, but presupposes and builds on previous utterances of God.

c) Any passage is to be read in the context of the entire Bible (the completed canon). God intended from the beginning that his later words should build on and enrich earlier words, so that in some sense the whole of the Bible represents one long, complex process of communication from one author.

17. This point is rightly emphasized by Kaiser, *Exegetical Theology,* 79–83.

For example, Ezekiel 34 is to be understood a) in terms of the immediate context of the Book of Ezekiel and the historical circumstances in which the book first appeared; b) in terms of its continuation of the word of God recorded in the law of Moses and the preexilic prophets; c) in terms of what we can understand in the light of the whole completed Bible, including the New Testament.[18]

In addition to these three analyses of the passage we may, in more fine-grained reflection, distinguish still other possibilities. In principle, we may ask what the passage contributes at any point during the progressive additions to canon through further revelation. For example, Bruce K. Waltke argues that in the case of the Psalms (and presumably many other Old Testament books), it is illuminating to ask about their meaning at the time when the Old Testament canon was complete but before the dawn of the New Testament era.[19] For simplicity we confine the subsequent discussion to the approaches (a), (b), and (c).

As we have said again and again, what we understand from a passage depends not only on the sequence of words of the passage, but the context in which it occurs. Hence the three readings (a), (b), and (c) can, in principle, lead to three different results. Some people might want to speak of three meanings. Meaning (a) would be the meaning obtained from focusing most on the human author and his circumstances. Meaning (c) would be the meaning obtained from focusing most on the divine author and all that we know about him from the whole of the Bible.

However, for most purposes I myself would prefer to avoid calling these three results three "meanings." To do that suggests that three unrelated and perhaps even contradictory things are being said. But these three approaches are complementary, not contradictory. The difference between these three approaches is quite like the difference between reading one chapter of a book and reading the whole of the book. After taking into account the whole book, we understand the one chapter as well as the whole book more deeply. But it does not mean that our understanding of the one chapter by itself was incorrect. Remember again the example of "Jesus Loves Me."

18. My approach is virtually identical with that of Bruce K. Waltke, "A Canonical Process Approach to the Psalms," in *Tradition and Testament: Essays in Honor of Charles Lee Feinberg*, ed. John S. Feinberg and Paul D. Feinberg (Chicago: Moody, 1981), 3–18. My arguments rest more on the general features of communication, whereas Waltke's arguments rely more on the concrete texture of OT revelation. Hence the two articles should be seen as complementary. See also William Sanford LaSor, "The *Sensus Plenior* and Biblical Interpretation," in *Scripture, Tradition, and Interpretation*, ed. W. Ward Gasque and William Sanford LaSor (Grand Rapids: Eerdmans, 1978), 260–77; Douglas Moo, "The Problem of *Sensus Plenior*," in *Hermeneutics, Authority, and Canon*, ed. D. A. Carson and John D. Woodbridge (Grand Rapids: Zondervan, 1986).
19. Waltke, "A Canonical Process Approach," 9.

Psalm 22:12–18 as an Example

To see how this works, let us consider Psalm 22:12–18. Let us begin with approach (a), focusing on the human author. The passage speaks of the distress of a person who trusts in God (22:2–5, 8–10), but is nevertheless abandoned to his enemies. In a series of shifting metaphors the psalmist compares his suffering to being surrounded by bulls (22:12–13), to being sick or weak in body through emotional distress (22:14–15), to being caught by ravening dogs (22:16), to being treated virtually like a carcass (22:17–18).[20] The psalmist's words evidently spring from his own experience of a situation of abandonment.

We encounter a special complexity in the case of psalms. The actual author (David, according to the title of Psalm 22)[21] and the collector or collectors who under inspiration included Psalm 22 in the larger collection both have a role. The psalm receives a new setting when it is included in the Book of Psalms. This provides a new context for interpretation. In my opinion, it means that the collector invites us to see Psalm 22 not simply as the experience of an individual at one time, but a typical or model experience with which the whole congregation of Israel is to identify as they sing and meditate on the psalm.[22] Hence, in the context of the Book of Psalms (the context with divine authority), we compare this psalm of lament and praise (22:25–31) with other psalms. We understand that there is a general pattern of suffering, trust, vindication, and praise that is to characterize the people of Israel.

Now we move to approach (b). We consider Psalm 22 in the light of the entire canon of Scripture given up until the time when the Book of Psalms was compiled. But there is some problem with this. The Book of Psalms may have been compiled in stages (e.g., many scholars think that Book 1, Psalms 1–41, may have been gathered into a single collection before some of the other psalms had been written). Whatever the details, we do not know exactly when the compilation of the book took place. Hence we do not know exactly what other canonical books had already been written.

---

20. See Charles A. Briggs and Emilie G. Briggs, *A Critical and Exegetical Commentary on the Book of Psalms* (ICC; Edinburgh: T. & T. Clark, 1906), 1:196–97; A. A. Anderson, *The Book of Psalms* (NCB; 2 vols; London: Oliphants, 1972), 1:190–91; Derek Kidner, *Psalms 1–72* (London: InterVarsity, 1973), 107–8; Joseph A. Alexander, *The Psalms* (reprinted from 1864 ed.; Grand Rapids: Zondervan, 1955), 101–3. Commentators have some disagreements over the details of the picture, particularly over the interpretation of v. 16, "they have pierced my hands and feet." But it is clear that in the original context the speech is dominated by metaphorical comparisons between the psalmist's enemies and fierce animals.

21. We need not at this point discuss whether the superscriptions are inspired.

22. See, e.g., Anderson, *Psalms*, 1:30.

We may still proceed in a general way. We read Psalm 22 in the light of the promise to David (2 Sam. 7:8–16) and its relation to the earlier promises through Abraham and Moses. Then we understand that the people of Israel are represented preeminently by a king in the line of David. The deficiencies and failures of David's immediate descendants also point to the need for a perfect, righteous king who will truly establish David's line forever. Old Testament prophecies make it progressively clear that the hopes centered in David's line will ultimately be fulfilled in a single great descendent, the Branch (Isa. 11:1ff.; Zech. 6:12; Isa. 9:6–7). The experiences of suffering, trust, and vindication expressed in Psalm 22 and other psalms we expect to be fulfilled in a climactic way in a messianic figure, the Branch who is a kingly Davidic representative of all Israel.[23]

What the messianic mediator will be like becomes progressively revealed in the course of the Old Testament. Yet it is never made very clear just how the experience of the Messiah ties in with Psalm 22 in detail. We know that Psalm 22 is related to the prophetic passages, but just how is not so clear.

Finally, let us proceed to approach (c). Let us consider Psalm 22 in the light of the completed canon. In this light, we know that Christ has come to fulfull all righteousness (Matt. 3:15), to fulfill all God's promises (2 Cor. 1:20; Rom. 15:8; Luke 24:45–48). We know too that Christ used the opening words of Psalm 22 when he was on the cross (Matt. 27:46). This already suggests that he is in a brief way indicating the relevance of the *whole* psalm to himself. If we remain in doubt, other New Testament passages assure us that that is indeed the case (Matt. 27:35; John 19:24; Heb. 2:12).

We proceed, then, to read through Psalm 22 afresh. We compare it with the accounts of the crucifixion in the New Testament, and with New Testament theology explaining the significance of Christ's death. We see that in 22:12–18 Christ describes his own distress, and in 22:25–31 he expresses the "fruit of the travail of his soul" (Isa. 53:11), the benefits that will follow. In particular, certain details in the psalm which appeared to be *simply* metaphorical in the original Old Testament context strike home with particular vividness (22:16, 18).[24]

---

23. See Waltke, "A Canonical Process Approach," 10–14.

24. See Kidner, *Psalms 1–71*, 107: "While verses 14–15, taken alone, could describe merely a desperate illness, the context is of collective animosity and the symptoms could be those of Christ's scourging and crucifixion; in fact verses 16–18 had to wait for that event to unfold their meaning with any clarity." Many commentators in the classical historical–critical tradition, by contrast, refuse in principle to let the NT cast further light on the implications of the verses, because they do not allow the principle of unified divine authorship to exercise an influence on interpretation.

What Is "in" a Verse

Now let us ask, "What is the *correct* understanding of what God is saying in a verse like Psalms 22:16, 22:18, or 22:1?" Is it the understanding that we gain from approach (a), or the understanding that we gain from approach (c)? The answer, I think, is both. If we simply confine ourselves to approach (a), or even to approach (b), we neglect what can be learned by reading the whole of the Bible as the word of the single divine author. On the other hand, if we simply confine ourselves to approach (c), we neglect the fact that God's revelation was progressive. We need to remember that God was interested in edifying people in Old Testament times. Moreover, what he made clear and what he did not make so clear are both of interest to us, because they show us the ways in which our own understanding agrees with and sometimes exceeds previous understanding, due to the progress in revelation and the progress in the execution of God's redemptive program.

Moreover, certain dangers arise if we simply confine ourselves to approach (a) or to approach (c). If we neglect approach (a), we miss the advantage of having the control of a rigorous attention to the historical particulars associated with each text of the Bible. Then we run the danger that our systematic understanding of the Bible as a whole, or our subjective hunches, will simply dictate what any particular text means.

On the other hand, if we neglect approach (c), we miss the advantage of having the rest of the Bible to control the inferences that we may draw in the direction of applications. Perhaps we may refuse to apply the text at all, saying to ourselves, "It was just written for those people back there." Or we may apply it woodenly, not reckoning with the way in which it is qualified by the larger purposes of God. We miss the Christocentric character of the Bible, proclaimed in Luke 24:45–48. We refuse to see the particulars in the light of the whole, and so we may repeat an error of the Pharisees, who meticulously attended to detail, but neglected "justice and the love of God" (Luke 11:42).

But how can these approaches be combined? They combine in a way analogous to the way in which a human son combined earlier and later understandings of "Jesus Loves Me." There is a complex interplay.

But I think that we can be more precise. In scholarly research, we may begin with approach (a) as a control. For Psalm 22, we focus narrowly on the original historical context, and what is known within that context. We do grammatical-historical exegesis as the foundation for all later systematizing reflection. We try to avoid simply "reading in" our total knowledge of Scripture, or else we lose the opportunity for the Bible to criticize our views. As a second, later step, we relate Psalm 22 to earlier canonical books and finally to the New Testament. Whatever we find at this stage must harmonize with the results of approach (a). But we come to "extra" insights and deeper understanding as we relate Psalm 22 to the New Testament. These extra things are not "in" Psalm 22 in itself. They are not somehow mystically hidden in the psalm, so that someone with some esoteric key to interpretation could have come up with them just by reading the psalm in isolation from the rest of the Bible. Psalm 22 in itself gives us only what we get from approach (a). The extra things arise from the *relations* that Psalm 22 has with earlier canonical books (approach b), with the New Testament, and with the events of Christ's death. These relations, established by God, provide the basis for our proceeding another stage forward in understanding.

Hence, we are not talking about some purely subjective process of letting one's imagination run wild. Nor are we talking about a traditional Roman Catholic view of authority, where church tradition provides extra input with divine authority to enrich biblical understanding.[25] Rather, the "extra" understanding comes from the biblical canon itself, taken as a whole.

But now suppose we consider the case of nonscholars, of ordinary people. Suppose that we are not scholars ourselves, but that we have been Christians for many years. Suppose that through the aid of the Holy Spirit we have been growing spiritually and studying the Bible diligently for the whole time. From our pastors and from other scholarly sources we have gained some knowledge of Old Testament and New Testament times, but not elaborate knowledge. But we have gained a thorough knowledge of the Bible as a whole. Much of this knowledge might be called unconscious or subconscious knowledge. Especially when it is a matter of large themes of the Bible, we might not be able to say clearly what we knew, and exactly what texts of the Bible had given us our knowledge.

---

25. My views have certain affinities with the idea of *sensus plenior*. See Raymond E. Brown, *The* Sensus Plenior *of Sacred Scripture* (Baltimore, Md.: St. Mary's University, 1955). But Roman Catholic discussions of *sensus plenior* sometimes appear to be interested in including church tradition, not simply the biblical canon, in their reckoning. For instance, Brown mentions that *sensus plenior* may be needed to account for the dogmas of the immaculate conception and the assumption of Mary (ibid., 74; see also Raymond E. Brown, "The *Sensus Plenior* in the Last Ten Years," *CBQ* 25 [1963]: 272). And his full definition of *sensus plenior* seems to leave an opening for the entrance of later church tradition. He speaks of studying biblical texts "in the light of further revelation [later canonical books] or development in the understanding of revelation" (Brown, *The* Sensus Plenior *of Sacred Scripture*, 92). The last phrase, "development in the understanding of revelation," might mean only that we should pay attention to the achievements and opinions of previous generations. But that is true of any scholarly investigation of any subject. Hence the phrase seems superfluous unless it implies a greater role for tradition than what Protestants would grant.

When we read Psalm 22, we read it against the background of all that unconscious knowledge of biblical truths. When we see the opening words of 22:1, we naturally assume that the psalm speaks of Christ's suffering. We read the rest of the psalm as a psalm about Christ. In each verse we see Christ's love, his suffering, his rejection by his enemies.

The results we gain may be very similar to the results gained by the scholar who goes through all the distinct "steps." But the scholar knows that his understanding arises from the relations of Psalm 22 to the rest of the Bible. He self-consciously distinguishes what arises from the psalm viewed more or less in itself, and what arises from other passages of the Bible as they illumine the significance of the psalm. Laypeople may have the same "results," but without being able to say exactly what all the stages were by which they could logically come to those results.

The psychological perception of what is "in" the text of Psalm 22 may also be different. Lay readers are not *consciously* aware of the immense and important role played by our general knowledge of the rest of the Bible. Hence it seems that all the depth of insight that laypeople receive as they read Psalm 22 comes from Psalm 22. It is all "in" the psalm. By contrast, the scholar knows where things come from, and prefers to speak of the depth of insight as arising from the relations between many, many individual texts of the whole Bible, as these are brought into relation to Psalm 22 in a systematizing process.

But now consider once more the central question: what is *God* saying in Psalm 22? Well, he is saying what he said to the original Old Testament readers of the psalm. He speaks the truth to them. Hence, scholars are correct in taking care to distinguish what comes from the psalm itself and what comes from the psalm seen in the light of the whole Bible.

But God also intends that we should read Psalm 22 in the light of the rest of what he says. Scholars are correct in going on to a second stage in which they relate the psalm to the whole Bible. And laypeople are correct when they do the same thing. Of course, we must suppose that the laypeople are sober, godly readers, well versed in the Scripture. Then, as they read Psalm 22, all the depth that they receive is a depth that God intends them to receive. God is saying all that richness to them as they read. But that means that their psychological perception is correct. All that richness is "in" the psalm as a speech that God is speaking to them now.

Hence, I believe that we are confronted with an extremely complex and rich process of communication from God. The scholarly psychological process of making the distinctions is important as a check and refinement of laypeople's understanding. But that lay understanding, at its best, is not to be despised. We are not to be elitists who insist that everyone become a self-conscious scholar in reading the Bible. Laypeople have a correct perception, even psychologically, of what God intends a passage like Psalm 22 to say. God does say more, now, through that passage, than he said to the Old Testament readers. The "more" arises from the stage of fuller revelation, and consequent fuller illumination of the Holy Spirit, in which we live.

All this is true without any need to postulate an extra, "mystical" sense. That is, we do not postulate an extra meaning which requires some esoteric hermeneutical method to uncover. Rather, our understanding is analogous to the way that a son's understanding of "Jesus Loves Me" arises and grows. At the end of a long period of reading and digesting a rich communication, we see each particular part of the communication through eyes of knowledge that have been enlightened by the whole. Through that enlightenment, each part of the whole is rich.

What relation does all this have to the discussions of *sensus plenior*?[26] Raymond E. Brown's dissertation defines *sensus plenior* as follows:

> The *sensus plenior* is that additional, deeper meaning, intended by God but not clearly intended by the human author, which is seen to exist in the words of a biblical text (or group of texts, or even a whole book) when they are studied in the light of further revelation or development in the understanding of revelation.[27]

My distinction between the intention of the human author and divine intention, as well as my discussion of the role of later revelation, shows affinities with this definition. But I am also concerned to distinguish, from a scholarly point of view, between what is "in" the passage and what arises from comparison of the passage with later revelation. This shows affinities with the rejection of *sensus plenior* by John P. Weisengoff.[28] Weisengoff rejects *sensus plenior* precisely in order to protect the idea that the added knowledge comes from the new revelation.[29] In fact, the situation is complex enough to include the major concerns of both points of view.[30]

---

26. Brown, *The* Sensus Plenior *of Sacred Scripture;* idem, "The History and Development of the Theory of a *Sensus Plenior*," *CBQ* 15 (1953): 141–62; "The *Sensus Plenior* in the Last Ten Years," 262–85; James M. Robinson, "Scripture and Theological Method: A Protestant Study in *Sensus Plenior*," *CBQ* 27 (1965): 6–27; LaSor, "The *Sensus Plenior* and Biblical Interpretation."

27. Brown, *The* Sensus Plenior *of Sacred Scripture,* 92.

28. Weisengoff, Review of *Problèmes et méthode d'exégèse théologique* by Cerfaux, Coppens, Gribomont, *CBQ* 14 (1952): 83–85.

29. Ibid. See the reply in Brown, *The* Sensus Plenior *of Sacred Scripture,* 123–26.

30. This synthesis may be anticipated in Waltke, "A Canonical Process Approach," 8–9.

New Testament Interpretation
of the Old Testament

Our reflections up to this point also throw light on some of the problems arising from New Testament interpretation of the Old Testament.[31] I would claim that the New Testament authors characteristically do *not* aim merely at grammatical-historical exegesis of the Old Testament. If we expect this of them, we expect something too narrow and with too exclusively a scholarly interest. The New Testament authors are not scholars but church leaders. They are interested in showing how Old Testament passages apply to the church and to the New Testament situation. Hence, when they discuss an Old Testament text, they consider it in the light of the rest of the Old Testament, in the light of the events of salvation that God has accomplished in Christ, and in the light of the teaching of Jesus himself during his earthly life. They bring all this knowledge to bear on their situation, in the light of all that they know about that situation. In this process they are not concerned, as scholars would be, to distinguish with nicety all the various sources that contribute to their understanding. Both they and their readers typically presuppose the context of later revelation. Hence, what they say using an Old Testament passage may not always be based on the Old Testament text *alone*, but on relations that the text has with this greater context. There is nothing wrong or odd about this process, any more than there is anything wrong with laypeople who read Psalm 22 in the light of their knowledge of the whole of Scripture.

Scholarly Use of Grammatical-Historical Exegesis

In conclusion, let us ask what implications we may draw concerning scholarly grammatical-historical exegesis. By grammatical-historical exegesis I mean an approach like approach (a), which self-consciously focuses on each biblical book as a product of a human author, in a particular historical setting. On the positive side, we have seen that grammatical-historical exegesis has an important illumining role. Several points can be mentioned.

1) In writing the Bible God spoke to people in human language, in human situations, through human authors. God himself in the Bible indicates that we should pay attention to these human factors in order to understand what he is saying and doing.

2) On a practical level, grammatical-historical exegesis serves to warn the church against being swallowed up by traditionalism, in

---

31. Cf. similar concerns in the discussion of *sensus plenior* in Brown, *The* Sensus Plenior *of Sacred Scripture*, 68–71; Moo, "The Problem of *Sensus Plenior*."

which people merely read in the system of understanding which afterwards is read out. It alerts us to nuances in meaning that we otherwise overlook or even misread.

3) It serves to sensitize us to the genuinely progressive character of revelation. God did not say everything all at once. We understand him better the more we appreciate the wisdom involved in the partial and preliminary character of what came earlier (Heb. 1:1).

On the other hand, grammatical-historical exegesis is not all that there is to responsible biblical interpretation. Again, we can summarize the results in several points.

1) If grammatical-historical exegesis pretends to pay attention to the human author *alone*, it distorts the nature of the human author's intention. Whether or not they were perfectly self-conscious about it, the human authors intend that their words should be received as words of the Spirit.

2) God meets us and speaks to us in power as we read the Bible. God's power and presence must be taken into account from the beginning, just as we take into account all that characterizes a human author of any human text. We cannot, with perfect precision, analytically isolate God's propositional content from his personal communion. To attempt to perform grammatical-historical exegesis by such an isolating procedure is impious.

3) It is legitimate to explore the relations between what God says in all the parts of the Bible. When we perform such a synthesis, what we conclude may go beyond what we could derive from any one text in isolation. Yet it should not be in tension with the results of a narrow grammatical-historical exegesis. (Of course, sometimes because of the limitations of our knowledge we may find no way to resolve all tensions.)

4) We are not to despise laypeople's understanding of the Bible. We are not to reject it just because on the surface it appears to "read in" too much. Of course, laypeople may sometimes have overworked imaginations. But sometimes their conclusions may be the result of a synthesis of Bible knowledge due to the work of the Holy Spirit. Scholars cannot reject such a possibility without having achieved a profound synthetic and even practical knowledge of the Bible for themselves.

5) When later human writers of Scripture interpret earlier parts of Scripture, they typically do so without making fine scholarly distinctions concerning the basis of their knowledge. Hence we ought not to require them to confine themselves to a narrow grammatical-historical exegesis. In many respects their interpretations may be similar to valid uses of Scripture by nonscholars today.

6) God intends that the Bible's words should be applied in people's lives today. In complex personal, social, and political situations, we

may not always be sure what the correct applications are. But applications genuinely in accord with God's word are part of God's intention. Hence, in a broad sense, they are part of what God is saying to us through the Bible as a whole. God continues to speak today. When we read the Bible, aware that it is God's word, we understand that he is speaking to us now. We are constrained to obey, to rejoice in him, and to worship.

6

The Formula-Quotations of Matthew 2 and the Problem of Communication

R. T. France

From R. T. France, "The Formula-Quotations of Matthew 2 and the Problem of Communication," *New Testament Studies* 27 (1981): 233–51. Reprinted with the permission of Cambridge University Press.

This chapter takes its cue from L. Hartman's study of "Scriptural Exegesis in the Gospel of Matthew and the Problem of Communication,"[1] and more specifically from two comments on that paper made by Professor M. D. Hooker.[2] The first was to the effect that the title of Hartman's study involved a promise which was not fulfilled, in that he did not in fact deal significantly with "communication," in the sense of discussing what the ordinary reader might have been expected to get out of Matthew's scriptural quotations and allusions. The second was the related question whether the ordinary Jew of New Testament times, as opposed to the professional theologians or the exegetes of Qumran, could be expected to have as full an acquaintance with the Old Testament as Hartman assumed. This last point reminded me of a principle set out in a recent article by Humphrey Palmer, which neatly articulated a persistent doubt which I have felt when reading suggestions of sophisticated midrashic developments in the Gospels: "The complexity

---

1. In M. Didier, ed., *L'Evangile selon Matthieu: rédaction et théologie* (Bibliotheca Ephemeridum Theologicarum Lovaniensium 29. Gembloux: Duculot, 1972), 131–52.
2. At a meeting of her New Testament Seminar in Cambridge, October 1977. The present chapter represents a paper read to the same seminar in the following month.

of allusion intelligible to a modern scholar with lots of books and little else to do is much greater than that accessible to any member of Jesus' audience."[3] A civilization based on the printed book may be in danger of forgetting that a scroll of even one Old Testament book was in the first century an inconvenient and expensive luxury, and so of assuming an ease of reference which is more appropriate to the age of the "pocket Bible" than to primitive Christianity.

I would like to take up this line of thinking with special reference to the second chapter of Matthew. I have chosen this passage not only as one which is conspicuously rich in Old Testament quotation and allusion, but also one whose explicit quotations are notoriously obscure and unconvincing to the modern reader. I am well aware that it is also a minefield littered with exegetical corpses, but I shall try to tread lightly across it by asking some relatively naïve questions, and concentrating on fairly general answers. I want to ask simply what the author is trying to get across by his selection of Old Testament texts in this chapter, how he goes about communicating his meaning in the way he introduces them into the narrative and the form in which he cites them, and how far we may judge him to have been successful in communicating his thought to his putative readers. So I shall not be concerned with the minutiae of textual variations except in so far as these are relevant to the question of what the author is trying to make the texts say to his readers. Nor shall I go into the very complex questions of the tradition- and composition-history of this chapter; my interest is in the significance of the quotations in the final form of the text, however they got there. And I shall further restrict the potentially huge scope of the question by concentrating on the explicit formula-quotations, which are after all the first use of the Old Testament to strike the ordinary reader, not on the many individual scriptural allusions particularly in the story of the Magi, nor even on the more sustained Moses typology which surfaces clearly in the allusion to Exodus 4:19 in the words of verse 20, "Those who sought the child's life are dead."[4]

Scripture and Tradition in Matthew 2

Matthew, unlike Luke, does not have, properly speaking, a birth-narrative. The birth of Jesus is merely hinted at in 1:25, and then presup-

---

3. *Nov. T.* 18 (1976): 257.
4. For a further (or alternative) suggested use of the traditions about Jacob and Laban see D. Daube, *The New Testament and Rabbinic Judaism* (London: Athlone Press, 1956), 189–92; idem, *N.T.S.* 5 (1958/9): 184–86. I have discussed these and other suggested models for the Matthean account in my paper "Herod and the Children of Bethlehem," *Nov. T.* 21 (1979): 1–23.

posed in chapter 2. Nor is there any attempt at an account of Jesus' childhood as such. While Jesus is certainly the center of interest in these chapters, the stories are not about the child himself, but about Joseph, the Magi, and Herod. Chapters 1–2 are rather a theological, and to some extent apologetic, introduction of Jesus the Messiah before the story proper begins in chapter 3; they explain in genealogical and narrative form some salient features of Jesus' origin, his γένεσις, and aim to answer, as Stendahl put it in 1960, the question "Quis et unde?"[5]

The structure of the chapters is fairly clear: the genealogy, itself a carefully structured composition, is followed by five narrative sections, each of which is centered on a formula-quotation. The four of these narrative sections which comprise chapter 2 deal with the visit of the Magi, quoting Micah 5:1; the escape to Egypt, quoting Hosea 11:1; the slaughter of the children, quoting Jeremiah 31:15; and the settlement in Nazareth, quoting the elusive "He shall be called a Nazarene."

With the exception of the location of Jesus' birth in Bethlehem and his later residence in Nazareth, and of the bare historical datum of the death of Herod and the succession of Archelaus, these stories find no echo in any independent source, Christian or non-Christian.[6] This in itself suggests that we are not dealing here with mere historical reporting, and the impression is strengthened when we note the contrast with Luke's infancy narrative. Luke presents us with memorable stories and living characters, in whom he appears to be interested for their own sake. Matthew does not really tell stories at all. Even the visit of the Magi, by far his most colourful narrative, is built around a succession of Old Testament allusions. And the accounts of Jesus' birth (or rather of Joseph's preparation for it) and of his family's movements during his infancy give only enough detail to show the historical application of his chosen scriptural texts and to draw out the Moses typology which forms a subplot to the main theme of the formula-quotations.

All this suggests that in the composition of Matthew 2 it is the narrative element which has been hung on the peg of the scriptural quotations and allusions rather than vice versa. Scriptural exegesis takes priority over historical reporting.

This is, I think, undeniable in view of the characteristics of the text itself. What I would question is the further step of labeling this chapter as "midrash," often with the implied assumption that the "facts" related in

5. K. Stendahl, "Quis et Unde?: an analysis of Mt. 1–2" in W. Eltester, ed., *Judentum, Urchristentum, Kirche: Festschrift für J. Jeremias* (Berlin: Töpelmann, 1960), 94–105.

6. I have discussed elsewhere the question of external attestation for one particular incident, Herod's killing of the children. See section 2 of my article, referred to in note 4, 17–22.

these chapters are merely the product of a scripturally activated imagination; that, in other words, the events of chapter 2 are not recorded elsewhere for the cogent reason that they did not happen outside the mind
of Matthew or his exegetical "school." This seems to me a *non sequitur.*

For one thing, there is an inherent danger in applying to the Gospels
terms such as "midrash," "haggadah," or "pesher" (even if these in
themselves admitted of clear definitions and were universally understood in the same sense!), that we will then judge the Gospels in terms
of hermeneutical patterns derived from another genre of literature,
rather than in terms of the actual phenomena of the Gospel text. Thus,
as G. M. Soares Prabhu has pointed out in his exhaustive study of this
chapter,[7] midrash is properly

> "Literature about literature": that is, it is literature which comments in
> some way, generally but not always in a creative way, upon a biblical text.
> As such it is not an appropriate description of the Infancy Narrative,
> which is not a commentary on the biblical quotations found in it, but is
> rather commented on by these quotations. In midrash . . . it is the scrip-
> tural text which is the object of investigation; in the Gospels it is always
> some past event, and Scripture is brought in merely to illuminate it.

This is a formal point, but it is an important one. Nowhere in the Gospels
(and seldom in the New Testament) do we find a sustained commentary
on a given biblical passage. The Evangelists did not, like the Qumran exegetes, sit down with an Old Testament book in front of them and work
out its relevance to their situation. Rather they drew freely from the
whole corpus of Old Testament literature (and beyond) whatever seemed
to them suitable texts to illustrate their account of Jesus. There was no
compulsion on them to comment on one text rather than another.

The point may be made with reference to Matthew 2 by asking two
of what Dennis Nineham delightfully calls "idiot-boy questions."

First, why did Matthew choose these particular Old Testament texts
for his formula-quotations? He had the whole Old Testament to choose
from. On the assumption that he was uncontrolled by a historical tradition, and could invent whatever stories he liked to fit his texts, why
these? Only one is clearly messianic in its Old Testament context (Mic.
5:1). Stendahl's answer is that all have explicit geographical reference,
and that Matthew's aim in this chapter is to construct an apologetic for
Jesus' geographical origin. This I believe is right, as we shall see. But if
so, I ask again: why *these* texts? One mentions a geographical location

---

7. *The Formula-Quotations in the Infancy Narrative of Matthew: An Enquiry into the
Tradition History of Matt. 1–2* (Analecta Biblica 63. Rome: Biblical Institute Press, 1976),
15–16.

which is in fact embarrassingly different from that of the narrative (Ramah instead of Bethlehem); and one is not even in the Old Testament at all ("He shall be called a Nazarene"). Any of us could have done much better in finding geographical messianic proof-texts and constructing stories around them if there were no historical controls. Isaiah 11:11–16, for instance, could provide a very rich source for stories about the travels of the infant Jesus from Assyria to Egypt and in all the lands between, and all arising out of a Davidic messianic prophecy. Why not, if Matthew was free to create his narrative around his texts? It would be a lot more convincing than Rachel weeping at Ramah and "He shall be called a Nazarene."

My second question is related. If the facts were negotiable, why need Matthew twist the wording of his chosen texts? Why not twist the facts to fit the wording? Micah 5:1 has undergone some careful surgery, and something so dreadful has apparently happened to whatever text lies behind 2:23 that no one can now be sure what it was. Outside chapter 2 the most striking instance of Matthew's textual surgery is of course the composite quotation of 27:9–10, and there, as here, it is hard to explain such drastic modification of the text unless there was a pre-existent narrative situation into which it had to be fitted.[8] The freedom with which Matthew finds it necessary to adapt his chosen texts to the narrative strongly suggests that the narrative was there first. It was the fact of Jesus' residence at Nazareth that made it necessary to concoct the quotation "He shall be called a Nazarene," and not vice versa.

It is not correct, therefore, to describe Matthew 2 as "midrash," if that means a commentary on a given scriptural text or texts, which may involve the creation of imaginative stories out of the text. Rather this chapter is using scriptural texts, freely chosen and adapted as necessary, to comment on given traditions about the origins of Jesus. The evangelist at least believed these stories to be factual, and hence felt it incumbent on him to illuminate them with Scripture.

Thus we have not a simple relation of either facts controlling texts or texts creating "facts," but a more complex dialectic. The Evangelist (if we may for the sake of the argument credit him with the composition of the chapter as we have it)[9] is aware of traditions which he believes to

---

8. Cf. K. Stendahl, *The School of St. Matthew and Its Use of the Old Testament* (Acta Seminarii Neo-testamentici Uppsaliensis 20. Uppsala, 1954), 196–97.

9. This is not of course to deny the pre-existing unity of the traditional material used by the evangelist, as argued, for example, by A. Vögtle, "Die mattäische Kindheitsgeschichte" in *L'Evangile selon Matthieu* (see note 1), 156ff., and by R. E. Brown, *The Birth of the Messiah. A Commentary on the Infancy Narratives in Matthew and Luke* (London: Geoffrey Chapman, 1977), 96–19. Cf. E. Nellessen, *Das Kind und seine Mutter. Struktur and Verkündigung des 2 Kapitels im Matthäusevangelium* (Stuttgarter Bibelstudien 39. Stuttgart: Verlag Katholisches Bibelwerk, 1969), 77–80.

be factual, and which seem to him to require explanation or comment. This he achieves not only by incidental allusions and by a carefully drawn parallel with the experiences of Moses (and perhaps the story of Balaam),[10] but by one selected proof-text for each episode of his narrative. The narrative then affects the texts, as each is adapted more or less drastically to fit its new context and to draw out the message which was the evangelist's purpose in including this incident in his account. Conversely, the text affects the narrative, in that it is structured around the text and related in such a way as to bring out the relevance of the text to that situation, so much so that in some cases it is little more than a framework for the text. In short, the narrative tradition is the motive for the selection and shaping of the texts, but the texts have become the organizing principle for the narrative.

The Purpose and Message of Matthew 2

We may now broach more directly our primary question: what was the message these formula-quotations were intended to convey? Or, in the light of what we have just been considering, it could be put the other way: why did the evangelist choose to include and provide scriptural comment on these particular narrative traditions in the introduction to his Gospel?

The answer lies primarily, Stendahl argued, in geography. It is not only that each of the four formula-quotations in chapter 2 contains a place–name, though that is true. After the birthplace of the Messiah has been established in the story of the Magi and its associated quotation, the whole narrative of the rest of the chapter is devoted to the geographical movements of the Messiah and their justification: why he left Bethlehem, where he took refuge, how he returned from there and was further directed to a new home. In short, how the baby of Bethlehem became the prophet of Nazareth. These movements are all presented not as the accidental results of uncontrolled events, but as divinely planned and guided; this point is made not only by the quotations, but by a series of dreams in which the angel of the Lord directs Joseph's successive moves, to Egypt, Judaea, and finally Galilee (vv. 13, 19, 22).

Moreover, beyond this specific series of adventures, there is a clear interest in geographical locations throughout chapters 2–4. (Chapter 1, which introduces the person and name of the Messiah, is by contrast devoid of place-names.) The Magi come "from the East" to Jerusalem, and from there to Bethlehem. After Jesus' settlement in Nazareth, John the Baptist begins preaching in the wilderness of Judaea, and wins a fol-

10. See Brown, op. cit. (note 9), 190–96.

lowing from "Jerusalem and all Judaea and all the regions about the Jordan." Jesus comes from Galilee to the Jordan and thence to the wilderness. He then withdraws to Galilee, leaves Nazareth, and goes to live "in Capernaum, by the sea, in the territory of Zebulun and Naphtali," giving rise to another geographically oriented formula-quotation. Subsequently his mission extends "about all Galilee," his fame spreads "throughout all Syria," and his following comes from "Galilee and the Decapolis and Jerusalem and Judaea and from beyond the Jordan."

But what is all this geographical material meant to communicate about Jesus? Chapter 1 has presented him as the Davidic Messiah in his genealogy and in the giving of his name; what do his geographical movements tell us about him?

Undoubtedly there is an apologetic element here.[11] The problem is that articulated in John 7:41–42: "Is the Christ to come from Galilee? Has not the scripture said that the Christ is descended from David, and comes from Bethlehem, the village where David was?" This was inevitably an embarrassment for anyone who made messianic claims for the prophet from Nazareth. The scandal (for Jewish orthodoxy) of a Galilean domicile is dealt with by the formula-quotation of 4:15–16; but in chapter 2 the requirement of an origin in Bethlehem is reaffirmed in the quotation of Micah 5:1, and Jesus *of Nazareth* is shown to meet it. Not only, however, does Jesus meet the generally recognized messianic requirement; even his home in Nazareth, the potential source of geographical embarrassment, is boldly claimed to be itself in fulfillment of the scriptural pattern. The whole itinerary of chapter 2 thus links these two fixed points of the geographical tradition, and culminates in the triumphant quotation, "He shall be called a Nazarene."

But if that were all Matthew wanted to communicate, it is not easy to see why he needed to introduce the escape to Egypt and Hosea 11:1. Nor would this account for the many other geographical references listed above. There is apparently some more positive purpose in Matthew's geographical interest than merely the explanation of embarrassing traditions.

Chapter 1 has been geared to showing Jesus as the Messiah of Israel, the son of David, by means of his name and genealogy. Chapter 2 is now providing a geographical argument for the same point, and at the same time extending it further to show that his mission is wider than even the ideal extent of Israel.

The geographical elements in chapters 2–4 listed above (which are additional to the formula-quotations) explicitly include the whole of the classical area of Israel; note especially 4:25: "Great crowds followed him

11. For this point see further K. Stendahl, "Quis et Unde?" (note 5), 97–99.

from Galilee and the Decapolis and Jerusalem and Judaea and from beyond the Jordan [i.e. Peraea]." There is only one notable geographical la-
cuna, and that is Samaria, which is conspicuously absent from the
whole Gospel of Matthew except to be bracketed with the Gentiles in
10:5 as a prohibited area for the disciples' mission. Samaria, then, is for
Matthew an apostate region, but otherwise the whole of Old Testament
Israel welcomes its Messiah. Moreover, his fame spreads "throughout all
Syria" (4:24), thus taking in much of the "greater Israel" of King David.

But chapter 2 spreads the net wider. The Magi come "from the East,"
and are presumably Gentiles from Mesopotamia. Their involvement
thus represents an ultimately wider role for Israel's Messiah, and the
probable echoes of Psalm 72 and Isaiah 60 in the account of their "worship" reinforce this theme of the homage of the Gentiles. Moreover,
both these passages refer to Sheba as the source from which gifts are
brought, and these are specified in Isaiah 60:6 as "gold and frankin-
cense"; the gifts of the Magi in Matthew 2:11 are therefore probably also
designed to echo those of the Queen of Sheba to Solomon, son of
David—"spices and very much gold and precious stones" (1 Kings
10:2). If so, Arabia is also brought within the scope of the influence of
the son of David.

After Arabia and "the East" there is one other major geographical
component of the Old Testament world to be taken into account, and
that is Egypt. This too finds its place in Matthew 2, not by a mere dep-
utation but by a personal visit from the son of David himself. The Messiah of Israel has thus been shown to be at home also in the wider Gentile world, and the places of Israel's exile in the Old Testament period,
Egypt and "the East," have played their part in the preparation for his
ministry.

Even if some details of this account are overdrawn, there is enough
to show that the geographical element in Matthew 2 serves not only an
apologetic but also a positive christological purpose, and that this geographical element is the main structural principle of the chapter. I
would thus not agree with Hartman's assertion that "its warp is something like a midrashic haggadah based on the Moses haggadah and the
first chapters of Exodus."[12] If I am right in thinking that the warp is the
primary framework of vertical strands into which horizontal strands
are then woven, I would maintain that the geographical theme is the
warp, the main organizing principle of the chapter, into which the woof
of the Mosaic and Exodus typologies (together with other possible
scriptural elements) is woven. Or, abandoning the metaphor, Matthew's primary purpose in chapter 2 is to teach about the Messiah

12. Art. cit. (note 1), 138–39.

through his geographical movements and associations, with the scriptural texts which these bring to mind. This is not to deny that he is also developing a Moses and Exodus typology, but this forms only a subplot, less conspicuous and even capable of being missed completely by the casual reader.

Preliminary Observations on the Problem of Communication

We now come at last to the problem of communication. If we may assume that the main thing Matthew was concerned to communicate in this chapter was an understanding of the geographical associations of Jesus as not only divinely directed and scripturally validated, but also as an indication of the universality of his role as Messiah, how successful may we adjudge him to have been in communicating this, and other subsidiary themes, to his putative readership? Specifically, how far do the four formula-quotations succeed in getting this across?

I would like first to defend Hartman's article against one of Professor Hooker's criticisms. He does try to deal with the problem of communication in at least one way which seems to me to be of value, and that is in a distinction which is not systematically spelled out, but which emerges at certain points in his article, between different levels of understanding. Thus he refers to "a nuance in the text" which is available to "the appreciative reader"[13] and to "what a sharp-eyed reader found in the text";[14] on the other hand he mentions what is "on the surface," "this surface meaning."[15] He then concludes his discussion of Matthew 2:18 with the statement, "Only one who shared or thoroughly understood the religious tradition out of which and in which (and for which) Matthew 2 was written, was able to grasp these subtle meanings and nuances added to a quotation that could be understood, otherwise, solely as a way of saying that mothers grieved for their slain children."[16] It is in this "religious tradition" common to author and readers that he sees the key to the problem of communication, and it is the attempt to discover such shared traditions which is the main object of the article.

Now this seems to me a legitimate way to approach the problem of communication, but it is hard to control in the absence of any direct independent evidence of the religious traditions available to Matthew's readers, even supposing that we could be sure who they were! Studies of interpretative traditions in first-century Judaism, even where we

13. Ibid., 139.
14. Ibid., 140.
15. Ibid., 141.
16. Ibid.

have the material from which to reconstruct them, can in the nature of the case never be exhaustive, and it is seldom that we dare claim that we have isolated such a tradition which would have been universally accepted in early Jewish Christianity. There are too many examples, both in the New Testament and in non-Christian Jewish literature, of variant and even conflicting exegetical traditions (as in the case of Daniel 7:13–14) to allow any such precision.

In fact the only direct evidence we have for the interpretative traditions accepted in the community for whom Matthew writes is the text of Matthew itself. In what follows I shall try to use this direct evidence to suggest what may be some of the background of shared understanding which Matthew exploits in the presentation of his formula-quotations in chapter 2. I shall do this on the assumption, which I hope need not be justified, that Matthew wrote to be understood, that he expected there was at least somebody who would derive from the words he wrote the message which he intended to communicate. But I shall also bear in mind Hartman's distinction between the "surface meaning," which any reasonably intelligent reader might be expected to grasp, and what we may call a "bonus" meaning accessible to those who are more "sharp-eyed," or better instructed in Old Testament Scripture, or who may have shared with the author certain traditions of interpretation which were not commonly followed.

I am sure that such a distinction between surface meaning and a bonus meaning for the initiated or alert is realistic; any adult reader of children's classics, or any adult viewer of some of the more sophisticated children's television shows, will be well aware that the surface meaning may be communicated to the great delight of the more naïve audience, while at the same time a whole world of more esoteric pleasure is in store for those who share the author's private adult viewpoint and erudition. It is a poor author who aims to communicate only with the lowest common denominator of his potential readership.

The Four Formula-Quotations of Matthew 2

Turning then briefly to the four formula-quotations, we consider first *Micah* 5:1. The surface meaning here is quite straightforward, that Bethlehem was the predicted place of origin of the Messiah, and that the birth of Jesus in Bethlehem duly fulfilled this prediction. There is nothing arbitrary or forced in this use of Micah 5:1, nor anything in the least esoteric. So far, communication is fully successful to anyone with the most elementary knowledge of the Old Testament—or even without, if he is prepared to take Matthew's word for it that there is such a prophecy to be found.

But to achieve this, Matthew had no need to alter the received wording. In any recoverable version Micah 5:1 clearly names Bethlehem as the place of origin of the future leader of Israel. Why then has Matthew found it necessary to introduce at least three deliberate changes into the wording? (The substitution of "chieftains" for "clans" may perhaps be explained by an independent vocalization of the Hebrew text, and does not significantly affect the impact of the quotation.)

The substitution of γῆ Ἰούδα for "Ephrathah," the ancient name of Bethlehem, is not likely to be designed solely for geographical precision,[17] to differentiate it from the Bethlehem in Galilee (Josh. 19:15), for the latter is not clearly mentioned outside the list in the Book of Joshua, and could not conceivably come to mind in this messianic connection in preference to the "city of David." It may be intended to emphasize the difference between the two geographical poles of the Messiah's itinerary in this chapter, from Bethlehem *in Judah* to Nazareth in Galilee. But more probably the double reference to Judah in Matthew's form of the quotation is reinforcing the christological point already stressed in the genealogy, that Jesus really did derive from the royal tribe, from which alone a truly Davidic Messiah could come. The second alteration, to οὐδαμῶς ἐλαχίστη, emphatically reversing the original description of Bethlehem's insignificance, is shown by the following addition of γάρ to be deliberate, and not just a reflection of a variant Hebrew text.[18] The effect is to call attention to the dramatic alteration in Bethlehem's role from the insignificant village of David to the birthplace of the great son of David. (This paradox was, of course, already the point of the mention of Bethlehem's insignificance in Micah 5:1 itself; what Matthew has done is, perhaps rather prosaically, to remove the paradox by substituting Bethlehem's ultimate status for its original condition.)[19] Thirdly, the substitution of the words from God's charge to David in 2 Samuel 5:2 (ποιμανεῖ τὸν λαόν μου τὸν Ἰσραήλ) for the last words of Micah 5:1, while it in no way alters the meaning, and in fact takes up the theme of shepherding which is already present in Micah 5:3, imports a further significant echo of the prototype king David.[20]

17. So Stendahl, *The School of St. Matthew*, 99–100.

18. For defence of the hypothesis of a variant text see R. H. Gundry, *The Use of the Old Testament in St. Matthew's Gospel* (Supplements to Novum Testamentum 18. Leiden: Brill, 1967), 92 n. 3; G. M. Soares Prabhu, op. cit. (note 7), 263–64.

19. Cf. Brown, op. cit. (note 9), 185. The addition of a qualifying כְּ in the Targum goes part of the way in the same direction.

20. An earlier correlation of Micah 5:1 with the Davidic dynastic oracles is suggested by the use of מוֹשֵׁל בְּיִשְׂרָאֵל in 2 Chron. 7:18 (replacing אִישׁ עַל כִּסֵּא יִשְׂרָאֵל in 1 Kings 9:5). See the discussion by H. G. M. Williamson in an article to be published in *Tyndale Bulletin* 28.

All these three alterations, then, while not at all necessary for the surface meaning of the text, combine to convey a deliberate christological message to those who can recognize them. The ordinary reader, who was not closely acquainted with the Old Testament text, might well miss them all, *as alterations*. In that case he might still notice the repeated word "Judah," and be confirmed in his belief that Jesus was the true king of Israel; this would be a small bonus point for the "sharp-eyed reader." But the other two alterations would escape him. οὐδαμῶς ἐλαχίστη achieves its force precisely *as* an alteration: in itself it would cause no surprise. As Hartman says in another connection: "A 'twisted' quotation can communicate very special nuances of meaning, just as twisted. To a reader or a writer who knows the original text the twisted words become salient and draw attention to a new, wise or shrewd interpretation."[21] Similarly the words from 2 Samuel 5:2 would only convey a special meaning if recognized as an intrusion. But to those who had the necessary detailed knowledge of Scripture, these variations of wording would powerfully reinforce the message of the Davidic character of the Messiah which has already been so strongly stressed in chapter 1. To them, and to them only, Matthew offers this bonus point, without in the least detracting from the surface meaning which was open to all his readers.

Hosea 11:1 does not present any clear alteration in the wording; it is apparently a straightforward, if independent, translation of the Hebrew text. The surface meaning here is again the geographical point that there is scriptural warrant for a connection of the "son of God" with Egypt, and the addition of ὑπὸ κυρίου to the introductory formula ensures that there can be no doubt whose son was meant.[22] (That it is the mention of Egypt itself which is the main point, rather than the phrase "*out of* Egypt," is suggested by the position of the quotation in verse 15, where Jesus' arrival and settlement in Egypt has just been mentioned, rather than in verse 21 where the departure from Egypt is narrated.)[23] The Christian reader, who already regarded Jesus as "son of God,"[24] could appreciate this surface meaning however little his knowledge of the Old Testament: there was a proof-text for this further geographical

21. Art. cit. (note 1), 138.
22. See, for this addition, R. Pesch, "Der Gottessohn im matthäischen Evangelienprolog (Matt. 1–2)," *Biblica* 48 (1967): 397ff.
23. This observation does not, however, necessitate the rendering of ἐξ Αἰγύπτου by "*since* Egypt" and the consequent belittling of an Exodus reference both in Hos. 11:1 and in Matthew's use of it, *pace* Gundry, op. cit. (note 18), 93–94. It is rather that the ἐξ is simply not important for the primary use of the quotation.
24. Without this agreed terminology the relevance of the quotation to Jesus would be quite obscure. Thus the divine sonship of Jesus, which Pesch (art. cit., esp. 411–14) presents as the main point of the quotation, is rather its presupposition.

connection of Jesus' childhood. The problem, so obvious to us, that the "son of God" in Hosea was Israel, not the Messiah, would only occur to those with a reasonable acquaintance with Hosea.

A fuller knowledge of the Old Testament, however, would immediately demand a more sophisticated interpretation. This must have involved, for Matthew himself and for the better instructed of his readers, an Israel–Jesus typology[25] such as we meet elsewhere, for instance, in the quotations in the temptation narrative.[26] The rich interpretative possibilities of such a typology, as they have been explored throughout Christian history, would be a strong bonus point for those who stopped to question the exegetical basis of Matthew's use of this Old Testament text, and there is no reason to doubt that Matthew so intended it. A further bonus point might be found in an exploration of the significance of the Exodus as a type of salvation, and this would be especially apparent to any readers sufficiently erudite to have noticed the parallels to the childhood of Moses, both in its Old Testament form and more explicitly in its developed form as seen in Josephus and the Palestinian Targum,[27] which have already occurred in the story of the Magi and of Herod's subsequent search for the child, and which will continue in the slaughter of the children, finally coming to the surface in the allusion to Exodus 4:19 in verse 20.[28] So here again, as in the use of Micah 5:1, we have both a surface meaning based on the central geographical term and also a variety of christological implications available to those with the scriptural knowledge and perceptiveness to dig deeper into Matthew's purpose.[29]

The quotation of *Jeremiah* 31:15 is more difficult, for its surface meaning is not at all apparent. There is a place-name, to be sure, but it has no obvious connection with the narrative; if there is any significance in the mention of Ramah, it is certainly not on the surface. The immediately apparent connection of the text with the narrative is in the

25. Thus W. D. Davies assumes it as self-evident that here "Matthew sees in the history of Jesus a recapitulation of that of Israel" (*The Setting of the Sermon on the Mount* [Cambridge University Press, 1963], 78).

26. See, e.g., J. Dupont, *N.T.S.* 3 (1956/7): 287–304; G. H. P. Thompson, *J.T.S.* 11 (1960): 1–12; J. A. T. Robinson, *Twelve New Testament Studies* (London: SCM Press, 1962), 53–60; B. Gerhardsson, *The Testing of God's Son* (Lund: Gleerup, 1966).

27. Josephus, *Ant.* 2. 205ff. (cf. *Ex. Rab.* 1.18); Targum Pseudo-Jonathan to Exod. 1:15. The parallels are conveniently set out by M. M. Bourke in *C.B.Q.* 22 (1960): 161–66.

28. See W. D. Davies, *The Setting of the Sermon on the Mount,* 78–82; G. M. Soares Prabhu, op. cit. (note 7), 288–92.

29. Cf. G. Strecker, *Der Weg der Gerechtigkeit: Untersuchung zur Theologie des Matthäus* (FRLANT 82. Göttingen: Vandenhoeck & Ruprecht, 1971), 58, who sees the "biographische Aspekt" (by which he means the geographical movements) as "das wesentliche Motiv der redaktionellen Einfügung, wenn sich auch die Christusprädikation (υἱὸς θεοῦ) selbstverständlich der theologischen Konzeption des Verfassers einpasst."

misery caused by the loss of children. But while this correlation may be the *excuse* for the quotation, it can hardly be the *point* of it, since one hardly needs a scriptural text to inform one that the loss of children causes unhappiness. Why is the Old Testament brought in here at all? Is it that the fact that there is an Old Testament precedent for such apparently senseless suffering shows that it is not outside the purpose of God, that in some mysterious way the wretched events at Bethlehem fit into a scripturally authenticated pattern? That much could, I think, be deduced from Matthew's quotation by even the most unlearned reader, so that it may be appropriately described as the surface meaning, and that alone would perhaps be enough to justify the inclusion of this text. But few commentators have been content to leave it at that, and we may well doubt whether that was all Matthew had in mind.

For one thing, this surface meaning stands out in this geographically oriented chapter as having, in contrast with the other three formula–quotations, no geographical application. Is there then, perhaps, a bonus geographical significance for the more inquisitive reader?

Nothing much can be derived from any alteration in the wording in this case, Matthew's version being independent, but a quite acceptable, if slightly abbreviated, rendering of the Hebrew test.

But the place-name Ramah immediately draws attention. *Why* was Rachel's weeping heard "in Ramah"? Probably because that was one of the traditional sites of her grave,[30] but it would hardly escape Matthew that it was also the site of the gathering of the exiles in 586 for the march to Babylon, Jeremiah himself being among them (Jer. 40:1); this connection is noticed also by the Targum of Jeremiah 31:15, which interprets Rachel's weeping as "the house of Israel weeping and sighing after the prophet Jeremiah when Nebuzaradan the chief slaughterer sent him from Ramah." The fact that Jeremiah, like Jesus, subsequently escaped to Egypt may also have occurred to him. Moreover, there were probably already rival traditions of the site of Rachel's grave, at Bethlehem and in Benjamin,[31] as we find debated among the rabbis in the third century,[32] so that Rachel's weeping in Ramah may not have appeared so irrelevant to a disaster in Bethlehem as it seems to us. These geographical associations would be completely lost on the more naïve reader, but might well have provoked (and been intended to provoke)

---

30. Gen. 35:16–20, 48:7 locates it "some distance from Ephrath" (identified with Bethlehem in 35:19) on the way from Bethel, and 1 Sam. 10:2 specifies that it was in the territory of Benjamin; the resultant site must be somewhere near Ramah, though Jer. 31:15 is the only evidence for this specific location.

31. See J. Jeremias, *Heiligengräber in Jesu Umwelt* (Göttingen: Vandenhoeck & Ruprecht, 1958), 75–76.

32. *Gen. Rab.* 82.10.

some fascinating lines of thought for those with the scriptural knowledge to discern them. The fact that Matthew chose to include the name "Ramah" in his quotation, when he could easily have eliminated it either by omission or by a translation along the lines of the Septuagint A text (φωνὴ ἐν τῇ ὑψηλῇ ἠκούσθη),[33] indicates that he intended it to communicate something, however recondite.

Apart from the place-name, a more obvious relevance of this passage to the geographical theme of chapter 2 is that Jeremiah 31:15 is about *exile.* Rachel's children "are not," not because they have all died, but because they have been taken away. Jesus' "exile" from his homeland thus has scriptural precedent. Of course the correspondence is not exact: in Matthew the one exiled is not the same as the ones mourned, but the cause of mourning and the exile are closely linked as cause and effect. This understanding of Matthew's quotation depends, of course, on an awareness of the context of the text in Jeremiah 31; the words quoted do not by themselves indicate the exile as the cause of the mourning (though this does become explicit in the Targum, where "they are not" becomes "they are exiled"). But if we are prepared to grant that Matthew intended this bonus meaning for those who were aware of the original context, then perhaps we may go further and note that in Jeremiah 31 verse 15 stands out conspicuously as the one note of gloom in a chapter of joy, and that its function in context is to throw in relief the joy of the promised *return* of Rachel's lost children. May we then believe that Matthew wanted his readers to summon up their knowledge of Jeremiah 31, and see in it not only a precedent for exile as a part of the purpose of God, but a pattern of exile *and return,* of loss and sorrow as a prelude to restoration and joy?[34]

This suggestion of a "respect for context" in the original intention of the quotation is made not on the basis of an all-embracing theory, but because of a strong feeling, perhaps irrational, that the surface meaning of this particular quotation is simply not enough to explain why Matthew bothered to include it. There *was* a not entirely insignificant surface meaning accessible to the scripturally illiterate, but can we credit Matthew with introducing a long quotation with a sonorous fulfillment-formula, in a chapter devoted to the scriptural significance of the childhood movements of Jesus, simply in order to illustrate the very general theme that there is a place for loss and sorrow in the purposes

33. This vocalization is adopted also by Aquila, the Targum (though with a mention of Ramah later in the verse) and the Peshitta, and is accepted as original by J. Simons, *The Geographical and Topographical Texts of the Old Testament* (Leiden: Brill, 1959), 446.

34. So for example M. M. Bourke, *C.B.Q.* 22 (1960): 171f.; Gundry, op. cit. (note 18), 210; Brown, op. cit. (note 9), 216–17. Note that in Lam. R. Proem 24 (end) Rachel's protestations have become the *cause* of the return from exile.

of God? Most interpreters assume that there is something more here than can be derived from the cited words themselves. The trouble is that they do not agree on what that "something more" is. It is salutary to notice that Hartman's search in his article for the "subtle meanings and nuances added to (the) quotation"[35] produces almost entirely different results from the bonus points I have suggested above.[36] None of us is privy to the mind of Matthew, or of his intended readers, to be able to say which of these answers (if any) he wanted us to derive from the puzzle he has set for us. But that he intended us to try seems to me certain, and it may be that he would have regarded the variety of possible answers as an enrichment rather than an embarrassment.

The fourth "quotation" presents us with a different problem. Here there can be no uncertainty about the surface meaning. It is the simple apologetic point that Jesus' upbringing in Nazareth was scripturally authenticated. This, as we have seen, was a point of some importance to the primitive church in its relations with mainstream Judaism, and it is the QED to which the whole chapter has been building up. The Messiah, correctly born at Bethlehem, has by a series of scripturally sanctioned movements arrived at his known domicile, and *this too*, contrary to orthodox belief, is in fulfillment of the announced purpose of God. It is an important point, and it deserves to be strongly made. Our problem is that we cannot see *how* Matthew is trying to make it. By alleging a quotation which is not in fact found anywhere in the Old Testament, is he not in fact giving the game away at the very point where he needs to play his strongest card?

Now it is difficult to know how far we may press the assumed naïveté and scriptural ignorance of the ordinary reader, but I suspect that the majority of ordinary readers today who come across Matthew 2:23 are prepared to take it on trust that there *is*, as Matthew seems to claim, an Old Testament text saying "He shall be called a Nazarene," and I wonder whether the same might not have been true in Matthew's day.[37] If so, his purpose is achieved, as far as the uninstructed reader is concerned. The surface meaning is plain enough, for those who are not disposed to question how he arrived at it.

35. Art. cit. (note 1), 141; they are set out on pages 138–41.

36. Cf. also the exegetical *tour de force* by which Vögtle (art. cit. [note 9], 173–74), following W. Rothfuchs, *Die Erfüllungszitate des Matthäus-Evangeliums* (BWANT 88. Stuttgart: Kohlhammer, 1969), 64–65, identifies Herod's action as representing Israel as a whole (on the strength of 2:3b) and the massacre therefore as Israel's rejection of the Messiah, resulting in their loss of their status as the people of God, for which "loss" Rachel is weeping! For further discussion of this exegesis see section 1 (*c*) of my article referred to in note 4, 14–16.

37. E. Schweizer, *Das Evangelium nach Matthäus* (NTD 2. Göttingen: Vandenhoeck & Ruprecht, 1973), 20, thinks that Matthew too believed this!

But if that was all Matthew intended, it was nothing more than a confidence trick, and one which could not hope to work with the more instructed readers whom we have elsewhere seen reason to believe that Matthew had in view. Nor can I believe that the Matthew to whom scriptural fulfillment was so important could have written 2:23 unless he was himself convinced that Jesus' residence in Nazareth really did in some way fulfill the Old Testament. Both the repetition of the fulfillment-formula and the explicit use of the term Ναζωραῖος in what is ostensibly a specific quotation indicate that Matthew had some new Old Testament datum in mind here, and was not just, as Rothfuchs suggests,[38] referring to Nazareth as the end result of the events validated by the three preceding formula-quotations.

Nazareth is not mentioned in the Old Testament. To find scriptural warrant for Jesus' residence there, rather than in Galilee in general (and that is the point of the next formula-quotation in 4:15–16), therefore required a more oblique approach, and Matthew gives warning of this by the phrasing of his introductory formula, which by speaking of "the prophets" in the plural[39] and substituting ὅτι for λέγοντος already indicates that he is not making a direct quotation, but rather introducing a theme of prophetic expectation.[40] What this theme was has been variously formulated, but some commentators who accept this approach think of Ναζωραῖος as an epithet conveying a sense of inferiority, a humble and obscure origin inconsistent with the expected royal dignity of the Messiah.[41] Whether or not Ναζωραῖος originated as a term for one from Nazareth,[42] by the time of Matthew it had clearly acquired this connotation, and the remoteness of Nazareth would thus give it a derogatory sense of "backwoodsman" particularly for the Judaean whose view of Galilee in general was not flattering.[43] In the application of this opprobrious term to Jesus (hence κληθήσεται) Matthew sees, it

38. Op. cit. (note 36), 66–67. This is apparently also the view of G. Strecker, op. cit. (note 29), 62–63, though he does not make it so explicit; see note 40 below.

39. Cf. Ezra 9:11 "by thy servants the prophets," introducing a "quotation" made up of various scriptural elements. Cf. also 26:56, where again no direct quotation is given.

40. Cf. Strecker, op. cit. (note 29), 61–62, though Strecker declines to identify the source of this theme in the Old Testament, preferring to speak enigmatically of Matthew "filling the gap himself" by the use of the term Ναζωραῖος.

41. So the commentaries of T. Zahn, 112–17 (cf. his Einleitung in das NT, 2:294); M.-J. Lagrange, 39; R. V. G. Tasker, 45; P. Bonnard, 30. Cf. J.-L. Leuba, New Testament Pattern (London: Lutterworth Press, 1953), 36–39. For some earlier supporters see S. Lyonnet, Biblica 25 (1944): 196 n. 3; he refers to them as "la majorité semble-t-il aujourd'hui." (This interpretation does not depend on Zahn's questionable translation of ὅτι as causal.)

42. See the discussion in G. M. Soares Prabhu, op. cit. (note 7), 193–201.

43. See, for example, John 1:46 (and cf. Gundry, op. cit. [note 18], 103). That this derogatory connotation was quickly lost in Christian writings is natural: cf. the history of "Methodist," or indeed, probably, of "Christian."

is suggested, the fulfillment of prophecies of a humble and unrecognized Messiah, "despised and rejected by men."[44] To put it a little whimsically, it is Nazareth's very absence from the Old Testament which makes it a fitting fulfillment of this Old Testament theme.

If this is pronounced exceedingly tortuous, I agree! But Matthew must have meant *something!* What is the alternative? To look, in defiance of the conspicuously irregular introductory formula, for a single passage sufficiently resembling Ναζωραῖος κληθήσεται to be recognized in those words. It is a forlorn hope. The נֵצֶר of Isaiah 11:1[45] suffers from the rather serious disability that there is no way a Greek-speaking reader of Matthew could spot the reference, nor does it offer any explanation of κληθήσεται. Judges 13:5, 7, the other main contender, does offer the Greek term ναζιραῖος in the A text of the Septuagint, but it is odd that Matthew should have substituted κληθήσεται for the no less suitable ἔσται of the Septuagint,[46] thus reducing the allusion to a single word, and that differing from any known Greek rendering of נְזִיר.[47] When one adds that Jesus was *not* a Nazirite, and was even known as a winebibber (Matt. 11:19), this suggested allusion seems no less tortuous than that proposed above, which did at least have the merits of taking the modified introductory formula seriously, and giving some reason for Matthew's use of κληθήσεται. It is possible, even probable, that a secondary allusion to Samson as the miraculously born savior figure could have been intended,[48] providing a further and yet more abstruse

44. Gundry, op. cit. (note 18), 103–4, who argues for an allusion to Isa. 11:1, points out that the "Branch" passages were interpreted in Qumran, the Targums and Rabbinic literature "as meaning the Messiah will come out of obscurity and a low estate," and believes that Matthew therefore saw the fulfillment of Isa. 11:1 in the contemptuous use of Ναζωραῖος for Jesus.

45. So, for example, P. Billerbeck, *Kommentar,* 1:92ff.; K. Stendahl, *The School of St. Matthew,* 103f., 198f.; Gundry, op. cit. (note 18), 103–4.

46. E. Zuckschwerdt, "Nazōraîos in Matt. 2, 23," *T.Z.* 31 (1975): 71, argues rightly that καλεῖσθαι *can* approximate in meaning to εἶναι (see Arndt Gingrich, p. 400a, û d), but can only explain Matthew's use of κληθήσεται rather than the more obvious LXX ἔσται by the suggestion that in so doing "schloss er zugleich das von ihm ebenfalls beabsichtigte Moment der Namensgebung mit ein"—a "Moment" which he in fact recorded at 1:21–5, and to which there has been no reference throughout chapter 2, not to mention that Ναζωραῖος bears no relation to the names in 1:21–5.

47. Apart from the fifteenth-century MS 59! Zuckschwerdt, art. cit. (note 46), 71–76 explains the form as a hybrid of the consonants נור with the vowels of a presumed Qere קָדוֹשׁ.

48. So, for example, H. H. Schaeder, *TDNT* 4:878–79; E. Schweizer, in *Judentum, Urchristentum, Kirche* (see note 5), 90–93; J. A. Sanders, *J.B.L.* 84 (1965): 169–72; M. D. Goulder, *Midrash and Lection in Matthew* (London: SPCK, 1974), 240f.; Soares Prabhu, op. cit. (note 7), 205–7; Zuckschwerdt, art. cit. (note 46). Brown, op. cit. (note 9), 218–19 (and for details 209–13) wants to allow both the נֵצֶר and Nazirite derivations as intended by Matthew, but sees the primary "quotation" as a combination of Isa. 4:3 and Judg. 16:17, connected by the Nazirite theme.

bonus point for the persistent searcher, but I think we are entitled to claim that if this reference had been Matthew's primary purpose he ought not to have placed so many gratuitous obstacles in its way.

Communication in Matthew 2—Conclusions

Our object in this very sketchy account of the formula-quotations in Matthew 2 has been to isolate what the author was in fact trying to communicate by his selection of quotations, and how he set about doing so in the way he introduced them into the narrative and in some cases adapted their wording to bring out his intended interpretation. The final stage is to ask how far he may be judged to have succeeded in communicating.

It is, of course, essentially an unanswerable question. It could only be answered by interviewing those for whom he wrote his Gospel. If there was a large element of subjectivity in our attempt to read the mind of Matthew, whose writing we do at least possess, there is a far larger element of subjectivity in any attempt to question his readers, who are not only inaccessible, but unidentifiable. All we may be sure of is that their background and outlook would be very different from ours. But a few general comments may be ventured.

Assuming that Matthew was writing for a Jewish Christian readership (and even that is not universally agreed), I imagine that even the most uninstructed reader would have had no difficulty in grasping the apologetic point which governs the overall structure of the chapter, that Jesus' obscure Galilean background was not a cause for embarrassment, but rather the end-result of a series of divinely directed movements, beginning as orthodox belief demanded in Bethlehem, but culminating in Nazareth, and that for each stage of this process there was appropriate scriptural authority. The "surface meaning" which we have postulated for the four formula-quotations would plainly convey this general, essentially apologetic, message. If Matthew had readers whose lack of scriptural knowledge and sophistication limited their appreciation of his purpose to this surface meaning, and who were prepared to take on trust that Scripture really did say what Matthew claimed that it said, this was a not insignificant contribution to their Christian education and testimony.[49]

But we have seen reason at each point to believe that Matthew had more in mind than the "surface meaning"; that he had bonus points to

---

49. It may be questioned, however, whether there would be many such *readers*. How many who had the education to *read* Matthew would be so lacking in scriptural knowledge? Palmer's very just caution against assuming too much exegetical sophistication in Jesus' *hearers* is not likely to be so applicable to Matthew's *readers*.

offer to those whose acquaintance with the Old Testament enabled them to spot his "deliberate mistakes" in Micah 5:1 and his sophisticated creation of the Nazarene text from a minor theme of Old Testament prophecy, or to recollect the context of Jeremiah 31:15 and the original identity of the "son" in Hosea 11:1. There were bonus points too for those with the theological inquisitiveness to dig into the associations of Ramah, or to follow up the assonance of Ναζωραῖος with ναζιραῖος. Those whose exegetical sophistication would enable them to appreciate the numerous scriptural allusions in the story of the Magi and the sub-plot of Mosaic typology would also find in the formula-quotations material for christological reflections on the Davidic elements in Jesus' background, the typology of the Exodus, the exile-and-return pattern of Jeremiah 31, and perhaps Samson as the prototype of the God-sent redeemer. More could be added, all of it admittedly speculative and inevitably subjective. For what any given reader will find in a chapter like Matthew 2 will vary with his exegetical background. What I want to suggest is that Matthew would not necessarily have found this regrettable, that he was deliberately composing a chapter rich in potential exegetical bonuses, so that the more fully a reader shared the religious traditions and scriptural erudition of the author, the more he was likely to derive from his reading, while at the same time there was a surface meaning sufficiently uncomplicated for even the most naïve reader to follow it. This surface meaning is essentially apologetic, but the bonus meanings convey an increasingly rich and positive understanding of the person and role of the Messiah, not integrated into a tidy theological scheme, but diverse and suggestive for those with eyes to see.

I am arguing, in other words, that Matthew was well aware of differing levels among his potential readership. I would want to say not so much with Professor Moule, that he "does not seem to discriminate between the more superficial and the more profound,"[50] but rather that he deliberately included both, that he was a sufficiently sophisticated author and communicator not to aim only for the lowest common denominator in his readership, nor to write an esoteric manual for initiates only, but to cater for the different levels of comprehension at the same time. And I believe that in so doing he was in the company of many of the most successful writers of all ages, whose work has an immediate impact without extensive academic analysis, but is not exhausted on a first reading and continues to delight and reward in successive encounters over the years.

The existence of the sophisticated and varied readership which I have described is not, of course, a firm historical datum. I have postu-

50. C. F. D. Moule, *The Origin of Christology* (Cambridge: University Press, 1977), 129.

lated it on the basis of the text itself. The procedure is inevitably circular in that one understands and criticizes the text in terms of the readership, and reconstructs the readership from the text. But if there is any validity in the initial assumption that Matthew wrote to be understood by somebody, there is some justification for this procedure, if carried out with a due awareness that the background and thought-processes of Matthew and his readers were different from ours. The only firm datum is the text itself, so that is where we must start. That Matthew wrote these words rather than any others must tell us something about both the man and his purpose. The more obscure and tantalizing his words may seem to us, the more they demand some explanation in terms of a cultural and religious tradition different from ours.

Thus it is not surprising that the use of the Old Testament by Matthew is, in Professor Moule's words, "to our critical eyes, manifestly forced and artificial and unconvincing."[51] Our cultural and religious traditions would not allow us to write like this, and do not allow us to read Matthew, initially at least, with the shared understanding which we must assume his original readers, or some of them, would have had. But the inevitable distance which cultural relativity puts between us and Matthew's original readers does not entitle us to write him off as obscurantist or incapable. And when we attempt to read him on his own terms, by putting ourselves in the place of his original readers, we may not only achieve a more respectful appreciation of his literary ability and his skill as a communicator, but we may also be in a position to discern those guiding principles of interpretation which need to find as appropriate an expression in our cultural situation as Matthew gave them in his.[52]

---

51. Ibid. 129.

52. Cf. Moule's argument, ibid., chap. 5 ("The Fulfillment Theme in the New Testament"), where he goes behind what he terms the "vehicular" use of Scripture in the New Testament ("the arbitrary use of words as a vehicle, simply, for something that is derived from elsewhere") to a "relational" understanding of the significance of Jesus as "the Fulfiller in a supreme sense."

Part 3

Did the New Testament Authors Respect the Context of the Old Testament Text?

Opposing Arguments

7

The Place of the Old Testament in the Formation of New Testament Theology

Prolegomena

Barnabas Lindars

From Barnabas Lindars, "The Place of the Old Testament in the Formation of New Testament Theology: Prolegomena," *New Testament Studies* 23 (1976): 59–66. Reprinted with the permission of Cambridge University Press.

In a recent article on the interpretation of the Old Testament in the New Testament Traugott Holtz[1] takes as his point of departure the twice repeated *kata tas graphas* of 1 Corinthians 15:3, 5. C. H. Dodd took the same words for the title of his influential book, *According to the Scriptures*. So we may suitably start with this for our consideration of the place of the Old Testament in the formation of New Testament theology. Paul's use of this phrase in the *credo* of 1 Corinthians 15 is remarkable. For one thing, it is the clearest possible case in the New Testament of appeal to the Scriptures in order to provide the basis of a theological interpretation of the Christ-event. This at once alerts us to expect the importance of the Old Testament for New Testament theology to be in the realm of Christology, or rather of the person and work of Christ. It

---

1. T. Holtz, "Zur Interpretation des Alten Testaments im Neuen Testament," *T.L Z.* 99 (1974): Nr. 1, Sp. 19–32.

can be expected to be the most important factor in the primitive church's understanding of its own faith. But another point about 1 Corinthians 15:3, 5 is even more significant. In this instance Paul does not even consider it necessary to adduce the relevant texts. It is implied that he could do so, if he wished, and scholars have made various suggestions about which texts he actually had in mind. But the point is that he can presuppose that it is sufficient for his argument merely to allude to the *possibility* of adducing Scriptures. And this implies that they are common ground between him and his readers. The Scriptures are, then, an agreed basis for discussion. They have an authority which is unquestioned. Consequently it can be taken as axiomatic that they will play a most important, indeed indispensable, part in the formation of New Testament theology.

I

The first thing that must be done is to decide what is denoted by "the Scriptures." At the time of the rise of Christianity no final decision had been taken on the limits of the canon. Study of the New Testament shows that almost all the books of the Hebrew canon were quarried for supporting texts. Also certain books were used which were eventually excluded from the canon, for example, Ben Sira and the Wisdom of Solomon, and even one or two of the Pseudepigrapha. Thus, though the limits are undefined, and a certain degree of fluidity must be presupposed concerning the status of some writings, it would be quite wrong to suggest that the canon shared by primitive Christianity with the contemporary Judaism was anything less than the complete Old Testament. This remains true, even though individual writers may not have had personal access to all the books of the Old Testament. Thus Holtz has argued, in his very full investigation of the scriptural citations in Luke–Acts,[2] that Luke was only able to quote directly from Isaiah, Minor Prophets, and Psalms. The rest of his quotations and allusions were found already in his sources. G. Reim has gone even further with regard to John.[3] He argues that the Evangelist did not normally make firsthand use of Scripture, and that he was only thoroughly familiar with the chapters of Isaiah which we know today as Deutero–Isaiah. These conclusions may be disputed, especially in the latter case, but even if they are correct, they only highlight more strongly the significance of the pervasive influence of all the Old Testament Scriptures

---

2. T. Holtz, *Untersuchungen über die alttestamentischen Zitate bei Lukas* (TU 104) (Berlin, 1968).

3. G. Reim, *Studien zum alttestamentlichen Hintergrund des Johannesevangeliums* (SNTS Monograph Series 22) (Cambridge, 1974).

upon New Testament theology. For in spite of the scarcity of books, which must have been a real problem as the church became separated from the synagogue, the Old Testament is woven into the fabric of the New Testament.

It would be a mistake, however, to generalize from these observations with regard to Luke and John, and to suppose that the New Testament writers as a whole were not in a position to make extensive use of the Old Testament. Paul at any rate knew his Bible well. But even with Paul false conclusions are possible. It has been pointed out that Paul only makes actual quotations from the Old Testament when he is arguing with opponents who are either Jews or Judaizing Christians. This might suggest that he does not depend on the Old Testament for his creative thought. Conzelmann, noting this suggestion, replies that the category of *fulfillment* is essential to Paul's constructive theology, so that the Old Testament cannot be excluded from this aspect of his work.[4] That Christ is the fulfillment of the Old Testament prophecies is a basic presupposition of his thought. This observation in its turn draws attention to the extent to which the Old Testament has been used without direct quotation. Besides literary allusions there are also major themes, such as creation, exodus, Israel, covenant, righteousness, life, et cetera, to name just a few at random. The conclusion easily follows that the Old Testament is the greatest single influence in the formation of New Testament theology.

II

The implications of this fact must now be considered. Numerous books have been written to show the immense debt of the New Testament writers to the Old Testament, and writers of theologies of the New Testament are not slow to acknowledge it. But this does not mean that the church by-passed contemporary Jewish interests and exegesis in making recourse to the Old Testament, though such a view could be expressed, for example, by F. C. Grant, some twenty-five years ago.[5] All recent studies tend to confirm the fact that contemporary Jewish exegesis is the proper background to the church's use of the Old Testament. In the first place, the debt to Judaism in the case of *liturgical forms* is obvious. This needs no further demonstration. Secondly, *rabbinic literature* has been combed not only to illuminate gospel teachings and customs, but also, and increasingly in recent years, to trace exegetical

4. H. Conzelmann, *An Outline of the Theology of the New Testament* (London, 1969), 166ff.

5. F. C. Grant, *An Introduction to New Testament Thought* (New York & Nashville, no date), 15–17.

techniques and midrashic themes in early Christian use of the Old Testament. Thirdly, *Targumic studies* have been going on apace, and have been given a strong impulse from the discovery of Neofiti I, which can be expected to yield much that is of value to the New Testament specialist. Thus, to mention just one example, the rabbinic exegesis of Jacob's dream, in which Jacob is joined to his heavenly archetype by the ladder between heaven and earth, and which formerly could not be traced with certainty into the Tannaitic period,[6] has now turned up in Targum Neofiti.[7] The possibility that in John 1:51 the author is exploiting a contemporary Jewish exegesis is accordingly strengthened.

Fourthly, there is obviously the extremely important biblical exegesis of the *Qumran sect*. The significance of this, by comparison with the rabbinic literature, consists not primarily in rules of interpretation, which are often shared with rabbinic exegesis, but in the sect's conviction that it was living in the crucial time before the transition of the ages, to which all Scriptures refer. Consequently the fulfillment of Scripture can be discerned in the sect's own history and experience. This differs from the characteristic timelessness of the rabbinic application of Scripture. There are really two points at issue here. First, there is the conviction that all Scriptures, not only the Prophets and Psalms, but even the Torah itself, have the end time as their proper point of reference. Secondly, there is the conviction that the present generation is actually the end time to which they refer. This conjunction of two convictions is characteristic of Qumran, and applies too to a fifth category of contemporary Jewish thought, the *apocalyptic literature*. It is true, of course, that the rabbis also share the tendency to refer Scriptures to the end time to some extent. But the point is that their timing tends to be indeterminate, and we miss altogether in their writings the sense of involvement of the present in the future—or, rather, of the future in the present—which is characteristic alike of Qumran, apocalyptic, and early Christianity.

Nevertheless there is also a fundamental distinction between early Christianity and these sources. For it is in the christological use of the Old Testament in the New Testament (to quote the title of Professor Black's Presidential Address in 1970)[8] that the links between early Christian and contemporary Jewish exegesis can be most clearly seen. This points to the fact that it was the Christ-event which stood at the center of the church's conviction of living in the end time. Hence this aspect of the matter is not simply due to contemporary influences. It is

6. Genesis Rabba 68.18, where it is attributed to R. Yannai (c. A.D. 240).
7. At Gen. 28.12 (A. Diez Macho, *Neophyti I*, Madrid & Barcelona, 1968).
8. *N.T.S.* 18 (1971/2): 1–14.

also due to the tremendous impact of the Christ-event itself. But, when all due allowances are made for this fact, it remains true that the rapid expansion of Christianity would really be inexplicable except against the background of a widespread feeling amongst Jews of the day that they were living in the end time. For it is, as Holtz has pointed out,[9] only because of the pre-understanding of the Bible in this eschatological sense, attested not only in Qumran and apocalyptic, but also to some extent in rabbinic sources, that the church's application of the whole range of the Old Testament to Jesus could be felt to be a plausible undertaking and find acceptance.

III

Turning now to the actual use of the Old Testament in the New Testament, we must first sound a warning note. Qumran and apocalyptic are undoubtedly very important for the New Testament, but it would be a mistake to press the comparison too far. There is very little evidence in the New Testament for a deliberate scholarly activity comparable to that of the writers of this contemporary literature. Early Christianity uses what can be styled for the sake of convenience (if incorrectly) the *pēsher* type of interpretation,[10] but there are no biblical commentaries in the New Testament and early Christian literature comparable to those of Qumran. Rather, the evidence of the Old Testament citations points to a process of selection and adaptation of proof-texts. This might suggest the existence of a testimony-book at a very early date, preceding the composition of the books of the New Testament and even of the letters of Paul, as Rendel Harris argued in his well-known monographs on the subject nearly sixty years ago.[11] The discovery of such documents as 4Q Testimonia and 4Q Florilegium has revived support for this theory. But the variations in the form of the citations in the New Testament do not permit the conclusion that the writers are making use of a common document. What we see in the New Testament is the beginning of a process which can be traced through the *Epistle of Barnabas* and Justin Martyr's *Dialogue with Trypho,* and eventually culminates in the testimony-books of the anti-Judaic literature. This starts with the christological application of texts already current in contemporary messianic speculation. Further texts, often unique to Christianity in this sense, are added to the common stock on an ad hoc basis in

9. Art. cit. Sp. 25.
10. Cf. K. Stendahl, *The School of St. Matthew and Its Use of the Old Testament* (Acta Seminarii Neotestamentici Uppsaliensis 20) (Uppsala, 1954), 183–202; B. Lindars, *New Testament Apologetic* (London, 1961), 15.
11. J. Rendel Harris, *Testimonies 1 and 2* (Cambridge, 1916–20).

a living situation. It is not credible that a scholarly Christian Jew raked through the Old Testament in order to write a handbook for Paul to carry around on his journeys. In fact Paul did not need one. With his thorough training as a Pharisee, he had his own vast store of knowledge both of the Old Testament itself and of contemporary exegesis, which he drew on constantly in the course of his missionary labors. He made use of texts already well established in Christian discourse, and also added to this much further biblical material, as the need arose.

Apocalyptic, as von Rad has shown,[12] is also very largely a scholarly activity, though very different in kind from that of Qumran and that of the rabbis. It is a matter of theorizing about the times of the end, on the basis of encyclopedic learning. Paul is aware of such speculations, as we know from 1 Corinthians 15 and the Thessalonian epistles. But the New Testament writers on the whole do not do the theorizing. They are content to accept current speculations. What they are concerned with is the application of them to Christ. They work in a real-life situation, marked by a sense of urgency. Their apocalyptic is not in the first instance worked out quietly in the study. At a slightly later stage a genuinely Christian creative apocalyptic can be discerned, as is evident in the Little Apocalypse of Mark 13 and the Book of Revelation. It is not to be denied that there was some scholarly activity of this kind in the early church. But the point is that this is not the primary setting in which the Old Testament came to be a fundamentally formative influence on New Testament theology. The use of the Old Testament in apocalyptic is much more a mode of expression than the support for a theological enterprise.

The same considerations apply to the Epistle to the Hebrews. The classification of this work has always been a problem, as it appears to oscillate between academic theological exposition and urgent exhortation to the readers. If Hebrews is taken to be a theological treatise, it is natural to conclude that the extensive use of Scriptures in it is the writer's method of formulating his Christology by references to Old Testament types, which are fulfilled in Christ. However, the view that the Epistle is primarily an exhortation is to be preferred. From this point of view the theology is not a christological exercise, but the grounds for appeal to the readers. In both theological and hortatory passages the Old Testament is woven into the structure of the argument in such a way that it represents God himself speaking to the readers. The Old Testament is God's living word (4:12), his mode of address to the readers in their actual situation. Thus we have here precisely the

---

12. G. von Rad, *Old Testament Theology* (Edinburgh and London, 1962–65), 1:446, 450; 2:301–8.

same presupposition as appears in Paul in 1 Corinthians 10:6, 11 (cf. Rom. 15:4): that the present age, which is the beginning of the end time, is the proper point of reference for the whole of Scripture. God's word only reaches its full meaning when it is understood in the light of the present age, so that—to quote Paul again—those who do not accept this fact remain blind, and the "veil remains unlifted, because only through Christ is it taken away. Yes, to this day, whenever Moses is read a veil lies over their minds; but when a man turns to the Lord the veil is removed" (2 Cor. 3:14–16).

I hope that these brief indications are sufficient to show that the use of the Old Testament—whether in direct quotations, in allusions, or in the employment of biblical themes—is primarily a mode of expression for early Christian thought, arising from a contemporary understanding of the meaning of Scripture. There is no sign of a direct interest in the Old Testament for its own sake, as at Qumran. The New Testament writers do not take an Old Testament book or passage, and sit down and ask, "What does this mean?" They are concerned with the kerygma, which they need to teach and to defend and to understand for themselves. Believing that Christ is the fulfillment of the promises of God, and that they are living in the age to which all the Scriptures refer, they employ the Old Testament in an ad hoc way, making recourse to it just when and how they find it helpful for their purposes. But they do this in a highly creative situation, because the Christ-event breaks through conventional expectations, and demands new patterns of exegesis for its elucidation. It has been reasonably argued that some of the intuitions which contribute to this process are to be traced back to Jesus himself.[13] But, just as there is no such thing as a systematic theology in the New Testament, so there is no sign of an attempt to construct a theology of the Old Testament as the pedestal on which a New Testament theology can be erected.

IV

Finally, a word must be said about typological theories. It is obvious that, given the attitude to the Old Testament which I have indicated in this chapter with its central emphasis on the fulfillment in Christ, typology plays an important part in the early Christian use of the Old Testament, and numerous examples can be cited. It can also be granted that it is more pervasive than appears on the surface, seeing that some allusions are so light that they can easily be missed. We can also allow that

13. So C. H. Dodd, *According to the Scriptures: The Sub-structure of New Testament Theology* (London, 1952), 110.

the writers could, in some cases at least, expect their readers" ears to be better attuned to pick up Old Testament allusions than could be expected in a Christian congregation today. But this does not warrant theories which attempt to discover the "real" meaning of a passage in the light of a supposed reference to the Old Testament, which the readers are not only expected to observe for themselves, but also expected to use as a basis for inferences which are not actually and openly expressed in the text which they are reading. Such theories have plagued Johannine studies, and continue to do so. Take, for example, the recent theory of A. M. Serra,[14] which has been enthusiastically espoused by B. Olsson in his dissertation *Structure and Meaning in the Fourth Gospel,* that the sequence of days in John 1:19–2:12 is to be elucidated from the events of the Sinai theophany, as expounded in the Targum Pseudo-Jonathan to Exodus 19–24. We may well ask what this is supposed to mean. The Johannine sequence does seem rather artificial, so that it is reasonable to ask whether symbolical considerations have been at work in its composition, and various theories have been produced. But what does John wish to communicate? Is his meaning lost if the supposed allusions to the Sinai narrative are missed? If they are essential, why has he not taken the trouble to make his point plain? One can say that the interpretation has already been made explicit in 1:17: "For the law was given by Moses; grace and truth came through Jesus Christ." But then what does the recognition of a "Sinai screen"[15] for the sequence which follows add to this? The text must be allowed to make its point for what it is in itself. In fact this kind of interpretation is far more likely to distort the author's meaning than to elucidate it. There is simply no firm evidence that the New Testament writers were accustomed to work in this way. It presupposes a process of superimposing a gospel narrative upon a corresponding Old Testament narrative in order to convey a deeper meaning. Alternatively, it presupposes the more radical conclusion that items of gospel tradition were entirely evolved out of Old Testament prototypes. The actual, provable use of the Old Testament in the New Testament does not support such a hypothesis. For the same reasons, lectionary theories, in which New Testament books are supposed to receive illumination from the use of synagogue readings in conjunction with them, need to be treated with considerable reserve.[16]

14. A. M. Serra, "Le tradizioni della teofania sinaitica nel Targum dello pseudo-Jonathan Es. 19. 24 e in Giov. 1,19–2,12," *Marianum* 33 (1971): 1–39. Summary in B. Olsson, *Structure and Meaning in the Fourth Gospel* (Coniectanea Biblica, New Testament Series 6) (Lund, 1974), 24–25.

15. The phrase is Olsson's.

16. E.g., most recently, M. D. Goulder, *Midrash and Lection in Matthew* (London, 1974).

In this chapter I have argued that the New Testament writers used the Old Testament for a variety of purposes, kerygmatic, apologetic, catechetical, hortatory, liturgical, et cetera, because it was the natural medium of expression in religious contexts. They understood the Old Testament to refer to their own generation, in common with the Qumran sect and some apocalyptic writers. This, then, is a contemporary attitude to Scripture, and contemporary methods of exegesis must be regarded as regulative for the primitive church. God speaks to their own generation through the Scriptures, which are therefore subservient to God's new declaration in his Son, Jesus. The place of the Old Testament in the formation of New Testament theology is that of a servant, ready to run to the aid of the gospel whenever it is required, bolstering up arguments, and filling out meaning through evocative allusions, but never acting as the master or leading the way, nor even guiding the process of thought behind the scenes. God's new word, the "yes," the "now," of the gospel is Jesus, who demotes the Scriptures from master to servant, as much as he changes the basis of religion from law to grace.

8

Matthew Twists the Scriptures

S. V. McCasland

From S. V. McCasland, "Matthew Twists the Scriptures," *Journal of Biblical Literature* 80 (1961): 143–48. Reprinted by permission of the Society of Biblical Literature.

The theme of this chapter was suggested by a remark of the author of 2 Peter (3:16) with reference to the way some persons of the early church dealt with the letters of Paul. He says, "There are some things in them hard to understand, which the ignorant and unstable twist to their own destruction, as they do the other Scriptures." Our modern critical study of the New Testament writings makes it possible to document this ancient author's observation in many interesting ways. The words of this man who wrote under the name of Peter throw light not only on the use of the Scriptures in the early church but also on the way some of the New Testament writings were actually produced. One of the important discoveries of recent biblical studies is the position the Old Testament Scriptures held in the worship and piety of Jews and early Christians and in their understanding of the events of history through which they were passing, indeed in some cases shaping their own actions according to patterns of conduct which they believed they saw prescribed for them in the Scriptures.

I have chosen for this chapter to document some of these practices among early Christians by observing how the author of the Gospel of Matthew interpreted the Old Testament, and then to suggest that his uses of the Old Testament give some indication of how he treated his immediate sources for the story of Jesus recorded in his Gospel.

Let us begin with Matthew's treatment of Scripture in the genealogy of Jesus (1:1–17). Here he constructs a genealogy beginning with Abraham. It is constructed on a scheme with three subdivisions, the breaks being at David and the captivity, and each division contains fourteen generations, making a total of forty-two from Abraham to Christ. Luke's genealogy covering the same period (3:23–34) lists fifty-six generations. Without attempting to decide which, if either, of these is correct, a discrepancy of fourteen generations is noteworthy; but the exact division of Matthew's genealogy into three groups of fourteen generations each, and four times fourteen in Luke's, is enough to put one on guard. Indeed we discover that, in order to obtain fourteen in the first division, Matthew omitted the names of Ahaziah, Joash, Amaziah, and Jehoiakim from the kings of Judah (Matt. 1:8, 11; 1 Chron. 3:11–15). To get fourteen in the second division and also in the third, Matthew counted Jeconiah in both groups. It is evident therefore that Matthew imposed an arbitrary pattern on the genealogy and adjusted the Old Testament data to fit the pattern.

In order to explain the mystery surrounding the personality of Jesus, in 1:23 Matthew quotes Isaiah 7:14, "Behold a virgin shall conceive and bear a son, and his name shall be called Immanuel," thus providing a basis in Scripture for the belief that Jesus was born of a virgin mother. Matthew is the only New Testament writer to quote Isaiah 7:14. It is now well known that this saying of Isaiah refers to an event of his own time, and that the Hebrew word *'almāh,* for the mother of the child, does not mean a virgin but only a young woman. This makes it evident that Matthew transfers the event to his own time and follows, not the Hebrew text, but a Greek translation, which renders the Hebrew by *parthenos,* usually meaning a virgin.

Matthew is also the only New Testament author to relate the flight of Joseph and Mary with the child Jesus to Egypt. He says that when the little family returned from Egypt after Herod's death, only to discover that his son Archelaus reigned in Jerusalem, they went and dwelt in Nazareth of Galilee, and remarks that they did this to fulfill the saying of the prophets, "He shall be called a Nazarene," a passage which no scholar has been able to locate with certainty in the Old Testament (2:19–23). It is clear that Matthew, not being close to the facts of the birth of Jesus, has assumed from another passage he quotes from Micah 5:2 that Joseph and Mary lived in Bethlehem before the child was born, and that they transferred their residence to Nazareth after returning from Egypt. Matthew's conclusion contradicts the testimony of Luke that the family lived in Nazareth before Jesus was born, and made the journey to Bethlehem because of a census.

Moreover, Matthew 2:15 interprets the return of Joseph and Mary with the child Jesus from Egypt as fulfillment of Hosea 11:1, "Out of Egypt I called my son," which in its original setting means the exodus of Israel from Egypt. As only Matthew records the flight to Egypt, there is a strong possibility that the entire episode is an inference from the misunderstood Hosea 11:1.

Matthew's account of the triumphal entry of Jesus into Jerusalem (21:1–11) radically changes Mark (11:1–11), the source he is following. He says that Jesus rode into the city, not on one donkey, but on two at the same time, thus changing Mark's simple, dignified narrative of this historic event into something like a circus spectacle. Matthew was led to make this extraordinary change by misunderstanding the Scripture he quoted from Zechariah 9:9, which he thought was fulfilled by this entrance of Jesus into the city. The passage says,

> Tell the daughter of Zion,
> Behold, your king is coming to you,
> humble, and mounted on an ass,
> and on a colt, the foal of an ass.

The study of Hebrew poetry by modern scholars enables us to see that the literary structure is the well-known parallelism in which the second line of a couplet repeats in slightly different words the same idea expressed in the first. Zechariah had no intention to say the king would come riding on two asses at the same time. Matthew's failure to understand the poetic lines caused him to say that the disciples "brought the ass and the colt, and put their clothes on them, and he sat thereon" (ἐπέθηκαν ἐπ᾽ αὐτῶν τὰ ἱμάτια, καὶ ἐπεκάθισεν ἐπάνω αὐτῶν). Matthew's unfamiliarity with the nature of Hebrew poetry caused him to alter Mark's statement so as to fit Mark's narrative into his twisted understanding of the poem.

Another example from Matthew is his famous quotation (12:40), "For as Jonah was three days and three nights in the belly of the whale, so will the Son of man be three days and three nights in the heart of the earth." Matthew is the only New Testament author to cite this Scripture in connection with the resurrection. It is obvious, however, according to Matthew's own account of the resurrection, that Jesus was buried on Friday evening, that he lay in the grave that night, Saturday, and Saturday night, and arose early Sunday morning. So the passage from Jonah, as Matthew quotes it, does not fit the narrative of the resurrection as all the Gospels give it.

With these passages before us, it is possible to make certain generalizations with reference to Matthew's use of the Scriptures. The arbitrary pattern he imposed on the genealogy, by means of actually dropping the names of certain kings, shows that Matthew was experimenting with his skill in literary arrangement based on numbers. He was evidently fascinated by the number seven; his genealogy presents this number in various multiples. Matthew's use of Isaiah 7:14 to explain the mystery of the birth of Christ not only shows the power exercised by the ancient Scriptures in forming Christian doctrine, but how a misinterpreted passage might be just as influential as one correctly understood. The effort to explain why the family of Jesus resided in Nazareth by deriving it from a postulated Scripture illustrates the belief that all events of the life of Christ were in some specific sense not only implicit, but explicit in the Old Testament, even though one did not know the precise passage of Scripture in which the ancient writers had concealed it. The interpretation of Hosea 11:1 not only illustrates how early Christians found a meaning entirely foreign to the original; it may also show how incidents in the story of Jesus have been inferred from the Old Testament. Twisting the story of Jesus' ride into Jerusalem by making him ride two animals at the same time shows Matthew's lack of literary appreciation; that he failed to recognize the literary character of the poetic passage before him. The application of the saying about Jonah's sojourn in the belly of the whale to the period during which Jesus lay in the grave between his death and resurrection, although it does not really fit the narrative of the resurrection, indicates how desperately early Christians searched the Scriptures to find proof for the things happening among them.

Distorting Contemporary Sources

What we have observed about the liberties Matthew took with passages of Scripture he quoted suggests that he may have done the same thing with his more contemporary sources of the life and sayings of Jesus. The writings of the Old Testament were one group of Matthew's sources, but, being holy Scripture, they possessed a quality of sanctity far beyond that of his more recent contemporary sources, such as Mark, Q, and other documents relating to Jesus. Since we have discovered that Matthew felt free in changing and distorting the Scriptures, it becomes a probability that he has used an even freer hand in modifying, rearranging, and shaping documents not protected by scriptural sanctity, sources of a popular character which he used in putting together his gospel. And that is just what we find on examining Matthew's Gospel in comparison with Mark and Luke, the other synoptic Gospels.

Using a harmony which sets the texts of these Gospels side by side, one can quickly see changes of various kinds which Matthew has made. His account of the triumphal entry, as we have already noted, changes Mark's record and makes Jesus ride on two donkeys into Jerusalem. The sequel to this episode is driving the money-changers out of the temple. In this case also Matthew has not hesitated to change Mark's account. According to Mark (11:1–11) Jesus went into the temple on Sunday, looked around to observe what was going on there, returned to Bethany that night, and came back the next day to drive the traders from the temple. Matthew tells Mark's story, repeating most of it almost word for word, but he has changed the time when Jesus drove the money-changers out. Matthew says Jesus drove the traders out immediately after his arrival in the temple, that is, on Sunday afternoon (21:12–17; Mark 11:15–19; Luke 19:45–48). In taking over Mark's account, Matthew dropped out Mark's clear statement that Jesus returned to Bethany and spent the night before he came back the next day to cleanse the temple. Mark says Jesus did this on Monday.

Matthew's readiness to distort Mark is shown also in the way he deals with Mark's account of the Gadarene demoniac (Mark 5:1–20; Matt. 8:28–34) relieved by Jesus. When Matthew tells the story, Mark's one demoniac becomes two.

A similar treatment appears in Matthew's retelling of Mark's story of the blind beggar Bartimeus at Jericho (Mark 10:46–52; Matt. 20:20–34; Luke 18:35–43). In this case also, according to Mark there was only one blind man; but when Matthew tells the same story, the one blind man becomes two.

When Matthew comes to the account of the resurrection (Matt. 28:1–10; Mark 16:1–8), he quite boldly changes what Mark says. Mark states that the women who came to the tomb of Jesus early that Sunday morning were frightened when they found the tomb empty, and fled in fear; that they did not say a word to anyone because they were afraid. On the other hand, Matthew says the women ran with great joy and reported to the disciples what they had seen.

Editing the Words of Jesus

It is also possible to demonstrate Matthew's editorial freedom with the sayings of Jesus. Many years ago it was pointed out that Matthew had grouped sayings of Jesus into five collections, creating the impression that Jesus gave extended lectures or sermons, contrary to what otherwise appears to be the fact. The first of these is the Sermon on the Mount (Matt. 5–7); second, instructions to the Twelve (10:5–42); third, a collection of parables of the kingdom (13:1–52); fourth, another group of parables (18:1–35); fifth, sayings about the end of the world (24–25). Professor E. J. Goodspeed thinks there are six of these collections (*Matthew, Apostle and Evangelist*, 1959, 29ff.). These groups show that Matthew has freely picked up sayings of Jesus from various places and put them together in convenient collections, showing no concern for preserving the integrity of any original sources from which he drew them.

It is clear that Matthew has relocated sayings in new contexts, where they may have lost their original meanings. This may be illustrated by a famous passage from the Sermon on the Mount (5:27–31) dealing with adultery. It goes,

[27]"You have heard that it was said, 'You shall not commit adultery.' [28]But I say to you that every one who looks at a woman lustfully has already committed adultery with her in his heart. [29]If your right eye causes you to sin, pluck it out and throw it away; it is better that you lose one of your members than that your whole body be thrown into hell. [30]And if your right hand causes you to sin, cut it off and throw it away; it is better that you lose one of your members than that your whole body go into hell.

[31]"It was also said, 'Whoever divorces his wife, let him give her a certificate of divorce.' But I say to you that every one who divorces his wife, except on the ground of unchastity, makes her an adulteress; and whoever marries a divorced woman commits adultery."

The two sayings about adultery and divorce fit well together, but in between them Matthew has sandwiched verses 29–30, beginning, "If your right eye causes you to sin, etc." This passage has been introduced here in a strange context. We know this because the saying about the eye, the hand, and foot was taken from Mark 9:43–48, where it occurs in entirely different material. Matthew copied this in its original context in 18:8–9; but apparently because of its use of the eye, he has transferred it to the Sermon on the Mount, connecting it with the saying about adultery and divorce, where Jesus says, "Whoever looks on a woman lustfully. . . ." The new context of the saying about the eye makes it refer to sexual lust, and suggests castration as the remedy for this impulse, but there is no indication in Mark that the saying of Jesus originally had that radical meaning. It is true that Jesus' saying about the lustful eye has rabbinic parallels, but that he prescribed the treatment Matthew implies does not follow.[1]

About a hundred years after Matthew was written, the famous Origen, finding himself embarrassed by sex desire, had himself emasculated. Undoubtedly this relocation of the passage by Matthew had something to do with Origen's unfortunate misinterpretation of the Scriptures about sex desire.[2]

The much debated Matthew 16:19, where Jesus gives Peter the keys of the kingdom of heaven and all power on earth to bind and loose, is

---

1. Cf. H. L. Strack and P. Billerbeck, *Kommentar zum NT aus Talmud und Midrasch,* vol. 1, 302–3; G. F. Moore, *Judaism,* vol. 2, 267–70.
2. Eusebius, *H. E.* 6.8.1–2; also for another similar misunderstanding, Justin, *Apol.* 1.29.

another problem which appears to have been created by Matthew's disregard of original contexts, transference, relocation, and rewriting of sayings on the basis of a superficial similarity, literary whim, or theological idea. In 18:18 Matthew quotes a saying of Jesus to all the disciples, "Whatever you bind on earth shall be bound in heaven, and whatever you loose on earth shall be loosed in heaven." This word of Jesus is reflected also in John 20:23, "If you forgive the sins of any, they are forgiven; if you retain the sins of any, they are retained." The conclusion appears inescapable that Matthew's admiration for Peter has caused him to transfer this saying to a new context and to rewrite it, so as to give to Peter alone authority which Jesus otherwise gives to all the disciples alike.

9

A Dissenting Opinion about Respect for Context in Old Testament Quotations

Richard T. Mead

From Richard T. Mead, "A Dissenting Opinion about Respect for Context in Old Testament Quotations," *New Testament Studies* 10 (1964): 279–89. Reprinted with the permission of Cambridge University Press.

A recent short study by S. L. Edgar claims that various New Testament writings show varied degrees of respect for the context of Old Testament passages which they quote.[1] This encourages him to draw conclusions about the historical sources of the materials. I find reason to take issue with his argument and to dissent from his conclusions.

Dr. Edgar's study proceeds by comparison. Several unarguable examples demonstrate a free approach to Old Testament context among writers like Paul, Matthew, and John. These writers quote, combine, and freely reapply isolated sentences; they divest Old Testament verses of their historical subjects and objects—and so forth. "When we come to the use Jesus made of the Old Testament we are confronted with a different respect for context."[2] That judgment must be scrutinized before one deals with the inferences drawn from it.

What are the data? Dr. Edgar offers to study "the words of Jesus, as recorded in the gospels . . . compared with the editorial comments of

---

1. S. L. Edgar, "Respect for Context in Quotations from the Old Testament," *N.T.S.* 9 (October 1962): 55–62. Unless noted otherwise, all references to Dr. Edgar are to this article.
2. Ibid., 59.

the evangelists"[3] and seems to imply that a red-letter New Testament would just about suffice for this. (In an earlier study he offered specific views on some of the pertinent passages.)[4] In order to stay with his argument as he presents it, we will keep within this definition of the data until (further along) some more specific comments are needed.

All but one of Dr. Edgar's cases for Jesus come from the synoptic Gospels, so we will keep to them. Even so, the amount of Old Testament material is so bulky as to need distinctions. One can exclude merely incidental references to Old Testament history or institutions (for example, the leper told to "show yourself to the priest" in Matt. 8:4: cf. Lev. 13:49).[5] One may also exclude passages for which the quoted Old Testament material is so brief, so fragmentary, or of such general biblical idiom as to throw doubt upon intention to quote.[6] (For example, in Matt. 24:6 the two words *dei* and *genesthai* do not prove that Dan. 2:28 is quoted, Nestle's black-face type notwithstanding.) The remaining passages show intention to quote that varies from crystal clear on down to probable. Do these sustain Dr. Edgar's propositions?

First let us look at synoptic passages which have Jesus quoting Old Testament words which are to be fulfilled in the future (however immediately or remotely future). References to Jonah and the queen of the south in Matthew 12:40–2 do respect the Old Testament contexts. Now we face a large group which must be judged to be, at best, *detached* from their Old Testament contexts. That is to say, the situation which Jesus would clarify by quoting may resemble the Old Testament situation in one or a few particulars; the quotation runs far enough to associate these particulars; but then it stops. His arrest is near because Jesus must be "reckoned with transgressors" (Luke 22:37/Isa. 53:12); when the shepherd is struck the sheep will be scattered (Matt. 26:31/Zech. 13:7). Jerusalem's dark hour will resemble that of ancient Samaria enough for mountains and hills to be addressed in Hosea's words (Luke 23:30/Hos. 10:8). So much (for now) for detached quotations. More interesting are several cases of *violated* Old Testament context. On the basis of Dr. Edgar's treatment of Paul, Matthew, and John we may say that *violation* has occurred when the historical Old Testament situation

---

3. Ibid., 55.

4. S. L. Edgar, "New Testament and Rabbinic Messianic Interpretation," *N.T.S.* 5 (October 1958): 47–54.

5. Here I classify Luke 4:25–7; Matt. 8:4; 17:12; 23:35; 24:38–9. Throughout this study I cite Matthew, the richest source for Old Testament quotation, in passages involving synoptic parallels, unless there is specific reason for calling attention to Mark and Luke. A parallel text ordered upon Matthew will quickly show how Mark and Luke stand.

6. Here I classify Matt. 7:12; 8:11; 10:21; Mark 4:29; Matt. 13:32, 41, 43; Mark 9:12b, 49; Luke 19:10, 44; Matt. 24:6, 7, 16; Luke 21:22, 35; Mark 14:18 (John 13:18 gives an explicit quotation); Matt. 26:38.

is thoroughly disregarded (e.g., Matt. 2:18, weeping at Ramah refers to the slaughter of the innocents under Herod) and/or when novel subjects or objects are substituted into the interpretation (e.g., 1 Cor. 14:21, where Paul replaces the Assyrians of Isa. 28:11–12 with speakers in tongues).[7] Whether other forms of violation exist, these two suffice to deal with: Capernaum's being brought from exaltation down to Hades, instead of the king of Babylon (Matt. 11:23/Isa. 14:13–15); instead of God, the Son of man who will requite each man his activities (Matt. 16:27/Ps. 62:12; Prov. 24:12); and the Son of man's coming into human ken rather than being presented "to the Ancient of Days" (Matt. 26:64/ Dan. 7:13). Most of all, what shall we say about the synoptic Apocalypse? Even if we set aside phrases for which any doubt exists of intention to quote,[8] we face serious disturbances of context. A good argument might be made for contextuality at Matthew 24:15 (the desolating sacrilege, Dan. 9:27 and 12:11) and Matthew 24:21 (an unmatched time of trouble, Dan. 12:1). Reference to seeing the Son of man coming (Matt. 24:30/Dan. 7:13) is more contextual than at the trial scene, because less entirely earthly, but it is still not free from the objection made above. We have three *detached* quotations (i.e. one or a few particulars are associated by means of each quotation, which for that reason often is merely a fragment): at Matthew 24:29c (Isa. 34:4) and Matt. 24:31a+c (Isa. 27:13; Deut. 30:4). Sprinkled among these are three others with *violated* contexts: use of an oracle explicitly against Babylon (Matt. 24:29a, b/Isa. 13:10), the tribes of the earth substituted for those of Israel (Matt. 24:30/Zech. 12:12); and an apocalyptic ingathering in place of return from Babylonia (Matt. 24:31b/ Zech. 2:10 [LXX]). In sum, Matthew 24:29–31 offers us a panorama of fragmentary quotations not superior in any way to the diversely based mixture of denunciations which Paul brings forward in Romans 3:10–18 to prove that all men are in the grip of sin.[9]

When we turn to the synoptic record for Jesus' use of Old Testament words which are *presently* being fulfilled, we do find less disregard for context. Violation of context (in the strict definition set forth earlier) does not occur at all. Two passages may be judged respectful of context, and each time for the same reason—that the Old Testament base itself is predictive and thus cannot prescribe what fulfilment it shall have. John the Baptist is Elijah (Matt. 17:11/Mal. 4:5, cf. the clear allusion to the same at Matt. 11:14), and the Last Supper is the (new) covenant (Matt. 26:28/ Exod. 24:8, cf. Jer. 31:31 and Zech. 9:11).

7. See Edgar, 9:57–8.
8. Luke 21:24 (Zech. 12:3?); Matt. 24:24 (Deut. 13:2?).
9. Dr. Edgar cites this one among his flagrant Pauline examples: Edgar, 9:56.

What flourishes among the presently fulfilled Scriptures is *detached* quotation, the technique of association by means of fragmentary particulars. In the Lukan sermon at Nazareth Jesus quotes most of Isaiah 61:1–2 (Luke 4:18–19)—appropriately so, many Christians would feel, in light of the patent rebirth of prophetic consciousness in Jesus. Yet the words *aposteilai tethrausmenous en aphesei* (Luke 4:18/Isa. 58:6) cannot have been read from a scroll open at "the place where it [Isa. 61:1–2] was written" (Luke 4:17)! This phrase, however suitable, is intrusive and detached. Jesus' reply to John's disciples involves a mixed blend of terms detached from three Isaianic promises of blessing for the afflicted (Matt. 11:4–5/Isa. 29:18–19; 35:5–6; 61:1). Following the parable of the sower, Jesus' use of parables is explained so as once again to connect his task with Isaiah's (Matt. 13:14–15/Isa. 6:9–10). The detached particulars here are three: 1) the prophetic task, and 2) the people's inertia, 3) within the overriding intentions of God. (The New Testament passage and Mark's parallel are themselves widely disputed, as we know.) In Matthew 11:10 the definition of John as God's "messenger" makes use of Malachi 3:1 but apparently adjusts it in the direction of Exodus 23:20 in order to say "before thee" instead of "before me." The sword which divides households evokes a broad paraphrase based upon Micah (Matt. 10:35/Mic. 7:6): here context is close to being violated, for Micah's family divisions spring from a dissolute society, not from conflicts of loyalty. Finally, the last articulate words of Jesus crucified are detached utterances (Matt. 27:46/Ps. 22:1; Luke 23:46/Ps. 31:5). They come, appropriately enough, from "individual lament" psalms (*die Klagelieder des Einzelnen*: Gunkel). Nonetheless, they are short quotations, isolated as they appear in their Gospel settings.[10]

On the basis of the material reviewed so far, I find it impossible to support Dr. Edgar's claim that Jesus showed exceptional respect for Old Testament context. The prophetic-fulfillment material has been reviewed simply because Dr. Edgar seems inclined to affirm Jesus' authorship of all that the Synoptics ascribe to him.[11] Many critics, however, will long since have ascribed such material to the early church. Therefore we must push our inquiry into uses of Old Testament context in passages which are not predictive. In this connection, let me antici-

10. In fairness one should concede that a crucified man near death would not likely recite psalms at any length. The several references to Ps. 22 in the crucifixion narrative suggest that 22:1 should be regarded as part of a larger context of fulfillment, for which see Martin Dibelius, *From Tradition to Gospel*, trans. B. L. Woolf (New York, 1935), 184–89, 193–94.

11. This is clear for Matt. 10:35; 26:31, and Luke 4:18–19; 22:37: cf. Edgar, 9:61–62 and his earlier article in *N.T.S.* 5:49–51. Since he refrains in both articles from consigning words of Jesus to church authorship, I presuppose a conservative tendency whenever specific comments are absent.

pate something. We will soon see that among the nonpredictive passages the Old Testament contexts are well respected when compared with predictive passages. (In fact, this is what gives Dr. Edgar's article its apparent cogency, for most of his examples are taken from nonpredictive materials.) Observing the difference, one might feel stimulated to leap for the conclusion that Jesus caused it. The detached and violated predictive contexts would indicate material dominated by church Christology, while by the implication of contrast other material would be credited "authentically" to Jesus. One should resist the stimulus, lest it vault him into presumptuous error. We must not neglect New Testament contexts as we study Old Testament contexts. That would be a curious error to make. I point this out due to its considerable bearing upon our data and because doing so may check leaping to conclusions.

The following list of nonpredictive synoptic items reported for Jesus will meet even rigorous modern standards of respect for context—excepting only Isaiah 35:5–6 (item 8) and Hosea 6:6 (item 9).[12]

Statements to the disciples

1. Matt. 5:21/Exod. 20:13; Deut. 5:17   Against murder
2. Matt. 5:27/Exod. 20:14; Deut. 5:18   Against adultery
3. Matt. 5:31/Deut. 24:1   On divorce
4. Matt. 5:33–4/Lev. 19:12; Isa. 66:1; Ps. 48:2   Against swearing
5. Matt. 5:38/Exod. 21:24; Deut. 19:21; Lev. 24:20 Against retaliation
6. Matt. 18:16/Deut. 19:15   Rule concerning witnesses

Statements to outsiders (who are often opponents)

7. Matt. 4:3–10, containing quotations from Deut. 8:3; Ps. 91:11–12; Deut. 6:16; Deut. 6:13   The temptation
8. Matt. 11:4–5/Isa. 29:18–19; 35:5–6; 61:1   Answer to John's disciples
9. Matt. 12:1–8 containing clear allusions to Deut. 23:25; Exod. 20:10; Deut. 5:14; 1 Sam. 21:1–7; Num. 27:9–10; Hos. 6:6   Plucking grain on Sabbath
10. Mark 10:2–9/ Gen. 1:27; 2:24; Deut. 24:1   Against divorce
11. Matt. 19:18–19/Exod. 20:12–16; Deut. 5:16–20; Deut. 24:14; Lev. 19:18   Rich young man
12. Matt. 22:38–9/Deut. 6:5 [+5:4 in Mark]; Lev. 19:18   The greatest commandments

12. In due time we will consider whether modern, critical standards of respect for context are appropriate. Since Dr. Edgar premised his study upon such standards, we will adhere to them for the purpose of the discussion.

If anything can, this extensive list upon important subjects should sustain Dr. Edgar's statement that "the Old Testament passages quoted by Jesus were used with a respect for the original context that is unmatched by other New Testament writers."[13] Let us cross-examine these important witnesses to see what may account for their respect of context.

Items 1 to 5 belong to the well-known set of contrasts between new law and old law found in Matthew 5:21–47. The governing principle here is transparent: valid commentary must begin from a true text. No more need be said.[14] The same principle controls Old Testament usage in item 11. Item 12 reflects the same principle in that to elevate certain commandments above others is to comment upon the Torah. For that reason accurate citation of texts should surprise no one. (Whether Jesus was doing a radical or a conventional thing is outside our subject.)

Item 6 occurs in a section stipulating legal procedure leading up to excommunication. Deuteronomy 19:15 is taken over, perhaps on the premise that the church is the New Israel. Defining admissible evidence is a procedural issue important enough in every earnest jurisprudence to account sufficiently for the Old Testament usage here.[15]

Four items remain: numbers 7, 8, 9, 10. In these cases we must notice the premises brought to the discussion by those who took part in it. In other words, the New Testament context must be honored.

Item 8 (Jesus' reply to John through his disciples) has already been considered briefly among our prophetic fulfillment passages, but the presence of "outsiders" leads us to discuss it more fully here. In this case the "outsiders" are more friendly than many who confronted Jesus, and we may suppose that they share with Jesus an interest in prophetic renewal and fulfillment anticipating the dawning of God's reign. This shared premise makes possible a generalized verbal reference to three Isaianic passages of renewal—29:18–9; 35:5–6; 61:1—in terms of Jesus' activity: the blind see, the deaf hear, the poor are preached good news. Matthew 11:5 does not literally represent any of the passages from Isaiah. One might say it is nonetheless "true to the spirit" of the Isaiah passages. What one then really has said is that he shares the premises: he sympathizes with the connection Jesus offers to make between his own deeds and the blessings mentioned in Isaiah. For that reason one does not raise literalistic quibbles about the contextuality of fragmentary quotation.

By contrast, item 9 provides a hostile audience who consider casual grain-picking an unlawful form of sabbath work. This is a "Pronounce-

---

13. Edgar, 9:62.
14. Matt. 5:43 can be included, we notice, so far as it follows Lev. 19:18. It provokes objection insofar as "and hate your enemy" is not a true Old Testament text.
15. Cf. Mishna Sotah 1.1–2.

ment Story" (Vincent Taylor), so we must note what functions our materials serve within the form. All but one of the Old Testament quotations and clear allusions belong to the narrative set-up which "merely supplies the necessary background for the question and answer."[16] The allusion to sabbath violation is made by the questioners, not Jesus, and it appeals to a clear Old Testament law—as it must, in order to pose a legitimate question. Jesus' reply alludes to David's violation of Torah. Matthew alone contains another allusion, to lawful sabbath violation for the sake of the sacrifices. Either way, the Old Testament material supports an *a fortiori* extension of freedom toward Torah—there David (and the priests), here how much more the Son of man. The presence of hostile questioners demands that examples which are to be developed *a fortiori* must be contextually unimpeachable.[17]

The divorce question (our item 10) again brings together hostile questioners and a Pronouncement Story. Scripture confronts Scripture in a clear collision of torah passages. This sufficiently explains careful respect for context. Jesus opposes a clear and well-known *halakah* based on Deuteronomy 24:1. As David Daube shows, even the example of what God did (Mark 10:6/Gen. 1:27) is not strong enough. Jesus must provide an opposing *halakah* based upon God's precept (Mark 10:7–8a/ Gen. 2:24).[18] In such a high-powered conflict, only the purest inferential materials will serve.

Our item 7, the temptation, is one for which Dr. Edgar makes considerable claim of contextuality. Although the devil's use of Psalm 91:11–12 is more ingenious than contextual, we will dismiss it as being not formally a quotation from Jesus. The three Old Testament statements which are quoted for Jesus all come from Deuteronomy 6–8, one of the most familiar scriptural sections in Israel. All three quotations state commonplace truisms of Jewish religion. If the temptation narrative is even remotely historical, it is noteworthy but not astonishing that

16. Vincent Taylor, *The Formation of the Gospel Tradition* (2d ed., London, 1957), 65: cf. Dibelius, 44–53, and Rudolf K. Bultmann, *Die Geschichte der synoptischen Tradition* (3d ed., Göttingen, 1957), 66–70.

17. The uniquely Matthean material (12:5–7, alluding to Num. 28:9–10 and quoting Hos. 6:6) reflects the compulsion. It seeks to improve the base with a specific case of sabbath-breaking based upon halakic precept from torah: this is clearly demonstrated by David Daube, *The New Testament and Rabbinic Judaism* (London, 1956), 67–71. What we may think is a misfit quotation—Hos. 6:6 in Matt. 12:7—puts added scriptural force behind the *a fortiori* argument: temple and sacrifice justify violation of sabbath law; the Son of man is weightier than the temple; and, to nail it down by Hos. 6:6, an act of mercy outweighs sacrifice. The Hosea quotation is not used to pose the spirit against the letter of the law, as Dr. Edgar suggests, 9:60.

18. See Daube, 76–79. I cite Mark for the divorce passage because Matthew shifts the issue over to grounds for divorce.

Jesus' responses are satisfyingly contextual: after all, they are ready portions of a heritage—direct comments upon familiar ancient situations with which he might easily have identified his own. If the truisms themselves gave rise to the temptation narrative, respect for Old Testament context is implicit and an appeal to it would be *petitio principii*.

This ends our review of the twelve passages listed above. I have suggested that the respect shown for Old Testament context in Old Testament quotation arose from the specific functions which quoted materials served in each synoptic case. Such were those functions that looser contextual standards would have weakened the argument and sometimes even destroyed it. There is nothing left over in the material which requires Dr. Edgar's suggestion that the personal influence of Jesus brought about respect for context.[19]

In order not to neglect material which might clarify any of the issues, we need turn finally to nonpredictive passages which have Jesus quoting Old Testament material in ways not satisfactory to modern, critical canons of context. The most prominent among these concern the resurrection, David's son, the parable of the wicked tenants, and opposition to the traditions of the Pharisees.

The general resurrection is treated in a Pronouncement Story containing two Old Testament quotations. The first (Matt. 22:24/Deut. 25:5–6; Gen. 38:8) simply paraphrases the basis for levirate marriage: it belongs to the narrative set-up; and it is satisfactorily contextual. The second (Matt. 22:32/Exod. 3:6) either is the pronouncement or stands integral to it; it quotes very closely; and we would say it flagrantly violates the Old Testament context if we did not know about pharisaic Judaism. The key, as we do know, is the exegetical stress upon God's being even now God of Abraham et al., therefore they live, therefore resurrection of the dead.[20] Acceptance of this "proof" depends altogether upon prior belief in the doctrine of resurrection.[21] Something similar happens in the argument whether the messiah can be David's son. Since everyone accepted David for the author of Psalm 110, its 5:1 ("The Lord says to my lord," cf. Mark 12:36) proves that three people are involved—David, the Lord [God], and David's lord. But who is meant by David's lord? The Messiah (Mark 12:35). The entire argument rests upon that voluntary equation. Apart from it the scriptural context is violated and the proof falls.

19. It is possible and even likely that Jesus faced situations demanding greater respect for context than the NT writers in general faced. But that is a different issue for it introduces a third factor and a different cause.

20. See George Foot Moore, *Judaism* (3 vols., Cambridge, 1954), 1, 381–3.

21. Ibid., 382, shows plainly how the Sadducees insist that respect for original context destroys proof-texts of this kind.

In other words, we have reached passages where respect for context depends upon a friendly judgment from the reader (or the hearer). Such is again the case with Jesus' condemnation of Pharisaic tradition (Matt. 15:1–9 and Mark 7:1–13). Once more we meet the familiar pattern of the Pronouncement Story: those Old Testament citations belonging to narrative introduction are quoted accurately and are respectful of context (Matt. 15:4/Exod. 20:12; Deut. 5:16; Exod. 21:17; Lev. 20:9). In the case at hand Jesus uses these citations to expose by midrashic methods an area in which the Pharisees depended almost altogether upon mishnaic methods (tradition) with the result that a way sometimes opened to abuses.[22] Jesus' accusation of respect for human tradition to the disrespect of God's word refers pointedly to Isaiah 29:13 (quoted Matt. 15:8–9). Here is the crucial quotation, integral to the pronouncement; it is contextual if you agree to equate the Pharisees with Isaiah's stupefied leaders; but a hostile hearer could raise endless contextual objections. The same holds for the crucial equation (Matt. 21:42/Ps. 118:22–3) in the parable of the wicked tenants. Here, however, the quoted verse is not integral to the decisive point of the parable (rejection of the *tenants*). Perhaps it comes in by association under the rubric of rejection. As it stands, the rejected cornerstone must have the rejected son (Matt. 21:38–9) for its antecedent and of course it does.[23] But that equation springs from the mind of a sympathetic reader, not from the context of Psalm 118.

For the remainder of Jesus' nonpredictive citations of the Old Testament we may revert to our category of *detached* material—that is, the situation clarified by Scripture does resemble the original situation in a few particulars and the quotation does not go beyond these. We may list two beatitudes (Matt. 5:5/Ps. 37:11 and Matt. 5:8/Ps. 24:4) and possibly the command to be perfect (Matt. 5:48/Deut. 15:13). The directions for praying secretly seem (Matt. 6:6) to show the content of Isaiah 26:20 [LXX] attracted into the model of Elijah (2 Kings 4:33) and thus brought into connection with prayer. At the calling of the tax-collector Hosea 6:6 occurs again, still only in Matthew (9:13). It functions more allusively than it does at Matthew 12:7. In Mark 8:17 Jesus' comment upon his undiscerning disciples runs close to Jeremiah 5:21, closer still to Ezekiel's statement (12:2) that the "son of man" is dwelling among those who will not use their eyes or ears. Mark 9:48 defines Gehenna by means of Isaiah 66:24—a detached usage and not a violation of context

---

22. See Mishna Hagigah 1.8 and the tractate Nedarim; cf. T. W. Manson, *The Teachings of Jesus* (2d ed., Cambridge, 1951), 315–19.

23. Cf. Acts 4:11; Eph. 2:20–1; 1 Pet. 2:7. The other OT material in the parable is Isa. 5:1–2. Its conscious echoes in the narrative introduction are satisfactorily contextual.

unless you posit a supernatural hell. When Jesus portrays temple conditions by the contrast between a "house of prayer" and "a den of robbers" (Matt. 21:13), he has detached and contrasted Isaiah 56:7 and Jeremiah 7:11. The Scripture cited by Matthew a few verses later (Matt. 21:16/Ps. 8:2 [LXX 8:3]) is detached and yet not violate, for God seems to remain the ultimate subject of praise.

I state conclusions. First: Dr. Edgar's finding, that Jesus quoted the Old Testament "with a respect for context that is unmatched by other New Testament writers *[sic]*,"[24] is unfounded. Only an atmosphere of selected evidences can keep such a generalization alive, for the instances of detached or violated context are too numerous to count as exceptions to rule. Therefore respect for Old Testament context is no "mark of authenticity" upon Gospel material. Second: the greater respect for Old Testament context in nonpredictive, as against predictive, synoptic words of Jesus does not give us a usable tool with which to distinguish "authentic" statements of Jesus from those which the early church "put in his mouth." (This conclusion is not, of course, directed at anything said by Dr. Edgar.) Respect for context appears to be a function of the uses to which Old Testament materials were put. High respect tends to appear in incidental narration and in places requiring either 1) a true text to comment upon, 2) a solid basis for valid inferences, or 3) attack upon or defence against hostile questioners. Therefore respect for context *may* be a useful companion to the study of forms within the Gospel tradition, but it does not supply independent proof that it was *Jesus* whose words the tradition preserved. Respect for context is neutral toward authorship. Disrespect for context might be less neutral but it is too widespread to support generalizations.

In order to keep my discussion in contact with Dr. Edgar's, I have used "respect for context" throughout in its modern, critical connotation. That done, "respect for context" as an approach must be condemned as inappropriate to the material being studied. Dr. Edgar's article would not merit a dissent had it not raised a claim about historical verification of Gospel materials. To use our current, scholarly sense of respect for context is to make unfair, modernized demands upon the biblical materials. The simple fact that such respect tends to appear as a function of only certain kinds of Old Testament uses suggests quite plainly that historical contextuality was not cherished on principle in New Testament times. The New Testament writers as well as their Palestinian Jewish contemporaries (who also had the Old Testament for their Scripture) move about in an atmosphere of revealed religion

---

24. Edgar, 9:62.

which regards scriptural statements as true both in whole and in various sized parts.[25] If we feel constrained to detach Jesus from that atmosphere and bring him into line with current tastes in context, are we not victimized by a desire to make him respectable through modernity, despite Schweitzer, Cadbury, and many others?

So far as I know, we have no critical history of the use of proof-texts in either the Christian or the Jewish tradition. Yet anyone reading, say, the New Testament, Justin Martyr, the Westminster Confession, and current Jehovah's Witnesses' literature might wish we had. Perhaps no generalizations are safe, yet one may risk some as *obiter dicta* inviting comment and clarification for a perennial problem. What makes for unrestrained proof-texting? We might find an answer by pursuing this premise: "context" depends upon consensus.[26] Consensus, however, can be affected from two directions: one, the ideas within a group; the other, the group's colloquy with outsiders. The latter tends to enforce restraint by putting every step of a demonstration under scrutiny.[27] Consensus within is not different in principle, but may be so in fact: the same loyalties which bind people together may lead them to think that certain assumptions and forms of demonstration stand beyond question.[28] However, if these common loyalties are shaken by other loyalties, interest in methods of proof and steps of a demonstration may quickly emerge.[29] In general, therefore, we should expect unrestrained proof-texting to flourish in groups marked by strong inner consensus shielded with an impenetrable parochialism. If so, it is not surprising to find that New Testament materials directed to tiny conventicles of recent Christian converts should contain a rich vein of (what we call) noncontextual proof-texts. Yet the contrast between such material and some other series of items does not in itself tell the precise cause of the contrast. Only careful study of evidence can clarify specific causes.

---

25. This atmosphere and its effects upon exegesis are superbly described by Moore, 1:247–50.

26. Current historical-critical scholarship offers a good example: for it, "context" denotes historical situation and the intention of the author. What quickly confuses our semantics is that such scholarship constantly *reports on* a lot of other ideas about context.

27. However, all groups may have agreed upon canons of context which are alien to later comers: in that case, so will their proofs seem "wild" although they were considered satisfactory at the time.

28. E.g. 1 Cor. 9:9, "Is it for oxen that God is concerned?" is put forth as a purely rhetorical question anticipating (Greek: *mē*) a "No" answer.

29. Notice how carefully Tertullian, *On Idolatry* 5–9 and 14–15, seeks to distinguish denotation (strict) from connotation (broad) in Scripture in order to support the rigorous side of disputes over church discipline.

Part 4

Did the New Testament Authors Respect the Context of the Old Testament Text?

Affirmative Arguments

10

The Old Testament in the New

C. H. Dodd

Any reader of the Bible who is accustomed to the salutary, if now somewhat old-fashioned, practice of using an apparatus of marginal references cannot fail to be aware of the immense extent to which writers of
the New Testament quote passages from the Old, or make unavowed
but unmistakable allusions to such passages. Sometimes the apposite-
ness of a quotation will set the reader at once upon a profitable train of
thought; sometimes, but by no means always. From time to time he will
have an uneasy feeling that there are links of association which elude
him, which indeed may perhaps never have existed except in the fancy
of an individual writer. When this is so, further study is discouraged.
And the whole mass of quotations and allusions is so unwieldly and
seemingly so amorphous that it is not easy to discover any system in it.
Our present task is to seek for some clue to the intention, and the methods, of New Testament writers which may perhaps help us to see the
relevance, not of this or that quotation, but, in some measure, of their
use of the Old Testament in general.

We must no doubt allow for the possibility that in some places we
have before us nothing more than the rhetorical device of literary allusion, still common enough, and even more common in the period when
the New Testament was produced. Such an allusion may stimulate the

fancy and give liveliness to an argument which threatens to drag; at its best it may give perfectly legitimate aesthetic satisfaction; but there is not necessarily any deeper significance in it. I believe that such writers as Paul and the author to the Hebrews, both of them accomplished in Greek rhetoric, were not above employing such a device occasionally. We must allow these two at least, and possibly other New Testament writers, rhetorical license; though I believe the number of places where they have in fact availed themselves of it is less than might appear at first sight.

Yet when we have made this allowance, it is clear that in many places the New Testament writers have a more serious purpose in view. In adducing passages from the Old Testament they are consciously appealing to an *authority*. A quotation may be introduced to provide an unassailable premise upon which an inference may be founded, or to test a conclusion drawn by logical argument or put forth as a corollary of experience. In such cases as these it is pertinent to enquire into the propriety of the interpretation offered, and the validity of its application to the matter in hand.

It is in the course of such enquiry that we may hope to come upon evidence of the principles upon which the early Christian use of the Old Testament was based.

In the Greek world of the New Testament period there was a widely recognized method of interpreting an ancient literature which was venerated as an authority while its antiquity presented difficulties to the "modern" commentator—the so-called allegorical method. It had apparently been devised for the purposes of Greek teachers who employed the Homeric poems as an authoritative textbook for the instruction of youth and the guidance of those who aimed at moral improvement. This method had been taken over by Jewish interpreters of the Hebrew Scriptures. Its best known exponent is Philo the Jew of Alexandria. He employed it, with great skill and subtlety, not only to circumvent certain stumbling blocks which the traditional text presented to the Greek public he wished to reach, but also to discover in this venerable literature "modern" philosophical ideas of which its authors hardly dreamed. The same method came into extensive use among the Fathers of the church in the early Christian centuries. It is not surprising that it is to be found also in the New Testament. What *is* surprising is that it is employed so seldom.

There are a few outstanding examples. Paul's treatment of the story of Hagar and Ishmael, in Galatians 4:21–31, is (as he expressly says) allegorical; and in fact it observes the strictest rules of the game. Hagar stands for Sinai, the mountain of the law; Ishmael her son for the Jews as "sons of the law"; Isaac, the child of promise, for the Christian church; and the whole story falls into line. Similarly, in the Epistle to the Hebrews (7:1–10) the story of Melchizedek in Genesis 14:17–20 is treated on allegorical principles closely similar to those on which Philo treats the same story, though to a different end.

In allegory proper, as we have it here, the historical setting of the original, and the intention of its author, go for nothing. The Old Testament supplies only the imagery through which an idea may be forcibly presented. The idea itself is not derived from it. Any fictitious personage would do as well as Hagar or Melchizedek.

But such examples of true allegory are far from common; and while occasional traits of allegory may be detected in passages which are not in the strict sense allegorical, the method is not characteristic of the New Testament. Here the contrast with Philo is instructive. For Philo the Old Testament presents a picture without perspective; it is two-dimensional, on the flat. The writers of the New Testament, in comparison, show themselves aware of the historical perspective. Thus Paul notes the conflict of Elijah with Baal-worship, and Isaiah's announcement of the "remnant," as successive stages in a continuous process of "purposive selection" which was in operation for many centuries, and prepared the stage at last for the coming of Christ. Farther back in history, he is impressed by the long lapse of time between the covenant with Abraham and the promulgation of the law on Sinai—430 years, he computes, and he is not so very far out by modern calculations. The author to the Hebrews, in spite of his Alexandrine proclivities, is acutely aware of the tedious centuries during which the fathers lived and died in faith, not having received the promises, because God had prepared some better thing for us. For him Abraham, Isaac, and Jacob are not lay figures upon which to hang an allegory, but human beings who played their obscure part in the early stages of a process not visible in its completion. The evangelist Matthew, again, is interested in the run of the generations, from Abraham to David, from David to the Babylonian exile, from the exile to the birth of Christ. His chronology, indeed, is symbolic rather than exact, but it is clearly his intention to present the coming of Christ as the culmination of a real process in history. In the Acts of the Apostles, the speech of Stephen before his judges is almost a *cento* of quotations from the Old Testament, but a *cento* curiously unlike the linked series of allegorically interpreted texts which we find in Philo. Stephen's quotations mark the strictly historical sequence of events, from the call of Abraham to the apostasy of Solomon, at which point the survey breaks off as tension rises and argument is swallowed up in violence.

I recall these passages—and there are others that might be placed alongside them—to point the contrast between the characteristic atti-

tude of the New Testament writers to the Old Testament and the attitude which underlies its thoroughgoing allegorical treatment by Philo
and his like. In the main, these early Christian writers are aware of the
Old Testament as history, that is to say as reflecting the process of God's
dealings with his people over many centuries. With such an attitude, although they may occasionally fall into the fashionable method of allegory, and although from time to time they may make use of a phrase
from Scripture simply for its aptness, without deeper consideration, yet
it is unlikely that they would be systematically indifferent to the historical setting or the original intention of the Scriptures which they quote,
as they understood it. In studying their quotations, it will at any rate be
worth while always to turn up the context in the Old Testament and ask
how far it is being kept in view.

We must begin, naturally, by noting what passages are actually
quoted in the New Testament. These are usually quite short, more often
than not confined to the limits of a single sentence, or even a single
phrase. Only rarely do we meet with a passage amounting to several
verses reproduced *in extenso*. But suppose we turn up each such quoted
passage in its Old Testament context, and mark it by underlining. We
soon begin to discover that there are some books, and some portions of
books, where such underlinings cluster thickly, while other long tracts
are almost or entirely devoid of them. Closer examination reveals that
sometimes a particular cluster of quotations may all be made by a single New Testament writer; as for example certain chapters of Exodus
and Leviticus will be thickly underlined with quotations in the Epistle
to the Hebrews. Such cases we may discount as representing no more
than the predilection of an individual author. But in other places references will accumulate from a considerable variety of New Testament
books, and here we must be on the track of something more significant.
It seems clear that certain portions of the Old Testament Scriptures
commanded greater interest among early Christian thinkers than others. I will presently give some examples. But for the moment let us suppose that we have before us a given passage of the Old Testament which
has been largely laid under contribution for quotation in the New. By
simple examination of the facts it should be possible to draw some inferences not without importance.

If it can be shown that one particular sentence has been quoted in
two or more writings of the New Testament, where we have no reason
to suspect literary dependence of one writer on another, there is surely
a fair presumption that the sentence had been recognized as having
special significance for Christians at a date earlier than the first such
quotation. If adjacent or contiguous sentences from the same context

are similarly quoted, it begins to be probable that something more than the single sentence had been thus early recognized. The probability is all the stronger if the sentences quoted are in the original context very closely connected. To take one example: Psalm 69:9 reads, "For zeal for thy house has consumed me, and the insults of those who insult thee have fallen on me." The first member of this verse is quoted by John (2:17), the second by Paul (Rom. 15:3). The possibility that Paul is dependent on the fourth Gospel, or that the Fourth Evangelist had read the Epistle to the Romans, is too remote to be seriously considered. Yet it would be too much of a coincidence if the two writers independently happened to cite the two halves of a single verse, unless they were both aware that at least this whole verse, if not any more of the psalm, formed part of a scheme of scriptural passages generally held to be especially significant.

Again, if within the same chapter there are several detached sentences, in different parts of it, quoted independently by two or more writers, it seems to be a probable inference that the whole chapter was before these writers as a unit from which they might profitably draw illustrative material for their argument or exposition of the gospel. For example, in the same sixty-ninth psalm, not only are the two halves of verse 9 independently quoted by John and Paul, but verse 4 is cited by John, verse 21 by Matthew, and verse 25 in the Acts of the Apostles.[1] It seems at least a plausible hypothesis that Psalm 69 belonged to a group of Scriptures which had already attracted the attention of Christian thinkers even before the date at which Paul wrote to the Romans—say A.D. 57–59. This hypothesis will need testing by the examination of a large number of similar cases. If the same order of facts is to be observed elsewhere, the probability of our tentative conclusion will grow accordingly.

As a matter of fact there are many portions of the Old Testament for which there is even weightier evidence of the same kind, and I believe it is possible, by using the method I have exemplified, to compile a list of fairly lengthy portions which formed, from a very early date indeed, a body of Scripture to which appeal might be made by Christian evangelists, teachers, and apologists for the elucidation and justification of the main themes of the gospel. I am not thinking of the kind of classified anthology of detached proof-texts which has come down to us in the shape of the later "testimony-books"—the earliest of them edited by Cyprian in the third century. There is no convincing evidence that any such book was compiled in the earliest period. I am not thinking of a book at all, but rather of something belonging to the body of instructions imparted, orally in the main, no doubt, to those whose duties in

---

1. John 15:25, Matt. 27:34 and parallels, Acts 1:20.

the church led them to Old Testament research; a sort of guide to the study of the Bible for Christian teachers.

I now proceed to give some examples of the phenomena in question. A very striking example is the poem upon the sufferings of the "Servant of the Lord" in the fifty-third chapter of Isaiah. Of the twelve verses in this chapter there is only one which does not reappear, as a whole or in part, somewhere in the New Testament. No one author quotes the chapter extensively; it is rarely that two or more writers quote the same verse; only one writer quotes as many as two successive verses—quoting them, however, in a way which shows that he had the whole chapter before him (Acts 8:26–40). But one sentence or another from the chapter is quoted, or unmistakably echoed, in all four Gospels, in Acts, Romans, Philippians, Hebrews, and 1 Peter. In fact, if the original text of Isaiah had been lost at this point, it would have been possible to restore almost the whole chapter (in a Greek translation, of course) out of the New Testament. This surely means that the writers of the New Testament, while one of them might choose one sentence for quotation and one another, all considered this chapter, taken as a whole, to have outstanding significance for the understanding of the gospel, and the significance it possessed as a whole has determined the sense in which extracts from it are employed.

Now let us look at the "plot" of the fifty-third chapter of Isaiah. It is the story of a character, distinguished as the Servant of the Lord, who voluntarily submits himself to contumely and suffering for the sake of others, endures the consequences of other men's sins without resistance or complaint, and is put to death, but after death achieves the glory of final achievement. Who the Servant was meant to be, whether an individual or a personified community, and if an individual, whether a historical character or an ideal figure of the future, is a point on which there seems to have been no agreement in antiquity, even as there is no agreement on the question among modern scholars.

A similar doubt arises about certain psalms which have some affinity with the fifty-third chapter of Isaiah. Their plot is similar, at least so far that they describe the troubles of someone who suffers undeservedly in unshaken loyalty to God, and is ultimately delivered and glorified through his grace and power. We may call them Psalms of the Righteous Sufferer, whether the sufferer is to be conceived individually or collectively. These psalms are largely laid under contribution by the writers of the New Testament, and applied in general to the sufferings of Christ: in Christian tradition they are often known as "Passion Psalms." For the moment we note the similarity of their "plot" to that of the Isaianic "Servant" poem, and the similar ambiguity between the individual and the collective in the description of the hero.

I now turn to another example, of a different kind: the vision of the Son of man in the seventh chapter of Daniel. Unmistakable allusions to this chapter are to be found in all four Gospels, in the Pauline epistles, and in the Revelation, and less clear but almost certain echoes elsewhere. Again we ask, what is the "plot"? The hero is a figure described as "like a son of man"—that is, a human figure in contrast to four beasts, red in tooth and claw, ramping over the earth. He has been (it is implied, though not directly stated) subject to the ravages of the beasts; but at last the tables are turned. The Son of man is called into the presence of the Eternal, enthroned at his side, and given an everlasting kingdom. The whole story is highly symbolic, borrowing its imagery from mythology. But the writer himself has supplied a key. The Son of man, he says, stands for "the people of the saints of the Most High," long oppressed by foreign powers, but called by God to victory and glory. A seemingly individual figure, who acts like an individual in the visionary drama, and yet represents a whole people, he clearly has affinities with the Servant of the Lord in Isaiah, who also appears in a guise which makes it doubtful whether he is an individual person or a community; and his fortunes are not widely different, when allowance is made for the different convention—in this case the apocalyptic convention—in which the matter is presented.

And here we may usefully compare two other Scriptures which in different ways speak of a "Son of man." The eightieth Psalm describes, in the kaleidoscopic imagery of oriental poetry, the fortunes of God's people in prosperity and adversity. They are the vine which he brought out of Egypt and planted. For a while it flourished, but then wild beasts entered the vineyard and ravaged it. "Look down from heaven," the poet prays, "and visit this vine." But then the imagery changes: "Let thy hand be upon the man of thy right hand, the Son of Man whom thou hast made strong for thyself." Here again, though the psalm is never expressly quoted, it has clearly supplied much of the standing imagery of the New Testament.

But we have not yet done with the "Son of man." The same expression occurs in Psalm 8, a poem to which there are numerous references in the New Testament, with one long quotation:

> What is man, that thou art mindful of him? or the son of man that thou visitest him? Thou madest him for a little while inferior to the angels; thou crownedst him with glory and honor, and didst set him over the works of thy hands; thou didst put all things in subjection under his feet.

This is quoted by the author to the Hebrews (2:6–8), after the Greek version, which this writer invariably follows, and which I have here translated. Here the Son of man is clearly no mere individual, nor does he any longer stand for any single people. He stands for man as such, for the human race, which is described as almost too insignificant for God to notice, and yet destined, through his sole grace, to be "crowned with glory and honor." Once again we have a variation upon the same plot: the Son of man, who is the Servant of the Lord, who is the Man of God's right hand, who is the people of the saints of the Most High, who is the vine which God brought up out of Egypt, who is in the end the whole human race, is first brought very low and then, by grace of God, exalted to glory. The parallel which the New Testament writers imply between man's dominion over the "beasts of the field" in Psalm 8, and the victory of the Son of man over the four beasts in Daniel 7, is surely more than a passing fancy. To follow it out might lead us to reflect on the relations between the realms of nature and of grace. But for that this is not the place.

We shall now look at some further Scriptures in which a similar plot is worked out in different terms.

In the short book of Joel, in chapters 2–3, we come, once again, upon a context where passages quoted or echoed in the New Testament are fairly thick on the ground, among them the long passage about the Spirit poured forth upon all flesh which is reported to have been quoted by Peter on the day of Pentecost, as a clue to the meaning of the surprising events of that day. These chapters contain a dramatic and highly colored picture of what the prophet calls "the Day of the Lord." It begins, "Blow the trumpet in Zion!" and goes on to depict in lurid imagery the terrors of a day of judgment—the ravages of a destroying army like demon locusts, the darkened sun, the quaking earth, and "multitudes, multitudes in the valley of decision." Out of the darkness and terror emerges the picture of a purified and renovated people of God with the Lord dwelling in Zion, and a spring of perennial waters giving life to the whole land. There is here no suggestion of an individual hero of the drama: the hero is Israel, the people of God: Israel as a community subjected to humiliation and suffering—this time as divine judgment on their sins—and yet destined, through the sheer grace of God, to final peace and blessedness. May we not say, it is the Son of man, the Servant of the Lord, in a new guise?

Once more, in Zechariah 9–14 we have a longer context full of passages which are either quoted or echoed in the New Testament. It is a group of prophecies whose interrelations are not too clear; but essentially it constitutes, like Joel 2–3, an apocalypse of the Day of the Lord, and it employs much the same stock of imagery. It begins with the King entering Zion, meek and riding upon an ass, to bring peace and to liberate the prisoners, and it ends with all the nations of the earth coming up to Jerusalem to worship Jehovah their King—in other words, with the proclamation of the universal kingdom of God. Between this beginning and this ending there is a complicated plot, in which Israel, the "flock" of God, passes through stages of rebellion against God and the punishment it entails, in the course of which the shepherd is smitten and the flock scattered. A drastic purge follows, which selects out of the whole nation a faithful nucleus called to be God's own people, with whom the future lies. Much of the story is obscure and mysterious, after the manner of apocalypse; yet we can recognize it as an elaboration of the general plot: humiliation and suffering turned into triumph by grace of God. Here the humiliation and suffering are in the main deserved by the unfaithfulness of God's people, as in Joel, and in contrast to Isaiah 53 and Daniel 7. But there are obscure hints of a martyred leader, or at least expressions which might be so understood.

I will take one more example, of a still more complicated kind: Isaiah 6:1–9:6. The opening scene is that of Isaiah's awe-inspiring vision of the glory of God, which carries a message at once of judgment and of forgiveness; for the prophet is stirred almost to despair with a sense of the impurity that clings to him and his people, and he is cleansed by the touch of fire from the altar of God. This tension between judgment and forgiveness strikes the keynote of all that follows. The prophet is moved to pronounce a terrible sentence of all but extinction upon a people whose heart is waxed fat and their ears dull of hearing. Yet almost immediately thereafter the names of two children—Shear-jashub, "a remnant shall turn," and Immanuel, "God with us"—hold out a gleam of hope. As terror falls darkly on the scene, the prophet separates his small circle of disciples to wait for the promised redemption. At last dawn breaks over the darkness of Galilee of the Gentiles, heralding the peaceful and perpetual reign of the Prince of Peace. The exact sequence, the true interpretation, and the primarily historical reference of many of these obscure prophecies are still matters of doubt and debate among scholars, but it is easy to see how for a first-century reader it all worked out as an elaboration and enrichment of the same broad plot of suffering and humiliation followed by triumph through grace of God. Here the suffering is wholly a deserved judgment upon the people's iniquities, and the triumph is granted, not directly to the people as a whole, but first to the faithful nucleus, and ultimately to the King whom God in his mercy sends them.

We have now to ask, with what intention, and in what sense, the New Testament writers adduce these and similar passages of the Old Testament for the consideration of their readers. We should evidently be far from their main intention if we supposed that their interest was confined to single verses or expressions where some coincidental similarity might be discerned to incidents in the gospel story, such as the fact that Jesus, like the peaceful king of Zechariah, rode into Jerusalem on an ass, or that, like the Servant of the Lord in Isaiah 53, he was silent—or almost silent—before his judges. Such similarities, though suggestive and often moving, are in themselves superficial, and they do not take us to the heart of our authors' intention. We have seen reason to suppose that they often quoted a single phrase or sentence not merely for its own sake, but as a pointer to a whole context—a practice by no means uncommon among contemporary Jewish teachers, as they are reported in the rabbinic literature. The reader is invited to study the context as a whole, and to reflect upon the "plot" there unfolded. In some way, an understanding of the plot will help him to see the significance of the strange events of the life and death of Jesus, and what followed.

In one of those passages of the Acts of the Apostles which appear most directly to represent the apostolic preaching (2:23), Peter is reported to have said that those events took place "by the determinate counsel of God." It is a challenging statement. The events, to all appearance, were tragic and even scandalous. The atrocious persecution of a good man to death under the forms of the two most advanced systems of law that then existed seemed to impugn both the decencies of human nature and the divine government of the universe. Yet these events, we are asked to believe, were under "the determinate counsel of God." Having said so much, Peter was bound to say more. To suppose him to have meant that the whole drama was a prearranged puppet show would go against the entire trend of biblical teaching. In what sense, then, was "the determinate counsel of God" at work in the events that took place under Pontius Pilate? It is this question which the church undertook to answer—and to answer out of the Old Testament. Where else, indeed, upon the basic assumptions of biblical religion, could it be learned what the counsel of God is? For that man cannot by searching find out God is axiomatic.

Now let us look at the specimen Scriptures which we have had before us. They may all be said to be in part a record of (or a commentary upon) events that happened in the course of the history of Israel—as for example, in Isaiah 6–9, the struggle of Judah against the northern coalition and the menace of Assyria, or in Daniel 7, the oppression of the Jews by Antiochus Epiphanes—and in part a forecast of events yet to come. The exact point in each case where historical record ends and a visionary future begins is often difficult to determine. But for these writers history and post-history are parts of one whole. In both it is the one purpose of God which is at work. In the swaying fortunes of war in which eighth-century Judea was involved, in the Seleucid assault upon the last sanctities of Jewish life in the second century and the conse-

quent flaring up of the Maccabean revolt, the principles of God's prov-
idential government of the universe are disclosed in part: in the final
upshot—in what Joel and other prophets call the Day of the Lord—they
will be fully and finally disclosed.

For the way in which these prophets of different periods interpret the
history of their own times, and forecast the future in its light, shows
that they conceive the course of events, with all its unpredictable vicis-
situdes, to exhibit certain universal principles, embedded in the structure of this world as governed by the law and providence of God. These
principles are permanent, and condition the results of human choice
and action at every period of history. Upon the assumptions of biblical
religion, they are most clearly to be perceived in the dealing of God with
Israel as interpreted by the prophets. In this interpretation, both the
comment upon contemporary events in the prophet's own time, and his
vision of the Day of the Lord, are equally relevant. The process is not to
be fully understood or valued apart from its consummation; but also,
the true meaning of the vision of the Day of the Lord is not to be understood apart from the process which finds fulfilment in it. For the Day of
the Lord, if unrelated to the moral and spiritual values recognized by
the prophets in the struggles, failures, and achievements of their people, might be no more than a compensation in fantasy for a too painful
reality, without spiritual worth—as Amos showed. Thus each of the different prophetic pictures of the changing experience of God's people,
with the hope at the end of the road, helps to illuminate in different aspects the one purpose of God running through it all to its fulfilment.

The early church believed that with the coming of Christ, his death
and resurrection, the Day of the Lord had dawned. To elucidate and justify this belief they appealed to prophetic descriptions, not only of the
Day itself, but of the essential elements in the process which led up to
it. Here *all* the various prophetic descriptions are relevant; for the Day
of the Lord is fulfillment, not merely in the sense that it is the end of a
process whose stages may now be put out of mind. It is fulfillment in
the sense that the true meaning of all the strange and often tragic experiences of God's people *in via* is now at last made clear, and those experiences in turn give depth and richness to the Christian understanding
of the consummation that Christ has brought.

All this seems to be implied in the New Testament appeal to prophecy. It is to be observed that its writers are not troubled by the variety,
or the seeming inconsistency, of the imagery employed, as we are apt
to be, with our more literal bent of mind. Being orientals they take symbolism in their stride. Nor do they make any difficulty about finding
their own situation reflected, or foreshadowed, in such different pictures as those which Isaiah, Joel, and Zechariah draw after the pattern

of historical situations in remote centuries before Christ. All these illustrate, in the last resort, varying aspects of the one divine plan now brought to its fulfillment in the events of the gospel story.

It seems clear that in recalling such Scriptures the New Testament writers imply that they and their contemporaries are in some sense living through the drama of disaster and glory, of death and resurrection, which in a variety of ways, and with greater or less elaboration, is the "plot" of them all. It is sometimes illuminating to note the precise point at which the writer conceived himself and his contemporaries to stand in the development of the plot. To take one example: in Joel's prophecy of the Day of the Lord the outpouring of the Spirit marks the transition from the first act of the drama to the second. In the first act Israel is purged by the terrible judgments of God and restored to favor. The second act is the judgment of the nations and the harvest of the world. The author of Acts, in quoting the prophecy of the outpouring of the Spirit, clearly intends to set the events of the day of Pentecost in this light, as the turning point of the drama. This explains the significance of the "Parthians, Medes, and Elamites," and the rest of the nations whose names roll so sonorously in the catalogue of Peter's audience on that memorable occasion: they are the first fruits of those "multitudes, multitudes in the valley of decision" whom the prophet summoned into the presence of the Eternal. In this setting, Joel's call, "Proclaim among the nations!" (3:9), becomes a direct command to the church to enter upon its missionary task, now seen to be an essential element in the fulfillment of the purpose of God, since through its faithful discharge the multitudes of the nations are in fact summoned into the presence of the King.

But if this is so, it seems to be implied that the first act of the drama is already over; and again, if so, the story of suffering, disaster, and recovery which occupies the second chapter of Joel must be held to find its fulfillment, in some sense, in the sufferings, death, and resurrection of Christ; and that in fact is the view taken by New Testament writers. To recognize it supplies an essential key to the fundamental teaching of the New Testament. There is no question of a literal "fulfillment" of apocalyptic traits such as the darkening of the sun and the shaking of the earth. This is well understood imagery suggesting the magnitude and horror of the situation; and all that horror is present in the events of Christ's conflict and death. The Gospels may be thought to hint as much when they say that at the crucifixion of Christ the sun was darkened and the earth quaked. We must always be prepared for this acute sense which the New Testament writers betray for the deep purport of imagery.

It is not always as easy as it is with the prophecy of Joel to determine the precise point in the development of the drama at which a New Testament writer conceives himself and his contemporaries to stand. The question deserves investigation in each case separately. But the general assumption clearly is that the course of events in which the early Christians are caught up—that is to say, the conflict, sufferings, and death of Jesus, his resurrection, and the emergence of the church as the witness and embodiment of his finished work—exhibits the essential traits of the prophetic drama of God's purpose, and is to be understood in its terms.

The plot of the drama turns, as we have seen, on what in Greek tragedy is called *peripetia,* a startling reversal of fortune: in this case the transformation of a scene of suffering and disaster into a scene of triumph for the good cause. There are many variations upon this theme. The various renderings differ about the identity of the hero, the cause and character of the sufferings through which he passes, the manner of his deliverance, and the nature of the ultimate triumph; they differ so widely sometimes that their inconsistencies seem hardly reconcilable. Yet it would not be wise to assume without long and careful consideration that the New Testament writers either did not observe the differences or forced them into harmony by arbitrary interpretations. I will call attention in particular to two of the most conspicuous points in which the prophecies seem to differ fundamentally. Both of them we have noted in passing.

First, there appears to be no agreement whether the hero of the drama is an individual or a people. In some passages it is apparently an individual hero who passes from disaster to triumph; in others it is clearly Israel as a whole, or some smaller circle within Israel deemed more fit to be a people of God; and sometimes it is difficult to say with certainty whether the conception in the author's mind was individual or collective.

Secondly, there is no agreement about the nature and cause of the disasters and sufferings that fall upon the hero. As is natural in any transcript from human experience there are unanswered questions. Is suffering the stern judgment of God upon the sin of an apostate people? Or the undeserved persecution of his faithful servant, or servants, at the hands of his enemies? Is the suffering to be put down altogether on the debit side of the account—sheer loss to be made good only by the intervention of God *ex machina*—or does it possess some positive value? Does it, for example, serve as a test and a purge, to determine who truly belongs to the people of God? Or as chastisement or discipline for the faithful? Or can the martyr-death of a leader conduce to the salvation of the whole people? Such questions, necessarily arising out of the situations depicted, are answered in different ways.

Yet all these variations of plot are applied by New Testament writers to the interpretation of the same series of facts, those comprised in the

Gospel story. I believe they did not so apply them irresponsibly, in mere carelessness, or without appreciation of the differences. On the contrary, the richness and depth of their interpretation of what happened "under Pontius Pilate" results largely from bringing together these apparently inconsistent features and superimposing them to form a single composite picture of the "determinate counsel of God" and its achievement.

Thus, in interpreting the passion of Christ the New Testament writers find in it not only the undeserved persecution of God's faithful Servant; they find also the element of judgment upon human sin: "Now," says John on the eve of the crucifixion, "now is the judgment of this world." They find the element of discipline: "Although a son, he learned obedience through the things he suffered," says the Epistle to the Hebrews, and draws inferences regarding the sufferings of God's people. They find the element of vicarious self-sacrifice, of which the classical expression is the fifty-third chapter of Isaiah. It is the drawing together of these separate strands, and others, all derived from the Old Testament, that provides the basis for the Christian theology of atonement. It would have been well if theologians had always remembered this.

Again, the New Testament doctrine of the person of Christ depends for its richness and depth, almost for its intelligibility, upon the inseparable fusion of two figures of prophecy: the leader and sovereign over God's people, and the "inclusive representative," or embodiment, of that people, and indeed, in the last resort, of redeemed humanity as a whole. All the ideal attributes of the church are assigned to it in the New Testament solely insofar as it is comprehended "in Christ," and as being "in Christ" is itself the true Servant of God and the suffering and exalted Son of man. All that is said about the significance of the work of Christ presupposes that he includes in himself the whole people of God, or redeemed humanity. His death and resurrection are not to be understood if they are thought of as no more than the death and miraculous resuscitation of an individual, but only if they are seen as the fulfillment of the whole purpose of God to raise up for himself, through suffering, tribulation, and disaster, a people made wholly one in him and devoted to his righteous purpose. Christ "rose the third day," says the ancient formula quoted by Paul in his first epistle to the Corinthians, "according to the scriptures." But in the Scriptures—*videlicet,* in Hosea 6:1–3— it is Israel whom God will raise on the third day. The bold application of that prophecy to the resurrection of Christ in the earliest Christian confession of faith known to us lies behind the Pauline doctrine of the church as dead and risen with Christ.

I have here only hinted at the significance for Christian theology of a right understanding of the treatment of the Old Testament in the New.

I believe it represents an intellectual achievement of remarkable originality, displaying penetration into the meaning that lies beneath the surface of the biblical text, and a power of synthesis which gathers apparently disparate elements into a many-sided whole, not unsuitable to convey some idea of the "manifold wisdom of God."

11

Response Against C. H. Dodd's View: On Testimonies

Albert C. Sundberg, Jr.

From Albert C. Sundberg, Jr., "On Testimonies," *Novum Testamentum* 3 (1959): 268–81. Reprinted by permission.

Until the publication of C. H. Dodd's *According to the Scriptures*,[1] interest in testimonies centered around J. Rendel Harris's theory of testimony books.[2] According to his theory, an enlarging collection of Old Testament proof-text prophecies fulfilled in Jesus and the Christian church were gathered into books of testimonies. The Old Testament texts, Harris supposed, were collected according to theological titles of particular interest to the church, for example, "that Jesus was the stone."[3] Having knowledge of such collections in a later period of the church,[4] Harris suggested that testimony collections have an intrinsic probability of representing the earliest Christian theological effort and, therefore, antedate all extant Christian writings.[5] Thus, testimony books served as sources for the writers of the New Testament and other early Christian works. That the New Testament writers actually used collections of testimonies is evinced, according to Harris, by such phenomena as: 1) identical mixed Old Testament quotations found in more than one Christian writer, 2) parallel misidentification of Old Testa-

---

1. New York, 1953.
2. *Testimonies*, 1, 2 (Cambridge, 1916–1920).
3. Ibid., 1:18–19, cf. p. 10.
4. E.g., in Cyprian's *Testimonia*, Tertullian's *Adversus Judaeos* and another work of the same title attributed to Gregory of Nyssa.
5. Op. cit., 1:21–25, 2:2.

ment passages cited, and 3) similar textual variants from all extant Old Testament texts in Old Testament citations in the New Testament.[6] These curiosities, Harris suggests, indicate common sources in which these errors were first made and from which they passed into our present Christian collection; they also support the supposition that many of the Old Testament passages cited in the New Testament belonged to such collections.

Harris presented his theory with much cogency and his work has been the basic work in the field.[7] Dodd tells us that he worked with Harris's hypothesis for many years and (like all subsequent students of the problem) is greatly indebted to Harris's work.[8] Dodd, however, has come to question Harris's theory, concluding that the theory outruns the evidence. If such a book existed and was used widely by the New Testament writers, how, Dodd asks, could it have been omitted from the canon of Christian Scriptures and never be referred to, unless by Papias's enigmatic reference to the *logia* of Matthew?[9] And why should it not have emerged as a substantive work until Cyprian edited it in the middle of the third century?[10] Actually, the earliest mention of such a collection of testimonies is found in Melito c. A.D. 170. However, either he knew no such collection or found known ones unsatisfactory since he made a collection of Old Testament testimonies for himself.[11] Moreover, Dodd remarks, the recurrence of the group of passages in which a "stone" is used as a symbol is striking; it corresponds to an established grouping in known testimony books. But it is almost the only group of its kind, certainly the only one which carries any particular weight.[12] Dodd's criticism continues, that the list of identical combinations of Old Testament passages occurring in more than one writer is comparatively short. They may be exceptional cases and are insufficient to prove a general theory.[13]

K. Stendahl has further subjected Harris's theory to critical examination.[14] Noting that Matthew's use of the Old Testament is crucial to Harris's theory, he asks, "did Matthew use testimonies?" Stendahl reached

6. Ibid., 1:18.

7. Cf. K. Stendahl, *The School of St. Matthew* (*Acta Seminarii Neotestamentici Uppsalienis*, 20, Uppsala, 1954), 207ff., for a summary of work on testimonies.

8. Op. cit., 26.

9. Cf. F. C. Burkitt, *The Gospel History and its Transmission*, 2d ed. (Edinburgh, 1907), 124–28, followed by Harris, op. cit., 124ff., thought Papias's reference (Eusebius, *H. E.* 4.26:13–14) was to the testimony book. Cf. Stendahl, op. cit., 209, note 2.

10. Dodd, op. cit., 26–27.

11. Eusebius, *H. E.* 4.26:13–14.

12. Op. cit., 26–27.

13. Idem.

14. Op. cit., 210ff.

a negative conclusion to his question. Findlay's study[15] had shown that known collections of testimonies do not follow Matthew either in word order or in language; he concluded that Matthew was not in the main testimony stream. Thus, Stendahl continues, the question reverts to Hatch's attempt to explain the composite quotations by the use of testimonies.[16] But, similar to Dodd, here Stendahl finds more simple alternatives than the testimony hypothesis. A hint as to how the intermingling of texts came about may be found in the *midrashim* where Old Testament quotations are brought together by the association of ideas and by the collection of passages from the Law, the Prophets, and the Writings. The ascription of passages to incorrect authors (and, no doubt, the mixture of some passages as well) must partly be due to the faulty memory of the authors. Thus, Stendahl concludes, the methods of the synagogue in dealing with the texts of the Old Testament, both in liturgical reading and in teaching, account for most of the features Harris wanted to explain by his Book of Testimonies.[17] These criticisms so weaken Harris's hypothesis as to destroy its usefulness.

A fresh approach to the problem of Old Testament citations in the New is made by Dodd in his recent study.[18] Dodd's method in this study is to isolate those elements which are so widely common to the New Testament books that they must be regarded as forming part of a central tradition, by which they were all more or less controlled.[19] This central tradition embodied the events of the *kerygma:* the ministry, suffering, and death of Jesus, the resurrection, the session, the infilling of the Holy Spirit, and the eschatological expectation.[20] These events, however, could have significance in the early church only as they were related to the Scriptures. "Thus the church was committed, by the very terms of its *kerygma*," says Dodd, "to a formidable task of biblical research, primarily for the purpose of clarifying its own understanding of the momentous events out of which it had emerged, and also for the purpose of making its Gospel intelligible to the outside public."[21] Therefore, Dodd turns his attention to collecting passages from the Old Testament which, "being cited by two or more writers of the New Testament in *prima facie* independence of one another, may fairly be presumed to

15. A. J. Findlay, *The First Gospel and the Book of Testimonies,* in *Amicitiae Corolla* (London, 1933), 57–71.

16. E. Hatch, *Essays in Biblical Greek* (Oxford, 1889), 203, 209–11.

17. Op. cit., 217.

18. *According to the Scriptures.* Cf., also, Dodd's earlier statement, *The Old Testament in the New* (London, 1952).

19. *Acc. to the Scripts.,* 11.

20. Ibid., 11–12.

21. Ibid., 14.

have been current as *testimonia* before they wrote."[22] Dodd makes this collection upon the assumption that where two separate writers cite the same passage from the Old Testament, unless there are definite reasons to the contrary, they represent to that extent a common tradition.[23] Dodd's collection of such passages consists of fifteen examples.[24] Dodd then turns, in a chapter entitled *The Bible of the Early Church,* to the problem of collecting Old Testament passages where two or more New Testament writers "have quoted or recalled, contiguous or adjacent sentences within a wider context," which, also, "may be supposed to be drawn from pre-canonical tradition."[25] Through the investigation of contiguous Old Testament passages cited in the New, Dodd would show that the unit of reference was intended to be wider than the usual brief quotation.[26] He, therefore, concludes, "these sections were understood as *wholes,* and particular verses or sentences were quoted from them rather as pointers to the whole context than as constituting testimonies in and for themselves."[27] The Old Testament sections therein discovered, Dodd would say, may be considered the bible of the early church.[28]

In the light of Dodd's thesis, it would seem reasonable to expect a considerable concentration of interest on the part of the New Testament writers in the special Old Testament sections indicated by Dodd. And this concentration should readily appear in indices of the Old Testament citations in the New that are impartial to Dodd's study. In this expectation table 1, on Old Testament chapters multiply cited in the New, was prepared from such an impartial index. The most evident fact displayed by this table is the absence of any real concentration of New Testament references to particular passages of the Old Testament. Forty-two percent of the four hundred twenty-three Old Testament chapters cited in the New Testament are cited by more than one New Testament writer. Fifty-six of Isaiah's sixty-six chapters are cited, seventy-one percent doubly. Of the one hundred one Psalms cited, more than a third are doubly cited. Dodd's listings of "Primary sources of testimonies," and of "Subordinate and supplementary sources,"[29] simply do not account for the greater portion of Old Testament citations in the New. This is true whether one compares a chapter by chapter count of Nestle's index or whether the comparison is made of doubly attested chapters, as in table 1.

22. Ibid., 29.
23. Ibid., 30.
24. Ibid., 31–57.
25. Ibid., 59.
26. Ibid., 61.
27. Ibid., 126. Cf. Stendahl, op. cit., 52.
28. *Acc. to the Scripts.,* 107–8.
29. Idem.

TABLE 1
Old Testament Chapters Multiply Cited in the New Testament*

Book	No. of Chaps. in OT Book	No. of Chaps. Cited in NT	No. of Chaps. Cited by NT Authors				
			Twice	Thrice	Four Times	Five Times	Six Times
Genesis	50	29	7	7	3		
Exodus	40	30	8	4	3		
Leviticus	27	12	1	1	1		
Numbers	36	12		1			
Deuteronomy	34	28	8	4	1		
Joshua	24	12	1				
Judges	21	2					
Samuel	55	19		1		1	
Kings	47	10	2	1			
Isaiah	66	56	17	14	6	1	2
Jeremiah	52	25	9	3			
Ezekiel	48	28	3	2			
The Twelve	67	42	15	4	1		
Psalms	150	101	23	7	3	3	
Proverbs	31	12	1		1		1
Job	42	7					
Canticles	8						
Ruth	4						
Lamentations	5	1					
Ecclesiastes	12						
Esther	10	2					
Daniel	12	12	6	1	1		
Ezra-Nehemiah	23	1					
Chronicles	65	2					

*The synoptic Gospels and Acts are counted as one because of interdependence. The index used is *"Index locorum," Novum Testamentum Graece*, ed. E. Nestle. Stuttgart (1948), 658–71.

A further test of Dodd's thesis that certain *sections* of the Old Testament served as a kind of "bible of the early church" may be had in comparison of the relative importance of each Old Testament book to each New Testament writer. A significant predominance, consistent through most of the New Testament authors, of those Old Testament books containing the passages Dodd suggests as part of the "bible of the early church" would tend to confirm Dodd's hypothesis. Such a comparison has been tabulated in table 2. The table shows the quotations per page in the New Testament authors of the Old Testament books, after the Old Testament books have been corrected to a common length.[30]

TABLE 2
The Relative Importance of Old Testament Books
Cited in the New Testament*

	N.T.	Mt.	Mk.	Lk.–Acts	Jn.	Paul	Cath.	Heb.	Jas.	1 Pet.	2 Pet.	1, 2, 3 Jn.	Jude	Rev.
W:														
Genesis	.64	.13	.13	.44	.05	.44		1.88	1.16	.27				1.79
Exodus	.45	.42	.37	.63	.13	.39	.16	.96	.35	.31				2.16
Leviticus	.26	.29	.26	.02		.13		.43	.93	.83				.44
Numbers	.10	.06	.05	.09	.06	.04	.15	.72						.19
Deuteronomy	.44	.52	.58	.34		.57	.50	.93	1.13					1.17
Total	1.89	1.42	1.39	1.52	.24	1.57	.81	4.92	3.57	1.41				5.75
PROPHETS														
Joshua	.03			.03										.34
Judges	.01			.02										.11
Samuel	.04	.02	.05	.09	.05	.05		.15						.14
Kings	.05	.06	.07	.04	.05	.03								.40
Isaiah	.95	.64	.33	.45	.19	.73	.09	.72	.65	2.89	1.19			4.45
Jeremiah	.19	.16	.10	.08		.01		.20	.22					1.66
Ezekiel	.33	.08	.17	.08		.14		.09		.50				3.18
The Twelve	.51	.50	.34	.24	.15	.22		.70		.50			1.92	2.35
Total	2.11	1.46	1.06	1.03	.44	1.18	.09	1.86	.87	3.89	1.19		1.92	12.63
WRITINGS														
Psalms	.67	.45	.34	.44	.28	.40	.36	1.75	.65	.88	.45			2.97
Proverbs	.47	.05		.02		.28	.22	.62	1.48	2.22	.69			.48
Job	.09	.04	.06	.04		.09		.81						.08
Five Scrolls	.01	.04	.07											
Daniel	1.79	.94	.99	.21		.05	.41		1.86					
Chronicles	.02		.01						.23				6.40	12.40
Ezra-Nehemiah				.03										
Total	3.05	1.52	1.47	.74	.28	.82	.99	3.18	4.22	3.10	1.14		6.40	15.93

*The Old Testament citations in the New Testament are taken from *Novum Testamentum Graece*, ed. E. Nestle and E. Nestle (Stuttgart: Würtembergische Bibelanstalt, 1948), 658–71. The values given are citations per page in the New Testament after the Old Testament books have been corrected to a common length.

30. A direct, book to book comparison would be of little value because of the inherent probability that longer books would be more frequently quoted than shorter books. By correcting the OT books to a common length the figures are made comparative.

Again, in table 2 we are met with multiplicity rather than uniformity. Among the thirteen New Testament author groups, one-quarter of the Old Testament books appear first in importance to a New Testament author group. If one asks, how many books would be included in a list of the five most important Old Testament books to each New Testament author group, we find one-half of the Old Testament books in this list (counting a twenty-four-book canon). Even among the Synoptics, where interdependence is presumed, an unexpected degree of variation is found. Daniel is the most important book to Mark and Matthew. But Exodus ranks first in Luke–Acts; Daniel does not even appear among the five most important books for this author. Isaiah is almost twice as frequently cited in Matthew as in Mark, moving from fifth in importance in Mark to second in Matthew. The material of Dodd's *Bible of the Early Church* is forty-three percent from Isaiah[31] but nowhere is such a preponderance of citations from Isaiah to be observed, except in 1 (31%) and 2 (52%) Peter. Otherwise Isaiah is the most important Old Testament book only to Paul (20.7%, followed by Deut.). Generally, in the New Testament, the substantial use of the Law, as compared with the Prophets and the Writings, is to be observed; the frequency ratio in the New Testament is within five percent of roughly contemporary Jewish usage (except Philo).[32] Greater clarity is indicated in the Old Testament books that tend to be neglected by the New Testament authors. These include the historical books (the Former Prophets, Chronicles, Ezra–Nehemiah), the Five Scrolls, and Numbers. Even the uniformity of disuse, however, is broken: the author of Revelation has made significant use of the Former Prophets. And Hebrews cites Numbers as frequently as Isaiah! Tables 1 and 2 significantly demonstrate the breadth with which the writers of the New Testament used the Old; Dodd has overlooked a remarkable absence of concentration.

Another point of Dodd's hypothesis that bears testing is his assertion that citations in the New Testament of a verse or phrase from the Old frequently constitutes an intended reference to a larger context in doubly attested passages.[33] Dodd would, thus, make the Old Testament passages cited in the New into a kind of early reference system (that could now be replaced by chapter references?). If the Old Testament citations in the New are frequently intended as mere references to a larger passage (as collected in *the Bible of the Early Church*), it would not be nec-

---

31. The material of Dodd's *Bible of the Early Church* (op. cit.), 107–8 fills about 46 pages of the *R.S.V.* of which about 20 pages are from Isaiah.

32. Cf. my article "The Old Testament of the Early Church," *Harvard Theological Review* 51 (1958): 211, note.

33. *Acc. to the Scripts.* 59, 61ff.

essary for the Old Testament portion cited to carry the weight of the argument or reference, but merely to indicate where the weight of the argument could be found. The New Testament text could be presumed to be fragmentary and incomplete at the points of Old Testament citation, which lack would be readily filled by referring to the context of the citation in the Old Testament. We may expect that such a dependence on *the Bible of the Early Church* would be generally self-evident in the New.

But do the citations of the Old Testament generally depend upon the context of the passage for their meanings in the New Testament citations? There are, to be sure, some few citations where a larger context seems to be implied.[34] But these passages are heavily outweighed by the atomistic citations of the Old Testament.[35] Of course, Dodd's field is more narrow and we must inquire whether the New Testament citations from those passages which Dodd suggests were *the Bible of the Early Church*[36] usually require the larger context that Dodd suggests. There is not space here for detailed examination of all of Dodd's passages; one or two examples will suffice.

Isaiah 40:1–11 is cited by five New Testament author-groups and may serve as one example. All four Gospels have citations from this passage as a proof-text for John the Baptist. And the motifs of Isaiah 40:1–10 compare well with the motifs of the Baptist's ministry in the Gospels: a call for preparation, the Lord is coming, and he brings judgment. When we examine the synoptic Gospels, however, the results are disappointing for Dodd's thesis. Though the motifs for the ministry of John the Baptist are to be found in this passage from Isaiah, the point of reference to Isaiah, through a curious alteration of the Septuagint text, is made to support only the wilderness preaching of John;[37] the prediction of a forerunner is found in Malachi 3:1.[38] Mark does not include the motif of judgment that will accompany the coming of the Lord; Matthew and Luke do not turn to Isaiah 40:10 for support of this motif.[39] Likewise, in John 1:19–23 the reference to Isaiah 40:3 carries only the weight that John the Baptist preached in the wilderness, calling for rectitude; its purpose is a rejection of the suspicion that John the Baptist was the Christ or Elijah (the forerunner?).[40]

---

34. E.g., Ps. 22:22 cited in Heb. 2:12; Isa 53:7 cited by Rev. 5:6, 12; 13:8; Isa. 53:4–5, 9, 12 cited by 1 Pet. 2:21–25. The latter citation is consistent with, though it does not require, a larger context of reference.

35. W. O. E. Osterley, *The Exegesis of the Old Testament,* in *Record and Revelation,* ed. H. W. Robinson (Oxford, 1938), 412.

36. *Acc. to the Scripts.*, 107–8.

37. Cf. Stendahl, op. cit., 47–48.

38. Mark 1:2; Matt. 11:10; Luke 7:27.

39. Matt. 3:12; Lk. 3:17.

40. Cf. Mark 9:11–13; Matt. 11:13–14; 17:11–13.

The Epistles of James and 1 Peter allude to Isaiah 40:6–8, which compares the transientness of life to the permanence of the word of God: physical existence (σάρξ) and human glory (πᾶσα δόξα ἀνθρώπου) are momentary as grass and its blossom but τὸ ῥῆμα τοῦ θεοῦ ἡκῶν μένει εἰς τὸν αἰῶνα, that is, the word given to the prophet will be fulfilled. This is, also, the meaning of the allusion in 1 Peter 1:23–25, where, however, the permanent ῥῆμα κυρίου is not the word given to the prophet but τὸ ῥῆμα τὸ εὐαγγελισθὲν εἰς ὑμᾶς which is σπορὰ ἄφθαρτος. James 1:9–11, on the other hand, alludes to this passage in Isaiah as indicative of the illusion of worldly values: in the heat of the sun the grass withers, its flower falls, and its beauty perishes; οὕτως καὶ ὁ πλούσιος ἐν ταῖς πορείαις αὐτοῦ μαρανθήσεται. Revelation 22:12 is apparently an allusion to Isaiah 40:10. As Isaiah (2) promised reward and recompense to the suffering Jews, so the Christian under persecution can look forward to the coming of the Lord who will recompense everyone for what he has done. To suggest that any of these New Testament writers, citing from Isaiah 40:1–11, is referring to the entire eleven verses is not consistent with the evidence. The precise portion cited in each instance is sufficient for the author's purpose.

Psalm 22 is cited by six New Testament author-groups and will serve as another point of testing of Dodd's thesis. The synoptic Gospels refer to verses 1, 7, 8 and 18 of this psalm in relating the crucifixion story and the fourth Gospel cites verse 18. Verse 1a, transliterated from the Hebrew and then translated into Greek, is a cry of Jesus from the cross in Mark 15:34 and Matthew 27:46. Mark 15:29 and Matthew 27:39 allude to verse 7a when they describe the spectators at the crucifixion deriding and wagging their heads at Jesus; the same context in Luke (23:35) attributes scoffing only to the rulers. The mocking of the rulers in Matthew 27:43, πέποιθεν ἐπὶ τὸν θεόν, ῥυσάσθω νῦν εἰ θέλει αὐτόν, is apparently an allusion to verse 8. Mark 15:24, Matthew 27:35, and Luke 23:34 allude to verse 18 in describing the soldiers dividing Jesus' clothing by casting lots; John 19:24 quotes this verse with the formula, ἵνα ἡ γραφὴ πληροθῇ, in describing the division of Jesus' garments among the soldiers and their casting lots over his tunic as a fulfillment of prophecy. However, while the Gospel writers show their acquaintance with Psalm 22 by their repeated use of it in the crucifixion story there is no indication in any single instance that a broader reference to the psalm is intended; the portion cited is sufficient to the author's purpose. The allusions in Romans 5:5 to verse 5, in 2 Timothy 4:17 to verse 21, and in Revelation 19:5 to verse 23 and 11:15 to verse 28 appear more like verbal likenesses, such as one finds among those well acquainted with the Scriptures, than intentional references to specific passages of Scripture: Hebrews 2:12, (17) quotes verse 22 in support of the argument that

Christians are brethren of Christ. Since Christians are sanctified through Christ they are related to him; the sanctifier and the sanctified have the same origin: δι' ἣν αἰτίαν οὐκ ἐπαισχύνεται ἀδελφοὺς αὐτοὺς καλεῖν, λεγων, the writer of the Hebrews continues, and quotes Psalm 22:22, ἀπαγγελῶ τὸ ὄνομά σου τοῖς ἀδελφοῖς μου, ἐν μέσῳ ἐκκλησίας ὑμνήσω σε. Here the writer has used the words of Psalm 22 as appropriate to Christ. The use presupposes the suffering of Christ and his resurrection. And the quotation from Psalm 22:22 only has relevance in Hebrews from its context of suffering and deliverance in the psalm. This appears to be an instance where understanding of the Old Testament citation depends upon its larger context in the Old Testament.

Such examples could be monotonously multiplied. Citations of contiguous Old Testament passages by more than one New Testament author do not of themselves indicate that such citations serve as a kind of index-reference to a larger context in the Old Testament. It must be shown that the multiply cited Old Testament passages regularly require the larger reference in order to understand the citation in its New Testament context. But such evidence is not to be had. Only a minority of Old Testament citations seem to imply a larger Old Testament context; they will not carry the weight of Dodd's thesis.

Another issue of Dodd's hypothesis, which is closely related to the multiple citation of contiguous passages, is his supposition that there existed, prior to the writing of any books of the New Testament, a traditional method of exegesis of Old Testament passages.[41] This supposition can mean only one thing: that the same Old Testament passage received the same interpretation whenever it was cited in the New. However, careful examination of doubly cited passages indicates that there is no such uniformity of Old Testament interpretation. Examples of varied interpretation of Old Testament texts related to the *kerygma* may be had in the following: 2 Samuel 7:14 is interpreted in Hebrews 1:5 as God speaking to Jesus, ἐγὼ ἔσομαι αὐτῷ εἰς πατέρα, καὶ αὐτὸς ἔσται μοι εἰς υἱόν; however, Revelation 21:7 relates this saying to faithful Christians. Psalm 2:1 is related in Acts 4:25–27 to the events of Jesus' trial and crucifixion; in Revelation 12:18 it is related to the final judgment. The preaching of peace from Isaiah 52:7 is depicted in Acts 10:36 as fulfilled by Jesus but Paul relates the saying to the preaching of the gospel by Christians (Rom. 10:15; cf. Eph. 6:15). More than one example of divergent exegesis is found in citations from Isaiah 53: Matthew 8:17 quotes verse 4, αὐτὸς τὰς ἀσθενείας ἡμῶν ἔλαβεν καὶ τὰς νόσους ἐβάστασεν, as fulfilled in Jesus' miraculous cures; 1 Peter 2:21–25 cites the same passage as fulfilled in Jesus' death.[42] Verse 9b, ὅτι

41. *Acc. to the Scripts.*, 11, 21–23, 57–58, 108–9, 126–27.

ἀνομίαν οὐκ ἐποίησεν, οὐδὲ δόλον ἐν τῷ στόματι αὐτοῦ, is used in 1 Peter 2:22 as a description of Jesus while Revelation 14:5 alludes to it as a description of Christians. Again verse 12 appears in Luke 22:36–38 as the scriptural prediction of whatever episode in Jesus' life that sinister passage implies; but to Paul (Rom. 4:24–25), the writer of Hebrews (9:28), and the writer of 1 Peter (2:24) the verse is considered a prediction of Jesus' death.[43] The prophecy in Zechariah 12:10 is quoted in John 19:37 as a prediction of the piercing of Jesus' side after his death, καὶ πάλιν ἑτέρα γραφὴ λέγει· ὄψονται εἰς ὃν ἐξεκέντησαν; Revelation 1:7 uses the same passage as a prediction of the second coming (cf. Matt. 24:30). The variation of exegesis in these passages suggests that, while the early church was convinced that the Old Testament contained predictions about Jesus and the church, there did not exist at the time of the composition of the New Testament books an established tradition of exegesis for Old Testament passages which the New Testament writers accepted and adopted.

Indeed, the direct application of Old Testament passages to New Testament meanings may not have been as primitive as either Harris or Dodd suppose. Double citation, upon which Dodd builds his case, must have relevance apart from its relation to the *kerygma* if it has usefulness as a historical tool. But doubly cited passages relate, also, to what is manifestly developed positions of the church. For example, the Jewish rejection of Jesus and the gospel appears as a fulfillment of prophecy doubly cited.[44] Our earliest evidences of Christianity were written against the background of Jewish rejection as an accomplished fact. Only the Gentile mission is treated seriously in the New Testament; the Jewish mission is perfunctory, to fulfill the prediction of rejection. But certainly the earliest Christian activity must have been preaching to Jewish hearers. Probably in the first instance this preaching did not presuppose rejection. The Jewish-Christian community that existed in Jerusalem until A.D. 68–70,[45] probably did not regard themselves as a lost cause. If Acts (15:1–29) may be trusted, the Jewish-Christian community was cautious in its attitude toward the Gentile mission. And, yet, our earliest sources regard the Jewish rejection as a *fait accompli*, according to the Scriptures; and there are doubly attested Old Testa-

---

42. Cf. Mark 9:12 which, also, appears to be an allusion to this passage.

43. Cf. also the rejected reading of Mark 15:28, καὶ ἐπληρώθη ἡ γραφὴ ἡ λέγουσα· καὶ μετὰ ἀνόμων ἐλογίσθη (EFGHSUVΩΘ), which can hardly be regarded as an interpolation from Luke 22:37.

44. Cf. 2 Kings 1:10 cited by Luke 4:54; Rev. 20:9; Isa. 29:13 cited by Mark 7:6–7 (Matt. 15:8–9); Col. 2:21–22; Isa. 45:14 cited by 1 Cor. 14:25; Rom. 3:9; Isa. 52:5 cited by Rom. 2:24; 2 Pet. 2:2; Dan. 8:13–14 cited by Luke 21:24; Rev. 11:2.

45. Eusebius, *H.E.* 3.5.3.

ment proof-texts attesting thereto. The conclusion that a process of development preceded this doubly attested tradition is inescapable.

Another feature reflecting theological development and doubly attested by references to the Old Testament is the concept of salvation by faith, which finds its chief example from the Old Testament in Abraham.[46] It is evident from New Testament usage that faith means faith in Jesus Christ. However, messianic anticipations in Judaism apparently did not stipulate that only those who properly identified the Messiah when he came would share in the redemption of Israel.[47] Probably the first Christians were Jews who had identified Jesus as the Messiah.[48] It seems likely that the earliest Christian preaching was of the glad news that the Messiah was identifiable. Faith in this identification of the Messiah with Jesus as a requirement for participation in the Messiah's reign soon to be instituted appears to be a development in Christianity resulting from Jewish refusal to receive the proclaimed good news, indeed, the Jewish attempt to suppress it. To verify this position the Christians turned to the Old Testament, as they did for proofs that Jesus was the Messiah, and found that Abraham was counted righteous because he believed God. The Christians claimed that they were inheritors of God's promises to Abraham because they, like Abraham, believed God's message, that is, that Jesus was God's Christ. This requirement of faith that the Christ was Jesus forms part of the message of our earliest sources; the Old Testament passages used to support it are doubly attested in our earliest Christian sources: Paul, Hebrews (and the speeches in Acts).

On the principle of double attestation these two features have as valid a claim to an existing tradition of primitive character as any of the features of the *kerygma*. It is only by hypothesis that the *kerygma* features may be separated as more primitive. That is to say, the earliest historical evidence of Christian beginnings already reflects these developments.

Dodd's theory of testimonia actually only represents a variation in form of Harris's hypothesis of testimonies. It is fraught with the same canonical problem Dodd found with Harris's: if the early church made such a collection of Old Testament passages and used it as the basic Old Testament reference for its preaching of the gospel, how could it have been omitted from the canon? Like Harris, Dodd's theory outruns the evidence. Kilpatrick's observations on Harris's hypothesis still remain: it is unlikely that the Christians of the first century had a testimony

---

46. Gen. 12:1 cited in Acts 7:3; Heb. 9:8. Gen. 12:7 (13:15; 48:4) cited in Acts 7:5; Gal. 3:16. Gen. 15:6 cited in Rom. 4:3, 9, 22–23; Gal. 3:6; James 2:3.

47. G. F. Moore, *Judaism* (Cambridge, 1927–30), 2:323ff.

48. A. N. Wilder, *Otherworldliness and the New Testament* (New York, 1954), 111.

book apart from the Greek Bible itself. "More truly it could be said that this was their testimony book and that, apart from the general view that Scripture *in toto et in partibus* was fulfilled by and in our Lord, homiletic exposition was accustomed to use certain quotations from the Old Testament regularly in connection with certain events of the Gospel story."[49]

---

49. G. D. Kilpatrick, *The Origins of the Gospel according to St. Matthew* (Oxford, 1946), 66.

12

Counter-Response in Favor of C. H. Dodd's View

An Assessment of Recent Developments

I. Howard Marshall

From I. Howard Marshall, "An Assessment of Recent Developments," in *It Is Written: Scripture Citing Scripture*, ed. D. A. Carson and H. G. M. Williamson (Cambridge: Cambridge University Press, 1988), 1–21. Reprinted with the permission of Cambridge University Press.

The distinguished scholar in whose honor [*It Is Written*] has been compiled has placed on record his view that "the Old Testament is the greatest single influence in the formation of New Testament theology" (Lindars, 1976, 60). The point is one that needs to be made and to be defended, since it is not certain that it would be universally accepted. The contents of some of the essays which follow in this book will demonstrate the pervasiveness and the variety of the use of the Old Testament in the New Testament. It should thus constitute both an elucidation and a defence of the position which Professor Lindars has stated and which he has done so much to commend as a scholar whose expertise stretches widely, though never superficially, over both fields.

The scope of this volume has admittedly been defined rather more broadly by its editors as the use of Scripture within *Scripture;* that is to say, it discusses not only the use of the Old Testament in the various parts of the New Testament but also the use of earlier parts of the Old Testament in later parts. But since the use of Scripture in the so-called intertestamental literature throws a flood of light on the New Testament use of the Old Testament, it is inevitable that this topic is also considered. However, the use of Scripture within Scripture in the sense of the use of earlier texts of the New Testament or of New Testament traditions within the New Testament is excluded from consideration.

This limitation of scope means that the book is not primarily concerned with such topics as the subsequent history of the Christian use of the Old Testament or how Christians today should understand and use the Old Testament, although it may be presumed that a study of how the New Testament writers used the Old Testament is of significance in answering these questions (Longenecker 1970; Hanson 1974, 225ff; 1983, 178ff). . . .Our task . . . will be to look at some of the general problems which arise in the study of the use of Scripture by Scripture. We shall, however, steer clear of one problem . . . , namely the use of the Old Testament in the Old Testament, which is the field of Old Testament specialists.

There have been several recent surveys of the whole field. These can be divided into two kinds. First, there are the works which survey the actual topic of the use of the Old Testament in the New Testament, usually advancing the author's own view of the subject but manifestly not without some attention to the work of other scholars. Here we may mention the works of Tasker (1946), Barrett (1970), Shires (1974), Longenecker (1975), Hay (1976), Ellis (1978), Vermes (1976), and Hanson (1983). Second, there are the works which survey recent scholarship on the subject rather than the subject itself. Here we have particularly the work of Smith (1972). Our discussion will fall more into this second pattern, and it will confine itself for the most part to study since 1946.

The questions to which we shall attempt to devote some attention include the following: to what extent is it correct to say that the use of the Old Testament was the decisive influence in the creation of Christian theology? What led the early Christians and the New Testament writers to specific texts in the Old Testament? To what extent did they pay respect to the meaning of these texts in their context? In what kind of church situation did the Christian use of the Old Testament develop? What kind of exegetical methods were used, and how far were these methods adopted from contemporary Judaism? In what ways did the use of the Old Testament shape the content and structure of the New Testament?

The Place of the Old Testament in New Testament Theology

The first major contribution to the study of the use of the Old Testament in the New Testament in the last forty years was that of Dodd (1952). The book has an importance out of all proportion to its brevity, and has been the starting point for a fair amount of discussion. Dodd's basic concern was with the process by which theology developed in the New Testament church. If it is correct to say "In the beginning was the kerygma," how did the early church move on to the development of a theology? He argued that the kerygma was understood in the light of the Old Testament, but this then raises the question of how the church used the Old Testament to elucidate the kerygma. He rejected the theory of Harris (1916, 1920) that it was done by the creation of an apologetic testimony book in the early days. Instead he argued that the appearance of the same Old Testament texts independently in different writers but often with the same peculiarities of wording suggested the use of a common stock of textual materials, and that these texts appeared to have been drawn from various specific areas or "fields" in the Old Testament which were systematically exploited for what they might yield, due attention being paid to context. So the principles of exegesis were established, and the way in which certain doctrines were developed was expounded. It will thus be apparent that Dodd was really concerned to answer three questions:

1. In what way did the early church develop a theology? It understood the kerygma in the light of the Old Testament.
2. How did the early church find its way round the Old Testament? It recognized certain fields which were of particular theological significance.
3. How did the early church use the material from these fields? On the one hand, it recognized the presence of common themes in the various fields and therefore drew materials from them with a certain regard for the context. On the other hand, it developed its theology by the incorporation of teaching that sprang from the Old Testament.

Dodd's first point, which is of major importance, is that the roots of the early church's theologizing lie in the illumination of the kerygma by the prophecies of the Old Testament (Dodd 1952, 135).

What might be regarded as a criticism of this hypothesis has come from Wilcox (1979) and has recently been taken up by Black (1986, 7–8). He insists that the procedures followed by the early Christians imply a common ground between them and their partners in discussion, namely a set of accepted exegetical traditions for understanding the Old Testament on the basis of which Christians could argue that the traditions found their correct interpretation and fulfillment in Jesus. It was, then, out of debates within the context of "messianic Judaism" that the kerygma emerged.

However, it is doubtful whether this is really a criticism of Dodd's position or the presentation of an alternative to it. Rather it is a reminder of an important factor in the process, namely that when the early Christians went to the Scriptures for evidence in favor of their view of Jesus it was necessary that their methods of interpretation should follow the accepted procedures of the time. But at the same time the point should be made that it was the use of the Old Testament which helped to shape the kerygma—a fact that Dodd would surely not have denied. Thus when the early summary of the kerygma in 1 Corinthians 15:3 declares that "Christ died for our sins according to the Scriptures," the fact that Christ died is a "given," and probably also the fact that his death had a significance of some kind. But did the early church go to the Scriptures to find evidence that he died "for our sins" or was it study of the Scriptures that led to the realisation that he died "for our sins"? The effect of Wilcox's argument is to remind us that the latter process went on alongside the former, and we may add that many times we must envisage a dialectical process with the influences going in both directions. Again, in 1 Corinthians 15:4 the event of the resurrection is probably primary—unless we are to assume that the phenomena of the empty tomb and the appearances of Jesus were interpreted by a category drawn from the Old Testament—and the scriptural backing either for the resurrection itself or for "on the third day" will have come later. Thus it seems that Wilcox has offered a refinement of Dodd's case rather than an alternative to it.

Dodd developed his theory in express contradiction to the view that Paul based his theology on religious experience, whether visions and revelations or even his conversion experience. Nor was theology based on speculation influenced by and incorporating the religious ideas of Hellenism; its fundamental content and way of thinking are biblical. In saying this Dodd was not arguing for an early church theology which was based purely on the "Word," but rather for one in which "the mighty acts of God" in history are understood in the context which is provided by the Old Testament.

Dodd's view may seem at first sight to stand in contrast to that of Kim who argues that the origins of Paul's gospel lie in his Damascus road experience with its vision of Jesus as the image of God (Kim 1981). But it seems rather that Kim is showing how Paul came to a realization of the truth of the kerygma, and nothing that he says contradicts the possibility that the development of early church theology and of Paul's own theology took place "according to the Scriptures."

The really important question which arises is whether Dodd is justified in his claim that it was the study of the Old Testament which formed the substructure of New Testament theology. I take "substructure" to mean the basic underlying presuppositions of thought which supply the basis or structure of the gospel. Is the influence of the Old Testament so far-reaching, or does it merely supply the background for a few aspects of the kerygma, the real and central impetus to the categories in which it is formulated coming from somewhere else? Is it possible to conceive of a different substructure? In order to do so it would be necessary to disprove the claim that the essential vocabulary and conceptualization and the basic structure of New Testament theology are drawn from the Old Testament. It is true that the theology of the New Testament approaches the Old Testament wearing the spectacles of Judaism, but this does not affect the basic fact that it was to the Old Testament and to the traditions inspired by it that the church turned when it began to do theology.

Dodd's view thus stands in sharp contrast to the view of Käsemann, for example, that the mother of Christian theology was apocalyptic (Käsemann 1969, 82–107). Käsemann appears to mean that its structure of thought was determined basically by the near expectation of the parousia and also that its content consisted of the kind of thoughts expressed in the Jewish apocalyptic literature. But this view is unacceptable, for, as various scholars have observed, it is the kerygma of the death and resurrection of Jesus which figures in the earliest expressions of the church's theology (Lohse 1971, 58).

Dodd's view that it was the Old Testament which was the inspiration of New Testament theology stands over against the view that we should look for another source in the Hellenistic world. We should not expect to find much influence from Hellenism in general. It is significant that, when Knox wrote on *Some Hellenistic Elements in Primitive Christianity* (1944), it was a remarkably slim volume which resulted, and there is no doctrine of central importance which can be shown to have been derived from Hellenism. Earlier, of course, Bousset (1921) had tried to show that the understanding of Jesus as Lord was derived from Hellenism, but it is quite clear that his attempt was a failure. A much greater challenge has come from attempts to derive essential elements of early Christian doctrine from Gnosticism (Bultmann 1952; cf. Schmithals 1971a; 1971b; Schottroff 1970), but these seem to me to be equally dubious. Nevertheless, there is here a field for continuing discussion.

The Problem of Textual "Fields"
in the Old Testament

The second part of Dodd's thesis was concerned with the way in which the early Christians found specific textual "fields" in the Old Testament.

The discovery of collections of texts at Qumran has made the alternative possibility of a testimony book more plausible than it was when Dodd advanced his thesis. These parallels certainly show that a testimony book was a possibility, but we have still to ask whether the internal evidence of the New Testament confirms that the texts are most plausibly to be explained in this way. The existence of an actual testimony book and of a set of "fields" side by side is of course quite possible, and the question is rather whether there is decisive evidence for the existence of either. Subsequent discussion has tended on the whole not to go back to the testimony book theory (Lindars, 1961, 14, 23–24).

Dodd's own theory has been strongly criticized by Sundberg, Jr. (1959). Against Dodd's concept of exegetical "fields" Sundberg argued, first, that the New Testament authors appear to draw their biblical citations from such a wide area of the Old Testament as to make it seem unlikely that they were following a tradition which directed attention to specific, limited fields. He also claimed, second, that the particular fields which Dodd isolated do not seem to be used particularly often in the New Testament.

Sundberg's arguments, however, must be tested. The statistics which he produced to prove his point are dubious. He worked from the list of "citations" in the index to the 1948 edition of Nestle's text, and was able to claim that out of 929 chapters in the Old Testament no less than 423 are cited in the New Testament. But the latter figure covers far more than express citations of Old Testament texts, and in this respect the figures in the index to the third edition of *The Greek New Testament* furnish a better guide. They show that texts from 162 chapters are cited in the New Testament. The books which show the greatest number of chapters from which citations are drawn relative to their size are Genesis, Exodus, Leviticus, Deuteronomy, Isaiah, the Twelve, and Psalms. Dodd's own list of fields included Genesis, Deuteronomy, Psalms, Isaiah, Daniel, and the Twelve. Only Exodus and Leviticus figure in the revised Sundberg list, which may suggest not that Dodd's list is wrong in principle but that it needs revision in detail. Sundberg then went on to list the relative importance of the various Old Testament books in terms of the number of "citations" from each (again using the Nestle list). But here in fact Sundberg's figures appear to support Dodd, for the books with the highest ratings are Genesis, Exodus, Deuteronomy, Isaiah, the Twelve, Psalms, Proverbs, and Daniel.

Sundberg next tries to establish his point by considering the relative usage of the different New Testament authors, but fails to observe that the different purposes and characters of the various writings make such a comparison futile. Nor does he recognize adequately that what Dodd was discussing was the fields used in the *earliest* stage of the church's study of the Old Testament. It is reasonable to assume that at the literary stage of composition of the New Testament the writers would not be tied to the specific fields and would feel free to explore more widely and to ignore materials that had earlier been of greater importance. This point may be relevant in dealing with the further objection that a study of the repetition of *allusions* to specific texts (rather than just the occurrences of actual citations) indicates that a larger area of material was being tapped; again the point may be made that the allusions are more of a literary phenomenon. Nevertheless, the point should be made that Dodd's theory need not require that the early church turned *only* to a limited list of fields. His view was that these fields developed in the earliest days of the church's theologizing rather than that they imposed limits throughout the New Testament period and prevented New Testament authors from looking outside them, especially to any well-known passages which were not in the fields.

Here we may take up Sundberg's next point which is that Dodd supposed that there was "a traditional method of exegesis of Old Testament passages" in the church which governed the meaning (Sundberg 1959, 278). Sundberg takes this to mean that the same Old Testament passage should have received the same interpretation whenever it was cited in the New, and he cites examples to show that this did not happen. But these examples are not wholly convincing, as when he finds texts that are applied both to Jesus and to his followers, and ignores the way in which what is true of Christ is also often true of his followers. There is no change in meaning here, only a shift in application. In any case Jewish exegesis was quite capable of finding multiple meanings in any one text (Brooke 1985, 354–55).

Sundberg (1959, 279) argues further that some doubly cited passages refer to "manifestly developed positions of the church," for example, the Jewish rejection of Jesus which cannot have existed from the beginning. But surely the evidence goes the other way and suggests that this was a problem to the church from an early date (1 Thess. 2:14–16).

Finally Sundberg argues that such a collection as Dodd presupposes should have been preserved in the New Testament canon. The reasons for this statement are not obvious, especially if the list of passages was oral and so short as to be easily memorable; one cannot see that such a list would be regarded as Scripture in the same way as the actual New Testament writings.

Sundberg's case against Dodd thus stands open to criticism at every point, and I judge that it is not successful in refuting his case. The hypothesis that the early church turned to specific fields in the Old Testament and used them can still be used as a starting point for investigation (Lindars 1961, 14). What still needs to be determined is how the church used the material from the Old Testament once it had found it.

The Problem of Attention to the Old Testament Context

A further problem is whether the New Testament writers pay attention to the context in their use of Old Testament materials. Certainly Dodd did not deny that there was what he called "a certain shift, nearly always an expansion, of the original scope of the passage" (Dodd 1952, 130), and he argued that great literature contains the potential of more meaning than the original author explicitly intended.

Again Sundberg attempts to contradict Dodd. He argues that the meanings given to the citations are not dependent upon the context of the original passages. There seem in fact to be two possible points here. One is whether there is an intended reference to the larger context in which the citation is found; the other is whether the meaning is related to that context. But is either of these quite what Dodd had in mind? He argued that the finding of an appropriate text in part of the Old Testament led the Christians to look in the same context for further appropriate texts, and that in some cases the choice of a text was dependent upon the assumption that the larger passage is christologically oriented. Thus, for example, the quotation of Psalm 69:25 with reference to the defection of Judas presupposes the belief that the psalm had already been seen to be christological and that therefore this text is relevant to the rejection of Christ. Now over against this Sundberg argues that the majority of texts are cited atomistically. But Sundberg's examination of cases where the New Testament authors cite several different texts from the same Old Testament passage does not disprove the fact that having found christological significance in one text the New Testament authors kept coming back to the same area. It is not a case so much of *understanding* the citation that is at issue (Sundberg 1959, 277) but of tracing how the Christians came to use it. In the broader sense all that was needed was a recognition that the passage was christological, so that the use of a text from within it was not arbitrary. This has not been disproved by Sundberg. The general question of whether respect for context in a narrower sense is preserved is a separate issue and deserves further investigation. The point may be made that the New Testament authors *thought* that they were respecting the context and original meaning, since they would have argued that the meaning which they found was the meaning which God intended.

The Context of the Use of the Old Testament in the New Testament

But before we discuss the question of how the early Christians determined the meaning of the Old Testament we must comment on the situation in which they did so and the effect which this had on their interpretation. The study of this aspect of our topic received a fresh impetus with the publication in 1961 of Professor Barnabas Lindars's book on *New Testament Apologetic*. Basically Lindars is arguing for two positions. The first is that we can trace shifts in the application of the Old Testament passages in different parts of the New Testament, and the second is that the starting point of this process lies in the apologetic activity of the early church. The early church was particularly concerned to answer Jewish objections to the messiahship of Jesus, and where such a concern can be detected we come up against the earliest uses of the texts in question. Lindars begins with the resurrection of Jesus and then turns to passion apologetic. He then moves on to a secondary development in the application of Scripture to events in the life of Jesus before the passion and to the question of his origins. Finally, he looks at developments in these lines of thinking by Paul.

The discussion is acute and full of penetrating observations. The apologetic use of Scripture by the early church is clearly documented. Nevertheless, it is open to some criticisms. These have been presented by Gundry (1967, 159–63) who lists six objections to Lindars's view before coming to his major point, which is that Lindars's case hangs on detecting *Tendenz* in the varied text forms which are used, whereas the evidence shows the existence of "mixed text-forms in the untendentious material of many allusive quotations throughout the synoptics." This is essentially the same objection as that which Gundry raises against the validity of Stendahl's discussion of the material in Matthew, and it is clear that much hangs or falls with the correctness of his interpretation of the material.

It seems to me that Lindars tends to make two assumptions in his work which need greater justification than he provides. One is the assumption, to which Gundry also draws attention, that the earliest use of Old Testament texts was apologetic rather than anything else. This is assumed rather than argued. Obviously much use of the Old Testament would be apologetic, and this need not be denied, and where texts were used apologetically Lindars has much that is helpful to say about them. But are we justified in assuming that in the earliest days there was no other type of use? There is a firm tradition that Jesus used the Old Testament to throw light on his mission, and there is no good reason to reject it (France 1971). Moreover, the New Testament shows clearly that the early church used the Old Testament in an explanatory manner as well as in a definitely apologetic and hence somewhat polemical context. We can also observe how the early church went to the Old Testament for the still-valid teaching which it gave and for the responsive material which it took over and used to provide the form and content of its own praise and prayer to God. There is a good deal of use of the Old Testament in the New Testament which can be labeled "liturgical," and this usage stems from the life of the church in its early days. Hence the field of use seems to be much wider than Lindars suggests.

Second, Lindars argues that it is probable that the very earliest apologetic would be concerned with the resurrection of Jesus, and he then attempts to find a putative resurrection-application as the starting point for the development of the use of any and every text. This begs the question of Jesus' own use of the Old Testament, to which we have already referred, and it further begs the question of the actual use of specific texts in the early church. Granted what lies beyond dispute, namely that resurrection-apologetic was an early phenomenon in the church, it was by no means the only form of apologetic, and it is a strange assumption that every text used in the earliest days of the church must have had an initial reference to the resurrection. Although Lindar's assumption at this point is thus a puzzling one, he has rendered an important service in stimulating further explorations of the kind of use, or rather the purposes for which use was made, of the Old Testament in the early church.

Types of Use of the Old Testament

We come now to the question of how the New Testament writers made use of the Old Testament and what understanding they had of it. If anything is clear, it is that a variety of types of use must be recognised. It may be helpful to offer a list of them before considering one or two of them in greater detail:

1) The influence of the language of the Old Testament on the diction of the New Testament authors, with the result that they write a "biblical Greek" distinguished by its secondary Semitisms (i.e. Semitisms which have been transmitted through the Septuagint).

2) The influence of the style of the Old Testament. This emerges specifically in the case of Luke whose use of a Septuagint style must raise the question whether he thought of himself as writing a work of the same kind and thus continuing the "salvation historical" story which he found in it.

3) The use of the Old Testament in a straightforward "literal" manner when reference is being made to events described in it. This use is so "obvious" that it is often passed over without comment, and yet it may demand further attention.

4. The use of the Old Testament again in a "literal" manner to refer to the divine commands, etc., which are found in it and which are believed to be still valid (or which may be cited in order to be brought up to date or even abrogated).

5) The use of the Old Testament yet again in a "literal" manner to refer to passages which were understood as prophecies and which found their literal meaning in the events now taking place. "About whom does the prophet say this?" Then Philip "told him the good news of Jesus" (Acts 8:34–35).

6) The use of the Old Testament typologically to show a correspondence between a contemporary event and an event in the Old Testament so that understanding of the former (and sometimes of the latter) may be enhanced.

7) The use of the Old Testament allegorically to draw parallels between an Old Testament story and a contemporary situation or piece of teaching.

The lines between these types of use are not always easy to draw. Our attention will centre on the problems of prophecy and typology in the light of Jewish usage.

Exegesis in the Dead Sea Scrolls

In their dialogue on "The Place of the Old Testament in the Formation of New Testament Theology" Lindars (1976) and Borgen (1976) list between them six areas of Jewish interest in, and exegesis of, the Old Testament which are relevant for understanding the use made in the New Testament. These are: Jewish liturgical forms; the rabbinic literature; the targums; the Qumran sect; apocalyptic literature; and Philo. Each of these will receive due attention later in this book. For our present purpose it may suffice to open up the question of Jewish influence on the New Testament use of the Old Testament by looking at some of the issues as they are raised by a consideration of the Qumran documents.

The first important work to show the influence of the Scrolls was Stendahl's book, *The School of St. Matthew* (1954; 2d ed. 1968), of which the author has been known to comment that people tended to quote the title rather than read the book. The thesis was concerned (obviously) with one limited area, namely the use of a specific set of quotations in the Gospel of Matthew, which appeared to stand out from the others for formal and textual reasons, and it had two main parts.

First, Stendahl argued that the character of these quotations and the implied interpretation of them resembled the kind of thing found in the use of Scripture at Qumran and specifically in the Habakkuk commentary; in particular, he drew attention to the use of variant readings in the text to promote a particular interpretation, and he labeled the kind of exegesis which was going on as "midrash pesher." The name was coined by analogy with midrash halakah and midrash haggadah which designate two other types of midrashic activity (Stendahl 1968, 184), and it is important to bear this fact in mind in view of later discussions of the suitability of the term. In all cases midrash refers to a manner of exegesis of the text which aims to bring out its contemporary significance, for instance by showing how the precepts of the Torah still apply in the commentator's own time. In the case of Qumran the type of midrash consists in a technique of quoting the text in a form appropriate to the meaning which is deemed to lie hidden in it and then explaining it in accordance with a set of principles of interpretation, thirteen of which are listed from Brownlee (1951); thus the interpretation lies partly in the text cited and partly in the interpretative comments in which it is embedded.

This led to the second part of the thesis which was that the activity thus demonstrated suggested the work of a "school" rather than of one specific individual.

The thesis was important for two reasons. First, there was the suggestion that some kind of corporate study of Old Testament Scriptures developed in the early church. The question whether we should speak of "school" activity in this connection was raised with specific reference to the phenomena in Matthew, and it is not necessarily implied that all early Christian exegesis was carried out in such a setting. Nevertheless, the character of the New Testament activity suggests the development of communally known and practiced methods of understanding, which it may be appropriate to call "school" activities. The activity of scriptural interpretation was not confined to a few individuals but was fairly widespread in the church and occupied a position of great importance.

But we must concentrate our attention on Stendahl's other claim, namely that in certain quarters at least the early church practiced a

form of scriptural exegesis hitherto unknown but now shown to be par-
alleled in one area of contemporary Judaism. The character of this so-
called pesher interpretation deserves some critical comment since it
has become something of a catch-phrase in subsequent study. The principles of "pesher" interpretation cited by Stendahl (1968, 191) may be
listed as follows:

1) What the prophets wrote has a veiled, eschatological meaning.
2) Since the meaning is veiled, the meaning may be discerned by
   what may appear to be a forced interpretation.
3) One may observe textual or orthographical peculiarities.
4) One may also make use of textual variants (for the light they
   shed on the text or to replace the text).
5) One may note analogous circumstances.
6) The text may be allegorized in an appropriate manner.
7) One may find more than one meaning in the words.
   One may assume that the author has hidden the meaning he intended in various ways and "undo" his techniques:
8) by substituting synonyms for the intended words,
9) by using anagrams,
10) by substituting similar letters for the ones he really intended,
11) by running words together, which must be split to get the
    meaning,
12) and by using abbreviations which must be spelled out in full.
13) One may find that other passages of Scripture illuminate the
    meaning of the text.

It is clear that a series of assumptions are operative here. The first is
that the prophet's message has a meaning which is "eschatological."
That is to say, it applies to a future period which the sect identified with
its own time and the immediate future. It found its own activities
prophesied and it looked forward to whatever else God would do in the
future. The question whether the passage had a meaning for the
prophet's own time is ignored. Thus the first of the thirteen principles
is a statement about the nature of prophecy rather than a method for
finding its meaning. It defines the kind of meaning that is presumed to
be there.

The second assumption is that this eschatological meaning is often
(but not always) "hidden" and needs to be recovered by suitable procedures which involve going beyond the apparent message of the text to a
hidden meaning which can be detected by noting abnormalities in the
text. In other words the abnormalities represent a deliberate coding of
the message which must now be decoded. Principles 3–13 are in effect

methods for apprehending this hidden meaning. The procedures were presumably justified by their "results." Some of them are more justifiable than others, such as recourse to analogous circumstances or to other passages of Scripture.

The question whether the method of "decoding" can be called charismatic seems to have more relevance to the self-understanding of the Qumran interpreters than to an objective assessment of their actual procedures. It seems probable that the Qumran interpreters did claim to have special insights given by revelation into the hidden meaning of Scripture, but there is no necessary tension between this consciousness and the view that there was a "science" of exegesis, by which a set of rules was applied to get at the meaning of the text. Indeed a cynic might suggest that the rules were so arbitrary that some kind of sense of "inspired interpretation" was necessary to justify the use of any particular rule at any given time.

Many scholars have suggested that we can find a kind of "pesher" exegesis in parts of the New Testament. But the recent discussion by Brooke (1981) makes some cogent criticisms against a slipshod use of this category. He draws attention to the fascination which the term "pesher" exerts upon scholars and complains that it is used loosely, and that it really means nothing different from midrash, which is the art of bringing the application of the Scripture up to date. However, this does not necessarily rule out the useful application of the term. The special meaning, if the term has one, can be applied to the kind of exposition which takes up a text and proceeds to quote it in sections and to comment on each phrase in turn using the term *pišrô* to introduce the identification of each significant element in the text and a justification or explanation of the identification—in short the method exemplified in the Habakkuk commentary. The ways in which the comments are "worked out" is found elsewhere in Qumran in discussions of brief texts grouped around themes rather than simply of continuous texts, but the actual method of commenting with the "pesher" formula remains distinctive, and it seems appropriate to recognize it as a specific genre of interpretation.

A further point made by Brooke (1985, chap. 1) is to ask whether the "rules" of the game at Qumran are any different from those of midrashic exegesis among the rabbis. This leads him into a discussion of the antiquity of the middoth, and to argue that while the formulations of them may be late, the practice of them is early. In point of fact there does not seem to be any great distinction between Qumran and rabbinic exegesis so far as methods are concerned. This means that the Qumran methods were not confined to Qumran and were presumably more widespread—so they could perhaps have influenced the early

Christians all the more readily. It should be remembered that the formulated middoth are very general and do not necessarily reflect the precise methods that are followed.

Qumran and the New Testament

It follows from what has been said that we need to distinguish between the presence of the more specific characteristics of pesher in the New Testament and the presence of the kinds of exegetical technique which were used at Qumran in pesher exegesis but which were broadly characteristic of Jewish midrash. The presence of the latter has been helpfully discussed by Doeve (1954), but the presence of what can strictly be called "pesher" is dubious. Even the language of "pesher" is absent, and the parallels which have been observed by Ellis (1978, 160) are not exact. Nevertheless, we can certainly say that the use of text in an appropriate textual form and the writing of the interpretation into the text are visible (Ellis 1957).

With regard to the actual methods used at Qumran we saw that they were in reality part of the general approach which has come to be called "midrashic." We can discover many parallels between Qumran and rabbinic methods of exegesis and the methods utilized in the New Testament. Ellis (1957) claims that the same Qumran-like method of exegesis, for which he took over the label "midrash pesher" from Stendahl, is to be found in some of the Pauline material. Thus the choice of appropriate wording among variant readings of a text or the deliberate alteration of the wording of a citation to fit a syntactical context or to make a theological point is easily demonstrated. However, many of the devices used at Qumran and listed by Brownlee simply do not function in the New Testament: the assumption that the Old Testament text has a hidden meaning and must be decoded by what may seem to us to be rather arbitrary procedures in order to reveal it is not present, and this marks a decisive difference between Qumran and New Testament interpretation of the Old Testament.

From their techniques we move to the first of the assumptions made by the Qumran sect, namely that the Scriptures were seen as having relevance to their own day, so that contemporary events formed a key to the understanding of passages taken to be prophetic. They also regarded their own days as being the last days, so that we can designate their interpretations as "eschatological" (in the sense of "having reference to the last days"). The New Testament writers share the view that at least some prophecy looks forward to the last days and that the coming of Jesus and the establishment of the church are parts of the events of the last days (indeed the most significant events) and are the object of prophecy. This means that both groups regarded themselves as having a "key" to understanding the Old Testament: they "know" that the text *must* apply to their own situation in the last days, and therefore they use their techniques to get at this meaning. The Qumran sect lived in the conviction that the life of their sect was prophesied in the prophets and Psalms. Consequently, when they came to an obscure passage the method was to ask: Granted that this text must refer to something in our recent history, can we identify a plausible event, and then see the text as a prophetic description of it? So when some genius decides that in one verse of Habakkuk there is a prophecy of the wicked priest, it is natural to look in other verses for further references and to clear away obscurity or lack of message by assuming that the verse must have something to say within this frame of reference. Thus light is thrown both on the career of the wicked priest and also on the problems of the text of Habakkuk by this means.

New Testament interpretation works in the same say by assuming that prophecy finds its fulfillment in the coming of Jesus and the history of his followers. A familiar way of putting this is: "Jesus as the Christ opens up the true meaning of the Old Testament" (Hay 1976, 443). But what does this mean? And does it apply to the whole of the Old Testament? Presumably the point is that to the early Christians it was "obvious" that some passages prophesied the coming of Jesus. Thus Jesus could be seen as, say, the Servant of Yahweh. The next step was to ask whether obscure verses about the Servant could make sense when seen as prophetic of him. Thus a "key" had been found, but the way in which the Scriptures were interpreted in the light of this conviction that they prophesied Jesus had still to be worked out. But how far can this method be applied throughout the Old Testament? Clearly it will work for passages that can be regarded as prophecy (but not necessarily for all prophecies). It will work for passages that can be interpreted typologically. It will also work for much of the Old Testament teaching, regarded as valid and still true for the church, because written for it (we are the true Israel). It works for praise and other appropriate materials for human address and prayer to God (Hay 1976, 444).

The use of this and other methods helps to draw out the continuity felt by the New Testament writers between the work of God in their own day and in Old Testament times and hence between themselves and the ancient people of God. But there is also the consciousness of differences, and it may be interesting to work out how far the early Christian use of the Old Testament as a court of appeal was affected by their readiness to do away with some of its teaching. Did they see themselves as abrogating it or rather as reinterpreting it to suit their own situations?

Finally, a question arises concerning the purpose of the Qumran exposition. Granted that we know something of the context in which it was carried on, we have still to ask why the sect did it? Was the purpose apologetic or controversial? Was it to mount a reasoned defense of themselves to others or to encourage themselves by showing that they were God's people and that what was happening to them was part of a plan that would not be thwarted? It is not obvious that the question should be answered with a simple either / or, and this should be borne in mind as we come to consider the aims and purposes of early Christian use of the Scriptures.

Space forbids discussion of the study of other Jewish exegesis of the time. In particular, recent study of the targums is of great importance in throwing light on Christian exegesis as regards both the methods used and some of the interpretations which were reached (Chilton 1984; Hanson 1974, 1980).

The Problem of Typology

However, some consideration must be given to the question of typology. Ellis in particular drew the attention of English-speaking scholars to the fact that a major element in Paul's interpretation of the Old Testament was typology, where a comparison is made between events in the New Testament and events in the Old Testament which are historical, which happened in accordance with a divine plea and which may have "a dispensational or economic relationship to the corresponding New Testament fact" (Ellis 1957, 128).

Ellis was here taking up the lead given by an earlier work which, strictly speaking, falls outside our period for comment, Goppelt's book *Typos*. Although it was published in 1939, it did not appear in English translation until 1982, and one hopes that from now on it will have a wider influence. Much has been written loosely and inexactly about typology, but it is Goppelt who gives the topic the careful study that it demands and who shows that typology is of central importance in the New Testament use of the Old Testament. Typology may be defined as the study which traces parallels or correspondences between incidents recorded in the Old Testament and their counterparts in the New Testament such that the latter can be seen to resemble the former in notable respects and yet to go beyond them. Redemption in Christ shows an analogy to the deliverance of Israel from Egypt but goes beyond it. Thus we see that God works on the same principles in both eras. The Old Testament incident can thus be said to point forward to the New Testament one, but it does not lose its own significance in and for its own time.

What remains uncertain is whether the Old Testament incident was thought to have been deliberately planned as a type for its antitype, so that a full exposition of the Old Testament passage recording it would have to say "and God did this *in order that* it would serve as a type for his later redemption of the world in Christ." It may serve as a type merely because God works consistently in Old Testament and New Testament times. That is to say: the fact that it points forward to the New Testament antitype is not part of the meaning of the type. Or, put otherwise, the fact that the New Testament sees an Old Testament event as a type does not throw light on its interpretation in its Old Testament context.

Or does it? Certainly the type is used to thrown light on the New Testament incident by providing a frame of reference or a metaphorical expression which helps to illuminate the New Testament incident. We can say: if you want to understand what happened in Christ, it was like what happened at the exodus. Thus we may be given what can border on an allegorical framework for understanding: just as the people of Israel were slaves in Egypt, so we were slaves to sin. Just as God delivered them by a mighty act, so now the death of Christ is the mighty act by which he delivers us. Just as at the same time God made a covenant with his people and sealed it with the blood of a sacrifice, so too he has made a covenant with us and sealed it with the blood of Jesus. But does the New Testament use the method in the opposite direction: just as we were slaves to sin, so too the Israelites were slaves in Egypt, and so on? Does the New Testament claim that certain Old Testament incidents happened *in order* to teach *us* lessons? In 1 Corinthians 10 we are told that certain things happened typically to the Israelites and were written for our instruction and as a warning. Here Paul appears to be saying that God caused the incidents in the wilderness to be recorded with the deliberate intent that we might profit from the record. Compare how he says that the commandment about not muzzling the ox was written for us. So we must ask whether typology is a means of interpreting both Old Testament and New Testament or just New Testament. Goppelt appears to be uncertain:

> Typology begins and ends with the present salvation. NT typology is not trying to find the meaning of some OT story or institution. It compares Jesus and the salvation which he has brought with the OT parallels in order to discover what can be learned from this about the new and then perhaps, what can be learned also about the old. (Goppelt 1982, 201)

Ellis, as we have noted, holds that "Divine intent is of essence both in their occurrence and in their inscripturation," so that "although the 'type' has its own historical value, its real significance typologically is revealed only in the 'anti-type' or fulfillment" (Ellis 1957, 127). Similarly, Walter Kaiser has argued that a passage of Scripture has only one meaning, that given it by God speaking through the original writer, and that consequently when a New Testament writer sees a passage in a given way, that way must correspond to the divinely-intended meaning. He insists that "there should be competent evidence of the Divine *intention* in the correspondence between it and the Antitype" (Kaiser 1985, 121, citing Van Mildert 1815, 239; see further the full discussion in Davidson 1981). On this view, it follows that the meaning detected by the New Testament author is the original meaning of the passage. The question is whether this view was that of the New Testament writers themselves.

The Structure of New Testament Argumentation in the Light of the Old Testament

An interesting feature of recent study has been the search for rabbinic patterns of argument in the New Testament. Research has been done on the way in which Jewish midrashic material, especially in the form of synagogue sermons, was structured in terms of its relation to the seder and the haftarah, and it has been claimed that similar structures can be found in the New Testament. We may refer particularly to the suggestions of Bowker and Ellis in this regard (Bowker 1967; Ellis 1978) who have discovered material of this kind in Acts, the Pauline epistles, and Jude. The view that some of the material in John derives from Christian sermons is especially associated with Lindars (Lindars 1971; 1972), but some of this sermon material is based on Old Testament texts, for example, John 6 (Borgen 1965), and it is worth asking how far early Christian sermons followed Jewish patterns.

The question of Jewish patterns influencing the structure of the New Testament has been raised in a more far-reaching way. On the Dodd hypothesis the earliest Christians concentrated their attention on certain specific "fields" in the Old Testament. We may presume, however, that they extended their search into "all the Scriptures," as Luke suggests, for material about Jesus. If they attended the synagogue, they would be familiar with some kind of regular pattern of reading the Old Testament which took them through the Torah and the Prophets section by section. Earlier scholars, among whom Guilding (1960) must especially be mentioned, argued that traces of the synagogue readings appropriate to specific occasions can be detected behind passages in the New Testament which are linked to such occasions (e.g., the various festivals mentioned in John). The claim that a lengthy section in Luke could be regarded as reflecting the content of successive pericopae in Deuteronomy was made by C. F. Evans (1954).

But the major contribution developing this approach is that of Goulder who has argued that much of the New Testament, especially the synoptic Gospels, can be shown to have been inspired, pericope by pericope, by the seriatim readings of the Scriptures in the synagogue (Goulder 1974; 1978). Goulder further argues that the Gospels themselves were composed in order to function as Christian lectionaries, a use to which they were put at later dates, as the section divisions in certain MSS would indicate. If this theory can be sustained, it indicates that the structure of parts of the Old Testament exercised an important influence on the structure and the content of much of the New Testament.

But can it be sustained? Reviewers in general have been content to marvel at Goulder's *tour de force* without attempting to evaluate his conclusions in a largely uncharted area of study. It seems to have been left largely to Morris and Hooker to challenge his hypothesis (Morris 1983; Hooker 1980; cf. Blomberg 1983). Goulder's work is in fact open to considerable criticism, but he has drawn attention to an important area where further research is required.

Conclusion

If this survey has demonstrated anything, it has shown the breadth of the field that will be traversed in much greater detail in the remaining chapters of this book. Even so we have not been able to discuss all the topics that might be raised, in particular the question of the kind of understanding of the Old Testament as Scripture which animated the minds of early Christians. In their dialogue, to which reference has already been made, Professor Lindars and Professor Borgen have suggested that the Old Testament may be regarded in some ways as servant and in some ways as master in the process of formation of New Testament theology. The paradox emerges that the Scriptures "have an authority which is unquestioned," and yet "the place of the Old Testament in the formation of New Testament theology is that of a servant, ready to run to the aid of the gospel whenever it is required" (Lindars 1976, 59, 66). Granted that Jesus Christ is the new master, we may perhaps remind ourselves that to be "a slave of Jesus Christ," as Paul so frequently called himself, is to occupy a position of humble service which is at the same time one of high authority and dignity.

Bibliography

Barrett, C. K. "The Interpretation of the Old Testament in the New" in *The Cambridge History of the Bible*, vol. 1 (Cambridge, 1970), 377–411.

Blakc, M. "The Theological Appropriation of the Old Testament by the New Testament." *SJTh* 39 (1986): 1–17.

Blomberg, C. L. "Midrash, Chiasmus, and the Outline of Luke's Central Section," in R. T. France and D. Wenham, eds., *Gospel Perspectives:* vol. 3. *Studies in Midrash and Historiography* (Sheffield, 1983), 217–61.

Bock, D. L. "Evangelicals and the Use of the Old Testament in the New." *BSac* 142 (1985): 209–93, and 143 (1985): 306–19.

Borgen, P. *Bread from Heaven*. SNT 10 (Leiden, 1965).

———. "The Place of the Old Testament in the Formation of New Testament Theology." *NTS* 23 (1976–77): 67–75.

Bousset, W. *Kyrios Christos* (Göttingen, 1921).

Bowker, J. W. "Speeches in Acts: A Study in Proem and Yellammedenu Form." *NTS* 14 (1967–68): 96–110.

Brooke, G. J. "Qumran Pesher: Towards the Redefinition of Genre." *RevQ* 10 (1979–81) (Dec. 1981): 485–503.

———. *Exegesis at Qumran: 4Q Florilegium in its Jewish Context* (Sheffield, 1985).

Brownlee, W. H. "Biblical Interpretation among the Sectaries of the Dead Sea Scrolls." *BA* 14 (1951): 54–76.

Bultmann, R. *Theologie des Neuen Testaments*. 9th ed. (Tübingen, 1953). ET *Theology of the New Testament* (London: 1952).

Chilton, B. *A Galilean Rabbi and His Bible: Jesus' Own Interpretation of Isaiah* (London, 1984).

Davidson, R. M. *Typology in Scripture. A Study of Hermeneutical* τύπος *Structures* (Berrien Springs, 1981).

Dodd, C. H. *According to the Scriptures* (London, 1952).

Doeve, J. W. *Jewish Hermeneutics in the Synoptic Gospels and Acts* (Assen, 1954).

Ellis, E. E. *Paul's Use of the Old Testament* (Edinburgh, 1957).

———. *Prophecy and Hermeneutic in Early Christianity* (Tübingen/Grand Rapids, 1978).

Evans, C. F. "The Central Section of St Luke's Gospel," in D. E. Nineham, ed., *Studies in the Gospels* (Oxford, 1955), 37–53.

France, R. T. *Jesus and the Old Testament* (London, 1971).

Goppelt, L. *Typos: Die typologische Deutung des Alten Testaments in Neuen* (Gütersloh, 1939). ET *Typos: The Typological Interpretation of the Old Testament in the New* (Grand Rapids, 1982).

Goulder, M. D. *Midrash and Lection in Matthew* (London, 1974). *The Evangelists' Calendar: A Lectionary Explanation of the Development of Scripture* (London, 1978).

Guilding, A. *The Fourth Gospel and Jewish Worship* (Oxford, 1960).

Gundry, R. H. *The Use of the Old Testament in St. Matthew's Gospel with Special Reference to the Messianic Hope*. SNT 18 (Leiden, 1967).

Hanson, A. T. *Jesus Christ in the Old Testament* (London, 1965). *Studies in Paul's Technique and Theology* (London, 1974). *The New Testament Interpretation of Scripture* (London, 1980). *The Living Utterances of God: The New Testament Exegesis of the Old* (London, 1983).

Harris, R. *Testimonies: Part 1* (Cambridge, 1916), *Part 2* (Cambridge, 1920).

Hay, D. "Interpretation, History of. C. NT Interpretation of the Old Testament," in *IDBSup*, 443–46.

Hooker, M. D. Review of M. D. Goulder, *The Evangelists' Calendar*, in *Epworth Review* 7 (1980): 91–93.

Käsemann, E. *Exegetische Versuche und Besinnungen*. 2d ed. (Göttingen, 1965). ET *New Testament Questions of Today* (London, 1969).

Kaiser, W. C. Jr. *The Uses of the Old Testament in the New* (Chicago, 1985).

Kim, S. *The Origin of Paul's Gospel* (Tübingen, 1981).

Knox, W. L. *Some Hellenistic Elements in Primitive Christianity* (London, 1944).

Lindars, B. *New Testament Apologetic* (London, 1961). "The Place of the Old Testament in the Formation of New Testament Theology: Prolegomena." *NTS* 23 (1976–77): 59–66.

Lohse, E. "Apokalyptik und Christologie." *ZNW* 62 (1971): 48–67.

Longenecker, R. N. "Can We Reproduce the Exegesis of the New Testament?" *TynB* 21 (1970): 3–38. *Biblical Exegesis in the Apostolic Period* (Grand Rapids, 1975).

Morris, L. "The Gospels and the Jewish Lectionaries," in R. T. France and D. Wenham, eds., *Gospel Perspectives*, vol. 3, *Studies in Midrash and Historiography* (Sheffield, 1983), 129–56.

Schmithals, W. *Die kirchliche Apostelamt: Eine historische Untersuchung*, FRLANT 81 (Göttingen, 1961). ET *The Office of Apostle in the Early Church* (London, 1971) (= 1971a). *Die Gnosis in Korinth: Eine Untersuchung zu den Korinherbriefen*, 2d ed. (1965); ET *Gnosticism in Corinth: An Investigation of the Letters to the Corinthians* (Nashville, 1971) (= 1971b).

Schottroff, L. *Der Glaubende und die feindliche Welt* (Neukirchen-Vluyn, 1970).

Shires, H. M. *Finding the Old Testament in the New* (Philadelphia, 1974).

Smith, D. M. Jr. "The Use of the Old Testament in the New," in J. M. Efird, ed., *The Use of the Old Testament in the New and Other Essays: Studies in Honor of William Franklin Stinespring* (Durham, N.C., 1972), 3–65.

Stendahl, K. *The School of St. Matthew and its Use of the Old Testament* (Lund, 1954; 2d ed., Philadelphia, 1968; the second edition published at Lund at about the same time is undated).

Sundberg, A. C. Jr. "On Testimonies." *NovT* 3 (1959): 268–81.

Tasker, R. V. G. *The Old Testament in the New Testament* (London, 1946).

Vermes, G. "Interpretation, History of. B. At Qumran and in the Targums," in *IDBSup*, 438–43.

Van Mildert, W. *An Inquiry into the General Principles of Scripture-Interpretation* (Oxford, 1815).

Wilcox, M. "On Investigating the Use of the Old Testament in the New Testament," in E. Best and R. McL. Wilson, eds., *Text and Interpretation: Studies in the New Testament Presented to Matthew Black* (Cambridge, 1979), 231–43.

13

The Old Testament Background of Reconciliation in 2 Corinthians 5–7 and Its Bearing on the Literary Problem of 2 Corinthians 6:14–7:1

G. K. Beale

From G. K. Beale, "The Old Testament Background of Reconciliation in 2 Corinthians 5–7 and Its Bearing on the Literary Problem of 2 Corinthians 4:14–7:1," *New Testament Studies* 35 (1989): 550–81. Reprinted with the permission of Cambridge University Press.

Introduction[1]

Few scholars have proposed that there is any *precise* Old Testament background for Paul's view of reconciliation, even though there has been much discussion about the formulation of the doctrine. There is no Hebrew word for "reconciliation" in the Old Testament; there is general agreement that Paul obtained this word from not only the Jewish but also the Greco-Roman world. The καταλλάσσω-διαλλάσσομαι word group is found in the Septuagint (rarely), 2 and 4 Maccabees and Josephus as well as in classical, Hellenistic and *koine* writings. The use of the word group in these writings has been well documented.[2]

---

1. This chapter was read in the fall term of 1987 at the New Testament Seminar at Cambridge University and at the Ehrhardt Seminar at the University of Manchester. I am grateful for comments made by members of these seminars, by M. D. Goulder of Birmingham, by my colleagues at Gordon-Conwell Theological Seminary and at Tyndale House Library, Cambridge, and by Professors Stuhlmacher and Hengel of Tübingen.

2. See J. A. Fitzmyer, *To Advance the Gospel* (New York: Crossroad, 1981), 164–65; I. H. Marshall, "The Meaning of 'Reconciliation,'" in *Unity and Diversity in New Testament Theology: Essays in Honor of G. E. Ladd* (ed. R. A. Guelich; Grand Rapids: Eerdmans, 1978), 117–21; R. P. Martin, *Reconciliation: A Study of Paul's Theology* (Atlanta: John Knox, 1981), 104–6, among others.

However, proposals that Paul derives his understanding of "reconciliation" from any specific Old Testament background are rare,[3] although there have been some more general suggestions along these lines.[4] That such a background has not been looked into more is perhaps due to a too narrow view of establishing parallels on a semantic basis, often to the exclusion of conceptual considerations. The primary purpose of this chapter is to propose a new, specific Old Testament background for reconciliation based on a fresh analysis of 2 Corinthians 5:17–7:6.

Paul seemingly links reconciliation with the idea of the new creation in 2 Corinthians 5:17–21, in which is found his most intense and longest excursus on the subject of reconciliation (where καταλλάσσω and καταλλαγή occur five times). However, although some commentators have acknowledged this apparent linkage on the exegetical level, none has been able to explain how reconciliation and new creation are conceptually related in this passage.[5] One goal of this study is to propose such a specific conceptual relationship. And even if this goal can be accomplished, there is the more difficult problem of relating chapter 6, especially 6:14–7:1, to 5:17–21 on both a literary and thematic level. Especially problematic is the awkward presence of the catena of Old Testament quotes in 2 Corinthians 6:16–18. Many commentators are convinced that 6:14–7:1 do not logically fit into the contextual flow of the argument and reflect a non-Pauline style. Consequently, this segment is often viewed as part of a non-Pauline interpolation. Therefore, another aim of the present discussion is to demonstrate that behind 2 Corinthians 5:17–7:1ff. there stands a common, precise Old Testament theme which best explains the presence of the series of Old Testament quotes there and especially why they are found in the same context as Paul's discussion of "reconciliation." In particular, the

3. The apparent exception to this is O. Hofius, "Erwägungen zur Gestalt und Herkunft des paulinischen Versöhnungsgedankens," *ZThK* 77 (1980): 186–99, who argues that 2 Cor. 5:18–21 is based on Isa. 52–53.

4. See P. Stuhlmacher, "Das Evangelium von der Versöhnung in Christus," in *Das Evangelium von der Versöhnung in Christus,* ed. P. Stuhlmacher and H. Class (Stuttgart: Calwer, 1979), 44–49, who proposes that the OT is the origin for the language of reconciliation in the NT (in particular he cites Isa. 2:2–4; 9:1ff.; 11:1ff.; 25:6ff.; 40:9–11; 43:1ff.; 52:13–53:12; 56:1ff.; 60–63; Jer. 23:7ff.; 31:31ff.; Zech. 9–13). However, he only cites these texts and conducts no exegetical analysis of them.

5. E.g., see the helpful albeit general discussions of F. C. Hahn, "Siehe, jetzt ist der Tag des Heils," *EvTh* 33 (1973): 244–53; Stuhlmacher, "Erwägungen zum ontologischen Charakter der *kaine ktisis* bei Paulus," *EvTh* 27 (1967): 1–35; Stuhlmacher, *Versöhnung, Gesetz und Gerechtigkeit* (Göttingen: Vandenhoeck and Ruprecht, 1981), 133–34, 238–39; Hofius, "Versöhnungsgedankens," 188; Martin, *Reconciliation,* 108–10; idem, *2 Corinthians* (Word Biblical Commentary; Waco: Word, 1986), 149–53, 58; H. J. Findeis, *Versöhnung-Apostolat-Kirche,* Forschung zur Bibel 40 (Würzburg: Echter, 1983), 157–64, 176, whose discussion is the best in this regard.

overarching thesis of this study is to show that Paul understands both "new creation" in Christ as well as "reconciliation" in Christ (2 Cor. 5:17–21) as the inaugurated fulfillment of Isaiah's and the prophets' promise of a new creation in which Israel would be restored into a peaceful relationship with God and that this theme extends through the beginning of 2 Corinthians 7.

Analysis of 2 Corinthians 5:17–21

Brief discussion of the broader literary context merits initial consideration in order to discern the function of this text in Paul's overall argument. The motivation for Paul writing this epistle is the readership's rejection of him as God's true apostle for the gospel (cf. 3:1; 5:12; 10:10; 11:6–8, 16–18; 13:3, 7). Paul's purpose throughout the epistle then is to demonstrate the authenticity of his divine apostleship so that those questioning it would fully reaffirm it. His claim of apostleship cannot be proved according to worldly standards of evaluation (cf. κατὰ σάρκα in 5:16; 10:3–7) but by means of perceiving that Paul's authority and spiritual power are present because of the past work God has accomplished through him among the Corinthians[6] and because of his perseverance through suffering and weakness, which is characteristic of his life in Christ (cf. 4:7–12, 16–18; 6:3–10; 10:2–7; 12:7–10; 13:3–7).[7] In the light of this overall purpose, the literary unit of 5:14–21 should best be understood as functioning to strengthen Paul's argument that the readership accept him as God's apostle, and the precise language of reconciliation is employed to underscore emphatically this idea of acceptance. That is, the Corinthians' reconciliation with Paul will also be their reconciliation with God and Christ, since Paul is the legal ambassador of both (cf. 5:20). And if they understand their past reconciliation rightly, they will respond to Paul's message favorably. As we will argue, this same theme continues in 6:1–7:6.

In verse 17 Paul states that an effect (ὥστε) which Christ's death and resurrection (vv. 14–15) have upon the readership is that they are a new creation: "If anyone is in Christ, *he is a new creation;*[8] the old things have passed away; behold, new things have come about." In the context of the argument, this idea of the new creation may even be incipient in the mention of Christ's death and resurrection of verses 14–15, so that

---

6. So S. Hafemann, "'Self-Commendation' and Apostolic Legitimacy in 2 Corinthians: A Pauline Dialectic?" *NTS* (1989).

7. I have found that S. Hafemann, *Suffering and the Spirit,* WUNT (Tübingen: Mohr [Siebeck] 1986), 58–87, has made the same point.

8. This phrase could also be translated "there is a new creation." Either translation does not affect our overall argument.

the new creation theme also provides the basis for Paul's exhortation in verse 16 (cf. further infra). Therefore, he exhorts the readership in verse 16 not to evaluate his claim of apostolic authority according to the unbelieving, fleshly standards of the old world which for them have passed away. They are a new creation in Christ and consequently should evaluate all things by the spiritual standards of the new world.[9]

Paul draws from Isaiah in explaining the reality of the readership's part in the new creation. Although the wording of verse 17 is not a verbatim quotation of any text, its wording has unique parallels traceable to Isaiah 43:18–19 and probably to Isaiah 65:17:[10]

Isaiah 43:18–19
μὴ μνημονεύτε τὰ πρῶτα,
καὶ τὰ ἀρχαῖα μὴ συλλογίζεσθε.
Ἰδοὺ ποιω καινά

Isaiah 65:17
ἔσται γὰρ ὁ οὐρανὸς καινὸς,
καὶ ἡ γῆ καινή καὶ οὐ μὴ
μνησθῶσιν τῶν προτέρων

2 Corinthians 5:17
εἴ τις ἐν Χριστῷ, καινὴ κτίσις.
τὰ ἀρχαῖα παρῆλθεν,
ἰδοὺ γέγονεν καινά

Especially striking is the contrast found nowhere else between τὰ ἀρχαῖα and καινά which is connected by ἰδού plus creation vocabulary.[11]

Commentators have generally acknowledged Paul's allusion to Isaiah, especially Isaiah 43:18–19 and 65:17,[12] but surprisingly there ap-

---

9. Although Stuhlmacher, *"kaine ktisis,"* 5–6, among a number of others (cf. infra n. 2 576), is right that v. 16 concerns Paul's conversion and apostolic call, its function in the overall argument of chapters 2–7 is to encourage the readers also not to evaluate "according to the flesh." This is evident from its syntactical dependence on vv. 14–15 and its parallelism with v. 17 (cf. ὥστε), which is clearly a general reference.

10. Among relevant Jewish texts the next closest parallels are 1 En. 91.16 and 1 QH 13.11–12, which also contrast the old creation with the new creation; the former text has only a generally parallel contrast, while the latter is so filled with lacunae that its original wording is questionable.

11. However, this combination does occur in post-NT Christian literature always in allusion to 2 Cor. 5:17 or Isa. 43:18–19 (cf. Clemens Alexandrinus, *Stromata* 3.8.62.1.4; 3.8.62.2.1–6; Origenes, *Commentarium in evangelium Mattaei* 17.33.104–6; 17.33.110–33; *Fragmenta in Psalmos* 1–150; Gregorius Nazianzenus, *In theophania* 36.313.9–12; *In novam Dominicam* 36.616.39–42; Gregorius Nyssenus, *Contra Eunomium* 3.2.53.5.5–8).

12. However, V. Furnish, *II Corinthians* (Anchor Bible; Garden City: Doubleday, 1984), 314–15, would be representative of a few in seeing 2 Cor. 5:17 as generally depen-

pears to have been no specific attempt to link this Old Testament background closely with the following discussion of reconciliation in verses 18–21. Only a general linkage is made between "new creation" and "reconciliation" in the sense that God's reconciliation of humanity in Christ has begun to reverse the alienation introduced at the fall, and a return to the peaceful conditions of the original creation has been inaugurated in the eschatological age of the new creation of Christ.[13] We can only suppose that there has been no discussion of the recognized links with Isaiah because commentators perhaps view Paul as merely using Isaiah's words to convey his own new thought which is foreign to the Old Testament context. The remainder of this discussion will try to show that although this is a possible view, it is improbable.

If Paul does have the context of Isaiah in mind, then in what manner is he developing this Old Testament context in verse 17 and how do verses 18–21 logically flow out of the thought of verse 17? Of course, it is conceivable that Paul's discussion of reconciliation in these verses is a separate and new subject unrelated to "new creation" in verse 17 to which Paul is now turning his attention, but this is unlikely, as is borne out by the majority of the literature on this text.

The primary text to which Paul alludes in verse 17 is Isaiah 43:18–19. The context of these two verses refers to God's promise that a time will

---

dent only on the concept of creation in apocalyptic Judaism. Nevertheless, Furnish adds that "the roots of the apocalyptic idea go back to Isa. 65:17–25 (cf. Isa. 42:9, 43:18–19; 48:6; 66:22)" (ibid., 315). But it could just as easily be said that Paul was aware that this apocalyptic tradition was based on Isaiah so that he also has Isaiah itself in mind (see Stuhlmacher, *"kaine ktisis,"* 10–13, 20, who understands this apocalyptic tradition as having been based on Isa. 43 and 65). This especially could be the case since a number of Jewish texts cited by Furnish stem from the end of the first century A.D. (1 En. 45.4–6; 72.1; 2 Bar. 32.6; 44.12; 57.2 and perhaps Joseph and Asenath 15.4) and some of the relevant texts allude to Isa. 43 or 65 (cf. likewise Stuhlmacher, ibid., 13, who cites 1 En. 106.13, 1 QS 4, 25 and 1 QH 13, 11 ff. in this latter regard). Indeed, it is highly likely that 1 En. 45.3–6 and 72.1 explicitly allude to Isaiah's creation theme since the former also develops Isaiah's "elect one" idea (cf. Isa. 41:8–9; 42:1; 43:10; 43:20; 44:1–2; 45:4; 49:7) and the latter context paraphrases Isa. 52:7 (cf. 1 En. 71.15–17). Likewise Jub. 1.29 reflects the same creation idea of Isaiah since 1.28 alludes to Isa. 24:23 and 1.29a refers to Isa. 63:9 (other texts which may be developing Isaiah's new creation theme are Jub. 4.26; 5. 12; 1 En. 91.16; 106.13; 2 Bar. 32.6; 44.12; 49.3; 57.2; 4 Ezra 7.75). Certainly Paul must be given the same liberty. Among those viewing either Isa. 43:18–19 or 65:17 (or 66:22), or both, as the basis for 2 Cor. 5:17, see Stuhlmacher, ibid., 6; H. Windisch, *Der zweite Korintherbrief* (Göttingen: Vandenhoeck & Ruprecht, 1924), 189; R. V. G. Tasker, *The Second Epistle of Paul to the Corinthians* (Grand Rapids: Eerdmans, 1958), 88; Martin, *2 Corinthians*, 152; Bruce, *1 and 2 Corinthians* (New Century Bible; London: Marshall, Morgan and Scott, 1971), 209; S. Kim, *The Origin of Paul's Gospel* (Grand Rapids: Eerdmans, 1982), 18 n. 2.

13. E.g., Martin, *2 Corinthians*, 149–53; P. E. Hughes, *Paul's Second Epistle to the Corinthians* (Grand Rapids: Eerdmans, 1962) 201ff. See similarly Hahn, "Tag des Heils," 244–53, and Furnish, *II Corinthians*, 335, who see a definite link between the two concepts but explain it only very generally.

come when he will cause the Israelites to return from Babylonian exile and to be *restored* to their land in Israel (Isa. 43:1–21). Isaiah 43:18–19 is an exhortation to Israel that they no longer reflect on their past sin, judgment and exile but on God's promise of *restoration*. This is a reiteration of the theme of Isaiah 43:1–13, which also expresses a promise of restoration not only back to the land but also into a relationship with Yahweh as their creator, redeemer, savior, and king (cf. 43:1, 3, 7, 10–11). Israel was to be God's "servant" "chosen" to be restored "in order that" they "may know and believe Me, and understand that I am He" (43:10). Furthermore, Israel's promised restoration is referred to both as an imminent "redemption" (43:1; cf. v. 14) and creation (43:6–7). In this context Yahweh's role as Israel's "creator" (43:1) is accentuated, as he is portrayed as the one who "created," "formed" and "made" the nation for his "glory" (43:7). The point of this emphasis upon God as creator is not to focus on the first creation nor primarily the first exodus when the nation was initially created, but the recreation of the nation through restoring it from exile to its homeland, as Isaiah 43:3–7 makes clear. Isaiah 43:14–21 repeats the same idea, where Yahweh again refers to himself as Israel's "creator" (43:15, 21), "redeemer," (43:14) and "king" (43:15), and the restoration from exile (43:14–17) is described with new creation language. Israel is exhorted not to reflect on her former condition of exile when she experienced divine wrath (43:18; cf. 65:16b–19) but on God's imminent new creation of her as his "chosen people" whom he "formed" for himself (43:19–21). This coming restoration is further highlighted as a new creation through describing Israel's return with paradisal imagery: "beasts . . . jackals and ostriches" glorify God because of the water which he has caused to gush forth in the desert for the sake of his returning people (43:19–20). This second creation is also referred to as a second exodus (43:2, 16–17).

It may well be the case that Isaiah 65:17 is also included in Paul's allusion. If so, the emphasis on restoration as a new creation would even be stronger, since this is the point of Isaiah 65:17–25 in its context (cf. Isa. 60:1–65:25; 64:8–65:16; see also 66:19–23).

Indeed, Isaiah 43:18–19 is but one of a series of pericopae in the so-called Book of Consolation (Isa. 40–55) which explains the restoration of exiled Israel as a new creation or at least integrally associates the two concepts of restoration and creation (Isa. 40:28–31; 41:17–20; 42:5–9; 44:21–23; 44:24–28; 45:1–8; 45:9–13; 45:18–20; 49:8–13; 51:1–3; 51:9–11; 51:12–16; 54:1–10 [cf. v. 5]; 55:6–13).[14] Isaiah 60:15–22,

---

14. See C. Stuhlmueller, *Creative Redemption in Deutero-Isaiah*, Analecta Biblica 43 (Rome: Biblical Institute Press, 1970), 66–98, 109–61, 193–208; W. J. Dumbrell, *The End of the Beginning* (Homebush West, Australia: Lancer, 1985), 97–100.

65:17–25 and 66:19–24 continue the same thematic emphasis. God's act of new creation as restoration is also described outside of chapter 43 as his "redemption" of Israel (e.g., 44:1–8; 44:24–45; 54:1–10)[15] and as a new exodus (cf. 40:3–11; 41:17–20; 44:24–28; 51:1–13; 52:7–10; see also 43:16–21).[16]

Moreover, Isaiah 40–66 describes Israel's exile as an expression of divine "wrath" (51:20; 60:10), "anger" (47:6; 51:17, 22; 54:8; 57:16–17; 64:5, 9), "forsakenness" (49:14; 54:6–7; 62:4), "rejection" (54:6), "hiddenness" (54:8; 57:17; 59:2; 64:7) and consequent "separation" between God and the nation (59:2). All these texts assume that sin or iniquity is *the* cause of Israel's forsaken condition and this cause is sometimes stated explicitly for the sake of emphasis (cf. 50:1; 57:17; 59:1–15; 64:5–9). God's restoration of Israel from this estrangement is described not only as a redemptive new creation but as a time when the nation will "not be forsaken" (62:12); it will be reunited with God (45:14) and "know" him (43:10) because of his gracious initiative in regathering them (54:6–8; 57:18). And God will "wipe out their transgressions" (43:25) and free them from the bondage resulting from sin (42:6–9; 49:8–9) by the sacrificial death of the Servant, who becomes the ʾāshām for the people (53:4–12). Therefore, the return from exile is a period in which there is a cessation of anger, and "peace" is re-established between the nation and its God (cf. 48:18; 52:7; 57:19), a peace which results from and is characteristic of the new creation, modeled on the original paradisal conditions (cf. 26:11–19; 27:1–6 [cf. Targum]; 32:15–18; 45:7–8 [cf. Targum]; 45:18–25 [Sym.]; 55:12 [MT]; 60:15–22; 66:12–14, 19–23). In fact, in the context of Isaiah 43 restoration and new creation are to be viewed as brought about through the payment of ransom (43:3ff.) and the forgiveness of sins (43:22ff.). The vicarious suffering of the Servant in Isaiah 53 probably has the same function.

Therefore the complex of ideas found in 2 Corinthians 5:14–21 can already be seen in Isaiah 40–66. In the light of the thematic overview of Isaiah 40–66 it is plausible to suggest that "reconciliation" in Christ is Paul's way of explaining that Isaiah's promises of "restoration" from the alienation of exile have begun to be fulfilled by the atonement and forgiveness of sins in Christ. The believer's separation and alienation from God because of sin have been overcome through the divine grace expressed in Christ, who has restored the believer into a reconciled relationship of peace with God. Paul's point in 2 Corinthians 5:14–21 is that if the Corinthians are truly partakers of the new creation and of a reconciled relationship with God (vv. 14–19), then they should behave like

15. Stuhlmueller, *Creative Redemption*, 112–34, 196–208.
16. Ibid., 66–73, 82–94; Dumbrell, *End of the Beginning*, 15–18, 97.

reconciled people (v. 20). They have been acting like people alienated from God since they have questioned the divine authority of Paul's apostleship. If this alienation between Paul and his readers continues, it will also be an alienation from God since Paul represents God's authority and it is actually God who is "entreating" through him (5:20; cf. 2:14–17; 3:6; 6:7; 10:8; 13:3). There is to be a connection between their identity as reconciled people and their behavior as such people. Therefore, Paul appends an imperative of καταλλάσσω (v. 20) after his previous four uses of the participial and nominal forms, which may connote the reality of the readership's participation in such a reconciled condition (vv. 18–19),[17] although the first person plurals ἡμῖν in verses 18b and 19b probably have primary reference to Paul and his circle (but the first person plural ἡμᾶς in v. 18a could well include the readers).[18]

Furthermore, it was evident from the above overview of Isaiah 40–66 that 43:18–19 (and perhaps 65:17) is but part of a broader theme of that segment which concerns a promise that Israel's restoration from exile is to be a redemptive new creation brought about by the payment of a ransom and the forgiveness of sins. This was to result in a cessation of divine wrath and in a peaceful relationship between Yahweh and the people. Paul alludes to Isaiah 43:18–19 and 65:17 in order to link this Isaianic promise with the work of Christ. Christ's death and resurrection are the fulfillment of this promise. As in the case of the Isaianic Servant's mission and in line with Jewish exegetical tradition, Paul explains the atonement not only as a negative means of doing away with sin but also as resulting in the reuniting and renewing of sinful people with God, which amounts to a new creation.[19] This is clear from observing

17. It is also possible that in 5:20 Paul is calling for unbelievers among the professing readership to be reconciled, as 2 Cor. 13:5 may bear out. This is not incompatible with our above view, i.e., Paul may well be exhorting believers to live according to their calling of reconciliation and for unbelievers to accept this calling.

18. Throughout 2 Cor. the first person plural almost always refers to Paul and his co-workers, although there is occasional ambiguity (cf. 1:21–22; 3:18; 5:4–10; 5:16; 5:21; 6:16a; 7:1). Since there is high probability that an inclusive reference is intended in 5:21, 6:16a, 7:1, and perhaps in 5:16, the same intention may also be present in 5:18 (cf. also the inclusive πᾶς of vv. 14–15 and κόσμος in v. 19). Whichever is the case, our overall argument is not significantly affected.

19. Kim suggests that to some degree in 2 Cor. 5:15–17 Paul may have in mind the rabbinic idea which compares forgiveness generally, as well as atonement for sin specifically on the New Year's Day or on the Day of Atonement with a new creation (*Origin of Paul's Gospel*, 17 n. 1 and 4, citing in support H. Strack and P. Billerbeck, *Kommentar zum Neuen Testament aus Talmud und Midrasch*, vol. 2, 421–22; vol. 3, 519, together with other secondary sources). The relation of atonement and new creation may have already been incipient in the OT concept of the Day of Atonement, which laid the basis for the development of the combination by Paul and Jewish tradition (so H. Gese, *Essays on Biblical Theology* [Minneapolis: Augsburg, 1981], 109–16). However, Kim thinks a closer parallel to Paul than the rabbinic ideas is the Qumran concept of new creation which was applied to a

that Paul understands the "new creation" of 2 Corinthians 5:17 to be a direct effect (ὥστε) of Jesus "death for all" mentioned in verse 15. Verse 17 also concludes that, in addition to Christ's death, his resurrection (also mentioned in v. 15) is a new creation, "so that" as one is identified with this resurrection, one also becomes a part of the new creation.[20] Therefore, the idea of the new creation may already be implicit in the mention of both the death and especially resurrection in verse 15. The ὥστε of verse 16 in dependence on verse 15 shows that a result of the readership being part of such a new creation through identification with Christ's death and resurrection is that they will evaluate Paul's apostleship according to the spiritual standards of the new creation (or new age [cf. νῦν]) and no longer by means of the fleshly standards of the fallen creation (if "indeed" they really are "in Christ," 2 Corinthians 13:5).

Therefore, in verses 18–21 Paul does not shift his thinking to a new, unrelated topic. In these concluding four verses Paul makes clear what lies beneath the surface of his allusion to Isaiah in verse 17. Christ's death for human sin (2 Cor. 5:14–15, 21) has removed the condition of separation between God and sinful people, and, against the Isaiah background, both his death and resurrection can be viewed as inaugurating true Israel, the church, into the presence of God. We suggest that just as Christ, the true Israel, was separated from the Father because of his vicarious death (cf. vv. 21, 14–15) and was restored to a relationship with God by means of the resurrection, so likewise is the church restored through corporate identification with Christ. Therefore, in the light of the Old Testament background, to say that the church is a new creation because of Christ's resurrection (v. 17) is also to speak of the church as being *restored* or *reconciled* to God from her former Gentile estrangement (vv. 18–20). Simply put, Paul understands both "new creation" in Christ as well as "reconciliation" in Christ (2 Cor. 5:18–20) as the fulfilment of Isaiah's promise of a new creation in which Israel would be restored into a peaceful relationship with Yahweh. And Israel's exile in Isaiah is seen as representative of humanity's alienation from God, since Paul is applying Isaiah's message for Israel to Gentiles.

The two concepts of new creation and reconciliation are explicitly linked in verse 18a by τὰ δὲ πάντα ἐκ τοῦ θεοῦ τοῦ καταλλάξαντος ἡμᾶς ἑαυτῷ διὰ Χρισ. The "new things" (καινά) of the "new creation" (v. 17)

---

person's entry into the eschatological community to picture cleansing and renewal (*Origin*, 17 n. 4, citing in support 1QH 3. 19–22; 11. 10–14; 1QS 11. 13ff. [?] and secondary sources).

20. Findeis, *Versöhnung*, 149, 156–60, also sees the death and resurrection of v. 15b as resulting in the new creation of v. 17. Christ's resurrection is also viewed as the beginning of the new creation elsewhere in the NT (cf. Col. 1:15–16 and 1:18; Eph. 1:20–23, 2:5–6 and 2:10; Rev. 1:5 and 3:14).

are seen as having their creative source in God who has brought the new world (πάντα)[21] into being and "reconciled" people to himself through Christ (v. 18a). The phrase διὰ Χριστοῦ can have no other reference here than Christ's death and resurrection (vv. 14–15), which means that the death and resurrection are a means both to the "new creation" (v. 17) and to "reconciliation" (vv. 18ff.). The two ideas then are almost overlapping concepts for Paul as for Isaiah. To be propelled into the eschatological new creation is to enter into peaceful relations with the Creator.

Analysis of 2 Corinthians 6:1ff.

So far our argument about Paul's view of reconciliation is based entirely on the suggested Isaiah background of 2 Corinthians 5:17. Indeed, if Hofius's argument that Isaiah 53 stands behind 2 Corinthians 5:18–21 can be sustained, then the links with Isaiah are even stronger.[22] In 2 Corinthians 5:18–21 he discerns a twofold pattern of a *Versöhnungstat* and a *Versöhnungswort*, which he sees as based on the portrayal of the Servant's salvific role in Isaiah 52:13–53:12 and the proclamation if Israel's coming salvation in Isaiah 52:6–10. In addition, he adduces a number of specific conceptual parallels between Isaiah 53 and 2 Corinthians 5:21. Hofius's proposal should be judged as plausible with respect to 2 Corinthians 5:21,[23] since the combined ideas of a sinless penal substitute, the imputation of sin to a sinless figure to redeem a sinful people and the granting of righteousness are uniquely traceable to Isaiah 53:4–12. As we observed earlier, chapter 53 functions in the argument of Isaiah as explaining the means Yahweh will employ to restore Israel, and Paul seems to have recognized this. It is probably not a coincidence that Paul has combined allusions to Isaiah 43 and Isaiah 53, since Werner Grimm has shown that references to these two chapters had already been utilized together by the Gospel writers (cf. the dual background of Isa. 43:3–7 and 53, especially with respect to the

21. The phrase τὰ δὲ πάντα functions as a reference to the new creation and in doing so likely also summarizes the preceding thought of 5:14–5:17 (cf. Windisch, *Korintherbrief*, 191). The identical phrase in 4:15 (although here with γάρ instead of δέ) and 12:19 may have the same literary function and conceptual meaning (however, Findeis, *Versöhnung*, 164, argues that no cosmic nuance is evident in the phrase in 5:18 but that it functions only in a literary manner to summarize). Perhaps on a first reading many readers may have discerned only the literary function, but on a re-reading some may have also noticed its significance as a creational reference.

22. Hofius, "Versöhnungsgedankens," 196–99.

23. Cf. Stuhlmacher, *Versöhnung, Gesetz und Gerechtigkeit*, 79–80, and O. Betz, *Wie Verstehen Wir das Neue Testament?* (Wuppertal: Aussaat, 1981), 56–57, who find Hofius's overall argument convincing. Cf. Furnish, *II Corinthians*, 351 (and authors cited therein), who sees Isa. 53 as standing behind 2 Cor. 5:21.

idea of a substitutionary sin offering and the *Stichwort* "seed").[24] This exegetical tradition may have influenced Paul to do the same. However, does Paul really have the *restoration context* of Isaiah in mind to the extent that we have argued? Any affirmative answer to this question perhaps could be considered somewhat tentative if the material examined is limited only to 2 Corinthians 5:14–21. Although we think the argument could stand on its own up to this point, consideration of the context of chapter 6 will strengthen our proposal.

In 2 Corinthians 6:1 Paul picks up his thought from 5:20. In 5:20 Paul defines his role as God's ambassador to be an office whereby "God exhorts through us" (ὡς τοῦ θεοῦ παρακαλοῦντος δι᾽ ἡμῶν) and the opening expression of 6:1 (συνεργοῦντες δὲ καὶ παρακαλοῦμεν) continues a description of this role. That is, since it is through Paul's ambassadorial office that God "exhorts" the readership to be reconciled (5:20), Paul logically views himself and his apostolic circle also as "working together with God" in exhorting the readership to be reconciled or to behave as reconciled people. However, rather than using the language of reconciliation as the object of the exhortation as in 5:20, Paul exhorts them "not to receive the grace of God in vain" (εἰς κενόν) (6:1). Paul's reference to χάρις here focuses on "the ministry of reconciliation" (5:18) and "the word of reconciliation" (5:19) God had committed to him to preach to the Corinthians,[25] which was probably an essential part of Paul's broader apostolic ministry to the Gentile world. Indeed, Paul's use of χάρις in 2 Corinthians 1–5 does not primarily refer to a work of divine grace in the readership but the manner in which Paul presented the gospel in word and deed (2 Cor. 1:12, 15; 4:15), as is also the case elsewhere in his writings.[26] In fact, 2 Corinthians 6:1b is typical language used by Paul when he reflects on whether or not his labor of proclaiming the gospel to Gentiles has had salvific effect.[27]

Therefore, in 6:1 Paul is directly developing the thought of 5:18–20 by emphasizing that his exhortation for the readership to be reconciled should not be heard in vain because it is not merely his exhortation but it is from God himself (5:20). Indeed, there should not be an unfruitful response to this imperative since the readership already claimed to be partakers of this reconciling "grace of God" (as implied by 5:14–15, 18–19).

24. W. Grimm, *Weil Ich dich liebe. Die Verkündigung Jesu und Deuterojesaja*, ANTI 1 (Bern and Frankfurt: Lang, 1976), e.g., 254, 267 (and 275 of the second edition).

25. See K. T. Kleinknecht, *Der leidende Gerechtfertigte*, WUNT (Tübingen: Mohr [Siebeck] 1984), 264, who has independently made the same point.

26. Cf. Rom. 12:3; 15:15; 1 Cor. 3:10; 15:10; Gal. 2:9; Eph. 3:2, 7–8, where χάρις refers to Paul's apostolic task of proclaiming the gospel to the Gentiles as originating from divine grace.

27. Cf. κενός in 1 Cor. 15:10, 14; Gal. 2:2; Phil. 2:16; 1 Thess. 2:1; 3:5.

Now, in 6:2 Paul appeals to Isaiah 49:8 in order to establish further (cf. γάρ) his claim to be a legitimate divine spokesman of the message of reconciliation.[28] We have noted above that Isaiah 49:8 is part of one of the sections in Isaiah which closely associates the restoration of exiled Israel with a new creation theme (cf. Isa. 49:8–13), and so its appearance here as a reinforcement of 2 Cor. 5:17–21 is not surprising. In fact, Isaiah 49:8 is an explicit reference to Israel's restoration: the first part of the verse (quoted by Paul) is in synonymous parallelism with the second part. That is, the "favorable time" and the "day of salvation" (v. 13a) are explained to be the time of coming restoration: "And I will keep you and give you for a covenant of the people to restore (להקים) the land, to make them inherit the desolate heritages (v. 8b)." Isaiah 49:8 is a repetition of the promise of restoration mentioned only two verses earlier, where the "Servant's" role was not only "to raise up the tribes of Jacob, and to restore (להשיב) the preserved ones of Israel" but also to extend salvific restoration "to the ends of the earth" (49:6). Isaiah 49:8 is Yahweh's answer to the "Servant's" future protestation of despair over the apparent failure of his mission to restore Israel (cf. 49:4–5). His efforts of restoration seemed to have been "in vain" (κενῶς) and to have resulted "in vanity" (εἰς μάταιον) and "in nothing" (εἰς οὐδέν). The answer in verse 8, which is a continuation of verse 6, is that although the Servant's work of restoring Israel has appeared largely to be in vain and has caused him to be despised and abhorred (v. 7a), there is nevertheless a significant effect of this work on some in Israel ("the preserved ones" or remnant, 49:6a, 8b [MT]), and especially with respect to the nations (49:6b). Although the majority of Israel would apparently reject the Servant's restoring efforts (49:4–6a, 7a), God would cause such efforts to have a cosmic effect, that is, the salvation of the Gentiles (Isa. 49:6b, 8b).[29]

Thus, Isaiah 49:8 is a divine reaffirmation of the Servant's calling to restore Israel (and the nations) through promising to the Servant and assuring him that God will make his efforts fruitful despite apparent failure. Isaiah 49:9 portrays the Servant attempting to restore Israel to their land by "saying to those who are bound, 'Go forth,' to those who are in darkness, 'Show yourselves'" (cf. 49:8–9), language which is similar to 2 Corinthians 6:14–18.

28. Cf. D.-A. Koch, *Die Schrift als Zeuge des Evangeliums,* Beiträge zur historischen Theologie 69 (Tübingen: Mohr, 1986), 263, 318. This OT citation may also be continuing the thought of 5:17 because of the following parallels: 1) emphasis on the inaugurated presence of the eschatological age; 2) the use of ἰδού; (3) both are references to Isaiah (cf. Koch, ibid., 263).

29. Isa. 49:8b is altered in the LXX to refer to the gathering of the nations and not Israel.

In radical fashion Paul applies to himself a prophecy of the Isaianic Servant, probably in order to identify himself with that figure. He is in some way the fulfillment of the righteous "Servant, Israel" (Isa. 49:3) who was to proclaim restoration to sinful Israel.[30] In line with the prophetic portrayal, Paul has proclaimed reconciliation to the Gentile, Corinthian church, the beginning of the fulfillment of latter-day promises of restoration to Israel, but many are apparently not responding because they are questioning the very legitimacy of Paul as God's spokesman. Although the readership claims to have begun to partake of the eschatological promises of restoration to God, they are in danger of forfeiting these blessings if they continue to reject Paul as the official, divine messenger of reconciliation, since to do so is also to reject Jesus. Such a rejection is a rejection of God himself, since God is really speaking through Paul. Hence, although Paul's ministry appears to be on the verge of being received "in vain" (εἰς κενόν; cf. Isa. 49:4), he appeals to Isaiah 49:8 in order to authenticate his legitimacy as an apostolic "servant" of restoration and to demonstrate that his ministry will bear fruit. The quote, according to the contours of the original Old Testament context, shows that God himself will aid Paul in this ministry in order to express a divine reaffirmation of his calling to proclaim reconciliation (cf. 2 Cor. 6:2, "I listened to you . . . I helped you"). The period in which Paul sees this "help" and reaffirmation being offered is referred to as καιρῷ δεκτῷ, usually translated as "acceptable time." However, because of the following parallel expression (ἐν ἡμέρᾳ σωτηρίας), this phrase is best translated as "time of acceptance," referring to the end-time period when God's offer of acceptance or "restoration-reconciliation" is extended to exiled Israel and the nations.[31]

Indeed, the MT's רצון ("pleasure, favor" = the LXX's δεκτός) is rendered in Isaiah 49:8 by the Aramaic equivalent רעוא in the Targum, which is further explained by the paraphrase "I will receive your prayer." The Aramaic רעוא (or רעותא) also refers elsewhere in the Isaiah Targum generally to God's "pleasurable acceptance" (Isa. 1:11; 1:15; 56:7; 60:7) and specifically to such "pleasurable acceptance" in the sense of restoration from exile (Isa. 34:16–17; 60:10; 62:4; 66:2). Isaiah 60:10 is noteworthy since רצון is not only rendered by the Targum's רעותא but also by διαλ-

---

30. It is possible though less probable that Paul applies the quote primarily to Christ and only secondarily to himself as Christ's ambassador. Of course, if the citation is used without regard for the thought of its OT context, which is improbable in the light of our overall argument, then all of the above-mentioned identifications of the quote could be called into question.

31. For this translation see Hughes, *Second Epistle to the Corinthians,* 220 and Furnish, *II Corinthians,* 342. The almost identical phrase of Isa. 61:2 in the restoration context of 61:1–9 supports our view of the expression in 49:8.

λαγή of Symmachus, which refers likewise to God's acceptance of Israel by restoring them ("for on account of my wrath I smote you, and on account of *reconciliation* I loved you").[32] These general Old Testament lexical associations in Isaiah may be suggested as the possible origin of Paul's use of the καταλλάσσω word group in 2 Corinthians 5:18–20 (and elsewhere in his letters) to express divine acceptance or reconciliation.[33] This suggestion may be plausible in the light of our cumulative argument that in 2 Corinthians 5:17–7:4 Paul's understanding of reconciliation is a result of his meditation on the Isaianic restoration context.

Therefore, the quote from Isaiah 49:8 and Paul's comment on it in 2 Corinthians 6:2b focuses primarily on the eschatological period of prophetic fulfillment (cf. the νῦν twice in 6:2) when the "servant," Paul, is given divine authority and reaffirmation in his work, and it is a call for the readership to accept this reaffirmation and to be reconciled, in the sense of "making complete" their profession to be partakers of the Old Testament promises of restoration (cf. 2 Cor. 13:5, 9b, 11a).[34]

It may seem unusual that Paul would apply to himself a prophecy which the early Christian community would likely have applied to Christ. However, this is not without precedent. In Luke 2:32 and Acts 26:23 Jesus is viewed as the fulfillment of Isaiah 49:6 (cf. Isa. 42:6), while in Acts 13:47 and 26:18a Paul is identified as the fulfillment respectively of Isaiah 49:6 and 42:7. The rationale for these dual identifications lies probably in the conception of corporate representation already found in the Old Testament[35] and elsewhere in Paul and the New Testament, which may well lie behind the Pauline expression of "the Christ who speaks in me" (2 Cor. 13:3; cf. 2:14–17; 12:9, 19). And it is this same idea of corporate representation which allows Paul in his own

---

32. Symmachus also renders רצון by διαλλαγή in Ps. 29:6 and 68(69):14 in the sense of "pleasurable acceptance" before God's presence in contrast to God "turning his face away" (cf. Ps. 29:6b; 68(69):17).

33. Although Paul uses only the καταλλάσσω word group, it is synonymous with the διαλλάσσω word group, so that the latter could have sparked off the former in Paul's mind.

34. After writing the first draft of this article I found W. L. Lane's study, "Covenant: the Key to Paul's Conflict with Corinth," *TynB* 33 (1982): 8–9, 19–22, who also discusses at some length Isa. 49:1–13 as a "paradigm" not only for the immediate context of 1 Cor. 6:2 but also for the themes of "comfort" and "affliction" elsewhere in the book. However, his focus is only on the theme of Paul as a prophetic messenger of a covenant lawsuit along the lines of the OT prophets.

35. See generally H. W. Robinson, *Corporate Personality in Ancient Israel* (Philadelphia: Fortress, 1964) and the bibliography therein; A. R. Johnson, *The One and the Many in the Israelite Conception of God* (Cardiff: Univ. Press, 1942). For applications in Paul see Robinson's bibliography, as well as E. E. Ellis, *Prophecy and Hermeneutic in Early Christianity* (Grand Rapids: Eerdmans, 1978), 170–71, who also applies the concept to 2 Cor. 6:2. I am not endorsing the idea of corporate "personality" also held by Robinson and Johnson, which is distinct from corporate "representation."

mind to understand how the very context of the Isaiah 49 Servant could apply to himself without distorting the way in which he thought it may have been intended originally. Furthermore, in that he was continuing the mission of Jesus, the Servant, he could easily apply this Servant prophecy to himself.

Therefore, Paul views the Corinthians as receiving the promises of Isaiah 40–66 concerning the redemption of the Gentiles which was to occur together with that of Israel's salvation. And from this perspective Paul's use is consistent with that of the context of Isaiah. However, Paul's new development in comparison to Isaiah is to view Jewish and Gentile Christians together in the Corinthian church as authentic Israelites when they are redeemed. But what is the explanation for this development? First, the prophets, including Isaiah, do not primarily define Israel along ethnic, nationalistic lines but in a religious or theological manner, according to their covenant loyalty to Yahweh (e.g., Hos. 1:10–11; 2:23).[36] Paul may well be applying this prophetic view as a rationale legitimizing his application of Israel's promises to Gentiles, as he does in Romans 9:24–26 in citing Hosea 1:9–10 and 2:23. Therefore the church is the true Israel in so far as they are now receiving the prophetic promises intended for Israel in the Old Testament. Furthermore, this rationale may have been enforced by Paul's understanding that Christ summed up Israel in himself and hence represented true Israel in a legal, corporate fashion (e.g., Isa. 49:3, 6 and Luke 2:30–32; Acts 26:23). Those, whether Jew or Gentile, who identify with him by faith become considered part of genuine Israel, receiving the promises which he inherited as the ideal Israel (2 Cor. 1:20–21).[37]

Therefore, the "appeal to *be reconciled* to God, 5:20, is re-emphasized in 6:1–2, where . . . it is no less emphatically stated that the apostles are serving God in extending it."[38] And this re-emphasis of reconciliation in 6:1–2 is expressed through the citation of a prooftext from Isaiah 49

36. Cf. A. R. Hulst, *Wat betekent de naam "Israel" in het Oude Testament?* Miniaturen No. 1, Bijlage Maandblad Kerk en Israel, Jrg. 16, No. 10 (Den Haag: Boekencentrum, 1962); idem, "Der Name 'Israel' im Deuteronomium," *OTS* 9 (1951): 65–106.

37. I found that N. T. Wright has also argued that the church inherited Israel's promises through Christ their representative, who sums up true Israel in himself, and he views this idea as the key to understanding the argument and theology of Romans ("The Messiah and the People of God. A Study in Pauline Theology With Particular Reference to the Argument of the Epistle to the Romans" [unpub. 1980 D.Phil. Thesis, Oxford University]). He sees the same concept as crucial for understanding 2 Cor. 5:17–21, although his discussion is brief (ibid., 222). Even more important is Wright's subsequent article "Adam in Pauline Christology," *SBL 1983 Seminar Papers* (Chico, Calif: Scholars Press, 1983), 359–89, which demonstrates throughout Pauline literature that Christ was viewed as representative of the ideal Israel (in relation to his role as the ideal Adam).

38. Furnish, *II Corinthians*, 352; cf. likewise Findeis, *Versöhnung*, 224–27.

concerning a promise of restoration to Israel. Since 6:1–2 is a continuation of the initial appeal to the Corinthians to be reconciled in 5:20, it must be seen as part of that appeal. This appeal itself in 5:20–6:2 is based on the *reality* of reconciliation as a new creation and the fact that the apostles (e.g., Paul) have been appointed as the official ambassadors to proclaim this reality (5:17–19). The focus of the appeal in 5:20–6:2 is that the readership accept Paul as a legitimate divine legate in the extension of the appeal, since to reject the messenger of reconciliation is to reject the God who reconciles.[39] Consequently, foundational to the argument of 5:17–6:2 are Isaiah's promises of restoration.

2 Corinthians 6:3–10 should be seen as a continuation of the appeal begun in 5:20 in that it offers further support for the appeal. Whereas in 6:2 Paul employs an Old Testament prooftext to support his apostolic legitimacy, in 6:3–10 he offers the integrity of his lifestyle as additional support. 2 Corinthians 6:3–4a is the topical summary for verses 4b–10 which demonstrates that the following material is to be seen as evidence testifying to his contention that his conduct and motives are not a cause of discredit to the "ministry of reconciliation" (cf. τὴν διακονίαν τῆς καταλλαγῆς of 5:18 with ἡ διακονία in 6:3)[40] but "commend" the truth of it. Paul commends his ministry for its endurance through difficulties (vv. 4b–5), for its evidence of God's power working through it (vv. 6–7) and by contrasting the world's view of his ministry with that of genuine believers (vv. 8–10).[41] Therefore, there is nothing in Paul's conduct which can be a basis for rejecting his message.

Now in 6:11–13 Paul re-issues the appeal of 6:1–2 concerning reconciliation to himself as God's authoritative ambassador, although again the technical language of the καταλλάσσω word group is not employed.[42] Accordingly, Paul utilizes metaphors of reconciliation to summarize the tension between himself and his readers: Paul has made overtures to reconcile through his message, actions and attitude ("our mouth is open to you . . . our heart is opened wide," v. 11) but the readership has begun to shut Paul and his proclamation out of their heart ("you are cramped in your affections" [toward us], v. 12). In verse 13 Paul appeals to the readership to accept his reconciling overtures ("now in a like exchange . . . open wide [to us] also").

39. On this point cf. more generally Lane, "Covenant," 19.
40. The article ἡ in 6:2 if anaphoric referring back to 5:18.
41. See Furnish, *II Corinthians*, 349, on which this division of 2 Cor. 6:4–10 is based. Cf. Kleinknecht, *Der leidende Gerechtfertigte*, 263–68, who proposes that vv. 4–10 are best seen against the background of the Jewish tradition of the suffering of the righteous (e.g., Slavonic Enoch 66.6; Test. Jos. 1 ff.; DSS; Pss. 118; 139) as given its ultimate definition by the suffering of Jesus.
42. Furnish, *II Corinthians*, 367.

The Place of 6:14–7:1 in the Argument

Second Corinthians 7:2 provides a clear interpretative conclusion to the argument of 6:3–13 by continuing the closing appeal of 6:11–12; "make room for us [in your hearts]; we wronged no one, we corrupted no one, we took advantage of no one." But this conclusion presents the well-known problem of why 2 Corinthians 6:14–7:1 intervenes between 6:11–13 and 7:2. This segment seems to be an abrupt interruption between 6:11–13 and 7:2. The apparent interruption consists of an opening exhortation to separate from unbelievers (v. 14a), which is emphasized by five rhetorical questions (vv. 14b–16) and a statement declaring that believers are a temple of God (v. 16b). Then a catena of Old Testament quotes is adduced to demonstrate the affirmation concerning the temple of God (vv. 16c–18). The problem is that the appeals of verses 14–18 do not appear to fit into the logical thought flow of the appeals in 6:11–13 and 7:2. Some commentators contend that whereas the main theme of the epistle and the immediate context is the Corinthians' relationship to Paul's apostleship, the apparent thrust of 6:14–7:1 is the relationship of the Corinthians to unbelievers.[43] The history of the exegesis of this text presents diverse proposals which attempt to explain the awkward presence of 6:14–7:1.

There is consensus among the majority of commentators that 6:14–18 is logically disruptive. Some argue that it is a segment from another Pauline letter, interpolated here when Paul's correspondence was finally edited for circulation. Others contend that 6:14–7:1 is an insertion of a non-Pauline or anti-Pauline source. Still others affirm that Paul is adapting testimonia already composed in a Jewish or Christian environment. In addition to the contextual problem, many doubt the literary integrity of this pericope for the following reasons: its unique theological emphasis on separation from the world, the number of *hapax legomena*, the unique introductory formula introducing the Old Testament citations, the informal manner in which these citations are linked and the thematic parallels with Qumran. A number of recent commentators view the text as from Paul's own hand and logically related to the context.[44] The arguments against integrity have been given viable responses by these recent commentators, but nevertheless some still view these arguments as having a cumulative force.

It does not serve our purposes to present a thorough *Forschungsgeschichte* of this debate, since this already has been done by others,[45]

---

43. Cf. ibid., 378–9.
44. Ibid., 368.
45. See Furnish, *II Corinthians*, 368–83, for an excellent survey of the recent history of interpretation, especially focusing on alternative viewpoints.

but to propose a new solution to the problem which argues for Pauline authenticity and claims that 6:14–18 functions as an essential logical link in the contextual argument. First, the assertion of some commentators that 6:14–18 concerns the relationship of believers with unbelievers, whereas the preceding context deals with the Christian Corinthians' relationship with Paul is a false dichotomy, since the latter may involve the former, especially in the light of such texts as 2 Corinthians 13:5. Accordingly, the theme of 5:16–6:13 and 6:14–18 is an exhortation to genuine believers to be reconciled by not being influenced by the worldly thinking of unbelievers who present themselves in the guise of professing believers.

Secondly, R. P. Martin's proposal is the most cogent among recent authors holding the position of Pauline authenticity and further amplifies our above remarks. He sees 6:14–7:2 as a reinforcement of the teaching on reconciliation begun in 5:14–21 and continued in 6:1 through 6:13.[46] It is a repeated appeal to be reconciled but now in the form of a warning "lest the Corinthians should range themselves with the world of unbelievers that is still hostile and unreconciled; and by continuing to disbelieve his [Paul's] integrity and his Gospel the Corinthians would fail to heed the call, Be reconciled to God (5:20). Hence the opening line compares them to unbelievers . . . to stab them awake to their condition and peril if they refuse to join him."[47] In particular, this pericope expresses Paul's conviction that the "temple of the living God" in Corinth had not broken all ties with the world and consequently was impure. The rejection of Paul as God's true apostle of reconciliation by some of the Corinthians was an expression of such worldly impurity and demonstrated that they had begun to evaluate in the same manner as the unbelieving world (cf. 5:16). Insofar as some among the readership were identifying with an unbelieving world which needed reconciliation, they also needed reconciliation both to Paul and the God represented by Paul. Therefore, in 2 Corinthians 6:14–7:2 "Paul enforces a single point: the call to reconciliation involves a whole-hearted commitment and pledge of loyalty to him and to his proclamation as the 'divine apostle.'"[48]

Martin's explanation is a viable attempt to tie in 6:14–7:1 with the preceding context and with 7:2. Our proposal is that 6:14–7:1 is an *intended* interruption of Paul's final appeal begun in 6:11–13 and repeats

---

46. See likewise Lane, "Covenant," 19–20, 24–25. The literary integrity of this section has most recently been argued on a different thematic basis by D. Patte, "A Structural Exegesis of 2 Corinthians 2:14–7:4 with Special Attention on 2:14–3:6 and 6:11–7:4," *SBL 1987 Seminar Papers* (Atlanta: Scholars Press, 1987), 40–49.

47. Martin, *2 Corinthians*, 194.

48. Ibid., 211.

the initial appeal of 5:20–6:2, a view which is also supported by J. Lambrecht and M. Thrall.[49] Lambrecht views 7:2–4 as an expression of Paul's self-conscious awareness that he has digressed in 6:14–18.[50] Thrall argues that 6:3–13 is a digression which interrupts the appeal of 6:2 and that this appeal is picked up again in 6:14–7:1, since the latter text contains the kind of specific injunctions one would expect to follow such an appeal.[51] This is viable although the appeal likely is picked up again even earlier in verses 11–13.[52]

These recent proposals, though probably essentially correct, emphasize mainly the negative aspect of the exhortations to be reconciled in 6:14–7:1 (cf. 6:14–16a, 17a), seeing the primary thrust to be a call to separate from unbelievers and their way of thinking. Although this is partially true, it does not account sufficiently for the presence of the Old Testament citations in 6:16c–18 and the positive summary of these texts in 7:1 as inherited "promises" upon which the readership is commanded to act, if indeed, they really possess them (cf. 2 Cor. 13:5).[53]

The inability of commentators to account for how verses 16–18 fit into the logical flow of the epistle may be due to the lack of any serious attempt to study the Old Testament quotes in their original contexts. *Almost without exception, the six generally agreed upon Old Testament references refer in their respective contexts to God's promise to restore exiled Israel to their land.* This observation is crucial in tracing Paul's argument, since it allows us to view verses 16–18 as a continuation of the restoration promises to Israel quoted by Paul in 6:2 and even earlier in 5:17, which were utilized as prooftexts to support Paul's appeal for the Corinthians to be reconciled. This analysis would lend further support to Thrall's argument that 6:3–13 is a parenthetical section interrupting the initial appeal of 6:1–2, which is then picked up again in 6:14–7:1, although we have qualified this by seeing it resumed beginning in 6:11–

---

49. Intriguingly, Clemens Alexandrinus, *Stromata* 3.8.62.1–2.6 quotes 2 Cor. 5:17 and then immediately cites the exhortations of 6:14–16a, 7:1, while omitting the OT references.

50. J. Lambrecht, "The Fragment 2 Cor. vi 14–vii 1. A Plea for its Authenticity," in *Miscellanea Neotestamentica*, 2, eds. T. Baarda, A. F. J. Klijn, and W. C. van Unnik, *Nov T Supp*. 48 (Leiden: Brill, 1978), 143–61.

51. Thrall, "The Problem of II Cor. vi.14–vii.1 in Some Recent Discussion," *NTS* 24 (1978): 144.

52. See J. Murphy-O'Connor, "Relating 2 Corinthians 6:14–7:1 to Its Context," *NTS* 33 (1987): 273.

53. Cf. Lane, "Covenant," 22–25, who does see the "promises" of 7:1 positively summarizing the OT quotes in 6:16–18 but referring only generally to blessings promised by God to Israelites who submit to the demands of the covenant. He never explains what blessings are in mind. He also argues that 6:14–7:1 is not an interpolation because it concerns the OT covenant motif as does also the preceding and following context. However, there is no substantial study of the OT citations nor any discussion of how they could relate to the OT theme of restoration or Paul's development of reconciliation in the context.

13 and continued in 6:14–7:1. Furthermore, the observation that verses 16–18 are Old Testament promises of Israel's restoration best explains why Paul summarizes them in 7:1 positively—not negatively—as "promises" which the Corinthian church, the true Israel, now possesses. Indeed, Paul can only issue negative imperatives not to identify with the unbelieving world on the positive basis that the readers are already possessors of these Old Testament restoration promises. In fact, the negative imperatives themselves assume a context of peaceful restoration. That is, the series of words μετοχή, κοινωνία, συμφώνησις, μερίς and συγκατάθεσις in 6:14–16 refer to a condition of peaceful existence which is incompatible with and contrasted to those worldly elements which cause sinful alienation (which are expanded upon in 12:20b).[54]

Verse 16b provides the basis (γάρ) for the antithetical warning of verse 16a: because the church is the temple of God, it should not live in peaceful coexistence with idolators and their idols. And verses 16a–b together are a metaphorical summary of the preceding antitheses. That is, the positive elements of the antitheses referring to a condition of peace are now described in Old Testament terms as conditions characteristic of God being present with his people in his temple. Indeed, the church is his temple because he is present in it, as the Old Testament restoration quotes in verse 16c establish. On the basis of the quotes in verse 16c, the Old Testament references in verse 17 reissue another imperative to separate from the ungodly. And the allusions in verse 18 restate the idea of God's presence among his people as a promise which will be fulfilled (or continue fulfillment) if they heed the previous exhortations.

Although there is general consensus about what precise Old Testament texts verses 16c–18 are based on, a comparison of some of the texts and brief discussion of the contexts of each reference is necessary in order to present a clear basis for the conclusions we reached above.

The first Old Testament reference is in verse 16b: "I shall dwell among them and I shall walk [among them], and I shall be their God and they shall be my people." There is apparent unanimous agreement that this text is a conflation of Leviticus 26:11–12 and Ezekiel 37:27. Some suggest that Leviticus is the primary text and its second person uses are changed to third persons under the influence of Ezekiel. But why would these two texts be combined, whether by Paul or an earlier tradition? The answer lies in recognizing, not only the obviously common wording, but also that the common theme of both is the restoration of Israel. Ezekiel 37:27 is clearly a divine promise that God will restore Israel from its alienated condition to its land and to a relationship of peace in-

---

54. This idea is based on a suggestion made to me by Otto Betz in a personal communication.

stead of hostility with himself (cf. 37:11–14; 37:21–23, 25–26). This restoration is also termed a "cleansing" and "sanctification" (Ezek. 37:23, 28; cf. 2 Cor. 6:17 and 7:1). At first glance Leviticus 26:11–12 does not appear to be concerned with Israel's restoration from exile but is a promise that God will grant them "peace" in their land if they continue to be faithful to his covenant. However, Leviticus 26:14–39 explains that the Israelites will be exiled from their land and experience divine "hostility" if they break the covenant (cf. esp. 26:15, 17, 21, 24, 28). But if they repent while in exile, God promises to remember his covenant and to restore them to the land (26:40–45), so that the nation again would enjoy a peaceful relationship with God in its land, as initially explained in 26:11–12. The connection with Ezekiel 37 then becomes obvious.

Second Corinthians 6:17a forms the next link in the series of quotations adduced: "Therefore, come out from their midst and be separate, says the Lord, and do not touch the unclean." Isaiah 52:11 is generally acknowledged as the undoubted basis for this statement, although it appears in paraphrastic form. While some have stressed that this quote is employed to express the idea of purification from cultic uncleanness, the primary sense in the context of Isaiah 52:1–12 is that of God's promise to restore Israel from its exile to "peace" in the land. And 52:11 is an exhortation for the nation to participate in this promise when it begins fulfillment and not to remain in Babylon, since this would demonstrate a lack of participation in the promise and an identity with the unbelieving world. Therefore, the presence of the Isaiah 52:11 reference in 2 Corinthians 6:17a is best explained because of its restoration theme, which continues to develop the same idea in the Leviticus and Ezekiel quotes.

The Isaiah 52:11 allusion is appended with the phrase κἀγὼ εἰσδέξομαι ὑμᾶς (v. 17b), which is from Ezekiel 20:34 (καὶ εἰσδέξομαι ὑμᾶς), although almost identical verbatim parallels from that context also may be included (cf. 20:41, καὶ εἰσδέχεσθαι ὑμᾶς, and 11:17, καὶ εἰσδέξομαι αὐτούς). In each of the Ezekiel contexts the quoted expression is part of the larger identical phrase, "I will gather you from the nations *and take you out* of the countries in which you have been scattered." That this phrase in 2 Corinthians 6:17b is, in fact, based on these Ezekiel texts and not a mere interpretative gloss on Isaiah 52 is borne out from the observation that all three contexts in Ezekiel are restoration promises to exiled Israel and the cited allusion a precise prophecy of God's restoration of the nation to their land. The rationale for including the Ezekiel wording again would be because its primary meaning is the same as the previous Old Testament allusions in verses 16b–17a.

Verse 18 concludes the series of quotes with another conflated reference. All agree that 2 Samuel 7:14 is the primary basis for the statement. This text, like Leviticus 26:11–12 above, does not seem on the surface to fit into the restoration theme of the previous Old Testament allusions. It is a promise to a descendant of David that God "will be a father to him and he will be a son" and his throne and kingdom would "be established forever" (2 Sam. 7:12, 16). However, included in the promise is that God in the future "will also appoint a place for . . . Israel and will plant them that they may live in their own place and not be disturbed again, nor will the wicked afflict them any more as formerly . . . and I will give you rest from all your enemies" (2 Sam. 7:10–11). Although the context has no explicit mention of exile, it is easy to see how this promise could easily—even legitimately—be viewed in the context of later Old Testament prophets as associated with the prophecies about restoration to the land from exile (e.g., Isa. 54:14; 57:13; 60:18; 61:7). In addition, part of the promise involves the future Davidic king building a temple for God to dwell in forever (2 Sam. 7:2, 5–7, 13), which is also a part of the restoration promise in Leviticus 26:11–12ff. and Ezekiel 37:26–28, and is also found emphasized in 2 Corinthians 6:16a. Also striking is the observation that the promise of restoration in Ezekiel 37 and 2 Samuel 7 included an oath that a Davidic king would reign over Israel's restored "kingdom" forever (Ezek. 37:22–25; cf. 2 Sam. 7:12–16). The 2 Samuel text likely was linked with the preceding Old Testament passages in 2 Corinthians 6:16–17 on the basis of the thematic associations. As in 6:2, the concept of corporate representation probably facilitated the shift of application from an original promise to an individual (Solomon) to a promise for the church.[55]

Many commentators seem persuaded that the influence of Isaiah 43:6 explains the change from the singular υἱός of 2 Samuel 7:14 to a plural, as well as the addition of θυγάτηρ. This Isaiah text is yet another promise of Israel's restoration to its land: "Bring my sons from afar, and my daughters from the end of the earth" (cf. 43:3–7). But what commentators formerly have failed to observe is that Isaiah 49:22 and 60:4 together with Isaiah 43:6 were probably fused together in Paul's mind with the 2 Samuel wording, since these two former texts also are promises that Israel's "sons" (υἱούς) and "daughters" (θυγατέρας) will be restored from exile (49:22, "and they will bring your sons in their bosom, and your daughters will be carried on their shoulders" [cf. 49:5–23]; 60:4, "your sons will come from afar, and your daughters will be carried on arms" [cf. 60:1–14]).[56]

55. So Ellis, *Prophecy and Hermeneutic*, 170–71. In the same manner the 2 Sam. 7 promise is applied to the Messiah in Heb. 1:5.
56. Some include Hos. 1:10 as part of the OT background which is possible but uncertain. However, its context also concerns restoration from exile.

2 Corinthians 7:1 summarizes (οὖν) the Old Testament quotes in 6:16b–18 as "promises"—not as negative warnings. In the light of the contexts of these Old Testament passages, the idea of "Israel's restoration promises" must be in mind. And it is with the presupposition that the readership together with Paul has begun to partake of the fulfillment of these promises (1:20–21) that he exhorts them in 7:1b to join with him in persevering and behaving in a manner consistent with such promises: *"let us cleanse ourselves*[57] from all defilement of flesh and spirit, perfecting holiness in the fear of God." This is an imperative which, although not verbatim, is based on the Isaiah 52:11 restoration quote of 6:17a.[58] The Corinthian church is being seen as beginning to participate in Israel's prophesied restoration and they are now exhorted to continue in this by not identifying with the unbelieving world.

The precise manner in which they are to separate from the world is by not evaluating Paul's apostleship according to the unbelieving standards of the world, as the preceding context indicates. Paul probably did not consider the "unbelieving world" which he refers to in 6:14–15 to be that which lay only outside the confines of the church, but viewed it as a force within the church (2 Cor. 13:5), against whose influence believers needed to be on guard. Far from being an interruption, 6:14–7:2 also anticipates the main opposition to be elaborated upon in chapters 10–13. A certain type of Jewish-Christian opponents is in the process of infiltrating the readership and doing what the Judaizers did in Galatia by opposing Paul's authority and preaching another type of Jesus than Paul preached (so 11:1–4, 13–15, 20–23; Gal. 1:6–8). They are trying to win the congregation to their teaching while Paul is absent. 2 Corinthians 6:14–7:2 then shows that the situation is so serious that their very salvation is at stake. Those who are influenced to resist Paul's authority are also resisting his gospel, and are thereby bringing into question their very standing as part of God's true people (cf. 13:5). This section of chapter 6 also anticipates the continuing problem of worldly behavior among some in the congregation (12:20–21), which is probably related in part to the false teachers' influence but not necessarily exhaustively so. Continued participation in the sins noted in 12:20–21 would also mean rejection of the apostle's authority, since he had already commanded the Corinthians in the past to cease such behavior.

---

57. Although it is possible that the first person plural is purely rhetorical and does not include Paul.

58. See Furnish, *II Corinthians*, 368, who sees the phrase "perfecting holiness" in 7:1 as a summary of the appeals of 6:14a and of the Isa. 52:11 quote in 6:17. Targ. Isa. 53:5 may also be relevant as background here: there it is said that the Servant "shall build the sanctuary that was polluted because of our transgressions" and that "by his teaching shall his peace be multiplied upon us."

Therefore, the ἄπιστοι of 2 Corinthians 6:14 is to be understood generally as emphasizing the worldly, *unbelieving standards* of evaluating Paul's authority used by the false apostles and those under their influence, as well as by some in the readership who were not repenting of sins of which Paul had earlier convicted them.[59] This warning about evaluating Paul's apostleship in such a worldly manner is likely a development of the same thought from 5:16 (cf. κατὰ σάρκα).

This contextual analysis is confirmed by 7:2 which further explains that the way the readership is to "cleanse themselves" (7:1) is by accepting Paul as God's apostle ("making room" for him)—being "reconciled" to Paul and ultimately to God. In fact 7:1ff. is a conclusion of a section stretching back to 5:17. The section of 6:16b–7:19 together with 5:17–19 and 6:2 are all based on Old Testament prophetic hopes of Israel's restoration and serve as the foundation for the imperatival segments of 5:20, 6:1, 6:13–16a, and 7:1b–2. Paul's statements in 7:3–4, 7 express his confidence that since the readership has begun to participate in these promises, they will respond positively to his exhortation to continue to grow in such promises.

We may speculate further, as Gordon Fee has argued, that the more precise way in which Paul wanted the readership to separate from the unbelieving world was not to participate with unbelievers at meals in an idol's temple.[60] In this regard, he sees 2 Corinthians 6:14–7:1 as in its original context and as picking up the same prohibition first given in 1 Corinthians 8–10. The reason that this exhortation reoccurs here is that although some of the Corinthians had heeded his exhortation, *some were still despising his authority by not submitting to this prohibition.* Fee adduces some persuasive parallels between the relevant segment in 1 Corinthians and the pairs of contrasts in 2 Corinthians 6:14–16a and proposes that the Old Testament references in verses 16b–18 function (1) to support the claim that the Corinthian believers are a temple of God (developing 1 Cor. 3:16–17) (2) "and because of that, to reinforce the church's absolute dissociation from idolatry."[61] However, although this is how the catena of quotes seems to function, Fee does not analyze the citations in their Old Testament context in order to inquire about why these particular references are used instead of others. He makes only general statements about the idolatry background of the wilderness generation and of Isaiah 52:11.

---

59. The same general meaning is to be attached to the synonyms for ἄπιστοι in 6:14b–15.

60. G. D. Fee, "II Corinthians VI. 14–VII. 7 and Food Offered to Idols," *NTS* 23 (1977): 140–61.

61. Ibid., 159.

Nevertheless, when such inquiry is made one finds that not only are these Old Testament citations associated with hopes of restoration and God dwelling among them in a temple (cf. Ezek. 37:26–28; 20:40; Lev. 26:11; 2 Sam. 7:2–7, 12–13; cf. Ps. 117[118]:17–18, 22–23, 26–27; cf. Isa. 52:11d) but also with prohibitions concerning idolatry, judgments on idolaters and promises to deliver Israel from idolatry when they are restored (Ezek. 11:18, 21; 20:28–32, 39; 37:23; Lev. 26:1, 30; 2 Sam. 7:23; and probably Isa. 52:11 is to be understood in this general manner). This observation adds more force to Fee's contention, although he himself admits that "the one real difficulty with this interpretation is that 'food offered to idols' is not specifically mentioned either in this passage or its immediate context."[62]

But even if Fee is not correct, the repeated temple and idolatry motifs in these Old Testament texts enhance their common restoration theme. The Corinthians are those among whom God's eschatological temple presence has come to dwell in fulfillment of the prophetic hopes of restoration, so that the mention of the temple and idolatry themes are not abrupt but arise naturally in conjunction with discussion of restoration. If God's presence really dwells among them as his temple, then they will respond and become reconciled with Paul who represents God's authoritative presence in word and Spirit. The contrasts would become figurative, stressing separation from unbelieving standards of evaluation, especially with respect to Paul (as already explained above). Indeed, the temple idea may also arise in conjunction with the new creation idea, since in Isaiah 56–66 this was part of the restoration–new creation complex of ideas.[63]

Our analysis of 6:16b–7:2 provides additional confirmation that Paul understands reconciliation in Christ to be the inaugurated fulfillment of the Old Testament prophecies of Israel's restoration from exile. While Paul would perhaps allow that this prophecy began fulfillment with the nation's return from Babylon, the escalated fulfillment occurred at Christ's death and resurrection. This is why the reference to Christ's death and resurrection in 5:14–15 introduces the segment on reconciliation. Christ suffered the extreme exile of death and was re-

---

62. Ibid., 161.
63. The Epistle of Barnabas 6:13 refers to Christ's redemption of believers (cf. 6:1–12) as a "second creation" and explains this as a typological fulfillment of Israel entering into the land after the first exodus (cf. Exod. 33:3), as well as a fulfillment of the prophecy of Israel's restoration to the land in Ezek. 11:19 and 36:26 (Ep. Barn. 6.13–14), two OT contexts cited in 2 Cor. 6:16–17 (see supra). Furthermore, the writer then explains that the Ezek. 36:26 prophecy has also been fulfilled by believers becoming a "holy temple" (ναὸς ἅγιος) and "habitation" (κατοικητήριον) for God "to dwell among us" (cf. Ep. Barn. 6.14–15; 2 Cor. 6:16).

stored to fellowship with God through the resurrection. Those who believe in Jesus become identified corporately with his death and resurrection and so partake of his exile and reconciliation. In reality, true Israel was summed up in the individual Christ so that he alone was the ultimate fulfillment of the nation's restoration promises. This is probably why Paul says in 2 Corinthians 1:20 that "the promises of God in him . . . are yes." God had already begun to "establish" the readership together *with* Paul in these restoration promises in Christ (1:21) and this was the basis for Paul's appeal in 2 Corinthians 5:14–7:3 that the readership continue to partake in such promises by being reconciled to Paul as God's official spokesman.[64]

This analysis of Old Testament usage in 2 Corinthians 5:17–7:1 may illuminate the role of other Old Testament allusions in the same context which have formerly been recognized but whose presence has not been adequately explained. For example, Isaiah 49:13 (θεὸς . . . τοὺς ταπεινοὺς τοῦ λαοῦ αὐτοῦ παρεκάλεσεν) is generally recognized as an allusion in 2 Corinthians 7:6 (ὁ παρακαλῶν τοὺς ταπεινοὺς παρεκάλεσεν ἡμᾶς ὁ θεός). Verse 6 together with verse 7 function to emphasize further the previous expression of Paul's confidence in his readers' ability to respond to his encouragement to be reconciled (vv. 3–4), since he sees in them signs that they are already in the process of being reconciled to him. Paul draws in the Isaiah allusion in order to explain that God has "comforted" him through this observation. In the Old Testament context Isaiah 49:13 is part of the same pericope introduced by 49:8, also quoted in 6:2, which concerns the topic of Israel's future restoration. 49:13 is an exclamation of joy because the restoration is none other than the coming time when God will comfort his people. Indeed, the restoration is none other than the coming time when God will comfort his people. Indeed, the restoration is divine comfort. Likewise, the Corinthians' beginning signs of reconciliation with Paul (vv. 6–7) provide him with joyous comfort that they together with him really are God's latter day Israel who are fulfilling the restoration promises.

Psalm 118[119]:32 (ἐπλάτυνας τὴν καρδίαν μου) is often adduced as lying behind 2 Cor. 6:11b (ἡ καρδία ἡμῶν πεπλάτυνται), although recently Deuteronomy 11:16 (μὴ πλατυνθῇ ἡ καρδία σου) has been proposed.[65] However, no one has discussed the possibility that Isaiah 60:5 may be in mind (ורחב לבבך), which is almost identical *in Hebrew* to the wording of Psalm 119 (תרחיב לבי). The Isaiah text refers to those living in Israel in the end-times "making wide their heart" and "rejoicing" be-

---

64. See supra, n. 1 p. 565.
65. See Thrall, "Problem of II Cor. vi.14–vii.1," 146, and especially Murphy-O'Connor, "Relating 2 Corinthians," 273–75.

cause the nations will stream to Israel (vv. 3–10), bringing back the exiled nation's "sons" and "daughters" (vv. 4, 9). Consequently, Isaiah 60:5 can be construed as a response whereby those living in the land at the time of the restoration will "open wide their hearts" to accept repentant Gentiles, as well as their returning Israelite "sons" and "daughters," referred to in Isaiah 60:4, a text also alluded to in 2 Corinthians 6:18. The phrase in Isaiah 60:5 may merely be a general figurative expression for Israel's joyous attitude in response to the Israelites returning from the dispersion along with the incoming Gentiles. Against the background of our study so far, Isaiah 60:5 should be seen as the most probable Old Testament text lying behind 2 Corinthians 6:11b. Regardless of the precise nuance of the figurative phrase in Isaiah 60:5, Paul's point in the allusion would be to exhort the readership to "open wide their hearts"—be reconciled—to him (6:13) as he has to them (6:11), since this is the accepting or joyful attitude prophesied to be expressed by those who are part of the eschatological community sharing in Israel's restoration promises.

If this conclusion about Isaiah 60:5 is correct, we may speculate that Paul's statement concerning the readership becoming "cramped" (στενοχωρεῖσθε, 2x), in their hearts toward him could likewise be based on Isaiah 49:19–20, where so many Israelites are seen as being restored to the land that they are "cramped" (στενοχωρήσει, στενός) for space. Since in 2 Corinthians 6:18 both Isaiah 60:4 and 49:22 are referred to, Paul may be making an ironic interpretative pun to the effect that the blessing of restoration-reconciliation should lead the readership not to "cramping" Paul out of their hearts but to "widening their heart" to let him in. Such an associative jump might not be too difficult for Paul to make since the common phraseology and theme of Isaiah 60:4 and 49:22 would have facilitated the link. Our speculation should not be viewed with too much skepticism since others have observed similar kinds of associative links between Old Testament texts elsewhere in 2 Corinthians.[66]

Another Old Testament reference often cited but whose significance is just as often not discussed is Psalm 117[118]:17–18 in 2 Corinthians 6:9 ("as dying yet behold, we live; as punished yet not put to death"). Although the precise historical occasion of the psalm is unclear, there is general acknowledgment that it reflects the cultic ex-

---

66. Such kinds of associative links where the sense is altered have been illustrated elsewhere in 2 Corinthians by J. A. Fitzmyer, "Glory Reflected on the Face of Christ (2 Cor. 3:7–4:6) and a Palestinian Jewish Motif," *TS* 42 (1981): 633–39. Indeed, Thrall and Murphy-O'Connor make a proposal virtually identical to ours for the use of Deut. 11:16 in 2 Cor. 6:11b (cf. supra, n. 2 p. 576).

perience of Israel and that its theme concerns the figure of a king who corporately represents his people undergoing affliction by the nations.[67] In spite of affliction Israel was not annihilated (vv. 10–13) because God's strength was with them (vv. 14–18). While Israel was "rejected" by the nations, God had chosen them to be his people and would preserve them as "the head cornerstone" to fulfill his purposes (v. 22). Verses 17–18 emphasize that Israel would "not die" as a result of their affliction "but live"; God has "severely disciplined" the nation but had "not given her up to death." It is possible that this portion of the psalm has the exile and subsequent restoration in mind. Regardless of whether or not this can be demonstrated, it is easy to see how Paul could have deduced such an idea and woven this reference into his argument. If so, he was generally applying the reference to himself in analogical fashion to show that just as Israel persevered through the suffering of exile until they began to be restored, so Paul's perseverance in suffering demonstrated that he was also a true Israelite and a genuine partaker of restoration blessings. The readership should take stock of this and regard him accordingly.

The Use of "Reconciliation" Language in Ephesians

Our overall conclusions may be corroborated by Ephesians 2:13–17, where in verses 13 and 17 the restoration promise of Isaiah 57:19 is quoted to explain the conception of "reconciliation" found in verse 16. In the original context "those far off" refers to the restoration of the Israelite exiles in captivity and "those near" to the people still living in the land who would be reconciled with the returning exiles. The former are now identified as believing Gentiles and the latter as ethnic Israelite believers in general. As in 2 Corinthians 5–7, so here the church is understood to be the fulfillment of Isaiah's restoration promises. This reconciliation of Jew and Gentile is also referred to as "creating the two in one new man," which is a continuation of the creation theme begun in Ephesians 2:10 ("we are His workmanship [ποίημα] created in Christ Jesus"). Indeed, this new "creation" has come about through Christ's death and, especially, resurrection (cf. Eph. 1:20–23; 2:5–6), as is also clear in 2 Corinthians 5:14–17. That this is the case is evident from the likelihood that ἐσμεν ποίημα κτισθέντες ἐν Χριστῷ (v. 10) is parallel to τοὺς δύο κτίσῃ ἐν αὐτῷ εἰς ἕνα καινὸν ἄνθρωπον (v. 15b), so that the

---

67. E.g., see A. A. Anderson, *The Psalms*, vol. 2 (New Century Bible; London: Marshall, Morgan and Scott, 1972), 792–802; A. Weiser, *The Psalms* (Philadelphia: Westminster, 1962), 725–27; A. R. Johnson, *Sacral Kingship in Ancient Israel* (University of Wales, 1967), 2–4, 126.

"new man" is none other than the resurrected Christ. That the concepts of new "creation" in verse 15b, "reconciliation" in verse 16 and the Old Testament promise of restoration in verses 17–18 are virtually synonymous in Ephesians 2 is indicated by their literary parallelism: 1) all three speak of the "two" (Jew and Gentile) existing in one organism ("one new Man," "one body," "one Spirit"); 2) each refers to the primary activity resulting in "peace" or the dissolving of enmity; 3) they all appear to be three purpose clauses dependent on the ἵνα of verse 15b, even though the introductory verb in verse 17 is an indicative and the previous two are subjunctives. The reason for the difference in mood may well lie in the author's intention to employ the Isaiah 57:19 citation in verses 17–18 both as a parallel with verse 15b and verse 16 and as a concluding parallel with the same Isaiah 57:19 allusion in verse 14, thus forming an inclusio.

Another point of similarity between Ephesians 2 and 2 Corinthians 5–7 is that the emphasis of reconciliation is upon both the restoration of alienated human relationships and the reconciliation of alienated people to God.

The same combination of reconciliation language with Old Testament restoration references and the idea of the new creation is probably also present in the contexts of Romans 5:1–6:11, 11:11–31 and Colossians 1:15–22, but the limits of the present article preclude exegetical discussion of these passages.[68]

Conclusion

In the light of 2 Corinthians 5–7, and Ephesians 2, the idea of reconciliation in these passages is to be understood as the beginning of fulfillment of the Old Testament promises of Israel's restoration. Such a perspective on the former passage aids in perceiving the segment of 2 Corinthians 5:14–7:7 as a literary unity. Hence, Paul views Christ's death and resurrection to be the basis of mankind's reconciliation in inaugurated fulfillment of the prophetic promises concerning restoration and the new creation. These promises have begun fulfillment but they have not been consummated. By faith people identify with and partake of the ultimate exile of death in Christ and his resurrection as the beginning of the new creation leading to reconciliation and peace with God. Through Christ's redemptive actions he represented the nation in himself and so began to fulfil the Old Testament's hopes for the nation. And, as we have seen, his Old Testament background is utilized to en-

---

68. I am presently writing a monograph in which these texts together with 2 Corinthians 5–7 and Ephesians 2 will receive fuller discussion.

force Paul's argument that the readership needs to be restored or reconciled to him as God's authoritative representative, which amounts to a reconciliation to God himself.[69]

But what could have motivated Paul to conceive of "reconciliation" through Christ's death and resurrection as the realization of the prophetic hopes of restoration, especially those from Isaiah 40–66? Such questions can be difficult because they often necessitate speculation about an author's psychology. However, our overall analysis will become more convincing if a cogent answer can be given to this question. In Acts 26:14–18 the author of Luke–Acts narrates Paul's account before Agrippa of the commission which the risen Christ gave to him on the Damascus road. In 26:18 there is common acknowledgement that clear reference is made to Isaiah 42:6–7, 16 in explaining the essence of Paul's commission: "to open their eyes so that they may turn from darkness unto light and from the dominion of Satan to God" (cf. Isa. 42:6–7:16: "I have given you . . . unto a light of the nations, to open blind eyes, to bring the bound and them that sit in darkness out of bonds and the prisonhouse" [vv. 6–7]; "I will bring the blind . . . I will make darkness into light for them" [v. 16]). This Isaiah text which speaks of the commission Yahweh gave to the Servant to restore exiled Israel is now applied by the risen Christ to Paul's apostolic commission. Consequently, if this part of the Acts narrative represents early Pauline tradition, it is plausible to suggest that this commission from Christ provided the foundation and spark for the development of Paul's subsequent understanding and explanation of reconciliation as the fulfillment of Isaiah's and the Old Testament's restoration promises. It likewise also accounts best for Paul's self-identification with the Isaianic Servant in 2 Corinthians 6:2.[70]

In this connection, the fact that many scholars have seen 2 Corinthians 5:16 as an allusion to Paul's Damascus road experience is not a coincidence. Likewise, many commentators have seen the same

---

69. In 2 Cor. 5–7 Paul is developing on the surface level who he is, what he is teaching and what the readers are to gain or lose from this. But Paul's thoughts here are not drawn exclusively from the situation in Corinth but from what may be considered the deeper level of the Isaianic background. Some readers (especially Jewish Christians) may have quickly discerned this, while others might have thought on this deeper level only through further reflection on the epistle, especially after positively responding to the "surface" message.

70. In 26:23 Christ is said "to proclaim light both to the people and to the Gentiles," which is most likely a reference to the similar phrases in Isa. 42:6; 49:6; 60:3 (so I. H. Marshall, *The Acts of the Apostles* [Tyndale New Testament Commentaries; Leicester: Inter-Varsity, 1980], 398; F. F. Bruce, *The Book of the Acts* [The New International Commentary on the New Testament; Grand Rapids: Eerdmans, 1954], 494). As suggested for 2 Cor. 6:2, this close contextual association of Isaiah Servant allusions in Acts 26 which are applied to Paul and Christ may betray an idea of corporate representation or solidarity.

allusion in 2 Corinthians 4:4–6, so that 5:16 may continue what was begun in chapter 4.[71] This may be confirmed further by noticing the common use of creation imagery in the midst of both the purported allusions, which points to Paul's understanding of his initial encounter with Christ as an event which was part of an inaugurated new creation (which we have argued is itself inspired by the associations of restoration with a new creation in Isaiah 40–66). Therefore, his discussion of reconciliation as fulfilling the Old Testament promises of restoration in 5:18–7:1ff. develops naturally out of this reflection upon the Damascus christophany together, no doubt, with the early Christian tradition about Jesus. In like manner, argument about reconciliation in connection with new creation and the Old Testament restoration hope in Ephesians 2:13–17 also may come to mind because in the immediately following context there is a recollection of the Damascus experience (see Eph. 3:2–11).[72]

71. For most recent discussion of these allusions see Kim, *Origin of Paul's Gospel*, 5–20, where also a survey of other commentators seeing the same allusions is found. It is also noteworthy to observe the striking parallel phraseology between 2 Cor. 4:4, 6 and Acts 26:18.

72. Cf. likewise Col. 1:23, 25, although there is no explicit reference to OT restoration texts.

14

Luke and Isaiah

David Seccombe

From David Seccombe, "Luke and Isaiah," *New Testament Studies* 27 (1981): 252–59. Reprinted with the permission of Cambridge University Press.

In the course of an inquiry into the origins of Luke's understanding of the poor I was forced to ask the question how far Luke might have been influenced not only by certain *texts* in Isaiah but also by wider *themes*. In answer to this question one is often referred to C. H. Dodd's *According to the Scriptures*, where he concluded that when New Testament authors quoted small Old Testament texts they often did so with knowledge of larger passages or collections of passages from which the text was drawn. This principle has become a commonplace and is frequently used illegitimately to find ideas in the New Testament which are not otherwise discernible.[1] The recent study of B. Lindars ("The Place of the Old Testament in the Formation of New Testament Theology: Prolegomena," *N.T.S.* 23 (1977): 59–66) argues that New Testament writers had no interest in the meaning of the Old Testament for its own sake, but simply quarried texts to support and illustrate a preexisting New Testament theology. Both these views need to be kept in mind. It may be that each is correct in different places. What is needed is a closer study of the practice of individual authors and their use of different parts of the Old Testament. Only then will it be possible to give any confident judgment of how much an New Testament author may

---

1. An example in connection with the present study: L. C. Crockett (*The Old Testament in the Gospel of Luke* (Brown Univ. Ph.D., 1966), 2: 277ff.) thinks the dominant idea in Luke's quotation of Isa. 61:1f. (Luke 4:18–19) is the messianic banquet (from Isa. 61:6 and elsewhere) which is not even mentioned.

have carried in the way of related ideas, theology, and contextual understanding when he quotes or alludes to the Old Testament.[2]

A preliminary question of obvious importance is which parts of the Old Testament were accessible to a particular author, for we cannot assume that he had a complete set of Law, Prophets, and Writings. T. Holz (*Untersuchungen über die alttestamentliche Zitate bei Lukas* [Berlin, 1968]) concluded that Luke must have had significant access to Isaiah and at least three Minor Prophets (Joel, Amos, Habakkuk) in a version akin to the Septuagint A-type, and that his interest centered on these and on the Psalms. Of Isaiah he asserts,

> Dass Lukas eine Jesaja-Rolle im Besitz oder doch wenigstens während seiner schriftstellerischen Arbeit zur Hand hatte, ist mir sicher (p. 41).

Turning to Luke's use of Isaiah the first thing which catches our attention is his citation of four extended passages (Luke 3:4–6 = Isa. 40:3–5; Luke 4:17–19 = Isa. 61:1–2; Acts 8:28–33 = Isa. 53:7–8; Acts 28:25–27 = Isa. 6:9–10). In the first of these he carries the quotation five lines further than Matthew (Q). His interest in the *book* of Isaiah should also be noticed (Luke 3:4; 4:17–30), as well as the fact that where most quotations in Luke–Acts occur in the course of speeches, in Luke 3 and Acts 8 the Isaiah passage is part of Luke's telling of the story. All this is a definite pointer to a particular interest in the Book of Isaiah.

The story of the Ethiopian eunuch leads us further. When Philip finds him he is reading *and seeking to understand* what he reads. His question has a modern ring about it. It displays a critical awareness of an interpretative *crux*: Does the prophet speak of himself, or of another? (Acts 8:34). Such a question betrays the author's familiarity and concern with such problems.

This is encouragement to inquire further. We are aware of Luke's interest in the fulfillment of Scripture, but how deep is his understanding of it? With respect to Isaiah, did he use it simply as a quarry for texts or was he influenced by a deeper appreciation of Isaianic themes? Examination of Luke's Nazareth story and his use of the Servant theme have convinced me that the latter is the case.

The Nazareth Sermon

Luke defines the person and mission of Jesus by means of a quotation from Isaiah 61:1–2/58:6. However, whereas Matthew might quote

---

2. See F. W. Young, "A Study of the Relation of Isaiah to the Fourth Gospel," *Z.N.W.* 46 (1955): 215–33; W. R. Farmer, "Matthew and the Bible," *Lexington Theol. Quart.* 11 (1976): 57–71.

the passage and leave it, content with having drawn attention to its fulfillment, Luke keeps returning to it. In his Great Sermon (Luke 6:20), in
Jesus' answer to the disciples of John (Luke 7:22), and in Peter's speech
to Cornelius (Acts 10:38) the same understanding of Jesus' mission re-
surfaces, indicating a significant depth of interest in these particular
Isaianic categories, and suggesting that Isaiah may have had a formative influence on Luke's theology. But we can go further, for it is possible to regard Isaiah 61:1–2 as a succinct summary of a number of different themes from the rest of Isaiah. Just as these themes are, so to
speak, focused in Isaiah 61:1–2 so do we find them spreading out from
it to form basic themes in Luke–Acts.

The Spirit of the Lord

Descriptions of the activity of the Spirit are frequent in Isaiah. In
11:1ff. the Spirit is to rest on a descendant of David conferring wisdom
and understanding to enable him to render righteous judgment on behalf of the poor and to usher in an age of peace and the knowledge of
God. In 42:1 the Spirit is given to God's Servant to empower him to establish God's sovereign will (*mishpat*) in the earth. He will comfort and
encourage those almost extinguished, establish justice–law for the Gentiles and lead the captive exiles home. These ideas are found elsewhere
in Isaiah and are summed up in Isaiah 61:1ff.: An anointed one is em-
powered with the Spirit to evangelize the poor, heal the weak, release
captives, and announce the time of salvation.

The prominence of the Holy Spirit motif in Luke–Acts is well recognized.[3] From his baptism onwards Luke emphasizes Jesus' *Spirit-filled*[4]
state and Spirit-empowered ministry (Luke 4:14, 18; 5:17b; Acts 10:38).
The Spirit is related to Jesus' person and works in the same way as he
is related to the Messiah–Servant–Anointed One of Isaiah.

Anointed One

Luke is the only evangelist who uses the word χρίειν (Luke 4:18; Acts
4:27; 10:38). He means to identify Jesus as Messiah but also to link his
messiahship with his endowment with the Holy Spirit. W. C. van Unnik
("Jesus the Christ," *N.T.S.* 8 (1961–62): 113) thinks Luke wants to explain the origin and meaning of the title χριστός to his Hellenistic read-

---

3. See G. W. H. Lampe, "The Holy Spirit in the Writings of St. Luke" in *Studies in the
Gospels*, ed. D. E. Nineham (Oxford, 1955); H. von Baer, *Der Heilige Geist in den Lukas-
schriften* (Stuttgart, 1926).

4. In Mark 1:12 the Spirit drives Jesus *into* the wilderness (τὸ πνεῦμα αὐτὸν ἐκβάλ-
λει εἰς . . .) (cf. Matt. 4:1). In Luke 4:1 he returns from the baptism πλήρης Πνεύματος
Ἁγίου and *was being* led *in* the wilderness in the Spirit (ἤγετο ἐν τῷ πνεύματι ἐν τῇ
ἐρήμῳ).

ers. It is significant that he does so by means of a concept which is to be found in the Old Testament explicitly only in Isaiah 61:2.[5]

Εὐαγγελίζομαι

It is a well-known oddity that Luke only twice uses the substantive εὐαγγέλιον, so much loved by Paul and Mark. Even then it is in speeches of Peter and Paul (Acts 15:7; 20:24). Otherwise he uses the verbal form εὐαγγελίζομαι which, according to P. Stuhlmacher (*Das paulinische Evangelium* [Göttingen, 1968], 1:233–34) is traceable to the influence of Isaiah 61:1. Although Isaiah is not the only Old Testament book to use this term, it is the only book which employs it in a significant theological manner. In Isaiah 40:9 the "evangelizer" of Zion announces the appearance of God's sovereign rule for the salvation of Israel. In 52:7 the "evangelizer" brings a message of "peace" and "good"; God will rule (save) Zion. In 61:1 he announces salvation to the poor.

Like Isaiah, but contrary to current usage,[6] Luke uses εὐαγγελίζομαι without an object almost as a technical term for the proclamation of salvation. As in Isaiah the recipients of the "evangel" are Israel (Luke 2:10; 3:18; Acts 10:36) and the poor (Luke 4:18; 6:20; 7:22), and the content of the message is the kingdom[7] (Luke 4:43)[8] and peace (Luke 2:14; Acts 10:36). The εὐαγγελίζομαι theme is of obvious importance to Luke and he also makes use of the motifs of the three main Isaiah passages which deal with it (preparation, the kingdom, peace, the poor). Within its compass he includes the message of John the Baptist, the work of Jesus, and the preaching of the apostles.

Doing Good

In Acts 10:38 Peter sums up the ministry of Jesus as "doing good and healing all those who were oppressed of the devil." The whole speech has much in common with the Nazareth sermon and it pinpoints Luke's interest in the *works* of Jesus the Messiah. Luke's characterization of the salvation which becomes present with the coming of Jesus is largely Isaianic. In addition to the messianic works of healing (cf. Luke 7:21–23 with Isa. 29:18; 35:5–6; also Acts 3:2ff.; 14:8ff.), there is light for those

---

5. Though note 1 Sam. 16:13; 2 Sam. 23:1–2. The Targum to Isaiah gives a messianic interpretation to Isa. 11:1 and 42:1.

6. Philo and Josephus always supply an object. One "evangelizes" something (the message with accusative or περί) to someone. Sometimes the object is supplied from the context.

7. In Isaiah this is expressed in terms of the coming of God (or his arm) to rule (save and judge). The Targum interprets this as the kingdom of God (e.g., Tg. Isa. 40:9).

8. It is instructive to compare Luke 4:43 with its source in Mark 1:38: εὐαγγελίσασθαι replaces κηρύξω and ἀπεστάλην replaces ἐξῆλθον. The formative influence of Isa. 61:1/Luke 4:18 is apparent.

in darkness (cf. Luke 1:79 with Isa. 9:1–2; Luke 2:32 with Isa. 42:7; Luke 4:18 with Isa. 61:1 and see Acts 26:18, 23), blessing for the poor (Isa. 29:19; 41:17; 61:1), and consolation for Israel (Luke 2:25; 16:25). The use of παράκλησις to describe God's salvation of Jerusalem is characteristic of LXX Isaiah (35:4; 40:1, 11; 49:10, 13; 51:3, 12; 57:18; 61:2; 66:10–13). The only comparable use in the Old Testament is in Lamentations but there it is negative: the fact that Zion has no lovers to comfort her. The idea of "comfort" as glorious eschatological salvation is Isaiah's.

Because of the complexity of the problems and the shortness of this chapter I have sidestepped the question of the Isaianic content of Luke's sources as well as Isaiah's influence on current Palestinian soteriological thinking. It is plain that the Gospels have been influenced by Isaiah at all levels, and this influence probably goes back to Jesus himself. The idea of the "comforting" of Zion, although first attested for the first-century period by Luke, was probably a standard Jewish category (see Targums on 2 Sam. 23:1, 4b; Isa. 4:3; 18:4; 33:20; Jer. 31:6 also 2 Bar. 44:7). Nevertheless, the concentration of Isaianic themes in Luke indicates his awareness of their origin and suggests that this book was influential in his selection of themes and categories from what was doubtless a much wider field.

The Servant

The launching point for this theme is probably the Nazareth sermon.[9] According to E. Franklin (*Christ the Lord* [London, 1975], 64), ". . . the Servant career provides a programme in the light of which the ministry of Jesus can be presented and clarified." He thinks the source of this is Isaiah 61:1–2 which Luke has taken as part of the whole Servant description.

The "Servant" (παῖς) is not a title which Luke employs with unequivocal reference to the Servant of Isaiah. In Acts 3:13, 26 he is clearly in mind, but 4:27, 30 refer to the messianic son of Psalm 2.[10] This, however, only serves to illustrate an important point: unlike us the New Testament writers were not interested in clearly differentiated Old Testament title-themes. They believed in the essential unity of Old Testament theology so that ultimately the messianic son of Psalm 2 and the suffering παῖς of Isaiah are identical. "Christ" is the dominant title for Luke; the Servant theme is subsumed under it.

Our interest, therefore, is not in the title but in Luke's presentation of Jesus as the fulfillment of Isaiah's Servant role. The story of the Ethi-

---

9. Many would see the Servant idea in Jesus' baptism (Luke 3:22).
10. So C. F. D. Moule, "The Christology of Acts" in *Studies in Luke–Acts,* ed. L. E. Keck and J. L. Martyn (Nashville, New York, 1966), 169–70.

opian eunuch highlights Luke's interest in this role, but it is possible to go further.

Suffering Servant

Though M. D. Hooker (*Jesus and the Servant* [London, 1959]) has urged caution before assuming that Jesus identified himself as the "Suffering Servant," there can be no doubt that Luke makes the identification and that it is important to him. As well as the story of the eunuch he cites Isaiah 53 in relation to Jesus in Luke 22:37: Jesus is to be treated as a criminal. In Luke 18:31–33 he reproduces from his source (Mark 10:33–34) a clear allusion to the sufferings of the Servant (ἐμπτύσουσιν, μαστιγώσουσιν; cf. Isa. 50:6) but differs from Mark in setting out these words as an explicit fulfillment of Scripture (καὶ τελεσθήσεται πάντα τὰ γεγραμμένα διὰ τῶν προφητῶν . . .). The discerning reader is thus prepared to interpret Jesus' sufferings in terms of scriptural paradigms, especially that of the Servant. Luke also adds ὑβρισθήσεται to the description of Jesus' sufferings (Luke 18:32), an apposite summary of the sufferings related in Isaiah 50:6 and 53). It is also possible that his statement about the disciples' lack of understanding (though similar statements are to be found in Mark) is meant to echo the lack of understanding which according to Isaiah 53 was to meet the Servant's mission.

Exalted Servant

In Acts 3 the healing of the lame man is described in Isaianic terms (cf. Acts 3:2, 8 with Isa. 35:6) and Peter points to the exaltation of the Servant Jesus in explanation (Acts 3:13–14, 26). Luke has in mind the Servant of Isaiah who, though humiliated and rejected, remained faithful and was glorified by God (Isa. 52:13ff.).

Luke's version of the parable of the strong man (Luke 11:21–22) is also probably related to this theme. He was familiar with two versions of this parable (Mark 3:27 and Q) so his own redaction cannot be discerned with any certainty. Nevertheless whether by choice of Q against Mark or by his own modification, the parable seems to have been influenced by the Servant theme. Both versions have been influenced by Isaiah 49:24–25 but Luke's makes this more plain by the replacement of σκεύη with σκῦλα (a NT hapax; σκεύη occurs in Luke 17:31). However, even more probable than that Luke has accommodated the parable more closely to Isaiah 49:24–25 is that he has been influenced by Isaiah 53:12 and its picture of the victorious Servant dividing up the spoil (καὶ τῶν ἰσχυρῶν μεριεῖ σκῦλα cf. Luke 11:22, καὶ τὰ σκῦλα αὐτοῦ διαδίδωσιν).[11] The out-

---

11. So J. M. Creed, *The Gospel according to St. Luke* (London 1957), 161.

come of the Servant's mission is that he divides up the spoil of the strong, exactly the picture in Luke's version of the parable. He has either chosen that form of the parable which accentuates the victory of the Servant, or has edited it to display more clearly its Servant significance.

The Righteous One

In Acts 3:14 Jesus is called τὸν Ἅγιον καὶ Δίκαιον, denied by his people. ὁ Ἅγιος probably originates in Psalm 15 (16):10, a much used messianic testimonium. It is more difficult to be sure of the origin of ὁ Δίκαιος because of the commonness of the idea, but, considering the presence of the Servant theme in this passage, the likelihood is that it echoes the "Just One" of Isaiah 53:11 (LXX has δικαιῶσαι δίκαιον εὐ δουλεύοντα πολλοῖς; but cf. MT which places the "Just One" in apposition to "my Servant"). The title occurs in Stephen's speech (Acts 7:52), again in relation to the murder of Jesus, and in Acts 22:14. No doubt this terminology belonged to the Christology of the early Palestinian Christian community.

J. A. T. Robinson ("The Most Primitive Christology of All?" in *Twelve New Testament Studies* [London, 1962], 152) calls the Christology of Acts 3 "the fossil of a bygone age." However, the fact that Luke has bothered to preserve this and two other such "fossils" is evidence of his continued interest in such Christology; a carefully preserved collection of fossils is witness to more than just the time in which the fossils were living!

Luke's Passion Narrative

It is curious that for all his interest in the role of Jesus as the Servant Luke does not make more of it in the actual account of his passion. This is told simply and without any adornment of fulfillment motifs or scriptural allusions. After his careful preparation of his readers for a scriptural and Servant understanding of the passion this demands some explanation.

Luke's passion narrative is not a martyr story,[12] nor is there any weaving in of theological themes (except perhaps 23:45 which is not emphasized). The distinctive positive characteristic of Luke's account is its presentation of Jesus' righteousness. His innocence is a feature of the other Gospels too, but in Luke it has become the unifying theme and, seemingly, an important purpose of the narrative. Thus:

    1)   Jesus heals the severed ear of the servant of the high priest (22:51).

---

12. Jesus' confession is simple and receives less emphasis than in the other Gospels. No alternative to death is seriously contemplated, no emphasis is given to the intensity of his sufferings, and there is no discourse from the cross.

2) Pilate's declaration of Jesus' innocence is thrice repeated (23:4, 14, 22; cf. Mark 15:14) and Luke adds the witness of Herod (23:15).

3) Jesus is forcefully contrasted with Barabbas who had been cast into prison for insurrection and murder (23:25).

4) He is declared innocent by the repentant thief who confesses his own guilt and the justice of his punishment (23:39–43).

5) There is no cry of dereliction; Jesus simply commends his spirit into God's hands (23:46).

6) The centurion confesses Ὄντως ὁ ἄνθρωπος οὗτος δίκαιος (cf. Mark 15:39—υἱὸς θεοῦ) ἦν (23:47).

7) The multitudes who have witnessed the sight return home "smiting their breasts," thus declaring that Jesus was innocent (23:48).

This emphasis is probably attributable to the situation of the early missionary church. One of the easiest charges to bring against Christians would have been that their "Christ" was an evildoer—witness the manner of his death.[13] It would have been of great importance to demonstrate Jesus' innocence, but further, his positive righteousness. For Luke's concern was not just to establish the *bona fides* of the founder of Christianity, but to manifest him as the Servant, a role which hinged on his righteousness.

Conceivably he might have proceeded in either of two ways. He could have given a theological explanation of the true meaning of the cross (as Mark and Paul), or he could simply have related what actually happened, depending on the "witness" of those present to establish his case. The latter, it seems, is what he has done. It explains why there is such emphasis on witness, as well as why there is so little allusion and interpretation. Anything of this nature would have tended to render the story suspect for the critical reader of his time (or the reader who was sensitive to critical issues). His readers may well have been aware of the Christian interpretation of Jesus' death. What they needed was assurance that the facts matched the interpretation.[14]

I am inclined, therefore, to agree with Vincent Taylor (*The Passion Narrative of St. Luke*, ed. O. E. Evans [Cambridge, 1972], 138) who

---

13. Cf. A. E. Harvey (*Jesus on Trial* [London, 1976], 1ff.) who makes similar observations in relation to the purpose of the fourth Gospel.

14. For a different interpretation of the same facts see W. J. Larkin, Jr., "Luke's Use of the Old Testament as a Key to His Soteriology," *J.E.T.S.* 20 (1977): 329–35. He thinks Luke has prepared his readers to puzzle over the anomaly of the innocent man suffering as a criminal in a God-ordained way by quoting Isa. 53:12 in Luke 22:37. This is meant to lead them to a soteriological understanding of Jesus' passion.

thinks Luke's passion narrative "depicts Jesus as the Servant of the Lord without using the name." What Luke gives his readers is not an abstract notion of the goodness of Jesus but an apologetic defense of his righteousness, designed to undergird his identity as the "Just One."

The Mission to the Nations

The ἕως ἐσχάτου τῆς γῆς of Acts 1:8 undoubtedly goes back to the characterization of the Servant's mission in Isaiah 49:6. This passage is quoted in Acts 13:47. The Twelve and Paul are seen to share in the Servant mission. They continue the work of Jesus as his appointed witnesses.[15] A Servant understanding is also clear in the account of Paul's commissioning (Acts 9:15f.; 26:16ff.).[16] However, Paul never becomes the Servant though he continues the Servant mission. He is not "anointed" but "selected" or "appointed" (προχειρίζεσθαι); he is ὑπηρέτης, μάρτυς ορ δοῦλος, but never παῖς. In his person he is at most σκεῦος ἐκλογῆς, the servant (ὑπηρέτης) of the Servant (παῖς).

Conclusions

The influence of Isaiah is apparent at many points in Luke–Acts.[17] In this chapter I have concentrated on just two themes which demonstrate the radical and searching nature of Luke's use of Isaiah. He is not the only one to have been so influenced. All the sources are permeated with Isaianic quotations and allusions. Non-Christian sources of the period also bear witness to the contemporary interest in Isaiah. What this study has shown is Luke's evident appreciation of this heritage as well as his thorough understanding of its source. Many of his major theological categories are drawn from Isaiah and he has a special consciousness of the relationship between the ministry of Jesus and the theological patterns of the Isaiah prophecies. No doubt his depth of understanding is attributable in some degree to the controversy which surrounded the proclamation of Jesus as Christ in the Hellenistic synagogues. It was necessary to convince skeptics from the Scriptures that Jesus answered to the pattern of the promised one (Acts 17:2–3, 11; 19:8).

I conclude, therefore, with some confidence that in approaching quotations from and allusions to Isaiah there is a presumption in favour of Luke's awareness of their context and wider meaning within Isaiah as a whole.

---

15. Acts 1:1. In Acts 3:1ff. Peter does messianic works in the name of the Servant. A similar thing is recorded of Paul in Acts 14:8–10. Cf. G. W. H. Lampe, op. cit., 194.

16. G. W. H. Lampe, "The Lucan Portrait of Christ," *N.T.S.* 2 (1955–56): 175.

17. Further studies: W. Grundmann "Der Bergpredigt nach der Lukasfassung," *Stud. Evang.* 1 (1957): 180–89; J. D. M. Derrett, "Midrash in the New Testament: The Origin of Luke xxii. 67–68," *Stud. Theol.* 29 (1975): 147–56.

15

The Use of the Old Testament in Revelation

G. K. Beale

From G. K. Beale, "Revelation," in *It Is Written: Scripture Citing Scripture*, ed. D. A. Carson and H. G. M. Williamson (Cambridge: Cambridge University Press, 1988), 318–36. Reprinted with the permission of Cambridge University Press.

Introduction

In comparison with the rest of the New Testament, the Apocalypse of John has not been given a proportionate amount of attention: merely two books (A. Schlatter 1912; and G. K. Beale 1984) and six significant articles have been dedicated to the topic (see A. Vanhoye 1962; A. Lancellotti 1966; L. P. Trudinger 1966; A. Gangemi 1974; B. Marconcini 1976; M. D. Goulder 1981; cf. also J. Cambier 1955 and E. Lohse 1961, which are of more limited value).

Otherwise, important discussion of this subject can be found only in portions of books and commentaries, the more valuable of which are H. B. Swete (1911, esp. cxl–clvi and passim), R. H. Charles (1920, esp. lxv–lxxxii and passim), L. S. Vos (1965, 16–53), G. B. Caird (1966, passim), C. van der Waal (1971, 174–241), G. R. Beasley-Murray (1981, passim), D. Ford (1982, 243–306), and to somewhat lesser degree G. Delling (1959), J. Comblin (1965), A. Farrer (1964) and T. Holtz (1971).

There is general acknowledgment that the Apocalypse contains more Old Testament references than any other New Testament book, although past attempts to tally objectively the total amount have varied.[1] The vari-

---

1. UBS³, 901–11 = 394; NA²⁶, 739–44 = 635; British and Foreign Bible Society Greek text, 734–87 = 493; E. Hühn, 1900, 269ff. = 455; W. Dittmar, 1903, 263–79 = 195; Swete,

ation in statistics is due to the different criteria employed to determine the validity of an Old Testament reference and the fact that some authors include "echoes" and parallels of a very general nature (cf. also the survey and evaluation of Vos 1965, 17–19 and Vanhoye 1962, 438–40). The range of Old Testament usage includes the Pentateuch, Judges, 1–2 Samuel, 1–2 Kings, Psalms, Proverbs, Song of Solomon, Job, major prophets and the minor prophets. Roughly more than half the references are from the Psalms, Isaiah, Ezekiel, and Daniel, and in proportion to its length Daniel yields the most (so Swete 1911, cliii, where numerical statistics are also given for many of the Old Testament books used).

The evaluation of Daniel as most used is supported by recent study (cf. Beale, 1984). Among the allusions to Daniel, the greatest number come from Daniel 7. Proportionally Ezekiel ranks second as the most used Old Testament book (cf. Vanhoye 1962, 473–75), although in terms of actual numbers of allusions Isaiah is first, followed by Ezekiel, Daniel, and Psalms (Although statistics cited by commentators differ; e.g., Swete cites Isaiah = 46, Daniel = 31, Ezekiel = 29, Psalms = 27) The Old Testament in general plays such a major role that a proper understanding of its use is necessary for an adequate view of the Apocalypse as a whole.

The Text Form of Old Testament References in the Apocalypse

The text form of the Old Testament references in Revelation needs in-depth discussion since there are no formal quotations and most are allusive, a phenomenon often making textual identification more difficult. However, unfortunately the scope of the present discussion is unable to include such important analysis (cf. further L. P. Trudinger 1966; G. K. Beale 1985, in addition to a forthcoming article), including criteria for discerning degrees of dependence (but see further L. P. Trudinger 1966; G. K. Beale 1984a, 43–259; 1985, in addition to a forthcoming study).

Preliminary Considerations for Studying Old Testament Usage in the Apocalypse

Problematic Use of Combined Allusions and the Issue of Literary Consciousness

We have already acknowledged the nonformal character of the Old Testament references in Revelation. Not only does this make Old Testament textual identification more difficult but it also renders it problem-

---

1911, cxl = 278; Charles, 1920, lxv–lxxxii = 226; C. van der Waal, 1971, 174–241 = 1000 (approx.).

atic to determine whether or not the author is consciously or unconsciously referring to an Old Testament text. This problem is
compounded since many, indeed most, of the Old Testament reminis-
cences are found in combination with one another. Sometimes four,
five, or more different Old Testament references are merged into one
picture. Good examples are the descriptions of Christ (1:12–20), God on
the throne and the surrounding heavenly host (4:1–11) and the diabolic
beast (13:1–8; for a thorough list of other examples see Vos 1965, 39–
40). How are such combined allusions to be studied? This phenomenon
would be particularly hard to analyze if, as some contend, it is less intentional and more the result of a memory so saturated with Old Testament language and ideas that they are unconsciously organized in the
author's visions "like the changing patterns of a kaleidoscope" (so
Swete 1911, cliv and Vos 1965, 38–39). In this case, the Old Testament
contextual meanings of the allusions need not be examined to comprehend better John's use, since he himself did not consciously reflect on
such Old Testament contexts. Indeed, many have concluded that the
lack of formal citation in the Apocalypse points in the same direction.

However, Caird sees conscious effort in such allusive combinations
for the purpose of expressing evocative and emotive power. Therefore,
it is unnecessary to attempt to comprehend the meaning of each reference in its Old Testament and New Testament context, since the whole
picture must be kept together—without separating and analyzing various strands—in order to maintain the desired emotional effect (1966,
25–26). Of course, in these mosaics there is always the possibility of a
mixture of conscious intention with unconscious activity.

But often a greater understanding is gained and emotive effect felt
when the various allusive parts of these visionary amalgamations *are*
studied separately in their Old Testament contexts. Vos cites Revelation
4:2–9 as a fitting illustration of unconscious mixing of Old Testament
allusions. However, when the Old Testament context of each allusion is
studied one finds that, without exception, they all are from descriptions
of theophany scenes, which function as introductory sections to an announcement of judgment either upon Israel or the nations (cf. Vos' parallels: 4:2 = *Isa. 6:1* and/or *1 Kgs. 22:19*; 4:3–4 = *Ezek. 1:28*; 4:5a = *Ezek.
1:13* and/or *Exod. 19:16*; 4:5b = *Ezek. 1:13* and *Zech. 4:2, 6* [omitted from
Vos]; 4:6a = *Ezek. 1:22*; 4:6b = *Ezek. 1:5* and *1:18*; 4:7 = *Ezek. 1:10*; 4:8a
= *Isa. 6:2*; 4:8b = *Isa. 6:3*; 4:9 = *Isa. 6:1*). This common denominator of
theophany—judgment is enhanced when one notes also the dominant
influence of Daniel 7:9–13 throughout Revelation 4–5 (see infra). This
clearly common motif in all the Old Testament allusions points toward
a more intentional thematic formation of texts to describe a similar
theophany scene in Revelation. This seems even more likely when one

considers that in the immediate contexts of 3 of the Old Testament allusions there appears the image of a "book" associated with judgment, as in Revelation 5:1 (cf. Dan. 7:10; Ezek. 2:9–10; Zech. 5:1–3). All of the common scenes and themes of these Old Testament contexts intensify the cognitive and emotive aspects of the picture in Revelation 4:2–9.

The same thing can be illustrated through Revelation 1:12–20, 13:1–8 and 17:1ff, other examples cited by Vos to support his proposal of unconscious clustering (see Beale 1984, 154–270).

Therefore, caution must be used in making claims of unconscious activity on the author's part, although this is a possibility. For example, it is possible, but speculative, to propose that the above-mentioned exegetical links were already intact in some previous tradition to which John makes unconscious allusion (e.g., a synagogue or Christian liturgical tradition). Such unconscious activity is more likely to have occurred with the less clear or nonclustered allusions, although exegetical analysis must determine this in each case. Furthermore, as Vanhoye has concluded, it is not typical for John to use Old Testament allusions in isolation but to fuse them together on the basis of their affinity with one another (Vanhoye 467), as illustrated above in Revelation 4–5.

Although space does not permit, it would be helpful to discuss in this section whether or not the Apocalypse is a literary stereotype or if it can be traced to a visionary experience, or is a combination of both (cf. further L. Hartman 1966, 106; Beale 1984, 7–9). If there was an experiential basis, probably descriptions of such visions were colored both unconsciously and consciously by the traditions which had exerted a formative influence on the author's thinking. Furthermore, actual visions would have been experienced in the author's own thought forms, so that it might be difficult to distinguish description of a visionary experience from that of a retelling of the experience through unconscious or conscious appeal to various traditions (OT, Jewish, etc.).

John's apparent self-identification with the line of Old Testament visionaries implies that he would be conscious of developing the ideas of the earlier prophets and, therefore, that the *clearer* Old Testament references in his work are the result of an intentional activity (cf. 1:1–3, 10; 4:1–2; 17:3; 21:10; Vos 1965, 52). Furthermore, the chain of associated texts in Revelation 1, 4–5, 13, and 17 discussed above, and evident elsewhere, confirms an intentional activity on the author's part. This conclusion is enhanced by the remaining evidence considered below.

A Consideration of Contextual and Non-Contextual Use of the Old Testament

Of course, if one concluded that John alluded to the Old Testament only unconsciously, there would be little possibility of studying his method of allusion, since such study assumes conscious activity. In light of our conclusion in favor of intentionality, however, we must first ask whether or not John uses the Old Testament in harmony with its broader contextual meaning.

There is unanimous consensus that John uses the Old Testament with a high degree of liberty and creativity. As a result, many conclude that he often handles numerous Old Testament passages without consideration of their original contextual meaning—even contradictory to it. This has been argued in a thoroughgoing way by Vos. Our comments will be focussed on an evaluation of his discussion as generally representative of those who hold this viewpoint.

Vos restricts most of his survey to what he considers to be the clearest Old Testament references in the Apocalypse (21–37, 41). He concludes that at least seven of the twenty-two passages discussed there show a "disregard for [the OT] context." Four of these concern references to heavenly beings. The first is the application of a description of Yahweh (Ezek. 43:2) to that of the Son of man figure (Rev. 1:15). But this is more of a change of application than non-contextual use, since the Son of man is clearly portrayed as a divine figure in Revelation 1. In Revelation 18:1 a description of Yahweh (Ezek. 43:2b) is applied to an angel descending from heaven, yet since angels in the Old Testament and Revelation are mere conveyers of divine decrees, so it is plausible that they would take on other theophanic characteristics besides that of the divine word. In addition, sometimes in the Old Testament God appears in the form of a heavenly being, and this may be the case also in Revelation (e.g., Rev. 10:1–6, which is based on the heavenly being of Dan. 10–12 who may be divine). Therefore, in spite of a possible change of application, the broad Old Testament idea of a heavenly being revealing a divine decree to a prophet remains intact. The same general conclusion can be reached with respect to the similar usage of Ezekiel 37:3 in Revelation 7:14. In Revelation 4:8a descriptions of the Isaiah 6 seraphim are merged with those of the Ezekiel 1 cherubim, but again the primary Old Testament framework of a heavenly being guarding God's throne is still retained.

Vos also argues for a disregard of context in the use of Ezekiel 37:10b in Revelation 11:11. The Ezekiel text uses the idea of resurrection as a metaphor for the future ingathering of Israel from throughout the nations, while John applies it to the resurrection of the two witnesses, who probably are symbolic of the witnessing church as the true Israel (so Caird, Sweet, etc.). This kind of reference may fit into the analogical usage category (see below) because of the common idea of *Israel's resurrection*. The shift of application to the church as the true Israel and the understanding of the Ezekiel language as apparently connoting a literal resurrection may represent eschatological escalation whereby the resurrection terminology now finds an eschatological—not merely historical—level. Although there is a possibility of disregard for context because of the different application and even somewhat changed meaning, a correspondence and sense of continuity can be discerned (note also in both passages that those "resurrected" have previously been slain among the nations; cf. Ezek. 37:9–14, 21–22/Rev. 11:7–10).

Vos also contends that the use of Isaiah 22:22 in Revelation 3:7 is non-contextual, since Eliakim's authority over the Israelite kingdom is applied to Christ's authority over God's kingdom. But, this can also be viewed as an escalated analogy wherein the human, earthly, political, and temporal rule over Israel by Eliakim finds a correspondence on a grander scale with Christ's divine, heavenly, spiritual, and eternal rule over the whole world (cf. Rev. 1–5). Additional points of note in Isaiah 22 are: 1) the possible priestly connotations of Eliakim's rule (22:21a); 2) Eliakim was to be like a "Father" for the Israelites in the exercise of his office (22:21b); 3) apparently Eliakim's authority was to be equal to that of King Hezekiah's (22:22); 4) the exercise of his office would bring glory to his relatives (22:23–24); 5) Eliakim is referred to as the "servant" of Yahweh (22:20). All of these elements, together with the messianic overtones of the "house of David" (22:22) enhance the idea that John was quite aware of the context of Isaiah 22:22 and intentionally escalated these aspects of Eliakim's reign to the grander scale of Christ's reign. Perhaps the correspondences were just too good to miss (cf. G. von Rad who argues cogently for a typological relationship between Isa. 22:22 and Rev. 3:7 [1965 373]).

We may therefore viably speak about changes of applications but need not conclude that this means a *disregard* for Old Testament context, since this is not a logically necessary deduction. It seems likely that Vos, and others, confuse disregard for context with change of application. That the above texts reflect disregard for Old Testament context is possible but other explanations are equally satisfactory. The passages we have discussed are test cases, the conclusions of which are applicable to other Old Testament references where it is probable that the author has made *intentional allusion*. Admittedly, it is sometimes difficult to know whether there has been conscious or unconscious activity. Non-contextual uses of the Old Testament can be expected to occur in those places where there is unconscious allusion. No doubt, the apocalyptist's mind was so saturated with Old Testament language from his learned tradition that when he described his vision he sometimes spontaneously used this language without much forethought. For example, the phrase "I turned *to see the voice which was speaking*" (Rev. 1:12a) is probably drawn from Daniel 7:11 (LXX), but there refers to the "boastful words" of the beast. This may have been drawn in unconsciously because of the clear influence of Daniel 7 in Revelation 1:7–14.

To clarify what is meant by "context" is important. What is usually meant is *literary* context—how a passage functions in the logical flow of a book's argument. But there is also *historical* context. For example, the *historical* context of Hosea 11:1 is the exodus and not the argument of the Book of Hosea. A New Testament author might reflect on only one of these contexts, he could focus on both or entirely disregard both. In the light of the passages discussed above, the author appears to display varying degrees of awareness of literary context, as well as perhaps historical context, although the former is predominant. Those texts with a low degree of correspondence with the Old Testament literary context can be referred to as semi-contextual, since they seem to fall between the opposite poles of what we ordinarily call "contextual" and "non-contextual" usages. The categories of use to be considered below should further clarify and illustrate these initial conclusions.

Various Uses of the Old Testament in the Apocalypse

The Use of Segments of Old Testament Scripture as Literary Prototypes

Sometimes the author takes over large Old Testament contexts or sequences as models after which to pattern his creative compositions (cf. E. Schüssler-Fiorenza 1980, 108). Such modeling can be apparent 1) through observing a thematic-structure which is uniquely traceable to only one Old Testament context or 2) by discerning a cluster of clear allusions from the same Old Testament context. Sometimes both are observable, thus enhancing the clarity of the Old Testament prototype. It has been argued in some depth that broad patterns from Daniel (especially chaps. 2 and 7) have been followed in Revelation 1, 4–5, 13, and 17, the former two sections in particular exhibiting both allusive clusters and structural outlines from segments of Daniel (Beale 1984, 154–305, 313–20). Incidentally, this would show further design in these chapters and point further away from an unconscious use of the Old Testament. The same use of Daniel as a midrashic *Vorbild* is also observable in Jewish apocalyptic, indicating that this kind of use of the Old Testament was not uncommon (e.g., 1QMI; 1 En. 90:9–19; 4 Ezra 11–13; 1 En. 69:26–71:17; 2 Bar. 36–40. So Beale, 67–153). The suggestion is also made that this influence of Daniel may even extend to the structure of the whole Apocalypse, since the same Daniel 2:28–29 allusion punctuates the book at major divisional transitions (1:1; 1:19; 4:1; 22:6). Furthermore, the five apocalyptic visions in Daniel (2, 7, 8, 9, 10–

12) cover the same time of the eschatological future, which may be the prototypical structure followed by Revelation in some of its purported synchronously parallel sections (Beale 1984a, 271–85; 1984b, 413–23).

In a somewhat similar vein, M. D. Goulder has argued that broad portions of Ezekiel have been the dominant influence on at least twelve major sections of the Apocalypse (Rev. 4; 5; 6:1–8; 6:12–7:1; 7:2–8; 8:1– 5; 14:6–12; 17:1–6; 18:9–24; 20:7–10; 21:22; cf. Goulder, 1981, 343–49). Goulder observes that these uses of Ezekiel are a dominant influence on the structure of Revelation since they are placed to a marked extent in the same order as they are found in Ezekiel itself (343–54), a somewhat similar observation to that made earlier by Vanhoye (442). However, Goulder proposes that a liturgical rather than literary explanation can be given to account better for the Revelation-Ezekiel parallel order. He attempts to demonstrate this by speculating that there is a general alignment of the Apocalypse with the Jewish calendar, especially with respect to the year of festivals and holy days, and that this liturgical-calendrical pattern is even more formative on the structure of Revelation than Ezekiel (349–64).

Others have also recognized Ezekiel's broad influence, especially in Revelation 20–22, where the order of events appears to have been taken from Ezekiel 37–48 (E. C. Selwyn 1902, 332–34; A. Wikenhauser 1932, 13–25; K. G. Kuhn 1933, 790–92; J. Lust 1980). And there are many commentators who, along with Goulder, see Ezekiel as the paradigm for Rev. 4:1–5:1 (e.g., Caird, Sweet).

In addition to Goulder's above liturgical view, others of paradigmatic significance for the book have also been proposed, which are based either on early Jewish or Christian liturgical tradition (cf. D. R. Carnegie 1978; S. Läuchli 1960 [see Carnegie's evaluation, 1982, 245]; P. Prigent 1964, 46–79 [see Beale's evaluation, 1984, 184]).

There is consensus that the plagues of the "trumpets" in Revelation 8:6–12 and those of the bowls in 16:1–9 follow the paradigm of the Exodus plagues (Exod. 8:12), although creatively reworked and applied (e.g., Beasley-Murray, Caird, Sweet). Already this exodus model had been used by Amos (chaps. 8–10) and creatively amplified in Wisdom of Solomon 11–19, the latter usage perhaps also exerting influence on John's application (Sweet, 1979, 161–62). J. A. Draper proposes that the eschatological scheme in Zechariah 14 "provides the basis for a midrashic development in Revelation 7" (1983, 133–47), while Sweet more tentatively suggests the same thing for Revelation 20–22 (1981, 112).

Mention should also be made of the synthetic use of the end-time woes from the synoptic eschatological discourse together with Leviticus 26:18–28, Ezekiel 14:13–23, and Zechariah 6:1–8 (cf. 1:8–15), all of which have served as the compositional paradigm for Revelation 6:2–8. Likewise, H. P. Müller has argued that the Sinai theophany, 1 Kings 22, Isaiah 6, Ezekiel 1, and Daniel 7 have been synthesized to provide the *Vorbild* for Revelation 4–5 (1962 and 1963; for evaluation see Beale 1984, 178–239).

All of the above proposed Old Testament models have woven within them allusions from other parts of the same Old Testament book and from elsewhere in the Old Testament corpus, and many of these are based upon common themes, pictures, catch-phrases, etc. Often these other references serve as interpretative expansions of an Old Testament prototype. On the reasonable assumption that these models were intentionally composed, two primary uses of them can be discerned. First, the Old Testament patterns appear to be used as forms through which future (sometimes imminent) eschatological fulfillment is understood and predicted (cf. Rev. 13:17. Also see the same employment of the Daniel models in 1QMI; 1 En. 46–47; 69:26–71:17; 90; 4 Ezra 11–13; 2 Bar. 36:1–42:2). Second, the *Vorbilden* are utilized as a lens through which past and present eschatological fulfillment is understood (cf. Rev. 1; 4–5). It is not always clear whether or not these Old Testament prototypes are the means or the object of interpretation, and perhaps there is an oscillation between the two.

Thematic Use of the Old Testament

In addition to alluding to specific Old Testament texts, the author of Revelation develops important Old Testament *themes*. Many of these themes are delineated throughout the major commentaries. Some special studies of note are D. Ford's tracing of Daniel's "abomination of desolation" theme (1979, 243–314), T. Longman's study of the Old Testament divine warrior motif (1982, 291–302), R. Bauckham's article on the Old Testament earthquake idea, recent articles on the employment of the A.N.E.–Old Testament covenant form in Revelation 2–3 and throughout the book (W. H. Shea and K. A. Strand) and the Old Testament concept of the "day of the Lord" (D. A. Gray 1974).

D. A. Carnegie has offered a most interesting study on the function of hymns in the Old Testament and their reuse in Revelation. He shows that the various songs in Isaiah 40–55 come at the end of subsections and round them off, not only by offering a concluding thanksgiving, but also by giving an interpretative summary of the theme of the whole previous section (cf. Isa. 48:20ff.; 52:9; etc.). The series of hymns in Revelation are seen to have the same function under the inspiration of the Isaianic songs (cf. Rev. 4:11; 5:13ff.; 7:9–12; 11:15–18; 19:1–8; so Carnegie 1982, 250–52).

Analogical Use of the Old Testament

This use can be considered the most general description of Old Testament usage in the Apocalypse, since the very act of referring to an Old Testament text is to place it in some comparative relationship to something in the New Testament. However, here we have in mind specific well-known persons, places, and events. The pictures undergo creative changes (expansions, condensations, supplemental imagery, etc.) and, of course, are applied to different historical situations (for a superb example of such alteration see Vos's discussion of the Exodus plague imagery in Revelation 8:6–12 and 16:2–15, 45–47). Nevertheless, a key idea in the Old Testament context is usually carried over as the main characteristic or principle to be applied in the New Testament situation (so Vos, 47–48). Therefore, even though John handles these Old Testament figures with creative freedom, almost always these pictures broadly retain an essential Old Testament association and convey principles of continuity between the Old Testament and New Testament (so J. Cambier 1955, 116–20; cf. A. Gangemi 1974, 322–39).

For example, the image of the deceiving "serpent of old" in Revelation 12:9 (cf. 20:2) evokes an episode of primitive religious history which maintains the same meaning for the final, eschatological phase of theological history (so Cambier, 118–19). The author's theological basis for maintaining such continuities lies in his conviction that Old Testament and New Testament history is but the working out of God's unified design of salvation and deals throughout with the unchanging principles of faith in God, God's faithfulness in fulfilling his salvific promises, the anti-theocratic forces attempting to thwart such promises and the victory of God's kingdom over that of Satan's (Cambier, 119–20).

The following is a sampling of these analogies with a brief description of the primary point of continuity: 1) *judgment*—theophanies introducing judgment (Isa. 6, Ezek. 1, Dan. 7/Rev. 4–5), books of judgment (Ezek. 2, Dan. 7, Dan. 12/Rev. 5:1–5 and Ezek. 2/Rev. 10), lion from Judah exercising judgment (Gen. 49:9/Rev. 5:5), "Lord of lords and King of kings" exercising judgment (Dan. 4:37 [LXX]/Rev. 17:14; 19:16), horsemen as divine agents of judgment (Zech. 1 and 6/Rev. 6:1–8), Exodus plagues inflicting judgment (Exod. 8–12/Rev. 8:6–12; 16:1–14), locusts as agents of judgment (Joel 1–2/Rev. 9:7–10), prophets giving testimony through judgment (Exod. 7:17; 1 Kgs. 17:1/Rev. 11:6), "Babylon" judged by God in "one hour" (Dan. 4:17a [LXX]/Rev. 18:10, 17, 19); 2) *tribulation and persecution of God's people*—10 days of tribulation (Dan. 1:12/Rev. 2:10), 3 1/2 years of tribulation (Dan. 7:25; 12:7/ Rev. 11:2; 12:1; 13:5), Sodom, Egypt, and Jerusalem as infamous places where persecution occurs (Rev. 11:8), persecuting rulers symbolized as beasts (Dan. 7/Rev. 11–13, 17) and "Babylon the Great" (Dan. 4:30, etc./ Rev. 14:8; 16:19; 17:5; 18:2); 3) *seductive, idolatrous teaching*—Balaam (Rev. 2:14) and Jezebel (Rev. 2:20–23); 4) *divine protection*—the tree of life (Rev. 2:7; 22:2, 14, 19), the "sealed" Israelites (Ezek. 9/Rev. 7:2–8) and the wings of the eagle (Exod. 19:4; Deut. 32:11/Rev. 12:14); 5) *victorious battle of God's people over the enemy*—Armageddon (Rev. 16:16; [19:19]. Cf. Gog and Magog in Revelation 20:8); 6) *apostasy*—the harlot (Ezek. 16:15; etc./Rev. 17); 7) *the divine Spirit as the power for God's people*—Zech. 4:1–6/Rev. 1:12–20; 11:4.

Some analogies are repeated in the book and creatively developed in different ways, though usually within the parameters of the Old Testament context to some degree.

Universalization of the Old Testament

Vanhoye is apparently the only author to discuss this as a formal category of Old Testament usage. The apocalyptist has a tendency to apply to the world what in the Old Testament was limited in reference to Israel or other things (cf. Vanhoye with reference to Ezekiel, 446–67). There are several examples of this phenomenon. The title which Yahweh gave Israel in Exodus 19:6 ("kingdom of priests") is applied in Revelation 1:6 and 5:10 to the church, composed of kingly priests "from every tribe and people and nation" (Rev. 5:9). Indeed, this very phrase of universality in Revelation 5:9 is most likely taken from Daniel 7:14, where it referred to the world nations subjugated to Israel's rule—now extended to the rule by all these very nations (cf. Rev. 5:10; Beale 1984, 214–19). The phrase in Revelation 1:7 "and every eye will see him, even those who pierced him; and all the tribes of the earth will mourn over him" refers in Revelation to the peoples throughout the earth, although in Zechariah 12:10 it is limited to the Israelite tribes. The same trend in this widening application of Zechariah 12:10 is also given in John 19:31–37, where one of the Gentile, Roman soldiers is viewed as a beginning fulfillment of this prophecy (so J. R. Michaels 1967, 102–9; Sweet 1981, 112).

Another classic example of this tendency is the extension of the Exodus plague imagery from the land of Egypt to the whole "earth" in Revelation 8:6–12 and 16:1–14 (e.g., in 8:8 a third of the sea, including fish and ships, is affected instead of merely a river and fish; in 16:10 rather than the sun being darkened, it is the kingdom of the satanic beast which becomes darkened). The "ten days of tribulation" experienced by Daniel and his friends (Dan. 1:12) and the 3 1/2 years of Israel's tribulation (Dan. 7:25; 12:7) both are extended to the tribulation of the church—the eschatological true Israel—throughout the world. And part of this tribulation is instigated by the eschatological "Babylon the Great" (Dan. 4:30) who persecutes not merely ethnic Israelite believers, but also saints throughout the earth (Rev. 17:5–8; 18:24), and harmfully affects "nations," "kings of the earth," and the world's economy (18:1–23). Therefore, when "Babylon the Great" falls rather than the effect being provincial, "the cities of the nations" also fall (16:19). Likewise, the former persecutors of God's people in the Old Testament (Sodom, Egypt, and Jerusalem) are now defined as "peoples and tribes and tongues and nations" (Rev. 11:8–10).

The Apocalypse concludes with references from the predicted eschatological temple reserved for Israel, although now its cultic benefits are extended to the Gentiles (cf. Ezek. 37:27, 44:9 and 48:35 in Rev. 21:3; cf. Rev. 22:2 where the "leaves of healing" foretold in Ezek. 47:12 to be an aid to the Israelites is transformed into "leaves . . . for the healing of the *nations*").

Sometimes the rationale for universalization is found already in the Old Testament contexts (cf. Ezek. 14:12–21 in Rev. 6:8) from which the allusions are drawn, although the inspiration can also arise from combining a narrowly designed Old Testament Israelite reference with another very similar Old Testament text which, however, is universal. For example, the Israelite-oriented book of judgment from Ezekiel 2:9 is given cosmic dimensions in Revelation 5:1 and 10:8–11 because it has been attracted to other Old Testament judgment-book allusions which have a wider cosmic application (cf. Dan. 7:10; 12:4, 9 in Rev. 5:1–5 and Dan. 12:4–9 in Rev. 10:1–6). Nevertheless, the primary reason for the extended applications is the New Testament's and John's presupposition concerning the cosmic dimensions of Christ's lordship and death (cf. Rev. 1:5; 5:9–10; for other examples of universalization see Revelation 19:7 [bride], 17:1ff. [harlot], 7:9, 15 [Ezek. 37:26], 18:9 [Ezek. 26:16ff.; 27:29–35], 1:12–13, 20 [lampstands], 2:17 [manna], 3:12 and 21:2 [Jerusalem]).

It is tempting to conclude that John does not handle the Old Testament according to its original contextual meaning when he universalizes. But Vanhoye's evaluation is plausible. He says that while this universalization is motivated by the Christian spirit to explain redemptive fulfillment, it is not contrary to the Old Testament sense. Although the author certainly makes different applications and executes developments beyond those of his Old Testament predecessors, he stays within the same interpretative framework and is conscious of being profoundly faithful to the overall parameters of their message (Vanhoye, 467). This is a viable analysis since all of these universalizations can be considered subcategories of the above-discussed analogical use of the Old Testament, where it was proposed that, although John creatively rewords the Old Testament and changes the application of it, his pictures retain significant points of correspondence with the Old Testament context and express salvation-historical principles of continuity. All of the cited examples of universalization appear to be harmonious developments of these principles as, for example, is the case with the Old Testament texts pertaining to ethnic Israel's redemption which are applied in Revelation to the world's redemption on the basis of defining the true people of God according to their faith in him. This is why the church comes to be viewed as the true Israel.

Possible Indirect Fulfillment Uses of the Old Testament

Although there are no formal Old Testament quotations (with introductory formulas) used as prooftexts to indicate prophetic fulfillment, it is still possible that some Old Testament texts were *informally* referred to in order to designate present or future fulfillment of Old Testament verbal prophecy. The determination of whether a text refers to future or present fulfillment often depends on one's overall view of the book (e.g., preterist, historicist, idealist, futurist).

Of special note is the introduction to the book (1:1), where allusion is made to Daniel 2:28–29, 45: δεῖξαι . . . ἃ δεῖ γενέσθαι followed directly by ἐν τάχει (cf. Dan. 2:28, ἐδήλωσε . . . ἃ δεῖ γενέσθαι ἐπ᾽ ἐσχάτων τῶν ἡμερῶν). John's "quickly" has been substituted for Daniel's "in the latter days" so that what Daniel expected to occur in the distant future—the defeat of cosmic evil and ushering in of the kingdom—John expects to begin in his own generation, and perhaps has already been inaugurated. Such imminence and even *incipient inauguration* is corroborated by the phrase—ὁ γὰρ χαιρὸς ἐγγυς in 1:3, which elsewhere includes *both* the "already" and "not-yet" element (so Mark 1:15; Matt. 26:45; Lam. 4:18; cf. Matt. 3:2 with 4:17 cf. Beale 1984b, 415–20).

Daniel 12:4, 9 is used likewise in 22:10: whereas Daniel is commanded to "conceal these words and seal up the book until the end of time" (12:4), John is given the consummatory command to "not seal up the words of the prophecy of this book, for the time is near." This use in 22:10 intensifies that of 1:1–3 since it is directly linked to a verbatim repetition of 1:1 in 22:6.

The reference to the *Son of man* (1:13–14) probably indicates John's belief that Jesus had begun to fulfill the Daniel 7:13 prophecy of the son of man's exaltation, although the similar reference in 1:7 refers to a further phase of the same prophecy which may still await realization. The same kind of already-and-not-yet idea is found in 2:26–27 where Jesus says he has started to fulfill the Psalm 2:7 prediction but that his followers will also take part in the fulfillment at a future time (probably at death).

If the argument that Revelation 1 and 4–5 are each modeled on Daniel 7 can be sustained (cf. Beale, 154–228), then John's intention may be to indicate that Jesus' death, resurrection, and gathered church is the inaugurated fulfillment of Daniel.

There is also evidence of expectations of exclusive future fulfillment, of which only the clearest examples are listed (Zech. 12:10/Rev. 1:7; Isa. 25:8/Rev. 7:17; Ps. 2:1/Rev. 11:18; Ps. 2:8/Rev. 12:5; 19:15; Isa. 65:17; 66:22/Rev. 21:1; Ezek. 47:1, 12/Rev. 22:1–2).

All of the illustrations so far have concerned fulfillments of Old Testament texts which are clearly direct verbal prophecies. It also seems possible that there are texts which John understands as prophetic but do not appear as such in the Old Testament. It is worthy to consider whether parts of certain Old Testament historical narratives are viewed as *indirect typological prophecies*. Many of the Old Testament passages listed in our above discussion of analogical uses are potential candidates in this category. That is, are all of these texts merely analogies? We have already found that the essence of the analogies has to do with a basic *correspondence* of meaning between Old Testament prophecy or *historical* narrative and something in the New Testament. Some of these Old Testament historical elements have also undergone an escalation, even a universalization, under John's hand. Perhaps there was a prophetic rationale in escalating these historical texts. At any rate, such uses are worthy of further inquiry in this direction, especially against the background of John's and the New Testament's awareness that the "latter days" had been inaugurated, that the church was the latter-day Israel and that the whole Old Testament pointed toward this climax of salvation history (for inaugurated eschatological language cf. Mark 1:15; Acts 2:17; Gal. 4:4; 1 Cor. 10:11; 2 Cor. 6:2; 1 Tim. 4:1; 2 Tim. 3:1; 1 Pet. 1:20; Heb. 1:2; 9:26; James 5:3; 1 John 2:18; Jude 18; *Rev. 1:1; 1:19; 4:1; 22:6, 10*—cf. Beale 1984b, 415–20). The precedent of overt typological-prophetic uses in Matthew, Hebrews, and elsewhere in the New Testament should leave open the same possibility in Revelation.

Inverted Use of the Old Testament

There are some allusions which on the surface are distinctly contradictory to the Old Testament contextual meaning. But further study again reveals the imprecise nature of such categories. The clearest example of this is Revelation 3:9, which collectively makes reference to the Isaianic prophecies that the Gentiles would come and bow down before Israel and recognize them as God's chosen people (Isa. 45:14; 49:23; 60:14). However, this Jewish hope from Isaiah has been turned upside down, since it is the Jewish persecutors of the Christians whom God will make to submit to the church. This reversal of Isaiah's language is most likely attributable to a conscious attempt to express the irony that the submission which unbelieving ethnic Jews hoped to receive from Gentiles, they themselves would be forced to render to the church (so also Vos, 25; R. H. Mounce 1977, 118). John concludes that ethnic Jews had become as unbelieving Gentiles—non-Jews—because of rejection of Christ and persecution of Christians. In fact, this ironic element is intensified at the end of verse 9 through John's reference to the Gentile church as the true Israel. This is accomplished by making a reverse application of Isaiah 43:4, which originally spoke of God's love and honor for Israel above the nations. Vos is therefore inconsistent in recognizing an irony in the first part of verse 9 but concluding with respect to the Isaiah 43:4 citation that "the context of the alleged quotation has been totally disregarded" (26). This rather shows a consistent ironic understanding of some of the major themes in Isaiah 40–66. And while such a view arises out of a contextual awareness of the Old Testament, the New Testament use is so diametrically opposite that it is best to categorize this as an inverted or ironic use.

The use of the cosmic universality terminology from Daniel 7:14 in Revelation 5:9 reveals an intended inversion. Whereas in Daniel the phrase refers to the nations subjugated to Israel's rule, now these very nations rule together with the Messiah.

A sampling of other such uses are noteworthy. Daniel 7:21 refers to an antitheocratic "horn" which "was waging war with the saints and overpowering them." This is applied in reverse fashion in Revelation 12:7–8 to describe the overthrow of Satan by Michael and his angels. Such reverse application probably doesn't reflect unconscious activity or an atomistic exegesis, but polemical irony is expressed by portraying the theocratic forces' defeat of the cosmic enemy through the same imagery from Daniel 7 which was used to describe how this enemy began to defeat God's forces. This may be a figurative way of expressing a *lex talionis* irony whereby the point is to show that the same way in which the enemy will try to subdue God will be used by God himself to subdue the enemy. That this language is intentionally drawn in reverse manner from Daniel 7:21 is evident not only by the verbal likeness (cf. Theod.) but also by the immediately following allusion to Daniel 2:35 (Rev. 12:8b) *and* by the same Daniel 7:21 reversal in Revelation 17:14, where the Danielic "Lord of lords and King of kings" (= Dan. 4:37 [LXX]) is the subject of the polemical overthrow.

The same kind of retributive ironies can be observed elsewhere in the Apocalypse: Daniel 8:10 in Revelation 12:4, 9, 10; Daniel 7:7ff. in Revelation 5:6–7 (so 1 En. 90:9–13, 16; Test. Jos. 19:6–8; Midr. Rab. 99:2; 4 Ezra 13:1ff.–cf. Beale, 1983); Daniel 7:14 in Revelation 13:7–8; Exodus 8:10 and 15:11, etcetera in Revelation 13:4; Exodus 3:14 (esp. Midr. Rab. Exod. 3:14) in Revelation 17:8 (cf. 1:4, 8; 4:8; 11:17; 16:5; cf. also Ezra 9:14b in 1QMI, 6b and Dan. 11:40, 44–45 in 1QMI, 4).

There may be other examples of this reversal phenomenon but those discussed should alert one to caution in making facile statements about non-contextual, atomistic, or straightforward contextual use, since the apocalyptic style is not always susceptible merely to such categories.

Nevertheless, all of the above cases studied here and throughout section 4 can be categorized, at least, as *broadly* contextual. Vanhoye has noted that John employs Old Testament references always with a view to making them contribute to the unified argument of his work (1962, 463–64), and that every page "witnesses to a penetrating intelligence of the ancient prophecies and of a perfect familiarity with their mode of expression" (1962, 462). A. Gangemi observes that John doesn't choose Old Testament allusions at random but in accord with the main themes of the Apocalypse: divine transcendence, redemption, Yahweh's servant, Babylon's judgment, and new creation of the heavenly Jerusalem (1974, 322–38). And it is clear that John drew these unifying themes of his work from the Old Testament (in this case Isaiah 40–66). Indeed, John is continuing to develop fundamental lines of Old Testament salvation history (Cambier 1955, 118–21; Gangemi 1974, 332–39).

Stylistic Use of Old Testament Language

This use represents the most general category so far discussed. It has long been recognized that the Apocalypse contains a multitude of grammatical solecisms. Charles claimed it contained more grammatical irregularities than any other Greek document of the ancient world (1920, cxliii). He accounted for this with his famous dictum *"while he writes in Greek, he thinks in Hebrew*, and the thought has naturally affected the vehicle of expression" (cxliii), a judgment which has met with subsequent agreement, especially recently (cf. Sweet 1979, 16–17, A. Y. Collins 1984, 47 and above all S. Thompson 1985, passim).

But was this intentional on the author's part or an unconscious by-product of his Semitic mind? It seems that his grammatical "howlers" are deliberate attempts to reproduce Semitic idioms in his Greek, the closest analogy being that of the Septuagint translations—especially Aquila (Sweet 1979, 16; see especially Thompson 1985, 108 and passim). The fact that most of the time the author does keep the rules further points to the solecisms being intentional.

Why did John write this way? His purpose was deliberately to create a "biblical" effect in the hearer and thus to demonstrate the solidarity of his work with that of the divinely inspired Old Testament Scriptures (Sweet 1979, 16). A polemical purpose may also have been included. John may have been expressing the idea that Old Testament truth via the church as the new Israel was uncompromisingly penetrating the

Gentile world, and would continue to until the final parousia (cf. somewhat similarly Collins 1984, 47; Thompson 1985, 108).

Conclusion

Perhaps one of the reasons for the high degree of Old Testament influence in the Apocalypse is that the author could think of no better way to describe some of his visions which were difficult to explain than with the language already used by the Old Testament prophets to describe similar visions. The above study, particularly of categories of usage in the Apocalypse, favors the evaluation of I. Fransen:

> The familiarity with the Old Testament, with the spirit which lives in the Old Testament, is a most essential condition for a fruitful reading of the Apocalypse (1956–1957, 67; cf. likewise J. P. M. Sweet 1981, 111).

This is a conclusion which runs counter to that of Barnabas Lindars's general evaluation of the primary role of the Old Testament in the majority of the New Testament corpus:

> The place of the Old Testament in the formation of New Testament theology is that of a servant, ready to run to the aid of the gospel whenever it is required, bolstering up arguments, and filling out meaning through evocative allusions, but never acting as the master or leading the way, nor even guiding the process of thought behind the scenes (1977, 66).

However, Lindars appears to exclude the Apocalypse from his analysis (cf. 1977, 63–64; 1961, passim). He expresses apparent openness to discovering more respect for Old Testament contextual meaning in the Apocalypse because he judges John's writing not to be the result of urgent, ad hoc apologetic concerns but to have arisen out of meditation worked out quietly in the study at a slightly later stage of Christian apocalyptic (1977, 63).

Therefore, the conclusion of this investigation is that the place of the Old Testament in the formation of thought in the Apocalypse is both that of a servant and a guide: for John the Christ event is *the* key to understanding the Old Testament and yet reflection back on the Old Testament context leads the way to further comprehension of this event and provides the redemptive-historical background against which the apocalyptic visions are better understood. Whether or not there is the same reciprocal relationship elsewhere in the New Testament is a question which cannot be addressed here. However, the observation that much of the New Testament was written not only with an apologetic motive but also in an apocalyptic atmosphere should cause us to be open to this possibility.

Bibliography

Bauckham, R. "The Eschatological Earthquake in the Apocalypse of John," *NovT* 19 (1977): 224–33.

Beale, G. K. "The Problem of the Man From the Sea in IV Ezra 13 and Its Relation to the Messianic Concept in John's Apocalypse," *NovT* 25 (1983): 182–88.

————. *The Use of Daniel in Jewish Apocalyptic Literature and in the Revelation of St. John* (Lanham, 1984) (= 1984a).

————. "The Influence of Daniel Upon the Structure and Theology of John's Apocalypse," *JETS* 27 (1984): 413–23 (= 1984b).

————. "The Origin of the Title 'King of Kings and Lord of Lords' in Revelation 17.14," *NTS* 31 (1985): 618–20.

Beasley-Murray, G. R. *The Book of Revelation,* New Century Bible Commentary (Grand Rapids, 1981).

Caird, G. B. *The Revelation of St. John the Divine,* HNTC (New York, 1966).

Cambier, J. "Les images de l'Ancien Testament dans l'Apocalypse de saint Jean," *NRT* (1955): 113–22.

Carnegie, D. R. "The Hymns in Revelation: Their Origin and Function," a dissertation submitted to the Council for National Academic Awards for the Degree Doctor of Philosophy-Research conducted under the supervision of the London Bible College (1978).

————. "Worthy Is the Lamb: the Hymns in Revelation," in H. H. Rowden, ed., *Christ the Lord: Studies Presented to Donald Guthrie* (Downers Grove, 1982), 243–56.

Charles, R. H. *A Critical and Exegetical Commentary on the Revelation of St. John* I, ICC (Edinburgh, 1920).

Collins, A. Y. *Crisis and Catharsis. The Power of the Apocalypse* (Philadelphia, 1984).

Comblin, J. *Le Christ dans l'Apocalypse* in Bibliothèque De Théologie, Théologie biblique-Série 3, 6 (Tournai, 1965).

Delling, G. "Zum gottesdienstlichen Stil der Johannes-Apokalypse," *NovT* 3 (1959): 107–37.

Dittmar, W. D. *Vetus Testamentum in Novo* (Göttingen, 1903).

Draper, J. A. "The Heavenly Feast of Tabernacles: Revelation 7:1–17," *JSNT* 19 (1983): 133–47.

Farrer, A. *The Revelation of St. John the Divine* (Oxford, 1964).

Ford, D. *The Abomination of Desolation in Biblical Eschatology* (Washington, 1979).

Fransen, I. "Cahier de Bible: Jésus, le Témoin Fidèle (Apocalypse)," *BiVi Chrét* 16 (1956–57): 66–79.

Gangemi, A. "L'utilizzazione del Deutero-Isaia nell' Apocalisse di Giovanni," *Eunt Doc* 27 (1974): 311–39.

Goulder, M. D. "The Apocalypse as an Annual Cycle of Prophecies," *NTS* 27 (1981): 342–67.

Gray, D. A. "The Day of the Lord and Its Culmination in the Book of Revelation," unpublished Ph.D. dissertation (Univ. of Manchester, 1974).

Hartman, L. *Prophecy Interpreted* in Coniectanea Biblica: New Testament Series 1 (Uppsala, 1966).

Holtz, T. *Die Christologie der Apokalypse des Johannes,* in Texte und Untersuchungen 85 (Berlin, 1971).

Hühn, E. *Die alttestamentlichen citate und Reminiscenzen im Neuen Testament* (Tübingen, 1900).

Kuhn, K. G. "God-Magog" in *TWNT* 1 (Stuttgart, 1933): 790–92.

Lancellotti, A. "L'Antico Testamento nell'Apocalisse," *Rivist Bib* 14 (1966): 369–84.

Läuchli, S. "Eine Gottesdienststruktur in der Johannesoffenbarung," *TZ* 16 (1960): 359–78.

Lindars, B. *New Testament Apologetic* (London, 1961).

———. "The Place of the Old Testament in the Formation of New Testament Theology," *NTS* 23 (1977): 59–66.

Lohse, E. "Die alttestamentliche Sprache des Sehers Johannes, Textkritische Bemerkungen zur Apokalypse," *ZNW* 52 (1961): 122–26.

Longman, T. "The Divine Warrior: The New Testament Use of an Old Testament Motif," *WTJ* 44 (1982): 290–307.

Lust, J. "The Order of the Final Events in Revelation and in Ezekiel," in *L'Apocalypse Johannique et l'Apocalyptique dans le Nouveau Testament,* Bibliotheca Ephemeridum Theologicarum Lovaniensium 53 (Gembloux, 1980): 179–83.

Marconcini, B. "L'utilizzazione del T.M. nelle citazione isaiane dell' Apocalisse," *RiVist Bib* 24 (1976): 113–36.

Michaels, J. R. "The Centurion's Confession and the Spear Thrust," *CBQ* 29 (1967): 102–9.

Mounce, R. H. *The Book of Revelation,* NICNT (Grand Rapids, 1980).

Müller, H. P. "Formgeschichtliche Untersuchungen zu Apc 4F," unpublished doctoral dissertation (Univ. of Heidelberg, 1962).

———. "Die himmlische Ratsversammlung. Motivgeschichtliches zu Apc 5:1–5," *ZNW* 54 (1963): 254–67.

Prigent, P. *Apocalypse et Liturgie,* Cahiers Théologiques 52 (Neuchatel, 1964).

———. "Une Tradition Messianique relative à Juda," *MDB* 11 (1979): 46.

von Rad, G. *Old Testament Theology* 2, translated by D. M. G. Stalker (New York: 1965).

Schlatter, A. *Das Alte Testament in der johanneischen Apokalypse* in *Beiträge zur Förderung christlicher Theologie* 16:6 (Gütersloh, 1912).

Schüssler-Fiorenza, E. "Apokalypsis and Propheteia. The Book of Revelation in the Context of Early Christian Prophecy," in *L'Apocalypse johannique et l'Apocalyptique dans le Nouveau Testament,* Bibliotheca Ephemeridum Theologicarum Lovaniensium 53 (Gembloux, 1980), 105–128.

Selwyn, E. C. "Dialogues of the Christian Prophets," *Expositor,* Sixth Series 5 (1902): 321–43.

Shea, W. H. "The Covenantal Form of the Letters to the Seven Churches," *AUSS* 21 (1983): 71–84.

Strand, K. A. "A Further Note on the Covenantal Form in the Book of Revelation," *AUSS* 21 (1983): 251–64.

Sweet, J. P. M. *Revelation* in SCM Pelican Commentaries (London, 1979).
————. "Maintaining the Testimony of Jesus: The Suffering of Christians in the Revelation of John," in W. Horbury, ed., and B. McNeil, ed., *Suffering and Martyrdom in the New Testament* (Cambridge, 1981), 101–17.
Swete, H. B. *Commentary on Revelation* (London, 1911).
S. Thompson *The Apocalypse and Semitic Syntax*, Society for New Testament Studies Monograph Series 52 (Cambridge, 1985).
Trudinger, P. "Some Observations Concerning the Text of the Old Testament in the Book of Revelation," *JTS* 17 (1966): 82–88.
van der Waal, C. *Openbaring van Jezus Christus* (Groningen, 1971).
Vanhoye, A. "L'utilisation du livre d'Ezéchiel dans l'Apocalypse," *Bib* 43 (1962): 436–76.
Vos, L. A. *The Synoptic Traditions in the Apocalypse* (Kampen, 1965).
Wikenhauser, A. "Das Problem des tausendjährigen Reiches in der Johannes-Apokalypse," *Römische Quartalschrift* 40 (1932): 13–25.

Part 5

Did the New Testament Authors Respect the Context of the Old Testament Text?

Two Perspectives on Paul's Use of Exodus 34 in 2 Corinthians 3

16

Beyond the Things That Are Written?

Saint Paul's Use of Scripture

Morna D. Hooker

From Morna D. Hooker, "Beyond the Things That Are Written? Paul's Use of Scripture," *New Testament Studies* 27: 295–309. Reprinted with the permission of Cambridge University Press.

It seemed appropriate that a lecture given to honor a scholar whose concerns have been centered on the Old Testament, by someone whose field is the New Testament, should link together these two topics. I have therefore chosen to consider one aspect of the problem of the way in which the Old Testament is interpreted by New Testament authors: more specifically, the authority ascribed by one of them—St. Paul—to the Old Testament in relation to the revelation of God in Christ.

Any New Testament scholar who is in any way interested in the problem of hermeneutics is well aware of the dichotomy between the approach of New Testament authors to "Scripture" and our own. A study of their methods of exegesis must surely make any twentieth-century preacher uncomfortable, for they tear passages out of context, use allegory or typology to give old stories new meanings, contradict the plain meaning of the text, find references to Christ in passages where the original authors certainly never intended any, and adapt or even alter the wording in order to make it yield the meaning they require. Often one is left exclaiming: whatever the passage from the Old Testament originally meant, it certainly was not this! Yet we cannot simply dismiss their interpretation as false, for they were certainly being true to the exegetical methods of their day. Moreover, although the biblical scholar's primary concern will always be with the original meaning of his material, the present tendency in hermeneutics is to emphasize that "meaning" can never be limited to the intentions of an author. We may consider that the meaning which Paul gave to the prohibition to muzzle an ox in Deuteronomy 25:4[1] would have seemed as foreign to the original author as it seems far-fetched to us; but it is at least worth asking *why* Paul interprets Scripture in this kind of way. What was his underlying hermeneutical principle?—if, indeed, he had one.

The phrase which I have borrowed as the title for this chapter is a well-known *crux interpretum* in Paul.[2] He tells the Corinthians that he wishes them to learn what this means: "not beyond what is written." Alas! If only we *knew* what it meant! The most ingenious theory is, of course, that the phrase is a gloss, so that to ask what Paul meant by it is to chase a red herring. My own hunch is that Paul means "You Corinthians must learn to keep to Scripture"—that is, you must not start trying to add philosophical notions to the basic Christian gospel.[3] If the phrase "nothing beyond what is written" seems an odd way of putting this, it is worth remembering that for Paul the death and resurrection of Christ were "in accordance with the scriptures," and that throughout these early chapters of 1 Corinthians, he is concerned to demonstrate—from Scripture—the folly of human wisdom, with which the Corinthians want to clothe the gospel. For Paul, to stick to *this* understanding of Scripture *is* to stick to the gospel.

But does Paul himself really stick to Scripture? Or can he in turn be accused of going beyond what is written? Does he not often use Scripture simply as a convenient peg on which to hang his arguments? Although he may frequently quote from Scripture, the interpretation he gives it often lies beyond the obvious meaning of the text. His somewhat artificial exegesis leaves one wondering whether there is anything which it would not be possible for him to argue on the basis of Scripture. Is there some unifying factor which explains his approach and sets limits to his imagination?

Perhaps the clearest example of Paul's apparent ability to do what he will with Scripture is seen in his arguments about the law. For in thumbing through the pages of a Greek text, one is soon aware of the fact that the greatest concentration of quotations from the law is to be found in those passages where Paul is arguing *against* the law. If Paul uses the law to refute the law, is he not quite blatantly wishing to have his cake and

---

1. 1 Cor. 9:9.
2. 1 Cor. 4:6.
3. M. D. Hooker, "'Beyond the Things which are Written': An Examination of 1 Cor. 4:6," *New Testament Studies* 10 (1963): 127–32.

eat it? Is he really following his own advice to "keep to what is written," or is he twisting its meaning to make it mean whatever he wants?

One of the key passages for understanding Paul's position on this matter is 2 Corinthians 3, and I would like to take some time in exploring this passage. Needless to say, it is full of problems, ambiguities, and pitfalls. Nevertheless, it certainly repays closer examination.

The chapter begins with a brilliant metaphor: brilliant because Paul, in trying to defend his apostleship, describes the Corinthians themselves as his own credentials; since they owe their Christian faith to Paul, they cannot deny his apostleship without denying their own Christian standing. It is not long, however, before Paul's metaphor—typically—becomes a mixed one. "*You* are our letter of recommendation," he says, "a letter written not with ink but with the Spirit of the living God; not on tablets of stone but on hearts of flesh." Paul has jumped from one image to another; put them together, and he is clearly in a mess, for while it is possible to speak metaphorically of the Spirit of God writing on men's hearts, it really is not much use trying to write on stone with ink! Nevertheless, we can see how he got there—via a clear echo of Jeremiah 31.

The chapter which follows is concerned with this same theme of Paul's ministry. Like other crucial passages in the Pauline epistles, the argument here is based on a comparison and contrast: not between law and gospel, nor between Moses and Christ, but between the ministry of Moses and that of Paul. With amazing audacity, Paul defends his own ministry, and his ability to fulfill that ministry—albeit an ability which is given to him by God—by comparing himself favorably with Moses. Paul is minister of a new covenant, ratified not by letters engraved on stones, but by the Spirit at work in men's hearts. The argument is of course based on Exodus 34, the story of Moses' descent from Mount Sinai with the two tablets of the law, and quickly becomes an exposition of that passage. New Testament scholars at the moment delight in applying the term *midrash pesher* in a multitude of inappropriate places; if anything may properly be described as *midrash pesher*, however, 2 Corinthians 3 certainly qualifies. Paul gives a running commentary on the passage from Exodus, explaining it, not in terms of Moses, but in terms of its fulfillment in Christ.[4] He begins, however, by contrasting the glory of Moses' ministry, which was concerned with letters en-

4. It has been argued that Paul is here adapting an earlier Jewish-Christian *midrash* on Exod. 34, which extolled the figure of Moses and the Mosaic law. See S. Schulz, "Die Decke des Moses, *Z.N.T.W.* 49 (1958): 1–30, D. Georgi, *Die Gegner des Paulus im 2 Korintherbrief* (Neukirchen, 1964), 274–82. But Paul's own Jewish background, together with his opposition to those who still gave a central role to the law, is sufficient to explain his argument here.

graved on stone—a ministry which, he says, brought only death—with that of the ministry of the life-giving Spirit: if the ministry of law, which was able only to condemn, was accompanied by glory, how much *more* glorious is the ministry of righteousness—so much so, that the glory of the former pales into insignificance by comparison. It will be noted that Paul does not *deny* glory to Moses; indeed, he reminds us that, according to the Exodus story, the glory which shone from his face when he came down Sinai was such that the children of Israel could not gaze at it.[5] Nevertheless, says Paul, this glory was καταργουμένη, verse 7—in the process of abolition, transient, temporary. Moreover, if one could measure the strength of glory with the appropriate instrument—a doxameter perhaps?—the glory seen on Moses' face is nothing by comparison with the glory which belongs to the ministry of the Spirit, a ministry which endures. After all, when one is plugged into the mains, candles seem a pretty inefficient form of lighting.

Well then, if the new glory is so much greater than the old, surely this, too, will be too dazzling for human eyes to bear? If Moses was forced to cover his face with a veil, will not the Christian minister also need to cover *his* face—since now the irradiation hazard must be infinitely greater? This would be the logical conclusion of Paul's argument, but in fact Paul makes precisely the opposite point. Unlike Moses, Paul does *not* cover his face; he is in no way ashamed, and makes no concealment, but acts boldly—a sign of the liberty that comes through the Spirit.[6] Earlier Paul's argument seemed to imply that he accepted the explanation for Moses' veil which is found in Exodus—that is, that it was worn to protect the children of Israel, because they were unable to gaze on the glory reflected from his face. Now, however, he gives a totally different explanation: Moses wore a veil in order to conceal the end of what was being done away with—by which he seems to mean the glory. It is true that some commentators try to reconcile these two explanations by understanding the second as meaning that Moses deliberately concealed from Israel "the fulfillment of the law"—that is, Christ, whose glory is greater than that of the law.[7] If the end of the law

5. A similar interpretation is given in Philo, *De Vita Mosis,* 2.70. Both Paul and Philo in fact go beyond what is said in Exodus, which is that the people were afraid to come near Moses.

6. For the link between boldness and the absence of a veil, see W. C. van Unnik, "'With Unveiled Face,' an Exegesis of 2 Corinthians III 12–18," *Novum Testamentum* 6 (1963): 153–69. Brevard S. Childs, *Exodus* (London: S.C.M. Old Testament Library, 1974), 623, suggests that meekness might have been associated with Moses via Num. 12:3, which is also an account of a theophany.

7. E.g. J. Héring, *The Second Epistle of Saint Paul to the Corinthians* (London: E.T., 1967), in loc.; R. P. C. Hanson, 2 Corinthians, London 1954, in loc.; A. T. Hanson, *Jesus Christ in the Old Testament* (London, 1965), 28–29.

is its fulfillment, this too will be too dangerous for human eyes. But there are great difficulties with this interpretation. Moreover, even if we were to accept it, we still would not have solved the basic inconsistency in Paul's picture. For he has told us that Israel could not gaze on Moses' glory: how, then, does it come about that Christians can now gaze on the overwhelming glory which belongs to Christ?

We need to recognize that Paul has—typically—moved in the course of his argument from one interpretation of the Old Testament image to another. In verses 7–11 he compares the glory of Moses and of Christian preachers, and maintains that the latter far exceeds the former; if he were to pursue the "how much more" theme he would be in trouble, for clearly Christian preachers ought to need much thicker veils than Moses ever wore! But in fact if we read Paul carefully we see that, like the narrative in Exodus itself, he does not mention Moses' veil at all at this stage of the argument—he simply refers to the dazzling glory which presumably necessitated the veil which is referred to later in the Exodus story. In this paragraph Paul concentrates on the superiority of the "new" covenant to the old, and he does not explain how it is that Christians can gaze without danger on the overwhelming glory which is now revealed. In verses 12ff., however, he concentrates on the theme of concealment, symbolized by the veil, and explains why it is that he, unlike Moses, does not wear a veil. He seems to have overlooked the fact that his opponents, following on from the logic of verses 7–11, might well give a very different explanation and retort: the reason why you, Paul, do not wear a veil is quite simply that you do not have any glory to conceal!

It is remarkable that none of the commentaries I have consulted acknowledges that there is a *non sequitur* in Paul's thought at this point—though several of them struggle to reconcile the conflicting motives which he attributes to Moses. But they cannot be reconciled—and they ought not to be. Paul is using the idea of glory in two different ways in the two paragraphs, and we shall misunderstand him completely if we try to combine the two arguments. And why *should* anyone expect Paul to apply the image consistently, after beginning the whole section with a glorious mixed metaphor? It is typical of Paul to explore an idea in this confusing but very rich way.[8]

In verses 6–11, then, Paul makes four basic contrasts between the ministry of the new covenant and the ministry of the old. The old one

---

8. These inconsistencies do not in themselves provide evidence for the view that Paul has taken over an earlier *midrash* and failed to adapt it sufficiently for his purpose. Indeed, if he were doing this, one might perhaps expect him to produce a more consistent interpretation than he would if he were composing the *midrash* himself and incorporating traditional Jewish interpretations of the Sinai story.

functions through letter, γράμμα, the new through spirit, πνεῦμα; the former kills, the latter gives life; the former brings condemnation, the latter justification or righteousness; the former is temporary and the latter permanent. If even the former is accompanied by glory, then of course the latter will possess much greater glory.

In verses 12ff., on the other hand, Paul explores the significance of the veil. Whereas Paul is bold (as indeed his opponents complain), Moses hid his face in order to conceal the end of what was being abrogated. But what was being abrogated? Is it the glory, as in verse 7? Now the logical answer to this question must be "yes," since what Moses hid was his shining face; it is therefore the end of the glory which Moses concealed. But the word meaning "glory," δόξα, is feminine, and the participle used here for "abrogated" is either masculine or neuter; so it seems that Paul must be thinking also of what that glory represented—namely the ministry of Moses and the old covenant. But the words for both covenant, διαθήκη, and ministry, διακονία, are also feminine! The answer to this grammatical puzzle may be that Paul has used the phrases τὸ καταργούμενον and τὸ μένον in verse 11 of "what is temporary" and "what is permanent," and he repeats one of those phrases here to sum up everything which belongs to the old covenant. Moses concealed everything that was on the way out. Or perhaps Paul is referring back to τὸ γράμμα, for that is certainly being abrogated.

So Moses hid his face. "But," says Paul, "the minds of Israel were hardened." Once again, we seem to have a strange *non sequitur* in Paul's exposition. Why the "but" at this point? And what is the logical connection between Moses' veil and the hardening of Israel's minds? The solution, I suggest, is found if we look back at the story of Moses' shining face in Exodus, and see how it is expounded by Paul in 2 Corinthians 3:14 and 15. According to the account in Exodus 34:29ff., Moses came down from Mount Sinai carrying the two tablets of the law, unaware of the fact that his face still shone as a result of his encounter with God. The people were naturally afraid to approach him, but Moses summoned them to him, and gave them all the commandments which the Lord had given to him. It is only at this stage, when the law has been delivered to Israel, that Moses is said to have covered his face. After that, we are told, Moses always wore a veil—except when he went in to speak with the Lord. Then he would take off the veil, and keep it off until he had come out—with shining face—to tell Israel whatever the Lord commanded him; only when that was done would he cover his face again. Now it is immediately obvious that there is something rather odd about this narrative in Exodus: the reason which it offers for Moses' veil—namely the splendor of his face—does not fit what actually happens, since he fails to wear it when he addresses Israel.[9] The picture given by the Exodus narrative seems to be of Moses wearing a veil *except* when he is receiving or passing on the commands of Yahweh—that is, when he is acting as the mediator of the law; at such times, the veil must be removed, presumably in order that nothing may impede the revelation of God to his people. It is perhaps not surprising to find Paul giving two contradictory interpretations of this story. The first, which seems to be assumed by Paul in his first paragraph, starts from the statement in Exodus 34:30 that Israel was afraid to come close to the glorified Moses; the veil conceals from them this terrifying symbol of the presence of God. This is probably the way in which the passage was understood by Paul's contemporaries, since there is a Jewish tradition which speaks of the glory of Moses as remaining until his death.[10] The other explanation is that which Paul offers in his second paragraph: when Moses is the "conductor" of divine revelation, then he cannot wear a veil; but the glory which shines from his face is the reflection of God's glory—a glory which is presumably renewed when he speaks with God, and which could therefore well be understood—though Exodus does not say so—to fade at other times. Since, according to the Exodus story, Moses veiled his face at those times when he was not being "charged" or passing the "charge" on, Paul's interpretation is at least logical, even if the notion of Moses concealing what did not exist is a little quaint. Paul's whole argument in both sections is in fact based on the assumption that the glory on Moses' face did not last, an assumption which he does not bother to prove, perhaps because he is not arguing with Jews in 2 Corinthians; it seems unlikely that Jews would have accepted his bald statement that the glory of Moses was in any way temporary.[11]

It is, then, this account of Moses removing and replacing his veil which Paul expounds in verses 14–15. The clue to Paul's statement "But their minds were hardened" is found in the words which follow: "for until this very day the same veil remains unlifted at the reading of the old covenant—for it is in Christ that it is done away with." What Paul is doing, I suggest, is to explain how it comes about that—contrary to the pattern set out in Exodus—the veil now obscures the old covenant when it is read. The reason, he says, is that the minds of Israel were hardened. *That* is why the veil could not be removed when the old covenant was read. Once again, we see how Paul makes a statement about Judaism which certainly would not have been accepted by his Jewish

9. Cf. Childs, *Exodus*, 618–19.
10. Targum of Onkelos, Deut. 34:7.
11. Childs, *Exodus*, 621–22, suggests that Paul does not argue the point because his exegesis reflects a well-known Jewish tradition. However, there is no evidence for this.

contemporaries—namely, that the true meaning of the old covenant is hidden from them. In talking about a veil which is not lifted at the reading of the old covenant, Paul would no doubt have in mind not only the veil on Moses' face in the Exodus story but the curtain which hid the Torah in the synagogue and which was of course removed whenever it was read.

What Paul describes is a two-way process—or rather nonprocess: the veil—the barrier which prevents something being seen—goes hand-in-hand with a refusal to see the truth. This same argument is used elsewhere in the New Testament of men's refusal to respond to the gospel, most notably in Mark 4 and Romans 11. So here: if Moses wore a veil, and if the veil remains unlifted from Scripture to this day, it is because Israel's minds were hardened. Paul repeats his argument in verse 16, but now the veil seems to have moved to Israel's heart; it is still the barrier which conceals the truth, however: "until this day, whenever Moses is read, a veil lies on their heart. But whenever he turns to the Lord, the veil is taken away." At this point Paul returns to the Exodus story, and actually quotes from it, but he does not explain whether it is Moses who turns to the Lord—as in the original story—or Israel or Christian believers or perhaps all three; nor does he explain whether "the Lord" means Yahweh (as in Exodus) or refers to Christ (as is normal in Paul). However, the close parallelism between verses 14 and 16 gives us a clue to this problem. The veil, says Paul, is done away with in Christ (v. 14); it is removed when someone turns to the Lord (v. 16). His statement is an exposition of Exodus 34:34: Moses removed the veil when he went in to the Lord. Insofar as the words refer to Moses, "the Lord" must refer to Yahweh. But Paul is also applying the passage to the present situation. And since the veil is now on the heart of Israel, he must be thinking also of Israel turning to the Lord—that is to Christ, with whom the veil is abolished. The text from Exodus is given a new meaning, as it is applied to the time of fulfillment: Israel turns away from the letter to the Spirit.

But just as it seems as if the veil is being lifted from our minds, too, and we think that we begin to grasp Paul's meaning, he confounds us all by declaring: "Now the Lord is the Spirit." Paul is not, of course, concerned here with the niceties of trinitarian theology. Rather, he is returning to the contrast with which he began—the contrast between letter and Spirit. The Lord is the Spirit who writes directly on men's hearts. In turning to the Lord, Israel not only experiences the removal of the veil, but moves from a relationship with God which is based on letter to one which is based on Spirit.

So the chapter concludes with a clear contrast between Moses and Israel on the one hand and Christian apostles and believers on the other; the latter gaze with unveiled face at the glory of the Lord, and are changed from glory to glory. At this point, we perhaps see at last what Paul is doing; returning to the theme of the contrast between the two kinds of glory, he now demonstrates that the first was derivative, the second direct. Moses caught a glimpse of God's glory, and it was this which was reflected from his face, and which was seen by Israel—until even that was hidden from them; but Christians gaze directly at the glory of the Lord—a glory which, as Paul goes on to explain in chapter 4, is seen in Christ, who is the image of God. Moses plays a mediating role; this is why he is compared with Christian apostles and not with Christ, who is the source of glory. Whereas Moses concealed the glory which was reflected from his face with a veil, Christians wear no veil, but reflect the glory of the Lord constantly, as though in a mirror,[12] as they become like him in character; nor does their glory fade, for they are made progressively more glorious, as they are transformed into Christ's image.

Those who are entrusted with this ministry, then, have renounced underhand ways and cunning; they do not tamper with God's word, but declare God's truth openly. One is somewhat surprised by Paul's vigorous language here; it seems more likely that he is defending himself against attack than bringing an accusation against Moses. Certainly he is defending himself when he goes on to say "even if our gospel *is* veiled, it is veiled only to those who are perishing." But if *his* gospel is veiled, is he not in the same situation as Moses? The answer seems to be that, as Paul puts it, "in their case the god of this world has blinded the minds of the unbelievers, to keep them from seeing the light of the gospel of the glory of Christ." In the case of the Jews it was Moses—presumably acting under divine instructions—who veiled his face; but now it is Satan who tries to hide the light of the gospel from men and women. Once again, Paul states his case, rather than arguing it. The gospel is nothing less than Christ himself, and the glory which we see in him is the glory of God himself, who at the creation said "Let light shine out of darkness." Paul here links the light of Genesis 1:3 with the glory revealed in Christ, which eclipses that of Moses. Interestingly enough, he is not the only New Testament author to do so. It is well known that the fourth Gospel begins with a clear echo of Genesis 1; the opening verses explore the themes of creation, of life and light. But the author then goes on to link this with the figure of Moses, and to explore the account

---

12. Many commentators understand κατοπτρίζεσθαι here to mean "behold," but the parallel with Moses suggests that it is used with its alternative meaning "reflect." The difference in meaning is not great. It is only as they *gaze* at Christ that Christians are able to *reflect* his glory. If they are said to be changed from glory to glory through *looking* at the glory of Christ, then they are clearly understood to be *reflecting* that glory.

of the theophany in Exodus 33 and 34;[13] he contrasts the giving of the law through Moses with God's self-disclosure in Christ. No one—not even Moses—has ever seen God, but the only Son has declared him to men, and we have seen his glory—a glory which makes known the character of God himself. The theme set out here is one which underlies the whole of John's gospel: Moses was the mediator of the law, the one through whom God made his glory known, but the Son has not only seen God's glory—he is himself the *source* of divine glory. Christ is a much greater figure than Moses—the real contrast is therefore between Christians and Moses, since both are the recipients of revelation. The glory of Christ is greater than that of Moses, but it is nevertheless continuous with it, and Moses therefore bears witness to Christ, the lesser to the greater.[14]

In John 1, then, we find ideas very similar to those which Paul is handling in 2 Corinthians 3–4. But whereas John begins with the light of creation in Genesis 1 and moves from that to the story of Moses on Sinai in Exodus, Paul begins with Moses and uses Genesis 1:3 as the climax of his argument. It seems likely that both authors are making use of a common tradition here, and it may well be that both of them are using the idea of wisdom, which has come to be associated in Jewish thought with the law. The divine plan was with God from the beginning, and was revealed to Israel on Sinai, just as the divine glory was reflected by Adam in the garden, and then glimpsed again when the law was given. Later rabbinic writings describe the Torah as having been hidden with God since before the creation.[15] It is clear that for Paul the secret wisdom of God, hidden from creation and now revealed, is not the law but Christ; he is the divine plan for mankind, the image to which we are being conformed, and the glory of God—and John expresses the same belief in his own terms. Over against the Jewish claim that God's eternal purpose was finally revealed at Sinai, we have the Christian claim that the Torah only pointed forward to the revelation made in Christ. As the result of a gigantic take-over bid, we find all the functions of the law attributed to Christ.[16]

2 Corinthians 3–4 is an important passage, not simply because it is an interesting example of Pauline exegesis, but because in its central section it raises the question of the role of Scripture. Now we must be careful at this point not to make too much out of what Paul says. His primary

13. See M. D. Hooker, "The Johannine Prologue and the Messianic Secret," *New Testament Studies* 21 (1974): 40–58.

14. John 5:39.

15. E.g., T. Bab. Shabbath 88b.

16. Cf. Rom. 8:3–4; 10:5ff.

concern is not, after all, with Scripture, but with the ministry of Moses. When he refers to the old covenant in verse 14 he of course means the account of the covenant made between God and Israel, not our Old Testament—though commentators sometimes fall into the trap of interpreting the phrase in this anachronistic way; nevertheless, Paul refers to the reading of the old covenant, and to Moses being read—so he is certainly thinking of the recital of Scripture. The covenant is, after all, based on obedience to the demands of Torah, which are written in "the book of the covenant"; in Paul's writings, "Moses" and "law" are almost synonymous. Yet it is clear that Paul—however inconsistent he may sometimes be—could hardly have referred to Scripture itself as "abolished," when Scripture provides him with his primary witness to Christ.

But if Paul's primary concern here is not the role of Scripture, neither is it the role of that part of Scripture which is more specifically known as the law—though part of the confusion in this passage arises, I believe, from Paul's ambivalent attitude to the law. Attempts have been made to find in rabbinic writings indications of an expectation that the Law would be abolished by the Messiah, or replaced by a new law;[17] but the whole idea runs counter to Jewish belief in the Torah as the revelation of God. If the Torah expresses God's eternal plan, set out in heaven before creation, it is scarcely likely that it will be subject to second thoughts! Paul himself, asked if he is abrogating the law, replies with a characteristic μὴ γένοιτο![18] Closer to Paul's attitude is the idea that the age of the law will be succeeded by the age of the Messiah, an idea which suggests fulfillment rather than cancellation. What is it, then, that is done away with in 2 Corinthians 3? What is it that possesses this characteristic of built-in obsolescence? It is not the law itself, but what Paul terms the ministry of Moses. Now it is undoubtedly true that if we were to unpack what Paul meant by this, we should find ourselves talking about a relationship with God which is based on works of the law, and of obedience to the letter of that law. But Paul is not concerned with that issue here, and there is no indication that his opponents in Corinth were demanding obedience to the Jewish law. His principal concern here is the nature of his ministry—which, like the gospel itself, is a matter of πνεῦμα, not γράμμα.

However, it is precisely because the question at issue is the nature of Christian ministry that the role of Scripture is fundamental: for Moses and Paul are both ministers of God's word. But whereas in the Mosaic dispensation the word is enshrined in the written page, in the Christian

17. A full discussion can be found in W. D. Davies, *Torah in the Messianic Age* (Philadelphia, 1952).
18. Rom. 3:31.

dispensation it is embodied in Christ. What the veil hides from Jewish eyes is the temporary character—not of Scripture, but of the Mosaic covenant; when the veil is removed, then at one and the same time the temporary aspect of the law and its abiding character are revealed—temporary, in so far as it is understood in terms of commands which claim to offer life to those who obey them, abiding in so far as it is seen as a witness to Christ. Christ has replaced the law in Paul's thinking as the expression of God's purpose, character and glory; but Paul cannot simply ditch the law. He transfers to Christ his former beliefs about the law without denying the law itself a role. If he seems to denigrate the law, it is because he is concerned to emphasize the superiority of Christ. "What once had splendor has come to have no splendour at all, because of the splendor that surpasses it." Moses was a minister of the law, Paul is a minister of Christ; Moses' ministry was temporary, not because the *law* was temporary, but because the law's *true* role is to be a witness to Christ—this is why, when Christ comes, the Mosaic ministry is superseded. At that stage it is abrogated, because the law takes on its true role.

In looking at this passage in 2 Corinthians, we have noted several times that there are blatant contradictions and *non sequiturs* in Paul's argument. From our point of view, his exposition is inconsistent. His arguments do not stand up logically, and he juxtaposes conflicting images and interpretations of the biblical text. Yet I have no doubt whatever that from his point of view, Paul's argument seemed proper and acceptable. He is, after all, using a well-known method of biblical exegesis; and in this particular case the apparent contradictions in what he says are in part due to the peculiarities of the text which he is expounding, peculiarities which do not worry him in the way that they would worry us—and no doubt, were *we* expounding the passage, we would feel bound to deal with them. In our terms, Paul's own arguments about glory do not hold together; in his terms, both are valid interpretations of the text of Exodus 34. New Testament scholars perhaps need to take warning from this example of one of the dangers into which we easily fall when interpreting Paul—the danger of presupposing that all his exegesis will be consistent, and furthermore, that *his* form of consistency will be similar to our own. In spite of warnings against the *Wörterbuch* approach, writers of monographs often tend to assume that Paul will always use words in the same way, always take a consistent line in handling a topic, always fight the same battles on the same basis. In fact, of course, there are plenty of examples of cases where Paul does nothing of the kind. The fact that in a single passage he can develop a clear line of argument and at the same time apparently tie himself in knots, can combine several images into a mixed meta-

phor, and apply one image in several different ways, is a salutary reminder that one should not try to force Paul into the straitjacket of a
systematic theologian.

There is something else which we can observe in this passage, and
that is Paul's way of approaching Scripture. Paul starts from Christian
experience and expounds Scripture in the light of that experience, quarrying the Old Testament where he will. It is perhaps not accidental that,
though Paul writes a *midrash* on this particular Exodus text, he does *not*
write a commentary on the Book of Exodus. In this respect, his approach is somewhat different from that of the sectarians of Qumran,
even though both employ the so-called *midrash pesher* method, and
both understand the text as fulfilled in their community. Once again,
Paul's method is radically different from that of a modern biblical
scholar, who will think it proper to try to discard all his presuppositions
when he approaches the text. The difference in our approach is, of
course, the result of our own conditioning, for we are trained in the historical method; we are quite confident that the Deuteronomic command to leave an ox unmuzzled was *not* intended as a hidden command
about Christian ministers, that the story of Moses' veil has nothing to
do with the refusal of Jews to recognize the truth of the gospel, that it
is improper to read back Chalcedonian definitions into New Testament
terminology. Paul's exposition of Exodus 34 illustrates clearly the difference between his approach and ours. For him it is axiomatic that the
true meaning of Scripture has been hidden, and is only now made plain
in Christ; for the modern biblical scholar it is axiomatic that the biblical
writings must be interpreted in relation to their contemporary setting,
not treated as secret texts which make sense only to later generations.
What seemed to Paul to be the true interpretation often seems to us to
be a bizarre reinterpretation.

In treating Scripture as holding a hidden meaning Paul was not, of
course, alone. Indeed, to some extent, much of Christendom took the
same view for centuries to come. Rabbinic exegesis presupposed meanings which had to be uncovered. Among Paul's contemporaries, Philo
expounded the allegorical meaning of Scripture, and the sect at Qumran adopted the technique of *midrash pesher* on the assumption that
Scripture contained a hidden eschatological meaning. The principle on
which they worked is summed up in this passage from the Habakkuk
commentary:[19]

> God commanded Habakkuk to write the things that were coming upon
> the last generation, but the fulfillment of the epoch he did not make

19. 1 Qp Hab. 7:1–5.

known to him. And as for the words, *so he may run who reads it,* their interpretation *(pesher)* concerns the Teacher of Righteousness, to whom
God made known all the mysteries *(razim)* of the words of His servants
the prophets.

A similar idea is reflected in apocalyptic writing, for the basis of apocalyptic is that what is written contains a hidden meaning; the fact that
apocalyptic writers wrote in the name of Old Testament characters,
using Old Testament material and deliberately concealing their message in symbolic language, suggests that they understood the prophets
also to have been writing material which contained secret meanings
which needed to be unlocked. We find the Book of Daniel, the one example of apocalyptic writing in the Old Testament, using the same
terms as those found in the Qumran writings. When Daniel interprets
the dream of King Nebuchadnezzar he says:[20] "this mystery *(raz)* has
been revealed to me in order that the interpretation *(p^{e}shar)* may be
made known to the king." Again, the king says to Daniel:[21] "I know that
the spirit of the holy gods is in you and that no mystery *(raz/*μυστήριον
LXX and Theodotion) is too difficult for you; here is the dream which I
saw; tell me its interpretation *(p^{e}shar)."* Daniel is full of riddles; my
guess is that the famous Son of man passages in 1 Enoch are attempts
to unlock the meaning of one of them—namely the vision in Daniel 7.[22]
   The significant difference between Paul and his contemporaries is
not, then, a question of method, since he uses techniques which would
have been familiar to them, even though they are strange to us. Rather
it is seen in his underlying assumption that Christ himself is the key to
the meaning of Scripture. It is not that Christ expounds the Scriptures—as did the Teacher of Righteousness at Qumran, and as was perhaps expected of the Messiah—but that he is himself the one about
whom all Scripture spoke. He is himself the μυστήριον, hidden by God
through all ages and now revealed to men;[23] he is the "Amen" to all
God's promises.[24] In 2 Corinthians 3, Paul has moved beyond the idea
of Christ as the passive *content* of Scripture, to seeing him as the active
agent; he is the Lord, whose glory is reflected in Scripture; he is τὸ
πνεῦμα, the life-giving spirit, the one who writes in men's hearts the
truth to which Scripture bears witness. The writers of the New Testament were convinced that God had acted in Christ; but they were convinced, too, that God had revealed himself in the Hebrew Scriptures. It

---

20. Dan. 2:30.
21. Dan. 4:9.
22. Cf. M. D. Hooker, *The Son of Man in Mark* (London, 1967), 43–47.
23. 1 Cor. 2:7; Col. 1:26.
24. 2 Cor. 1:20.

was necessary for them to hold together the divine origin, both of what they had received from the past, and of what they were experiencing in the present. One way was to see Christ as the fulfillment of Scripture. Another was to see Christ as the blueprint, and regard the law as the witness to him; the roles of the law and the Messiah are then in effect reversed, for though Christ followed the law in time he is understood to have preceded it and ordered it. When this second approach is adopted, it means that Christ is seen as the key to the whole Old Testament; all Scripture can be used, because it is all christological. This is why one does not need to go beyond the things that are written. And it is why Paul himself, however fanciful his interpretation may appear to us, would not consider his exegesis to be eisegesis, for his interpretation of the text accords with his experience of Christ, and therefore does not stray beyond what is written.

I promised to look at Paul's use of Scripture, and I have looked at only one passage: time has been too short for more than one exploratory dig. But, one may ask, does this particular academic exercise have any relevance to our own situation, and our own problems in interpreting the Bible? The two tasks must not, of course, be confused. I cannot use Paul's first-century methods of exegesis, and I therefore inevitably read and use the Old Testament in a different way. Yet the way in which New Testament authors tackled the problem of hermeneutics will necessarily be of concern to Christians.

In Brevard Childs's commentary on Exodus, I came across this comment on Paul's use of Exodus 34:[25]

> Paul's interpretation of 2 Corinthians 3 is a classic example of genuine theological dialectic. He brings to the text the perspective of faith which had learned to hope in Christ . . . but he brings from the text a witness which conversely forms his understanding of God and shapes the Christian life through his Spirit.

When I read these words I found myself saying "Snap!" for in a lecture given last year I had written these words:[26]

> We judge the Bible—but we ourselves are judged *by* it; our Christian experience and attitudes are themselves shaped by the Bible, so that though we interpret the Bible from our own standpoint, that standpoint is itself a response to the Bible. The Bible and the believer are engaged in a continuing dialogue.

25. *Exodus*, 624.
26. "The Bible and the Believer," Peake Memorial Lecture 1978, *Epworth Review* 6 (1979): 88.

It is no accident that for Paul, as for us, Scripture exercises this function of standing over against us, representing the givenness of the past, the otherness of God. What has often happened in the course of history, however, is that there has been no genuine dialectic between the text and experience. Sometimes enthusiastic eisegesis has run riot without any check—and as I typed these words, my front-door bell was rung, with a splendid sense of timing, by a member of the Jehovah's Witnesses! But let us not imagine that it is only the fringe sects that misuse Scripture in this way: it is all too easy for Christians to misrepresent Scripture by reading back into it the beliefs of later age. Sometimes, again, the text has been interpreted in a rigid way which has left no room for ongoing Christian experience: it has been understood, not as a witness to the truth, but as the embodiment of truth. One of the ironies of history is that Paul's own writings have often been fossilized—turned to stone and treated as τὸ γράμμα. Paul's own exposition of Scripture demonstrates the absurdity of using him in this way. For him, God's word is living, not static, and Scripture is the witness to that word, not its embodiment. As for his own words, they were addressed to particular Christian communities; he certainly did not imagine that he was writing universal principles which would be treated as valid in all ages and in every circumstance.

Like Paul, we need to learn *from* the text all that it can teach us, but we need to bring *to* the text our own experience of the ongoing activity of God. Only in this way can the dialogue continue.

17

The Glory and Veil of Moses in 2 Corinthians 3:7–14

An Example of Paul's Contextual Exegesis of the Old Testament—A Proposal[1]

Scott J. Hafemann

From Scott J. Hafemann, "The Glory and Veil of Moses in 2 Cor. 3:7–14: An Example of Paul's Contextual Exegesis of the OT—A Proposal," *Horizons in Biblical Theology* 14 (1992): 31–49. Reprinted by permission.

As Morna Hooker expressed it almost a decade ago, when modern readers of the New Testament encounter its adoption and adaptation of Old Testament texts, "often one is left exclaiming: whatever the passage from the Old Testament originally meant, it certainly was not this!"[2] Ever since the work of Hans Windisch (1924) and Siegfried Schulz (1958),[3] nowhere has this reaction been more universal than to Paul's

1. This chapter is a brief excerpt and summary of various sections of a forthcoming monograph on this subject tentatively entitled *Paul and Moses, The Letter/Spirit Contrast and Argument from Scripture in 2 Cor. 3*. The bulk of this project was written during a year's sabbatical at the University of Tübingen, which was made possible to a large degree by a generous research grant from the Alexander von Humboldt-Stiftung, to whom I am deeply indebted. A shortened form of this chapter was read in the Pauline Epistles Section of the 1990 SBL Annual Meeting.

2. "Beyond the Things That Are Written? St. Paul's Use of Scripture," *NTS* 27 (1981): 295–309, 295.

3. Cf. H. Windisch, *Der Zweite Korintherbrief,* KEK Bd. 6, edited as the ninth ed. in 1970 by G. Strecker, pp. 113ff.; Siegfried Schulz's essay, "Die Decke des Moses, Untersuchungen zu einer vorpaulinischen Überlieferung," *ZNW* 49 (1958): 1–30.

interpretation of the glory and veil of Moses from Exodus 34:29–35 in 2 Corinthians 3:7–14. The reason for this is readily apparent. According to the virtually unanimous opinion of biblical and post-biblical Jewish tradition, the glory on Moses' face as he descended from Mount Sinai after the second giving of the law was not only brilliant, but permanent. The only possible divergence from this opinion is found in Pseudo-Philo's *Antiquities* 19:16, though even this text probably supports the overwhelming consensus.[4] Opinions in early Jewish literature vary concerning exactly why Moses consequently veiled himself, but both the Masoretic Text and later tradition agree that it was to protect the people in some way, not to cover up some deficiency in Moses or the glory he reflected. In contrast, Paul is seen to assert both that the glory on Moses' face was "fading" (*katargeo*; cf. 3:7, 13) and that Moses thus veiled himself to hide this fact and/or its implications from Israel (cf. *pros to . . . eis to telos tou katargoumenon;* 3:13). Paul's argument has therefore been construed not only to be internally inconsistent (cf. 3:13 with 3:7), but also inherently anti-Jewish in its apparent attribution to Moses of duplicitous motives and deceptive activity, while Paul portrays himself as both forthright and honest.

The recent responses to this common conclusion by P. von der Osten-Sacken (1989), Stockhausen (1989), Hays (1989), and Hofius (1989) vary greatly in their approaches and conclusions.[5] Nevertheless, all of these studies share the conviction that Paul's argument, though perhaps not an expression of a willful misreading of the Old Testament, can nevertheless be justified only on the basis of his own distinctively Christian presuppositions. Moreover, it has become common in recent discussions to suggest that, although Paul's interpretation of Exodus 34:29ff. is not acceptable by modern historical-critical standards, it can be justified on the basis of the exegetical practices and presuppositions of his day. Such an assumption has led Brevard Childs to posit, against the lack of evidence, that since Paul read Exodus 34 in this way, there must have been some prior Jewish tradition which also did so; and

4. For an argument in favor of reading this text to refer to the fading of the glory on Moses' face, see Linda L. Belleville's soon to be published work, *Paul's Polemical Use of the Moses-Doxa Tradition in 2 Corinthians 3:12–18* (Ph.D. Diss., University of St. Michael's College, 1986), 37–42.

5. Peter von der Osten-Sacken, "Die Decke des Moses, Zur Exegese und Hermeneutic von Geist und Buchstabe in 2 Korinther 3," in his *Die Heiligkeit der Tora, Studien zum Gesetz bei Paulus* (1989), 87–115; Kern Stockhausen, *Moses' Veil and the Glory of the New Covenant, The Exegetical Substructure of II Cor. 3:1–4:6* (AB 116, 1989); Richard B. Hays, *Echoes of Scripture in the Letters of Paul* (1989), 122–53; Otfried Hofius, "Gesetz und Evangelium nach 2. Korinther 3" in his *Paulusstudien* (WUNT 51 1989), 75–120 (now also found in *"Gesetz" als Thema Biblischer Theologie,* Jahrbuch für Biblische Theologie 4, [1989], 105–49).

more recently Belleville has tried to rediscover such a trail of thought in order to provide a necessary backdrop to Paul's thinking conceptually or methodologically.[6]

Against this backdrop, the thesis of this chapter is that Paul's argument in 2 Corinthians 3:7–14 takes Exodus 34:29ff. seriously within its original context (Exod. 32–34) and that it is precisely this context, not Paul's apostolic experience or Christian convictions *per se*, that provides the background and key for Paul's "exegesis" of the glory and veil of Moses. In the past, however, the vast majority of students of Paul have been content to look merely at the one verse that Paul quotes from Exodus 34:29–35 (cf. Exod. 34:34 in 2 Cor. 3:16) or to the allusions to Exodus 34:30, 33, 35 in 2 Corinthians 3:7, 13, rather than taking Exodus 34 seriously as part of the larger biblical narrative in which it is anchored.[7] The implications of a critical reading of biblical narratives have thus inadvertently carried over into the interpretation of Paul's own reading of the biblical tradition.

The Theological Meaning of Exodus 32–34

Unfortunately, we do not have the space here to consider the entire narrative of Exodus 32–34, but will have to jump in at the climax to the story, which is found in the text Paul cites in 2 Corinthians 3, namely Exodus 34:29–35. At this juncture in the account the turning point of the narrative, which was reached with the granting of Moses' petition in 33:19–23, now finds its fulfillment in Moses' descent from the mountain. For as 34:29 makes clear, Moses does in fact return as the "answer to his own prayers" in that he not only brings the reestablishment of the covenant, but unknowingly becomes himself the *means* of its continuation.[8] The former is stressed by the emphasis in the text on Moses as

6. Cf. Brevard S. Childs, *The Book of Exodus, A Critical, Theological Commentary* (1974), 621 and Belleville, *Polemical Use*, 10–103.

7. For this same critique of past scholarship and a similar call to reinvestigate the content and function of Exod. 34:29–35 within the "thematic covenant unit, Exod. 19–34," as the backdrop to 2 Cor. 3:7ff. see now William J. Dumbrell, "Paul's Use of Exodus 34 in 2 Corinthians 3," in *God Who Is Rich in Mercy, FS for D. B. Knox*, ed. Peter T. O'Brien and David G. Peterson (1986), 179–94, 180. Recently, Stockhausen, *Moses' Veil*, 96, has also emphasized the importance of remembering that Exod. 34:29–35 is a narrative so that Paul's "verbal echoes call to mind the whole *story* and not just isolated snatches of it" (emphasis hers, cf. p. 101 n. 30 for the same point). It is surprising, then, that she limits her reading to Exod. 34:29ff., which has serious implications for her understanding of 2 Cor. 3:7ff.

8. Herbert Chanan Brichto, "The Worship of the Golden Calf: A Literary Analysis of a Fable on Idolatry," *HUCA* 54 (1983): 1–44, p. 36, suggests that the role of Moses as the one who will mediate God's presence in the midst of the people is already expressed in 34:10 with YHWH's statement that he will perform his wonders for the people "in whose

the one who brings the two tablets with him "in his hand" (b^{e}yad-Moshe,
v. 29a), an allusion to the fact that Moses was also the one who earlier
broke the tablets by throwing them "from his hands" (miyyado, 32:19).
The one who mediated the breaking of the covenant is the one who also
mediates its restoration. The latter, and now more important theme, is
expressed in the reference to Moses not knowing that his face was
"shining" (qaran) because he had been speaking with YHWH (34:29b).
The translation of qaran has been a matter of much debate. But regardless of its etymology or use elsewhere, the present context, with its emphasis on Moses' role as the mediator of YHWH's presence among the
people, together with the explicit reference to the "skin of (Moses') face"
('or panayw) as its subject, demand that it be rendered "shine."[9] More-

midst Moses is." Brichto interprets this to mean that YHWH will be present in Moses
"and will thereby be present in the midst of the people." But Brichto's further attempt to
identify Moses with the angel promised in Exod. 23:20–24 remains unconvincing to me.

9. So too R. W. L. Moberly, At the Mountain of God, Story and Theology in Exodus 32–
34 (JSOT Supplement Series 22; 1983), 107; Childs, Exodus, 609. The attempt to render
it as a reference to "having horns" (of a priestly mask) is based on the verbal form mqrn
in Ps. 69:32 and the corresponding noun form throughout the OT. For an insightful study
of the issue in support of the position taken here, see Karl Jaros, "Des Mose 'Strahlende
Haut': Ein Notiz zu Exod. 34:29; 30:35," ZAW 88 (1976): 275–80 and Menahem Haran,
"The Shining of Moses' Face: A Case Study in Biblical and Ancient Near Eastern Iconog-
raphy," in In the Shelter of Elyon, Essays on Ancient Palestinian Life and Literature, FS
G. W. Ahlström, ed. W. Boyd Barrick and John R. Spencer (JSOT Supplement Series 31;
1984), 159–73, pp. 159–60, 163–65; for the opposing view, see esp. Anton Jirku, "Die
Gesichtsmaske des Mose," in his Von Jerusalem nach Ugarit, Gesammelte Schriften
(1966), 347–49. The recent article by William H. Propp, "The Skin of Moses' Face—
Transfigured or Disfigured?" CBQ 49 (1987): 375–86, pp. 375–83 provides an extensive
bibliography of sources and literature on both basic interpretations from antiquity to the
present and a helpful analysis of the Hebrew text and its reception in the LXX, Targumic,
and other early Jewish literature. Propp's own thesis is that Exod. 34:29 should be translated "the skin of his face was burnt to the hardness of horn" (p. 386), so that the text refers to an injury or disfigurement suffered by Moses (i.e., "some kind of light or heat
burn, p. 385). For Propp, the Israelites thus fled from Moses because of his disfigured
face, while the veil functioned "to spare the people the gruesome sight" (following B. D.
Eerdmans, p. 384). But Moses' glimpse of YHWH's back not only disfigured him by hardening his skin, it also consequently rendered him "invulnerable to divine radiance"
(p. 386). Moses can therefore take the veil off in YHWH's presence to "renew . . . his im-
munity" (p. 386). Exod. 34:29ff. "has no ritual significance," rather, "the story honors
Moses as the human most intimate with Yahweh, but it also specifies the price he paid"
(p. 386). But just as Propp accuses those who advocate that Moses was wearing a horned
ritual mask with a "disregard for the present form of the biblical text" that "diminishes
the plausibility" of their theory (p. 383), so may it be said of Propp's own suggestion. For
apart from the fact that there is no direct evidence of qrn being used metaphorically of a
skin disease, Propp's view also fails to do justice to the cultic role of Moses in the larger
context of Exod. 32–34, where in addition to Moses' role as mediator of God's presence
in 34:29ff., the narrative also stresses in 33:18–23 that YHWH hid Moses to protect him,
not to disfigure him. And, as we shall see, Israel's fear in 34:29ff. is to be understood
against the backdrop of 33:3, 5.

over, this is certainly the way it was understood in the LXX, where *qaran* in 34:29f., 35 (MT) is rendered by *dedoxastai, en dedoxasmene,* and *dedoxastai* respectively. This is further highlighted in the LXX by its use of *he opsis* ("the appearance") and *chromatos* ("color") in reference to Moses' face, which have no equivalents in the MT, but call attention to the fact that Moses now appeared glorified. Some image of a shining or radiance upon his face thus lies close at hand, as indicated by the direct reference to the glorification of Moses' face in 34:35 rather than to the "skin of the face of Moses" *('or p^{e}ne Moshe)* as in the MT.[10] The use of the perfect tenses and periphrastic construction to describe the glorification of Moses' face as a permanent condition in 34:29–30, 35 and the explicit reference to the repeated action of removing and replacing the veil in 34:34–35 (cf. *henika d' an, heos an* and the use of the imperfect tense in vv. 34–35) further highlight this emphasis on the glorification of Moses' face. Finally, within the context of Exodus 32–34, the choice of *doxazein* throughout 34:29–35 naturally recalls the development of the theme of the glory of God introduced earlier in 33:5, 16b, 19 and the thematic parallel in 33:13. Hence, as the LXX makes explicit, Moses now becomes the vehicle through which the presence of the glory of God, lost by the people as a result of their sin with the golden calf, is restored, albeit now in a mediated manner. The shining on Moses' face in 34:29ff. is the shining of the glory of God itself which he reflects as a result of his theophanic experience in Exodus 34:5–8; cf. 33:19. The point of 34:29 is thus made by way of contrast. Never before, although Moses had earlier been in the presence of God on several occasions, did his face shine as a result. Now, however, as a result of the unique experience of God's glory in 34:1–9, Moses himself bears the glory of God with him back to camp. This then is the means by which YHWH will place his presence in the midst of his people. Moses becomes not only the mediator of the covenant law, but of the covenantal presence of God.[11]

10. Contra Propp, "The Skin of Moses' Face," p. 377, who takes the lack of an explicit reference to radiance and the wide semantic range of *doxazo/doxa* to be a sign of a lack of clarity concerning this point. But the context alleviates this ambiguity. For his explanation of the origin of the LXX rendering of 34:30a as a result of reading the MT 'or ("skin") as ᵓor ("light") and a possible redivision of *ki qrn,* see his pp. 379–80. But the simplest solution is to see the LXX as an interpretation of the MT in terms of Moses' skin shining.

11. Contra George W. Coats, "The King's Loyal Opposition: Obedience and Authority in Exodus 32–34," in *Canon and Authority, Essays in Old Testament Religion and Theology,* ed. G. W. Coats and Burke O. Long (1977), 91–109, p. 105, who interprets the glory on Moses' face not in terms of the reflection of the glory of God, but as a symbolic expression of the authority of Moses. But although Moses' speaking with the glory of God on his face certainly substantiates his authority, against the backdrop of the problem of God's presence in 33:1ff., this is a secondary motif.

The fact that Moses now mediates the very glory of God in the midst of the people thus becomes the key to explaining both the reason and nature of the people's fear in 34:30 and the purpose of the veil in 34:33–35. At the first theophany and giving of the law in Exodus 19:16–20:18a the people also responded with fear at seeing the revelation of YHWH on the mountain (cf. 20:18b–21). But this fear is interpreted *positively* as the sanctifying means employed by YHWH to keep the people from sinning (Exod. 20:20).[12] Moreover, Moshe Greenberg has shown that, according to Exodus 20:20, the purpose of the original Sinai revelation was not only to legitimize Moses' authority (cf. Exod. 19:9), but to accomplish this sanctifying purpose by giving Israel a "direct palpable experience of God."[13] Moses thus commands the people not to be afraid because of God's terrifying presence, but to accept it as part of the ratification of the covenant itself (20:22, cf. Exod. 24:9–11). Of course, the people as a whole cannot approach God's presence directly, but are represented by Moses and the elders (cf. Exod. 19:24; 20:21; 24:1f, 9–11). This is not because of a broken relationship with YHWH, however, but because of their own mortal nature. Hence, the people are encouraged to remain as close as possible to the theophany and to hear YHWH's voice directly as an integral part of their new covenant relationship with him (Exod. 20:22).

In stark contrast, the people's fear in response to Moses' shining face in 34:30ff. must be interpreted in view of YHWH's earlier statements concerning the effect of his presence after their idolatry with the golden calf. Rather than sanctification, God's presence in the midst of his people now means judgment for the people (cf. Exod. 33:3, 5). While earlier the people feared YHWH because of their mortality, now they must fear him because of their sinful condition. Even though YHWH can no longer speak to the people directly, but only through Moses as mediator, and in spite of the fact that now the radiance of God himself can only be seen "second hand" on the face of Moses, the people's response in 34:30 thus testifies to the genuine nature of Moses' role on the one hand, and to their own *altered* relationship to YHWH on the other hand.

---

12. So too Childs, *Exodus*, on Exod. 20:18–22.

13. Moshe Greenberg, "*nsh* in Exodus 20:20 and the Purpose of the Sinaitic Theophany," *JBL* 79 (1960): 273–76, p. 275. His argument is based on the structural parallels between Exod. 20:20 and Deut. 4:10 and 5:29 and the use of *nsh* elsewhere to mean "to have/cause to have an experience" (cf. 1 Sam. 17:39; Deut. 28:56; 2 Chron. 32:31; Judg. 3:1–3). Israel is thus not being "tested" at Mt. Sinai, but being brought into the presence of God (p. 276). Even if Childs, *Exodus*, p. 344 n. 20 is correct that this factitive use of the verb has not been demonstrated, Greenberg's basic view of v. 20 seems to hold inasmuch as the giving of the law and the theophany, by "testing" Israel, would lead also to their obedience. Childs is thus right in emphasizing that there is no need to separate the giving of the law from the theophany, as Greenberg seems to do (p. 372).

YHWH now only comes to them mediated through Moses. But even this is still too much for the people to bear in their hardened condition.

Moses therefore responds with an act of grace in compensation for their stiffnecked nature. He first calls the leaders (34:31a) and then the people (34:32a) to him in order to deliver YHWH's covenant commands. In this way, the legitimacy of the message and the authority of the messenger are again authenticated through a "tangible confirmation of the fact that it is God's word that is being spoken to them when they see the light radiating from Moses' face"[14] (cf. 34:31f. with Exod. 19:9). But after speaking the words of YHWH to the people, Moses veils himself. Against the backdrop of the explicit statements of Exodus 32:9, 22 and 33:3, 5 and the function of the tent of meeting itself in 33:7–11, this act should be seen as an act of mercy on Moses' part in order to keep the people from being destroyed by the reflected presence of God.[15] The veil of Moses makes it possible for the glory of God to be in the midst of the people, albeit now mediated through Moses, without judging them. In view of the people's "stiff-neck" and idolatry with the golden calf, Moses' veil is thus the final expression of the theme of YHWH's judgment and mercy, which runs throughout this narrative and from the theological perspective ties it together.

The Significance of Moses' Veil

The veil of Moses is thus the theological corollary to the sinful nature of Israel and the demonstration of the character of YHWH as declared in 34:6–7. Moses veils himself, not to make up for some deficiency in the glory or in himself,[16] not as an expression of his humility and modesty,[17] not to keep the glory of God from being wasted,[18] nor even to

---

14. M. Haran, "The Shining of Moses," 162. Haran is thus correct in emphasizing that it is not the veil *per se* which is the main point of the text, but the fact that the glory of God can now be seen once again. Coats, *Moses. Heroic Man, Man of God* (JSOT Supplement Series 57; 1988), 131, misses this point when he suggests that the veil itself functions, like Moses' rod, as "a visible and concrete symbol of Mosaic authority derived from his intimacy with God" (cf. too pp. 138, 190). It is the shining, not the veil, which results from Moses' experience of the theophany. The veil results from Israel's hardened condition.

15. Thus, though Moberly, *Mountain of God,* 108 is correct that "no reason is given" for the purpose of the veil in the text, the context indicates its function clearly enough that we need not "but speculate" concerning its function.

16. Contra Brichto, "Golden Calf," 37; there is no indication that the veil exists to hide the fact that the glory was fading or to compensate for Moses' own human "concerns and aspirations." On the permanent nature of the glory on Moses' face, see J. Morgenstern, "Moses with the Shining Face," *HUCA* 2 (1925): 1–27, pp. 4–5.

17. Contra Cassuto, *Exodus,* 450.

18. Contra Haran, "The Shining of Moses' Face," 162.

keep it from being profaned.[19] Rather, the veil makes it possible to bring the glory of God into the midst of the rebellious people. Moreover, the switch to the frequentative nature of the action regarding the veil in 34:34–7 indicates that this protective function of the veil continued from this point on as the people moved on in their wilderness wanderings. As long as he lives, Moses remains the one who mediates God's presence in the midst of his people and who, not only as an act of divine judgment, but even more so of divine mercy, veils himself in their midst. The restoration of the covenant in Exodus 32–34 therefore finds its climax, possibility, and means of fulfillment in Moses as the mediator of both the law and the glory of God. It is not saying too much, therefore, to conclude with Wilms that as it now stands the theology of the *"Mittleramt"* of Moses determines the main points of chapter 34,[20] and, beyond that, chapters 32–33 as well. Moreover, from the perspective of the narrative, the eventual filling of the tabernacle with the glory of God in Exodus 40:34, behind the curtain (!), is thus the logical extension and fulfilment of Moses' experience in the tent of meeting and of his role as mediator between YHWH and Israel.[21]

This then is the key to understanding the theological significance of Moses' veil. Just as Moses had to be kept from God's direct presence in 33:22 because of his mortality, now the Israelites must be veiled even from God's indirect presence because of their sinful state (34:33–35). Due to her "stiff-neck," Israel cannot bear to see the radiance of God's glory (cf. 32:9, 22; 33:3, 5 with 34:30). Hence, in both cases, the barrier is an expression of YHWH's protection and mercy, the first in regard to mankind's finitude, the latter in regard to Israel's sin. But in Israel's case, the veil on Moses' face also embodies the theme of God's judgment, which together with his mercy runs both implicitly and explicitly throughout the narrative (cf. 33:19; 34:6–7). Whereas Moses experiences protection from God's direct presence as an act of mercy in response to the favor he has found before YHWH, Israel is kept from continually seeing the glory of God as an act of both mercy and judgment in response to her sinful nature.

The problem of God's presence in the midst of a rebellious people is finally solved, therefore, as a result of the fact that God's mercy overshadows his judgment. For within the flow of the narrative, the answer

19. Contra O. Eissfeldt, "Das Gesetz ist zwischeneingekommen. Ein Beitrag zur Analyse der Sinai-Erzählung Ex. 19–34," now in his *Kleine Schriften IV* (1968), 209–14, p. 210.

20. Frank Elmar Wilms, *Das Jahwistische Bundesbuch,* 183.

21. The historical relationship between the tent of meeting and the tabernacle is a matter of much dispute; but for their identification in the final redaction of the text, see M. Haran, *Temple and Temple Service,* 271f. In support of this he points to Exod. 38:21; Num. 1:50, 53; 9:15; 10:11; 17:23; 18:2; and esp. Exod. 39:32, 40; 40:2, 6, 29.

to the problem of God's presence in the midst of a sinful people is Moses himself as the mediator of the will and splendor of God in anticipation of the establishment of the tabernacle. This is reflected in the fact that in Exodus 39:33–14 the articles for the tabernacle are first presented to Moses, who then inspects them and blesses the people prior to the tabernacle's establishment (39:42–43).[22] In this way, Israel is reminded, above all, of her cultic obligations (as in 34:10–26), while the theological significance of Exodus 32–34 as a whole is summarized and embodied in Moses' descent from the mountain with the light of God's glory shining on his face, a glory which must then be veiled from the people due to their stiff-necked condition. In this context, the veil on Moses' face is not only part of YHWH's judgment against his people; but more importantly, it is an expression of his grace.[23]

With these specific themes found in Exodus 32–34 in mind, we can now turn our attention to Paul's argument in 3:7ff. in order to posit a thesis for consideration. What does Paul's argument in 2 Corinthians 3:7ff. look like against this backdrop?

The Argument from Scripture in 2 Corinthians 3:7–14

First, Paul's references to the "fading" glory of Moses' face in verses 7, 13, and the Sinai covenant which it represents in 3:11 must be rethought. The use of *katargeo* in the ancient world apart from the New Testament and the literature dependent upon it is rare. A partial search of the stem *katarg.* in the literature from the 4th century B.C. to 4th century A.D. provided by the Thesaurus Linguae Graecae Project at the University of California, Irvine produced over 1300 occurrences of the verb.[24] Of these occurrences, only 16 are found in literature outside the New Testament and its circle of influence.[25] In particular, the vast majority of other references throughout the literature are dependent ei-

---

22. For this point and the chiastic relationship between Exod. 25–31 and 35–40, as well as the loss of the structural role of the creation motifs in chaps. 35–40, facts which can only be explained by the influence of chapters 32–34, see Peter J. Kearney, "Creation and Liturgy: The P Redaction of Ex. 25–40," *ZAW* 89 (1977): 375–87, esp. pp. 380–81.

23. Though it is beyond the scope of this paper to develop this, my forthcoming work demonstrates how in the LXX this reading of Exod. 32–34 is not only supported, but strengthened.

24. Because of the focus on the present passive form of the verb, the Aorist and Perfect Indicative forms were not included, but have been surveyed in the LXX and NT. But cf. Polybius, *Fragmenta* 176 for the use *katergekenai.* The papyri have not been surveyed.

25. Besides the texts explicitly referred to below, see *Scholia in Homerum* 19:157–8:3 (no canon yet available) and the *Cyranides* (ante 1st/2nd cent. A.D.) 10:101 (designations, dates, and references to editions given according to Luci Berkowitz and Karl A. Squitier, *Thesaurus Linguae Graecae, Canon of Greek Authors and Works*, 1986²).

ther by allusion or quotation on Paul's writings, especially his statements in Romans 3:3, 31; 6:6, 1 Corinthians 1:28; 2:6; 15:24, 26,
Ephesians 2:15, and 2 Thessalonians 2:8. This is not surprising in view
of the fact that of the 27 times the verb appears in the New Testament,
25 are found in the Pauline corpus.[26] The only exceptions are Luke 13:7
and Hebrews 2:14. Hence, as the lexicons testify and the TLG search
confirms, our evidence for these meanings must largely be drawn from
Paul's use itself.[27]

Yet there is little, if any, doubt concerning the semantic field encom-
passed by the *active* forms of the verb *katargeo* in these non-Christian
sources. The few sources that we do have outside the Christian sphere
in ancient literature, including the LXX, all testify to the meanings "put
to an end," "abolish," or "destroy" as adequate equivalents for *katargeo*.

The same lack of uncertainty is true for Paul's writings as well. Paul
uses the active forms of *katargeo* figuratively in the sense of "to make
(something) ineffective, powerless, idle," or "to nullify (something)"
(Rom. 3:3, 31; 1 Cor. 1:28; Gal. 3:17; Eph. 2:15; cf. Luke 13:7); and in the
related sense they can mean "to abolish, wipe out, set aside something"
(1 Cor. 6:13; 13:11) or "bring (something) to an end" (1 Cor. 15:24;
2 Thess. 2:8; 2 Tim. 1:10; cf. Heb. 2:14).[28] This is confirmed not only by
the larger contexts in which these occurrences are found, but also by
the specific verbs which are used in parallel constructions in several of
the passages.[29]

26. 6x in Rom., 9x in 1 Cor., 4x in 2 Cor., 3x in Gal., and 1x in Eph., 2 Thess and 2 Tim.
See *Vollständige Konkordanz zum Griechischen Neuen Testament, Bd. II Spezialübersich-
ten*, ed. K. Aland (1978), 148–49.

27. Including the LXX, W. Bauer, *A Greek-English Lexicon of the New Testament and
Other Early Christian Literature*, revised and augmented by F. Wilbur Gingrich and
Frederick W. Danker from Bauer's fifth edition (1979²) 417 list the same 3 non-Christian
literary sources found in Liddell, Scott, and Jones, *A Greek-English Lexicon* (1958; 1940⁹),
908; W. Bauer, K. Aland, and B. Aland, *Griechisch-deutsches Wörterbuch* (1988⁶), 848–49,
add the *Ascension of Isaiah* 3:31 (which, however, is part of the Christian addition to the
composite work sometimes called the Testament of Hezekiah found in *Ascen. Is.* 3:13–
4:22; cf. M. A. Knibb, "Martyrdom and Ascension of Isaiah," *OTP*, 143).

28. So accurately BGD, *A Greek-English Lexicon*, 417, BAA, *Griechisch-deutsches
Wörterbuch*, pp. 848f., give the same three basic meanings: "auBer Wirksamkeit, Geltung
setzen, entkräften" and from this "wirkungslos machen, zunichte machen;" "vernichten,
vertilgen, beseitigen," and "aus d. Verbindung mit jmdm. oder mit etw. gelöst
werden . . ." LSJ, *A Greek-English Lexicon*, 908 supplies the basic meaning, "leave unem-
ployed or idle."

29. Cf. the contrast between *katargoumen* and *histanomen* in Rom. 3:31; the parallel
between *ouch . . . kleronomesousin* and *ho theos katargesei* in 1 Cor. 6:10, 13; the use of
pausontai as a parallel to *katargeo* in 1 Cor. 13:8, 11; the parallel between *akaroi* and *ka-
targesai* in Gal. 3:17; the synonymous use of *lusas* and *katargesas* in Eph. 2:14f. and of
anelei and *katargesei* in 2 Thess. 2:8; and finally, the antithetical use of *katargesantos* and
photisantos in 2 Tim. 1:10.

Furthermore, in the case of Romans 3:3; 1 Corinthians 1:28; 13:11; 15:24; Galatians 3:17; Ephesians. 2:15; and 2 Thessalonians 2:8 this act of nullification is explicitly linked to the consequent abolishment of the *effects* of that which has been brought to an end. In Romans 3:3 the fact that the faithfulness of God is not nullified results in the continuation of the truthfulness and justice of God in judgment in 3:4–8. In 1 Corinthians 1:28 God nullifies the things that are "so that (*hopos* + subjunctive) no one may boast before God" (1 Cor. 1:29). The abolishment of "childish things" in 1 Corinthians 13:11 results in the putting away of speaking, thinking, and reasoning as a child. According to 1 Corinthians 15:24–25, Christ abolishes every rule, authority, and power in order to eliminate the rebellion that still remains against the Father and as a result can then turn the kingdom over to God. The fact that in Galatians 3:17 the law does not nullify the promise means that the effects of the promise remain valid, that is, that the inheritance of God still comes "from the promise" (*ex epaggelias*, 3:18). As the modal use of the participle *katargesas* indicates, the point of Ephesians 2:15 is that Christ establishes peace *by means of* abolishing in his death the enmity which existed between Jew and Gentile. For the result of this destruction is the creation of Jews and Gentiles into "one new man," which in turn establishes peace on the basis of their mutual reconciliation to God through the cross (Eph. 2:15b–16). And finally, in 2 Thessalonians 2:8 the Lord will bring to an end "the Lawless One," which in the context means bringing to an end the false power, signs, and wonders, and the deception which these things caused among those who are perishing (2 Thess. 2:9–10). It is important to see, therefore, that in developing his use of *katargeo* Paul intends not simply to call attention to the fact that something has been definitively abolished, but to raise the question of the consequences of these acts of nullification.

In those texts where no explicit result is mentioned, as in 2 Corinthians 3, Romans 3:31, 1 Corinthians 6:13, and 2 Timothy 1:9–10, it is thus consistent with Pauline usage, and confirmed by the surrounding context, that here too, Paul is directing his attention to the ramification of the act of abolishing. In asserting that the gospel does not "nullify" (*katarguomen*) the law in Romans 3:31, Paul is thus also implying that its past failure among the Jews and its continuing validity among Christians must be explained (cf. Rom. 7:1–8:4; 9:30–10:4; 13:8–10). Similarly, though not explicitly stated, the implications of the fact that God will "abolish" (*katargesei*) food and the stomach in 1 Corinthians 6:13 for the ethical admonitions and warnings of the impending judgment in the surrounding context are clear. Christians are now to act already in the present as if the effects of the lure of appetite have already been destroyed (cf. 6:9–20). This is also the point of

2 Timothy 1:9–10, though now applied to the willingness to suffer with
Paul for the sake of the gospel (2 Tim. 1:8). Hence, when Paul speaks of
"abolishing," "nullifying," or "bringing something to an end," he also
consistently speaks, either explicitly or implicitly, of the corresponding
effects of that which has or has not been made ineffective. The active
sense "rendering something inoperative" thus captures both the act and
the effect expressed by the verb *katargeo*.[30] But in no case is it appropriate to translate *katargeo* with the sense of a gradual "fading away" of
that which is said to be brought to an end. Of most significance for our
study is the fact that these same three observations also hold true of the
passive use of *katargeo* in Paul's writings. Of the 25 appearances of the
verb in Paul, 14 are passive, including the four occurrences in
2 Corinthians 3:7, 11, 13, 14. And in each of these cases, a rendering
equivalent to the active force of the verb captures the meaning well: "to
be brought to an end, made powerless, or rendered inoperative in regard to its effects." But in no case, either active or passive, does *katargeo*
refer to the gradual "fading away" of some aspect of reality.

In returning to the argument of 2 Corinthians 3:7–11, the question
now before us, therefore, is whether this consistent Pauline use of *katargeo* found throughout the Pauline corpus is also found in
2 Corinthians 3:7ff., or whether Paul has in fact, as past students of
Paul have assumed, introduced a distinctive meaning for the verb in
this one context. Clearly, the burden of proof will now be on those who
wish to render it in any way different from the range of meaning established by Paul in the rest of his writings. My thesis is that here too Paul
is referring to the fact that the veil of Moses brought the glory of God to
an end in terms of that which it would accomplish if not veiled, that is,
the judgment and destruction of Israel. This corresponds exactly to
what we find in the Exodus narrative. The result clause in 3:7 can thus
be rendered in this way: the ministry of death came in glory, "so that as
a result, the sons of Israel were not able to gaze into the face of Moses
because of the glory of his face, which was being rendered inoperative
as to its effects . . ." Paul's statement in 3:7 merely reflects the point of
Exodus 34:29ff. concerning both the fear of the Israelites in response to
the glory of God after their sin with the golden calf and Moses' response. Paul's interpretation of Exodus 34:29ff. is thus faithful to the
original context and none of the various attempts to "redeem" his reading by recourse to contemporary exegetical methods or an attempt to

---

30. Cf. Kenneth Willis Clark, "The Meaning of *ENERGEO* and *KATARGEO* in the
New Testament," now in his *The Gentile Bias and Other Essays*, selected by John L.
Sharpe III (Supplements to Novum Testamentum vol. 54; 1980), 183–191, pp. 190f., who
suggests that it ought to be translated "render powerless" as the antonym of *energeo*.

take the attributive participle as referring to some time other than that of the Exodus narrative are necessary.

Second, contrary to the overwhelming consensus, the purpose of the veil in 3:13 also corresponds to its function in Exodus 34:29–35 read against its original context. Moses must continually veil himself "in order that (taking *pros to* plus the infinitive to indicate a final rather than a result clause, in contrast to Paul's use of *hoste* plus the infinitive in 3:7) the sons of Israel might not look into the *telos* of that which was being rendered inoperative as to its effects." Moses' purpose is not to hide something from the Israelites, either intentionally or unintentionally. In Exodus 34:29ff., Moses veils himself in order that the glory of God might not produce its intended result, that is, the judgment of the people because of their "stiff-necks." In 2 Corinthians 3:13 Paul is simply repeating this point. As such, *telos* ought to be rendered, "goal" or "result" as a reference to what the glory would have brought about had it not been veiled.

But Furnish is right in objecting that those who argue that *telos* means "aim" or "outcome" in 2 Corinthians 3:13 "have in general not been persuasive in their explanations of *why* Paul thought Moses wanted to hide the aim of the old covenant—that is Christ—from Israel . . . or *how* the veil could have done that."[31] Furnish's objection, however, points to the heart of the problem itself, *since the problem with past attempts to read telos in this way has been their assumption that its referent in this context is Christ,* either the pre-existent Christ or the future coming of Christ in Paul's day. Yet the parallel between *telos* in 3:13b and "the face of Moses because of the glory of his face" in 3:7b indicates that Paul is now simply summarizing in one word what he described at length earlier. Though not to be preferred, the introduction of the textual variant *to prosopon* as an attempt to relieve verse 13b of its ambiguity is an indication that this was the case.[32]

Hence, Moses is not keeping Israel from seeing either that the glory is fading, nor is he keeping Israel from seeing that the law really points to Christ as its goal. In 3:13, as in 3:7, the time reference is still that of the Exodus narrative, as the imperfect verb *etithei* in 3:13a indicates. 2 Corinthians 3:14a thus provides the theological rationale for Moses' action as implied in Exodus 34:29ff. Paul is merely making the tie explicit between Exodus 32:9, 33:3, 5; 34:9 and 34:29–35 that is so crucial in the original context of the narrative. Only in 14b does Paul switch back to his present situation, and he indicates this explicitly. Again, Paul's exegesis therefore proves to be a sober and careful contextual in-

---

31. *II Corinthians*, 207.
32. Cf. A *pc* b f* vg (bo^mss).

terpretation of his tradition rather than a paradigmatic example of Paul's supposedly presuppositional re- (or mis-) reading of his tradition in which he "starts from Christian experience and expounds Scripture in the light of that experience, quarrying the Old Testament where he will."[33]

Viewed from this perspective, the "how" and "why" of Paul's statement in 3:13 now becomes apparent. In turning his attention from the glory on Moses' face to the purpose of the veil which it made necessary in 3:13, Paul is calling explicit attention to the unexpressed presupposition which we posited undergirded his earlier statement in verse 7b. Specifically, Moses veiled himself in order that the sons of Israel might not gaze "into the outcome or result" *(to telos)* of that which was being rendered inoperative, that is, the death-dealing judgment of the glory of God upon his "stiff-necked" people as it was manifested in the old covenant.[34] For *unlike* Romans 10:4, the *telos* in 2 Corinthians 3:13b takes place within the time frame of Moses' activity, rather than referring to the future time of Christ from Paul's perspective, since in 3:13, as in 3:7, the time reference is *still* that of the Exodus narrative. For this reason, in 3:13 Paul explicitly does *not* identify the *telos* of the old covenant with Christ as he does in Romans 10:4, even though the two statements are related theologically within Paul's overall perspective. It is precisely because Moses had to veil the purpose *(telos)* of the glory of the old covenant from Israel due to their hard hearts (2 Cor. 3:13b) that Christ eventually must become the *telos* of the law, whatever *telos* means in Romans 10:4. The *telos* kept from Israel's view in 2 Corinthians 3:13 was the outcome or consequence of the glory of God itself as it encounters a rebellious people, and as such of the purpose of the old covenant as a whole (cf. 3:7, 9), had it not been veiled. Hence, far from duplicity, Moses' merciful *intention* was to keep Israel from being judged by the glory on his face, which was the *telos* of that glory in response to the continuing hardened nature of the people.

Once again, therefore, Paul's meaning in 3:13 is best recaptured when read in the context of Exodus 34:29–35. There is no compelling exegetical basis for concluding that it is the expression of a foreign, specifically "Christian" rereading of the text, whether based upon Paul's supposedly negative view of Moses and the old covenant, his introduction of the idea of the "fading" glory not found in the biblical account, the postulating of some hidden referent in Exodus 34:29ff. imported

---

33. Hooker, "Beyond the Things," 305.

34. This use of *telos* to refer to the outcome or consequence of a given action in 2 Cor. 3:13 corresponds to Paul's undisputed use of *telos* with this same meaning in Rom. 6:21–22; 2 Cor. 11:15; Phil. 3:19. Cf. too 1 Tim. 1:5; James 5:11; 1 Pet. 1:9; 4:17.

into the present context on the basis of Romans 10:4, or in the case of those who argue for the veiling of the pre-existent Christ, from 1 Corinthians 10:4.

Moreover, Paul has not ignored nor reinterpreted the fact that Israel could in fact see the glory of God on the face of Moses during those periods of revelation in which Moses removed the veil as is often maintained. Rather, as his careful choice of *atenisai* in verses 7 and 13 indicates, it is precisely this periodic and limited access to the glory of God which Paul presupposes as indicative of Israel's problem. They were not able to "gaze" into the glory of God, but could only encounter it briefly. When seen in this light, rather than being in tension with, or even a contradiction of verse 7, verse 13 is its natural complement, just as verse 12 is Paul's equally natural response to his own ministry of the glory of God. Again, Paul's exegesis proves to be a sober and careful contextual interpretation of his tradition.

Against this backdrop, it may not be surprising if the rest of Paul's argument in 3:7–18 can also be shown to derive from his understanding of Exodus 34:29–35 within its original context. Paul can be bold, where Moses had to veil himself (3:12–13), precisely because Paul can expect that instead of destruction, those whose hearts have been changed will be *transformed* by their encounter with the glory of God on the face of Christ (3:18; 4:4–6). Paul's reason for this confidence and boldness (3:4, 12; 4:1) is clear. In the preaching of the gospel God is at work through his Spirit to change people's hearts (3:8, 17–18; 4:2–6). In contrast to Moses, Paul need not "veil himself" before a people whose disposition toward God and his will has been radically changed. For where the Spirit is, there is freedom (3:17), not from the law, or from the old covenant, or from judgment *per se,* but from the veil as a metonymy for the hard heartedness that continues to characterize those outside of Christ and which, when removed by the power of the Spirit, makes a Spirit-empowered obedience to the law of God possible. For now, in Christ, God's people once again are brought near to God so that, with unveiled faces, they too, like Moses before them, may see the glory of God, albeit still dimly (3:18). Moreover, this transformation, as the promises of the new covenant in Jeremiah 31:31ff. and Ezekiel 11 and 36 make clear, is a moral transformation in accord with the Torah as the stipulations of the new covenant. The dawning of the new covenant is thus the beginning of that obedience to God in response to his merciful redemption and restoration which characterizes the new creation (2 Cor. 3:18; 5:17).

Part 6

How Did the New Testament Authors Use Typology?

18

Typology and
the Christian Use
of the Old Testament

David L. Baker

From David L. Baker, "Typology and the Christian Use of the Old Testament," *Scottish Journal of Theology* 29 (1976): 137–57. Reprinted by permission.

The Question of Definition

It is necessary first of all to consider what is meant by the word "typology." There is a world of difference between the use of τύπος (type) in the Bible and many of the fanciful interpretations which were called "types" in the early church,[1] or between the use of typology in modern biblical scholarship and in modern church life. Two main conceptions of typology are to be found today. Recently a number of biblical scholars, notably Gerhard von Rad, have used the term to describe the interpretation of history involved in the "promise-fulfillment" approach to the relationship between the Testaments. Alongside this there are those who perpetuate fanciful kinds of biblical interpretation closely related to allegory and symbolism, referring to them as typology. The place of typology in the Christian use of the Old Testament depends entirely therefore on what is meant by the word.

A term with such diverse connotations stands in need of replacement or more precise definition. Some scholars have chosen the former alter-

---

1. By no means all the early church's interpretation was fanciful; cf. J. Daniélou, *From Shadows to Reality: Studies in the Biblical Typology of the Fathers* (ET: London, 1960; French, 1950).

native and rejected the idea of typology for the modern church.[2] Others have suggested alternative terms such as "homology,"[3] "analogy,"[4] patterns,"[5] or "parallel situation."[6] Nevertheless, although there are problems in retaining the term "typology," a word originating in the Bible and well recognized in modern scholarship cannot be dropped so easily simply because it has been misused in some periods of history and is popularly misunderstood today.[7] Like it or not the term "typology" is firmly established in theological vocabulary and in the present chapter the latter alternative is chosen in an attempt to define the word more precisely. This is done on the basis of the meaning of τύπος and its cognates in biblical Greek and the meaning of "type" in modern English. It will be seen that this results in an understanding of typology which is more satisfactory than that in most modern writing on the subject, being consistent with the nature of the biblical literature and offering a basis of interpretation for the Christian use of the Old Testament.

There is however a great deal to be learnt about typology from modern scholarship and this will first be briefly surveyed.

Modern Study of Typology

Definitions

In modern scholarship many definitions of typology have been proposed and they fall into two main categories. The first category com-

2. E.g., W. A. Irwin, "The Interpretation of the Old Testament," *ZAW* 62 (1949–1950): 1–10 and "A Still Small Voice . . . Said, What are You Doing Here?" *JBL* 78 (1959): 1–12; F. Baumgärtel, *Verheissung: Zur Frage des evangelischen Verständnisses des Alten Testaments* (Gütersloh, 1952), 138–43 and "The Hermeneutical Problem of the Old Testament," ET in *Essays on Old Testament Interpretation* (*EOTI*; ed. C. Westermann; ET: London, 1963), 143–44 (German: *TLZ* 79 [1954]); J. D. Smart, *The Interpretation of Scripture* (London, 1961), 129–33; J. Barr, *Old and New in Interpretation: A Study of the Two Testaments* (London, 1966), 103–48; G. Fohrer, "Das Alte Testament und das Thema 'Christologie'" *EvTh* 30 (1970): 293–94.

3. W. J. Phythian-Adams, *The Way of At-one-ment: Studies in Biblical Theology* (London, 1944), 11; followed by A. G. Hebert, *The Authority of the Old Testament* (London, 1947), 218–22.

4. So Barth, according to Smart, *The Interpretation of Scripture*, 125–29; cf. H. U. von Balthasar, *Karl Barth: Darstellung und Deutung seiner Theologie* (Cologne, 1951), 93–181; W. Pannenberg, "Zur Bedeutung des Analogiegedankens bei Karl Barth," *TLZ* 78 (1953): 17–24; H. G. Pöhlmann, *Analogia entis oder Analogia fidei? Die Frage der Analogie bei Karl Barth* (Göttingen, 1965). See also G. von Rad, *Old Testament Theology*, 2 (ET: Edinburgh, 1965; German: 1960), 363–64; H. W. Wolff, "The Hermeneutics of the Old Testament," ET in *EOTI* (German: *EvTh* 16 [1956], 167–81).

5. H. H. Rowley, *The Unity of the Bible* (London, 1953), 19–20.

6. A. T. Hanson, *Jesus Christ in the Old Testament* (London, 1965), 162.

7. cf. Wolff's defence of the retention of the term "typology": *EOTI*, 181n. Also, G. von Rad, "Typological Interpretation of the Old Testament," ET in *EOTI* (German: *EvTh* 12 [1952–53]), 38–39.

prises definitions centering on the idea of "prefiguration," and these date mainly from more than twenty years ago. An example is the definition given by C. T. Fritsch: "a type is an institution, historical event or person, ordained by God, which effectively prefigures some truth connected with Christianity."[8] The second category comprises definitions centering on the idea of "correspondence," and these date mainly from the past twenty years. An example is G. W. H. Lampe's definition of typology as being "primarily a method of *historical* interpretation, based upon the continuity of God's purpose throughout the history of his covenant. It seeks to demonstrate the correspondence between the various stages in the fulfillment of that purpose."[9] Both kinds of definition have in common a historical basis and both are clearly distinguished from fanciful interpretation. There seems to be general agreement among modern scholars that typology is a form of historical interpretation, based on the Bible itself.[10]

Old Testament

A number of writers claim that typology originated in the Old Testament itself, especially in the prophetic writings: Isaiah uses the garden of Eden as a type for the new paradise (Isa. 9:1(2); 11:6–9), Hosea predicts another period in the wilderness (Hos. 2:16–17 (14–15); 12:10 (9); cf. Jer. 31:2), Second Isaiah expects a new exodus (e.g., Isa. 43:16–21;

---

8. C. T. Fritsch, "Biblical Typology: IV: Principles of Biblical Typology," *BS* 104 (1947): 214. Cf. J. C. Lambert, "Type," *HDAC* 2 (1918), 623; L. Goppelt, *Typos: Die typologische Deutung des Alten Testaments im Neuen* (Gütersloh, 1939, reprinted Darmstadt, 1969), 18–19; W. G. Moorehead, "Type," *ISBE* (1939), 3029; S. Amsler, "Où en est la typologie de l'Ancien Testament?" *ETR* 27 (1952): 80 and "Prophétie et typologie," *RThPh* 3 (1953): 139.

9. G. W. H. Lampe, "Typological Exegesis," *Theology* 56 (1953): 202. Cf. H. L. Ellison, "Typology," *EQ* 25 (1953): 161; K. J. Woollcombe in *Essays on Typology* (by G. W. H. Lampe and K. J. Woollcombe, London, 1957), 39–40; von Rad, *Old Testament Theology*, 2, 272, 329, et al.; H. W. Wolff, "The Understanding of History in the Old Testament Prophets," ET in *EOTI* (German: *EvTh* 20 [1960]), 344; A. B. Mickelsen, *Interpreting the Bible* (Grand Rapids, 1963), 237; R. T. France, *Jesus and the Old Testament* (London, 1971), 40.

J. H. Stek ("Biblical Typology Yesterday and Today," *CTJ* 5 [1970]: 133–62) contrasts the use of "typology" in Patrick Fairbairn's *The Typology of Scripture: Viewed in Connection with the Whole Series of Divine Dispensations* (Edinburgh, 1863[3], 1870[5]) and in volume two of Gerhard von Rad's *Old Testament Theology*. The former he characterizes as "a divine *pedagogical instrument* for progressive revelation of a system of spiritual truths about heavenly and earthly realities" and the latter as "a useful *theological method* by which men appropriate for themselves and proclaim to others their experiences of the self-revelation of God in history."

10. It is true that these definitions, like the term "typology" itself, are theological rather than biblical (cf. Lambert, *HDAC*, 2:623), but the Bible's general lack of abstraction makes this inevitable (cf. H. D. Hummel, "The Old Testament Basis of Typological Interpretation," *BR* 9 (1964): 40).

48:20–21; 51:9–11; 52:11–12; cf. 11:15–16; Jer. 16:14–15), and many of the prophets see David as typical of the king who is to come in the future (Isa. 11:1; 55:3–4; Jer. 23:5; Ezek. 34:23–4; Amos 9:11).[11] Eichrodt and von Rad also see typology within the Pentateuch, so that Abraham is a type of the faithful (Gen. 15:6),[12] Moses a type of the prophets (Deut. 18:15, 18),[13] and even the story of the manna has the typological significance that God gives to each according to his need (Exod. 16:9–27).[14]

Francis Foulkes, in *The Acts of God*, sets out to show that the "theological and eschatological interpretation of history" which is called typology originates in the Old Testament.[15] He argues that, since the prophets assumed that God would act in the future in the same way that he had acted in the past (e.g., call of Abraham; exodus; reign of David), the concept of God's acts in history being repeated is fundamental to the Old Testament. However, Israel hoped not simply for a repetition of God's acts but for a repetition of an unprecedented nature (e.g., new temple; new covenant; new creation). This hope was fulfilled in the New Testament and was the basis of the New Testament's typological interpretation of history.

Horace Hummel, in an article in *Biblical Research* (1964), asserts even more emphatically that typology is based in the Old Testament, stating that "the *typical* is a dominant concern of the O.T., its historiography, its cultus, its prophecy, etc."[16] He surveys "typical" thinking (which he identifies with "typological" thinking) in the Old Testament and finds examples in the presentation of historical events (e.g., Exodus), individuals (e.g., Abraham; Moses; David), groups (e.g., the righteous; Israel; the wise man), laws (e.g., Pss. 15 and 24), nations (e.g., Israel; Edom, especially in Obadiah; Babylon, especially in Nahum; Gog and Magog), places (e.g., holy land; Jerusalem; temple), legends (creation; flood; Jonah) and the cult (in its very nature: re-enaction of God's redemptive acts). Thus he defends his proposition that "Israel's fundamental concern behind all the personages, events, and scenes of

11. See Amsler, *ETR* 27: 80–81; W. Eichrodt, "Is Typological Exegesis an Appropriate Method?" ET in *EOTI* (German: *SVT* 4 [1957]), 234–35; Lampe in *Essays on Typology*, 26–27; B. W. Anderson, "Exodus Typology in Second Isaiah" in *Israel's Prophetic Heritage: Essays in honor of James Muilenburg* (ed. B. W. Anderson and W. Harrelson; London, 1962), 177–95; cf. Smart, *The Interpretation of Scripture*, 102–3.
12. W. Eichrodt, *Theology of the Old Testament*, 2 (ET: London, 1967; German: 1964[5], 1935–9[1]), 227–28, cf. p. 244.
13. Von Rad, *Old Testament Theology*, 1 (ET: Edinburgh, 1962; German: 1957), 294–95; cf. Eichrodt, *EOTI*, 235.
14. Von Rad, *Old Testament Theology*, 1:282.
15. F. Foulkes, *The Acts of God: A Study of the Basis of Typology in the Old Testament* (London, 1958), 7.
16. Hummel, *BR* 9: 38–50 (quote is from p. 40).

her history was typical, and intended to point to the basic realities of all existence."[17]

New Testament

In the New Testament the typical element is even clearer than in the Old, especially in its interpretation of the Old Testament. The standard work on this subject is still that of Leonhard Goppelt, *Typos*.[18] Goppelt examines in detail those passages in the New Testament which involve a typological use of the Old Testament, against the background of the contemporary Jewish understanding of Scripture and in contrast to the "typology" of the letter of Barnabas. His conclusion is simple and important: typology is the dominant and characteristic method of interpretation for the New Testament use of the Old Testament.[19] It is not only when the Old Testament is actually cited that this is apparent but in all the allusions to the Old Testament, many of which do not refer to specific texts. There is a double aspect to the typology: correspondence and increase. The New Testament writer recalls Old Testament parallels to Jesus and the salvation which came through him and depicts both the similarity and the difference. In contrast, the use of a typological correspondence to expound the meaning of an Old Testament text is rare in the New Testament. **Typology is not a method of interpretation which functions according to fixed rules but a way of thinking.** It is primarily directed to the understanding of the New Testament, both with respect to individual passages and to theological ideas. It is an aspect of the New Testament's own awareness of being part of the history of salvation: **the New Testament is both a typological fulfillment of the Old Testament salvation history and a typological prophecy of the consummation to come.** In contemporary Jewish biblical interpretation typology is relatively unimportant and where it occurs it is comparatively superficial. In the letter of Barnabas "typology" is used to make the Old Testament a collection of Christian teaching, instead of the New Testament's view of the Old Testament as a unity which is valid in its own right. So, according to Goppelt, the New Testament views the Old Testament by means of typology, in a historical and not a mystical sense.

17. Ibid., 47.
18. L. Goppelt, *Typos: Die typologische Deutung des Alten Testaments im Neuen* (Gütersloh, 1939). He has also written two important articles: "Apokalyptik und Typologie bei Paulus," *TLZ* 89 (1964): 321–44, reprinted as appendix to the reissue of *Typos* (Darmstadt 1969); "τύπος," *TDNT* 8 (ET: 1972; German: 1969), 246–59.
19. Goppelt, *Typos*, 239–49. Cf. A. Richardson, *Christian Apologetics* (London, 1947), 190–91; R. M. Grant, *The Bible in the Church: A Short History of Interpretation* (New York, 1948), 31–42; G. E. Wright, *God Who Acts: Biblical Theology as Recital* (London, 1952), 61. Contrast Hanson, *Jesus Christ in the Old Testament*, 8, 172–77.

Among other studies of New Testament typology the works of E. Earle Ellis, K. J. Woollcombe, Samuel Amsler, and R. T. France are particularly important.[20] Although it is impossible here to consider these in detail, it can be stated that each in its own way confirms that the historical understanding of typology is fundamental to the New Testament.

The Relationship Between the Testaments

Hans Walter Wolff develops the idea of typology as the analogy between the Old and New Testaments, centering his argument on the special starting point of Old Testament interpretation.[21]

First, he rejects any suggestion that ancient Near Eastern religion is this starting point. The Old Testament is quite distinct from its ancient Near Eastern environment: in spite of parallels in detail the substance is essentially different. Its distinctive characteristics, including its divine law and its prophecy (which are more important than the cult) and especially the unique nature of Yahweh, the God of Israel, show that it is a stranger in the ancient Orient. It follows that the essence of the Old Testament cannot be understood by analogy to its religious environment.

Secondly, he asks, if studies of the ancient Near East are not the key to the Old Testament, will rabbinic studies unlock its meaning? There is an apparent continuity between the Old Testament and Judaism,[22] but the fact is that from the Christian standpoint Judaism has not properly understood the Old Testament. Whether the synagogue reads its Bible as law or as the source of all wisdom, the full meaning of the Old Testament is to be sought elsewhere.

Thirdly, the question of whether the New Testament can show the meaning of the Old Testament remains for consideration. Wolff points out that Paul addresses the church as the Israel of God (Gal. 6:16) and throughout the New Testament Israel is a type of the church of Jesus Christ (e.g., Mark 3:14; Rom. 11:17ff; James 1:1; Rev. 21:12–14). Here, he says, is a fundamental analogy: "the Church of Jesus Christ can understand itself aright only as the eschatological Israel of God."[23] There

20. E. E. Ellis, *Paul's Use of the Old Testament* (Edinburgh, 1957), 126–35; Woollcombe in *Essays on Typology*, 39–69, 75; S. Amsler, *L'Ancien Testament dans l'Église* (Neuchâtel, 1960), esp. pp. 141–47, 215–27; R. T. France, *Jesus and the Old Testament*, 38–80 and "'In all the Scriptures'—a Study of Jesus' Typology," *TSFB* 56 (spring 1970): 13–16.

21. Wolff, *EOTI*, 167–81.

22. K. H. Miskotte considers that there are two sequels to the Old Testament: the New Testament and the Talmud. Neither Jews nor Christians alone are Israel but together they form one congregation of God (*When the Gods Are Silent* [ET: London, 1967; Dutch: 1956; revd. German edn.: 1963], 77–78, 165–67).

23. Wolff, *EOTI*, 174.

is also an analogy between the basis and method of salvation in the two Testaments. Although there are obvious differences the fundamental pattern is the same: the people of God is formed through God's saving activity, the covenant is kept intact only through the forgiveness of sins, and God's kingship over the members of the people demands their obedience to his law. Finally, there is a third analogy between God's gifts in the Old and New Testaments. In both cases there are material and spiritual gifts, and although there are differences the analogy is dominant: "the new covenant in Christ corresponds to the covenant will of Yahweh as its fulfillment in the same way that marriage corresponds to engagement."[24] Wolff concludes in these words:

> the old Oriental environment and the Jewish successors of the Old Testament Israel, while presenting us with numerous aids to understanding details, still do not provide anything comparable to the essential total meaning of the Old Testament. *Only the New Testament offers the analogy of a witness of faith to the covenant will of God—a witness founded on historical facts—who chooses out of the world a people for himself and calls it to freedom under his Lordship.*[25]

This analogy Wolff calls "typology."

To sum up, the conclusion of not a few modern scholars is that typology is far from being a fanciful method of interpretation to be dismissed as an illegitimate way of understanding the Bible. On the contrary it is historically based, originates in the Bible, and is still valid today. In order to define the place of typology in Christian use of the Old Testament its basis, nature, and practical value will be considered. It should be noted that there are two aspects to Christian use of the Old Testament: the manner in which a Christian should use the Old Testament and the purpose for which he should use it. In each case the New Testament is important, both because it contains examples of how the Old Testament may be used and because one of the most important uses of the Old Testament is to form a basis for the message of the New Testament.

The Basis of Typology

The Biblical Basis

A more precise definition of the biblical meaning of "typology" necessitates an examination of the biblical use of the word τύπος and its

---

24. Ibid., 179–80.
25. Ibid., 180; cf. A. B. Davidson, *Old Testament Prophecy* (ed. J. A. Paterson; Edinburgh, 1903), 239–40.

cognates τυπικός (typical), ἀντίτυπος (antitype) and ὑποτύπωσις (type). There is no biblical equivalent to the word "typology" for the simple reason that the biblical writers did not analyze or systematize types. For the same reason "typical" is a more appropriate translation of τυπικός than "typological." "Type" is a common word in modern English but in the Septuagint and New Testament τύπος is used only 17 times. In both languages however there is one basic meaning.

The word τύπος in the Bible usually means "example" or "pattern" (12 times); and the occasional meanings "mark" (John 20:25, twice), "image" (Amos 5:26; Acts 7:43) and "to this effect" (Acts 23:25) are related to the basic meaning. Its cognates also relate in every case to the meaning "example" or "pattern." To show this clearly the biblical occurrences of τύπος and its cognates are set out in full. The basic text is the RSV and the translations in brackets are from the RSV, NEB, and NIV respectively (except for LXX, RSV, NEB, and Bagster).

The Use of the τύπος Word-Group in the LXX (OT) and NT
τύπος

Exod. 25:40	"the (pattern, design, pattern) . . . shown you on the mountain"
Amos 5:26	"your (images, images, images)"
John 20:25	"(print, marks, marks) of the nails"
(twice)	"mark, place, where (the nails were) of the nails"
Acts 7:43	"(figures, images, idols) which you made to worship"
Acts 7:44	"the (pattern, pattern, pattern) that he had seen"
Acts 23:25	"a letter (to this effect, to this effect, as follows)"
Rom. 5:14	"Adam, who was a (type, foreshadows, pattern)"
Rom. 6:17	"obedient . . . to the (standard, pattern, form) of teaching"
1 Cor. 10:6	"these things are (warnings, symbols to warn, examples) for us"
Phil. 3:17	"as you have an (example, model, pattern) in us"
1 Thess. 1:7	"an (example, model, model) to all the believers"
2 Thess. 3:9	"an (example, example, model) to imitate"
1 Tim. 4:12	"set the believers an (example, example, example)"
Titus 2:7	"show yourself . . . a (model, example, example) of good deeds"
Heb. 8:5	"the (pattern, pattern, pattern) . . . shown you on the mountain"
1 Pet. 5:3	"being (examples, an example, examples) to the flock"

τυπικός

1 Cor. 10:11	"happened to them as (a warning, symbolic, examples)"

ἀντίτυπος

Heb. 9:24   "a (copy, symbol, copy) of the true one"
1 Pet. 3:21   "Baptism, which (corresponds) to this" (RSV)
               "This water (prefigured, symbolises) baptism" (NEB, NIV)

ὑποτύπωσις

1 Tim. 1:16   "(example to, typical of, example for) those who . . . believe"
2 Tim. 1:13   "Follow the (pattern, outline, pattern) of the sound words"

The τύπος word-group is closely related in meaning to the word-group which includes δεῖγμα (Jude 7) and its cognates δειγματίζω (Col. 2:1–5), παράδειγμα (Exod. 25:9; 1 Chron. 28:11, 12, 18, 19), παραδειγματίζω (Matt. 1:19; Heb. 6:6) and ὑπόδειγμα (John 13:15; Heb. 4:11; 8:5; 9:23; Jas. 5:10; 2 Pet. 2:6). Here again the meaning is "example" or "pattern" in almost every case.[26]

In no instance is any member of either of these word-groups used in the Bible as a technical term.[27] The conclusion is straightforward: the evidence of biblical terminology suggests the meaning "example, pattern" for "type."

The Theological Basis

Typological thinking is part of all human thought, arising out of man's attempt to understand the world on the basis of concrete analogies,[28] so there is nothing surprising about the application of this method to the biblical world. Archbishop Trench once wrote:

the parable or other analogy to spiritual truth appropriated from the world of nature or man, is not merely illustration, but also in some sort

26. The only exception is Heb. 6:6, where the meaning of παραδειγματίζω is "to hold up to contempt."

27. It is sometimes thought that the word τύπος has a technical sense in 1 Cor. 10:6 (cf. v. 11) and Rom. 5:14 (e.g., Goppelt, *TDNT* 8:251–53). However, translators generally agree that the meaning is "foreshadow" (NEB), "prefigure" (JB) or "pattern" (NIV) in Rom. 5:14 and "example" (NIV) or "warning" (RSV, JB) in 1 Cor. 10:6, 11. In both cases the usual biblical meaning "example, pattern" is entirely appropriate and it is unnecessary to suggest a technical use. It is presumably to prevent any implication of a technical term that the English versions avoid the translation "type" for τύπος.

28. As von Rad points out (*EOTI*, 17–18 and *Old Testament Theology*, 2:364). Contrast R. Bultmann ("Ursprung und Sinn der Typologie als hermeneutische Methode," *TLZ* 75 [1950]: 205–12) who rejects typology because it is based on the idea of repetition. According to him this is derived from the cyclic view of history of the ancient Near East and classical Greece, whereas, the Old Testament has a linear view of history, a history whose course is divinely-directed and moves toward a definite conclusion. Von Rad disputes the validity of this view (*EOTI*, 20).

proof. It is not merely that these analogies assist to make the truth intelligible. . . . Their power lies deeper than this, in the harmony unconsciously felt by all men, and which all deeper minds have delighted to trace, between the natural and the spiritual worlds, so that analogies from the first are felt to be something more than illustrations, happily but yet arbitrarily chosen. . . . They belong to one another, the type and the thing typified, by an inward necessity; they were linked together long before by the law of a secret affinity.[29]

It is the conviction that there is such a "secret affinity" within God's created order, shared by the biblical writers and many of their interpreters throughout the centuries, which lies at the root of the idea of typology. Some use typology cautiously, others use it extravagantly, but all base their use of typology on the conviction that there is a secret affinity between the natural and spiritual orders, as well as between different events in the same order.

Thus it is natural for those in biblical times to see a close relationship between the tabernacle and the heavenly pattern shown to Moses (Exod. 25:40; Acts 7:44; Heb. 8:5), between the life of Christ or a Christian leader and the way Christians ought to live (1 Tim. 1:16; Phil. 3:17; 1 Pet. 5:3), between events in Israel's history and events in the life of the church (1 Cor. 10:6, 11; 1 Pet. 3:21), between an idol and the spiritual reality it symbolizes (Amos 5:26; Acts 7:43), and between the man who brought sin into the world and the man who took it away (Rom. 5:14). In each case the presupposition is that God acts consistently so that there are correspondences between different parts of his created order. Typology rests on the basic assumption that "the history of God's people and of his dealings with them is a single continuous process in which a uniform pattern may be discerned."[30]

There are two main kinds of correspondence here: vertical (archetype and antitype, that is, the relationship between heavenly and earthly realities) and horizontal (prototype and antitype, that is, the relationship between earlier and later historical facts).[31] In practice how-

29. R. C. Trench, *Notes on the Parables of our Lord* (London, 1870[11]; first ed. c. 1850), 12–14; cf. C. H. Dodd, *The Parables of the Kingdom* (rev. ed. London, 1961; 1935[1]), 20.

30. Lampe, *Theology* 56:201. Cf. C. T. Fritsch, "Biblical Typology: I: New Trends in Old Testament Theology," *BS* 103 (1946): 293; R. A. Marcus, "Presuppositions of the Typological Approach to Scripture," *CQR* 158 (1957): 448; Wolff, *EOTI*, 344n.; Hummel, *BR* 9, 41.

31. On this distinction see Hummel, *BR* 9, p. 39; C. T. Fritsch, "TO ANTITYTTON" in *Studia Biblica et Semitica: Theodoro Christiano Vriezen dedicata* (Wageningen, 1966), 100–177.

ever the Bible is more interested in horizontal than vertical typology, as is most modern writing on the subject.

The Interpretative Basis

It has been shown that Christian typical understanding of the Old Testament is based on the biblical meaning of τύπος (example, pattern) and the consistency of God which leads to correspondences within creation and history. Yet there is something even more basic about the idea of analogy or typology: it is the way in which almost any biblical text (Old Testament or New Testament) addresses us. The Bible does not generally contain propositions but stories and these can only be relevant in the sense of being typical. What significance would Abraham or Moses have for us if they were not typical? It is of no relevance to us that a frog can hop or that a snake can bite (except to get out of its way!). It is because Abraham and Moses were men like us (cf. James 5:17) and as such encountered the same God as we do, in other words because they were typical, that their experiences are directly relevant to us.

At the end of John's Gospel it is noted that "Jesus did many other signs in the presence of the disciples, which are not written in this book; but these are written that you may believe that Jesus is the Christ . . ." (John 20:30–31). The implication is that certain signs were chosen to be recorded because they were typical. In chemistry a "type" is a "compound whose structure illustrates that of many others" (Concise Oxford Dictionary). Hydrochloric acid for example is a type of the acids. It is no more an acid than any other but is typical because it shows clearly the essential nature of an acid in its structure: H-Cl. Sulphuric acid (H_2SO_4) and acetic acid (CH_3COOH) have the same basic structure but it is not so clear. The structure of hydrochloric acid is also a pattern for such compounds as NaCl and HBr and so it may be termed a type of the haloids too. In a similar way certain signs are recorded in John because they show some aspect or aspects of the gospel message especially clearly and thus can serve as types.

This provides at least one reason why so much is made of the affair between David and Bathsheba. There is no question of reveling in the sins of others: it is rather that the temptation, sin, attempt to conceal, rebuke, repentance, forgiveness, punishment, and restoration are recorded because they are typical of what happens frequently in the life of a believer. Jonah may be chosen as a type of the Christian because like so many he was led from sin through despair to eventual salvation. He is also a type of Christ who bore the sins of the world, was brought to the point of despair and descended to the lowest state possible before he was raised from death to life.

The Nature of Typology

Some False Ideas of Typology

It has been seen that typology is based on the consistency of God's activity in the life of the world and his chosen people. A more precise definition of its nature will now be attempted: what are the characteristics of something which is typical? It is necessary first to distinguish a number of incorrect uses of the word typology.

1. Typology is not exegesis.[32] The biblical text has only one meaning, its literal meaning, and this is to be found by means of grammatical-historical study. If the author intended a typical significance it will be clear in the text. And if we see a typical significance not perceived by the original author it must be consistent with the literal meaning. Typology is not an exegesis or interpretation of a text but the study of relationships between events, persons and institutions recorded in biblical texts.

2. Typology is not prophecy.[33] The two are related since both presuppose continuity and correspondence in history but typology is retrospective whereas prophecy is prospective. It is true that recognition of the fulfillment of prophecy is retrospective but this is concerned with the fulfillment of *words* in the Old Testament whereas typology discerns a relationship between the *events, persons*, and *institutions* recorded in the Bible.

3. Typology is not allegory.[34] The distinction between typology and allegory was formulated as early as 1762 by J. Gerhard: "Typology consists in the comparison of facts. Allegory is not so much concerned in facts as in their assembly, from which it draws out useful and hidden doctrine."[35] In spite of one or two objections[36] modern scholars have gener-

---

32. See, e.g., Goppelt, *Typos*, 19–20; Amsler, *ETR* 27: 77–79; von Rad, *EOTI*, 37–38; H. W. Wolff, "The Old Testament in Controversy: Interpretive Principles and Illustration," ET in *Interpn* 12 (1958): 285 (German of section "On the Method of Typological Interpretation of the Old Testament" originally in *ZdZ* 10 [1956]); France, *Jesus and the Old Testament*, 4–12. Contrast Woollcombe, in *Essays on Typology*, 39–40.

33. See, e.g., Amsler, *RThPh* 3:139–48; Wolff, *EOTI*, 188–89; Eichrodt, *EOTI*, 229; Woollcombe in *Essays on Typology*, 41–42.

34. See, e.g., Goppelt, *Typos*, 19; Richardson, *Christian Apologetics*, 189–90; G. Florovsky, "Revelation and Interpretation," in *Biblical Authority for Today* (ed. A. Richardson and W. Schweitzer; London, 1951), 173–76; Amsler, *ETR* 27: 77; Eichrodt, *EOTI*, 227–28; Lampe, Woollcombe in *Essays on Typology*, 29–35, 40–42; R. E. Nixon, *The Exodus in the New Testament* (London, 1963), 11; D. Lys, *The Meaning of the Old Testament: An Essay on Hermeneutics* (Nashville/New York, 1967), 54–75.

35. Quoted by Goppelt, *Typos*, 8 and translated by Wright, *God Who Acts*, 61.

36. Barr (*Old and New in Interpretation*, 103–11) denies the validity of the distinction; P. K. Jewett ("Concerning the Allegorical Interpretation of Scripture," *WTJ* 17 (1954–55): 1–20) thinks they are much the same thing; and Bright (*The Authority of the Old Testament*, 79–80) points out that it is difficult to distinguish between the two in the Fathers.

ally accepted this distinction, laying stress on the historical nature of typology in contrast to the fanciful nature of allegory which often entirely ignores the historical situation. Typology requires a real correspondence between the events, persons, and institutions in question, but allegory can find "spiritual" significance in unimportant details or words.

4. Typology is not symbolism.[37] Symbolic interpretation involves understanding objects as expressions of a general truth but typical interpretation is concerned to see relationships between historical facts.

5. Typology is not a method or system.[38] In the church fathers an elaborate typological method was developed but in the Bible the typical approach is so unsystematic that it does not even have a fixed terminology. The Bible gives no exhaustive list of types and implies no developed method for their interpretation. On the contrary there is great freedom and variety in the outworking of the basic presupposition that the Old Testament is a model for the New.

Some Suggested Characteristics of Types

There have been numerous attempts to define the characteristics of types but many make the mistake of treating typology as a fixed system rather than a basic approach to the Bible.

1. It is suggested for instance that an essential characteristic of a type is that it is designed by God.[39] At first sight this is very plausible and it may be thought that it is self-evident. But surely the whole Bible was designed by God. "If David could have been placed where he was, and been what he was, without God's design, he would still have been typical. But, of course, without God's intervention, neither he nor his dispensation could have come into existence."[40]

2. Another suggestion is that the limits of typology should be defined by giving a series of standards to which a type must conform[41] or by limiting types to those found in the New Testament.[42] But although it is possible to describe what is meant by "typical" it is arbitrary to limit its occurrence in the Bible by a set of rules. The New Testament gives

---

But none have really gainsaid the fundamental distinction that typology is generally historical whereas allegory is fanciful.

37. Goppelt, *Typos*, 19.

38. Ibid., 243–44; Eichrodt, *EOTI*, 229–31; France, *Jesus and the Old Testament*, 76–77; cf. Amsler, *L'Ancien Testament dans l'Église*, 141, 144.

39. Goppelt, *Typos*, 18–19; Moorehead, *ISBE*, 3029; Fritsch, *BS* 104: 214; L. Berkhof, *Principles of Biblical Interpretation (Sacred Hermeneutics)* (Grand Rapids, Michigan, 1950), 145; Amsler, *ETR* 27:79.

40. Davidson, *Old Testament Prophecy*, 237; cf. A. Calmet, "Type" in *Calmet's Dictionary of the Holy Bible* (London, 1837⁶), 2:769.

41. Moorehead, *ISBE*, 3029–30; Amsler, *ETR* 27:81; cf. Eichrodt, *EOTI*, 244.

42. Wright, *God Who Acts*, 66.

guidelines but does not pretend to give a definition or exhaustive list of types.[43] Since typology is not concerned only with certain parts of the Old Testament but with the whole Bible there are an unlimited number of possible types.[44] It is not a matter of finding types in a fixed system: rather, many events and persons may usefully serve as typical for one purpose or another.

3. It is sometimes suggested that types are always concerned with Christ[45] or with God's redemptive activity.[46] But then much of the Bible is concerned with God's redemptive activity and thus with Christ! It is not surprising if this is the dominant concern of types in the Bible; but the Bible is interested in creation and the kingdom of God as well as redemption, and these have typical aspects too.[47]

4. A further suggestion is that types prefigure something future.[48] But this implies that they have some meaning other than that which is apparent at the time. It is only in retrospect that an event, person, or institution may be seen as typical.[49] The existence of types necessitates there being other events, persons, or institutions (earlier or later) of which they are typical.

5. It is often suggested that there is an "increase"[50] or "progression"[51] from the type to its antitype. But this is simply an aspect of the progression from Old Testament to New Testament and not a necessary characteristic of a type. The essence of a type is that it is exemplary and it would be theoretically possible for something which is more advanced to be typical of something which is less advanced. Moreover it is possible for one thing to be a type of its opposite: for example, the entry of sin into the world by the first Adam and the entry of grace by the second.[52]

43. Fritsch, *BS* 104: 220.

44. Von Rad, *EOTI*, 36; cf. J. Sailer, "Über Typen im Neuen Testament," *ZKT* 69 (1947): 490–96.

45. Amsler, *ETR* 27: 79–80 and *L'Ancien Testament dans l'Église*, 144–45.

46. Fritsch, *BS* 104: 220–21; Woollcombe in *Essays on Typology*, 75; J. B. Payne, *The Theology of the Older Testament* (Grand Rapids, Michigan, 1962), 357–58.

47. Cf. A. A. van Ruler, *The Christian Church and the Old Testament* (ET: Grand Rapids, Michigan, 1966; reissued: 1971; German: 1955), 62–73; P. A. Verhoef, "Some Notes on Typological Exegesis," in *New Light on Some Old Testament Problems: Papers read at 5th Meeting of Die O.T. Werkgemeenskap in Suid-Afrika* (Pretoria, 1962), 63.

48. Moorehead, *ISBE*, 3029; Berkhof, *Principles of Biblical Interpretation*, 145; cf. von Rad, *EOTI*, 36.

49. Von Rad, *Old Testament Theology*, 2:384; Bright, *The Authority of the Old Testament*, 92–93; Lys, *The Meaning of the Old Testament*, 71.

50. *Steigerung* (Goppelt, *Typos*, 19, 244).

51. Davidson, *Old Testament Prophecy*, p. 240; Amsler, *L'Ancien Testament dans l'Église*, 145–47; Verhoef in *New Light on Some Old Testament Problems*, 64; France, *Jesus and the Old Testament*, 78–9; cf. von Rad, *EOTI*, 37.

52. Amsler, *ETR* 27:80.

Principles and Definitions

So far the argument has taken the form of negative criticism. It has been argued that typology is not exegesis, prophecy, allegory, symbolism, or a system. Moreover the suggestions that divine design, specific limits, connection with Christ and redemption, prefiguration of the future and progression from type to antitype are necessary characteristics of typology have been rejected. On the positive side there are two basic principles of typology which must be adhered to if it is not to result in fanciful or trivial biblical interpretation.

First, typology is historical.[53] Its concern is not with words but with historical facts: events, people, institutions. It is not a method of philological or textual study but a way of understanding history.[54] The fundamental conviction which underlies typology is that God is consistently active in the history of this world (especially in the history of his chosen people) and that as a consequence the events in the history tend to follow a consistent pattern. One event may therefore be chosen as typical of another or of many others.

Secondly, typology implies a real correspondence.[55] It is not interested in parallels of detail but only in an agreement of fundamental principles and structure. There must be a correspondence in history and theology or the parallel will be trivial and valueless for understanding the Bible.

On the basis of these two principles some working definitions may be suggested:

> a *type* is a biblical event, person, or institution which serves as an example or pattern for other events, persons, or institutions;

53. Goppelt, *Typos*, 18; Florovsky in *Biblical Authority for Today*, 175; Amsler, *ETR* 27: 80; G. W. H. Lampe, *Theology* 56, 202 and "Hermeneutics and Typology," *LQHR* 190 (1965): 24; Woollcombe in *Essays on Typology*, 75; Wolff, *EOTI*, 344; cf. von Rad, *EOTI*, 36–37. Barr (*Old and New in Interpretation*, 103–48) rejects the attempt to rehabilitate typology on a historical basis.

54. Cf. Amsler, *ETR* 27: 78; but contrast S. N. Gundry, "Typology as a Means of Interpretation: Past and Present," *BETS* 12 (1969): 233–40. The question may be raised whether Jonah or Job, for instance, must be historical in order to be typical. It may be suggested that although typology is essentially historical it is possible to have correspondences between an imaginary person and a real person. Even if such a type is somewhat artificial it could still have educative value. There is undoubtedly a correspondence between Hamlet or Macbeth and real people: the significance of these characters is not lessened by the fact that they are merely fictional. Likewise, whether or not they ever lived, there remains a fundamental correspondence between the lives of Jonah and Job as portrayed in the biblical story and those of Christians.

55. Berkhoff, *Principles of Biblical Interpretation*, 145; Amsler, *ETR* 27: 79; Woollcombe in *Essays on Typology*, 75; France, *Jesus and the Old Testament*, 40–41; G. F. Hasel, *Old Testament Theology: Basic Issues in the Current Debate* (Grand Rapids, Michigan, 1972), 73–74.

typology is the study of types and the historical and theological correspondences between them; the *basis* of typology is God's consistent activity in the history of his chosen people.

The Confusion of Typology with Fanciful Interpretation

One of the basic issues mentioned at the beginning of the present article was that typology in church history and today has frequently been taken to be a fanciful kind of biblical interpretation. It may be suggested that in most cases it has been a neglect of the principles just stated which has led to this confusion of history and fancy. Too often typology has been used as a method of exegesis: there is all the difference between finding the real meaning of Genesis 37–50 to be a prefiguration of Christ and seeing Joseph as a typical character whose life reveals basic principles of God's activity which are also true for the life of Christ and Christians. The former is exegesis, the latter is typology. Sometimes the word "typology" has been used for what is really symbolism or allegory but the most common failing is to find correspondences in trivial details. There is no historical or theological correspondence between Rahab's scarlet cord and the death of Christ, nor between the axe Elisha retrieved from the river and the cross.[56] There is a consistency in God's created order which makes it possible for there to be red or wooden objects in both Old and New Testaments; but that does not mean that these things have any typical or exemplary importance for the Christian! Nevertheless the fact that the term "typology" has been applied to trivial correspondences, confused with allegory and symbolism, and misused in the exegesis of the Old Testament does not invalidate it as a principle if properly used. And although we should certainly not adopt such exegetical methods neither should we despise those who used them; it was the allegorical school in the early church who preserved the Old Testament for the Christian church.[57]

The Value of Typology for the Christian Use of the Old Testament

It has been argued that typology is not a method of exegesis or interpretation but the study of historical and theological correspondences between different parts of God's activity among his people in order to find what is typical there. The function of typology is therefore not to give a procedure for using the Old Testament but to point to the consistent working of God in the experience of his people so that parallels may

56. *I Clement*, 12; Justin, *Dialogue*, 86.
57. Cf. Grant, *The Bible in the Church*, 52, 72.

be drawn between different events, persons, and institutions and indi-vidual events may be seen as examples or patterns for others. Typology cannot be used for exegesis, because its concern is not primarily with the words of the text but with the events recorded in it. This means also that Old Testament exegesis is freed from the pressure to be relevant: often the narrator had recorded only a bare event, but in this very lack of interpretation it may have typical and thus theological significance.[58] The exegete has to find the meaning of the text and its witness to an event and for this the tool is grammatical-historical exegesis. To relate it to other events recorded in the Bible is the task of the biblical theolo-gian and historian; to relate it to modern Christian experience is the task of the preacher. For these typology has its value but it must be used judiciously and in accordance with the principles previously outlined. There are two main ways in which typology may serve Christian use of the Old Testament and they will be considered in turn.

First, typology points to the fundamental analogy between different parts of the Bible. Every part of the Bible is an expression of the consis-tent activity of the one God. This means that the Old Testament illumi-nates the New Testament and the New Testament illuminates the Old Testament. It is not the New Testament's use of the Old Testament or parallels in details which are in question but a fundamental analogy be-tween the Old Testament and New Testament as witnesses to God's ac-tivity in history. In this way, although it is not a method of exegesis, ty-pology supplements exegesis by throwing further light on the text in question. The most closely related discipline to the study of the Old Tes-tament is therefore that of the New Testament: ancient Oriental and Jewish studies clarify details of the Old Testament but lack the intrinsic analogy of New Testament studies to Old Testament studies. The corol-lary is that the most closely related discipline to the study of the New Testament is that of the Old Testament: Jewish and Hellenistic studies are important but do not have a fundamental analogy to New Testa-ment studies in the way that Old Testament studies do. This shows a double aspect to the Christian use of the Old Testament: on the one hand correct understanding and use of the Old Testament depends on the New Testament, and on the other hand one of the primary uses of the Old Testament is to be the basis for correct understanding and use of the New Testament. Some of the examples of this kind of interpreta-tion given by Wolff are worth mentioning.[59] The Sermon on the Mount and Paul's exhortations give insight into the Old Testament law as God's covenant gift, the concept of witness in Luke and John illuminates that

58. Von Rad, *EOTI*, 38.
59. Wolff, *EOTI*, 181–99.

in Ezekiel, and God's salvation of his people by the judges may be seen as one aspect of his continual saving activity throughout their history. Moreover, the primeval history witnesses to God's intention for the world (without which Jesus Christ would not be understood properly), the Day of Atonement ritual shows God's principles in dealing with sin (which are the presupposition for the coming of Jesus and apart from which his death would be inexplicable), and Exodus 14 and Ezekiel 37 show the nature of the divinely-constituted people of God (and thus the self-understanding of the church).

Secondly, typology is an aid to practical application of the Bible in the Christian church. It must be emphasized again that typology is not exegesis but a supplement to exegesis. Although the present concern is with the application of the Old Testament, typology is equally valid for the New Testament: the whole Bible is typical. It has been shown that the essence of the biblical concept of "type" is "example, pattern," and one of the primary values of the Bible for the Christian is that it presents examples and patterns of the experience of men and women with God which correspond to the experience of modern men and women.

Events, persons, and institutions offer the Christian types for his life. The flood (cf. 1 Pet. 3:20–21), the oppression and exodus (cf. 1 Cor. 10) and the exile and restoration (cf. Jer. 23:7–8) are typical of God's saving activity among his people, and thus patterns of the salvation which the Christian experiences in Christ. Noah and Job (cf. Ezek. 14:14, 20), Moses (cf. Heb. 3:2), and David (cf. 1 Kings 3:14; 15:3, 11) are examples of how the believer should live. Balaam (cf. 2 Pet. 2:15; Jude 11; Rev. 2:14) and Jeroboam (cf. 1 Kings 15:26, 34; 16:2–3, 19, 26, 31), in contrast, are examples of how he should not live. These examples could easily be multiplied (cf. Heb. 11). The correspondence between Israelite and Christian institutions (e.g., Passover and Lord's Supper; psalms and hymns) and the spiritual application of Old Testament material realities (e.g., the temple and the Christian church as dwelling-places of God, cf. 1 Cor. 3:16; sacrifices and offerings and the Christian's "living sacrifice," cf. Rom. 12:1) are further ways in which typology may aid use of the Old Testament to understand the Christian life. All these examples (and many others which could be adduced) apply also and especially to Christ himself, which is why typology is often thought to be concerned with types of Christ.

One final thought: is not the Lord Jesus Christ the supreme "example" and "pattern" for Christians (Matt. 11:29; John 13:15; Phil. 2:5; 1 Pet. 2:21)? Perhaps those interested in typology should concern themselves less with looking for types *of* Christ and more with presenting Christ *himself* as the supreme "type" for Christians and the world.

19

Introductory Notes on Typology

G. P. Hugenberger

Typology and Critical Scholarship

After nearly half a century of denigration and deliberate neglect, in the past few decades the subject of typology (broadly defined) has enjoyed a remarkable resurgence of interest among biblical scholars.[1] For evangelicals this renewed interest presents both a serious challenge and a welcome opportunity. It brings a challenge because of the problematic presuppositions, methods, and conclusions of some of the newer varieties of typology. Nevertheless, this interest is welcome for the more congenial atmosphere in which evangelical scholarship can function as it attempts to rediscover, develop, and refine the balanced typological method represented within our heritage by an earlier generation of scholars such as A. B. Davidson,[2] E. W. Hengstenberg,[3] M. S. Terry,[4] F. Delitzsch,[5] B. F. Westcott,[6] and especially P. Fairbairn.[7]

---

1. This interest in typology extends to the history of interpretation, as is evidenced in such works as Joseph A. Galdon, *Typology and Seventeenth Century Literature* (The Hague and Paris: Mouton, 1975); Sacvan Bercovitch, ed., *Typology and Early American Literature* (Amherst, MA: The University of Massachusetts Press, 1972); James M. Kee, "Typology and Tradition: Refiguring the Bible in Milton's *Paradise Lost*," *Semeia* 51 (1990): 155–75; and the recently published collection of sermons on typology preached by the colonial poet and minister, Edward Taylor, *Upon the Types of the Old Testament,* 2 vols. (ed. Charles W. Mignon; Lincoln, Nebraska and London: University of Nebraska Press, 1990).

2. A. B. Davidson, *Old Testament Prophecy* (Edinburgh: T. & T. Clark, 1904 [published posthumously]).

3. E. W. Hengstenberg, *Christology of the Old Testament*, 2 vols. (1836–39 [reprinted by McLean, VA: MacDonald Publishing Company, n.d.]).

4. Milton S. Terry, *Biblical Hermeneutics* (New York: Phillips & Hunt, 1883 [reprinted 1974]), 244–303.

5. Franz Delitzsch, as presented in his commentary on Genesis (English translation, 1888) and throughout the Keil and Delitzsch commentary series.

6. B. F. Westcott, *The Epistle to the Hebrews* (London and New York: Macmillan, 1892)—see his "Additional Notes" on the use of the OT in Hebrews.

7. Patrick Fairbairn, *The Typology of Scripture*, 2 vols. (New York: Funk and Wagnalls Co. [Zondervan reprint 1963], 1900 [original edition 1845–1847]).

Several factors have played a role in the current revival of interest in typology. Prominent among these is the inescapable need to take account of the New Testament's own use of typology in any attempt to relate the New Testament to the Old.[8] Accordingly, in his seminal work on the subject, L. Goppelt considers typology to be the characteristic method of interpretation of the Old Testament within the New.[9] Of course, the New Testament utilized typology no less in the period before Goppelt. This was hardly noticed, however, between 1880 and 1920, when as Goppelt notes, the question of the relation of the Testaments and the study of hermeneutics in general were being all but ignored in critical circles.[10]

A second, rather general, stimulus for typology has come from the desire to make Old Testament theology more relevant to modern Gentile readers who are disinclined or unable to offer animal sacrifices at a literal temple in Jerusalem, etc. This concern for relevance is apparent in the recent appeals in support of typology offered by G. von Rad,[11] W. Eichrodt,[12] and H. W. Wolff,[13] among others.

Finally, a third major impetus for this resurgent interest in typology may be found in a renewed awareness of the Old Testament's own use of typology, as it relates protology, the patriarchal narratives, Moses, the exodus, the Davidic period, and other redemptive-historical events to other Old Testament characters and events and especially, to its own eschatology.[14] This awareness has been heightened by the current

8. Cf., e.g., E. Earle Ellis's stress on the role of typology in the writings of Paul (*Paul's Use of the Old Testament* [Grand Rapids, MI: Baker, 1957]) and the similar conclusions of R. T. France regarding the teachings of Jesus (*Jesus and the Old Testament* [London: InterVarsity Press, 1971]).

9. Leonhard Goppelt, *Typos. The Typological Interpretation of the Old Testament in the New* (Grand Rapids, MI: Eerdmans, 1982 [translation of Goppelt's 1939 dissertation]), 246. Cf. the summary of Goppelt in D. L. Baker, *Two Testaments: One Bible* (Downer's Grove, IL: InterVarsity Press, 1977), 246.

10. L. Goppelt, op. cit., 14f.

11. Cf. G. von Rad, "Typological Interpretation of the Old Testament" in *Essays on Old Testament Hermeneutics* (ed. Claus Westermann; Atlanta: John Knox Press, 1960), 17–49 [reprinted in *A Guide to Contemporary Hermeneutics. Major Trends in Biblical Interpretation* (ed. Donald K. McKim; Grand Rapids, MI: Eerdmans, 1986), 28–46] and idem, *Old Testament Theology* (1965), 319–429.

12. W. Eichrodt, "Is Typological Exegesis an Appropriate Method?" in *Essays on Old Testament Hermeneutics* (ed. Claus Westermann; Atlanta: John Knox Press, 1960), 224–45.

13. H. W. Wolff, "The Hermeneutics of the Old Testament," in *Essays on Old Testament Hermeneutics* (ed. Claus Westermann; Atlanta: John Knox Press, 1960), 160–99.

14. Cf., e.g., G. von Rad, "Typological Interpretation of the Old Testament" in *Essays on Old Testament Hermeneutics* (ed. Claus Westermann; Atlanta: John Knox Press, 1960), 17–49, at 19; G. W. H. Lampe, "The Reasonableness of Typology," in G. W. H. Lampe and K. J. Woollcombe, *Essays on Typology,* Studies in Biblical Theology, No. 22 (Naperville, IL: Alec R. Allenson, 1957), 9–38, at pp. 26f. Cf. also Michael Fishbane, *Biblical Interpretation in Ancient Israel* (Oxford: Clarendon Press, 1985), 350–79.

On the use of the patriarchal narratives, cf., e.g., R. Clements, *Abraham and David; Genesis XV and its Meaning for Israelite Tradition* (London: SCM Press, 1967).

scholarly fashion to give greater attention to the literary artfulness, narrative typology, and unity of the Bible in its final form. So, for example, D. Daube's study, *The Exodus Pattern in the Bible* (London, 1963) argues for the centrality of the exodus as a self-conscious model for biblical authors treating the themes of redemption and eschatology.[15]

While many exegetical insights have resulted from these efforts, it is crucial to note that the new "typology," in contrast to traditional typology, is often little more than a purely literary or theological artifact which no longer presupposes a Christian philosophy of history (where a sovereign God ordains and structures the underlying analogies between persons, objects, and events in redemptive history) or even the facticity of the type or antitype in question. M. D. Goulder, for example, offers impressive evidence that Luke's account of the apostles in the Book of Acts is deliberately modeled on the life of Jesus—exemplifying Luke's claim that in the Gospel he had only written about what "Jesus *began* to do and to teach."[16] While evangelicals may be grateful for Goulder's insistence on the propriety of typology as an interpretive method in twentieth-century exegesis and can be impressed rightfully with the catenas of correspondence which he enumerates as a safeguard against subjectivism in typological exegesis, there is little to commend Goulder's assumption that "the more completely an incident or detail falls into pattern as an antitype, the more suspicious we shall have to be of its historicity . . .: the thicker the types, the less likely is the passage to be factual."[17] A similar disregard for the historicity of the underlying events comprising the history of redemption in preference to a history of theological ideas expressed in terms of types and antitypes characterizes the amalgam of typology and the traditio-historical method defended by G. von Rad.[18]

Typology and Evangelical Scholarship

In more conservative circles, a substantial number of evangelical scholars have argued in favor of a controlled typology (modeled on the

---

15. Cf. also Jacob J. Enz, "The Book of Exodus as a Literary Type for the Gospel of John," *JBL* 76 (1957): 208–15; and Meredith G. Kline, *The Structure of Biblical Authority*, 2d ed. (Grand Rapids, MI: Eerdmans, 1972), 174–203; and Rikki E. Watts, "The Influence of the Isaianic New Exodus on the Gospel of Mark," PhD. dissertation (University of Cambridge, 1990).

16. M. D. Goulder, *Type and History in Acts* (London: SPCK, 1964). Cf. also A. M. Farrer, who argues that Matthew 1–5 is modeled on Genesis and Exodus in a manner which is more profound than might be suggested by the use of quotation or verbal allusion. (*St. Matthew and St. Mark*, 2d ed. [London: Dacre Press, 1966], chap. 10).

17. M. D. Goulder, op. cit, 182.

18. Cf. G. von Rad, "Typological Interpretation of the Old Testament" in *Essays on Old Testament Hermeneutics* (ed. Claus Westermann; Atlanta: John Knox Press, 1960) and idem, *Old Testament Theology* (1965), 319–429.

sober typological method of the New Testament) as part of the modern exegetical encyclopedia. These include G. Vos,[19] L. Berkhof,[20] M. G. Kline,[21] P. A. Verhoef,[22] A. B. Mickelsen,[23] B. Ramm,[24] D. L. Baker,[25] S. L. Johnson,[26] J. A. Meek,[27] M. H. Woudstra,[28] M. Silva,[29] R. R. Nicole,[30] D. J. Moo,[31] G. R. Osborne,[32] and E. P. Clowney,[33] among many others.[34]

Needless to say, however, this cautious appreciation for typology has not been universally shared. In some cases a lack of confidence in the validity of typology as a modern interpretive method may reflect the influence of dispensationalism and its historic conviction that typology has no basis in a grammatico-historical exegesis of the underlying Old

19. Geerhardus Vos, *Biblical Theology. Old and New Testaments* (Grand Rapids, MI: Eerdmans, 1948), 144ff.

20. L. Berkhof, *Principles of Biblical Interpretation* (Grand Rapids, MI: Baker, 1950), 142–48.

21. Cf., e.g., Meredith G. Kline, *The Structure of Biblical Authority*, 2d ed. (Grand Rapids, MI: Eerdmans, 1972), passim.

22. P. A. Verhoef, "Some Notes on Typological Exegesis," in *New Light on Some Old Testament Problems. Papers read at the 5th Meeting of OTWSA* (Pretoria, 1962), 58–63.

23. A. Berkeley Mickelsen, *Interpreting the Bible* (Grand Rapids, MI: Eerdmans, 1963), 236–64.

24. Bernard Ramm, *Protestant Biblical Interpretation*, 3d ed. (Grand Rapids, MI: Baker, 1970), 215–40.

25. D. L. Baker, *Two Testaments: One Bible* (Downer's Grove, IL: InterVarsity Press, 1977).

26. S. Lewis Johnson, Jr., *The Old Testament in the New. An Argument for Biblical Inspiration* (Grand Rapids, MI: Zondervan, 1980), 53–79.

27. James A. Meek, "Toward a Biblical Typology," Th.M. dissertation (Westminster Seminary, 1981).

28. M. H. Woudstra, *The Book of Joshua*, The New International Commentary on the Old Testament (Grand Rapids, MI: Eerdmans, 1981), 31–32; 37 n. 13.

29. Moisés Silva, "The New Testament Use of the Old Testament: Text Form and Authority," in *Scripture and Truth* (ed. D. A. Carson and John D. Woodbridge; Grand Rapids, MI: Zondervan, 1983), 147–65.

30. Roger R. Nicole, "Patrick Fairbairn and Biblical Hermeneutics as Related to the Quotations of the Old Testament in the New," in *Hermeneutics, Inerrancy and the Bible. Papers from ICBI Summit II* (ed. Earl D. Radmacher and Robert D. Preus; Grand Rapids, MI: Zondervan, 1984), 767–76, with supportive responses by Ronald F. Youngblood, 779–88, and S. Lewis Johnson, Jr., 791–99.

31. Douglas J. Moo, "The Problem of Sensus Plenior," in *Hermeneutics, Authority, and Canon* (ed. D. A. Carson and John D. Woodbridge; Grand Rapids, MI: Zondervan, 1986), 179–211.

32. G. R. Osborne, "Type, Typology" in *The International Standard Bible Encyclopedia*, IV (ed. Geoffrey W. Bromiley, et al.; Grand Rapids, MI: Eerdmans, 1988), 930–32.

33. Edmund P. Clowney, *The Unfolding Mystery. Discovering Christ in the Old Testament* (Colorado Springs, CO: NavPress, 1988), passim.

34. Cf. also John Goldingay, *Approaches to Old Testament Interpretation*, Issues in Contemporary Theology (Leicester, England: InterVarsity Press, 1981), 97–115 and R. M. Davidson, *Typology in Scripture* (Berrien Springs, MI: Andrews University, 1981), 193–297.

Testament texts.[35] Although dispensational scholars concede the use of typology within the New Testament (such as when the New Testament authors identify Christ or the church as the New Israel), this is "viewed by them as New Testament *application* of the Old Testament, not the literal fulfillment of the Old Testament in its Old Testament meaning."[36]

Other evangelical scholars appear distrustful of typology largely because of the apparent subjectivism of this approach, its unfalsifiable and contradictory results, and the indisputable record of interpretive excess (such as G. von Rad's identification of the angel who sought out Hagar as a type of Christ[37] or J. Jordan's interpretive "maximalism," which leads him to identify the attempted Sodomite rape of the Levite in Judges 19 as a type of Christ's sufferings,[38] to note only two recent examples). Especially unconvincing have been the various extensions of biblical typology to encompass the "nature typology" of Calvin and Edwards, among others, (where roses, lambs [not just the Passover lamb], and the sun, etc., are "types" of Christ)[39] or "the New England theocratic typology" of the Puritans (cf., e.g., William Bradford's comparison of the dunes of Plymouth to the top of Pisgah and his identification of America as the new Promised Land).[40]

Finally, exacerbating this distrust of typology has been a tendency to

---

35. Cf., e.g., Vern S. Poythress, *Understanding Dispensationalists* (Grand Rapids, MI: Zondervan, 1987), 111–17.

As an example of this conviction that grammatico-historical exegesis is antithetical to typological interpretation ("spiritualizing"), cf. Paul Feinberg, "Hermeneutics of Discontinuity," in *Continuity and Discontinuity: Perspectives on the Relationship Between the Old and New Testaments. Essays in Honor of S. Lewis Johnson, Jr.* (ed. John S. Feinberg; Westchester, IL: Crossway, 1988).

36. So Mark W. Karlberg, "Israel and the Eschaton," *WTJ* 52:1 (1990): 117–30, at p. 123.

S. Lewis Johnson, Jr., *The Old Testament in the New*, as indicated above, appears as a happy exception to this characterization of the dispensational approach to typology.

37. Gerhard von Rad, *Genesis. A Commentary* (Philadelphia: Westminster Press, 1972), 193–94.

38. James B. Jordan, *Judges. God's War Against Humanism*, Trinity Biblical Commentary (Tyler, TX: Geneva Ministries, 1985), xiiff., 301.

Favorite ancient examples of the misuse of typology include the supposed correspondence between Rahab's scarlet cord and the death of Christ (1 Clement 12) or the axe recovered by Elisha from the river and the cross (Justin, *Dialogue* 86).

39. Cf. Calvin, *Inst.*, 1.5.6; 2.10.20; 3.25.1. Cf. also the discussion in Diana Butler, "God's Visible Glory: The Beauty of Nature in the Thought of John Calvin and Jonathan Edwards," *WTJ* 52 (1990): 13–26.

40. Cf. Sacvan Bercovitch, ed., *Typology and Early American Literature* (The University of Massachusetts Press, 1972).

The use of typology by the cults, such as the Unification Church which identifies Rev. Moon as the "third Adam" (arguing, e.g., that since the first Adam was born of no human parents and the second Adam of only one human parent, the third Adam should be born of two human parents—a condition which was met, indisputably, by Rev. Moon) similarly has not endeared this method to many.

confuse typology with allegory, with the inevitable result that the former is charged with all the deficiencies of the latter.[41]

Nevertheless, the abuse of an interpretive method does not disprove its validity. What are needed are a more precise definition of typology, a more exacting (and sympathetic) analysis of the New Testament's own typological method, and greater rigor in the application of adequate controls in any modern use of typology.[42]

With respect to the New Testament's typological method, G. E. Ladd,[43] D. Beegle,[44] and especially R. N. Longenecker,[45] among others, have argued that the New Testament authors not infrequently misunderstood the context of the Old Testament texts they cite and consequently distorted their meaning for typological and other purposes. If so, then, naturally the modern interpreter cannot benefit from following the exegetical/typological methodology of the New Testament, which would be at variance with the method of grammatico-historical exegesis. Against this claim for misunderstanding and distortion, however, see P. Fairbairn, C. H. Dodd,[46] R. Youngblood,[47]

---

41. Cf., e.g., James Barr, *Old and New in Interpretation: A Study of the Two Testaments* (London, 1966), 103–11.

In spite of the presence of ἀλληγορέω in Galatians 4:24, S. Lewis Johnson argues that Paul's use of Sarah and Hagar is an instance of typology and not true allegory (defined as "the expression by means of symbolic fictional figures and actions of truths or generalizations about human existence"). Cf. also E. Earle Ellis, *Paul's Use of the Old Testament* (Grand Rapids, MI: Eerdmans, 1957), 53.

More convincing are the comments of P. Fairbairn, *The Typology of Scripture*, and R. Nicole, "Patrick Fairbairn and Biblical Hermeneutics," 770, who consider that Paul is merely drawing a parallel without implying any prophetic significance.

42. Cf., e.g., the four suggested controls or "rules of interpretation" of types offered by B. Ramm, *Protestant-Biblical Interpretation*, 3d ed., 229–31.

43. George E. Ladd, "Historic Premillenialism," in *The Meaning of the Millennium: Four Views* (Downers Grove, IL: InterVarsity Press, 1977), 20f., as cited by S. Lewis Johnson, "A Response to Patrick Fairbairn and Biblical Hermeneutics as Related to the Quotations of the Old Testament in the New," in *Hermeneutics, Inerrancy and the Bible. Papers from ICBI Summit II* (ed. Earl D. Radmacher and Robert D. Preus; Grand Rapids, MI: Zondervan, 1984), 791–99, at p. 793.

44. Dewey Beegle, *Scripture, Tradition, and Infallibility* (Grand Rapids, MI: Eerdmans, 1973), 237, as cited by S. Lewis Johnson, "A Response to Patrick Fairbairn," at p. 793.

45. R. N. Longenecker, "Can We Reproduce the Exegesis of the New Testament?" *Tyndale Bulletin* 21 (1970): 3–38; idem, "'Who Is the Prophet Talking about?' Some Reflections on the New Testament's Use of the Old," *Themelios* 13:1 (1987): 4–8.

46. C. H. Dodd, *According to the Scriptures* (London: Nisbet, 1952).

47. Ronald Youngblood, "A Response to Patrick Fairbairn and Biblical Hermeneutics as Related to the Quotations of the Old Testament in the New," in *Hermeneutics, Inerrancy and the Bible. Papers from ICBI Summit II* (ed. Earl D. Radmacher and Robert D. Preus, Grand Rapids, MI: Zondervan, 1984), 779–88. Youngblood reviews Fairbairn's treatment of the five Old Testament quotations in Matthew 1–2, agreeing with Fairbairn concerning their legitimacy and appropriateness, though differing from Fairbairn in his treatment of the quotation of Is. 7:14 in Matt. 1:23.

R. E. Clements,[48] and G. K. Beale.[49]

Working Definitions for "Typology"

Although the Septuagint and the New Testament employ τύπος in a non-technical fashion to refer to various kinds of examples, patterns, and correspondences (including cosmological, as in Exod. 25:40 and Heb. 8:5, for example), it is convenient to limit the identification of a "type," understood as a theological term, to any "biblical event, person, or institution which serves as an example or pattern for other [biblical] events, persons or institutions [which are designated as the "antitype"]; *typology* is the study of types and the historical and theological correspondences between them; the *basis* of typology is God's consistent activity in the history of his chosen people."[50]

Obviously not every scholar would agree with the above redemptive-historical definition of typology. The two major competing views are:[51]

1) The "literary view" of Goulder, where a type is simply a person, event, or institution in Scripture, in terms of which a later biblical author presents his account.

2) The "historical interpretation view" of von Rad, where a type is simply an event in Scripture perceived by the modern interpreter to correspond to a later event.

Even among those who essentially agree with a redemptive-historical approach to typology, there are important differences of emphasis of which to be aware. Although it may be deemed largely a matter of taste, some scholars prefer to limit the vocabulary of typology to those events, persons, or institutions which find their antitype in Christ alone, while others would limit the antitype to the New Testament alone, while still others would allow the antitype to be located in either Testament, so long as the type provides a convincing model.[52] If this last definition is permitted, then it is possible, for example, to identify Abraham's despoiling of Egypt, the plagues, etc., which are recorded in Genesis 12, as a type of the exodus.

48. R. E. Clements concludes that NT interpretation used meanings that had already been attached to OT predictions ("The Messianic Hope in the Old Testament," *JSOT* 43 (1989): 3–19)!

49. Gregory K. Beale, "Did Jesus and His Followers Preach the Right Doctrine from the Wrong Texts? An Examination of the Presuppositions of Jesus' and the Apostles' Exegetical Method," *Themelios* 14 (1989): 89–96.

50. D. L. Baker, *Two Testaments: One Bible*, 267.

51. Cf. also J. Meek, "Toward a Biblical Typology," 100.

Major Characteristics of Types

L. Berkhof offers three major characteristics of types (in the redemptive-historical sense):

1) "There must be some notable real point of resemblance between a type and its antitype. Whatever differences there may be, the former should be a true picture of the latter in some particular point."

Related to this requirement, P. Fairbairn already insisted, "The typical is not properly a different or higher sense, but a different or higher application of the same sense."[53]

2) "The type must be designed by divine appointment to bear a likeness to the anti-type. Accidental similarity between an Old and New Testament person or event does not constitute the one a type of the other. There must be some Scriptural evidence that it was so designed by God."

3) "A type always prefigures something future. Moorehead correctly says: 'A Scriptural type and predictive prophecy are in substance the same, differing only in form.' . . . This distinguishes it from a symbol. It is well to bear in mind, however, that the Old Testament types were at the same time symbols that conveyed spiritual truths to contemporaries, for their symbolical meaning must be understood before their typical meaning can be ascertained."[54]

While Berkhof's observation regarding the symbolic character of types is widely supported, his insistence on "prefigurement," in the sense of prediction, is less certain. While types must necessarily be related to their antitypes by the notion of fulfillment, in the sense that the type provides a model, pattern, or example for the antitype (as well as a correspondence of meaning and historicity), not all types appear to be inherently predictive of their antitype, as noted by J. Wenham, for example, with respect to the citation of Jeremiah 31:15 in Matthew 2:18.[55]

---

52. For these options, cf., e.g., the discussion in D. L. Baker, *Two Testaments: One Bible,* 261. The following are examples of more restrictive definitions:

C. T. Fritsch offers, "A type is an institution, historical event or person, ordained by God, which effectively prefigures some truth connected with Christianity" ("Biblical Typology," *Bibliotheca Sacra* 104 [1947]: 214).

K. J. Woollcombe writes, "typology, considered as a method of exegesis, may be defined as the establishment of historical connexions between certain events, persons or things in the Old Testament and similar events, persons or things in the New Testament. Considered as a method of writing, it may be defined as the description of an event, person or thing in the New Testament in terms borrowed from the description of its prototypal counterpart in the Old Testament" (G. W. H. Lampe and K. J. Woollcombe, *Essays on Typology* [Naperville, IL: Alec R. Allenson, 1957], 39–40).

53. P. Fairbairn, *The Typology of Scripture,* 1:3.

54. L. Berkhof, *Principles of Biblical Interpretation,* 145.

55. John W. Wenham, *Christ and the Bible* (Downers Grove, IL: InterVarsity Press, 1977), 99. S. Lewis Johnson, Jr. terms such a case a "typical fulfillment" (*The Old Testament in the New,* 37).

Should Types be Confined to Those Examples Explicitly Identified as Such within the New Testament?

Perhaps as a safeguard against interpretive excess, some scholars have suggested that "types" should be limited to those examples which are explicitly identified as such within the New Testament. Such was the view, for instance, of Bishop Marsh, as discussed by P. Fairbairn. While attractive for its restraint, this approach would fail to recognize several already mentioned examples for which there is impressive literary evidence of deliberate parallelism (i.e., Abraham's sojourn into Egypt in relation to the exodus, or the careers of Stephen and the apostles in Acts in relation to Christ). To this observation, Fairbairn's own objection may be added:

> . . . nothing could be more arbitrary and inexplicable than this Scriptural Typology [that proposed by Bishop Marsh]. For, what is there to distinguish the characters and events, which Scripture has thus particularized, from a multitude of others, to which the typical element might equally have been supposed to belong? Is there any thing on the face of the inspired record to make us look on *them* in a singular light, and attribute to them a significance altogether peculiar respecting the future affairs of God's kingdom? So far from it, that we instinctively feel, if these really possessed a typical character, so also must others, which hold an equally, or perhaps even more prominent place in the history of God's dispensations. Can it be seriously believed, for example, that Sarah and Hagar stood in a typical relation to gospel times, while no such place was occupied by Rebekah, as the spouse of Isaac, and the mother of Jacob and Esau? What reason can we imagine for Melchizedek and Jonah having been constituted types—persons to whom our attention is comparatively little drawn in Old Testament history—while such leading characters as Joseph, Samson, Joshua, are omitted? Or, for selecting the passage through the Red Sea, and the incidents in the wilderness, while no account should be made of the passage through Jordan, and the conquest of the land of Canaan?[56]

The Clowney Rectangle[57]

It may be useful to conclude the present study with a diagram, first suggested by Edmund Clowney, which attempts to distinguish the

56. P. Fairbairn, *The Typology of Scripture*, 1:23.
Other scholars who recognize the propriety of discovering types beyond those explicitly identified in the New Testament include, among others, B. Ramm, A. B. Mickelsen, L. Berkhof, D. Moo, M. Silva, and S. L. Johnson. Cf. Gregory K. Beale, "Did Jesus and His Followers Preach the Right Doctrine from the Wrong Texts? An Examination of the Presuppositions of Jesus' and the Apostles' Exegetical Method," *Themelios* 14 (1989): 89–96, at p. 96 n. 37.
57. The present diagram is a slight elaboration of one related to the writer in private communication by Edmund Clowney.

method of controlled typology from other less responsible interpretive approaches.

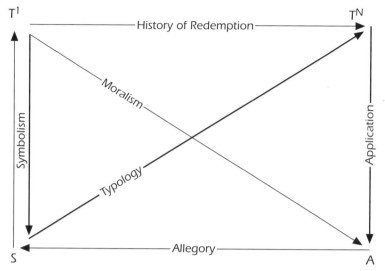

T^1 is some truth (to the first power), that is, some fact(s) regarding a person, event, or institution revealed in its Old Testament setting.

T^N is some truth (to the nth power), that is, some fact revealed in its fullness in Christ and his work.

S is the symbolic value (or significance) of T^1.

A is a contemporary application.

Moralism occurs when an exegete or preacher begins with an Old Testament account and moves directly to the contemporary need for an application, failing to interpret the Old Testament account in the light of redemptive history and especially Christ. An example would be to preach on David's battle with Goliath and conclude that God wants little boys to be brave.

Allegory occurs when an exegete or preacher begins with a contemporary application and discerns symbolic values within an Old Testament account which an original reader is unlikely to have detected, but which fit the desired application. An example may be seen in Origen's treatment of Abraham's marriage with Keturah (*Hom. vi.* in *Genes.*): "The death of Sarah is to be understood as the perfecting of virtue. But he who has attained to a consummate and perfect virtue, must always be employed in some kind of learning—which learning is called by the divine word his wife. Abraham, therefore, when an old man, and his body in a manner dead, took Keturah to wife. . . . Keturah, whom he married in his old age, is by interpretation *incense*, or sweet odor. For he said, even as Paul said, 'We are a sweet savor of Christ.'"[58]

Typology, on the other hand, begins with a fact related to a person, event, or institution, as recorded in the Old Testament, which is then understood in the context of redemptive history. It proceeds by way of discovering that symbolism or significance which the *original* reader of the biblical record, or observer, would have been justified in attaching to this fact.[59] It then correlates this significance to a later fact within redemptive history which, the typologist must establish, shares an analogous meaning to the first fact (not merely a superficial resemblance) and also fulfills or is modeled on the pattern of the first fact. Support for this claim may be discovered in patterns in the structure of redemptive history, in the existence of narrative typologies, or in other catenas of correspondence, etc. With these conditions met, the significance of the first fact, the type, illumines the second fact, the antitype.[60]

As an example, one may consider the case of Joshua renewing the covenant and leading the people of God into the promised land. Since the original reader/observer would have been justified in interpreting Joshua as a second Moses figure (cf. Deuteronomy 31, Joshua 1; 3:7), and since Jesus may also be viewed as a second Moses, it is possible to correlate the significance of Joshua's acts of salvation and conquest of the promised land to the work of Christ.[61]

---

58. P. Fairbairn, *Typology of Scripture,* 1:4.

59. This formulation is intended to avoid the "intentional fallacy." Cf. Philip B. Payne, "The Fallacy of Equating Meaning with the Human Author's Intention," *JETS* 20 (1977): 243–52 and Vern Sheridan Poythress, "Divine Meaning of Scripture," *WTJ* 48 (1986): 241–279; idem, "Analyzing a Biblical Text: What Are We after?" *Scottish Journal of Theology* 32 (1979): 19–31; idem, "Analysing a Biblical Text: Some Important Linguistic Distinctions," *Scottish Journal of Theology* 32 (1979): 113–37.

60. There is also bound to be a degree of reciprocal illumination as the antitype draws the attention of the interpreter to previously unnoticed facets of the type.

61. For a fuller development of Joshua as a type of Christ, cf. C. J. Goslinga, *Joshua, Judges, Ruth,* The Bible Student's Commentary (Grand Rapids, MI: Zondervan, 1987), ad loc.; S. G. de Graaf, *Promise and Deliverance,* 1 (St. Catharines, Ont.: Paideia Press, 1977), 397 and M. H. Woudstra, *The Book of Joshua,* The New International Commentary on the Old Testament (Grand Rapids, MI: Eerdmans, 1981), 31–32.

If there is special significance in Jesus' name ("Jesus" = "Joshua"), it appears more likely that this choice was dictated by an interest in relating Christ to the promised Jesus/Joshua of Zechariah 3 and 6, rather than to the Joshua of the conquest.

20

The Acts of God

A Study of the Basis of Typology in the Old Testament

Francis Foulkes

From Francis Foulkes, *The Acts of God: A Study of the Basis of Typology in the Old Testament* (London, 1958). Reprinted by permission.

For many years the typological study of the Old Testament was left to a very large extent on one side, and dismissed as allegorical and improper interpretation. But the revival of biblical theology has brought a new interest in it, as the theological literature of the past ten or twenty years evidently shows.[1] There is, however, among many Christian scholars a fear of typology because so frequently it has been contaminated by allegory.[2] The purpose of this chapter is to try to show that such a theological and eschatological interpretation of history has its roots deep down in the Old Testament itself.

1. Between the time of the delivery of this lecture and its publication an important reassessment of the validity of typological interpretation has been made by Professor G. W. H. Lampe and Mr. K. J. Woollcombe in *Essays on Typology,* 1957. Only the decision that this monograph should stand substantially as the lecture was delivered prevents reference to a number of the arguments of their work.

2. Indeed, among those who give greatest place to the typological study of the Old Testament there is still a danger of the confusion of typology and allegory. See P. K. Jewett, "Concerning the Allegorical Interpretation of Scripture" in the *Westminster Theological Journal* (Philadelphia), vol. 17, 1954, pp. 1–20.

Our study will be divided into three parts. First, we shall try to show the way in which the prophets and the writers of the Old Testament had, as the very basis of their understanding of the work of God in history, the conviction that his acts could be and were repeated, that as he had done, so he could and would do again—and this because he acts in accordance with principles of unchanging righteousness and mercy.

Secondly, we find in the Old Testament the hope and the conviction, not only that the past acts of God will be repeated, but that in the future they will be repeated on a scale greater and more wonderful than that of the past.

Finally we shall consider briefly what is typological, as distinct from allegorical interpretation, and try to understand how we should read the Old Testament in the light of the fulfillment in Christ of its history, as well as of its direct prophecy.

The Repetition of the Acts of God

One of the deepest convictions that the prophets and historians of Israel had about the God in whom they trusted, and whose word they believed they were inspired to utter, was that he was not like the gods of other nations, whose actions were totally unpredictable, who had to be appeased by sacrifice when things went wrong, and under whose rule the people could never know what would happen next. They believed that he had not left them in ignorance of his nature and purpose. Rather he had revealed himself to them, and had shown himself to be a God who acted according to principles, principles that would not change as long as the sun and moon endured. They could assume, therefore, that as he had acted in the past, he could and would act in the future. By such an assumption the whole of the Old Testament is bound together and given unity. Men may be fickle and unfaithful, but he does not change.[3] He dwells in the midst of his people and always cares for them.[4] Each succeeding generation could know that he would be with them as he had been with their fathers.[5] He keeps his word and his promise to a thousand generations.[6] For to him the passing of time is not as it is to men.[7] It produces no change in him; he was at the beginning and he will be at the end, and he is in the whole course of history in between.[8]

3. See Num. 23:19; 1 Sam. 15:29; Mal. 3:6.
4. See Num. 35:34; Deut. 11:12.
5. See Josh. 1:5; 1 Kings 11:38; 2 Kings 2:14ff.
6. See Exod. 20:6; Deut. 7:9; Mic. 7:20.
7. See Ps. 90:1–4; Ps. 102:12, 26–27.
8. See Isa. 44:6.

It is true of course that this understanding of Yahweh as the God of history stands out more clearly from some parts of the Old Testament than from others; for as he revealed himself in the history of Israel, a growing apprehension of him as the Lord of history becomes apparent. Yet there is evidence that in very early stages of the national life of Israel there was a looking back to what God had done for them in making them a nation and to the way in which he had covenanted with them that he would be their God and they would be his people. They came to look back in particular to three great "moments" in their history, the call of Abraham, the exodus, and the reign of David.

Their God was the "God of Abraham,"[9] or the "God of Abraham, and of Isaac and of Jacob,"[10] because of what he had done for the patriarchs,[11] and in particular because he had entered into covenant with them.[12] They saw that their existence as a people depended on the promises given to Abraham. "I will make of thee a great nation, and I will bless thee, and make thy name great; and be thou a blessing; and I will bless them that bless thee, and him that curseth thee will I curse."[13] "Unto thy seed will I give this land."[14] "In blessing I will bless thee, and in multiplying I will multiply thy seed as the stars of the heaven, and as the sand which is upon the sea shore; and thy seed shall possess the gate of his enemies; and in thy seed shall all the nations of the earth be blessed."[15]

So also they spoke of their God as the God who brought them up out of the land of Egypt,[16] and again and again they referred back to the exodus. That was the great act of Yahweh that made of them a free nation. It was with them as a nation that he had entered into covenant. We will return to this later, but again it is the recalling of the mighty act of God in past days and of the covenant made that is significant.

Then thirdly, they looked back on the way that God had set up David on his throne, given him victories by which the monarchy was established,[17] and promised that he would be with his seed after him on the throne.[18]

9. See Gen. 26:24, 28:13.
10. See Exod. 3:6, 16; 1 Kings 18:36; 1 Chron. 29:18; 2 Chron. 30:6. Cf. also references to the God of Jacob (Ps. 46:7), or the God of Bethel (Gen. 31:13).
11. See Isa. 29:22, and 51:2.
12. Gen. 35:12, 1:24; Exod. 6:8, 32:13, 33:1; Deut. 1:8, 6:10.
13. Gen. 12:2–3.
14. Gen. 12:7.
15. Gen. 22:17–18.
16. See Exod. 29:46; Lev. 11:45, 19:36, 22:33, 25:38; Num. 15:41; Dan. 9:15; Amos 2:10, 3:1. It was the greatest deception possible to ascribe the exodus to other gods. See Exod. 32:4; 1 Kings 12:28.
17. See 2 Sam. 7:1.

Such was the importance to Israel of their past history, the history of God's dealings with them, at these most fundamental points, and also at many others. Prophets and historians, sages and psalmists, looked in many different ways to what God had done in the past, and insisted that the past could be and was repeated.

The Repetition of the Acts of Divine Grace

The greatest act of God's grace and power to which Israel looked back was the exodus. Because of its special significance, and the way in which Israel experienced a release from bondage which they thought of as a repetition of the exodus, we must return later to deal with it separately. Independent of this particular significance of the actual exodus, God's victory given to them over Pharaoh was taken as an assurance that he would lead them to triumph over all their enemies.[19] Then, after the exodus, there was the provision for Israel during the time spent in the wilderness, where Yahweh supplied all his people's needs and led them in the way that they should go.[20] This could be recalled by prophet and psalmist to strengthen the conviction that, as he had provided when there was obviously no other means of help, so they could trust him to do again in every time of their need.[21] The conquest of Canaan was a repetition of the way that God gave victory over Sihon and Og,[22] and all these victories gave the assurance that he could always lead his people to triumph over their enemies. Like the victories over Midian, and over Jabin and Sisera, or over Oreb and Zeeb,[23] so could be the future victories of the people over their enemies. The Psalms repeatedly use what God has done in history in giving deliverance and victory to his people, as reasons for the praise of his mercy and might, but also as a basis of faith in his power to deliver from present enemies, and to continue to guard and to guide whatever the problems and difficulties of the future might be.[24] A man of faith might always say that, as God has delivered in the past, so he will for the future.[25]

The Repetition of the Acts of Divine Judgment

Yet not only could the deliverances of God be repeated; his judgments might also be repeated. The great judgments that stood at the be-

18. See 2 Sam. 7:13ff.; 1 Kings 11:12, 34; 2 Chron. 21:7; Isa. 37:35; Jer. 33:17, 20–21.
19. Deut. 7:18–19, 20:1ff.
20. See Deut. 2:7, 8: 2ff., 15–16, 29:3ff., 32:8ff.
21. See Ps. 78:52, 114:8; Isa. 4:6.
22. See Deut. 3:2–3, 21, 31:4.
23. See Ps. 83:9, 11.
24. See Ps. 78, 80, 114, 136, 145, 146.
25. See 1 Sam. 17:35ff.

ginning of biblical history were reminders of the righteousness of God, and warnings that he will judge those who utterly reject his ways. When, because Israel is under judgment, her enemies are said to come in like a flood, there is sometimes a reference to the deluge.[26] In the apocalyptic language of Isaiah 24 the deluge clearly is taken as the type of judgment. "Behold, the Lord maketh the earth empty and maketh it waste . . ." (v. 1). Verse 18 uses the language of Genesis 7:11 when it says that "the windows on high are opened." Then the following verse speaks of the consequences, which are those of a flood: "The earth is utterly broken, the earth is clean dissolved." Future judgment will be on the pattern of the past. There is also the warning that, as God judged Sodom and Gomorrah, so he would judge his own people if they were persistently unfaithful.[27] Similarly this act of judgment is put forward as an example of the way in which he would judge the nations.[28] When men are spoken of as like Sodom and Gomorrah, it is implied that they deserve such judgment as befell those cities.[29] So also it is said that the judgment of God would be as the plagues of Egypt.[30] Or it is said that, as he judged the nations that were in Canaan before Israel because of their gross immorality, so he would judge again; he would even judge his own people as he judged them,[31] if they persisted in making themselves like the heathen instead of living up to their calling as the elect people of God. Like the judgment at Baal-peor,[32] like the destruction of Shiloh,[33] like the judgment of the house of Ahab,[34] so would future judgments be. His past judgments were recalled to show that he is unchangingly a God of righteousness, and men must know that he will yet do as he has done in the past.[35]

26. See Isa. 28:2. In some cases the reference is to the waters of the Nile (Jer. 46:7–8 and cf. Amos 8:8, 9:5) and in others it is uncertain. In Ps. 18:6–16 features of the description of the deluge and the theophany at the exodus seem to be combined. In Ps. 29:10, however, the Psalmist expresses his confidence that everything in history is under the control of Yahweh, and he makes explicit reference to the deluge, and this is the only use of the Hebrew word *mabbul* other than in the Genesis narrative.

27. Deut. 29:23; Amos. 4:11.

28. Isa. 13:19; Jer. 1:40.

29. Isa. 1:9; Jer. 23:14; Ezek. 16:46ff.

30. See Deut. 7:15, 28:27, 60; also Amos 4:10 where a repetition of such judgment is said to have taken place.

31. Lev. 18:28; Deut. 8:19–20; cf. 2 Kings 21:2, 9, 12ff. and 1 Chron. 5:25–26 where it is said that the abominations of Israel were like those of the Canaanites before them, and consequently they were in the same way under God's judgment.

32. Deut. 4:3–4.

33. Jer. 7:12ff., 26:6, 9.

34. 2 Kings 9:9.

35. For similar warning of future judgment being like specific judgments of the past, see Isa. 10:26, and cf. 1 Sam. 6:6.

God's chastening of his own people has a repetitive nature about it because the faithlessness and rebellion of his people are so tragically recurrent. Israel again and again vainly relied on other nations instead of on the Lord. Repeatedly, therefore, they had to learn the consequences of their infatuation.[36] Repeatedly they turned to serve other gods instead of the One who had so often saved them in their national history: and repeatedly they had to learn the futility of such actions.[37] Time and again in their history it had been shown that unfaithfulness and rejection of Yahweh led to failure and judgment;[38] for Yahweh is unchangingly a holy God who rules Israel and all the nations in righteousness.

Nevertheless the very fact that God judges his people again and again indicates that he is not only a God of judgment but of infinite mercy. "The gifts and the calling of God are without repentance."[39] He seeks constantly to bring his people back to himself, and to forgive them. It is this interplay of mercy and judgment that shows most clearly the repetitive nature of Israel's history, or rather of the acts of God on their behalf.

This is nowhere in the Old Testament made more clear than in the Book of Judges. Here there is a pattern running through the book that is shaped by this understanding of history. Unfaithfulness leads to failure and defeat; repentance leads to renewed victory; and in this way history repeats itself. So there is the reiteration of this sequence: rebellion, judgment, repentance, and then victory through the God-given savior.[40] The standard by which Israel was always measured, was the covenant; and to the significance of this for the Old Testament understanding of history we must now turn.

The Significance of the Covenant

All of Israel's relationships with the God whom they worshipped were determined by the covenant that they had with him. This was in essence the Abrahamic covenant, but no doubt they looked above all to the covenant that was made with the nation at the exodus. There the Lord had promised to Israel that he would be their God and they would be his people. On their side they had promised to obey him, and remain true to him.

The promises of God in the Old Testament are taken back to Abraham (and to Isaac and Jacob, after him), to Moses at the time of the exodus,

---

36. See 2 Kings 17:4; 2 Chron. 16:7ff.; Isa. 30:1ff., 31:1ff.; Jer. 2:18. 36; Hos. 5:13, 7:11.

37. See 1 Kings 11:32–33; Amos 5:26–27.

38. For the sequence of unfaithfulness and judgment see the formula in 1 Kings 14:21ff., 15:3ff., 26ff., 16:18–19, etc.

39. Rom. 11:29.

40. See Judg. 2:11–23, 3:7–11, 12–30; 4, 5, 6, 7, 8:33; 9, 10:6, 12:7, 13, 16. Cf. also 1 Sam. 7:2–3, 12:2; 2 Kings 13:2ff; 2 Chron. 12, 15, 33:1–13.

and then, in the days when the kingdom was established, to David. Later generations depended on the word of God's promise given especially at those times. And his word was pledged that he would never fail on his side of the covenant.[41] He would never fail to be Israel's God, and to protect and deliver and bless them as his people, so long as they on their side were faithful. The blessings promised if the covenant is fulfilled are manifold.[42] Moreover, it is said that, if they have been unfaithful and return in true repentance,[43] they will always find his mercy. Israel might always appeal to the covenant, and to the grace of God pledged in it.

On the other hand, if the covenant were not kept, and the people refused to acknowledge and repent of their unfaithfulness, then they had no claim on the grace and the blessing of God.[44] The covenant judged them and found them wanting.[45] The Old Testament history of Israel is in fact one long story of the nation's unfaithfulness to the covenant; and at intervals along that history God sent his prophets, "rising up early and sending them."[46] There were judgments, repeated judgments; and the prophets sought to show the people that their failures and defeats and distresses did not happen by chance. If they looked back into their history, they would see the same thing repeatedly happening.

This aspect of the Old Testament understanding of history is shown especially in the records of the monarchy. The reigns of the whole succession of kings of Israel and Judah are described simply on this basis of faithfulness or unfaithfulness to Yahweh. There are several standards of comparison; there is the rule of David,[47] who kept faith with his God, and there is the standard of Jeroboam or Ahab,[48] who rejected the Lord and despised the covenant. And the issues of the various reigns are shown to be in accord with this faithfulness or unfaithfulness. There is mercy and deliverance and victory and peace; or there is judgment with consequent failure, disorder and defeat. The covenant determined the history; repetition of the acts of divine judgment or deliverance came naturally because Yahweh was an unchanging God.

The Possibility of Prediction

It follows from this that the predictions of Israel's prophets were not just mysterious or ambiguous utterances as those of the Delphic

---

41. Deut. 4:31, 8:18, 9:5; 1 Kings 8:23–24; 1 Chron. 16:15ff.; 2 Chron. 21:7.
42. Lev. 26:3–13; Deut. 7:12–26, 11:13–15, 22–25, 28:1–14, 30:20.
43. Deut. 4:30–31, 30:1–10; 1 Kings 8:30ff.
44. Lev. 26:14–35; Deut. 4:25–28, 11:16–17, 28, 28:15–68; 1 Kings 9:6–9; Jer. 11:1ff.
45. Ezek. 17:19.
46. See Jer. 7:25–26, 25:3ff., 26:5, 44:4; also 1 Sam. 8:8.
47. 2 Kings 14:3, 16:2, 18:3, 22:2, etc.
48. 2 Kings 8:18, 27, 10:31,13:2, 6, 11; 14:24, 15:9, 18, 24, 28, etc.

or other ancient oracles. The prophets saw clearly that history never followed a merely fortuitous course. When they warned of God's impending judgments, they were not beating the air; their words contained inspired predictions of future events. The prophet was not always given to see the time in which, in the purpose of God, the inevitable judgment or deliverance would come. Prophet and psalmist alike, as they shared the same understanding of history, were baffled by continuing successes of wicked men and nations.[49] But basically they understood the factors that determined the history of their own and other nations. They understood the principles of divine action that already had been revealed in history, and which would work themselves out in the future as they had done in the past.[50] A prophet might sometimes speak in ecstasy, and his own powers of thought and understanding, at least in part, be transcended, in order that he might be an instrument of divine revelation, but far more often prophetic inspiration consisted essentially in God's giving his servants clear understanding of the way in which he had acted in the past in accordance with his own nature and his covenant, and therefore of the way in which he would act in the future. None of the great prophets of the Old Testament was simply a medium or an ecstatic. If the prophets saw men stubbornly rebelling against him, and utterly refusing to repent and turn back to him, then they knew that judgment must come. If they saw a people willing to return in repentance to obey him, they could assure them that God would give them victory and prosperity, and encourage them with the promise of the good things that he has prepared for them that love him. The possibility of such prediction thus depended largely on the warnings and the promises of the covenant, and on the fact that prophets were convinced that, as God had done in the past, so he would do in the future. And repeatedly the prophetic word was vindicated.

Often, however, the prophet's prediction was not absolute. The judgment he announced was conditional. He still preached and implored and pleaded that men might return to God and so avert the judgment.[51] Only when the prophet was given to see repentance as no longer possible unless God's chastening came, did he preach the inevitability of judgment. It was on the nation's attitude to the covenant that the prophet's predictions were based.

49. Ps. 73:3ff.; Jer. 12:1ff.; Hab. 1:8; and cf. Job 12:6, 21:7ff.
50. See J. Marsh, *The Fulness of Time*, 1952, 54f.
51. This is well illustrated in Jeremiah. He brought to the people of his day a message of judgment and doom (e.g., 4:6–7, 11–18; 6:1–7); but he still exhorted them to repent and put away their iniquity, that they might be saved from ruin and desolation (4:1–2, 14; 6:8; 7:1–7).

The Basis of Prayer

The covenant was also the basis for prayer. Prayer in the Old Testament derives its meaning from the conviction that Yahweh's covenant with his people will not fail; he has pledged his word and he is an unchanging God. Prayer is not an attempt to persuade or propitiate an unwilling God, a God who is to be prevailed upon by the intensity of man's prayers, or simply by the requisite offerings. Prayer is a turning to God in the confidence that those who come in repentance and faith, will receive the things that they ask. There is confidence because God has given his word, and because of what he has done in fulfillment of his word in the past.

One could pray: "Remember Abraham, Isaac and Israel, thy servants to whom thou swarest by thine own self, and saidst unto them, I will multiply your seed as the stars of heaven, and all this land that I have spoken of will I give unto your seed, and they shall inherit it for ever."[52] Or similarly: "Remember thy congregation, which thou hast purchased of old, which thou hast redeemed to be the tribe of thine inheritance."[53] We see repeatedly in the Psalms that the acts of God in the past are the grounds of faith for present and future deliverances.[54] It is realized, too, that, as in the past, so in the present, an individual or the nation, having sinned against the Lord, can seek his favor only by the way of repentance.[55]

Law and History

It is significant also that for Israel the law is not just a statement of abstract principles, a carefully worked out code of behavior formulated as such. The law is the expression of the righteousness and mercy of God. It is the statement of the principles of the covenant. The Old Testament setting of the law is the giving of the covenant at the exodus.[56] The Decalogue begins, "I am the Lord thy God, which brought thee out of the land of Egypt, out of the house of bondage."[57] Many of the individual laws have also direct reference to the exodus. In some cases they referred back to the experiences of Israel in bondage. For example, there was an obligation to care for the stranger and the poor and the widow because in Egypt they themselves knew what it was to be in adversity, and God in his mercy set them free.[58] Or the laws might imply

---

52. Exod. 32:13; cf. 2 Sam. 7:28–29.
53. Ps. 74:2.
54. See esp. Pss. 9, 44, 48, 58, 74, 77, 80, 83.
55. See Ps. 81:8ff.
56. See 1 Kings 8:9, 21.
57. Deut. 5:6; cf. Deut. 6:20ff., 7:11ff.
58. See Lev. 19:34, 25:38; Deut. 10:19, 24:18, 22.

simply the obligation of obedience because of what Yahweh had done, and because of the covenant at the exodus. For example, with the laws that commanded the details of the way offerings were to be made went the words: "Ye shall not profane my holy name; but I will be hallowed among the children of Israel; I am the Lord which hallow you, that brought you out of the land of Egypt to be your God; I am the Lord."[59]

The law, therefore, contains not just a code for Israel to keep, but the principles of God's actions in the past, which remain the same for the present and the future. Such principles we have also in the Psalms and in the Wisdom literature. The significant fact is that they are never divorced from history to become mere abstractions. Yahweh is a living God, and the same yesterday, today and for ever. The law as well as history and prophecy, furnishes examples of the way that history must repeat itself, or rather of the way in which God's judgments and deliverances will be repeated. This is made most clear in the sections of the Holiness Code of Leviticus and in the parts of Deuteronomy where the blessing and the curse are given, the promises of the blessings of obedience, and the warnings of the tragic consequences of disobedience. These bear reference to past history, and show how that past history can be repeated.

Memorials and Feasts

The law stood constantly before Israel, and the righteous man was to meditate in it day and night.[60] But there were other reminders of what God had done. There were names such as Bethel, Gilgal, Achor, Ebenezer, Perez-uzzah and a host of others.[61] The associations of these names for the ancient Israelites are not weakened by modern discussions of their etymologies. There were also "visual aids" to the memory of Israel of various acts of God described in their written traditions: the stones at the Jordan, the heaps of stones at Achan's grave, and at the grave of the king of Ai, the stone where the ark rested when it was returned by the Philistines.[62] The Old Testament is full of such examples—each a visual reminder of the acts of God which were described in the written traditions of their history.[63]

Most important of all, there were the feasts. Once again, we are not concerned with their origins, nor with their agricultural aspect. For the Old Testament, what is important is that they had historical associa-

59. Lev. 22:32–33; cf. Num. 15:41; Deut. 5:15.
60. Ps. 1:2; cf. Josh. 1:8.
61. See Gen. 28:19; Josh. 5:9, 7:26; 1 Sam. 7:12; 2 Sam. 6:8.
62. See Josh. 4:4ff., 7:25–26, 8:29; 1 Sam. 6:18.
63. E.g., see Num. 16:40; Josh. 10:27, 22–24ff.; 1 Kings 8:9; 2 Chron. 5:10; Isa. 8:1ff., 30:8.

tions,[64] and, because of this, they renewed and kept alive constantly the faith of Israel in the God of history, the living and unchanging God.

Such was the Passover, and the feast of unleavened bread. Even if this feast began as an agricultural festival[65]—the festival that Moses asked Pharaoh for permission for the people to keep by going three days' journey into the wilderness[66]—it came to be associated inseparably with the exodus.[67] Its significance came to be much more than agricultural; it was national and historical. We know little about the observance of the Passover in the days of the monarchy, and it does not seem always to have been given prominence. But the occasions on which its observance is particularly recorded were times of great national religious revival in the days of Hezekiah and Josiah.[68] Through the traditions and records of the exodus the faithful Israelite kept the Passover in remembrance of what God had done then in redeeming his people from their bondage. As Pedersen says, "The Passover meant a re-living of the old common history."[69] It was a "feast through which the people re-experienced the event on which their existence as an independent nation was based."[70] They ate it in haste, with staff in hand, taking only unleavened bread, all in order to live over again the history of their deliverance. And, in so doing, "the people fortified itself by commemorating its history."[71] Faith was stimulated to believe that, as God had done at the exodus, so he could continue to deliver his people from their enemies.

Similarly the feast of weeks called to mind the fact that Israel was in bondage in Egypt.[72] The year of jubilee recalled that the Lord set free his people and did not intend them to be in bondage again.[73] The offering of the firstfruits and the consecration of the firstborn[74] recalled the exodus and the possession of the land. The feast of tabernacles recalled the period that Israel spent in the wilderness, and God's provision for them there.[75] The much later feast of Purim is given its historical associations.[76] Whatever their original significance, and however much or

64. See J. Marsh, *The Fulness of Time,* 40–41.
65. See J. Pedersen, *Israel,* 1926, 3–4:384 ff., and G. B. Gray, *Sacrifice in the Old Testament,* 1925, chaps. 21–24.
66. Exod. 3:18, 8:28, and see J. Pedersen, op. cit., 3–4:398ff.
67. Exod. 12:1–13:10, 23:15, 24:18–19.
68. See especially the record of these in 2 Chron. 30:1ff., and 35:1ff. See also Ezra 6:19–22 for the celebration of the Passover after the return from the exile.
69. J. Pedersen, op. cit., 3–4:85.
70. Ibid., 401.
71. Ibid., 502.
72. Deut. 16:12.
73. Lev. 25:42, 55.
74. Exod. 12:12–13, 13:11ff.; Num. 3:11–13, 8–17–18; Deut. 26:1ff.
75. See Lev. 23:43; Deut. 16:13–17; Neh. 8:13ff.
76. Esther 9:26ff.

little of this was retained, it is true to say that the feasts of Israel as a whole were historically orientated; they were orientated to recall the acts of God in history. In each one there was a reliving of the old national history, and consequently the strengthening of faith in the living and unchanging God.

The Interpretation of History

For Israel, history was never simply the narration of past events. Throughout the Old Testament history is written theologically; and behind the actual writing of this history lay the practice, its roots far back in the nation's past, of the rehearsal of the former acts of God.[77] The people were held responsible for making these acts known to each succeeding generation.[78] In particular they were not to fail to pass on the story of what God had done at the exodus.[79] They were to tell the meaning of the memorials that were set up to commemorate what God had done.[80] The true Israelite should always have been able to say with the psalmist: "We have heard with our ears, O God, our fathers have told us, what work thou didst in their days, in the days of old."[81] As we have noted, many of the psalmists rehearsed the national history[82] to stimulate faith in and praise of the God who had acted in their nation's past. The Old Testament historians do not simply record facts, nor do they simply relate what the great men of the past did. They are concerned to show what *God* did. Victory is attributed to the deliverance of God: defeat is to be explained by the unfaithfulness of man and his failure to rely on the strength of his God.

The people are urged to know and to remember history,[83] because history is instruction in the ways of God.[84] The history books of the Old Testament are "the former prophets." Whether we think of the writers of these books, or those whom we more naturally call prophets, we see that the task of the prophets was not only to denounce the sins of their own day, and to speak of what the future held in the judgment and the mercy of God, but also, and as a basis for what they said about the

---

77. See Num. 33; Deut. 1:19ff., 29:2ff., 32:7ff., 33; Josh. 23–24; Judg. 5:4ff.; 1 Sam. 12; 2 Sam. 22; 1 Chron. 16:8, 12, 15ff.; 2 Chron. 20:6ff.; Neh. 9:6ff.; Mic. 6:3ff.; Hab. 3. In the Song of Deborah we have reference to a custom that may well have gone back a very long way: " . . . in the places of drawing water, there shall they rehearse the righteous acts of the Lord . . ." (Judg. 5:11).

78. Deut. 4:9f., 9:19.

79. Exod. 12:8, 14f.; Deut. 6:20ff.

80. Josh. 4:6f., 21f.

81. Ps. 44:1.

82. See Pss. 44; 74; 77; 78; 80, etc.

83. See Deut. 5:15, 7:18, 8:2ff., 16:3, 24:9, 25:17ff., 29:2ff., 32:7ff.

84. See Ps. 78:1–11.

present and the future, to show God's judgment and mercy in the past. They were interpreters of history, and they made the past speak to the contemporary situation. God had judged unfaithfulness in the past, he had blessed his people when they turned to him and relied on him. The narration of history is prophetic; it is "less an account than an address, not an *it* but a *thou*, not a *once upon a time* but a *now*."[85] Judgment is pronounced on all the past, so that it may become instruction, a very word from God for the present. As God has acted, so he is acting in the contemporary situation in judgment or in mercy, and so he will act in all his future dealings with his people.[86]

The importance of this as a background for typology is obvious. History is recorded because history may be repeated, not of course exactly in detail, but according to the principle of the past acts of God among men. There is one case, however, in which the Old Testament writers saw a very close repetition of the past, and because of the importance of this for the development of typology it needs to be considered more carefully. The bondage of the nation in Egypt, the deliverance of the exodus, the period in the wilderness, and the re-occupation of the land, were repeated in the exile and the return.

The Second Exodus

When in the days of the monarchy the prophets saw the moral and spiritual decline of the nation, and with it the increasing threat of aggression from the great powers that surrounded them, they gave warning that the consequences of rebellion against God and failure to depend on his strength would be a new captivity. "They shall not return to Egypt,"[87] Hosea said, and he implied not simply a new bondage, but that the nation had to begin again to learn to know the Lord; it had to be dispossessed of its land, and go back to the simplicity of living in tents, and in another wilderness experience relearn the lessons of trust and obedience. "Therefore, behold, I will allure her, and bring her into the wilderness, and speak comfortably unto her. And I will give her her vineyards from thence, and the valley of Achor for a door of hope; and she shall make answer there, as in the days of her youth, and as in the day when she came up out of the land of Egypt."[88] Jeremiah lived through the pe-

---

85. See E. Sauer, *The Dawn of World Redemption*, 1947, 148f. Cf. A. Richardson, *Christian Apologetics*, 1947, 188.

86. "Toute l'oeuvre des Prophètes, qui est la charnière de l'Ancien Testament. repose sur un double mouvement. Elle rappelle les grandes oeuvres de Dieu dans le passé; mais elle ne les rappelle que pour fonder la foi dans ses grandes oeuvres à venir. Elle est à la fois indissolublement mémorial et prophétie." (J. Daniélou. *Sacramentum Futuri*, 1950, 4).

87. Hos. 8:13–14, cf. 7:16, 9:3, 6; 6: 11:1, 5, 11; cf. Deut. 28:68.

88. Hos. 2:14–15, cf. 11:1 and 12:9.

riod when the capture of Jerusalem and Judah by Babylon was imminent, but he saw through from despair to faith and hope, and the hope
was in the God of the exodus. "The days come, saith the Lord, that they
shall no more say, As the Lord liveth which brought up the children of
Israel out of the land of Egypt, but, As the Lord liveth, which brought up
and which led the seed of the house of Israel out of the north country,
and from all the countries whither I had driven them; and they shall
dwell in their own land."[89] In that second captivity, that second experience of "Egypt," this hope began to burn in the hearts of the people.
Dwelling among the nations, Israel came to know her God in a deeper
sense than ever before as the God of all the nations of the earth, the God
who rules and overrules in history, and to whom the nations are as "a
drop of a bucket." What God has done in the past, he will not merely do
again; he will do a new and greater thing. In the former days the Lord
led Israel out of Egypt, and "dried up the sea, the waters of the great
deep," he "made the depths of the sea a way for the redeemed to pass
over." He would do this again, the prophet said, "The ransomed of the
Lord shall return, and come with singing into Zion."[90] The power of
Babylon would be overthrown, as the horses and chariots of Egypt.[91]
There would be a new exodus,[92] though with a difference, "For ye shall
not go out in haste, neither shall ye go by flight; for the Lord will go before you; and the God of Israel will be your rearward."[93] They would find
in the wilderness the wonderful provision that God had made before,
and more than that, the way would be prepared for the people there,[94]
and the glory of the Lord would be revealed, as he led his people by a
way that they had not known, giving them springs of water in the
desert.[95] Waters would gush out from the rock again[96] and he would
protect them from hunger and thirst and from the heat of the sun.[97]

In Ezekiel the thought of the repetition of the experience in the wilderness recurs, but in a way more akin to Hosea's prophecies already
quoted. The prophet in exile gave as the Lord's word to his people, "I
will bring you out from the peoples . . . and I will bring you into the wilderness of the peoples, and there will I plead with you face to face. Like
as I pleaded with your fathers in the wilderness of the land of Egypt, so

89. Jer. 23:7–8, and cf. 16:14–15.
90. Isa. 51:10–11; cf. Isa. 11:15.
91. Isa. 43:17.
92. Isa. 52:3–4.
93. Isa. 52:12.
94. Isa. 40:3.
95. Isa. 43:19–20, cf. 41:18–19, and 35.
96. Isa. 48: 21.
97. Isa. 49:10.

will I plead with you, saith the Lord God" (Ezek. 20:34–36). Some of those wilderness experiences may be spiritualized as they are realized a second time, but as the dealings of God with his people they are repeated, in principle as they were before.

Thus the prophets spoke of the repetition of the captivity, release, and of the spiritual experiences of the wilderness. Here is that repetition of history which is the basis of typology; and here too is an indication of that other fundamental of typology, the difference of degree between the former acts of God and the new.

The Greater Glory of the Future Acts of God

The second great fact on which typology is based is that hope of Israel that not only would God act on the principles of his past action, but that he would do so on an unprecedented scale.[98] The faith of Israel as we see it in the Old Testament is constantly forward-looking. There was the promise made to Abraham, the promise that the covenant at the exodus involved, and the promises made to David. As long as the inheritance that God had for his people was not fully possessed, as long as they suffered defeat or were confined by their enemies and failed to enjoy peace and security and prosperity, they could feel that the promises were not completely fulfilled. Conscious of the failures and defects of the past, the more enlightened in Israel "felt that it required a more perfect future to render it altogether worthy of God, and fully adequate to the wants and necessities of His people."[99] At least from the time of the earliest of the writing prophets, the people began to look forward to something more than a repetition of God's acts of grace and judgment. They looked forward to a coming "day of the Lord," when his people would be exalted more gloriously than ever before, and other nations would be judged. We find reference made by Amos to a popular expression of this hope in the eighth century B.C.[100] In this case, as the prophet points out, the hope is perverted, and divorced from the understanding of God's moral demands on his people; but at least it was the hope of a climax of history, and of God's revelation of himself. We find it as an important part of the message of some of the later prophets. It is in Haggai and Zechariah, and is prominent in Zephaniah, Joel, and Malachi.

Yet even though the prophets and people believed that this "day of the Lord" would be unique, they could not help but think of it in terms of the past. As Fairbairn puts it, "the expectations cherished of what

---

98. This is what Bultmann calls the "eschatologizing" of typology. (R. Bultmann, *Ursprung und Sinn der Typologie als hermeneutischer Methode*).

99. P. Fairbairn, *The Typology of Scripture*, 1953 reprint. Pt. 1, 74.

100. See Amos 5:18–20.

was to be, took very commonly the form of a new and higher exhibition of what had already been."[101] They thought of the future in terms of the greatest leaders that God had previously given them, and the greatest acts of God on the behalf of Israel.

The Davidic Messiah

The most important, and most obvious expression of this was the hope of the Davidic Messiah. Without doubt this was associated with the promises made to David, and God's blessing of David's reign. Part of the promise was that the line of David would continue;[102] God had entered into covenant with him that there would not fail one to sit on his throne,[103] though it was said that the abiding line of David depended on the faithfulness of those who followed him.[104] In comparison with David,[105] few of the kings who followed him could be said to walk in his ways, and thus to enjoy the blessings and triumphs of his reign. Men longed for another David, for the reestablishing of the house of David, for a second David of his line who would be the Savior of his house and of the nation.[106] And, though there is a diversity in the prophetic understanding of the person and work of the Messiah, this anointed one of the line of David was often spoken of in terms which made him greater than David. For example in Isaiah 4:6–7 it is said of him, "The government will be upon his shoulder, and his name will be called Wonderful Counsellor, Mighty God, Everlasting Father, Prince of Peace. Of the increase of his government and of peace there will be no end, upon the throne of David, and over his kingdom, to establish it, and to uphold it with justice and with righteousness from this time forth and for evermore" (RSV). Or we may compare the words of Micah 5:2–5, "But thou, Bethlehem Ephrathah, which art little to be among the thousands of Judah, out of thee shall one come forth unto me that is to be ruler in Israel; whose goings forth are from of old, from everlasting . . . And he shall stand, and shall feed his flock in the strength of the Lord, in the majesty of the name of the Lord his God; and they shall abide: and now shall he be great unto the ends of the earth. And this man shall be our

101. P. Fairbairn, op. cit. Pt. 1, 73. He says further: "In giving promise of the better things to come, prophecy to a large extent availed itself of the characters and events of history. But it could only do so on the twofold ground, that it perceived in them essentially the same elements of truth and principle which were to appear in the future; and in that future anticipated a noble exhibit of them that had been given in the past."

102. 2 Sam. 7; 1 Chron. 17.

103. 2 Sam. 7:16; 1 Kings 11:12, 34ff.; 2 Kings 19:34, 20:6; 2 Chron. 21:7; Ps. 89:3–4, 132:11; Jer. 33:17, 20–21.

104. Ps. 130:12; Jer. 22:4, 30.

105. See p. 14 above.

106. See Jer. 23:5ff., 30:9, 33:14ff.; Ezek. 34:23–24, 37:24–25.

peace . . ." In Isaiah 11:1–9 the reign of the one who is described as "a shoot out of the stock of Jesse, and a branch out of his roots" is described in such a way as makes clear how exceedingly more glorious his reign is to be than that of the David of their history. In Isaiah 55:3–4 the fulfilling of the "everlasting covenant," the granting of "the sure mercies of David," is described in terms that make the coming ruler "a witness to the peoples," "a leader and commander" not just for Israel but "to the peoples." The hope of a personal Messiah is based firmly on the experiences and the traditions of the greatest anointed king that Israel had ever had; like David, he would be, but far greater than David.

A New Melchizedek, a New Moses, a New Elijah

There are other places in which figures of the present or the future are referred to in terms of personalities of the past; and even if these were in no sense messianic in their original context, they became messianic in interpretation. Whatever the date of Psalm 110, there is here clearly the description of one who can be called a new Melchizedek, one who like the Melchizedek of Genesis 14 would exercise the functions of priest and king at the same time.[107] If the picture this Psalm presents of the rule and victories and judgments of the priest-king is an idealized picture of the reign of a historical king of Israel, at least it could be applied more truly to the coming Messiah. Similarly Deuteronomy 18:15–19 speaks of another Moses bringing God's word to his people, "The Lord thy God will raise up unto thee a prophet from the midst of thee, of thy brethren, like unto me; unto him ye shall hearken . . . And the Lord said unto me . . . I will raise them up a prophet from among their brethren, like unto thee; and I will put my words in his mouth, and he shall speak unto them all that I shall command him." From the following verses it seems clear that simply the typical prophet of Israel is intended. But in later times—as is seen in the New Testament[108]—it is evident that the hope that was based on this passage was for a prophet greater than Moses, even the Messiah himself: and it must be said that the weighty words of verse 19 lend themselves to such an interpretation of the passage: "And it shall come to pass, that whosoever will not hearken unto my words which he shall speak in my name, I will require it of him."[109]

---

107. See R. V. G. Tasker, *The Old Testament in the New Testament* (2d ed.). 1954, 111.
108. See esp. John 1:21 and 6:14, 7:40.
109. "The terms of the description are such that it may be reasonably understood as *including* a reference to the ideal prophet, who should be "like" Moses in a pre-eminent degree, in whom the line of individual prophets should culminate, and who should exhibit the characteristics of the prophet in their fullest perfection." S. R. Driver, *A Critical and Exegetical Commentary on Deuteronomy,* 1895, 229. Cf. H. L. Ellison, *The Centrality*

In Malachi 4:5 there is the hope of the coming of Elijah the prophet in the context of the hope of the great and terrible day of the Lord. Chapter 3:1 is commonly associated with this, "Behold, I send my messenger, and he shall prepare the way before me; and the Lord, whom ye seek, shall suddenly come to his temple. . . ." Whether this was to be thought of as the return of the prophet of the 9th century, or whether of the coming of a new Elijah, there is the sense of the repetition of past history, but in the setting of the glory of the coming "day of the Lord."

The Feast of Tabernacles

The feasts of Israel were given an eschatological meaning. The Feast of Tabernacles was not only an agricultural festival, a thanksgiving for the land and its harvest: it recalled the dwelling in tabernacles in the wilderness days, and God's provision for the people before they entered their land. The Fourth Gospel probably reflects the ceremonies that later Jewish practice added to the celebration of the feast, as well as the fulfillment of its meaning in Christ. But there is an eschatological hope connected with the Feast of Tabernacles even in Old Testament days. In Zechariah 14 the thought of the feast as the harvest is connected with the ingathering of the nations. All the nations and families of the earth are summoned to go up to Jerusalem to keep it. Whether or not it can be said to be evident from this passage, it is clear that before the time of Christ, there was, connected with the Feast of Tabernacles, the hope of the future tabernacling of God in the midst of his people in a more glorious way than ever before. It has been sufficiently well established that the Jewish lectionary antedates the Christian era,[110] and in this Zechariah 14 and 1 Kings 8, Solomon's prayer at the dedication of the temple, were coupled as readings for the Feast of Tabernacles.[111] There can be little doubt of the significance of this fact. The presence of the Lord with his people in the wilderness and in the temple was a picture, or a type, of that more glorious tabernacling in their midst in the day that was yet to be, when the ingathering of the nations would be fulfilled.

The Passover

We may be certain also that long before New Testament times such a future hope was connected with the observance of the Passover. Again it is difficult to find direct evidence for this from the Old Testament itself. From the Gospels, however, we learn that the hope of a new re-

---

of the Messianic Idea for the Old Testament, 1953, 18, where also the suggestion is adopted that the Servant of Isa. 49:1–9 is presented as a new Moses.

110. See H. St. John Thackery, The Septuagint and Jewish Worship, 1923, 43ff.

111. Ibid., 64, 76–77.

demption or deliverance glowed in the hearts of devout Israelites before the coming of Christ and the preaching of his salvation,[112] and the thought of redemption must have taken their minds back to the exodus. To the quietists the redemption that was sought was a spiritual deliverance; to the Zealots redemption was an intensely political hope. But for both we can understand that it burned most brightly at Passover time. We have already dwelt on the way in which the exile was regarded as a new exodus. We should also notice that the prophets "spiritualize" some aspects of the exodus and the wilderness experiences in a way which prepared for the hope of a deliverance of a spiritual nature. Hosea said that the new captivity would be in "Egypt," but not in the literal "Egypt."[113] In Ezekiel especially we see how Egypt is regarded as the place of moral and spiritual temptation and bondage.[114] And the new bondage was, in a way that the old bondage in Egypt had not been, a punishment or chastening because of the nation's sin. Hence, as we have seen, the people were to re-learn through their experiences the knowledge and fear of the Lord, even as the nation of old had learnt to depend on him in the wilderness. The second exodus was a repetition of the first, but it was in a much fuller sense a spiritual deliverance. This must have affected the keeping of the Passover, so that its place in the religious life of Judaism, especially in postexilic times, must have been such that, with its observance, there was a hope of eternal deliverance, of deliverance from all the bondage of evil, for which those of the Pharisaic tradition in particular hoped. Dalman says of the Passover:

"Every thought of the redemption from Egypt, of which it is a memorial, must have led to a comparison between what had taken place and the present. Everything imperfect in the latter and not quite in tune with that redemption from slavery, must have awakened the hope of new redemption. The reality of God's act at the Exodus, in so far as it was believed and perceived as the foundation of the character of Israel as a People of God, was an assurance of the fact that the second divine act could not but take place, when the success of the former one seemed to have been made void through human sin."[115]

There is good ground, therefore, for the belief that, for devout Israelites, the feasts were not only witnesses to the fact that what God had done in the past he could do again; but that they also made vivid the hope that God would step into their history in a new way; the messianic age would dawn in which there would be a new deliverance, greater and

---

112. See Luke 2:38.
113. See Hos. 7:16, 9:3, 11:5, 11.
114. See Ezek. 19:4, 20, 23 and especially 29.
115. See G. Dalman, *Jesus–Jeshua* (English trans.), 1929, 124.

deeper than anything before. It is this hope that provides the background for the true relationship between type and antitype.

The New Temple

We may illustrate this further by considering Israel's institutions and in particular that of the temple. When, in Old Testament days, Israel thought of the presence of God in the midst of his people, they thought of the tent of meeting and of the temple. Before the days of the monarchy the ark and the tent of meeting were the particular symbols of God's presence; the loss of the ark was felt to be the loss of the glory of the Lord from amongst his people.[116] Then the temple was built, and it was regarded as in a unique sense the place of the Lord's dwelling in Israel. When God's judgment came on the nation, and the temple was destroyed, the prophet Ezekiel saw in his vision the glory of the Lord departing from the city.[117] The return from the exile saw the building of a second temple. To those who knew the old temple, and who saw the construction of a new and less magnificent structure, there could be only disappointment. But the answer of the prophet Haggai to them in their discouragement was that this new temple would be of more glory than that which had been destroyed.[118] In the latter days God would come to his temple. In the coming day of the Lord he would shake all nations, and cause them to bring their riches into the temple. Because of his acts then, which would surpass any of his acts on behalf of his people in the past, it would be a more glorious house than they had before.

In a different way we find in Ezekiel 40–48 the vision of a new and finer temple than that which had been destroyed. The temple of the prophet's vision was to be greater in dimensions and grander in structure than the old. But the one fact of transcendent importance was that to this house the glory of the Lord's presence would return[119] and consequently the city would be called "The Lord is there."[120] In various parts of the Old Testament, however, we find the expression of the hope that, since the Lord's presence cannot be thought of as limited in any way to the temple, his tabernacling presence would in future be known in a more glorious way than could be realized in the temple. God's dwelling is apart from men, and "heaven" is the place of his temple;[121] and no earthly shrine can adequately express or manifest the presence

116. 1 Sam. 4:20ff.
117. See Ezek. 4:3, 10:4–5, 18–19, 11:22–23.
118. Hag. 2:1–9.
119. Ezek. 43:1ff.
120. Ezek. 48:35.
121. E.g., see Ps. 11:4; Isa. 57:57a.

of God. In 1 Kings 8:27, in the prayer of dedication of the temple, we have these words, "But will God in very deed dwell on the earth? behold, heaven and the heaven of heavens cannot contain thee; how much less this house that I have builded." The prophet Isaiah clearly felt this as, in his vision, he saw that just the "skirts" or the "train" of the Lord filled the temple, and as he heard the seraphs cry, "The fulness of the whole earth is His glory."[122] Yet perhaps the greatest expression of this in the Old Testament is in the words of Isaiah 66:1, "The heaven is my throne, and the earth is my footstool; what manner of house will ye build unto me? and what place shall be my rest?" As the sense of God's transcendence grew, so developed the awareness that the tabernacling of the holy and omnipotent God among men was yet to be more wonderful than the temple could express.

From a different direction, some of the Old Testament prophets reached the verge of the hope that the tabernacling presence would not be thought of as in a place or a building, but in the hearts of men. Prophets could look for the day when the Lord would give his Spirit to his people in a new way, indwelling them and so giving new life and inspiration;[123] they could speak of a new covenant under which there would be a new desire to obey the Lord and do his will, because the law would be set in their hearts[124] or because his sanctuary would be in the midst of them in a new way.[125] It needed, however, the fulfillment to bring together the understanding that was already there of the indwelling Spirit and of the tabernacling presence of God. In both there was a hope for the future, expressed in terms of what had been realized in the past, but which was to be experienced in a more glorious way.

The New Covenant

This last point leads us to the thought of the new covenant. We have seen already that the basis of all the institutions of Israel, and all God's dealings with Israel, was the covenant. There was the old covenant made with the fathers and with Israel in all their generations, and there was nothing imperfect in the divine side of that covenant, no failure at any time in God's promises. Yet Israel had failed constantly. From time to time they were led back to renew the covenant and to make afresh their promises to their God who had pledged himself to them.[126] The

---

122. Isa. 6:3 (Sir G. A. Smith's translation). See W. J. Phythian Adams, *The People and the Presence*, 1942, 51.
123. Joel 2:28ff., and Exek. 37:9ff.
124. Jer. 31:31ff.
125. Ezek. 37:26ff.
126. E.g., under Hezekiah (2 Chron. 29), under Josiah (2 Kings 23), and later under Nehemiah (Neh. 9–10).

prophet Jeremiah saw such a renewal of the covenant under Josiah; but he lived to see its failure, for the people could not keep it from their hearts. He was enabled to see that God in his grace would give a new covenant,[127] in which man's part would not be just a law written on tables of stone. "But this is the covenant that I will make with the house of Israel after those days, saith the Lord, I will put my law in their inward parts, and in their hearts will I write it . . . and their sin will I remember no more."[128] Thus the Old Testament's own understanding of the covenant provides the basis of the later New Testament antitype: the new covenant fashioned on and foreshadowed by the old, but far surpassing it.

A New Creation and a New People

The point of Jeremiah's words, however, is not just that there will be a new covenant, but new men who will obey God from their hearts. Those of the Old Testament prophets and psalmists who were led to understand most deeply the nature of man's sin and of man himself, saw that only in new men, in a new creation, could the purpose of God be realized, and his people live in dependence on him and in the victory and peace and obedience that he had planned for them. And here we are brought again to the repetition of the acts of God. For those who believe their God to be Lord of all, the supreme act of the past is the act of creation itself. He was at the beginning, he is author of all things. The action whereby God would overcome all the limitations and failures and sins of men is thus described in terms of a new creation. The word of the Lord through the prophets is, "Behold I create new heavens and a new earth; and the former things shall not be remembered, nor come into mind . . ."[129] The messianic age, whether with or without reference to the personal Messiah, can be described as a return to the conditions of paradise.[130]

We should associate also with this—although the themes are slightly different—the renewing or reviving of God's people, their re-creation. Where it is said in Ezekiel that "this land that was desolate is become like the garden of Eden,"[131] it is said in the same context, "A new heart also will I give you; and a new spirit will I put within you; and I will take away the stony heart out of your flesh, and I will give you an heart of flesh."[132] The individual is to be made new, and so is the nation. This

127. Cf. Isa. 61:8 and Ezek. 37:26.
128. Jer. 31:33–34.
129. See Isa. 65:17ff.; cf. Isa. 66:22.
130. See Isa. 11:1ff., 65:23ff.; Jer. 31:27–28; Ezek. 34:25ff., 36:35.
131. Ezek. 36:35.
132. Ezek. 36:26.

same prophet looked on the Israel of his day, and saw them, as it were, as dry bones; but he was enabled to see the Spirit of the Lord come and bring new life to the bones. They said, "Our bones are dried up, and our hope is lost; we are clean cut off." But the answer was, "Thus saith the Lord God: Behold I will open your graves, and cause you to come up out of your graves, O my people; . . . And I will put my spirit in you, and ye shall live, and I will place you in your own land: and ye shall know that I the Lord have spoken it, and performed it, saith the Lord."[133]

We can understand some of the Servant passages of Isaiah 40–55 best as we see there a people redeemed by the new exodus, made anew the servant of the Lord to carry out his purpose among the Gentiles as they have never carried it out before. The repetition of the old work of redemption and the re-creating of a people come very close together here. The prophet passes from speaking of Israel as a nation and speaks of the Servant in terms that could never have been used of Israel in their past history. But the purpose of God for the Servant is based on the purpose of God for his people in the past.[134] Thus we have the two basic elements of typology that we have noted elsewhere brought before us again. And at the heart of the great statement of the work of the Servant in Isaiah 53 is the revelation that his life is to be made an offering for sin; his is a sacrifice with all the meaning of the old "guilt offering"; but the victim is now not an animal, but the righteous Servant of the Lord, a greater sacrifice than any that had been known before.

Thus we find in the Old Testament the twofold basis of typology. We find that the belief in the unchanging God who is Lord of history leads to the understanding of the repetition of the acts of God. We find also that the Old Testament itself points forward to divine acts more glorious than any in the past. The Old Testament is an incomplete book; it is revelation developing towards a climax. There is the constant prediction of a "day of the Lord," a consummation, a unique revelation of the power and glory of God in the person of the Messiah or in a messianic age. Then God will reveal himself in mercy and in judgment more fully than ever before. This hope is expressed in terms of the past, yet exceeds anything experienced in the past. There is to be a new David, but a greater than David; a new Moses but a greater than Moses; a new Elijah or Melchizedek, but one greater than those who stand out from the pages of the old records. There is to be a greater and more wonderful tabernacling of God, as his presence comes to dwell in a new temple.

133. Ezek. 37:11–14.
134. See P. Fairbairn, op. cit. Pt. 1, 74, and also the conclusions of H. H. Rowley on the person of the Servant in *The Servant of the Lord*, 1952, 49ff.

There is to be a new creation, a new Israel, redeemed, revived, a people made up of those to whom a new heart and a new spirit are given that they may love and obey their Lord.

Old Testament prophecy, as we have seen, depended for much of its expression on the actualities of Old Testament history, and of its record. Its conviction of an unchanging God was the basis of that confidence that he would act in the future as he had done in the past. Its hope of a messianic age provided for the relation between type and antitype, the latter greater and more excellent than the former. It needed only the coming of the One in whom all the prophecies of the Old Testament would be fulfilled, in whom all those themes of hope in the Old Testament would be gathered up and realized, the Fulfillment and the Fulfiller of all the types that the Old Testament history presented. The unity of the Old Testament depends on the changing nature of the God who is there revealed. The unity of Old and New Testaments provides the justification for typology as we understand it, as the theological interpretation of history. The superiority of the New is to provide the antitype, the fulfillment in Christ himself, of the Old Testament type or foreshadowing.

Typology as the Christological Interpretation of History

Typological interpretation, strictly speaking, is not concerned with those parts of the Old Testament which have the form of messianic prediction in the narrower sense. It is the interpretation of history. Predictive prophecy often, indeed, depends on the interpretation of a particular historical situation in the light of the revealed character of God; but the writing of history was itself "prophecy" in the broader sense of the understanding of God's action in history. Old Testament history, as we have seen, is the record of the acts of God in judgment and mercy; it is history with a purpose and a goal. Manifestly incomplete, it is pointing forwards to a climax of the manifestation of God among men.

It is thus that the New Testament interprets the Old. It interprets not only its prediction but also its history, which is itself revelation because it describes the acts of God, in the light of the revelation of him who is the Word Incarnate. It is only in him that the partial revelation that is foreshadowing (and the confessed fact that it is partial), is able to be understood. Speaking of the use that the earliest Christians made of the Old Testament, Professor Tasker says: " . . . it is the events recorded in the historical books, particularly the call of Abraham, the redemption from Egypt, the giving of the law on Sinai, and the triumphant establishment of the worship of the true God in the Holy Land in spite of much backsliding and many an attempt to compromise with paganism, which are represented as foreshadowing the final salvation wrought in the life, death, and resurrection of Jesus. Apart from these concluding actions the previous incidents remain unexplained and have no abiding significance . . . "[135]

We may look at this in two different ways. First, we may look at it from the point of view that history is itself prophetic. It is prophetic in the sense that all history, if understood *sub specie aeternitatis*, teaches us the principles on which God rules and will rule as Lord of history. Moreover the Old Testament record of history is prophetic in the particular sense that it describes a revelation and divine action which are shown to be incomplete. A divine purpose of judgment and mercy is revealed in the history; but it is yet to be fulfilled or fully wrought out in history. Alternatively, we may look at it from the point of view of God preparing the world, granting partial revelation as preparatory to the incarnation of the Word himself, instructing a people in his ways of dealing with men, working towards the fulness of time when he would send forth his Son to be the Savior of the world and the One by whom he will judge all men.

We may interpret the Old Testament typologically from either point of view, and, of course, fundamentally the two are one. Revelation is wrought out in history, and to the eyes of faith history is revelation.

Typology and Allegory

Typological interpretation of the Old Testament, therefore, is not to be dismissed as allegory. It is essentially the theological interpretation of the Old Testament history. It is the interpretation of the divine action in history, in the same way as the Old Testament itself sought to show that divine action, but in the fuller light of him in whom alone history has its full meaning, Jesus Christ.[136] All the action of God in the Old Testament history foreshadows his unique action and revelation in Christ. We may say that a type is an event, a series of circumstances, or an aspect of the life of an individual or of the nation, which finds a parallel and a deeper realization in the incarnate life of our Lord, in his provision for the needs of men, or in his judgments and future reign.[137] A type thus presents a pattern of the dealings of God with men that is followed in the antitype, when, in the coming of Jesus Christ and the set-

---

135. R. V. G. Tasker, op. cit., 12. Cf. J. Marsh, *The Fulness of Time*, 15.

136. A. Richardson, *Christian Apologetics*, 1947, 189: "Typological interpretation of the biblical history is based upon the actual course of that history, as recorded and interpreted by the prophetic and apostolic witness; it grows, as it were, out of the history itself and is not imposed upon history by the reading into it of fanciful meanings of our own."

137. Cf. M. J. Lagrange, *Saint Paul, Épître aux Galates*, 1942, 123.

ting up of his kingdom, those dealings of God are repeated, though with a fullness and finality that they did not exhibit before. Typology depends on the fact that "The same God offers in the two Testaments the same salvation. Both Testaments record certain divine acts in history, different indeed in execution and import, but one in their basic aim, viz., to create a people of whom God can say, 'I am their God, they are my people' . . . The salvation that is offered in both Testaments is the same—life with God through the forgiveness of sins."[138] There is unity in principle and in purpose between the Old Testament type and the New Testament antitype. The difference lies in the incomplete and preparatory nature of the type compared with the completeness and finality of the antitype.

In our usual ways of speaking, allegory involves something different from this, and it is best to define it in such a way as to distinguish it from typology as a method of interpretation. We may call that method of interpretation allegorical which is concerned, not with the interpretation of history, but simply of words that are believed to be inspired symbols. It may completely ignore the context and the principles of God's dealings with man that are revealed in a passage. Allegory is an exegetical[139] or philological method rather than an interpretation of events and of principles of divine action.[140] Allegory is based on the conviction of the inspiration of the words of the narrative or passage of Scripture in question; but its danger is that it does not proceed from the understanding of the context, and it may easily be guided by the interpreter's own whims and fancies. The danger of tracing a symbol through Scripture is seen most clearly in the early Fathers to whom "water," wherever it occurred in the Old Testament, might be taken to speak of baptism,[141] and references to "wood" or "a tree" to the cross.[142] The result of such interpretation may be the complete negation of the true theological understanding of a passage in its context. This is not the case with typological interpretation as we have defined it. Typology always depends on the context, and on the natural and historical sense of the context.

We say, therefore, that typology is not to be dismissed as allegory, like the foregoing. When St. Paul used the word ἀλληγορέω (in the one

138. J. Marsh in *Biblical Authority for To-day*, 1951, 186f.

139. Exegetical, in the sense of explanatory of words rather than interpretative of context; but in a stricter sense such allegory has been called *eisegesis*. See H. E. W. Turner, *The Pattern of Christian Truth*, 1954, 186.

140. See J. Massie on "Allegory" in *Hastings Dictionary of the Bible*, vol. 1, 64. B. F. Westcott, *The Epistle to the Hebrews*, 1892, 200. G. Florovsky in *Biblical Authority for To-day*, 175f. A. Richardson, *Christain Apologetics*, 190.

141. See Tertullian *Bapt.* 8–9; Cyprian *Ep.* 63.8.

142. See Justin, *Dial.* 86.6, 138.2–3, Tertullian, *Jud.* 13, Origen, *Hom.* 7:3 *in Ex.*

place in which it is used in the New Testament), he meant something
different from what we commonly mean by allegorizing. He said of
Abraham's two sons of the bondwoman and the free, ἅτινά ἐστιν ἀλλη-
γορούμενα,[143] and he meant that he was speaking, or interpreting, with
a meaning other than the literal, but neither to deny the reality of the
literal (as was often the case with Greek allegories), nor to reject the
principles of the context. St. Paul is taking the principles behind the differences between the children of Hagar and Sarah and applying them
to another (ἄλλος) setting, that of the children of promise under the
gospel and those who do not possess the promise but remain in bondage. This can rightly be classed as typological interpretation, because
the theological principles involved in the old narratives are simply
taken up and shown to find a new, and a deeper, meaning in Christ.[144]

Of allegorical interpretation, as we have defined it, we find very little
in the New Testament. We cannot say that it is completely absent from
the New Testament, but it is doubtful if it ever exists except as an elaboration of genuine typology. That is to say, there is first an interpretation of the theological principles of the Old Testament narrative, and
then elaboration based on the symbolism of words. This is probably the
case with the interpretation of Melchizedek in Hebrews 7. The basis of
this interpretation seems clearly to be that Melchizedek stands out
from the pages of the Old Testament as one who was priest and king,
and the combination of these functions was perfectly fulfilled in Christ,
of whom therefore Melchizedek may be called a type. Yet in the interpretation of his name "king of Salem," we have the use and interpretation of words and symbols rather than the interpretation of the work
and functions of the Old Testament character. So also when the writer
of the Epistle to the Hebrews speaks of him as "without father, without
mother, without genealogy, having neither beginning of days nor end
of life, but made like unto the Son of God"[145] he does so apparently because he believes that these facts about Melchizedek, through the inspiration of the Spirit of God, have been left out of the sacred narrative in
order that the picture of Christ as Priest-King, and as the Son of God,
might be made more perfect.[146] This is a dependence on words, or lack
of words, rather than the principles of the context; but it is to be noted
that the interpretation begins with typology. There are one or two other
cases of the use of the Old Testament in the New where the same ap-

143. Gal. 4:24.
144. See P. K. Jewett in "Concerning the Allegorical Interpretation of Scripture," in
the *Westminster Theological Journal* (Philadelphia) vol. 17, 1954, 18–20.
145. Heb. 7:3.
146. See A. G. Hebert, *The Throne of David*, 1941, 203, and R. V. G. Tasker, op. cit.,
112.

pears to be true, but it is not possible to deal with them in detail here. What matters is that regularly we have the Old Testament interpreted by the interpretation of its history and of the principles of its institutions in the purpose of God, and not simply by using its words as inspired symbols in the way the Fathers so often did.

This is not to say that the words do not matter, or to deny the operation of the Holy Spirit in guiding and inspiring the writer of the history. Revelation in the Old Testament can never depend simply on the events, but on the prophetic interpretation of the events. It is not only the acts of God that matter, but the record of the acts, if we are to understand their meaning. So the history is rightly given the title of the "former prophets"; men with prophetic insight and understanding of the ways of God wrote the history. So Saint Paul, speaking of the Old Testament revelation, says, "Whatsoever things were written aforetime, were written for our learning."[147] None the less it is necessary to distinguish typology from that allegorizing which has no concern with the revelation of the acts of God given in the particular passage of Scripture which it is treating. To take a word as symbolic of some spiritual truth without regard for the context in which it is found is always perilous as a method of interpretation.

Typological Interpretation and the Literal Sense

In one way it is true to say that typological interpretation involves a reading into the text of a meaning extrinsic to it. It takes more than the literal sense of a passage. The New Testament does this when it sees Christ as the theme and fulfillment of all the Old Testament, without limiting this to what is explicitly messianic prophecy. It sees the antitype foreshadowed by the types, and interprets the types accordingly. It sees in the Old Testament "by divers portions and in divers manners"[148] what is revealed uniquely in the Word Incarnate, in whom all the fragments of the past revelation are brought together. Typological interpretation shows that the partial and fragmentary revelation in the Old Testament pointed forward to Christ. It interprets the types by referring them to the Antitype, and by showing that their meaning can be understood fully only in relation to him and in the light of the knowledge of him.[149] Typology reads into Scripture a meaning which is not there in that it reads in the light of the fulfillment of the history. This is not ex-

---

147. Rom. 15:4; cf. 1 Cor. 10:11 and see J. K. Mozley on 1 Cor. 10:6–11 in *A New Commentary on Holy Scripture* (edit. Gore), 1928, 501, and C. H. Dodd in *Biblical Authority for To-day*, 159.

148. Heb. 1:1.

149. See A. Richardson, *Christian Apologetics*, 189–90. C. H. Dodd, *According to the Scriptures*, 1952, 128–29.

egesis, drawing out from a passage what the human author understood and intended as he wrote. Nevertheless it does not read a new principle into the context; it interprets the dealings of God with men from the literal context, and then points to the way in which God has so dealt with men in Christ. It does not necessarily say that the writer was conscious of presenting a type or foreshadowing of the Christ, although we have seen that there was sometimes in the Old Testament the consciousness that the acts of God in the past pointed forward to similar but much more glorious acts in the future. We, therefore, do not necessarily read the Old Testament, and say as Origen was prone to say, that the Old Testament writers spoke consciously of Christ. Nor do we read in such a way as to lift the Old Testament to the level of the New as the Fathers of the mid-second century were in danger of doing. But we read, recognizing the incompleteness of the Old Testament, and the true relationship of type and antitype. Then it is right to see the Old in the light of the revelation that we have in Christ, to see it as partial, a foreshadowing of what is revealed in Christ.[150]

Thus, also, it is not true to say that typological interpretation is a static method of interpretation which views the Old Testament simply as a closed corpus of inspired writings, and disregards the living faith of Israel and the experience of the prophets, and the way in which those of old time were led to the knowledge of God that was given to them. Allegory, when it takes up words as symbols, and disregards the context is always in this danger. True typology, on the other hand, involves the study of the living faith and growing apprehension of Israel, and the prophetic experience of God in order to understand more intimately the knowledge of God and of his ways that the prophets had, and which they were given in order to teach to men. It takes the history of Israel, wrought out in the trials and failures and triumphs that they as a nation experienced in the grime of battle and in the enticements of heathen cults around them; and it follows the Old Testament historians in seeing the hand of God in all of these, revealing itself in judgment and in mercy. It sees the Old Testament as a progressive and as an incomplete revelation. But because God was then revealing in part what he revealed uniquely in Christ, it finds in that history, as recorded, foreshadowings of the Christ.

This, in fact, is the way in which we as Christians must read the Old Testament, following the precedent of the New Testament interpretation of the Old, and supremely the use that our Lord himself made of the Old Testament. We should not look back to this part of the Bible just for the history of the Jewish religion, nor just for moral examples, nor

---

150. See H. Cunliffe Jones, *The Authority of the Biblical Revelation,* 1945, chap. 5.

just for its messianic prophecy, nor to see the excellence of the faith of Israel in contrast to the religious faith and understanding of other nations of antiquity. In actual fact Israel was often faithless, and it is God seeking to show himself to man, rather than man searching after God, that we need most to see. We look to the Old Testament to see God in his grace revealing himself in the history of Israel in preparation for the sending of his Son, the Incarnate Word and the Savior of the world.

If we understand typology in this way, it does not mean that we are limited to following the particular cases of typological interpretation that the New Testament gives to us. We have there a method of interpretation for which we have the background in the Old Testament itself. It is a method of interpretation of history. Its basis is in the Old Testament understanding of the unchanging nature of God and his unchanging covenant and principles of dealing with men; but for us that unchanging nature of God is made more clear in "Jesus Christ the same yesterday, and to-day, yea and for ever."[151] Its basis is also in the Old Testament hope that the acts of God in the past would be repeated in yet greater glory; but for us—although we still wait for its final manifestation and the summing up of all history in Christ—that great glory has been revealed. Therefore we study the Old Testament typologically, for we study it to gain a theological understanding of history; and that theological understanding is christological understanding, for it is only in Christ that the history of Israel, or of any nation or individual, past or present, is able to find its meaning.

151. Heb. 13:8.

Part 7

Should the Exegetical Methods of the New Testament Authors Be Reproduced?

21

Negative Answer to the Question

"Who is the Prophet Talking About?"
Some Reflections on the New Testament's Use of the Old

Richard N. Longenecker

From Richard N. Longenecker, "Who Is the Prophet Talking About? Some Reflections on the New Testament Use of the Old," *Themelios* 13 (1987): 4–8. Reprinted by permission.

The question of the Ethiopian eunuch in Acts 8 is that asked by every inquiring person when reading what has come to be known as the Old Testament: "Who is the prophet talking about, himself or someone else?" (v. 34). And Philip's answer is the definitive response of Christian proclamation: "Jesus" (v. 35). The movement from Scripture to Jesus, however, while seemingly simple, is a matter that requires careful delineation. For it is all too easy to reason in some deductive manner as to how early Christians must have viewed matters, given certain basic commitments, than to investigate inductively how they actually worked out their convictions in the context of the presuppositions and methodologies of the day. Three matters, in particular, call for reflection when we attempt to understand the New Testament's use of the Old Testament: 1) the concept of fulfillment in the New Testament; 2) the exegetical procedures of the early Christians; and 3) the normativity of then current hermeneutical practices for Christian faith, both in that day and today.

Fulfillment in the New Testament

The concept of fulfillment is at the heart of biblical theology. This is true, first of all, for the Old Testament, where God's purposes were to be fulfilled through his covenant people Israel and where the latter prophets often explicate the former prophets. It is pre-eminently true for the New Testament, where the focus is on Jesus of Nazareth as the fulfillment of God's redemptive purposes for mankind.

The question is, however, as to what exactly is meant by fulfillment in the biblical sense. One answer is to assert that fulfillment has to do with direct prediction and explicit verification. Indeed, a primary test of a prophet in Old Testament times was that his predictions could be precisely validated at a later time (Deut. 18:22; cf. 1 Sam. 9:6). And this same expectation is carried on in the New Testament, as witness Jesus' statement on fulfillment in Matthew 5:17–18 (even the most minute features of the prophetic vision shall be fulfilled) and many of the quotations of Scripture by the evangelists (e.g., Mark 1:2–3, par.; Matt. 2:5–6; John 12:14–15). It is, in fact, this understanding of fulfillment that Justin Martyr used to excess in his *Dialogue with Trypho*. It appears also in extreme form in many of the church fathers; for example, in Tertullian's claims that Genesis 49:27 ("Benjamin is a ravening wolf; in the morning he devours the prey, and in the evening he distributes food"). 1 Samuel 18 (Saul's pursuit of David, but later repentance), and Isaiah 3:3 ("I will take away from Judah . . . even the wise master-builder") are veiled predictions of Saul of Tarsus, who was from the Judean tribe of Benjamin, and so were fulfilled in Paul's life and ministry (*Adv Marc* 5.7.10).

So-calledproof from prophecy of a direct nature has always been a factor in both a Jewish and a Christian understanding of fulfillment. Sadly, however, some see this as the only factor, and so lay out prophecy-fulfillment relations in a manner approximating mathematical precision. Starting from such basic theological axioms as that there is a God in charge of human affairs and that historical events happen according to his will, they point to a few obvious instances where explicit predictions have been literally fulfilled (as Mic. 5:2, quoted with variation in Matt. 2:5–6) and move on from there to construct an often elaborate and ingenious "biblical" apologetic that is usually more "gnostic" than biblical.

What a "proof from prophecy" approach fails to appreciate is that other factors are involved in the New Testament's understanding of fulfillment. For example, there are times when an Old Testament text in its own context is enigmatic, yet is used in the New Testament with christological significance. Such a passage is Psalm 110:1 ("The Lord says to my Lord: 'Sit at my right hand until I make your enemies a footstool for your feet'"), which was variously understood in early Judaism—usually of God speaking to Abraham, or to David, or even to Hezekiah, but not as having messianic relevance by the rabbis until about 260 c.e.—yet was explicated by Jesus to clarify the nature of messiahship and to point to himself (Mark 12:36, par.). Stemming from Jesus' usage, this verse in fact became the scriptural bedrock of early Christian proclamation (most clearly seen in Acts 2:34–35) and the basis for further Christological reflection in the Christian church (e.g., anchoring the catena of passages in Heb. 1:5–13 as to the nature of Christ's Sonship, and triggering the use of Ps. 110:4 in Heb. 5:6–7:28 as to the nature of Christ's priesthood). There are also times when the New Testament quotes the Old Testament in ways that appear quite out of context yet claims fulfillment by Christ or in Christian experience for those passages. Romans 10:6–8 ("The word is near you; it is in your mouth and in your heart") is one such case, for Deuteronomy 30:12–14 (used proverbially) surely has in mind the Mosaic law, whereas Paul interprets it to mean "the word of faith which we preach." Likewise, Paul's use of a number of Old Testament texts in Galatians 3–4 can be cited as not being in strict accord with their original contexts. And though the biblical argument of Galatians 3–4 is telling when understood in terms of Paul's Christian perspective and polemical purpose, his use of Scripture cannot be said to be in line with a direct prediction-explicit verification model.

Furthermore, the concept of fulfillment in the New Testament often has more to do with ideas of "corporate solidarity" and "typological correspondences in history" than with direct prediction. For example, the editorial comment of Matthew 2:15, quoting Hosea 11:1 ("So was fulfilled what the Lord had said through the prophet: 'Out of Egypt I called my son'"), seems to be a rather clear case of the Evangelist thinking along the lines of what has been called corporate solidarity (i.e., the interchange between the nation and its representative, with the Messiah being the embodiment of Israel's hopes and the ultimate recipient of God's promises to his people) and of rereading his Old Testament from an eschatologically realized and christological perspective. For while in Hosea 11 "my son" appears as a collective synonym for the nation (LXX: "his [Israel's] children") which from childhood was loved by God (v. 1) but drifted into idolatry (vv. 2–7), the Evangelist's point—without taking up any of the other features in the passage, many of which would have been entirely inappropriate for his purposes—is that what was prefigured in the nation's exodus from Egypt finds its ultimate focus in the experiences of Jesus, Israel's Messiah. Likewise, Matthew 2:17–18, quoting Jeremiah 31:15 (Rachel weeping for her children), and Matthew 4:14–16, quoting Isaiah 9:1–2 (a great light appearing to the people of Zebulun and Naphtali), use certain events of the nation's history as prefigurements of Jesus' life and ministry, seeing these events as fulfilled in 1) Herod's killing of the young boys at Bethlehem (so Jer. 31:15) and 2) Jesus' preaching in Capernaum (so Isa. 9:1–2). Similarly, Paul invokes ideas of corporate solidarity and typological correspondences in history when he argues that Christ is Abraham's "seed" (Gal. 3:16; cf. Gen. 12:7; 13:15; 15:18; 17:7–8; 22:17–18; 24:7, where "seed" as a generic singular refers to Abraham's posterity as an entity), and that "that rock [which followed the Israelites in the wilderness] was Christ" (1 Cor. 10:4, probably alluding to traditions based on Num. 21:17 and Deut. 32:1ff.).

The passages cited above are only some of the more obvious instances of where the New Testament's understanding of fulfillment overflows any simple prediction-verification model. More elusive still, yet of great significance, are the currents of fulfillment that flow almost everywhere throughout the substrata of the New Testament writings. For example, as Leonhard Goppelt has spelled out in detail, underlying the common narrative of our canonical gospels are all sorts of typological connections between God's activity among his covenant people Israel and his working in the life and ministry of Jesus—connections which the earliest believers in Jesus, whose lives were lived in the ethos of Scripture, saw more clearly than we do today. Likewise, in each of the Evangelists' portrayals there are redactional features that speak of fulfillment: in Matthew, of Jesus as *the* Jew who recapitulates the experiences of Israel and the one "like" Moses whom the people are to "listen" to (cf. Deut. 18:15–18); in Mark, of Jesus who leads his people out of the wilderness; in Luke, of Jesus as the prophet of eschatological promise; and in John, of Jesus as the centre of the nation's social and religious life, the fulfillment of what was typified in the nation's festivals, and the true paschal lamb. Paul also carries on such motifs in his portrayals of Christ as the obedient Son whose faithfulness to the Father in the context of Jewish covenantal nomism is the basis for mankind's redemption (e.g., Gal. 4:4–5; Rom. 5:19).

Much has been written on each of the passages and themes referred to above (see appended bibliography for some helpful books and articles), and much more need be said for any full treatment. The point to be made here, however, is that the concept of fulfillment in the New Testament is broader and more profound than usually thought. Certainly it includes direct prediction and explicit verification. We would be surprised if it didn"t. But direct prediction that explicitly comes to pass is only one factor in a biblical understanding of fulfillment—and one not as prominent or prevalent as is often popularly thought. To be included as well are matters having to do with the clarification of the enigmatic, with corporate solidarity, and with typological correspondences in history, as we have suggested above.

Yet behind all our analyses of individual passages and basic to any proposed characterization of what is taking place in the New Testament's use of the Old Testament stands a vitally important couplet of ideas that needs to be brought to the fore if we are ever to understand what fulfillment in a biblical sense signifies: 1) that God's plan for mankind has to do with "achieving a truly personal relationship between himself and his people," and 2) that "God's personal relations with man assume, for those who are sensitive to personal values, a recognizable pattern" (quoting C. F. D. Moule, "Fulfillment-Words in the New Testament," *New Testament Studies* 14 [1968]: 194, 198). What the New Testament tells us is that in Jesus of Nazareth the early Christians saw the culmination or fulfillment of God's redemptive purposes for mankind, not principally because they could verify each of the prophecies recorded in their Scriptures but "because they found reflected in Jesus a perfect filial relationship with God" (ibid., 298). So they were able to look back over God's pattern of personal relationships in the past—particularly those with his covenant people Israel—and see all of those relationships coming to finality in the life, ministry, death, and resurrection of Jesus. Or, as Moule aptly puts it: "They had come to estimate Jesus, in his ministry, his crucifixion, and his resurrection to life, as the climax, the coping-stone, of an entire edifice of relationship. He was the inaugurator of a new and decisive covenant" (ibid.).

Having, then, such a view of God's purposes and their culmination, the early Christians looked to their Scriptures for prefigurements of what they had seen and experienced in Jesus. In so doing, they spelled out those prefigurements in terms of what we have categorized as 1) direct prophecy explicitly verified, 2) enigmatic passages clarified, 3) corporate solidarity, and 4) typological correspondences in history—though, admittedly, such a precise demarcation of categories would have seemed to them overly pedantic. In effect, they began with Jesus as the epitome of the divine pattern of personal relationships and worked from that estimate of him to prefigurements of such a pattern in the Old Testament. From their Christocentric and so new revelational perspective they laid stress on "fulfillment"—with fulfillment being understood to include everything from direct prediction precisely enacted on through typological correspondences in history.

Exegetical Procedures of Early Christians

In addition to understanding the concept of fulfillment in the New Testament, it is necessary to give attention to the exegetical procedures used by early Christians in working out their convictions. Scholarship of late has focused more and more on the exegetical methods of the New Testament vis-à-vis those of early Judaism. And this is entirely as it should be. For though the gospel is supra-historical in its origin and effect, it comes from a God who always incarnates his word (as witness the incarnation *par excellence,* Jesus Christ) and who uses current historical modes as vehicles for his grace (as witness, for example, the sacraments). Why, then, should it be thought unusual or un-Christian for early believers in Jesus to have interpreted their Scriptures by means of the hermeneutical canons then at hand? Indeed, how could they have done otherwise?

Jewish exegesis of the first century can generally be classified under four headings: literalist, midrashic, pesher, and allegorical. Admittedly, such a fourfold classification highlights distinctions of which the early Jewish exegetes themselves may not have always been conscious. In dealing with a system of thought that thinks more holistically, functionally, and practically than analytically—one that stresses precedent over logic in defense of its ways—any attempt at classification must necessarily go beyond that system's explicit statements as to its own principles. Nevertheless, we still maintain, Jewish interpretations of Scripture fall quite naturally into one or other of these four categories.

A literalist (*peshaṭ*) type of exegesis is to be found in all stands of early Jewish interpretation. While midrashic exegesis may characterize the Talmud, rabbinic literature also contains many examples of Scripture being understood in a quite straightforward manner, with the result that the natural meaning of the text is applied to the lives of the people—particularly in applying Deuteronomic legislation. The situation is somewhat similar in the Dead Sea Scrolls, where preoccupation with pesher interpretation so overshadows all other types of exegesis that one could easily get the impression that the men of Qumran never understood Scripture literally. Yet the opening lines of the Manual of Discipline commit the members of the community to a literal observance of both "the rule [order, *serek*] of the community" and what God "commanded through Moses and through all his servants the prophets" (1QS 1.1–3). Deuteronmic legislation, in fact, while adapted somewhat to their unique situation, was taken by the Qumran covenanters, for the most part, quite literally—even hyperliterally. Likewise Philo, while known most for his allegorical interpretations, understood certain biblical passages in a literalist fashion. Most familiar in this regard is his insistence that though allegorical exegesis is proper, it must not set aside the literal practice of the Law (*De Migrat Abr* 89–94). Philo believed, for example, that circumcision should be allegorically under-

stood, yet practiced literally (*De Migrat Abr* 92); he insisted on the eter-
nality of the Law (*De Vita Mos* 44) and rebuked those who did not keep
it (*De Exsecrat* 138–39).

The central concept in rabbinic exegesis, and presumably that of earlier Pharisees as well, was "midrash." The word comes from the verb *derash* (to resort to, seek; figuratively, to read repeatedly, study, interpret), and strictly denotes an interpretive exposition however derived
and irrespective of the type of material under consideration. In the
Mishnah, the Palestinian Gemaras, and the earlier Midrashim the verbs
peshaṭ and *derash* are used in roughly synonymous fashion, for the earlier rabbis (the Tannaim) did not see any difference between their literal interpretations and their more elaborate exegetical treatments.
Only among the Amoraite rabbis, sometime in the fourth century C.E.,
were literalist exegesis and midrash exegesis consciously differentiated.
But while not recognized as such until later, midrashic exegesis can be
seen in retrospect to have differed from literalist exegesis among the
Pharisaic teachers of the New Testament period.

Midrashic exegesis ostensibly takes its point of departure from the
biblical text itself (though psychologically it may have been motivated
by other factors) and seeks to explicate the hidden meanings contained
therein by means of agreed-upon hermeneutical rules (e.g., Rabbi Hil-
lel's seven *Middoth;* Rabbi Ishmael ben Elisha's later set of thirteen; or
Rabbi Eliezer ben Jose ha-Galili's thirty-two). The purpose of midrashic
exegesis is to contemporize the revelation of God given earlier for the
people of God living later in a different situation. What results may be
characterized by the maxim: "That has relevance for This"—that is,
what is written in Scripture has relevance for our present situation. In
so doing, early Judaism developed what George Foote Moore once aptly
defined as "an atomistic exegesis, which interprets sentences, clauses,
phrases, and even single words, independently of the context or the historical occasion, as divine oracles; combines them with other similarly
detached utterances; and makes large use of analogy of expressions,
often by purely verbal association" (*Judaism in the First Centuries of the
Christian Era*, 1.248).

The expositions in the texts from Qumran are usually introduced by
the term "pesher," which stems from the Aramaic word *pishar* meaning "solution" or "interpretation." There are also instances where "midrash" appears in the texts (e.g., 1QS 6.24; 8.15, 26; CD 20.6; 4QFlor
1, 14), though in these cases the word is used in a nontechnical sense
to mean only "interpretation" generally. The Dead Sea sectarians considered themselves to be the elect community of the final generation
of the present age, living in the last days of "messianic travail" before
the eschatological consummation. Theirs was the task of preparing

for the coming of the messianic age. And so to them applied certain prophecies in Scripture that were considered to speak of their present situation.

While the rabbis sought to contemporize Holy Writ so as to make God's Torah relevant to their circumstances, the Dead Sea covenanters looked upon Scripture from what they accepted was a revelatory perspective (based on the interpretations of the Teacher of Righteousness) and emphasized imminent, catastrophic fulfillment. Their maxim seems to have been: "This is That"—that is, our present situation is depicted in what is written in Scripture. Qumran's pesher interpretation of the Old Testament, therefore, is neither principally "commentary" nor "midrashic exegesis," though it uses the forms of both. As Cecil Roth pointed out: "It does not attempt to elucidate the Biblical text, but to determine the application of Biblical prophecy or, rather, of certain Biblical prophecies; and the application of these Biblical prophecies in precise terms to current and even contemporary events" ("The Subject Matter of Qumran Exegesis," *Vetus Testamentum* 10 [1960]: 51–52).

The most prominent Jewish allegorist of the first century was Philo of Alexandria, whose expositions of Scripture were produced during the life of Jesus and the earliest days of the church. Though a Jew, Philo was the inheritor of Stoic and Platonic ideas. And though a critic of the content of these philosophies, he used their basic categories of thought and methods in presenting to his Grecian audience what he believed to be the truth of the Jewish Torah. So he usually treated the Old Testament as a body of symbols given by God for man's spiritual and moral benefit, which must be understood other than in a literal or historical fashion. The *prima facie* meaning must normally be pushed aside— even counted as offensive—to make room for the intended spiritual meaning underlying the obvious; though, as noted above, at times he seems willing to consider literalist and allegorical exegesis as having a parallel legitimacy. In the main, however, exegesis of Holy Writ was for Philo an esoteric enterprise which, while not without its governing principles, was to be disassociated from literalist interpretation.

But though Philo was the most prominent Jewish allegorist of the first Christian century, he was not alone. The Letter of Aristeas includes one instance of a mild allegorical treatment in its portrayal of the High Priest Eleazer's defence of the Jewish dietary laws (see 150–70; esp. 150: "For the division of the hoof and the separation of the claws are intended to teach us that we must discriminate between our individual actions with a view to the practice of virtue"). Jacob Lauterbach has identified two groups of Palestinian Pharisees active prior to the time of Rabbi Judah "the Prince" (the compiler of the Mishnah in the latter part of the second century c.e.), the *Dorshe Reshumot* and the *Dorshe*

Hamurot, who used a type of allegorical exegesis in their interpretations of Scripture ("Ancient Jewish Allegorists," *Jewish Quarterly Review* 1 [1911]: 291–333, 503–31). And Joseph Bonsirven and David Daube have presented significant data in support of the thesis of an early Pharisaic allegorical exegesis within Palestine itself (Bonsirven, "Exégèse allégorique chez les rabbins tannaites," *Recherches de Science Religieuse* 23 [1933]: 522–24; Daube, "Rabbinic Methods of Interpretation and Hellenistic Rhetoric," *Hebrew Union College Annual* 22 [1949]: 239–64). In addition, the Dead Sea Scrolls include a number of examples of allegorical interpretation, representative of which is the treatment of Habakkuk 2:17 in 1QpHab 12:3–4: "'Lebanon' stands here for the Communal Council; 'wild beasts' for the simple-minded Jews who carry out the Law" (see also 1QpMic. 8–10; CD 6.2–11; 7.9–20). But though allegorical exegesis was widespread amongst Jews of the first century, it was not dominant in Palestine.

The Jewish roots of Christianity make it *a priori* likely that the exegetical procedures of the New Testament would resemble to some extent those of then contemporary Judaism. This has long been established with regard to the hermeneutics of Paul vis-à-vis the Talmud, and it is becoming increasingly clear with respect to the Qumran texts as well. Indeed, there is little indication in the New Testament itself that the canonical writers were conscious of varieties of exegetical genre or of following particular modes of interpretation. At least they seem to make no sharp distinctions between what we would call historico-grammatical exegesis, midrash, pesher, allegory, or interpretations based on "corporate solidarity" or "typological correspondences in history." All of these are used in their writings in something of a blended and interwoven fashion. Yet there are discernible patterns and individual emphases among the various New Testament authors.

In almost all of the New Testament authors one can find some literalist, straightforward exegesis of biblical texts. Occasionally some allegorical interpretation is also present. The pesher method, however, dominates a certain class of material, namely that representative of Jesus' early disciples: principally Peter's preaching recorded in the early chapters of Acts, the Gospels of Matthew and John, and 1 Peter. Here these authors seem to be taking Jesus' own method of using Scripture as their pattern. By revelation they had come to know that "this" manifest in the work and person of Jesus "is that" of which the Old Testament speaks. Yet other New Testament writers, notably Paul and the author of Hebrews, can be characterized by a midrashic type of biblical interpretation (except where Paul uses a pesher approach in describing his own apostolic calling). Midrashic interpretation in the hands of these authors starts with Scripture and seeks to demonstrate christological relevance by means of a controlled atomistic exegesis. Thus the interplay of Jewish presuppositions and exegetical procedures on the one hand, with Christian commitments and perspectives on the other, has produced on the pages of our New Testament a distinctive interpretation of the Old Testament.

Constraints of space and time prohibit any detailing here of the New Testament's use of the Old Testament as to specifics. That is what I have attempted to do in my *Biblical Exegesis in the Apostolic Period* (1975), and what can be found in many of the works listed at the end of this chapter. Suffice it here to say regarding the nature of New Testament exegesis: 1) that the early Christians used many of the same exegetical procedures as were common within the various branches of then contemporary Judaism, and that they did so quite naturally and unconsciously; 2) that they seem to have looked to Jesus' own use of Scripture as the source and initial paradigm for their own use; and 3) that they believed themselves to be guided by the exalted Christ, through the immediate direction of the Holy Spirit, in their continued understanding and application of the Scriptures.

The Normativity of Then Current Hermeneutical Practices

Any attempt to spell out the nature of the New Testament's use of the Old Testament raises the question of the normativity of then current hermeneutical practices for Christian faith, both in that day and today. Most evangelicals and many "constructive" theologians have been at least sympathetic to the view that the New Testament's exegetical procedures are so bound up with the New Testament's proclamation that they together constitute one package, so to speak, with both being in some manner normative for the exposition of the gospel in that day and for the church's exegetical endeavors today—though exactly how those exegetical procedures should be considered normative and exactly how they should be worked out is often left unanswered. Recently, for example, S. L. Johnson, Jr., in taking up my question of 1970, has insisted (in somewhat extreme fashion):

> "Can we reproduce the exegesis of the New Testament?" Unhesitatingly the reply is yes, although we are not allowed to claim for our results the infallibility of the Lord and His apostles. They are reliable teachers of biblical doctrine and they are reliable teachers of hermeneutics and exegesis. We not only *can* reproduce their exegetical methodology, we *must* if we are to be taught their understanding of Holy Scripture. Their principles, probably taught them by the Lord in His post-resurrection ministry, are not abstruse and difficult. They are simple, plain, and logical. The things

they find in the Old Testament are really there, although the Old Testament authors may not have seen them fully (*The Old Testament in the New: An Argument for Biblical Inspiration* [Grand Rapids: Zondervan, 1980], 93–94, emphases his).

Yet despite Johnson's ringing assurance, I am forced by the data alluded to above to respond: Really? Are we able? Ought we to try?

Evangelical Christians are committed to receiving, defending, proclaiming, and living out the faith and doctrine of the New Testament. But are we also committed to reproducing the exegetical procedures of the New Testament? We have always distinguished between the normative and the descriptive in other areas as presented in the New Testament—for example, in matters pertaining to church government, on the issue of apostolic doctrine and apostolic office, and regarding spiritual gifts and specific charismatic expressions, to name only a diverse few. Furthermore, the authors of the New Testament themselves at times suggest that their exegesis should be taken as more circumstantial and *ad hominem* in nature, in accord with their purposes then in view, than universally normative (e.g., Paul's catena of polemically motivated passages in Gal. 3:10–13, or his argument on the generic "seed" in Gal. 3:16, or his allegorical treatment of Hagar and Sarah and their sons in Gal. 4:21–31).

It is my contention that, unless we are "restorationists" in our attitude toward hermeneutics, Christians today are committed to the apostolic faith and doctrine of the New Testament, but not necessarily to the apostolic exegetical practices as detailed for us in the New Testament. What the New Testament presents to us in setting out the exegetical practices of early Christians is how the gospel was contextualized in that day and for those particular audiences. We can appreciate something of how appropriate such methods were for the conveyance of the gospel then and of what was involved in their exegetical procedures. And we can learn from their exegetical methods how to contextualize that same gospel in our own day. But let us admit that we cannot possibly reproduce the revelatory stance of pesher interpretation, nor the atomistic manipulations of midrash, nor the circumstantial or *ad hominem* thrusts of a particular polemic of that day—nor should we try. For various reasons, neither we nor our audiences are up to it. Ours, rather, is to contextualize the gospel in our own day and for our own circumstances, speaking meaningfully to people as they are and think today. Ours is to reproduce the faith and doctrine of the New Testament in ways appropriate to the apprehension of people today, not to attempt to reproduce—or to feel guilty about not being able to reproduce—the specific exegetical procedures contained therein.

Bibliography

Baker, D. L., *Two Testaments, One Bible: A Study of Some Modern Solutions to the Theological Problem of the Relationship between the Old and New Testaments* (Downers Grove: InterVarsity, 1977).

Bandstra, A. J., "Interpretation in 1 Corinthians 10:1–11," *Calvin Theological Journal* 6 (1971): 5–21.

Black, M., "The Christological Use of the Old Testament in the New Testament," *New Testament Studies* 18 (1971): 1–14.

Bruce, F. F., *Biblical Exegesis in the Qumran Texts* (London: Tyndale, 1960); *This Is That. The New Testament Development of Some Old Testament Themes* (Exeter: Paternoster, 1968).

Caird, G. B., "The Exegetical Method of the Epistle to the Hebrews," *Canadian Journal of Theology* 5 (1959): 44–51.

Dodd, C. H., *According to the Scriptures: The Sub-structure of New Testament Theology* (London: Nisbet, 1952).

Doeve, J. W., *Jewish Hermeneutics in the Synoptic Gospels and Acts* (Assen: Van Gorcum, 1954).

Ellis, E. E., *Paul's Use of the Old Testament* (Grand Rapids: Eerdmans, 1957); *Prophecy and Hermeneutic in Early Christianity* (Grand Rapids: Eerdmans, 1978).

France, R. T., *Jesus and the Old Testament* (London: Tyndale, 1971).

Goppelt, L., *Typos. The Typological Interpretation of the Old Testament in the New*, translated by D. H. Madvig (Grand Rapids: Eerdmans, 1982).

Hanson, A. T., *Studies in Paul's Technique and Theology* (London: SPCK, 1974).

Hay, D. M., *Glory at the Right Hand: Psalm 110 in Early Christianity* (Nashville/New York: Abingdon, 1973).

Longenecker, R. N., "Can We Reproduce the Exegesis of the New Testament?" *Tyndale Bulletin* 21 (1970): 3–38; *Biblical Exegesis in the Apostolic Period* (Grand Rapids: Eerdmans, 1975); "Three Ways of Understanding Relations Between the Testaments—Historically and Today," in *Tradition and Interpretation in the New Testament* (*Festschrift* E. E. Ellis), edited by G. F. Hawthorne (Grand Rapids: Eerdmans, 1987).

Moule, C. F. D., "Fulfillment-Words in the New Testament: Use and Abuse," *New Testament Studies* 14 (1968): 293–320.

Thiselton, A. C., *The Two Horizons: New Testament Hermeneutics and Philosophical Description* (Grand Rapids: Eerdmans, 1980).

Wenham, J. W., *Christ and the Bible* (London: Tyndale, 1972).

22

Positive Answer to the Question

Did Jesus and His Followers Preach the Right Doctrine from the Wrong Texts? An Examination of the Presuppositions of Jesus' and the Apostles' Exegetical Method

G. K. Beale

From G. K. Beale, "Did Jesus and His Followers Preach the Right Doctrine from the Wrong Texts?" *Themelios* 14 (1989): 89–96. Reprinted by permission.

The degree of continuity and discontinuity in both theology and interpretative method between Christianity and its Jewish environment has been a point of much debate in New Testament studies. This has especially been the case with the issue of the use of the Old Testament in Judaism and in the New Testament.

One widely-held position is that Jesus and the writers of the New Testament used non-contextual and atomistic hermeneutical methods such as were used by their Jewish contemporaries. We today would regard such methods as illegitimate. But, we are assured, they were guided in their interpretation by the example of Christ and by the Spirit, and so, although we cannot imitate their methods today, we can trust their conclusions and believe their doctrine.[1] This chapter is in-

---

1. For a lucid and sympathetic presentation of this sort of view see, for example, the writings of Richard Longenecker, including his recent article "'Who Is the Prophet Talking About?' Some Reflections on the New Testament's Use of the Old," *Themelios* 13 (1987): 4–8.

tended to raise questions about this approach and to offer a possible alternative.

The Issue of Noncontextual Exegesis in Postbiblical Judaism and Its Relation to the New Testament Methodology

Our starting-point is to observe that it is not at all clear that non-contextual midrashic exegesis was as central to earlier Pharisaic and Qumran exegesis as is suggested by scholars favoring the approach we have described. First, it may not be appropriate to speak of a non-contextual *rabbinic* method in the pre-A.D. 70 setting, since most examples come from after A.D. 70 and those which can be dated with probability before that do not appear to reflect such an atomistic approach.[2] Second, concern for contextual exegesis is found not uncharacteristically both in Qumran and in Jewish apocalyptic.[3] This analysis has far-reaching implications for the argument of those who believe that early Christian exegetes were influenced by a prevalent atomistic Jewish hermeneutic.

But even this assumption of influence may be questioned. It sounds *a priori* plausible that the exegetical procedures of the New Testament would resemble those of contemporary Judaism. And yet, since early Christianity had a unique perspective in comparison with early Judaism, one should not assume that Jewish and Christian hermeneutical approaches will necessarily have been identical in every way.[4] It is necessary to look at the New Testament itself, without prejudice about methodological continuity or discontinuity, in order to assess the issue.

It is often claimed that an inductive study of the New Testament reveals a predominantly non-contextual exegetical method. But, in fact, of all the many Old Testament citations and allusions found in the New

2. On this latter point D. Instone Brewer has identified all the exegetical examples representing this early period (approx. 100) of purported pre-A.D. 70 proto-rabbinic exegesis. He has attempted to demonstrate every example shows that, while these Jewish exegetes may not have always succeeded, they attempted to interpret the Old Testament according to its context, and they never supplanted the primary meaning by a secondary or allegorical one. Even if his conclusions are judged to be overstated, they nevertheless reveal an early concern for context to varying significant degrees which previously has not been sufficiently acknowledged (see "The Hermeneutical Method of Early Judaism and Paul," [published as *Techniques and Assumptions in Jewish Exegesis before 70 c.e.* (Tübingen: Mohr [Paul Siebeck], 1992).].

3. In Qumran, e.g.,1QM1; 1QS A 1; in Jewish apocalyptic, e.g., Enoch 36–72; 4 Ezra; 2 Baruch; The Testaments of the Twelve Patriarchs. See my own *The Use of Daniel in Jewish Apocalyptic Literature and in the Revelation of St. John* (Lanham: University Press, 1984); L. Hartman, *Prophecy Interpreted* (Lund: C. W. K. Gleerup, 1966).

4. E.g., as Longenecker surprisingly assumes ("NT's Use of the Old"; 7), since he points out the same kind of presuppositional fallacy on the part of others (ibid., 1).

Testament, only a very few plausible examples of non-contextual usage have been noted by critics. These include:[5]

1. *ad hominem* argumentation: the role of angels revealing the law in Galatians 3:19; the Exodus "veil" theme in 2 Corinthians 3:13–18.
2. non-contextual midrashic treatments: the understanding of baptism and the "following rock" in 1 Corinthians 10:1–4; Deuteronomy 30:12–14 in Romans 10:6–8; Genesis 12:7ff. in Galatians 3:16; Psalm 68:18 in Ephesians 4:8.
3. allegorical interpretations: Deuteronomy 25:4 in 1 Corinthians 9:9; the use of the Old Testament in Galatians 4:24; Genesis 14 in Hebrews 7.
4. atomistic interpretation: Isaiah 40:6–8 in 1 Peter 1:24ff.

Two things need to be said about such examples. First, it is by no means certain that even these examples are actually non-contextual. A number of scholars have offered viable and even persuasive explanations of how they could well be cases of contextual exegesis.[6] But, second, even if it is granted that they are convincing examples of non-contextual hermeneutics, it does not necessarily follow that they are truly representative of a wider hermeneutical pattern in the New Testament.[7] They may be exceptional rather than typical.

5. Here I am using Longenecker's examples from his "Can We Reproduce the Exegesis of the New Testament?" *Tyndale Bulletin* 21 (1970): 3–38, and *Biblical Exegesis in the Apostolic Period* (Grand Rapids: Eerdmans, 1975).

6. On 1 Cor. 10 and Gal. 3–4 see E. E. Ellis, *Paul's Use of the Old Testament* (Grand Rapids: Baker, 1957), 51–54, 66–73; R. M. Davidson, *Typology in Scripture* (Berrien Springs, Michigan: Andrews University, 1981), 193–297, and D. A. Hagner, "The Old Testament in the New Testament," in *Interpreting the Word of God*, FS in honor of S. Barabas, ed. S. J. Schultz and M. A. Inch (Chicago: Moody, 1976), 101–2, who sees a broad, contextual and typological approach in these texts.

On 2 Cor. 3 see W. J. Dumbrell, *The Beginning of the End* (Homebush West, Australia: Lancer, 1985), 107–13, 121–28, and S. Hafemann's forthcoming work in progress on 2 Cor. 3:13–18.

On 1 Cor. 9:9 cf. A. T. Hanson, *Studies in Paul's Technique and Theology* (London: SPCK, 1974), 161–66; S. L. Johnson, *The Old Testament in the New* (Grand Rapids: Zondervan, 1980), 39–51; D. J. Moo, "The Problem of Sensus Plenior," in *Hermeneutics, Authority, and Canon*, ed. D. A. Carson and J. D. Woodbridge (Grand Rapids: Zondervan, 1986), 179–211.

On Rom. 10 cf. M. A. Seifrid, "Paul's Approach to the Old Testament in Romans 10:6–8," *Trinity Journal* 6 (1985): 3–37, who sees a contextual and typological use.

7. But Longenecker has most recently contended that among NT writers there can be found only "some literalist, straightforward exegesis of biblical texts," that the *pesher* method (which he defines as an atomistic approach and which includes typology) "dominates" Matt., John and the early chapters of Acts and 1 Pet., and that midrashic interpretation (which he also views as a non-contextual method) "characterizes" Paul and Heb. ("NT's Use of the Old," 6–8; cf. his *Biblical Exegesis*, 218–19). He does qualify this by saying that NT authors employed a "controlled atomistic exegesis" (ibid., 7), but this is unclear and he never explains what he means by this.

The Contribution of C. H. Dodd

A substantial and often neglected argument against the view that the New Testament uses the Old Testament atomistically is C. H. Dodd's classic work, *According to the Scriptures* (London: Nisbet, 1952). In brief, Dodd observed that throughout the New Testament there are numerous and scattered quotes that derive from the same few Old Testament contexts. He asks the question why, given that the same segment of the Old Testament is in view, there are so few identical quotations of the same verse, and secondly, why it is that different verses are cited from the same segments of the Old Testament. He concludes that this phenomenon indicates that New Testament authors were aware of broad Old Testament contexts and did not focus merely on single verses independent of the segment from which they were drawn. Single verses and phrases are merely signposts to the overall Old Testament context from which they were cited. Furthermore, he concludes that this was a *unique hermeneutical phenomenom* of the day. He goes on to assert that since this hermeneutical phenomenon can be found in the very earliest strata of the New Testament traditions, and since such innovations are not characteristic of committees, then Christ was the most likely source of this original, creative hermeneutic and it was from him that the New Testament writers learned their method.[8]

Some disagree with Dodd; indeed, many scholars in this field affirm that the New Testament writers often employ a non-contextual exegetical method.[9] Nevertheless, others have supported Dodd's thesis about the New Testament's unique and consistent respect for the Old Testament context, rightly in our opinion.[10]

---

8. Dodd, *According to the Scriptures,* 110, 126–27.

9. E.g., A. C. Sundberg, "On Testimonies," *NovT* 3 (1959): 268–81; B. Lindars, *New Testament Apologetic* (London: SCM, 1961); S. V. McCasland, "Matthew Twists the Scripture," *JBL* 80 (1961): 143–48; S. L. Edgar, "Respect for Context in Quotations from the Old Testament," *NTS* 9 (1962–63): 56–59; A. T. Hanson, *The Living Utterances of God* (London: Darton, Longman and Todd, 1983), 184–90; M. D. Hooker, "Beyond the Things That Are Written? St. Paul's Use of Scripture," *NTS* 27 (1981–82): 295–309; B. Lindars, "The Place of the Old Testament in the Formation of New Testament Theology," *NTS* 23 (1977): 59–66; for other references in this respect consult Longenecker's bibliography in *Biblical Exegesis*, 223–30.

10. In addition to the sources cited above in this regard, see also, e.g., S. Kistemaker, *The Psalm Citations in the Epistle to the Hebrews* (Amsterdam: Van Soest, 1961); R. Rendell, "Quotation in Scripture as an Index of Wider Reference," *EQ* 36 (1964): 214–21; Hartman, *Prophecy Interpreted;* R. T. France, *Jesus and the Old Testament* (Grand Rapids: Baker, 1971); idem, "The Formula-Quotations of Matthew 2 and the Problem of Communication," *NTS* 27 (1980–81): 233–51; D. Seccombe, "Luke and Isaiah," *NTS* 27 (1980–81): 252–59; Johnson, *The Old Testament in the New;* Moo, *The OT in the Passion Narratives;* W. C. Kaiser, *The Uses of the Old Testament in the New* (Chicago: Moody, 1985); Moo, "The Problem of Sensus Plenior"; Beale, "The Influence of Daniel Upon the

To accept Dodd's view is not to deny that New Testament authors display varying degrees of awareness of literary context, as well as perhaps of historical context. Those texts with a low degree of correspondence with the Old Testament literary context can be referred to as semi-contextual, since they seem to fall between the poles of what we ordinarily call "contextual" and "non-contextual" usages.[11] Indeed, there are instances where New Testament writers handle Old Testament texts in a diametrically opposite manner to that in which they appear to function in their original contexts. Often, upon closer examination such uses reveal an ironic or polemical intention.[12] In such examples it would be wrong to conclude that an Old Testament reference has been interpreted non-contextually. Indeed, awareness of context must be presupposed in making such interpretations of Old Testament texts. On the other hand, non-contextual uses of the Old Testament may be expected to occur where there is unintentional or unconscious allusion. Caution should be exercised in labeling Old Testament usages merely either as contextual or non-contextual, since other more precisely descriptive interpretative categories may be better.

The Distinctive Presuppositions of the Apostles' Exegetical Method

But neither Dodd nor his followers have inquired deeply enough into the more fundamental issue concerning the reason why the New Testament is different from Judaism in its contextual approach (assuming for the sake of argument that a non-contextual method was an inherent trait of Jewish exegesis, a position we have tentatively questioned). Therefore, what were the presuppositions which inspired what Dodd and others believe to be a unique, consistent contextual approach to the Old Testament?

The answer which makes most sense of the data is that Jesus and the apostles had an unparalleled redemptive-historical perspective on the Old Testament in relation to their own situation (there are some parallels with Qumran but there is not space to discuss the reasons for its

---

Structure and Theology of John's Apocalypse," *JETS* 27 (1984): 413–23; idem, "The Use of the OT in Revelation," in *It Is Written: Scripture Citing Scripture*, FS for B. Lindars, ed. D. A. Carson and H. Williamson (Cambridge: University Press, 1988), 318–36; idem, "The Old Testament Background of Reconciliation in 2 Cor. 5–7 and Its Bearing on the Literary Problem of 2 Cor. 6:14–7:1," *NTS* (1989); I. H. Marshall, "An Assessment of Recent Developments" in *It Is Written: Scripture Citing Scripture*, 1–21. Although more nuanced than Dodd, see now also Richard B. Hays, *Echoes of Scripture in the Letters of Paul* (New Haven: Yale University Press, 1989).

11. Cf. Beale, "OT in Revelation."
12. Cf. Beale, ibid., 330–32.

methodological differences with the New Testament, except to note the following assumptions of the New Testament writers). This perspective involved a framework of five hermeneutical and theological presuppositions:

1. the assumption of *corporate solidarity* or *representation*.[13]
2. that Christ is viewed as representing the *true Israel* of the Old Testament and true Israel, the church, in the New Testament;[14]
3. that *history is unified* by a wise and sovereign plan so that the earlier parts are designed to correspond and point to the latter parts (cf. Matt. 11:13–14);[15]
4. that the age of *eschatological fulfillment* has come in Christ;[16]
5. as a consequence of (3) and (4), the fifth presupposition affirms that the latter parts of biblical history function as the broader context to interpret earlier parts because they all have the same, ultimate divine author who inspires the various human authors, and one deduction from this premise is that Christ as the centre of history is the *key to interpreting the earlier portions of the Old Testament and its promises*.[17]

It is only in the light of this fifth presupposition that we may legitimately speak of a *sensus plenior* of Scripture, although it is probably best not to use this phrase since it is not often understood in this precise manner (*sensus plenior* is typically defined as the full meaning of Scrip-

13. E.g., H. W. Robinson, *Corporate Personality in Ancient Israel* (Philadelphia: Fortress, 1964; as qualified by later critics) and his bibliography; E. E. Ellis, *Prophecy and Hermeneutic in Early Christianity* (Grand Rapids: Eerdmans, 1978), 170–71.

14. E.g., Isa. 49:3–6 and the use of 49:6 in Luke 2:32, Acts 13:47 and Acts 26:23; note how Christ and the church fulfill what is prophesied of Israel in the OT; see also France, *Jesus and the OT*, 50–60, 75; N. T. Wright, "The Paul of History and the Apostle of Faith," *TynBull* 29 (1978): 66–71, 87; H. K. LaRondelle, *The Israel of God in Prophecy* (Berrien Springs: Andrews University, 1983); Beale, "The Old Testament Background of Reconciliation."

15. Dodd, *According to the Scriptures*, 128, 133; and F. Foulkes, *The Acts of God*, Tyndale Monographs (London: Tyndale, 1958); cf. the significance of the temporal merisms applied to God's—and Christ's—relation to history in Eccles. 3:1–11; Isa. 46:9–11; Rev. 1:8, 17; 21:6; 22:13; see likewise Rev. 1:4; 4:8; cf. Eph. 1:11.

16. E.g., Mark 1:15; Acts 2:17; Gal. 4:4; 1 Cor. 10:11; 1 Tim. 4:1; 2 Tim. 3:1; Heb. 1:2; 9:26; 1 Pet. 1:20; 2 Pet. 3:3; 1 John 2:18; Jude 18. Longenecker has a brief discussion of these first four presuppositions but he does not relate them to the issue of contextual exegesis (cf. *Biblical Exegesis*, 93–95, and "NT's Use of the Old," 4–5). Likewise, see the forthcoming brief article by E. E. Ellis, "Biblical Interpretation in the New Testament Church," in *Mikra. Text, Translation and Interpretation of the Hebrew Bible in Ancient Judaism and Early Christianity* (Minneapolis: Augsburg Fortress, 1989).

17. Cf. 2 Cor. 1:10–21; Matt. 5:17; 13:11, 16–17; Luke 24:25–27, 32, 44–45; John 5:39; 20:9; Rom. 10:4.

ture of which an author was likely not cognizant: there is a wealth of literature discussing the legitimacy of seeing such meanings).[18] On this view it is quite possible that the Old Testament authors did not exhaustively understand the meaning, implications, and possible applications of all that they wrote. Subsequently, New Testament Scripture interprets the Old Testament Scripture by expanding its meaning, seeing new implications in it and giving it new applications.[19] I believe, however, that it can be demonstrated that this expansion does not contravene the integrity of the earlier texts but rather develops them in a way which is consistent with the Old Testament author's understanding of the way in which God interacts with his people—which is the unifying factor between the Testaments. Therefore, the canon interprets the canon; later parts of the canon draw out and explain more clearly the earlier parts.[20]

LaSor has explained well the fifth presupposition of canonical contextual interpretation:

> In one sense, it [the sensus plenior or fuller meaning] lies outside and beyond the historical situation of the prophet, and therefore it cannot be derived by grammatico-historical exegesis. But in another sense, it is part of the history of redemption, and therefore it can be controlled by the study of Scripture taken in its entirety.
>
> Perhaps an illustration will make [this] clear. . . . An ordinary seed contains in itself everything that will develop in the plant or tree to which it is organically related: every branch, every leaf, every flower. Yet no amount of examination by available scientific methods will disclose to us what is in that seed. However, once the seed has developed to its fullness, we can see how the seed has been fulfilled . . . [and] we have sufficient revelation in the Scriptures to keep our interpretations of *sensus plenior* from becoming totally subjective.[21]

18. For one of the most recent surveys of significant literature discussing *sensus plenior* see G. Reventlow, *Problems of Biblical Theology in the Twentieth Century* (London: SCM, 1986), 37–47.

19. For a partial exegetical demonstration of this see the representative literature in favor of a contextual interpretation of the OT in the NT cited throughout the present chapter.

20. So also Moo, "The Problem of Sensus Plenior," 204–11; V. S. Poythress, "Divine Meaning of Scripture," *WTJ* 48 (1986): 241–79; W. S. LaSor, "Prophecy, Inspiration, and Sensus Plenior," *TynBull* 29 [1978]: 54–60; idem, "The 'Sensus Plenior' and Biblical Interpretation," *Scripture, Tradition and Interpretation,* FS for E. F. Harrison, ed. W. W. Gasque and W. S. LaSor (Grand Rapids: Eerdmans, 1978), 272–76; D. A. Carson, *Matthew,* in *The Expositor's Bible Commentary* 8 (Grand Rapids: Zondervan, 1984), 92–93; J. I. Packer, "Infallible Scripture and the Role of Hermeneutics," in *Scripture and Truth,* ed. D. A. Carson and J. D. Woodbridge (Grand Rapids: Zondervan, 1983), 350; see Moo and LaSor for examples of how this method can be applied.

21. "Prophecy, Inspiration and Sensus Plenior," 55–56.

The biblical basis for each of these presuppositions needs more elaboration than the limits of this chapter allow. Nevertheless it is within this framework that we are to understand why the early church believed that through identification with Christ it was the continuation of the true Israel, living in the inauguration of the latter days. As such it was beginning to fulfill the Old Testament prophecies and promises about eschatological Israel.

It is within this framework too that the whole Old Testament was perceived as pointing to this eschatological age both via direct prophecy and the indirect prophetic adumbration of Israel's history. This latter point is especially significant. Old Testament history was understood as containing historical patterns which foreshadowed the period of the eschaton. Consequently, the nation Israel, its kings, prophets, priests and its significant redemptive episodes composed the essential ingredients of this sacred history. This is what scholars sometimes call "typology," which is often defined as the study of correspondences between earlier and later events, persons, institutions, etc., within the historical framework of biblical revelation, and which from a retrospective viewpoint are perceived to have a prophetic function. Ideal or even enigmatic depictions in the Old Testament became "ideal" candidates to select for descriptions of features in the eschatological period which had finally arrived. These came to be considered as typical or ideal prophetic portraits.

I would argue that this broad redemptive-historical perspective was the dominant framework within which Jesus and the New Testament writers thought, serving as an ever-present heuristic guide to the Old Testament. In fact, it is this framework which should be seen as the wider literary context within which the New Testament authors interpreted Old Testament passages. Consideration of the immediate literary context of Old Testament verses, which is what most exegetes affirm as an essential part of the historical-grammatical method, should therefore be supplemented with the canonical literary context.

But when these five presuppositions are related closely to the New Testament's exegetical method, they provide the best explanation for Dodd's observations and conclusions, especially why the New Testament does not focus on verses independent of their contexts. Their selection of Old Testament texts was determined by this wider, overriding perspective, which viewed redemptive history as unified by an omnipotent and wise design. Throughout this plan are expressed the unchanging principles of faith in God, God's faithfulness in fulfilling promises, the rebellion of the unbelieving, God's judgment of them and his glory. Therefore, there was an emphatic concern for more overarching historical patterns or for significant persons (e.g., prophets, priests, and kings), institutions and events which were essential constituents of such patterns. Such an emphasis was probably facilitated by the belief that Christ and the church now represented the true Israel, so that it would have been attractive to see various segments and patterns of Israel's history from the Old Testament as recapitulated in the New Testament. This then was a holistic perspective guiding them away from concentrating on exegetically or theologically insignificant minutiae in passages and quoting individual references as signposts to the broad redemptive-historical theme(s) from the immediate and larger Old Testament context of which they were a part. Is not this the most likely explanation for the phenomenon in the New Testament of so few identical quotations but different citations from the same segments of the Old Testament?

One reason why many see the New Testament typically interpreting the Old Testament non-contextually is often because the New Testament applies the Old Testament to new situations, problems, and people which were not in the minds of the Old Testament authors. Interestingly, many of the cases where such misuse is cited are passages where what was intended for Israel (or leaders or righteous individuals in Israel) in the Old Testament is now applied often by a typological method to either Christ or the church.[22] One aspect of this is that many see typology as an arbitrary method which typically involves allegory and therefore it is also viewed as a good example of non-contextual exegesis. But most scholars today agree that typology is not allegory because it is based on the actual historical events of the Old Testament passage being dealt with and because it essentially consists of a real, historical correspondence between the Old Testament and New Testament event. Typological interpretation involves an extended reference to the original meaning of an Old Testament text which develops it but does not contradict it. Put another way, it does not *read into* the text a different or higher sense, but *draws out* from it a different or higher application of the same sense.[23] Indeed, the five presuppositions of early Christian exegesis cited earlier undergird the typological method and distinguish it from allegory which not only disregards historical context but reads in a new, unrelated meaning to passages.[24]

---

22. Cf. the typical examples noted by McCasland, "Matthew Twists the Scriptures"; Edgar, "Respect for Context in Quotations from the Old Testament," 56–59.

23. P. Fairbairn, *The Typology of Scripture* 1 (Edinburgh: T. & T. Clark, 1876), 19.

24. This is an important distinction which cannot be developed further here, but for more discussion in agreement with our distinction see, e.g., L. Goppelt, *Typos* (Grand Rapids: Eerdmans, 1982); Hanson, *Studies in Paul's Technique and Theology*, 186; Foulkes, *Acts of God*, e.g., 35; O. Cullmann, *Salvation in History* (London: SCM, 1967), 132–33.

Typology is also faulted for being non-contextual because it some-times refers to purely historical events as being prophetically fulfilled (cf. the introductory πληρόω formula) when they are clearly not in-tended as prophecies from the Old Testament author's perspective. This occurs mostly in Matthew but appears as well in the other Gospels. But as we have discussed above this is partly explicable on the basis of the early Christian community's presupposition that Christ and the church (believing Jews and Gentiles) now represented true Israel, so that the various characteristic segments and patterns of God's interaction in Is-rael's history now apply to Christ and the church as the new people of God in the New Testament. Alternatively, such an approach is under-standable because of its foundational assumption that history is an in-terrelated unity and that God had designed the earlier parts to corre-spond and point to the latter parts, especially to those events which have happened in the age of *eschatological fulfillment* in Christ. Conse-quently, the concept of prophetic fulfillment must not be limited to ful-fillment of direct verbal prophecies in the Old Testament but broad-ened to include also an indication of the "redemptive-historical relationship of the new, climactic revelation of God in Christ to the pre-paratory, incomplete revelation to and through Israel."[25]

Typology therefore indicates fulfillment of the indirect prophetic ad-umbration of events, people and institutions from the Old Testament in Christ who now is the final, climactic expression of all God ideally intended through these things in the Old Testament (e.g., the law, the temple cultus, the commissions of prophets, judges, priests, and kings). Everything which these things lacked by way of imperfections was pro-phetically "filled up" by Christ, so that even what was imperfect in the Old Testament pointed beyond itself to Jesus.[26] Romans 5:12–21 is a classic example of this, where Christ is not only contrasted with Adam but is said to have accomplished what Adam failed to do, that is, to obey righteously. This is why Adam is called a τύπος in Romans 5:14. Therefore, it is a too narrow hermeneutic which concludes that New Testament writers are being non-contextual when they understand passages from historical or overtly non-prophetic genre as typologi-cally prophetic.[27]

25. Moo, "The Problem of Sensus Plenior," 191, who cites others such as Moule, Banks, Metzger, Meier, and Carson in support.
26. On this point see G. von Rad, *Old Testament Theology* 2 (New York: Harper and Row, 1965), 372–73.
27. Cf., however, France, *Jesus and the Old Testament*, 38–40, and D. Baker, "Typol-ogy and the Christian Use of the Old Testament," *SJT* 29 (1976): 149, who do not conclude that typology includes a prophetic aspect. But the πληρόω formulas prefixed to citations

In addition, changed applications of the Old Testament in general, whether or not typology is involved, do not necessitate the conclusion that these passages have been misinterpreted. For example, Matthew applies to Jesus what the Old Testament intended for Israel (e.g., Matt. 2:4–22)[28] or Paul does the same thing with respect to the church (e.g.,Rom. 9:24–26). What should be challenged is not their interpretation of the Old Testament but the validity of the above-mentioned framework through which they interpreted the Old Testament, especially the assumption that Christ corporately represented true Israel and that all who identify with him by faith are considered part of true Israel. If the validity of these presuppositions be granted, then the viability of their interpretation of the Old Testament must also be viewed as plausible. Of course, many do not grant the legitimacy of these assumptions and consequently view the New Testament as distorting the original intention of the Old Testament. But whatever conclusion one reaches, it is not based only on raw exegetical considerations but on the theological presupposition of the individual interpreter! For example, Hanson affirms that modern interpreters cannot reproduce the typological exegesis of the New Testament writers because essential to such exegesis was belief in the actual historicity of the events of the Old Testament texts being referred to, a belief purportedly no longer tenable to postcritical thinking.[29]

Further, changes of application need not mean a *disregard* for Old Testament context. Given the viability of the presuppositions, although the new applications are technically different, they nevertheless stay within the conceptual bounds of the Old Testament contextual meaning, so that what results often is an extended reference to or application of a principle which is inherent to the Old Testament text.[30] Of course, it would be possible to hold these presuppositions and still interpret the Old Testament non-contextually, but the point we are attempting to make here is that when a case by case study is made, our recognition of

---

from formally non-prophetic OT passages in the gospels decisively argue against this. See in general agreement Fairbairn, *The Typology of Scripture* 1:46; Johnson, *OT in New*, 55–57; Goppelt, *Typos*, 18, 130, passim; Davidson, *Typology in Scripture*, passim; Moo, "The Problem of Sensus Plenior," 196–98; Foulkes, *Acts of God*, 35–40, although he is sometimes cited wrongly as not holding this position.

28. Cf. France's good discussion of this context in "The Formula-Quotations of Matthew 2."

29. *Studies in Paul's Technique and Theology*, 229–35.

30. For examples of these kinds of changes of application see France, *Jesus*; Beale, "The Use of the OT in Revelation"; idem, "The OT Background of Reconciliation"; for further discussion of the legitimacy of this principle of extension see the section below entitled "The normativity versus descriptive debate."

such presuppositions among the New Testament writers nevertheless helps us to see *how* their interpretations could have been contextual from their particular perspective and *why* they would have been more sensitive to respecting contexts.[31]

Even when there is use of the Old Testament with no apparent interest in prophetic fulfillment, there appears to be a redemptive-historical rationale at work behind the scenes. For example, when an Old Testament reference is utilized only for the perceptible purpose of making an analogy, a key idea in the Old Testament context is usually in mind as the primary characteristic or principle applied to the New Testament situation. These comparisons almost always broadly retain an essential association with the Old Testament context and convey principles of continuity between Old Testament and New Testament even though they are handled with creative freedom. This is true even in the Apocalypse,[32] which is often seen as creatively handling the Old Testament in a hermeneutically uncontrolled manner.[33]

In the light of our overall discussion, the proposal of many that the New Testament's exegetical approach to the Old Testament is characteristically non-contextual is a substantial overstatement. It would take more space than allowed in this article to discuss all the relevant cases where the Old Testament is used in the New Testament, but the present aim has been to focus on methodological and presuppositional issues which often influence the exegetical task itself. I remain convinced that once the hermeneutical and theological presuppositions of the New Testament writers are considered, there are no clear examples where they have developed a meaning from the Old Testament which is inconsistent or contradictory to some aspect of the original Old Testament intention.[34] However, there will probably always remain some enigmatic passages that are hard to understand under any reading.

31. Again, for numerous examples of inductive case studies where this can be argued see the literature supporting a contextual approach cited throughout this chapter.

32. For examples of this see Beale, "OT in Revelation," 321–32; J. Cambier, "Les images de l'Ancien Testament dans l'Apocalypse de saint Jean," *Nouvelle Revue Théologique* (1955): 114–21; A. Vanhoye, "L'utilisation du livre d'Ezéchiel dans l'Apocalypse," *Biblica* 43 (1962): 462–67; "L'utilizzazione del Deutero-Isaia nell'Apocalisse di Giovanni," *Euntes Docete* 27 (1974): 322–39.

33. E.g., see L. A. Vos, *The Synoptic Traditions in the Apocalypse* (Kampen: J. H. Kok, 1965), 21–37, 41.

34. This conclusion is corroborated by the articles of Moo, "The Problem of Sensus Plenior"; R. Nicole, "The New Testament Use of the Old Testament," in *Revelation and the Bible,* ed. C. F. H. Henry (Grand Rapids: Baker, 1958), 135–51, and idem, "The Old Testament in the New Testament," in *The Expositor's Bible Commentary* 1, ed. F. E. Gaebelein (Grand Rapids: Zondervan, 1979), 617–28.

The Normative versus Descriptive Debate

The conclusion of those who see the New Testament use of the Old Testament as non-contextual is that twentieth-century Christians should not attempt to reproduce the exegetical method of the New Testament writers, except when it corresponds to our grammatical-historical method.[35] There are usually two major reasons given for this assertion. First, we do not have the revelatory inspiration which the New Testament writers had in their *pesher* (and other non-contextual) interpretations (direct prophetic fulfillment and typological fulfillment are typically included as subcategories of the *pesher* method, which can be defined as an *inspired application*[36]). But it is not necessary to claim that we have to have such inspiration to reproduce their method or their conclusions. The fact that we don"t have the same "revelatory stance" as the New Testament writers only means that we cannot have the same epistemological certainty about our interpretative conclusions and applications as they had. *Exegetical method* should not be confused with *certainty* about the conclusions of such a method, since the two are quite distinct.

One reason for discouraging imitation of the New Testament's exegesis is a justified fear of an uncontrollable typological exegesis, since typology has been misused throughout church history. How can we today look at the apparently non-prophetic portions of the Old Testament and try to make the same kind of correspondences between them and the New Testament which the inspired authors were able to make? However, the wrong use of a method should not lead to the conclusion that the method itself is wrong but only that great caution should be exercised in using it. Yet should not such care be taken with all the methods we employ in interpreting the Bible, since it is God's Word? Although we cannot reproduce the certainty the biblical authors had about their conclusions, should we not try to interpret the Old Testament in the same way as they did, as long as we keep in mind the presuppositions which guided their approach to the Old Testament and as long as we are ever cautious, in the light of the way such a method has been misused in past church history?[37]

35. E.g., see Longenecker, "Can We Reproduce the Exegesis of the New Testament?" *TynBull* 21 (1970): 38.

36. Longenecker, *Biblical Exegesis*, 99–100.

37. See likewise Moo, "The Problem of Sensus Plenior," 197, 206–10; Fairbairn, *Typology* 1:42–44; M. Silva, "The NT Use of the OT: Text Form and Authority," *Scripture and Truth*, 162–63; Johnson, *OT in New*, 23, 67, 77–79; who generally hold that it is plausible to attempt to discern with caution OT types beyond those mentioned in the NT.

Uppermost among the presuppositions to be aware of is the concern for broad historical patterns or significant individuals (prophets, priests, kings, etc.), institutions and events which integrally formed a part of such patterns.[38] Such a perspective should steer us away from illegitimately focusing on minutiae as typological foreshadowings (like the scarlet thread which Rahab hung out of her window in Joshua 2 being a type of Christ's blood, or the trees which Israel cut down in the promised land as a type of Satan whom Christ would slay).

Therefore, typology by nature does not necessitate a non-contextual approach (although like any method it can be misused in that way), but it is an attempted identification of Old Testament contextual features with similar escalated New Testament correspondences (many evangelical scholars would want to restrict the identification of what Old Testament texts are typological only to those so referred to by New Testament writers, yet, on the other hand, they would not be willing to acknowledge these as non-contextual uses of the Old Testament). Whether or not we have made a legitimate connection is a matter of interpretative possibility or probability. One may not reply that this is an inappropriate method on the basis that the authorial intention of Old Testament writers, especially of historical narratives, would never have included such New Testament identifications. This is because we are also concerned with divine intention discernible from a retrospective viewpoint, which is fuller than the original human intention but does not contradict its contextual meaning. The larger context of canonical, redemptive history reveals how such narrow human intentions are legitimately and consistently developed by other biblical writers (and ultimately the divine author) to include wider meaning, so that the whole canon of Scripture becomes the ultimate context for interpreting any particular passage.[39] Other controlling, heuristic guides helpful for typological exegesis may also be suggested. Repeated historical events, phrases or pictures may provide hints of typological correspondences both within the Old Testament and between the Testaments.[40] Nevertheless, these are only general parameters and will not be infallible guards against misuse and misinterpretation. We must also remember that the conclusions of all biblical exegesis are a matter of degrees of possibility and probability, and the conclusions of typology must be viewed in the same way.

38. For one of the most recent surveys of significant literature discussing typology, see G. Reventlow, *Problems of Biblical Theology in the Twentieth Century*, 14–37.

39. See on this point the above discussion of the fifth presupposition of early Christian exegesis of the OT.

40. E.g., see Foulkes, *The Acts of God*.

Some dispute that typology should be referred to as a method of exegesis since exegesis is concerned with deriving a human author's original intention and meaning from a text.[41] But this question is also bound up with the prior question of whether or not typology is prophetic.[42] If typology is classified as partially prophetic, then it can be viewed as an exegetical method since the New Testament correspondence would be drawing out retrospectively the fuller prophetic meaning of the Old Testament type which was originally included by the divine author. One's presuppositions also can determine how typology is classified. For example, if we concede that God is also the author of Old Testament Scripture, then we are not concerned only with discerning the intention of the human author but also the ultimate divine intent of what was written in the Old Testament, which could well transcend that of the immediate consciousness of the writer.[43] The attempt to draw out the divine intention of a text is certainly part of the exegetical task. And above all, if we assume the legitimacy of an inspired canon, then we should seek to interpret any part of that canon within its overall canonical context (given that one divine mind stands behind it all and expresses its thoughts in logical fashion).

In this regard, typology can be called contextual exegesis within the framework of the canon, since it primarily involves the interpretation and elucidation of the meaning of earlier parts of Scripture by latter parts. If one wants to refer to such canonical contextual exegesis instead as the doing of biblical or systematic theology, or even as scriptural application, it would seem to be but a purely semantic distinction. Rather than exegeting a text only in the light of its immediate literary context within a book, we are now merely exegeting the passage in view of the wider canonical context. The canonical extension of the context of a passage being exegeted does not by itself transform the exegetical procedure into a non-exegetical one. Put another way, the extension of the data base being exegeted does not mean we are no longer exegeting but only that we are doing so with a larger block of material. Even those

41. E.g., France, *Jesus and the OT,* 40–41, and Baker, "Typology," 149.
42. France, ibid.
43. On the fallacy of equating meaning exhaustively with authorial intention see P. B. Payne, "The Fallacy of Equating Meaning with the Human Author's Intention," *JETS* 20 (1977): 243–52, in contrast to the more extreme position of W. Kaiser, "The Eschatological Hermeneutics of 'Evangelicalism': Promise Theology," *JETS* 13 (1970): 94–95; "The Present State of OT Studies," *JETS* 18 (1975): 71–72; who thinks that discerning only the human author's intention exhausts the *full meaning* of an OT text and that the NT provides no fuller meaning of OT texts than the OT authors would not also have been completely cognizant of; the unusual interpretations which result from this view can be seen in Kaiser's *The Uses of the OT in the NT* (Chicago: Moody, 1985).

rejecting typology as exegesis employ exegetical language to describe typology.[44]

The plausibility of the suggestion that typological interpretation is normative and that we may seek for more Old Testament types than the New Testament actually states for us is pointed to by the observation that this method is not unique to the New Testament writers but pervades the Old Testament.[45] The fact that later Old Testament writers understand earlier Old Testament texts typologically also dilutes the claim that the New Testament writers' typological method was unique because of their special charismatic stance.[46] It is nevertheless still true that we today cannot reproduce the inspired *certainty* of our typological interpretations as either the Old Testament or New Testament writers could, but the consistent use of such a method by biblical authors throughout hundreds of years of sacred history suggests strongly that it is a viable method for all saints to employ today.

A second reason given for rejecting the normativity of New Testament exegetical method is because of their supposed non-contextual use of the Old Testament.[47] But we have already seen reason to question whether such use was characteristic of the New Testament writers. According to some scholars, the New Testament writers' methods were wrong according to twentieth-century standards but their conclusions from this method were right because they were inspired. Of course, if this assessment about the New Testament approach is correct, one is forced to conclude that we should not imitate their methods. However, if an inductive study of the New Testament yields the results that the New Testament method is contextual, then we may imitate their approach. This is the answer to the question sometimes posed about "how those exegetical procedures [of the New Testament] should be considered normative and exactly how they should be worked out."[48]

I am prepared to accept the possibility of non-contextual, Jewish *ad*

---

44. E.g., Baker, "Typology," 155, says that "although it is not a method of exegesis, typology supplements exegesis by throwing further light on the text in question"; cf. Goppelt, *Typos*, 152, 198, who, although referring to typology as not "a systematic exposition of Scripture, but as a spiritual approach," says it "is the method of interpreting Scripture that is predominant in the NT."

45. So Foulkes, *Acts of God*, passim; e.g., 40.

46. In addition to Foulkes, *Acts of God*, cf. M. Fishbane, *Biblical Interpretation in Ancient Israel* (Oxford: Clarendon, 1985), 350–79, and sources cited therein for discussion of such topological exegesis within the OT itself; see likewise H. G. Reventlow, *Problems of Biblical Theology in the Twentieth Century*, 28–29; H. D. Hummel, "The OT Basis of Typological Interpretation," *Biblical Research* 9 (1964): 38–50.

47. E.g., Longenecker refers to their "atomistic manipulations of midrash . . . the circumstantial or [Jewish] *ad hominem*" polemical argumentation ("NT's Use of the Old," 8) and "their allegorical explications" (*Biblical Exegesis*, 218).

48. Longenecker, "NT's Use of the Old," 7.

hominem argumentation used polemically by New Testament writers, although I am unconvinced that this occurs anywhere in the New Testament. If it did occur, it might best be understood as the author's intention not to exegete the Old Testament but to beat the Jews at their own game. This would not be imitated by us as a method of exegeting the Old Testament since it plausibly would not have been originally intended as a method of exegesis but as a manner of polemicizing. This is not to say that the New Testament writers were not influenced by Jewish exegetical methods, interpretations, and theology. Indeed, such influence pervades the New Testament but the influential methods consist of varieties of contextual approaches (which include *degrees* of contextual consideration) and the interpretative and theological traditions upon which they relied can be seen viably as consistent though quite creative developments of the Old Testament.

A possible response to part of what has here been said is that it is incorrect to label the New Testament's (or the Jewish) interpretative method as "wrong" according to twentieth-century criteria of logic, since first-century Judaism thought more holistically and employed less analytical and logical ways of thinking. We may only say that what applied in that culture and time no longer applies to ours, which can appear equivalent to saying that methodology is culturally determined and therefore relative (the same argument is sometimes appealed to in the biblical authority debate). But this response is a philosophical one (part of which James Barr in his studies on semantics has rightly criticized), arguing that our laws of logic underlying our evaluative standards were not the same laws of thought governing ancient, Semitic writers. The inductive historical evidence for this is negligible and, therefore, the assertion takes the form of a presupposition (although some have proposed that the purported presence of "error" in biblical literature supports the contention, a proposal which itself has met with much response in recent discussions concerning the nature of scriptural inspiration). Moreover, it is unlikely that it is logically legitimate to separate method in this instance from conclusions derived from the method.

Finally, the significance of this discussion should not be limited to exegetical method because it also has a bearing on theology and theological method, since the use of the Old Testament in the New Testament is the key to the theological relation of the Testaments, which many scholars have acknowledged.[49] If we are limited to understanding

49. E.g.,see G. Hasel, *Current Issues in NT Theology: Basic Issues in the Current Debate* (Grand Rapids: Eerdmans, 1978); D. L. Baker, *Two Testaments, One Bible: A Study of Some Modern Solutions to the Theological Problem of The Relationship between the Old and New Testaments* (Downers Grove: InterVarsity, 1977); Reventlow, *Problems of Biblical Theology in the Twentieth Century.* So also Longenecker, "NT's Use of the Old," 1.

this relation only by the explicit conclusions concerning particular Old Testament passages given by New Testament writers, vast portions of the Old Testament are lost to us. We can use the "contextual method" of interpreting these portions but we have to remember, according to some scholars, that this was not the dominant hermeneutical approach of the New Testament writers. Therefore, a hiatus remains between the way they linked the Testaments both exegetically *and* theologically and the way we should. If the contemporary church cannot exegete and do theology like the apostles did, how can it feel corporately at one with them in the theological process? If a radical hiatus exists between the interpretative method of the New Testament and ours today, then the study of the relationship of the Old Testament and the New Testament from the apostolic perspective is something to which the church has little access. Furthermore, if Jesus and the apostles were impoverished in their exegetical and theological method and only divine inspiration salvaged their conclusions, then the intellectual and apologetic foundation of our faith is seriously eroded. What kind of intellectual or apologetic foundation for our faith is this? M. Silva is likely correct when he states that "if we refuse to pattern our exegesis after that of the apostles, we are in practice denying the authoritative character of their scriptural interpretation—and to do so is to strike at the very heart of the Christian faith."[50] Indeed, the polemical and apologetic atmosphere of early Christian interpretation also points to an intense concern for correctly interpreting the Old Testament (e.g., Acts 17:2; 18:24–28; 1 Tim. 1:6–10; 2 Tim. 2:15).

Thus, I believe a positive answer can and must be given to the question, "Can we reproduce the exegesis of the New Testament?" True, we must be careful in distinguishing between the normative and descriptive (and this is an area in which there is disagreement in many areas among evangelicals in general), but in the case of the New Testament's method of interpreting the Old Testament the burden of proof rests upon those attempting to deny its normativity.

---

50. "NT's Use of the OT," 164, although he does slightly qualify this assertion; so likewise Johnson, *Use of OT in NT*, 67.

Select Bibliography of the Old Testament in the New Testament
(partially annotated)

For supplements to this bibliography (e.g., more special technical studies, relevant studies of Jewish exegesis, and other pertinent works in German and French) consult the sources listed marked with an asterisk and the sources discussed throughout the essays in the book. A number of the works cited are briefly summarized or evaluated in some of the essays preceding (e.g., see Snodgrass, Sundberg, Marshall, and the concluding essay by Beale).

Tools: Books Comparing Various Old Testament Versions with Old Testament Quotes in the New Testament

Archer, G. L., and G. Chirichigno. *Old Testament Quotations in the New Testament.* Chicago: Moody, 1983.

Bratcher, R. G., ed. *Old Testament Quotations in the New Testament.* London: United Bible Societies, 1961 (reprint, 1984).

Dittmar, W. *Vetus Testamentum in Novo: Die alttestamentlichen Parallelen des Neuen Testament im Wortlaut der Urtexte und der Septuaginta.* Göttingen: Vandenhoeck und Ruprecht, 1899. 2 vols.

Hühn, E. *Die alttestamentlichen Citate und Reminiscenzen im Neuen Testament.* Tübingen: Mohr (Paul Siebeck), 1900.

Toy, C. H. *Quotations in the New Testament.* New York: Scribner's, 1884.

Turpie, D. M. *The Old Testament in the New.* London: Williams and Norgate, 1868.

Books and Essays

Aageson, J. W. *Written Also for Our Sake: Paul and the Art of Biblical Interpretation.* Louisville: John Knox, 1993.

Allison, D. C. *The New Moses: A Matthean Typology.* Minneapolis: Fortress, 1993.

*Baker, D. L. *Two Testaments, One Bible.* Leicester: InterVarsity, 1976.

Barrett, C. K. "The Interpretation of the Old Testament in the New." In *The Cambridge History of the Bible,* ed. by P. R. Ackroyd and C. F. Evans, 1:377–

411. Cambridge: The University Press, 1970. [Vol. 1: *From the Beginnings to Jerome*].

———. "The Old Testament in the Fourth Gospel." *Journal of Theological Studies* 48 (1947): 155–69.

Barth, M. "The Old Testament in Hebrews. An Essay in Biblical Hermeneutics." In *Current Issues in New Testament Interpretation*, ed. by W. Klassen and G. Snyder, 53–78. New York, Evanston, and London: Harper & Row, 1962.

Bauckham, R. *The Climax of Prophecy*. Edinbugh: T. & T. Clark, 1993.

Beale, G. K. *The Use of Daniel in Jewish Apocalyptic Literature and in the Revelation of St. John*. Lanham: University Press of America, 1984.

———. "The Origin of the Title 'King of Kings and Lord of Lords' in Revelation 17:14." *New Testament Studies* 31 (1985): 618–20.

———. "The Old Testament Background of Rev. 3.14." *New Testament Studies* (forthcoming).

Betz, O., and G. F. Hawthorne, eds. *Tradition and Interpretation in the New Testament: Essays in Honor of E. Earl Ellis for His Sixtieth Birthday*. Grand Rapids: Eerdmans, 1987.

Black, M. "The Christological Use of the Old Testament in the New Testament." *New Testament Studies* 18 (1971): 1–14.

———. "The Problem of the Old Testament Quotations in the Gospels." *Journal of the Manchester University Egyptian and Oriental Society* 23 (1942): 4.

———. "The Theological Appropriation of the Old Testament by the New Testament." *Scottish Journal of Theology* 39 (1986): 1–17.

Bock, D. L. *Proclamation from Prophecy and Pattern: Lucan Old Testament Christology*. Journal for the Study of the New Testament Supplement Series 12. Sheffield: JSOT, 1987.

———. "Evangelicals and the Use of the Old Testament in the New. *Bibliotheca Sacra* 142 (1985): 209–23, 306–19.

Bruce, F. F. *New Testament Development of Old Testament Themes*. Grand Rapids: Eerdmans, 1968.

———. "Paul's Use of the Old Testament in Acts." In *Tradition and Interpretation in the Old Testament*, ed. G. F. Hawthorne with O. Betz, 71–79. Grand Rapids: Eerdmans, 1987.

Caird, G. B. "Exegetical Method of the Epistle to the Hebrews." *Canadian Journal of Theology* 5 (1959): 44–51.

*Carson, D. A., and H. G. M. Williamson, eds. *It Is Written: Scripture Citing Scripture: Essays in Honour of Barnabas Lindars*. Cambridge: Cambridge University Press, 1988. See especially the introductory essays by I. H. Marshall and M. Wilcox, as well as the essays on the use of the Old Testament in the respective New Testament books by G. Stanton, M. Hooker, C. K. Barrett, D. A. Carson, D. M. Smith, A. T. Hanson, R. Bauckham, and G. K. Beale; consult bibliographics at the end of each article.

Childs, B. S. "Prophecy and Fulfillment: A Study of Contemporary Hermeneutics." *Interpretation* 12 (1958): 259–71.

Clowney, E. *Preaching and Biblical Theology*. Grand Rapids: Eerdmans, 1961. This work discusses typology.

————. *The Unfolding Mystery: Discovering Christ in the Old Testament.* Colorado Springs, Colo.: NavPress, 1988.

Combrink, H. J. B. "Some Thoughts on the Old Testament Citations in the Epistle to the Hebrews." *Neotestamentica* 5 (1971): 22–36.

Danielou, J. "The New Testament and the Theology of History." *Studia Evangelica* 1 (1959): 25–34.

————. *From Shadows to Reality: Studies in the Typology of the Fathers.* London: Burns and Oates, 1960.

*Davidson, R. M. *Typology in Scripture.* Andrews University Seminary Doctoral Dissertation Series 2. Berrien Springs, Mich.: Andrews University Press, 1981.

Dodd, C. H. *According to the Scriptures, The Sub-Structure of New Testament Theology.* London: Nisbet, 1952.

Doeve, J. W. *Jewish Hermeneutics in the Synoptic Gospels and Acts.* Assen: Van Gorcum, 1954.

Drane, J. W. "Typology." *Evangelical Quarterly* 50 (1978): 195–210.

Edgar, S. L. "New Testament and Rabbinic Messianic Interpretation." *New Testament Studies* 5 (1958–59): 47–54.

Efird, J. M., ed. *The Use of the Old Testament in the New and Other Essays. Studies in Honor of William Franklin Stinespring.* Durham, N.C.: Duke University Press, 1972.

Eldridge, V. J. "Typology—the Key to Understanding Matthew's Formula Quotations?" *Colloquium* 15 (1982): 43–51.

————. "Second Thoughts on Matthew's Formula Quotations." *Colloquium* 16 (1983): 45–47.

Ellis, E. Earle, "How the New Testament Uses the Old." In *New Testament Interpretation: Essays on Principles and Methods,* ed. by I. Howard Marshall, 199–219. Grand Rapids: Eerdmans, 1977.

————. "Biblical Interpretation in the New Testament Church." In *Mikra,* ed. by M. J. Mulder, 691–725. Minneapolis: Fortress, 1990.

————. *Paul's Use of the Old Testament.* 1957; reprint ed., Grand Rapids: Baker, 1981.

*————. *The Old Testament in Early Christianity.* Grand Rapids: Baker, 1991. Consult the good bibliography on pp. 63–74.

————. *Prophecy and Hermeneutic in Early Christianity.* Grand Rapids: Eerdmans, 1978.

————. "Midrash, Targum and New Testament Quotations." In *Neotestamentica et Semitica: Studies in Honour of Matthew Black,* ed. by E. Earle Ellis and Max Wilcox, 199–219. Edinburgh: T. & T. Clark, 1969.

Eslinger, Lyle. "Inner-Biblical Exegesis and Inner-Biblical Allusion: The Question of Category." *Vetus Testamentum* 42 (1992): 47–58.

Evans, C. A. "On the Quotation Formulas in the Fourth Gospel." *Biblische Zeitschrift* 26 (1982): 79–83.

————. "Paul and the Hermeneutics of 'True Prophecy': A Study of Romans 9–11." *Biblica* 65 (1984): 560–70.

———. *To See and Not Perceive. Isaiah 6.9–10 in Early Jewish and Christian Interpretation.* Journal for the Study of the Old Testament Supplement Series 64. Sheffield, JSOT, 1989.

*———. "Old Testament in the Gospels." In *Dictionary of Jesus and the Gospels,* ed. by J. B. Green, S. McKnight, and I. Howard Marshall, 579–90. Downers Grove, Ill.: InterVarsity, 1992.

Evans, C. A., and J. A. Sanders. *Luke and Scripture. The Function of Sacred Tradition in Luke–Acts.* Philadelphia: Fortress, 1993.

Evans, C. A., and W. R. Stegner, eds. *The Gospels and the Scriptures of Israel.* JSNT Supplement Series 104. Sheffield, JSOT, 1994.

Evans, C. A., and J. A. Sanders, eds. *Paul and the Scriptures of Israel.* Journal for the Study of the New Testament Supplement Series 83. Studies in Scripture in Early Judaism and Christianity 1. Sheffield: JSOT, 1993.

Evans, C. A., and W. Stinespring, eds. *Early Jewish and Christian Exegesis.* Studies in Memory of William Hugh Brownlee. Atlanta, Ga.: Scholars, 1987.

Fairbairn, P. *The Typology of Scripture.* 2 vols. 6th ed. New York: Funk and Wagnals, 1876.

Farrer, A. "Typology (Ancient Hypotheses Reconsidered)." *Expository Times* 67 (1956): 228–31.

*Feinberg, J. S., ed. *Continuity and Discontinuity. Perspectives on the Relationship Between the Old and New Testaments. Essays in Honor of S. Lewis Johnson, Jr.* Westchester, Ill.: Crossway, 1988.

Fekkes III, J. *Isaiah and Prophetic Traditions in the Book of Revelation.* Journal for the Study of the New Testament Supplement Series 93. Sheffield: JSOT, 1994.

Fishbane, Michael. *Biblical Interpretation in Ancient Israel.* Oxford: Clarendon, 1985. See especially pp. 350–79.

Fitzmyer, Joseph A. "The Use of Explicit Old Testament Quotations in Qumran Literature and in the New Testament." *New Testament Studies* 7 (1960–61) : 297–333.

France, R. T. *Jesus and the Old Testament: His Application of Old Testament Passages to Himself and His Mission.* Tyndale, 1971; reprint ed., Grand Rapids: 1982.

———. "'In All the Scriptures'—A Study of Jesus' Typology." *Theological Students Fellowship Bulletin* 56 (1970): 13–16.

Freed, E. D. *Old Testament Quotations in the Gospel of John.* New Testament Supplements II. Leiden: Brill, 1965.

Gaston, Lloyd. "Theology of the Temple: The New Testament Fulfillment of the Promise of Old Testament Heilsgeschichte." In *Oikonomia: Festschrift for O. Cullman,* ed. by F. Christ, 32–41. 1967.

Gertner, M. "Midrashim in the New Testament." *Journal of Semitic Studies* 7 (1962): 267–92.

Glasson, T. F. *Moses in the Fourth Gospel.* Studies in Biblical Theology no. 40. London: SCM, 1963.

Goppelt, Leonhard. *Typos: The Typological Interpretation of the Old Testament in the New.* Grand Rapids: Eerdmans, 1982.

Goulder, M. D. "The Apocalypse as an Annual Cycle of Prophecies." *New Testament Studies* (1981): 342–67.

———. *Type and History in Acts.* London: S.P.C.K., 1964.

Gundry, R. H. *The Use of the Old Testament in St. Matthew's Gospel.* New Testament Supplements 18. Leiden: Brill, 1967.

*Hafemann, Scott J. *Paul, Moses, and the History of Israel. The Letter/Spirit Contrast and the Argument from Scripture in 2 Corinthians 3. Wissenschaftliche Untersuchungen zum neuen Testament.* Tübingen: Mohr (Paul Siebeck), forthcoming.

Hagner, Donald A. "The Old Testamment in the New Testament." In *Interpreting the Word of God: Fetschrift in Honor of Steven Barabas,* ed. by Samuel J. Schultz and Morris A. Inch, 78–104 [notes on 275–76]. Chicago: Moody, 1976.

Hanson, A. T. "Christ in Old Testament According to Hebrews." *Studia Evangelica* 2 (1964): 393–407.

———. *Jesus Christ in the Old Testament.* London: S.P.C.K., 1965.

———. *The Living Utterances of God: the New Testament Exegesis of the Old.* London: Darton, Longman and Todd, 1983.

*———. *The New Testament Interpretation of Scripture.* London: S.P.C.K., 1980.

*———. *Studies on Paul's Technique and Theology.* Grand Rapids: Eerdmans, 1974.

Hanson, R. P. C. *Allegory and Event.* Richmond, Va.: John Knox, 1959.

Harris, R. J. *Testimonies.* 2 vols. Cambridge: University Press, 1916, 1920.

Hartmann, L. *Prophecy Interpreted.* Coniectanea Biblica: NT Series 1, Uppsala, 1966.

———. "Scriptural Exegesis in the Gospel of Matthew and the Problem of Communiction." In *L' évangile selon Matthieu: Rédaction et Théologie,* ed. by M. Didier, 132–58. BEThL 29. Gembloux: Duculot, 1972.

Hays, R. B. *Echoes of Scripture in the Letters of Paul.* New Haven and London: Yale University Press, 1989.

Hengstenberg, E. W. *Christology of the Old Testament.* 4 vols. Edinburgh: T. & T. Clark, 1856–1858; reprint, Grand Rapids: Kregel, 1956.

Hillyer, N. "Matthew's Use of the Old Testament." *Evangelical Quarterly* 36 (1964): 12–26.

Howard, G. "Hebrews and the Old Testament Quotations." *Novum Testamentum* 10 (1968): 208–16.

Hughes, G. *Hebrews and Hermeneutics.* Society of New Testament Studies Monograph Series 36. Cambridge: Cambridge University Press, 1979.

Hummel, H. D. "The Old Testament Basis of Typological Interpretation." *Biblical Research* 9 (1964): 38–50.

*Instone Brewer, David. *Techniques and Assumptions in Jewish Exegesis before 70 CE.* Texte und Studien zum Antiken Judentum 30. Tübingen: Mohr (Paul Siebeck), 1992.

Johnson, L. T. "The Use of Leviticus 19 in the Letter of James." *Journal of Biblical Literature* 101 (1982): 391–401.

Johnson, S. E. "The Biblical Quotations in Matthew." *Harvard Theological Review* 36 (1943): 135–53.

Johnson, S. L. *The Old Testament in the New.* Grand Rapids: Zondervan, 1980. This is a work demonstrating a good method for interpreting the Old Testament in the New Testament.

Jones, P. R. "The Apostle Paul: Second Moses to the New Covenant Community." In *God's Inerrant Word*, ed. J. Montgomery. Minneapolis: Bethany Fellowship, 1974.

Juel, D. *Messianic Exegesis.* Philadelphia: Fortress, 1988.

Kaiser, Walter C., Jr. *The Uses of the Old Testament in the New.* Chicago: Moody, 1985.

Katz, P. "The Quotations from Deuteronomy in Hebrews." *Zeitschrift für die neutestamentliche Wissenshaft* 49 (1958): 213–23.

Kee, H. C. "The Function of Scriptural Quotations and Allusions in Mark 11–16." In *Jesus und Paulus: Festschrift für W. G. Kümmel zum 70. Geburtstag*, ed. by E. Earle Ellis and E. Grässer, 165–88. Göttingen: Vandenhoeck und Ruprecht, 1975.

Kimball, C. A. *Jesus' Exposition of the Old Testament in Luke's Gospel.* JSNT Supplement Series 94. Sheffied: JSOT, 1994.

Kistemaker, S. *The Psalm Quotations in the Epistle to the Hebrews.* Amsterdam: van Soest, 1961.

Kline, M. "The Old Testament Origins of the Gospel Genre." *Westminster Theological Journal* 38 (1975): 1–27.

*Knowles, M. *Jeremiah in Matthew's Gospel. The Rejected Prophet Motif in Matthean Redaction.* Journal for the Study of the New Testament Supplement Series 68. Sheffield: JSOT, 1993.

Koch, D. A. *Die Schrift als Zeuge des Evangeliums: Untersuchungen zur Verwendung und zum Verständnis der Schrift bei Paulus.* Beiträge zur Historischen Theologie 69. Tübingen: J. B. Mohr, Paul Siebeck, 1986.

Krause, A. E. "Historical Selectivity: Prophetic Prerogative or Typological Imperative." In *Israel's Apostasy and Restoration: Essays in Honor of Roland K. Harrison*, edited by Avraham Gileadi, 175–212. Grand Rapids: Baker, 1988.

Lampe, G. W. H. "Hermeneutics and Typology." *London Quarterly and Holborn Review* 190 (1965): 17–25.

———. "The Reasonableness of Typology." In *Essays on Typology*, ed. by G. W. H. Lampe and K. J. Woollcombe, 9–38. Studies in Biblical Theology 22. Naperville, Ill.: Allenson, 1957.

———. "Typological Exegesis." *Theology* 56 (June 1953): 201–8.

LaRondelle, H. K. *The Israel of God in Prophecy.* Berrien Springs, Mich.: Andrews University, 1983.

LaSor, W. "The Sensus Plenior and Biblical Interpretation." In *Scripture, Tradition, and Interpretation*, ed. by W. Ward Gasque and W. S. LaSor, 260–77. Grand Rapids: Eerdmans, 1978.

Lindars, B. *New Testament Apologetic: The Doctrinal Significance of the Old Testament Quotations.* London: SCM, 1961.

———. "Place of the Old Testament in the Formation of New Testament Theology: Prolegomena." *New Testament Studies* 23 (1976–77): 59–66. See P. Borgen's response on pp. 67–75.

Longenecker, Richard N. *Biblical Exegesis in the Apostolic Period.* Grand Rapids: Eerdmans, 1975.

———. "Can We Reproduce the Exegesis of the New Testament?" *Tyndale Bulletin* 21 (1970): 3–38.

Longman, T. "The Divine Warrior: The New Testament Use of an Old Testament Motif." *Westminster Theological Journal* 4 (1982): 290–307.

Mánek, J. "New Exodus in the Books of Luke." *Novum Testamentum* 2 (1957): 8–23.

———. "Composite Quotations in the New Testament and Their Purpose." *Communio Viatorum* 13 (1970): 181–88.

Manson, T. W. "The Argument from Prophecy." *Journal of Theological Studies* 46 (1945): 129–36.

———. "The Old Testament in the Teaching of Jesus." *Bulletin of the John Rylands University Library of Manchester* 34 (1951–52): 312–32.

Markus, J. *The Way of the Lord: Christogical Exegesis of the Old Testament in the Gospel of Mark.* Louisville: John Knox, 1992.

Markus, R. A. "Presuppositions of the Typological Approach to Scripture." *Church Quarterly Rreview* 158 (1957): 442–51.

Mauser, U. *Christ in the Wilderness: The Wilderness Theme in the Second Gospel and Its Basis in the Biblical Tradition.* Studies in Biblical Theology 39. Naperville, Ill: A. R. Allenson, 1963.

McCartney, Dan G. "The New Testament's Use of the Old Testament." In *Inerrancy and Hermeneutic,* ed. Harvie M. Conn, 101–16. Grand Rapids, Baker, 1988.

McCartney, D. "The New Testament Use of the Pentateuch: Implications for the Theonomic Movement." In *Theonomy: A Reformed Critique,* ed. by W. S. Barker and W. R. Godfrey, 129–49. Grand Rapids: Zondervan, 1990.

McCullough, J. C. "The Old Testament Quotations in Hebrews." *New Testament Studies* 26 (1980): 363–79.

Meeks, W. A. *The Prophet–King: Moses Traditions and the Johannine Christology.* Leiden: Brill, 1967.

Metzger, Bruce M. "The Formulas Introducing Quotations of Scripture in the New Testament and the Mishnah." *Journal of Biblical Literature* 70 (1951): 297–307.

Michel, O. *Paulus und seine Bibel,* Beiträge zur Forderung christlicher Theologie, 2. Reihe, B. 18. Gütersloh, 1929.

Miller, Merrill P. "Targum, Midrash, and the Use of the Old Testament in the New Testament." *Journal of Semitic Studies* 2 (1971): 29–82.

Moo, D. J. *The Old Testament in the Gospel Passion Narratives.* Sheffield: Almond, 1983.

———. "The Problem of *Sensus Plenior.*" In *Hermeneutics, Authority and Canon,* ed. by D. A. Carson and J. D. Woodbridge, 179–211 (footnotes on pp. 397–405). Leicester: InterVarsity, 1986.

Moessner, D. P. *Lord of the Banquet.* Minneapolis: Fortress, 1989. This book is about the use of the Old Testament in Luke.

Moule, C. F. D. "Fulfillment-Words in the New Testament: Use and Abuse." *New Testament Studies* 14 (1967–68): 293–320.

*New, D. S. *Old Testament Quotations in the Synoptic Gospels, and the Two–Document Hypothesis.* Society of Biblical Literature Septuagint and Cognate Studies Series 37. Atlanta: Scholars, 1993.

Nicole, Roger R. "Patrick Fairbairn and Biblical Hermeneutics as Related to the Quotations of the Old Testament in the New." In *Hermeneutics, Inerrancy, and the Bible.* Papers from ICBI Summit II, ed. by E. D. Radmacher and R. D. Preus, 767–76. Grand Rapids: Zondervan, Academie Books, 1984. Responses also by Ronald R. Youngblood (779–88) and S. Lewis Johnson (791–99).

Oesterreicher, M. M. *The Israel of God. On the Old Testament Roots of the Church's Faith.* Englewood Cliffs, N.J.: Prentice-Hall, 1963.

O'Rourke, J. J. "The Fulfillment Texts in Matthew." *Catholic Biblical Quarterly* 24 (1962): 394–403.

———. "Explicit Old Testament Citations in the Gospels." *Studia Montis Regii* 7 (1964): 37–60.

*Osborne, G. R. "Type, Typology." In *International Standard Bible Encylopedia, Revised,* 4:930–32. Grand Rapids: Eerdmans, 1988.

Packer, J. I. "Unfolding the Unity of Scripture Today." *Journal of the Evangelical Theological Society* 25 (1982): 409–14.

Patte, D. *Early Jewish Hermeneutic in Palestine.* Society of Biblical Literature Dissertation Series 22. Missoula, Mont.: Scholars, 1975.

Piper, J. "Prolegomena to Understanding Romans 9:14–15. An Interpretation of Exodus 33:19." *Journal of the Evangelical Theological Society* 22 (1979): 203–16.

Poythress, V. *The Shadow of Christ in the Law of Moses.* Brentwood, Tenn.: Wolgemuth and Hyatt, 1991.

Rad, G. von. "Typological Interpretation of the Old Testament." *Interpretation* 15 (1961): 174–92.

Reim, G. "Jesus as God in the Fourth Gospel: The Old Testament Background." *New Testament Studies* 30 (1984): 158–60.

Rendall, Robert. "Quotation in Scripture as an Index of Wider Reference." *Evangelical Quarterly* 36 (1964): 214–21.

———. "The Method of the Writer to the Hebrews in Using Old Testament Quotations." *Evangelical Quarterly* 27 (1955): 214–20.

Sanders, J. A. "Isaiah in Luke." *Interpretation* 36 (1982): 144–55.

Sandmel, S. "Parallelomania," *Journal of Biblical Literature* 81 (1962): 1–13.

Scott, J. M. *Adoption as Sons of God. An Exegetical Investigation into the Background of* ΨΙΟΘΕΣΙΑ *in the Pauline Corpus.* Wissenschaftliche Untersuchungen zum neuen Testament 2. Reihe 48. Tübingen: Mohr (Paul Siebeck), 1992.

Schuchard, B. G. *Scripture within Scripture. The Interrelationship of Form and Function in the Explicit Old Testament Citations in the Gospel of John.* Society of Biblical Literature Dissertation Series 133. Atlanta: Scholars, 1992.

Selwyn, E. G. "The Authority of Christ in the New Testament." *New Testament Studies* 3 (1956): 83–92.

Shires, H. M. *Finding the Old Testament in the New.* Philadelphia: Westminster, 1974.

Silva, Moises. "The New Testament Use of the Old Testament. Text Form and Authority." In *Scripture and Truth,* ed. by D. A. Carson and J. D. Woodbridge, 147–65 (notes on pp. 381–86). Grand Rapids: Zondervan, 1983.

*———. "Old Testament in Paul." In *Dictionary of Paul and His Letters,* ed. by G. F. Hawthorne, R. P. Martin, and D. G. Reid, 630–42. Downers Grove, Ill.: InterVarsity, 1993.

Smart, James D. *The Interpretation of Scripture.* Philadelphia: Westminster, 1961.

Smith, D. Moody, Jr. "The Use of the Old Testament in the New." In *The Use of the Old Testament in the New and Other Essays: Studies in Honor of Wm. Franklin Stinespring,* ed. by James M. Efird, 3–65. Durham, N.C.: Duke University Press, 1972.

Soares Prabhu, G. M. *The Formula Quotations in the Infancy Narratives of Matthew: An Enquiry into the Tradition History of Mt. 1–2.* Analecta Biblica 63. Rome: Pontifical Biblical Institute, 1976.

Sperber, A. "New Testament and Septuagint." *Journal of Biblical Literature* 59 (1940): 193–293.

*Stanley, C. D. *Paul and the Language of Scripture: Citation Technique in the Pauline Epistles and Contemporary Literature.* Society of New Testament Studies Monograph Series 70. Cambridge: Cambridge University Press, 1993.

Stendahl, Krister. *The School of St. Matthew, and Its Use of the Old Testament.* Acta Seminarii Neotestamentici Uppsaliensis, 20. Lund: C. W. K. Gleerup, 1954.

Stuhlmacher, P. *Biblische Theologie des neuen Testaments.* Band I, Grundlegung von Jesus zu Paulus. Göttingen: Vandenhoeck und Ruprecht, 1992.

Sutcliffe, Edmund F. "The Plenary Sense as a Principle of Interpretation." *Biblica* 34 (1953): 333–43.

Tasker, R. V. *The Old Testament in the New Testament.* Philadelphia: Westminster, 1947.

Thomas, K. J. "The Old Testament Citations in Hebrews." *New Testament Studies* 11 (1965): 303–25.

———. "Torah Citations in the Synoptics." *New Testament Studies* 24 (1977): 85–96.

Thomson, J. G. "Shepherd-Ruler Concept in the Old Testament and Its Application in the New Testament." *Scottish Journal of Theology* 8 (1955): 406–18.

Trudinger, P. "Some Observations Concerning the Text of the Old Testament in the Book of Revelation." *Journal of Theological Studies* 17 (1966): 82–88.

Van Groningen. *Messianic Revelation in the Old Testament.* Grand Rapids: Baker, 1990.

Vermes, G. "Jewish Literature and New Testament Exegesis: Reflections on Methodology." *Journal of Jewish Studies* 33 (1982): 361–76.

Vischer, W. *The Witness of the Old Testament to Christ.* London: Lutterworth, 1949.

Waltke, B. K. "Is It Right to Read the New Testament Into the Old?" *Christianity Today* 27, no. 13 (1983): 77.

Wilcox, M. "Upon the Tree: Deuteronomy 21:22–23 in the New Testament." *Journal of Biblical Literature* 96 (1977): 85–99.

———. "On Investigating the Use of the Old Testament in the New Testament." In *Text and Interpretation,* ed. E. Best, 231–43. Cambridge: Cambridge University Press, 1979.

Wood, J. E. "Isaac Typology in the New Testament." *New Testament Studies* 14 (1968): 583–89.

Woollcombe, K. J. "The Biblical Origins and Patristic Development of Typology." In *Essays on Typology,* ed. by G. W. Lampe and K. J. Woollcombe, 39–75. Studies in Biblical Theology 22. Naperville, Ill.: A. R. Allenson, 1957.

Young, F. W. "Study of the Relation of Isaiah to the Fourth Gospel." *Zeitschrift für neutestamentliche Wissenschaft* 46 (1955): 215–33.

Zimmerli, Walther. "Promise and Fulfillment." *Essays on Old Testament Hermeneutics,* ed. by Claus Westermann, 89–122. English edition edited by James Luther Mays. Richmond, Va.: John Knox, 1963.

Index of Authors

Index of Subjects

Abrahamic covenant, 344, 347
Accomodation, 20
Ad hominem exegesis, 385, 389, 402–3
Adam, 396
Alexandrian school, 33
Alienation, 223–24
Allegory, 33, 84–85, 291–92, 340, 395
    arbitrariness, 49–50, 81, 87, 95, 395
    in Jewish exegesis, 380, 382–83
    in New Testament, 168–70, 205, 212, 279, 389
    v. typology, 313, 324–25, 328, 336, 342–43, 366–69, 370
Allusions, 13, 22, 35, 45–46, 167–68, 201, 258–60, 265, 270
    intentional, 262
    unconscious, 73–74, 262
    See also Quotations
Analogy, 270, 314, 321–22, 323
    of faith, 67
    of Scripture, 68, 81
Ancient Near East
    covenants, 265
    cyclical view of history, 321n
    religion, 318–19
Antiochean school, 33
Antitype, 212–13, 322, 337–38, 341, 370
Apocalyptic literature, 140–41, 142, 145, 199, 205, 221n, 273, 292, 388
Apocrypha, 14, 35n
Apologetics, 120, 132–33, 203–4, 273
Apostasy, 267
Application, 26, 85–88, 90–91, 112–13, 201, 262, 330, 340, 397, 401
    inspired, 399
Aramaic, 24, 29
Archetype, 322
Ark of the covenant, 361
Atomistic exegesis, 203, 381, 384, 385, 387, 389, 390
Atonement, 180
Audience, 72
Authorial intention. *See* Intention
Autographs, 19, 24

Babylon, 267–68, 355
Bethlehem, 123–24
Bible
    authority, 17, 79, 138
    difficulties, 27–28
    divine author, 15–16, 59, 70, 82–83
    dual authorship, 55, 83–84, 93–96
    genres, 98
    human authors, 15–16, 70–72, 76, 81, 85, 98–99, 111–12
Biblical theology, 68, 329, 342, 371, 401

Caiaphas, 26, 59–61, 77
Canon, and interpretation, 82n, 83, 87, 103–4, 108, 393–94, 400–401
Chalcedon, 95
Church, as true Israel, 271, 392, 395, 396
Circular reasoning, 80, 90
Circumcision, 32, 65
Communication, 88–91
Community, 37
Consensus, 163
Consummation, 364, 381. *See also* Fulfillment
Context, 67, 70–71, 80, 103–5, 153–63, 202–3, 263, 336, 377
    disregard for, 261–63
    historical, 71, 263
    literary, 71, 263
    New Testament on, 279
    regard for, 397
    social, 71–72
    and typology, 367–69, 370
Contextual meaning. *See* Meaning, original
Continuity, and discontinuity, 30, 34–35
Corporate representation, 230
Corporate solidarity, 37, 40, 48, 49, 377, 379, 383, 392
Correspondence, 315, 317, 322, 325, 327, 328
    in history, 37–38, 40, 48, 50, 377, 379, 383. *See also* Typology
    vertical and horizontal, 322

Index of Scripture